11-00
Donated
VER

The illustrated 3D studio quick reference
TR 897.7 .Z57 1997

Zirbel, Jay H.
WRIGHT LIBRARY

T5-CFU-319

DATE DUE 15726

Demco, Inc. 38-293

3D ... O®

Qui... R4

JAY ... MBS

Autodesk®
Press

I(T)P An International Thomson Publishing Company

Albany • Bonn • Boston • Cincinnati • Detroit • London • Madrid
Melbourne • Mexico City • New York • Pacific Grove • Paris • San Francisco
Singapore • Tokyo • Toronto • Washington

NOTICE TO THE READER

Publisher does not warrant or guarantee any of the products described herein or perform any independent analysis in connection with any of the product information contained herein. Publisher does not assume, and expressly disclaims, any obligation to obtain and include information other than that provided to it by the manufacturer.

The reader is expressly warned to consider and adopt all safety precautions that might be indicated by the activities herein and to avoid all potential hazards. By following the instructions contained herein, the reader willingly assumes all risks in connections with such instructions.

The publisher makes no representation or warranties of any kind, including but not limited to, the warranties of fitness for particular purpose or merchantability, nor are any such representations implied with respect to the material set forth herein, and the publisher takes no responsibility with respect to such material. The publisher shall not be liable for any special, consequential, or exemplary damages resulting, in whole or part, from the readers' use of, or reliance upon, this material.

Trademarks

AutoCAD® and the AutoCAD® logo are registered trademarks of Autodesk, Inc.
Windows is a trademark of the Microsoft Corporation.
All other product names are acknowledged as trademarks of their respective owners

Cover Credits

Front cover: upper left – Brendon Perkins; upper right and lower left - reprinted with permission of and under the copyright of Autodesk Inc; lower right – courtesy of Sony Pictures/Imageworks.
Back cover: courtesy of AYRES GROUP/Animation: architect ADP Flourdaniel

COPYRIGHT © 1997
By Delmar Publishers
Autodesk Press imprint
an International Thomson Publishing Company

The ITP logo is a trademark under license

Printed in the United States of America

For more information, contact:

Delmar Publishers
3 Columbia Circle , Box 15015
Albany, New York 12212-5015

International Thomson Publishing Europe
Berkshire House 168-173
High Holborn
London, WC1V7AA
England

Thomas Nelson Australia
102 Dodds Street
South Melbourne, 3205
Victoria, Australia

Nelson Canada
1120 Birchmont Road
Scarborough, Ontario
Canada M1K 5G4

International Thomson Editores
Campos Eliseos 385, Piso 7
Col Polanco
11560 Mexico D F Mexico

International Thomson Publishing Gmb
Königswinterer Strasse 418
53227 Bonn
Germany

International Thomson Publishing Asia
221 Henderson Road
#05 -10 Henderson Building
Singapore 0315

International Thomson Publishing -Japan
Hirakawacho Kyowa Building, 3F
2-2-1 Hirakawacho
Chiyoda-ku, Tokyo 102
Japan

All rights reserved. No part of this work covered by the copyright hereon may be reproduced or used in any form or by any means - graphic, electronic, or mechanical, including photocopying, recording, taping or information storage and retrieval systems - without written permission of the publisher.

1 2 3 4 5 6 7 8 9 10 xxx 01 00 99 98 97 96

Library of Congress Cataloging-in-Publication Data

Zirbel, Jay H.
The illustrated 3D studio quick reference / Jay H. Zirbel, Steven B. Combs.
p. cm.
ISBN 0-8273-7189-6
1. Computer animation. 2. 3D studio. 3. Computer graphics.
I. Combs, Steven B. II. Title
TR897.7 .Z57 1996
006.6--dc20 96-14155
CIP

Table of Contents

SECTION 3: 3D EDITOR

SECTION 4: KEYFRAMER

SECTION 5: MATERIALS EDITOR

SECTION 6: PULL-DOWN MENUS

SECTION 7: ICONS

Preface

We live in a three dimensional world filled with wondrous sights and colors. The ability to create these realistic sights and colors on a computer has traditionally been very difficult. In the past it took a lot of computing power along with expensive and often difficult to use software. When Autodesk first released 3D Studio, the power to create virtual *realistic* worlds on a personal computer became a reality. 3D Studio gave the average computer user the tools to create astounding images and animation's.

3D Studio has a great deal of flexibility, allowing the user to create infinite combinations of geometry, materials, lights, and cameras. While there are several good books available on 3D Studio, they only cover small portions of the program. Many of the intricacies and details had to be omitted, just to keep the book to a reasonable size! In the *Illustrated 3D Studio Quick Reference*, we covered *every* command. Where applicable we included actual screen shots from 3D Studio, illustrated to explain a particular command or procedure.

The beginner, experienced, and expert users of 3D Studio will all find this book helpful. For the beginner, basic commands such as creating and opening a file are covered in detail. The experienced user will find the grouping of commands helpful. By paging through a section, such as Modify in the 3D Editor, you can easily see the effect different commands (such as Skew, Bend, or Taper) have on a selected object. The advanced user will appreciate the complete coverage of *all* 3D Studio commands, even those seldom used.

By covering all 3D Studio commands, it is our attempt to stimulate your creative energies by covering all commands in a concise, easy to follow manner. The commands are listed by section, broken down in the same order that they appear on the menu. We sincerely hope you enjoy this book, and wish you happy world building!

Acknowledgments

The authors would like to express their gratitude and appreciation to Elizabeth Combs for her assistance in page layout and continued support during this project. They would also like to thank Krissy, Cody, and Cory Zirbel for their support and understanding during this project.

Using The Illustrated 3D Studio Quick Reference

This book is designed to provide the user of 3D Studio (Release 3 and 4) with a complete reference of all 3D Studio commands. To help the reader locate information easily, this book is broken into 7 sections: the 2D Shaper, the 3D Lofter, the 3D Editor, the Keyframer, the Materials Editor, the Pull-Down Menus, and the Icons. Also included on the inside front cover is a keyboard equivalent reference.

Features

Each command is listed at the top of the page followed by a keyboard shortcut (if applicable). To the right of the command is the menu or toolbar location for the command. Beneath the command is a definition followed by a short tutorial that is designed to show the reader how the command is used. For further clarification, a figure is included. Finally, related commands are listed that will help the reader locate commands that are similar or are necessary compliments to the command.

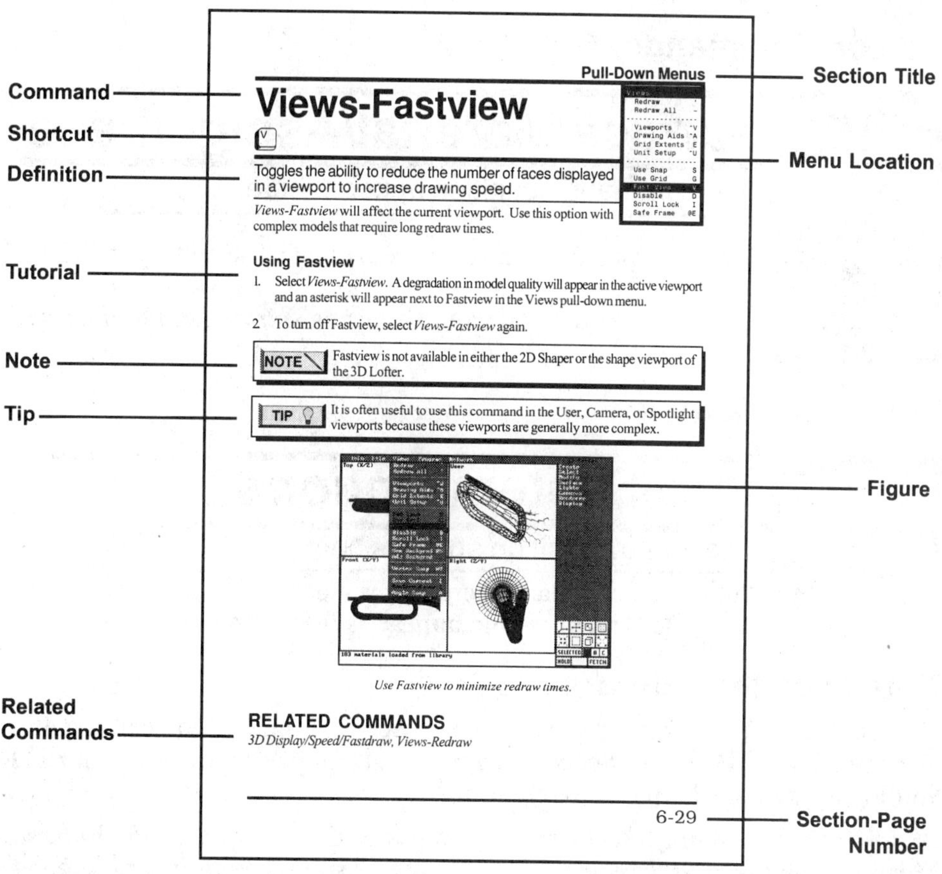

Conventions

The following conventions are used throughout this book.

Notes

NOTE — Notes provide the reader with additional information that is important to the proper use of the command. They also provide the reader with important warnings that help overcome problems while using the command.

Tips

TIP — Tips provide the reader with information that makes the command more efficient. They also provide the reader with insight as to how the command is used or for getting the most out of a command.

Screen Commands

```
Modify
Surface
Cameras
  Material...
  Smoothing...
  Normals...
  Mapping...
    Library
    Assign...
    Box...
      Face
      Element
      Object
      By Name
      By Color
      Update
```

Surface/Material/Assign/Face

The command definition appears here.

Screen command hierarchy is separated by a / and are italicized.

This screen command would appear as *Surface/Material/Assign/Face.*

Pull-Down Menus

```
Info
  About 3D Studio
  Current Status
  Configure
  System Options
  Scene Info
  Key Assignments
  Gamma Control
```

Info-System Options

The menu definition appears here.

Pull-down command hierarchy is separated by a - and are italicized. This menu would appear as *Info-System Options*.

Note from the Authors

We encourage you to keep this reference close at all times. Dog ear, tag and mark up this book so that it becomes a personal companion in all of your 3D Studio endeavors. Happy world creating!

Dr. Jay H. Zirbel, Murray, Kentucky
jzirbel@msumusik.mursuky.edu

Steven B. Combs, Evansville, Indiana
stevencombs@earthlink.net

Create/Line

Create
Select
Modify
Shape
Display
Line
Freehand...
Arc
Quad
Circle
Ellipse
N-gon...
Copy
Open
Close
Connect

Used to create open or closed spline polygons one vertex at a time. The segments making up the polygon can be either curved or straight. Can also be used to insert vertices into existing polygons.

Creating Individual Line Segments

1. When creating individual line segments, you must right-click to end the Line command after *each* segment.
2. To create the next segment, select a new start point. If you begin a new segment too close to the end vertex of another segment, it is added to the end of the previous segment.

NOTE Lines in the 2D Shaper are continuous linked segments. All segments created with a single command belong to the same polygon. You can use the screen cursor to locate a vertex, or enter exact vertex coordinates at the keyboard. See also *Views–Drawing Aids.*

Adding Additional Segments to a Polygon

1. Place the cursor on the first vertex you want to attach to and click.
2. When the mouse is moved, the first vertex remains unchanged and a "rubberband" line follows the cursor.
3. When you click again, a new vertex is inserted. See also *Create/Connect, Create/Polyconnect,* and *Display/First/Choose.*

Inserting a Vertex into an Existing Polygon

1. Place the cursor over the existing polygon at the point you want the vertex inserted at and click.
2. Click again to insert the vertex, or move cursor to modify the shape of the polygon. See also *Modify/Segment/Refine*, which will allow you to insert vertices without altering the polygon.

TIP The *Create/Line* command can be used to trace over an existing polygon. To do this, first freeze the original polygon to prevent the line tool from automatically inserting vertices on it. After it is frozen, trace over the existing polygon. See *Display/Freeze.*

Creating Curved Segments

1. When placing a vertex, press and hold down the left mouse button. This will display the direction arrows.
2. While holding down the left mouse button, drag the mouse to alter the size and rotation position of the direction arrows. When the direction arrows are displayed, you can also use the Ctrl and Alt keys to modify the spline further. The Ctrl key allows you to adjust the vertex position. The Alt key allows you to modify the angle between the directional arrows.

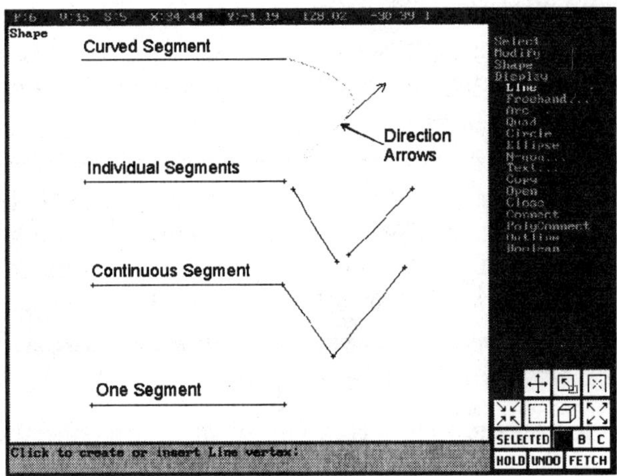

Creating line segments.

RELATED COMMANDS

Views–Drawing Aids, Create/Connect, Create/Polyconnect, Display/First/ Choose, Modify/Segment/Refine, Display/Freeze

Create/Freehand/Draw

Create
Select
Modify
Shape
Display
Line
Freehand...
Arc
Quad
Circle
Ellipse
N-gon...
Copy
Open
Draw
Setting

Creates a freehand polygon.

Creating a Freehand Polygon

1. After selecting *Create/Freehand/Draw*, the cursor changes appearance and becomes a pencil.
2. Hold down the left mouse button and move the pencil-shaped cursor. Release the mouse button to stop drawing.
3. Right-click the mouse to complete the drawing.

Creating a Straight-Segment Polygon

1. Instead of holding down the left mouse button when creating a freehand polygon, click anywhere to place a vertex.
2. A straight line segment is drawn, and the pencil-shaped cursor remains attached to the last vertex.

NOTE After creating a freehand polygon or straight-segment polygon, you have the following options:

1. Right-click the mouse to end the polygon.
2. Move the mouse and left-click, which will create vertices and straight-line segments.
3. Hold down the left mouse button and create a freehand polygon.
4. Click on the first vertex in the polygon to close the polygon.

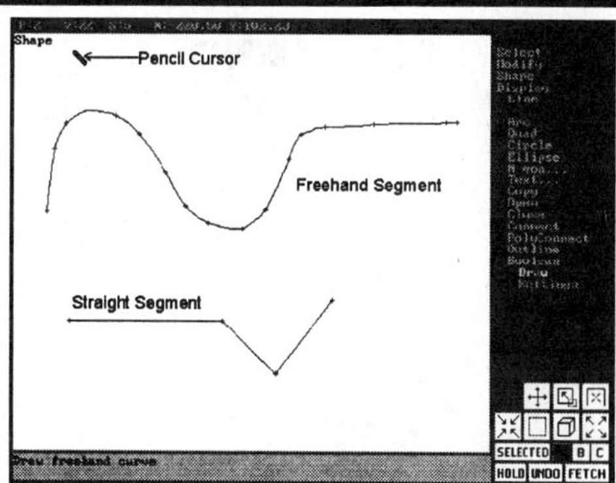

Creating straight– segment and freehand polygons.

RELATED COMMANDS

Create/Freehand/Settings, Create/Line, Views–Drawing Aids, Create/Connect, Create/Polyconnect

Create
Select
Modify
Shape
Display
Line
Freehand...
Arc
Quad
Circle
Ellipse
N-gon...
Copy
Open
Draw
Setting

Create/Freehand/Setting

Specifies the smoothness of a freehand polygon by setting the number of vertices in the polygon.

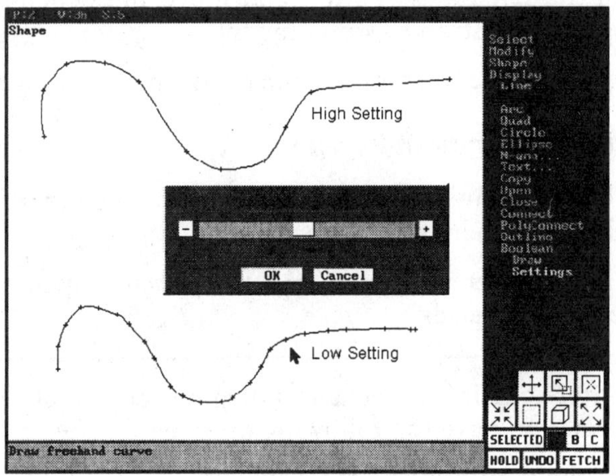

Effect of changing the number of vertices in a polygon.

A high setting inserts fewer vertices, resulting in a smoother polygon. A low setting inserts more vertices, and results in a rougher polygon.

RELATED COMMAND

Create/Freehand/Draw

Create/Arc

Create
Select
Modify
Shape
Display
Line
Freehand..
Arc
Quad
Circle
Ellipse
N-gon...
Copy
Open
Draw
Setting

Creates an arc by specifying a center point, radius, start angle, and end angle.

Creating an Arc

1. Specify the center point, either with the cursor or by entering the coordinates at the keyboard.
2. Move the mouse in any direction to set the start angle and radius. The start and end angles are based on degrees. The 0 position is at 3 o'clock, with 12 o'clock 90 degrees and 9 o'clock 180 degrees.
3. Move the mouse clockwise or counterclockwise to draw the arc. The status line at the top of the screen displays the end angle and total angle of the arc.

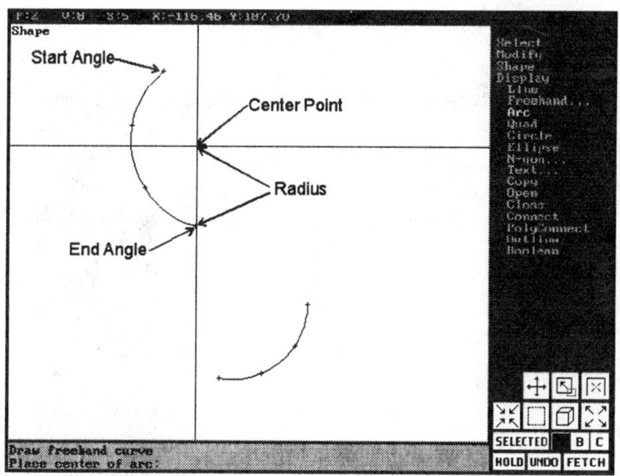

Creating an arc by specifying the center, start angle, radius, and end angle.

RELATED COMMAND

Views–Drawing Aids

Create
Select
Modify
Shape
Display
Line
Freehand...
Arc
Quad
Circle
Ellipse
N-gon...
Copy
Open
Close
Connect

Create/Quad

Creates a *quadrilateral*, more commonly called a square or rectangle.

Creating a Rectangle

1. Select the first corner of the rectangle, and move the mouse in any direction. The status line will show the current width and height of the rectangle in brackets, as well as the X and Y coordinates.
2. Click to create the rectangle, or right-click to cancel the operation.

Creating a Square

1. To create a square, hold down the Ctrl key when placing the first corner.
2. When the mouse is moved in any direction, a square with equal sides will be created.

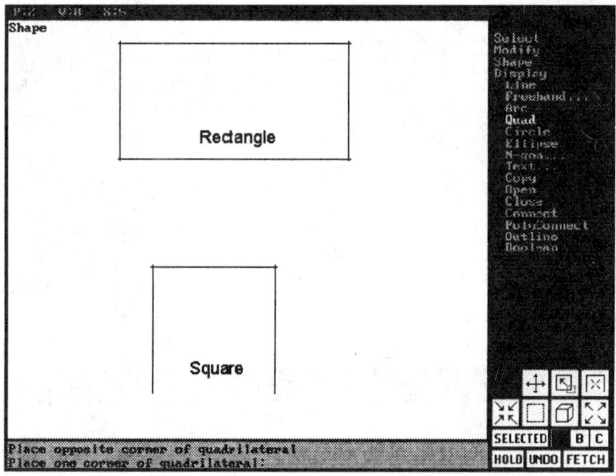

Creating a rectangle and square.

> **NOTE** You also have the option of entering the coordinates of a rectangle or square at the keyboard. When using the keyboard, however, all coordinates must be entered at the keyboard. You cannot mix using the mouse and keyboard when creating a square or rectangle.

RELATED COMMAND

Views–Drawing Aids

Create/Circle

Create
Select
Modify
Shape
Display
Line
Freehand...
Arc
Quad
Circle
Ellipse
N-gon...
Copy
Open
Close
Connect

Creates a circle by specifying the center point and radius.

1. Locate the center point of the circle with the mouse. The status line displays the X and Y locations.
2. Set the circle radius by moving the mouse away from the center point. The status line displays the radius.

NOTE You also have the option of entering the center point and radius of the circle at the keyboard. When using the keyboard, however, you must input *both* the center point and radius at the keyboard. You cannot mix using the mouse and keyboard when entering the values for the circle center point and radius.

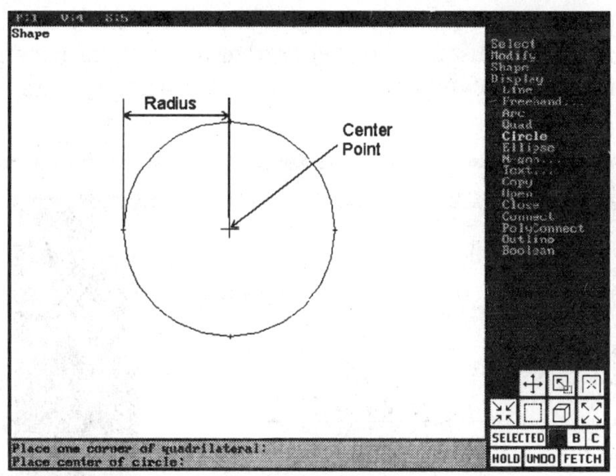

Creating a circle by specifying the center point and radius.

The number of vertices in a circle can be controlled using *Create/N-gon/Circular*. By default, a circle has 4 vertices.

RELATED COMMANDS

Views–Drawing Aids, Create/N-gon/Circular

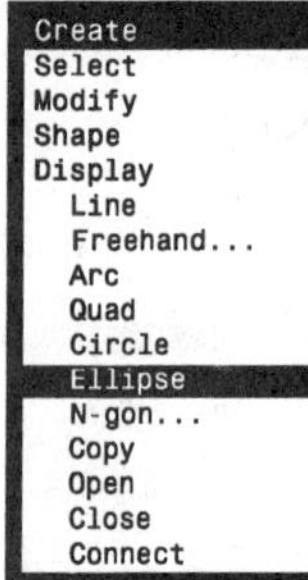

Create/Ellipse

Creates an ellipse by defining the major and minor axis.

Creating an Ellipse

1. First, set the center point of one of the arcs on the ellipse. The status bar at the top of the screen will show the X and Y coordinates.
2. Set the radius and angle of the axis by moving the mouse in any direction and clicking. The status bar will show the radius and angle of the axis.
3. Move the mouse to draw the ellipse by specifying the radius of the second axis. The status line will show the radius of the second axis.
4. Click at the appropriate radius to create the ellipse, or right-click to cancel the command.

NOTE You can also set the values for the ellipse at the keyboard. However, you must use the keyboard to input all information about the ellipse. You cannot mix keyboard and mouse entry when creating an ellipse.

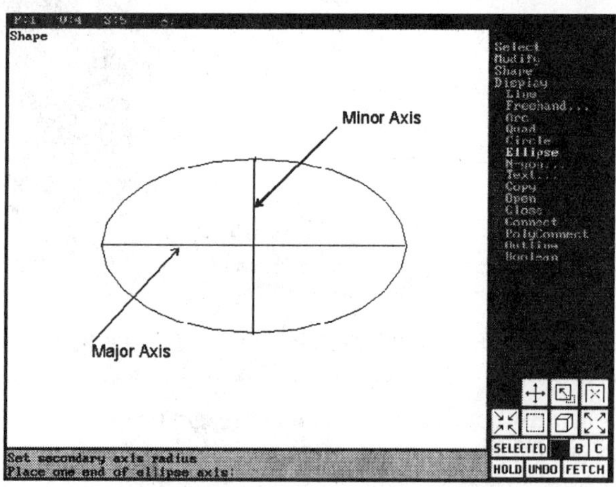

Creating an ellipse by defining the major and minor axis.

RELATED COMMAND

Views–Drawing Aids

Create/N-gon/Flat

Create
Select
Modify
Shape
Display
Line
Freehand...
Arc
Quad
Circle
Ellipse
N-gon...
Copy
Flat
Circular
Sides

Creates a closed polygon with three or more equal *flat* sides.

Creating a Flat, Closed Polygon

1. Select the number of sides by choosing *Create/N-gon/# Sides*.
2. Select the center point. The X and Y coordinates are displayed at the top of the screen.
3. As you move the mouse, the cursor is attached to the first vertex of the polygon. The status line displays the radius of the polygon, and the angle of the cursor relative to the X axis.
4. You can adjust the radius of the polygon by moving the cursor away from the center point. You can adjust the angle by moving the cursor around the center point.
5. After adjusting the radius and angle, click to create the polygon, or right-click to cancel the operation.

NOTE You can also enter the center point, radius, and angle of the polygon at the keyboard. However, you cannot mix keyboard and cursor input during the creating of a polygon.

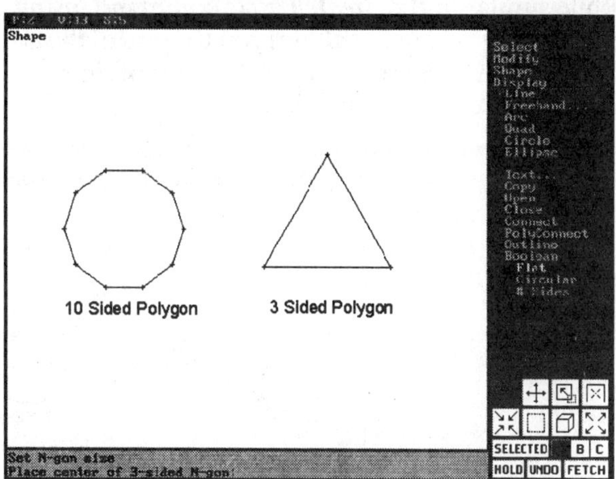

Creating a closed polygon with equal flat sides.

RELATED COMMANDS

Create/N-gon/# Sides, Create/N-gon/Circular, Views–Drawing Aids

Create
Select
Modify
Shape
Display
Line
Freehand...
Arc
Quad
Circle
Ellipse
N-gon...
Copy
Flat
Circular
Sides

Create/N-gon/Circular

Creates a closed polygon with three or more equal *curved* sides.

Creating a Circular Polygon

1. Select the number of *curved segments* in the circle by choosing *Create/N-gon/#Sides.*
2. Select the center point of the circle. The X and Y coordinates are displayed at the top of the screen.
3. Set the circle radius by moving the mouse away from the center point. As you move the mouse, the cursor is attached to the first vertex of the circle. The status line displays the radius of the circle, and the angle of the cursor relative to the X axis.
4. After adjusting the radius and angle, click to create the circle, or right-click to cancel the operation.

NOTE You can also enter the center point and radius of the circle along with the angle of the first vertice at the keyboard. You cannot mix keyboard and cursor input during the creating of the circle.

TIP While similar to the *Create/Circle* command, using the *Create/N-gon/Circular* command allows you to control the number of vertices in a circle. This is done when selecting the number of sides in the Set N-Gon Sides dialog box under *Create/N-Gon /#Sides.*

Controlling the number of vertices in a circle.

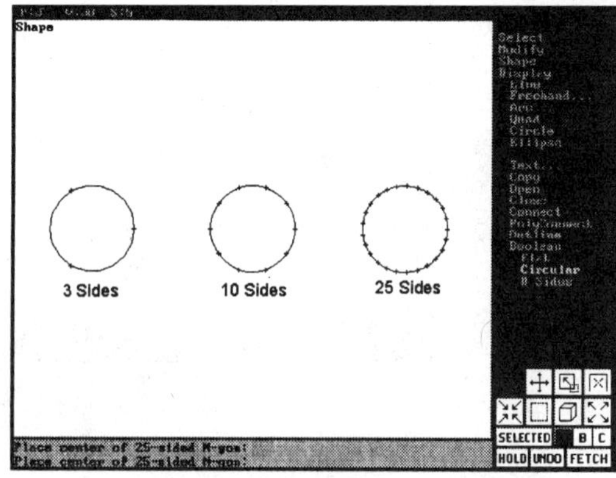

RELATED COMMANDS

Create/Circle, Create/N-gon/#Sides, Create/N-gon/Flat

Create/N-gon/# Sides

Controls the number of sides when creating flat and circular n-gons.

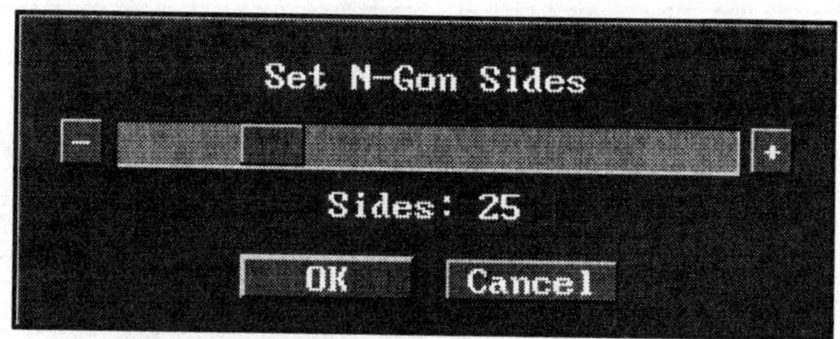

Set N-Gon Sides dialog box.

NOTE The value specified in the Set N-Gon Sides dialog box applies to all future polygons, unless you change the setting again or quit 3D Studio. Valid range is from 3 to 100.

RELATED COMMANDS

Create/N-gon/Circular, Create/N-gon/Flat

Create
Select
Modify
Shape
Display
Freehand...
Arc
Quad
Circle
Ellipse
N-Gon...
Text...
Copy
Font
Enter
Place

Create/Text/Font

Accesses a dialog box that sets the font used by the Create/Text/Enter and Create/Text/Place commands.

Examples of sample .pfb fonts.

Examples of sample .fnt fonts.

NOTE The fonts available for use in 3D Studio include URW Bezier fonts (*.fnt and *.be) and Postscript Type 1 fonts (*.pfb). All text can be treated like any other polygon created in the 2D Shaper. The figures above show examples of the sample .fnt and .pfb fonts included with 3D Studio.

RELATED COMMANDS

Create/Text/Enter, Create/Text/Place

Create
Select
Modify
Shape
Display
Freehand...
Arc
Quad
Circle
Ellipse
N-Gon...
Text...
Copy
Font
Enter
Place

Create/Text/Enter

Accesses a dialog box used to enter the desired text.

Entering the Desired Text

1. Set the font for the desired text with *Create/Text/Font*.
2. Select *Create/Text/Enter* and type the desired text in the dialog box.
3. Press ←Enter or click on **OK**.

Type the desired text in the dialog box.

Entering the desired text does not place the text on the screen. See *Create/Text/Place* to position the text on the screen.

RELATED COMMANDS

Create/Text/Font, Create/Text/Place

Create
Select
Modify
Shape
Display
Freehand...
Arc
Quad
Circle
Ellipse
N-Gon...
Text...
Copy
Font
Enter
Place

Create/Text/Place

Places and sizes the text defined with Create/Text/Enter, using the font set in Create/Text/Font.

Placing Text

1. Define the font with *Create/Text/Font* and enter the desired text with *Create/Text/Enter*.
2. Click to place the first corner of the selection box. Moving the mouse in any direction will draw the selection box.
3. After defining the chosen area, click to display the text, or right–click to cancel the operation. The resulting text is forced within the boundaries of the selection box.

NOTE Postscript Type I fonts (**.pfb*) weren't designed for 3D modeling. For this reason, many of them create overlapping polygons in the 2D Shaper. You can use *Shape/Check* to see if this condition exists. If you receive an error message, move them apart with *Modify/Polygon/Move*.

Maintaining Font Aspect Ratio

To maintain the correct aspect ration between the character height and width of the text, hold down the Ctrl key when setting the first corner of the selection box. This will force the selection box to maintain the correct aspect ratio for the current font.

Lofting Fonts

Many of the Bezier fonts are complex polygons with many vertices. To avoid creating highly complex mesh objects in the 3D Lofter, use a low step value such as 3 or 4. See *Shape/Steps* in the 2D Shaper. Also, make sure the Optimization button is on in the Object Lofting Controls box in the 3D Lofter. See *Objects/Make* in the 3D Lofter.

TIP For more accurate measurements while creating text and for placing multiple lines of text, turn on the snap and grid. See *Views–Drawing Aids*.

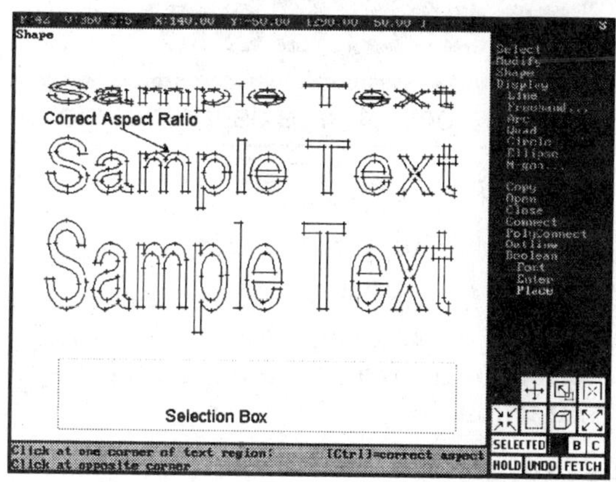

Maintaining the text aspect ratio.

NOTE When 3D Studio calculates text height, it is the height of a box that encloses the entered text string. Individual letter heights vary depending on whether they are lowercase or uppercase. You can compensate for this and ensure that your text is of a consistent height by entering your text with two dummy letters. Use an uppercase dummy letter at the beginning of the text string, and a lowercase descending dummy letter (such as a g or q) at the end of the string. Delete the dummy letters after placing the text.

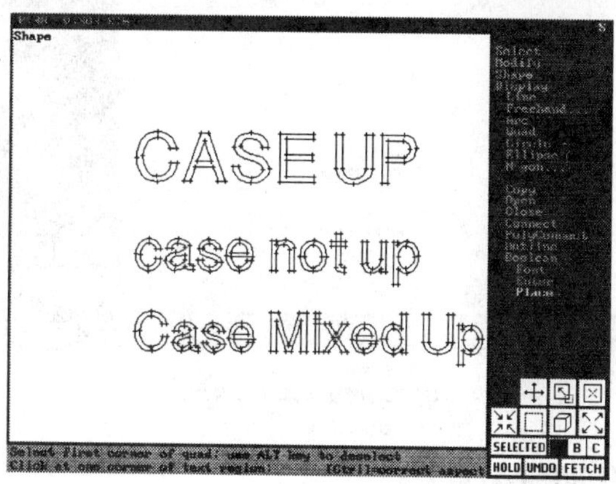

Varying text heights.

RELATED COMMANDS

Create/Text/Enter, Create/Text/Font, Shape/Check, Modify/Polygon/Move, Shape/Steps, Views–Drawing Aids, Objects/Make (3D Lofter)

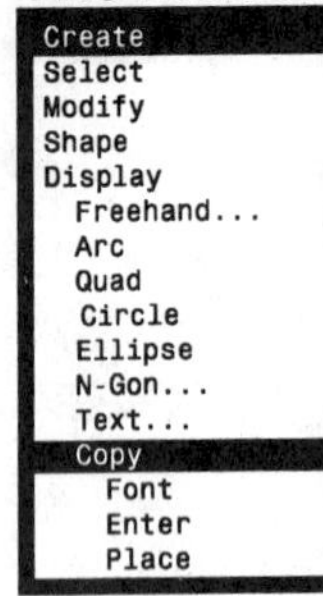

Create/Copy

Creates a copy of an existing polygon.

Copying Single Polygons

1. Select the polygon you want to copy.
2. Move the copy attached to the cursor to the chosen location in the drawing. You can use the Tab key to select a directional cursor to move the selected object in a specific direction.

Copying Multiple Polygons

1. Create a selection set containing two or more polygons. See *Select/Polygon.*
2. Select the *Create/Copy* command, and click on the **Selected** button at the bottom of the screen. A copy of all selected polygons will then be attached to the cursor.
3. Place the polygons in the desired location and click again.

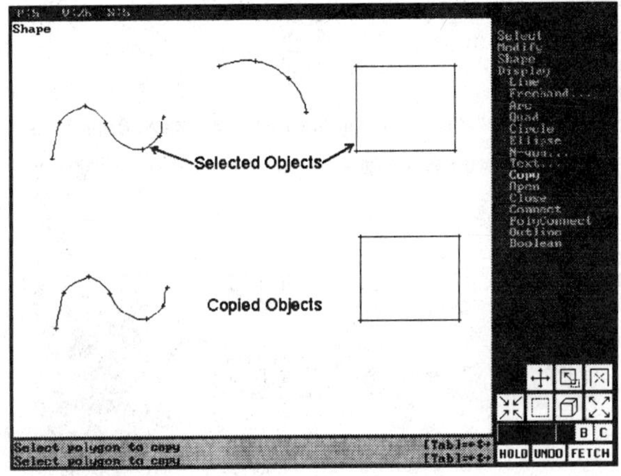

Copying more than one polygon.

RELATED COMMANDS

Select/Polygon, Views–Drawing Aids

Create
Select
Modify
Shape
Display
Circle
Ellipse
N-Gon...
Text...
Copy
Open
Close
Connect
Polyconnect
Outline
Boolean

Create/Open

Deletes a segment from an existing polygon.

Deleting a Segment from a Polygon

Place the cursor over the segment you want to delete and click.

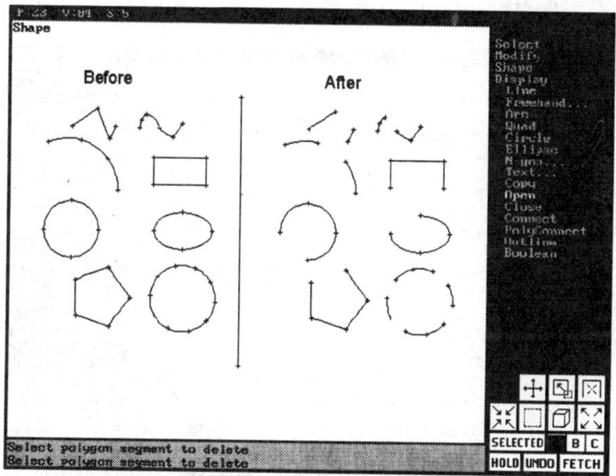

Deleting segments from existing polygons.

To restore a deleted segment, click on the **Undo** button *immediately* after deleting the segment.

RELATED COMMAND

Modify/Segment/Break

Create
Select
Modify
Shape
Display
Circle
Ellipse
N-Gon...
Text...
Copy
Open
Close
Connect
Polyconnect
Outline
Boolean

Create/Close

Creates a straight-line segment between two end vertices of an open polygon.

Closing a Polygon

1. To close an open polygon, simply select it.
2. A straight line is drawn between the end vertices.

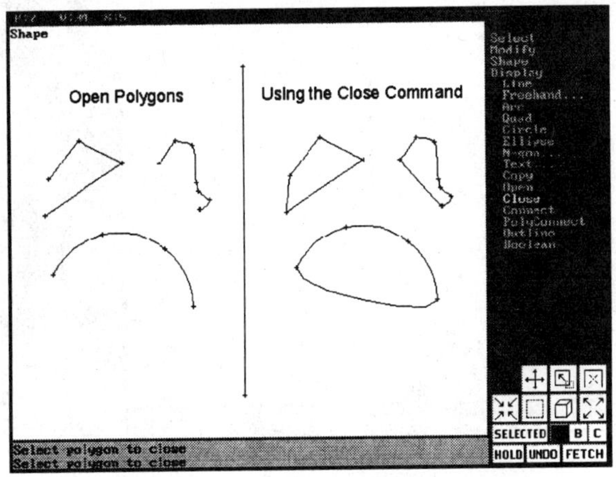

Open and closed polygons.

RELATED COMMAND

Create/Connect

Create/Connect

Create
Select
Modify
Shape
Display
Circle
Ellipse
N-Gon...
Text...
Copy
Open
Close
Connect
Polyconnect
Outline
Boolean

Connects two end vertices by drawing a line between them.

Connecting Two End Vertices

1. Click on the end vertex of an existing polygon.
2. Move the mouse to draw the connecting segment
3. Click on the end vertex.

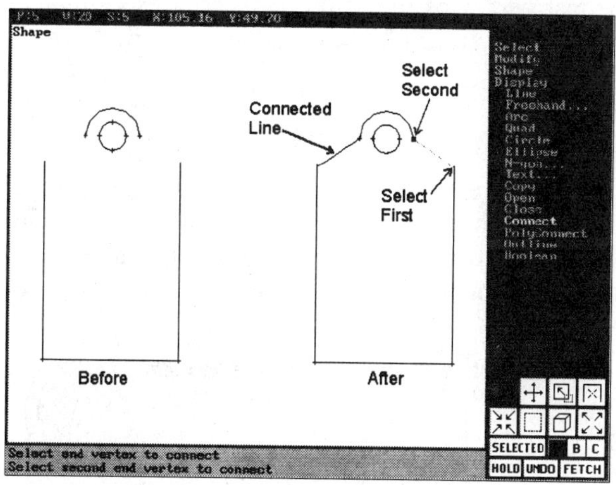

Connecting two end vertices.

> **TIP** The connect command can be used as an alternative to the *Create/Line* command to chain multiple open polygons into a single complex polygon quickly.

RELATED COMMANDS

Create/Line, Create/Polyconnect

VRJC LIBRARY

Create
Select
Modify
Shape
Display
Circle
Ellipse
N-Gon...
Text...
Copy
Open
Close
Connect
Polyconnect
Outline
Boolean

Create/Polyconnect

Connects two open polygons, creating one closed polygon.

Connecting Two Polygons

1. Click on the first open polygon
2. Click on the second open polygon.
3. Two linear segments are created, connecting the first vertex of each polygon with the last vertex of the other. This creates a single closed polygon. See *Display/First* for an explanation of first vertices and how to display them.

Using the ALT Key with Polyconnect

In certain instances the created segment may cross, depending upon the order of the vertices in the open polygons. If this occurs, click on **Undo**, and repeat the operation while holding down the a key. Using the Alt key connects the two first vertices with the two last vertices, as shown in the following example.

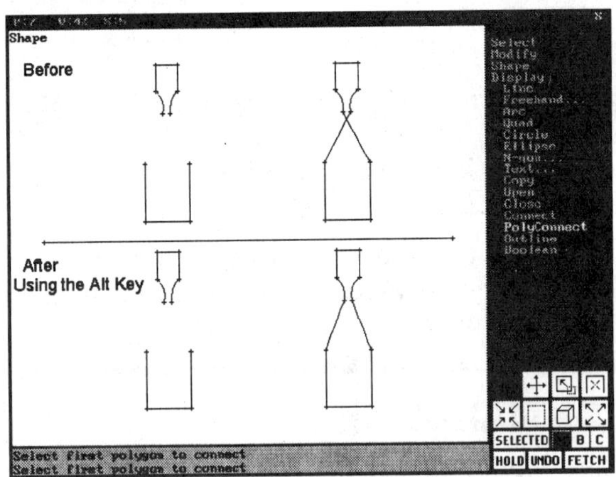

Using the Alt key with Polyconnect.

RELATED COMMANDS

Display/First, Create/Connect

Create/Outline

Create
Select
Modify
Shape
Display
Circle
Ellipse
N-Gon...
Text...
Copy
Open
Close
Connect
Polyconnect
Outline
Boolean

Creates an outline of an existing polygon. The thickness of the resulting polygon is determined by drawing a *definition* line.

Outlining a Polygon

1. Select the polygon you want to create an outline of.
2. Create the definition line. The definition line is the distance the outline polygon will be from the original polygon. Move the cursor anywhere in the drawing area and click to set the first point. To obtain an accurate line, use the Snap and Grid under *Views–Drawing Aids.*
3. Move the cursor the desired distance to set the definition line. The status line displays the length of the line.

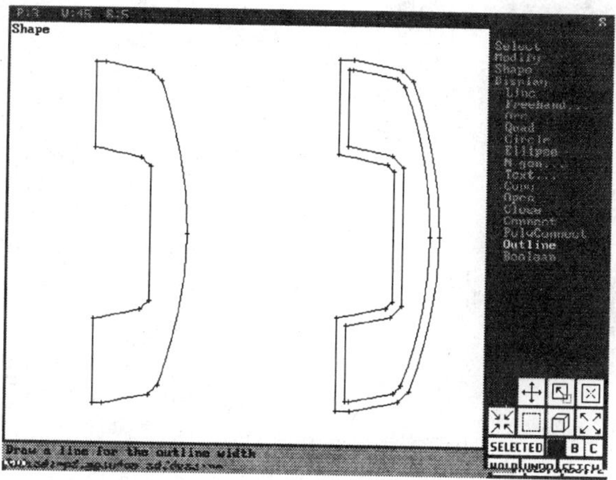

Using the outline command.

TIP When using the *Outline* command, your source polygon is *always* deleted. After specifying the definition line, the source polygon is deleted and concentric copies are created one-half the width distance on either side of the source polygon. To keep the source polygon after using the *Outline* command, do the following:

1. Create a copy of the source polygon and place it exactly on top of the original polygon. For accurate placement, turn Snap on. See *Views–Use Snap*.
2. Use the *Outline* command as described above. The selected polygon is deleted, but the copy remains intact.
3. Redraw the screen (*Views–Redraw*). You should see two outlined polygons, and a copy of the original polygon.

RELATED COMMANDS

None

Create
Select
Modify
Shape
Display
Circle
Ellipse
N-Gon...
Text...
Copy
Open
Close
Connect
Polyconnect
Outline
Boolean

Create/Boolean

Combines two closed polygons by performing a Boolean (union, subtraction, intersection) operation. The first polygon is altered, and the second polygon is deleted.

Types of Boolean Operations

Union

The two selected polygons are combined by removing the segments in the overlapping portions.

Subtraction

The overlapping portion of the second polygon is subtracted from the first polygon. The remainder of the second polygon is deleted.

Intersection

Only the overlapping portion of the two polygons is retained.

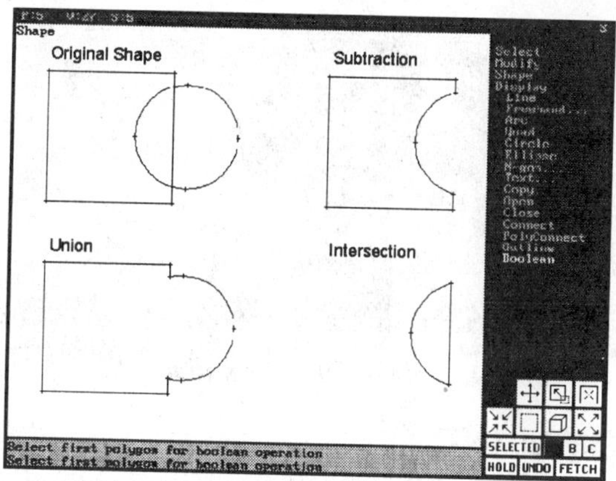

Boolean operations.

NOTE The following restrictions are placed on the source polygons:

1. Both polygons must be closed.
2. No polygon can intersect itself.
3. The polygons must overlap each other. A polygon totally enclosed within another is not considered to be overlapping.

Performing a Boolean Operation

1. Select the polygon to alter.
2. Select the second polygon. The 2D Boolean Operation dialog box appears.
3. Select the Boolean operation to perform. You are given the following options:

   Weld Polygons: Determines if the coincident vertices resulting from the Boolean operation are welded together, resulting in one or more closed polygons.

   Hold: Clicking on this button will store the current geometry in the Hold buffer. Clicking on the **Fetch** button will allow you to restore your original geometry after performing a Boolean operation. You can also restore your original geometry by clicking on the **Undo** button immediately after performing the Boolean operation.
4. After setting the appropriate options, click on **OK** to perform the Boolean operation.

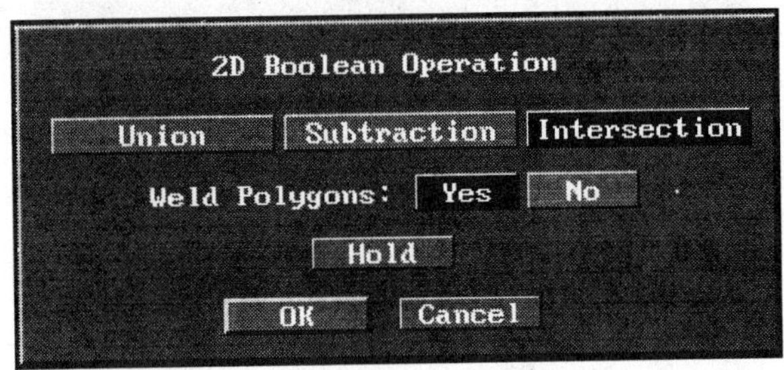

The 2D Boolean Operation dialog box.

RELATED COMMAND

Create/Object/Boolean in the 3D Editor for performing Boolean operations on 3D objects.

Select/Vertex/Single

Create
Select
Modify
Shape
Display
Vertex...
Polygon...
All
None
Invert
Single
Quad
Fence
Circle

Assigns individual vertices to a selection set.

Creating a Selection Set of Individual Vertices

1. Activate an icon letter (A, B, or C) at the bottom of the screen. All selected vertices will be assigned to whichever letter is highlighted.
2. Click on each vertice you want added to the selection set. Selected vertices appear in red.
3. Clicking on selected (red) vertices will remove them from the selection set.

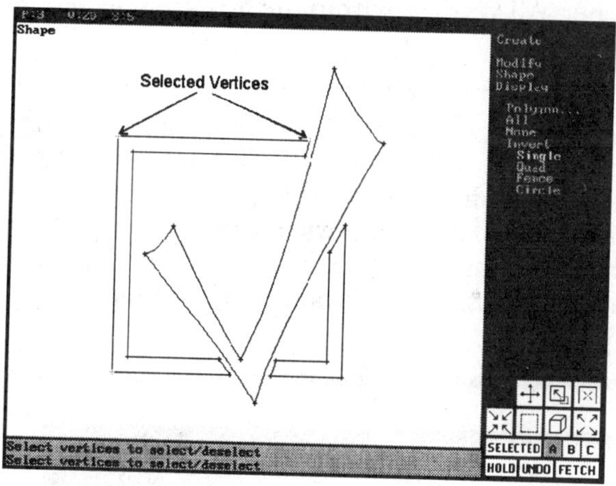

Selecting single vertices.

RELATED COMMANDS

Select/Vertex/Quad, Select/Vertex/Fence, Select/Vertex/Circle

Create
Select
Modify
Shape
Display
Vertex...
Polygon...
All
None
Invert
Single
Quad
Fence
Circle

Select/Vertex/Quad

Assigns vertices to a selection set by defining a box around the vertices.

Creating a Selection Set with Quad

1. Activate an icon letter (A, B, or C) at the bottom of the screen. All selected vertices will be assigned to whichever letter is highlighted.
2. Define a box around the vertices by clicking to place one corner of the box.
3. Move the mouse diagonally to enclose the vertices, then click to set the opposite corner. All vertices within the box are selected. Selected vertices appear in red.

NOTE Deselecting vertices with the Quad option is affected by the Region–Toggle option. See *Info–System Options*. By default, Region Toggle is set to **ON**, meaning vertices switch state each time you select them. If you turn Region Toggle **OFF**, vertices will not be deselected. You can hold down the [Alt] key while defining the Quad, however. This will deselect all vertices within the Quad, regardless of the Region Toggle setting.

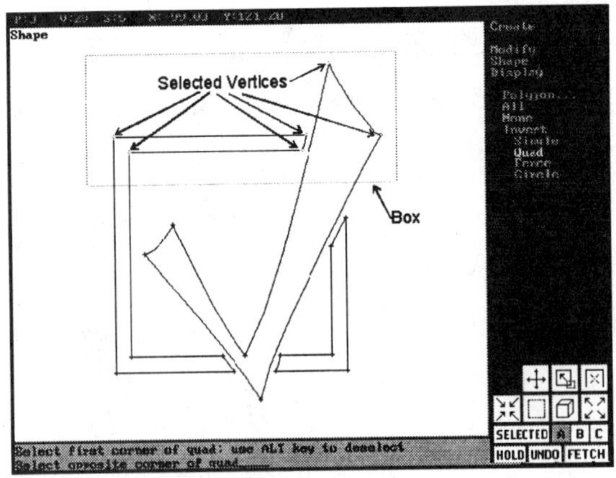

Selecting vertices with a box.

RELATED COMMANDS

Select/Vertex/Single, Select/Vertex/Fence, Select/Vertex/Circle

Select/Vertex/Fence

Create
Select
Modify
Shape
Display
Vertex...
Polygon...
All
None
Invert
Single
Quad
Fence
Circle

Assigns vertices to a selection set by defining a polygon around the vertices.

Creating a Selection Set with Fence

1. Activate an icon letter (A, B, or C) at the bottom of the screen. All selected vertices will be assigned to whichever letter is highlighted.
2. Define a polygon around the vertices. Begin by clicking to set a point. Click the mouse to create a segment, then click to set a second point.
3. Continue setting points and creating segments until all vertices you want selected are enclosed within the polygon.
4. Close the polygon and complete the selection set by either clicking at the first point in the polygon or pressing the **Spacebar**. All vertices within the polygon are selected. Selected vertices appear in red.

> **NOTE** When deselecting vertices, the Fence option is affected by the Region-Toggle option. See *Info–System Options*. Region Toggle is set to **ON** by default, meaning vertices switch state each time you select them. If you turn Region Toggle **OFF**, vertices will not be deselected. Holding down the [Alt] key while defining the Fence will deselect all vertices within the polygon regardless of the Region Toggle setting.

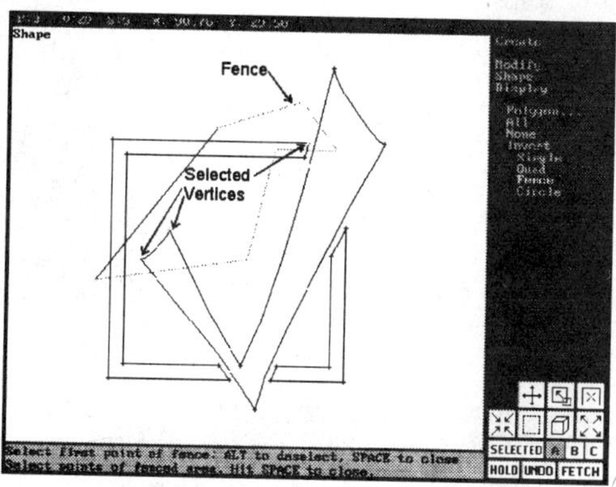

Selecting vertices with a fence.

RELATED COMMANDS

Select/Vertex/Single, Select/Vertex/Quad, Select/Vertex/Circle

Create
Select
Modify
Shape
Display
Vertex...
Polygon...
All
None
Invert
Single
Quad
Fence
Circle

Select/Vertex/Circle

Assigns vertices to a selection set by defining a circle around the vertices.

Creating a Selection Set with Circle

1. Activate an icon letter (A, B, or C) at the bottom of the screen. All selected vertices will be assigned to whichever letter is highlighted.
2. Define a circle around the vertices by first clicking to set the center of the circle.
3. Move the mouse to define the diameter of the circle. All vertices within the circle are selected. Selected vertices appear in red.

> **NOTE** The Circle option is affected by the Region-Toggle option. See *Info–System Options*. By default, Region Toggle is set to **ON**, meaning vertices switch state each time you select them. If you turn Region Toggle **OFF**, vertices will not be deselected. Holding down the Alt key while defining the circle will deselect all vertices within the Circle, regardless of the Region Toggle setting.

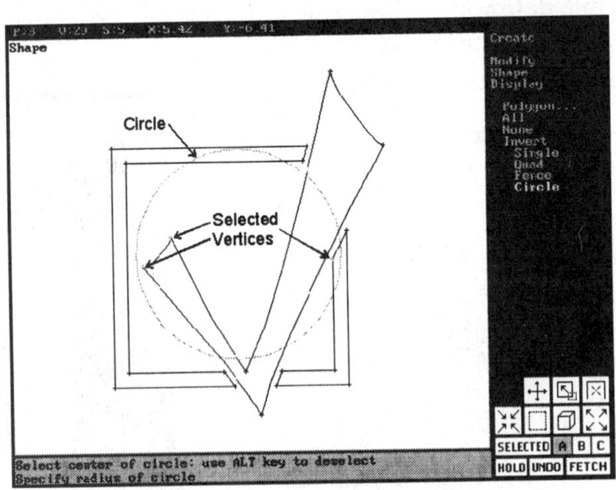

Selecting vertices with a circle.

RELATED COMMANDS

Select/Vertex/Single, Select/Vertex/Quad, Select/Vertex/Fence

Create
Select
Modify
Shape
Display
Vertex...
Polygon...
All
None
Invert
Single
Quad
Fence
Circle
Window
Crossing

Select/Polygon/Single

Assigns individual polygons to a selection set.

Creating a Selection Set of Individual Polygons

1. Activate an icon letter (A, B, or C) at the bottom of the screen. All selected vertices will be assigned to whichever letter is highlighted.
2. Click on each polygon you want added to the selection set. Selected polygons appear in red.
3. Clicking on selected (red) polygons will remove them from the selection set.

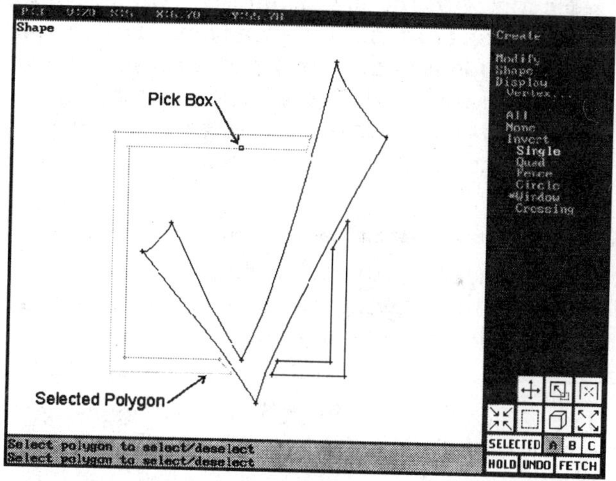

Selecting single polygons.

RELATED COMMANDS

Select/Polygon/Quad, Select/Polygon/Fence, Select/Polygon/Circle

Create
Select
Modify
Shape
Display
Vertex...
Polygon...
All
None
Invert
Single
Quad
Fence
Circle
Window
Crossing

Select/Polygon/Quad

Assigns polygons to a selection set by defining a box around the vertices.

Creating a Selection Set with Quad

1. Activate an icon letter (A, B, or C) at the bottom of the screen. All selected vertices will be assigned to whichever letter is highlighted.
2. Define a box around the polygons by clicking to place one corner of the box.

NOTE Selection with the Quad option is affected by the Window and Crossing options. Only one option can be active at a time. When the Window mode is active, only polygons *totally enclosed* within the defined region are included in the selection set. when the Crossing mode is active, all polygons *enclosed*, *crossing* or *touching* the defined region are included in the selection set. See *Select/Polygon/Window* and *Select/Polygon/Crossing*.

3. Move the mouse diagonally to enclose the polygons, then click to set the opposite corner. With the Window mode active, all polygons within the box are selected. Selected polygons appear in red.

NOTE The Quad option is affected by the Region-Toggle switch. See *Info–System Options*. By default, Region Toggle is set to ON, meaning polygons switch state each time you select them. If you turn region toggle OFF, polygons will not be deselected. You can hold down the [Alt] key while defining the Quad, however. This will deselect all polygons within the Quad, regardless of the Region Toggle setting.

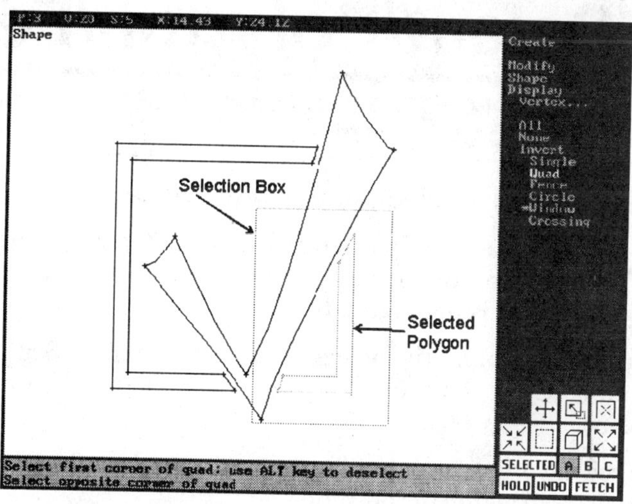

Selecting a polygon with the Quad–Window option.

RELATED COMMANDS

Select/Polygon/Single, Select/Polygon/Fence, Select/Polygon/Circle, Select/Polygon/Window, Select/Polygon/Crossing

Create
Select
Modify
Shape
Display
Vertex...
Polygon...
All
None
Invert
Single
Quad
Fence
Circle
Window
Crossing

Select/Polygon/Fence

Assigns polygons to a selection set by defining a polygon around the vertices.

Creating a Selection Set with Fence

1. Activate an icon letter (A, B, or C) at the bottom of the screen. All selected polygons will be assigned to whichever letter is highlighted.
2. Define a polygon around the objects you want to select. Begin by clicking to set a point. Click the mouse to create a segment, then click to set a second point.
3. Continue setting points and creating segments until all objects you want selected are enclosed within the polygon.

> **NOTE** Selection with the Fence option is affected by the Window and Crossing options. Only one option may be active at a time. When the Window mode is active, only polygons *totally enclosed* within the defined region are included in the selection set. When the Crossing mode is active, all polygons *enclosed*, *crossing* or *touching* the defined region are included in the selection set. See *Select/Polygon/Window* and *Select/Polygon/Crossing*.

4. Close the polygon created with the fence and complete the selection set by either clicking at the first point in the fence or pressing the **Spacebar**. With the Window mode active, all objects within the fence are selected. Selected objects appear in red.

> **NOTE** The Fence option is affected by the Region-Toggle switch. See *Info–System Options*. Region Toggle is set to **ON** by default, meaning polygons switch state each time you select them. If you turn Region Toggle **OFF**, polygons will not be deselected. Holding down the [Alt] key while defining the Fence will deselect all polygons within the fence regardless of the Region Toggle setting.

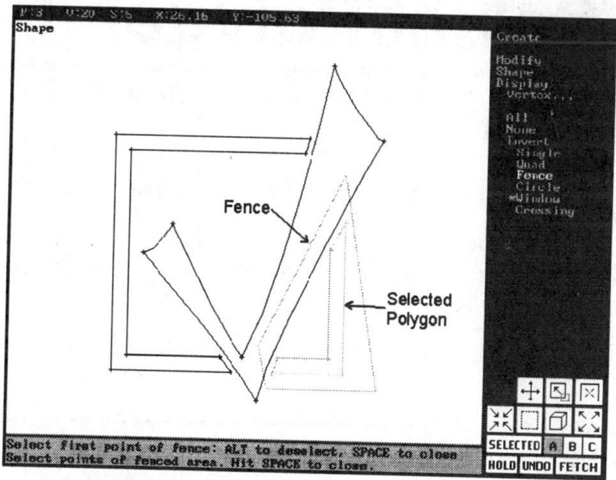

Selecting polygons with the Fence–Window option.

RELATED COMMANDS

Select/Polygon/Single, Select/Polygon/Quad, Select/Polygon/Circle, Select/Polygon/Window, Select/Polygon/Crossing

```
Create
Select
Modify
Shape
Display
  Vertex...
  Polygon...
  All
  None
  Invert
    Single
    Quad
    Fence
    Circle
    Window
    Crossing
```

Select/Polygon/Circle

Assigns polygons to a selection set by defining a circle around the polygons.

Creating a Selection Set with Circle

1. Activate an icon letter (A, B, or C) at the bottom of the screen. All selected polygons will be assigned to whichever letter is highlighted.
2. Define a circle around the polygons by first clicking to set the center of the circle.

> **NOTE** Selection with the Circle option is affected by the Window and Crossing options. Only one option may be active at a time. When the Window mode is active, only polygons totally enclosed within the defined region are included in the selection set. When the Crossing mode is active, all polygons enclosed, crossing or touching the defined region are included in the selection set. See *Select/Polygon/Window* and *Select/Polygon/Crossing*.

3. Move the mouse to define the diameter of the circle. With the Window mode active, all polygons within the circle are selected. Selected polygons appear in red.

> **NOTE** The Circle option is affected by the Region-Toggle switch. See *Info–System Options*. By default, Region Toggle is set to ON, meaning polygons switch state each time you select them. If you turn Region Toggle OFF, polygons will not be deselected. Holding down the a key while defining the circle will deselect all polygons within the Circle, regardless of the Region Toggle setting.

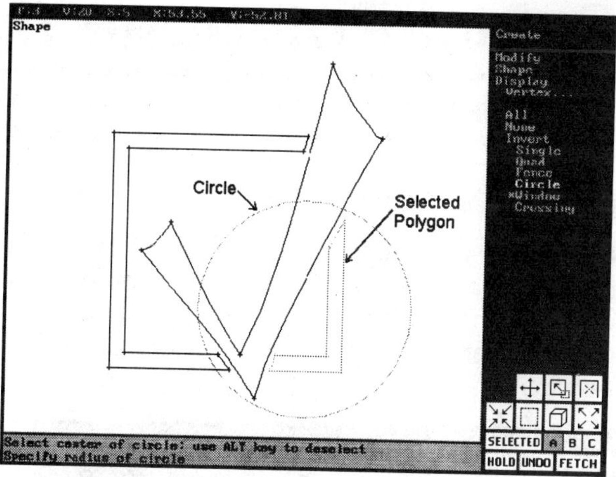

Selecting polygons with the Circle–Window option.

RELATED COMMANDS

Select/Polygon/Single, Select/Polygon/Quad, Select/Polygon/Fence, Select/Polygon/Window, Select/Polygon/Crossing

Create
Select
Modify
Shape
Display
Vertex...
Polygon...
All
None
Invert
Single
Quad
Fence
Circle
Window
Crossing

Select/Polygon/Window

Affects regional selection by only selecting objects that are totally enclosed within the defined region.

Using the Window Option

Used in combination with the *Select/Polygon/Quad, Select/Polygon/Fence,* and *Select/Polygon/Circle* commands. When the Window mode is active, all objects *totally enclosed* within the region defined by any of the previous commands are included in the selection set.

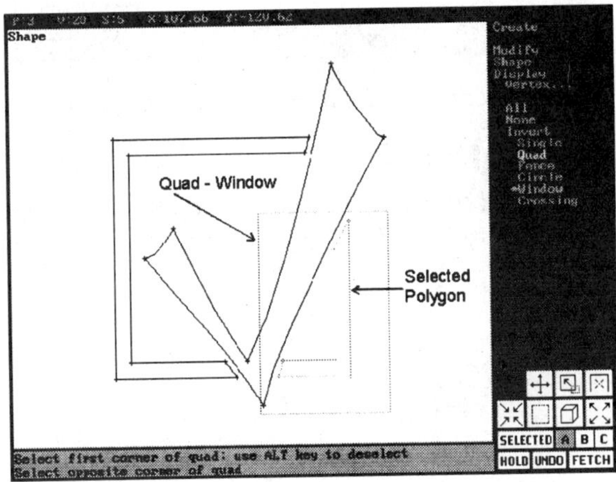

Selecting a polygon with the Quad–Window option.

RELATED COMMANDS

Select/Polygon/Quad, Select/Polygon/Fence, Select/Polygon/Circle, Select/Polygon/Crossing

Create
Select
Modify
Shape
Display
Vertex...
Polygon...
All
None
Invert
Single
Quad
Fence
Circle
Window
Crossing

Select/Polygon/Crossing

Affects regional selection by selecting objects that touch, are enclosed by, or cross the defined region.

Using the Crossing Option

Used in combination with the *Select/Polygon/Quad, Select/Polygon/Fence,* and *Select/Polygon/Circle* commands. When the Crossing mode is active, all objects *touching, crossing,* or *inside* the region defined by any of the previous commands are included in the selection set.

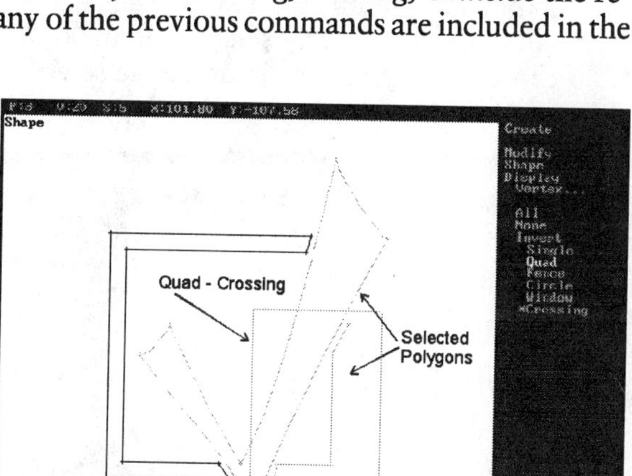

Selecting a polygon with the Quad–Crossing option.

RELATED COMMANDS

Select/Polygon/Single, Select/Polygon/Quad, Select/Polygon/Fence, Select/Polygon/Circle, Select/Polygon/Window

Create
Select
Modify
Shape
Display
Vertex...
Polygon...
All
None
Invert

Select/All

All polygons are assigned to the current selection set.

Using the All Option

When you use the *Select/All* command, all polygons in the 2D Shaper turn red, indicating they are selected.

> **NOTE** The current state of all selected objects is ignored when using *Select/All*. Any previously selected items do not toggle to an unselected state. If there are any objects in an active selection set, the set is replaced by a new selection set containing all polygons.

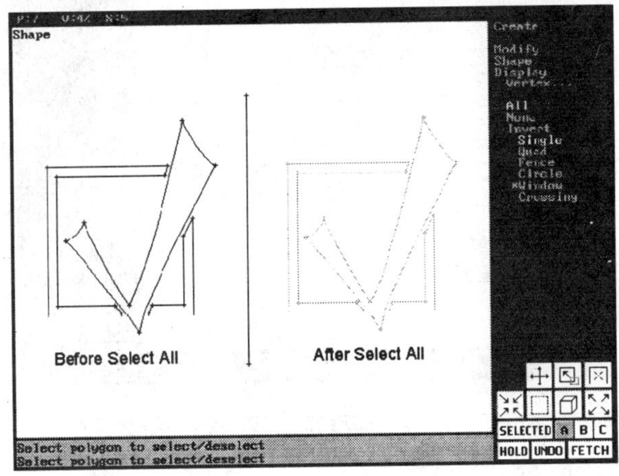

Selecting all polygons.

RELATED COMMANDS

Select/None, Select/Invert

Select/None

Create
Select
Modify
Shape
Display
Vertex...
Polygon...
All
None
Invert

Any previously selected polygons are deselected.

Using the None Option

When you use *Select/None*, all polygons in the 2D Shaper turn white, indicating they are not selected.

> **NOTE** The current state of all selected objects is ignored when using *Select/None*. Any previously selected items do not toggle to an unselected state. If there are any objects in an active selection set, the set is replaced by a new selection set containing all polygons.

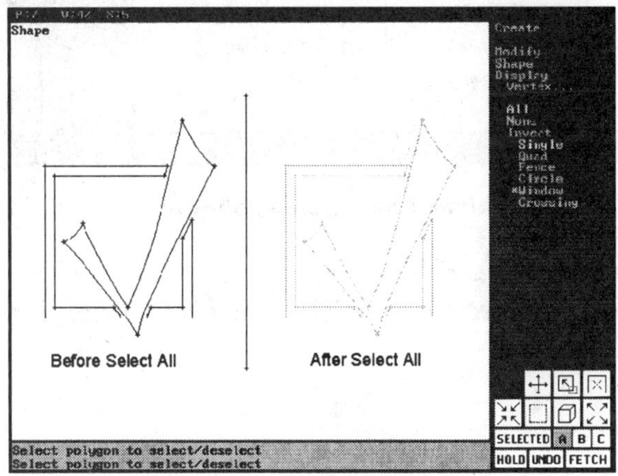

The Select/None option.

RELATED COMMANDS

Select/All, Select/Invert

Create
Select
Modify
Shape
Display
Vertex...
Polygon...
All
None
Invert

Select/Invert

The selection state of all geometry is reversed, with selected objects becoming unselected and vice versa.

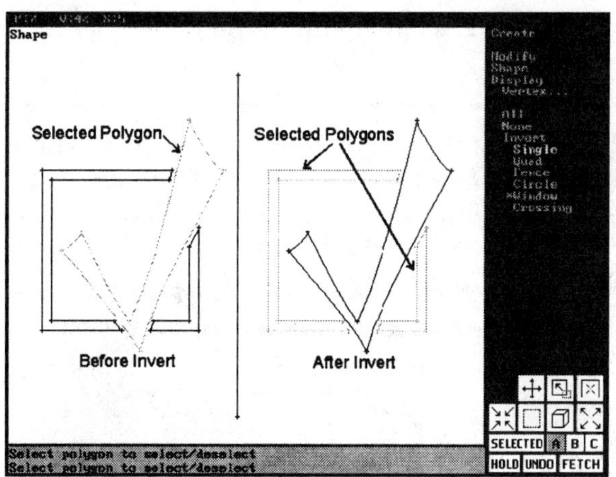

Inverting selected polygons.

RELATED COMMANDS

Select/Polygon/Single, Select/Polygon/Quad, Select/Polygon/Fence, Select/Polygon/Circle

Modify/Vertex/Move

Create
Select
Modify
Vertex...
Segment...
Polygon...
Axis...
Move
Rotate
Scale
Skew
Adjust
Linear
Curve
Weld
Delete

Moves a vertex and adjusts its spline values.

How to Move a Vertex

1. Select the vertex you want to move. You can select more than one, or create a selection set of vertices. See *Select/Vertex/Quad, Select/Vertex/Fence,* and *Select/Vertex/Circle.*
2. As you move the mouse, the selected vertices will move. You can use the [Tab] key to control horizontal and vertical movement.
3. Click to place the vertex, or right-click to cancel the operation.

TIP While the vertex is attached to the mouse, you can alter the curvature of the segments on both sides of the vertex by holding down the mouse button. This displays the directional arrows, allowing you to alter the curvature of the segments on both sides of the vertex.

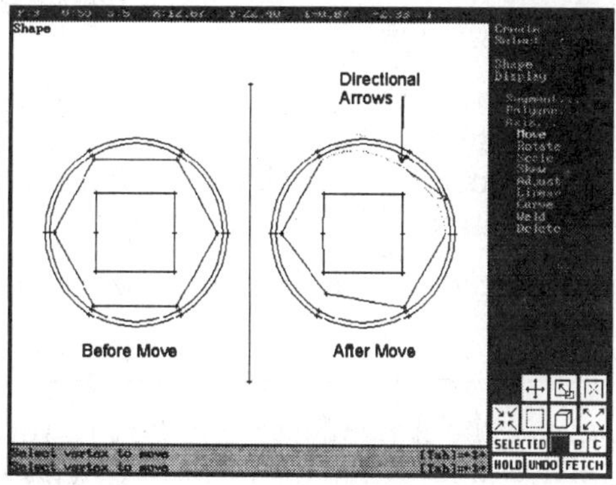

The directional arrows used to alter segment curvature on both sides of the vertex.

NOTE If you move an end vertex of an open polygon over the other end vertex of the *same* polygon, the polygon is automatically closed. If you move an end vertex of an open polygon over the end of a *different* polygon, 3D Studio responds with an alert box, asking you if you want to connect the vertices. Select **Yes** if you want the vertices connected; **No** to leave them unconnected.

RELATED COMMANDS

Select/Vertex/Quad, Select/Vertex/Fence, and Select/Vertex/Circle

Create
Select
Modify
Vertex...
Segment...
Polygon...
Axis...
Move
Rotate
Scale
Skew
Adjust
Linear
Curve
Weld
Delete

Modify/Vertex/Rotate

Rotates a single vertex around the global axis, and multiple vertices around the local or global axis.

Rotating a Single Vertex

1. Select the vertex to rotate.
2. As you move the mouse, the vertex is rotated about the global axis. The global axis is positioned at the 0X, 0Y origin of the 2D Shaper (the center of the drawing area). You can display the global axis by selecting *Modify/Axis/Show*. It appears as a small black X. You can also reposition the global axis. See *Modify/axis/Place* and *Modify/Axis/Center*.
3. Click to place the vertex in its new location, or right-click to cancel the command.

Rotating Multiple Vertices

1. Create a selection set of the vertices you wish to rotate and turn on the **Selected** button in the icon panel. See *Select/Vertex/Quad*, *Select/Vertex/Fence*, and *Select/Vertex/Circle*.
2. You can rotate the selected vertices about the global axis or the local axis. The local axis is positioned at the center of the selected vertices. To rotate the vertices about the local axis, click on the Local Axis icon in the icon panel. The local axis cannot be displayed.
3. Click to place the selected vertices in their new location, or right-click to cancel the command.

> **TIP** You can use the Angle Snap function to rotate single or multiple vertices a specified distance. See *Views–Drawing Aids* and *Views–Use Snap*.

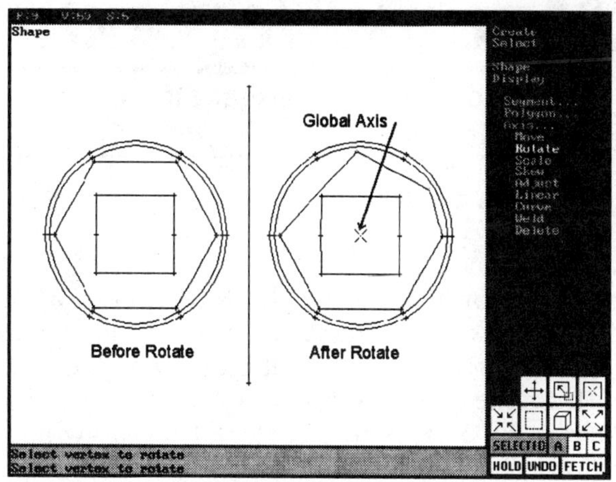

Rotating selected vertices about the global axis.

RELATED COMMANDS

Modify/Axis/Show, Modify/Axis/Place, Modify/Axis/Center, Select/Vertex/Quad, Select/Vertex/Fence, Select/Vertex/Circle, Views–Drawing Aids, Views–Use Snap.

Create
Select
Modify
Vertex...
Segment...
Polygon...
Axis...
Move
Rotate
Scale
Skew
Adjust
Linear
Curve
Weld
Delete

Modify/Vertex/Scale

Used to compress or expand portions of a polygon by selecting single or multiple vertices.

Scaling a Single Vertex

1. Select the vertex to scale.
2. As you move the mouse and scale the vertex, portions of the polygon attached to the vertex are compressed or expanded. You can use the Tab key to control horizontal and vertical movement. The compression and expansion is from the global axis. The global axis is positioned at the 0X, 0Y origin of the 2D Shaper (the center of the drawing area). You can display the global axis by selecting *Modify/Axis/Show*. It appears as a small black X. You can also reposition the global axis. See *Modify/Axis/Place* and *Modify/Axis/Center*.
3. Click to place the vertex in its new location, or right-click to cancel the command.

Scaling Multiple Vertices

1. Create a selection set of the vertices you wish to scale and turn on the **Selected** button in the Icon panel. See *Select/Vertex/Quad*, *Select/Vertex/Fence*, and *Select/Vertex/Circle*.
2. You can scale the selected vertices about the global axis or local axis. The local axis is positioned at the center of the selected vertices. To scale the vertices about the local axis, click on the Local Axis icon in the icon panel. The local axis cannot be displayed.
3. Click to place the selected vertices in their new location, or right-click to cancel the command.

You can use the Snap function to scale single or multiple vertices a specified dsistance. See *Views–Drawing Aids* and *Views–Use Snap*.

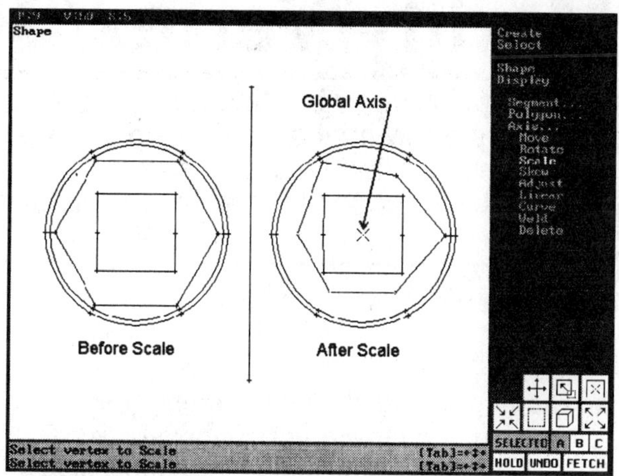

Scaling selected vertices about the global axis.

RELATED COMMANDS

Modify/Axis/Show, Modify/Axis/Place, Modify/Axis/Center, Select/Vertex/Quad, Select/Vertex/Fence, Select/Vertex/Circle, Views–Drawing Aids, Views–Use Snap.

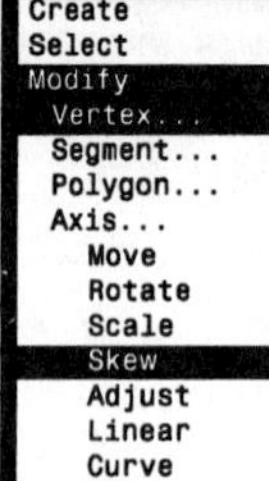

Modify/Vertex/Skew

Modifies a polygon by deforming one or multiple vertices on a plane with the local or global axis. When skewing, all vertices that lie on the same plane maintain their relationship to each other; only their distance to the axis changes.

Skewing a Single Vertex

1. Select the vertex to skew.
2. As you move the mouse and skew the vertex, portions of the polygon attached to the vertex are moved horizontally or vertically. You can use the [Tab] key to control horizontal and vertical movement. The horizontal and vertical movements are from the global axis. The global axis is positioned at the 0X, 0Y origin of the 2D Shaper (the center of the drawing area). You can display the global axis by selecting *Modify/Axis/Show*. It appears as a small black X. You can also reposition the global axis. See *Modify/Axis/Place* and *Modify/Axis/Center*.
3. Click to place the vertex in its new location, or right-click to cancel the command.

Skewing Multiple Vertices

1. Create a selection set of the vertices you wish to skew and turn on the **Selected** button in the Icon panel. See *Select/Vertex/Quad*, *Select/Vertex/Fence*, and *Select/Vertex/Circle*.
2. You can skew the selected vertices on a plane parallel to the global or local axis. The local axis is positioned at the center of the selected vertices. The greater the distance the plane of vertices is from the axis, the farther away it moves. To scale the vertices about the local axis, click on the Local Axis icon in the icon panel. The local axis cannot be displayed.
3. Click to place the selected vertices in their new location, or right-click to cancel the command.

You can use the Snap function to skew single or multiple vertices a specified distance. See *Views–Drawing Aids* and *Views–Use Snap*.

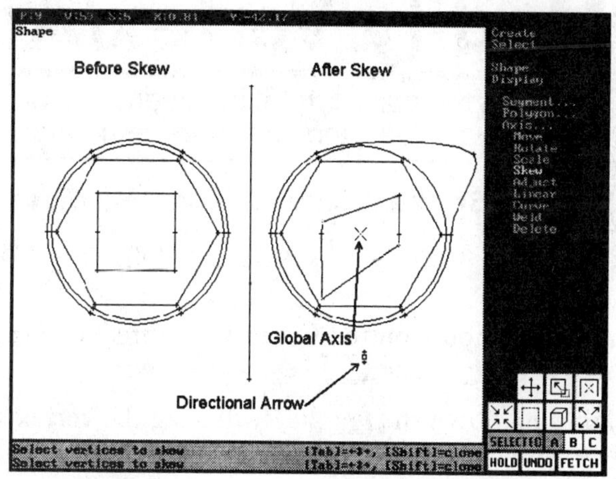

Skewing selected vertices about the global axis.

RELATED COMMANDS

Modify/Axis/Show, Modify/Axis/Place, Modify/Axis/Center, Select/Vertex/Quad, Select/Vertex/Fence, Select/Vertex/Circle, Views–Drawing Aids, Views–Use Snap.

```
Create
Select
Modify
  Vertex...
   Segment...
   Polygon...
   Axis...
     Move
     Rotate
     Scale
     Skew
     Adjust
     Linear
     Curve
     Weld
     Delete
```

Modify/Vertex/Adjust

Changes the curvature of the segments on either side of a vertex, or alters the curvature of multiple vertices.

Altering Segment Curvature on Both Sides of a Vertex

1. Select a vertex whose connecting segments you want to alter.
2. Hold down the left mouse button to cause the direction arrows to appear. You can also use the Ctrl and Alt keys as follows:

   Ctrl Key: Holding down the Ctrl key will drag the vertex without rotating the arrows.

   Alt Key: Holding down the Alt key will alter the angle of the yellow vector.
3. As you move the mouse, the arrows change size and rotate, altering the curvature of the segments.
4. After obtaining the desired curvature, release the left mouse button. If the resulting curvature is not what you wanted, press the **Undo** button.

Altering Segment Curvature with Multiple Vertices

1. Create a selection set of the vertices you wish to adjust and turn on the **Selected** button in the Icon panel. See *Select/Vertex/Quad*, *Select/Vertex/Fence*, and *Select/Vertex/Circle*.
2. Place the cursor on any one of the selected vertices and press and hold the left mouse button. This causes the direction arrows to appear.
3. Alter the curvature of the selected vertices by moving the mouse. You can also use the Ctrl and Alt keys modify the vertices further.
4. Once you have obtained the desired curve, release the left mouse button. Pressing the **Undo** button will undo the modification.

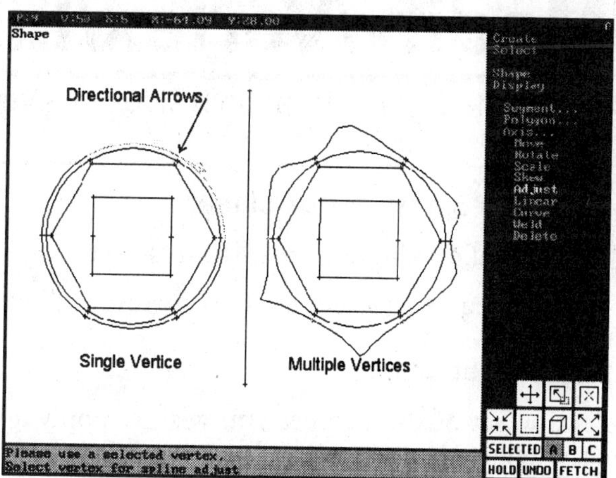

Adjusting single and multiple vertices.

RELATED COMMANDS

Select/Vertex/Quad, Select/Vertex/Fence, Select/Vertex/Circle

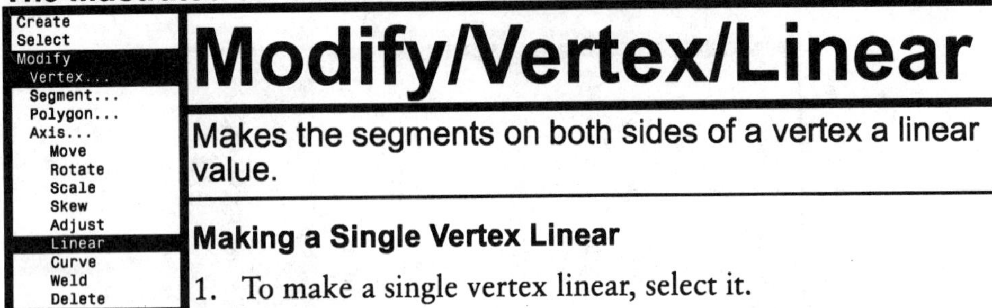

Modify/Vertex/Linear

Makes the segments on both sides of a vertex a linear value.

Making a Single Vertex Linear

1. To make a single vertex linear, select it.
2. To make a straight segment, select the two corresponding vertices.

Making Multiple Vertices Linear

1. Create a selection set of the vertices you wish to apply a linear value to and turn on the **Selected** button in the Icon panel. See *Select/Vertex/Quad*, *Select/Vertex/Fence*, and *Select/Vertex/Circle*.
2. Select any vertex. Clicking **Undo** will undo the Linear operation.

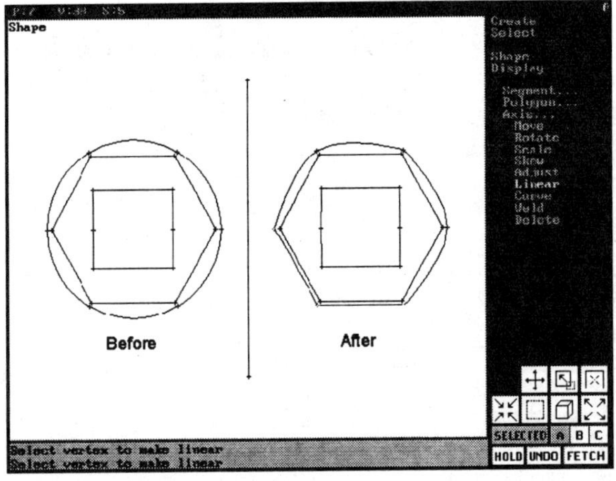

Applying a linear value to selected vertices.

RELATED COMMANDS

Select/Vertex/Quad, Select/Vertex/Fence, and Select/Vertex/Circle

Modify/Vertex/Curve

Create
Select
Modify
Vertex...
Segment...
Polygon...
Axis...
Move
Rotate
Scale
Skew
Adjust
Linear
Curve
Weld
Delete

Applies a default curve value to single or multiple vertices.

Applying a Curve to a Single Vertex

1. To apply a curve segment to a vertex, select it.

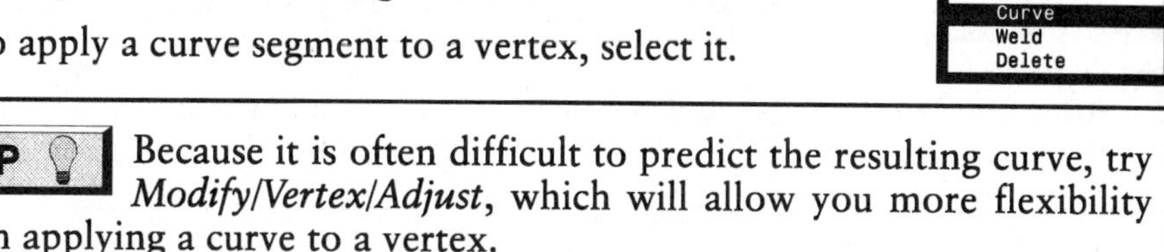

TIP Because it is often difficult to predict the resulting curve, try *Modify/Vertex/Adjust*, which will allow you more flexibility when applying a curve to a vertex.

Applying a Curve to Multiple Vertices

1. Create a selection set of the vertices you wish to curve and turn on the **Selected** button in the Icon panel. See *Select/Vertex/Quad*, *Select/Vertex/Fence*, and *Select/Vertex/Circle*.
2. Select any vertex. Clicking **Undo** will undo the Linear operation.

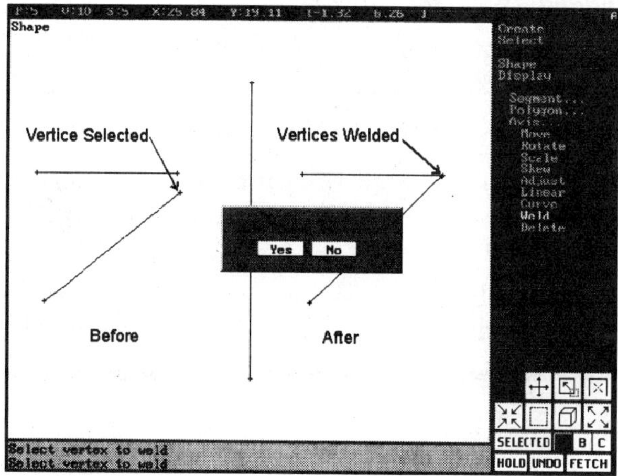

Applying a curve to single and multiple vertices.

RELATED COMMANDS

Modify/Vertex/Adjust, Select/Vertex/Quad, Select/Vertex/Fence, and Select/Vertex/Circle

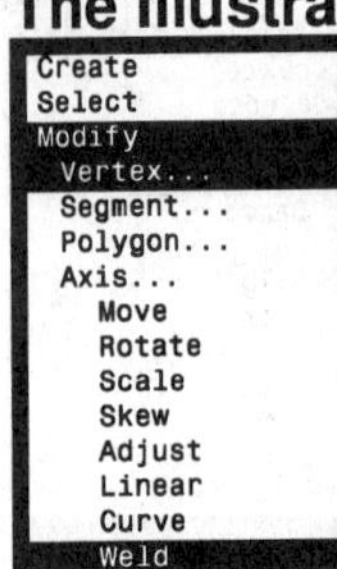

Modify/Vertex/Weld

Welds coincidental vertices together.

Welding Two Adjacent Vertices

1. Select a vertex and drag it to the position of another vertex and click.
2. After confirming you want the vertex welded, one vertex is deleted. Any faces that became collinear as a result of the operation are also deleted.

> **NOTE** To weld vertices together, they must be within the area specified by the Weld Threshold parameter. This can be set in the System Options dialog box, located in *Info–System Options*.

Welding Multiple Vertices

1. Create a selection set of the vertices you wish to weld together and turn on the **Selected** button in the Icon panel. See *Select/Vertex/Quad*, *Select/Vertex/Fence*, and *Select/Vertex/Circle*.
2. Select anywhere on the screen, and confirm you want the vertices welded.

> **TIP** You can use the *Modify/Vertex/Weld* option for the following:
>
> 1. Clean-up imported **.dxf* files. First use *Select/All*, then use *Modify/Vertex/Weld* with the Selected button turned on. This will clean up the object, welding all vertices and deleting duplicates.
> 2. Selecting an entire object and performing a weld can minimize the object size by deleting duplicate vertices and ensuring the object integrity.

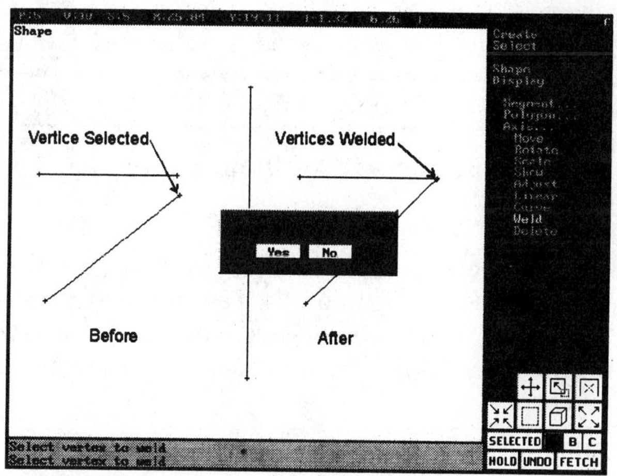

Welding vertices, with the corresponding dialog box.

RELATED COMMANDS

Info-System Options, Select/Vertex/Quad, Select/Vertex/Fence, and Select/Vertex/Circle, Select/All

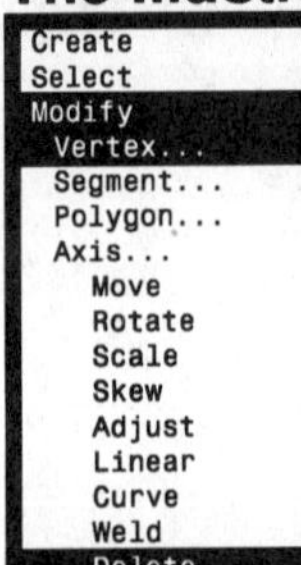

Modify/Vertex/Delete

Deletes one or more vertices.

Deleting Single and Multiple Vertices

1. To delete a single vertice, select it.

2. To delete multiple vertices, first create a selection set of all the vertices you wish to delete. Turn on the **Selected** button in the Icon panel. See *Select/Vertex/Quad*, *Select/Vertex/Fence*, and *Select/Vertex/Circle*. Clicking anywhere on the screen will delete the selected vertices. Selecting **Undo** will replace the vertice.

When you delete a vertex from a polygon, you also decrease the number of segments.

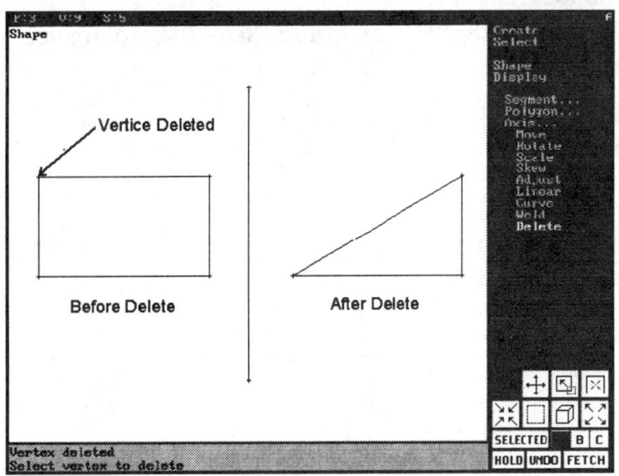

Deleting a vertex decreases the number of segments.

RELATED COMMANDS

Select/Vertex/Quad, Select/Vertex/Fence Select/Vertex/Circle

Modify/Segment/Adjust

Create
Select
Modify
Shape
Display
Vertex...
Segment...
Polygon...
Axis...
Adjust
Linear
Curve
Break
Refine
Delete

Alters the curvature of a segment along with the vertices at each end of the segment.

Adjusting a Segment

1. Select the desired segment you want to adjust.
2. Continuing to hold down the left mouse button causes the direction arrows to appear. You can also use the Ctrl and Alt keys as follows:

   Ctrl Key: Holding down the Ctrl key will drag the vertex without rotating the arrows.

   Alt Key: Holding down the Alt key will alter the angle of the yellow vector.
3. As you move the mouse, the arrows change size and rotate, altering the curvature of the selected segment along with the two segments connected to the vertices of the selected segment.
4. After obtaining the desired curvature, release the left mouse button. If the resulting curvature is not what you wanted, press the **Undo** button.

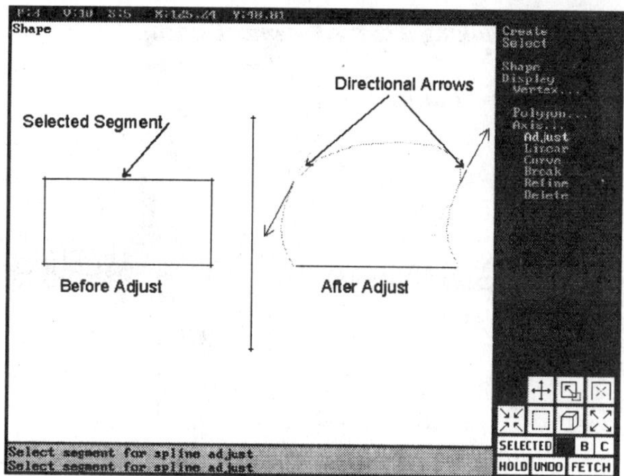

Adjusting a segment.

RELATED COMMANDS

None. Adjusting a segment is like no other command in the 2D shaper. It gives you the ability to manipulate segments in unique ways.

Create
Select
Modify
Shape
Display
Vertex...
Segment...
Polygon...
Axis...
Adjust
Linear
Curve
Break
Refine
Delete

Modify/Segment/Linear

Makes a curved segment linear.

Making a Segment Linear

1. To make a segment linear, select it.

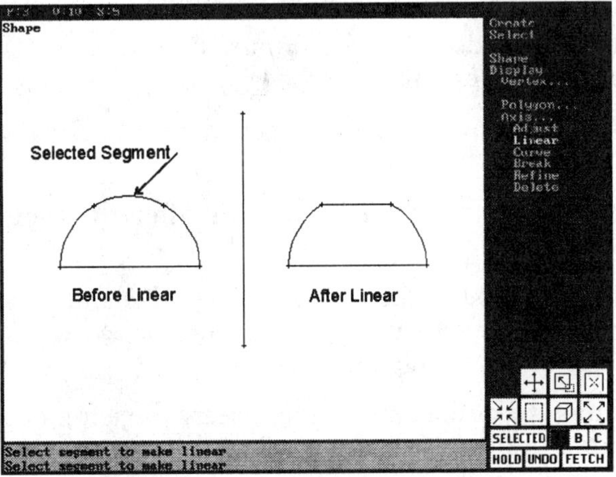

Making a curved segment linear.

RELATED COMMAND

Modify/Vertex/Linear

Modify/Segment/Curve

Applies a curve value to a segment.

Applying a Curve to a Segment

1. To apply a curve to a segment, select it.

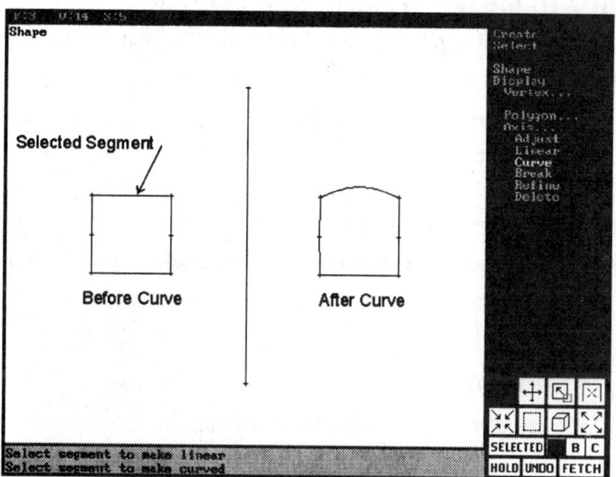

Making a linear segment curved.

RELATED COMMAND

Modify/Vertex/Curve

Create
Select
Modify
Shape
Display
Vertex...
Segment...
Polygon...
Axis...
Adjust
Linear
Curve
Break
Refine
Delete

Modify/Segment/Break

Two vertices are inserted at the selected location, dividing the segment into two parts.

Breaking a Segment

1. To break a segment into two parts, place the cursor at the location where you want it broken and click.

NOTE

Using *Modify/Segment/Break* inserts *two* vertices at the selected location. Because the inserted vertices are on top of each other, they appear as a single vertice. Breaking a single polygon results in two separate polygons; breaking a closed polygon results in an open polygon.

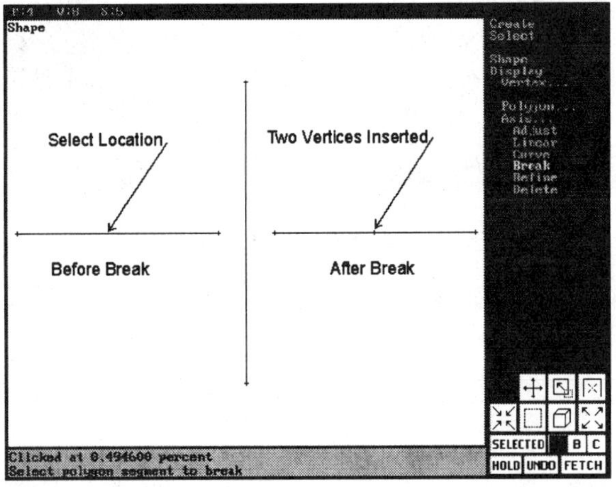

Breaking a segment inserts two vertices at the selected location.

To insert vertices without breaking a segment into separate parts, use *Modify/Segment/Refine.*

RELATED COMMAND

Modify/Segment/Refine

Modify/Segment/Refine

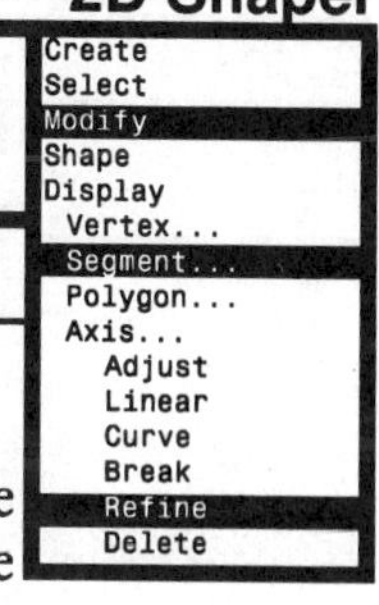

A single vertex is inserted into a segment.

Inserting a Vertex into a Segment

1. To insert a vertex into a segment, place the cursor at the point where you want the vertex inserted and click. The curvature of the segment is not altered.

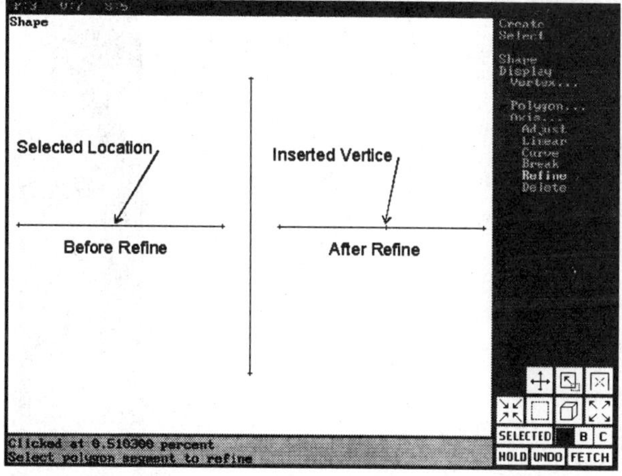

Refining a segment inserts one vertice at the selected location.

> **TIP** You can add selected vertices into the curved portion of a polygon to increase its smoothness. This can be especially effective with text shapes in preparation for lofting.

RELATED COMMAND

Modify/Segment/Break

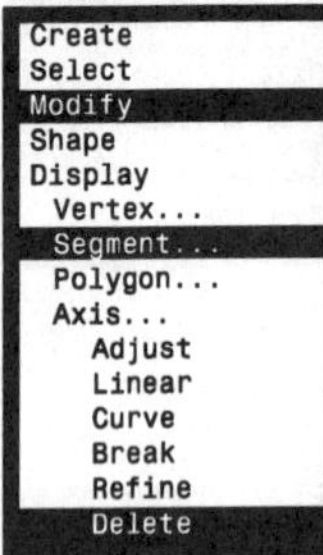

Modify/Segment/Delete

Permanently removes a segment from a polygon.

Deleting a Segment

1. To remove a segment permanently, select it. To restore the deleted segment, select the **Undo** button immediately after completing the deletion.

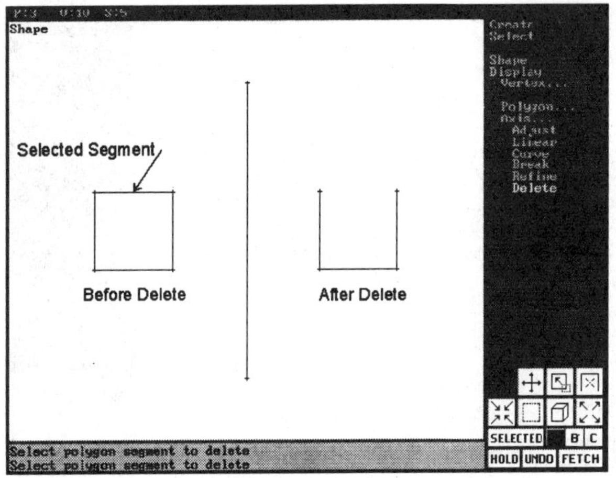

Deleting a segment.

RELATED COMMANDS

Undo, Modify/Vertex/Delete

Modify/Polygon/Move

Select
Modify
Shape
Display
Vertex...
Segment...
Polygon...
Move
Rotate
Scale
Skew
Mirror
Adjust
Linear
Curve
Delete

Moves one or multiple polygons.

Moving a Single Polygon

1. Select the polygon you want to move.

   Ctrl Key: Holding down the [Ctrl] key when selecting the polygon causes it to turn red, indicating that it is in the selected state.

   Shift Key: When selecting the polygon to move, hold down the [⇧Shift] key to create a clone or copy of the polygon. This will leave the original polygon in place, and move a copy of it.

2. Move the polygon to the desired location. You can use the [Tab] key to control horizontal and vertical movement.

3. When the polygon is in the correct location, left-click, or right-click to cancel the move.

NOTE If you move the end vertices of an open polygon over the end vertices of another polygon, you will be prompted to connect the vertices. Select **Yes** to connect the vertices, **No** to leave the vertices unconnected.

Moving Multiple Polygons

1. Create a selection set of the polygons you wish to move and turn on the **Selected** button in the Icon panel. See *Select/Polygon/Quad*, *Select/Polygon/Fence*, and *Select/Polygon/Circle*.

2. You can also create clones or copies of the selected polygons. This will leave the original polygons included in the selection set in place and move a copy. Before you begin the move on the selection set, hold down the [⇧Shift] key.

3. When the selected polygons are in the correct location, left-click the mouse, or right-click to cancel the command.

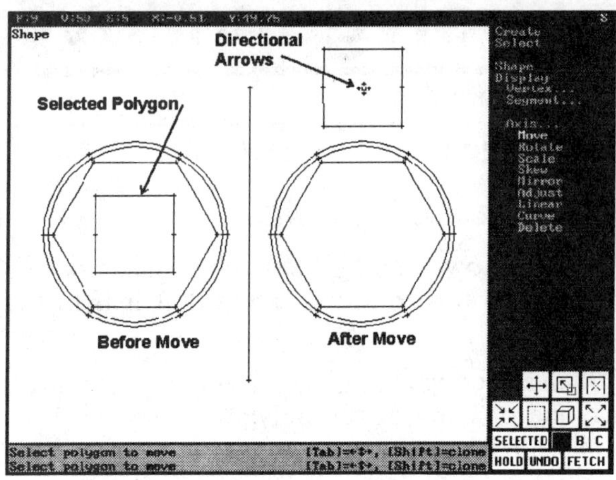

Moving a single polygon.

RELATED COMMANDS

Views–Drawing Aids, Select/Polygon/Quad, Select/Polygon/Fence, Select/Polygon/Circle

Modify/Polygon/Rotate

Select
Modify
Shape
Display
Vertex...
Segment...
Polygon...
Move
Rotate
Scale
Skew
Mirror
Adjust
Linear
Curve
Delete

Rotates single or multiple polygons about the global or local axis.

Rotating a Single Polygon

1. Select the polygon to rotate. Holding down the Ctrl key when selecting the polygon will cause it to turn red, indicating that it is in the selected state.
2. You can rotate the selected polygon about the global axis or local axis. The global axis is positioned at the 0X, 0Y origin of the 2D Shaper (the center of the drawing area). You can display the global axis by selecting *Modify/Axis/Show*. It appears as a small black X. You can also reposition the global axis. See *Modify/Axis/Place* and *Modify/Axis/Center*. The local axis is positioned at the center of the selected vertices. To rotate the polygon about the local axis, click on the Local Axis icon in the icon panel. The local axis cannot be displayed.
3. As you move the mouse, the polygon is rotated around the selected axis. You can also create a clone or copy of the polygon. This will leave the original polygon in place and move a copy. When selecting the polygon to rotate, hold down the ⇧Shift key.
4. Rotate the polygon to the desired location. When the polygon is at the correct rotation, left-click, or right-click to cancel the move.

> **NOTE** If you rotate the end vertices of an open polygon over the end vertices of another polygon, you will be prompted to connect the vertices. Select **Yes** to connect the vertices, **No** to leave the vertices unconnected.

Rotating Multiple Polygons

1. Create a selection set of the polygons you wish to rotate and turn on the **Selected** button in the icon panel. See *Select/Polygon/Quad*, *Select/Polygon/Fence*, and *Select/Polygon/Circle*.
2. Set the local or global axis to rotate the polygon. As you move the mouse, the selected polygons are rotated about the selected axis. You can also use the ⇧Shift key and create clones or copies of the selected polygons.
3. After rotating the selected polygons to the correct location, left–click. You can also right-click to cancel the rotation.

You can use the Angle snap to rotate single or multiple polygons a specific distance. See *Views–Drawing Aids* and *Views–Angle Snap*.

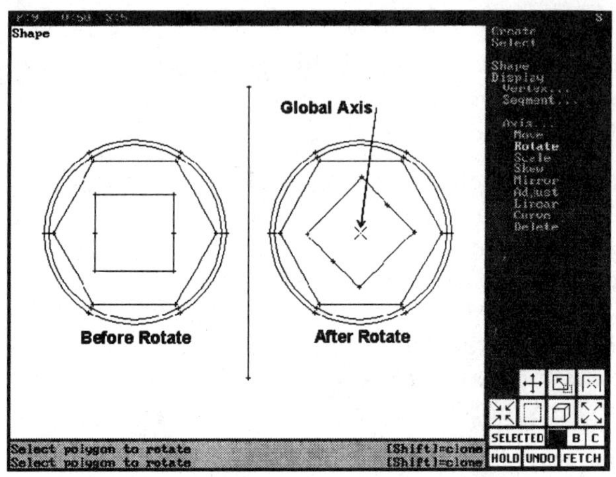

Rotating a polygon about the global axis.

RELATED COMMANDS

Modify/Axis/Show, Modify/Axis/Place, Modify/Axis/Center, Select/Polygon/Quad, Select/Polygon/Fence, Select/Polygon/Circle, Views–Drawing Aids, Views–Angle Snap

Modify/Polygon/Scale

Select
Modify
Shape
Display
Vertex...
Segment...
Polygon...
Move
Rotate
Scale
Skew
Mirror
Adjust
Linear
Curve
Delete

Scales single or multiple polygons to and from the local or global axis.

Scaling a Single Polygons

1. Select the polygon to scale. You can also hold down the [Ctrl] key when selecting the polygon that causes it to turn red, indicating that it is in the selected state.
2. As you move the mouse to scale the polygon, it increases in size as it is moved away from the axis, and decreases in size as it moves toward the axis. You can use the [Tab] key to control horizontal and vertical scaling. You can of scale the selected polygon from the global axis or local axis. The global axis is positioned at the 0X, 0Y origin of the 2D Shaper (the center of the drawing area). You can display the global axis by selecting *Modify/Axis/Show*. It appears as a small black X. You can also reposition the global axis. See *Modify/Axis/Place* and *Modify/Axis/Center*. The local axis is positioned at the center of the selected vertices. To scale the polygon about the local axis, click on the Local Axis icon in the icon panel. The local axis cannot be displayed.
3. You can also create a clone or copy of the polygon. This will leave the original polygon in place and scale a copy. When selecting the polygon, hold down the [Shift] key. After scaling the polygon, left-click, or right-click to cancel the scale.

NOTE If you scale an open polygon and its end vertices are over the end vertices of another polygon, you will be prompted to connect the vertices. Select **Yes** to connect the vertices, **No** to leave the vertices unconnected.

Scaling Multiple Polygons

1. Create a selection set of the polygons you wish to scale and turn on the **Selected** button in the Icon panel. See *Select/Polygon/Quad*, *Select/Polygon/Fence*, and *Select/Polygon/Circle*.
2. Set the local or global axis to scale the polygon around. As you move the mouse, the selected polygons are scaled about the selected axis. You can also use the [Shift] key and create clones or copies of the selected polygons.
3. After scaling the selected polygons to the correct size, left-click. You can also right-click to cancel the scale.

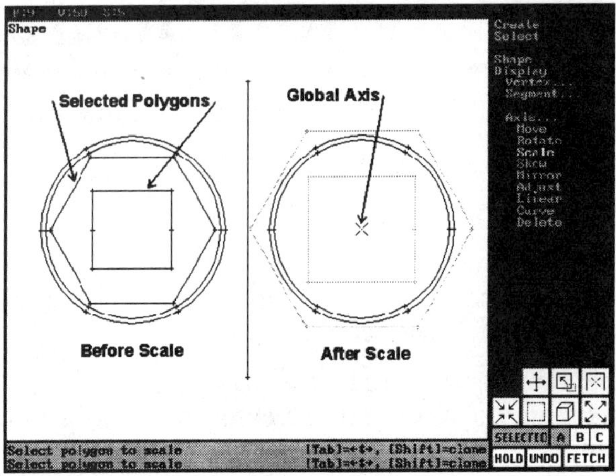

Scaling selected polygons about the global axis.

RELATED COMMANDS

Modify/Axis/Show, Modify/Axis/Place, Modify/Axis/Center, Select/Polygon/Quad, Select/Polygon/Fence, Select/Polygon/Circle

Modify/Polygon/Skew

Select
Modify
Shape
Display
Vertex...
Segment...
Polygon...
Move
Rotate
Scale
Skew
Mirror
Adjust
Linear
Curve
Delete

Modifies a polygon by deforming it on a plane parallel to the local or global axis.

Skewing a Single Polygon

1. Select the polygon to skew. You can also hold down the Ctrl key when selecting the polygon which causes it to turn red, indicating that it is in the selected state.

2. As you move the mouse to skew the polygon, it distorts horizontally and vertically. You can use the Tab key to control horizontal and vertical skewing. You can of skew the selected polygon about the global axis or local axis. The global axis is positioned at the 0X, 0Y origin of the 2D Shaper (the center of the drawing area). You can display the global axis by selecting *Modify/Axis/Show*. It appears as a small black X. You can also reposition the global axis. See *Modify/Axis/Place* and *Modify/Axis/Center*. The local axis is positioned at the center of the selected vertices. To skew the polygon about the local axis, click on the Local Axis icon in the icon panel. The local axis cannot be displayed.

3. You can also create a clone or copy of the polygon. This will leave the original polygon in place, and skew a copy. When selecting the polygon, hold down the Shift key. After skewing the polygon, left-click, or right-click to cancel the scale.

> **NOTE** If you skew an open polygon and its end vertices are over the end vertices of another polygon, you will be prompted to connect the vertices. Select **Yes** to connect the vertices, **No** to leave the vertices unconnected.

Skewing Multiple Polygons

1. Create a selection set of the polygons you wish to skew and turn on the Selected button in the Icon panel. See *Select/Polygon/Quad, Select/Polygon/Fence,* and *Select/Polygon/Circle.*

2. Set the local or global axis to skew the polygon around. As you move the mouse, the selected polygons are skewed horizontally or vertically about the selected axis. You can also use the Shift key and create clones or copies of the selected polygons.

3. After skewing the selected polygons to the correct size, left-click. You can also right-click to cancel the scale.

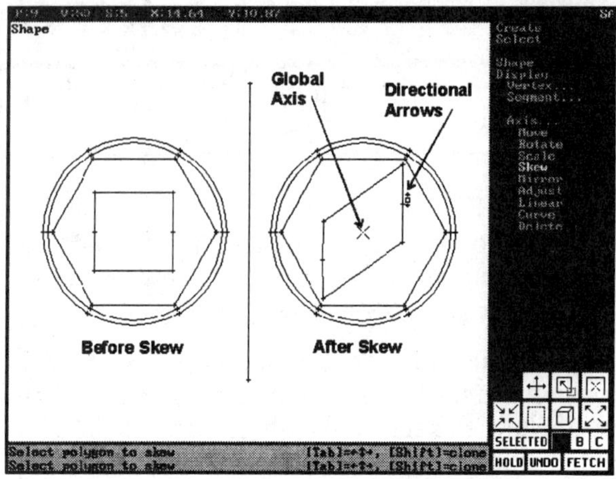

Skewing a polygon about the global axis.

RELATED COMMANDS

Modify/Axis/Show, Modify/Axis/Place, Modify/Axis/Center, Select/Polygon/Quad, Select/Polygon/Fence, Select/Polygon/Circle

Modify/Polygon/Mirror

Select
Modify
Shape
Display
Vertex...
Segment...
Polygon...
Move
Rotate
Scale
Skew
Mirror
Adjust
Linear
Curve
Delete

Flips single or multiple polygons about an imaginary mirror line.

Mirroring a Polygon

1. Select single or multiple polygons. To select multiple polygons, create a selection set of the polygons you wish to mirror and turn on the **Selected** button in the Icon panel. See *Select/Polygon/Quad*, *Select/Polygon/Fence*, and *Select/Polygon/Circle*.
2. Use the arrows to mirror the selected polygons.

   Vertical Arrows: Flip the selected polygons vertically about a horizontal mirror line.

   Horizontal Arrows: Flip the selected polygons horizontally about a vertical mirror line.

   Four Arrows: Flip the selected polygons about a 45–degree angle.
3. Use the [Tab] key to cycle through the arrows. Move the flipped image into position with the mouse. Click to place the flipped image, or right-click to cancel the operation.

Creating a Symmetrical Shape

1. Select the desired open polygons.
2. Hold down the [Shift] key and left-click on the selected polygon.
3. Use the [Tab] key to cycle through the different mirroring options. Move the mirrored copy until its end vertices are directly over the end vertices of the original polygon.
4. Click to place the mirrored copy. You are then prompted to connect the vertices. Select **Yes** to weld the vertices.

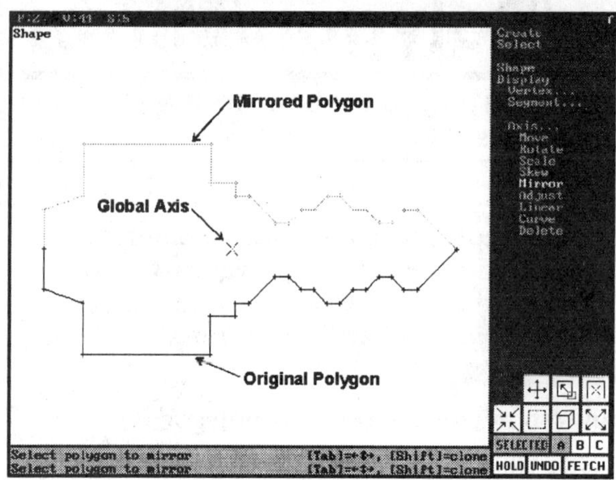

Creating a symmetrical shape with the mirror option.

RELATED COMMANDS

Select/Polygon/Quad, Select/Polygon/Fence, Select/Polygon/Circle

Modify/Polygon/Adjust

Select
Modify
Shape
Display
Vertex...
Segment...
Polygon...
Move
Rotate
Scale
Skew
Mirror
Adjust
Linear
Curve
Delete

By selecting a vertex on a single or multiple polygons, you can alter the curvature of all connected segments.

Altering a Single Polygon

1. Select any vertex in the polygon you want to alter.
2. Holding down the left mouse button causes the direction arrows to appear.
3. While continuing to hold down the mouse button, move the mouse in any direction to size and move the arrows. Although the direction arrows are displayed only for the vertice selected, all non-linear vertices and segments within the polygon are affected.
4. You can use the Ctrl and Alt keys to affect the polygon further while the direction arrows are displayed.
5. After obtaining the desired modification, release the mouse button. Click the **Undo** button to revert the polygon to its previous shape.

NOTE When using the *Modify/Polygon/Adjust* command only *curved* segments are altered. If you select a vertex with a straight segment, its connecting segments are altered, but any other straight segments are not altered.

Altering Multiple Polygons

1. Create a selection set of the polygons you wish to alter and turn on the **Selected** button in the Icon panel. See *Select/Polygon/Quad*, *Select/Polygon/Fence*, and *Select/Polygon/Circle*.
2. Select any vertex on any of the polygons you want to alter and hold down the left mouse button.
3. While continuing to hold down the mouse button, move the mouse in any direction to size and move the direction arrows. All non-linear vertices and segments within all selected polygons are affected. Use the Ctrl and Alt keys to affect the selected polygons further while the direction arrows are displayed.
4. After obtaining the desired modification, release the mouse button. Click the **Undo** button to revert the selected polygons to their previous shape.

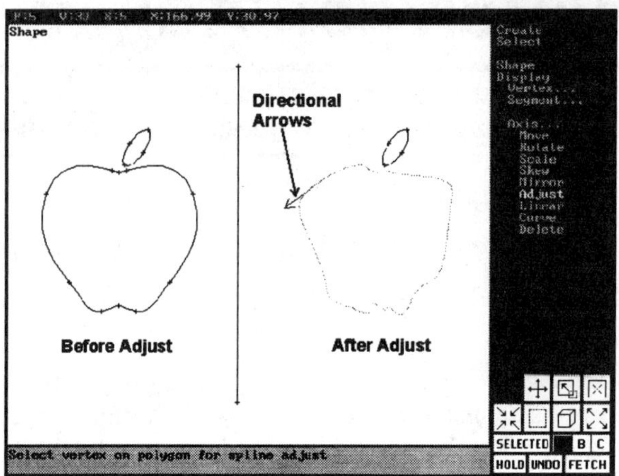

Altering the shape of a selected polygon.

RELATED COMMANDS

Select/Polygon/Quad, Select/Polygon/Fence, Select/Polygon/Circle

VRJC LIBRARY

Modify/Polygon/Linear

Select
Modify
Shape
Display
Vertex...
Segment...
Polygon...
Move
Rotate
Scale
Skew
Mirror
Adjust
Linear
Curve
Delete

Makes all segments of single or multiple polygons linear.

Making a Single Polygon Linear

1. To make a single polygon linear, select it. The resulting polygon will have all straight segments.

Making Multiple Polygons Linear

1. Create a selection set of the polygons you wish to apply a linear value to and turn on the **Selected** button in the Icon panel. See *Select/Polygon/Quad*, *Select/Polygon/Fence*, and *Select/Polygon/Circle*.
2. Select any polygon. Clicking **Undo** will undo the Linear operation.

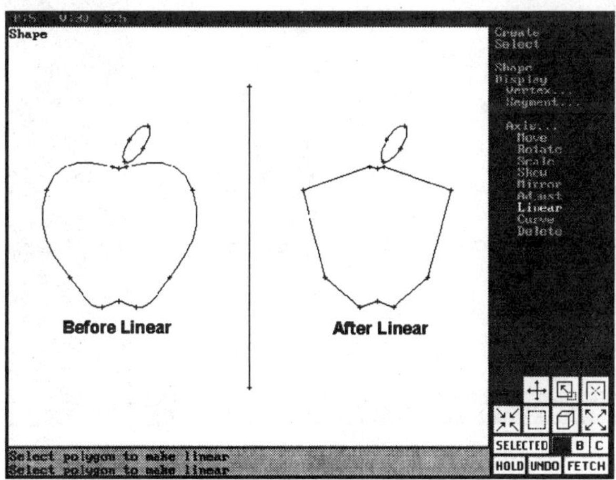

Applying linear values to a single polygon.

RELATED COMMANDS

Select/Polygon/Quad, Select/Polygon/Fence, Select/Polygon/Circle

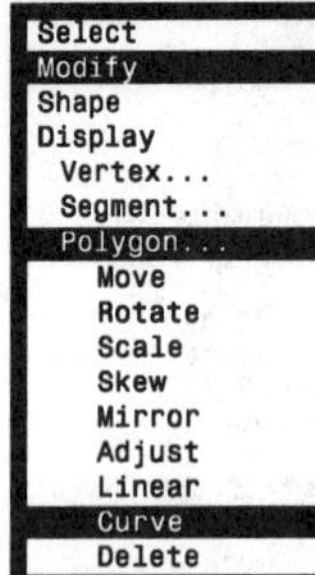

Modify/Polygon/Curve

Applies a curve value to single or multiple polygons.

Applying a Curve to a Single Polygon

1. To apply curves to all segments of a polygon, select it.

Applying a Curve to Multiple Polygons

1. Create a selection set of the polygons you wish to apply curves to curve and turn on the **Selected** button in the Icon panel. See *Select/Polygon/Quad*, *Select/Polygon/Fence*, and *Select/Polygon/Circle*.
2. Select any polygon. Clicking **Undo** will undo the Linear operation.

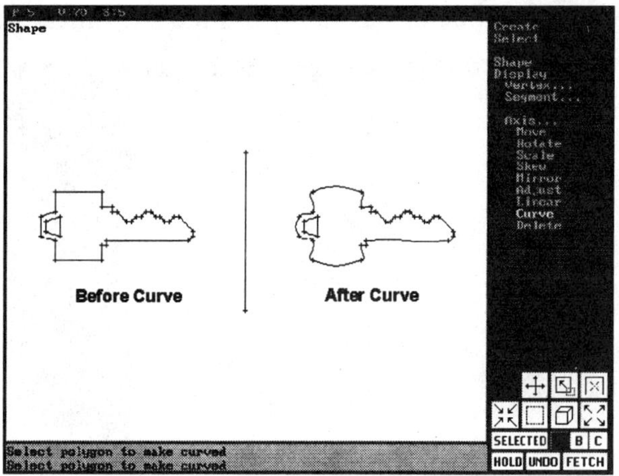

Applying curves to a single polygon.

RELATED COMMANDS

Modify/Polygon/Adjust, Select/Polygon/Quad, Select/Polygon/Fence, Select/Polygon/Circle

Modify/Polygon/Delete

Select
Modify
Shape
Display
Vertex...
Segment...
Polygon...
Move
Rotate
Scale
Skew
Mirror
Adjust
Linear
Curve
Delete

Deletes one or more polygons.

Deleting Single and Multiple Polygons

1. To delete a single polygon, select it.
2. To delete multiple polygons, first create a selection set of all the vertices you wish to delete. Turn on the **Selected** button in the Icon panel. See *Select/Polygon/Quad*, *Select/Polygon/Fence*, and *Select/Polygon/Circle*. Clicking anywhere on the screen will delete the selected polygons. Selecting **Undo** will replace the polygons.

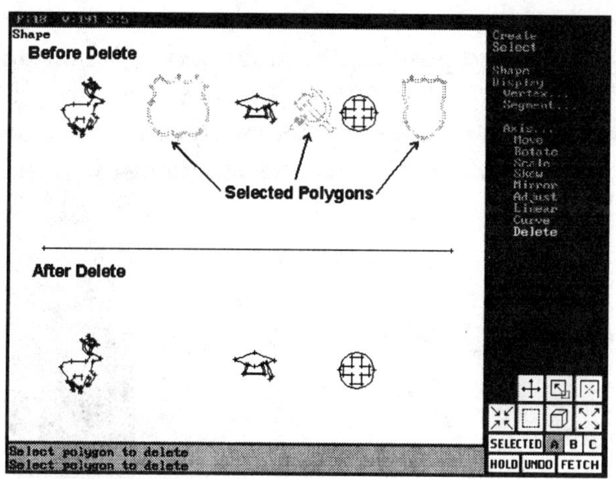

Deleting multiple polygons.

RELATED COMMANDS

Select/Polygon/Quad, Select/Polygon/Fence Select/Polygon/Circle

Create
Select
Modify
Shape
Display
Vertex...
Segment...
Polygon...
Axis...
Place
Center
Show
Hide
Home

Modify/Axis/Place

Repositions the global axis.

Moving the Global Axis

1. To move the global axis, move the cursor to the desired location and click. The axis will appear as a small black X.

If you do not want the axis displayed, you can turn it off with the *Modify/Axis/Hide* command.

You can also position the global axis by entering coordinates directly from the keyboard.

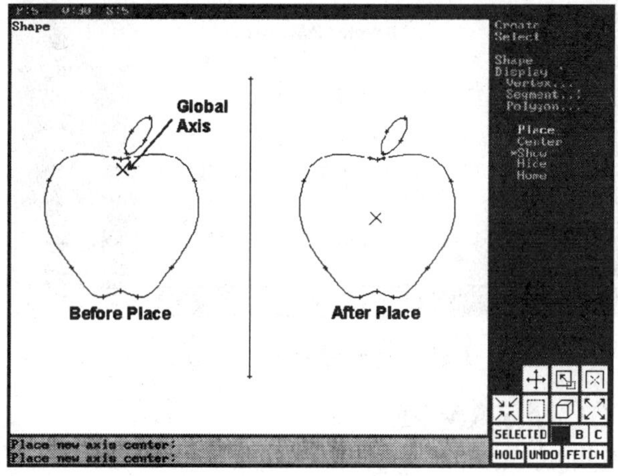

Placing the global axis.

RELATED COMMANDS

Modify/Axis/Hide, Modify/Axis/Center, Modify/Axis/Show, Modify/Axis/Home

Modify/Axis/Center

Create
Select
Modify
Shape
Display
Vertex...
Segment...
Polygon...
Axis...
Place
Center
Show
Hide
Home

Places the global axis at the center of a single polygon or at the center of a selected group of polygons.

Centering the Global Axis in a Single Polygon

1. Select the polygon to center the global axis in.
2. The axis appears as a small black X in the center of the polygon.

Centering the Global Axis in Multiple Polygons

1. Create a selection set of the polygons you wish to center the axis in and turn on the **Selected** button in the Icon panel. See *Select/Polygon/Quad*, *Select/Polygon/Fence*, and *Select/Polygon/Circle*.
2. Click anywhere on the drawing area. The axis appears in the center of an invisible box surrounding the selected polygons.

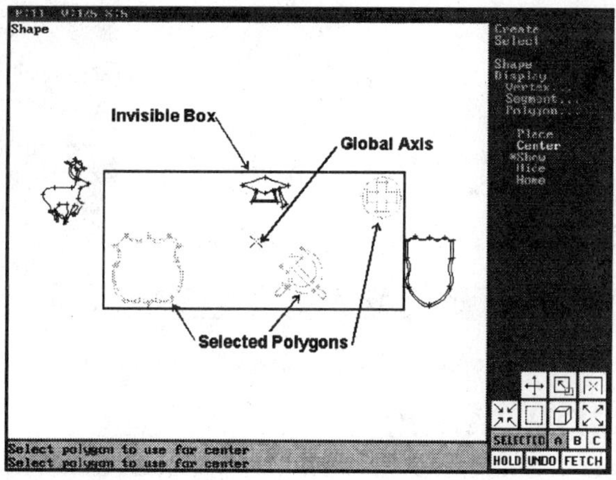

Centering the global axis in a selected group of polygons.

RELATED COMMANDS

Modify/Axis/Place, Modify/Axis/Show, Modify/Axis/Home, Modify/Axis/Hide

Create
Select
Modify
Shape
Display
Vertex...
Segment...
Polygon...
Axis...
Place
Center
Show
Hide
Home

Modify/Axis/Show

Displays the global axis.

Displaying the Global Axis

1. To display the global axis, select *Modify/Axis/Show*.

NOTE After selecting *Modify/Axis/Show*, an asterisk appears next to the command. If you still do not see the global axis, click on the Zoom Out icon.

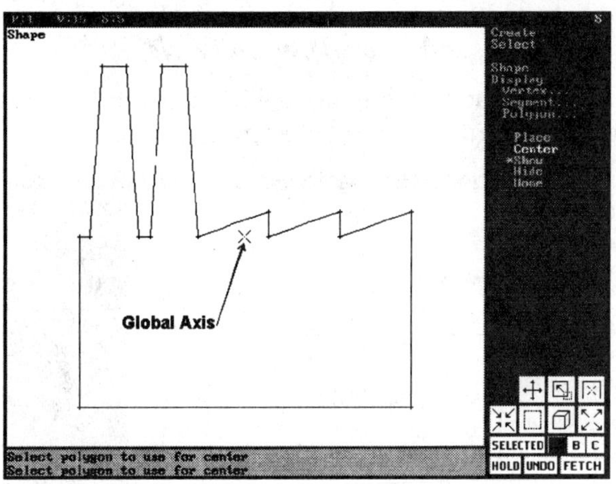

The global axis appears as a small black X.

RELATED COMMANDS

Modify/Axis/Place, Modify/Axis/Center, Modify/Axis/Home, Modify/Axis/Hide

Modify/Axis/Hide

Create
Select
Modify
Shape
Display
Vertex...
Segment...
Polygon...
Axis...
Place
Center
Show
Hide
Home

Hides the global axis if it is currently displayed.

Hiding the Global Axis

1. To hide the global axis, select *Modify/Axis/Hide*

> **NOTE** Hiding the global axis has no effect on any commands that use it.

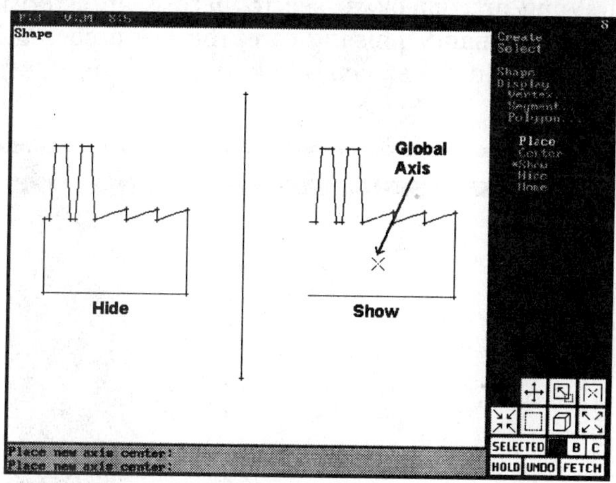

Hiding the global axis.

RELATED COMMANDS

Modify/Axis/Place, Modify/Axis/Center, Modify/Axis/Show, Modify/Axis/Home

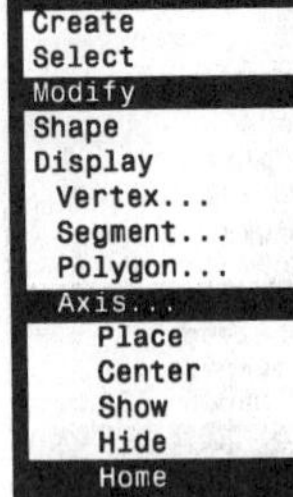

Modify/Axis/Home

Resets the global axis to the 0X, 0Y location, the origin of 2D Shaper space.

Sending the Global Axis Home

1. To reset the global axis to the default location of 0X, 0Y, select *Modify/Axis/Home.*

NOTE If the global axis does not appear as a small black X in the drawing are, check to see if there is an asterisk before the *Modify/Axis/Show* command. This indicates the axis is currently displayed. If it still is not visible on the screen, click on the Zoom Out icon until it becomes visible.

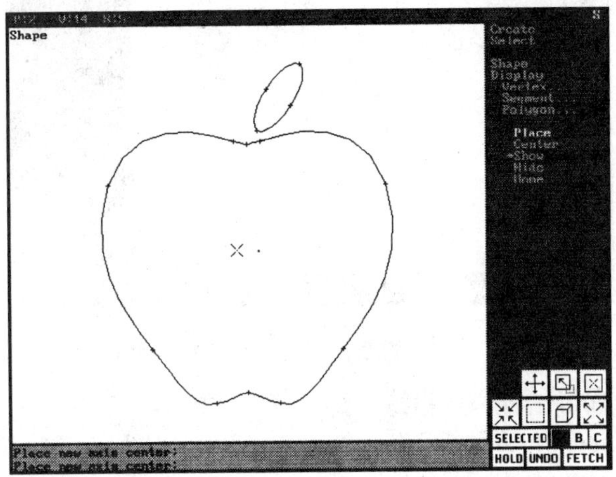

Resetting the global axis to its default position.

RELATED COMMANDS

Modify/Axis/Place, Modify/Axis/Center, Modify/Axis/Show, Modify/Axis/Hide

Shape/Assign

Assigns one or more polygons as the current shape, used before sending anything to the 3D Lofter.

Assigning Polygons to a Shape

1. To assign single polygons as a shape, simply click on them. When selected, they will turn yellow.
2. You can also create a selection set of the polygons you wish to assign as shapes. first click on a letter button (A, B, or C). Next, create a selection set of the desired polygons you want to assign as shapes. See *Select/Polygon/Quad*, *Select/Polygon/Fence*, and *Select/Polygon/Circle*.
3. Choose Shape/Assign, and click on the **Selected** button in the icon panel. Clicking anywhere on the screen assigns all of the selected polygons to the current shape. Polygons selected in this manner turn orange.
4. To unassign a polygon, make sure the selected button is off and click on the polygon you want to unassign.

NOTE If you only have one polygon in the 2D Shaper, or want all polygons in the 2D Shaper sent to the 3D Lofter, you do not need to assign them as shapes.

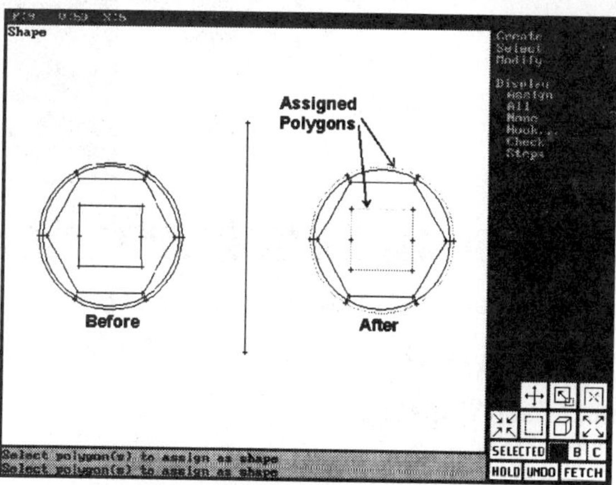

Polygons assigned to a shape.

RELATED COMMANDS

Select/Shape/All, Select/Shape/None, Select/Polygon/Quad, Select/Polygon/Fence, Select/Polygon/Circle

Create
Select
Modify
Shape
Display
Assign
All
None
Hook...
Check
Steps

Shape/All

Assigns all polygons currently in the 2D Shaper as one shape.

Assigning All Polygons as One Shape

1. Select *Shape/All*, and every polygon will be assigned as one shape. All polygons will turn yellow, and all red polygons (included in an active selection set; see *Select/Polygon/Quad*, *Select/Polygon/Fence*, and *Select/Polygon/Circle*) will turn orange.
2. To unassign a polygon, make sure the **Selected** button is turned off and click on the polygon you want to unassign.

Frozen polygons are not assigned as part of the shape. See *Display/Freeze/Polygon*.

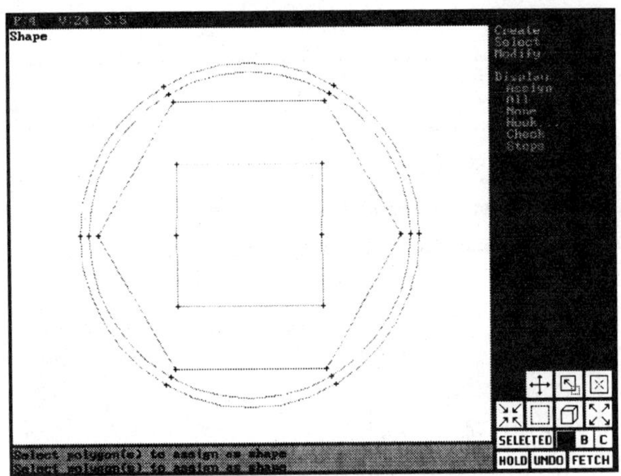

All polygons are assigned as one shape.

RELATED COMMANDS

Select/Shape/None, Select/Shape/Assign

Shape/None

Removes all polygons from the selected shape.

Removing the Assignment of All Polygons

1. Choose *Shape/None*, and all polygons assigned as shapes are deselected.

> **TIP** Using *Shape/None* before assigning polygons as the selected shape is a good technique to delete any previously assigned polygons. Assigned polygons may be off the screen, and can lead to unanticipated results when you attempt to bring them into the 3D Lofter.

> **NOTE** Any shapes that were assigned and then frozen will be reassigned when thawed, even after using *Shape/None*.

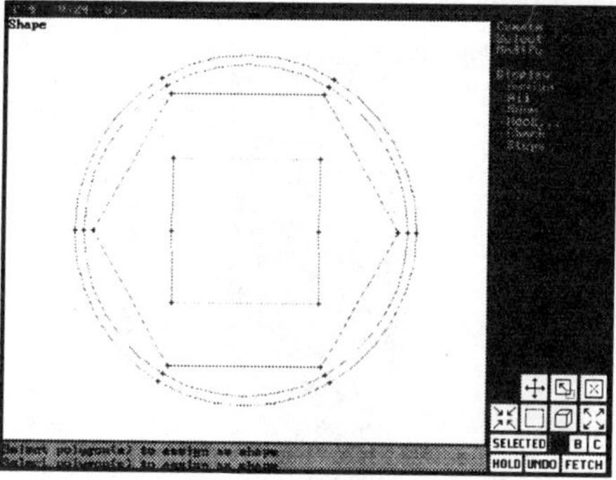

All polygons are assigned as one shape.

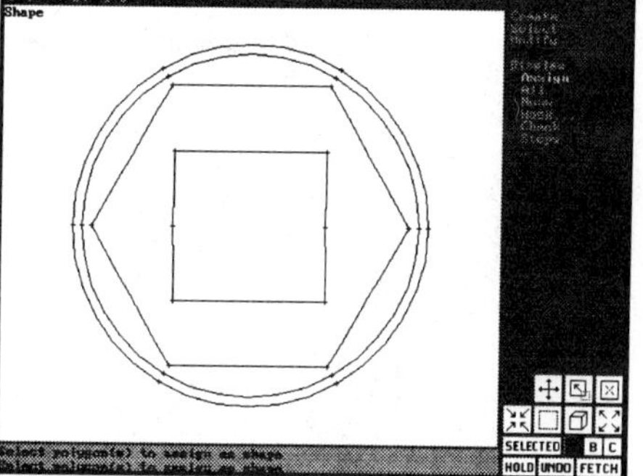

All polygons are removed as assigned shapes.

RELATED COMMANDS

Shape/All, Shape/Assign

Create
Select
Modify
Shape
Display
Assign
All
None
Hook...
Check
Steps
Place
Center
Show
Hide
Home

Shape/Hook/Place

Moves a shape's hook to a new location. The hook determines where the shape is placed in relation to the path when imported into the 3D Lofter.

Moving a Shape's Hook

1. By default, the hook is positioned at 0X, 0Y, the origin of 2D Shaper space. To see the current location of the hook, select *Shape/Hook/Show*. The hook will appear as a small yellow cross.
2. To relocate the hook, move the cursor to the new location and click. If you do not want to see the hook, select *Shape/Hook/Hide*.

You can also relocate the hook by entering coordinates at the keyboard.

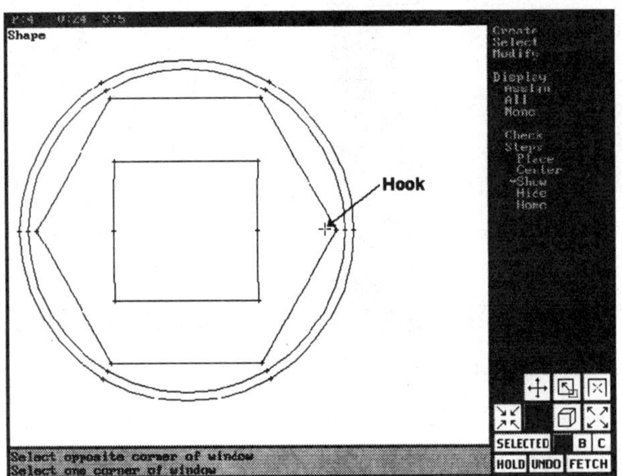

You can place the hook with the cursor or keyboard coordinate entry.

RELATED COMMANDS

Shape/Hook/Hide, Shape/Hook/Show, Shape/Hook Center, Shape/Hook/Home

Shape/Hook/Center

Locates the hook at the center of a bounding box surrounding the currently assigned shape. The hook determines where the shape is placed in relation to the path when imported into the 3D Lofter.

Centering the Hook in Assigned Shapes

1. Define the shape with the *Shape/Assign* command.
2. Select *Shape/Hook/Center* and click anywhere on the drawing screen.
3. The hook appears as a small yellow cross in the center of an invisible box surrounding the assigned shapes.

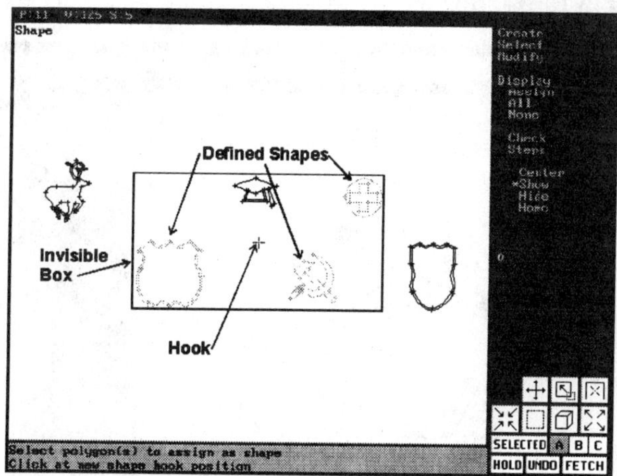

Centering the hook in a defined shape.

RELATED COMMANDS

Shape/Assign, Shape/Hook/Hide, Shape/Hook/Show, Shape/Hook Place, Shape/Hook/Home

Create
Select
Modify
Shape
Display
Assign
All
None
Hook...
Check
Steps
Place
Center
Show
Hide
Home

Shape/Hook/Show

Displays the hook for a defined shape. The hook determines where the shape is placed in relation to the path when imported into the 3D Lofter.

Displaying the Hook

1. To show the hook, choose *Shape/Hook/Show*. The hook appears as a small yellow cross.

> **NOTE** After selecting *Shape/Hook/Show*, an asterisk appears next to the command. If you still do not see the Hook, continue clicking on the Zoom Out icon.

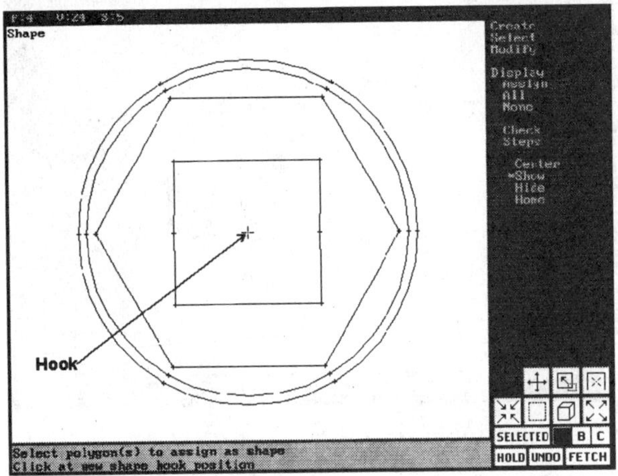

The hook appears as a small yellow cross.

RELATED COMMANDS

Shape/Assign, Shape/Hook/Place, Shape/Hook/Center, Shape/Hook/Hide, Shape/Hook/Home

Shape/Hook/Hide

Create
Select
Modify
Shape
Display
Assign
All
None
Hook...
Check
Steps
Place
Center
Show
Hide
Home

Hides the hook if it is currently displayed. The hook appears as a small yellow cross, and determines where the shape is placed in relation to the path when imported into the 3D Lofter.

Hiding the Hook

1. To hide the hook, select *Shape/Hook/Hide.* An asterisk appears next to the command.

> **NOTE** Hiding the hook has no effect on any commands that use it.

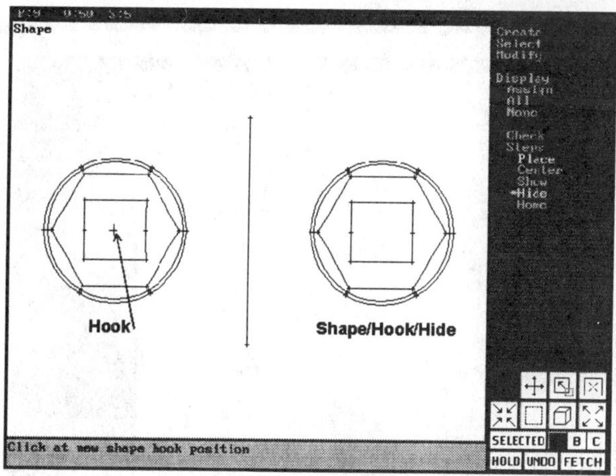

Hiding the hook.

RELATED COMMANDS

Shape/Hook/Place, Shape/Hook/Center, Shape/Hook/Show, Shape/Hook/Home

Create
Select
Modify
Shape
Display
Assign
All
None
Hook...
Check
Steps
Place
Center
Show
Hide
Home

Shape/Hook/Home

Resets the hook to the 0X, 0Y location, the origin of 2D Shaper space.

Sending the Hook Home

1. To reset the hook axis to the default location of 0X, 0Y, select *Shape/Hook/Home*.

> **NOTE** If the hook axis does not appear as a small yellow cross in the drawing are, first check to see if there is an asterisk before the *Shaper/Hook/Show* command. This indicates the hook is currently displayed. If it still is not visible on the screen, click on the Zoom Out icon until it becomes visible.

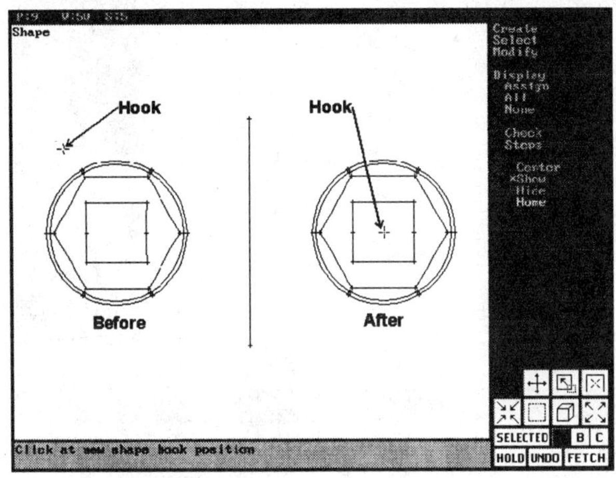

Resetting the hook to its default position.

RELATED COMMANDS

Shape/Hook/Place, Shape/Hook/Center, Shape/Hook/Show, Shape/Hook/Hide

Create
Select
Modify
Shape
Display
Assign
All
None
Hook...
Check
Steps

Shape/Check

Checks the validity of the currently assigned shape.

Checking an Assigned Shape's Validity

1. Define the polygon or polygons that make up the assigned shape. See *Shape/Assign, Shape/All.*

2. Select *Shape/Check.* 3D Studio performs the following checks on the assigned shape:

   Closed Polygons: After selecting *Shape/Check*, the 2D Shaper first checks to see if the assigned shape is closed. 3D Studio displays an alert box if the assigned shape contains one or more open polygons. You can close all open polygons with the *Create/Close* command.

   Intersecting Segments: If the assigned shape does not contain any open polygons, 3D Studio will check the assigned shape for intersecting segments. An alert box will be displayed if the assigned shape contains vertices or segments that intersect or overlap. Small red boxes appear where the segments intersect each other or the vertices overlap.

   Valid Shapes: If the shape does not contain any overlapping vertices, intersecting segments, or open polygons, 3D Studio responds with a Shape OK box, listing the number of vertices.

> **NOTE** Only valid shapes can be exported to the 3D Editor, or used as a loft shape in the 3D Lofter. Both the 3D Lofter and Keyframer can accept open shapes as paths, however.

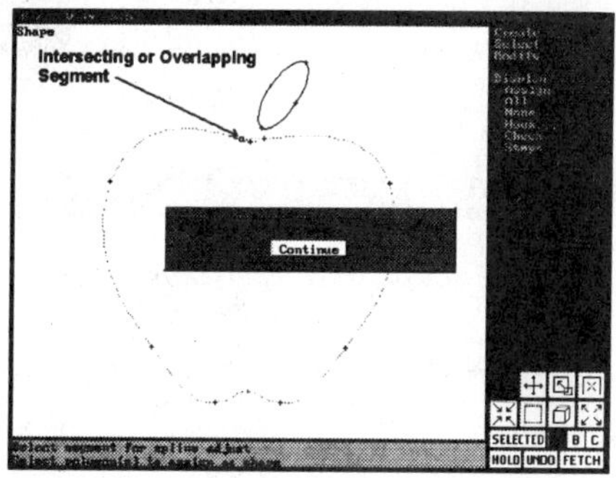

Small red boxes appear where segments intersect or vertices overlap.

RELATED COMMANDS

Shape/Assign, Shape/All, Create/Close

Create
Select
Modify
Shape
Display
Assign
All
None
Hook...
Check
Steps

Shape/Steps

Alters the number of steps used to define a curve between vertex points. The more steps in a segment, the smoother the curve and the more complex the resulting mesh object will be

Altering the Number of Steps

2. After selecting *Shape/Steps*, the Set Steps dialog box appears. Values may range from 0 to 10.
3. The new value is applied to all polygons in memory, as well as all future polygons you create. This value can be changed at any time while creating objects in 3D Studio.

TIP Because the step value affects the complexity of the resulting mesh object created in the 3D Lofter, set the step value as low as possible while still retaining the shape you want.

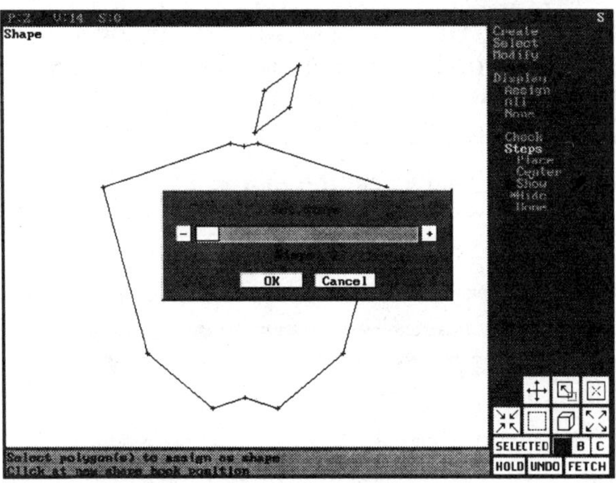

The apple shape with the steps set to 0.

RELATED COMMANDS

None

Display/First/Choose

Create
Select
Modify
Shape
Display
First...
Tape...
3D Display...
Freeze...
Choose
On
Off

Allows you to specify which vertex in a polygon is the first vertex.

Specifying a New First Vertex

1. When a polygon is created, the vertices are numbered from 1 to the total number created, in the order in which they were created. The first vertex is black, and can be displayed with *Display/First/On*.
2. To change the first vertex, select any vertex in a closed polygon, or any end vertex in an open polygon.

NOTE When bringing shapes into the 3D Lofter, the first vertex is commonly used as an alignment marker. When shapes are placed on different paths without aligning the vertices, the resulting mesh object is twisted. To avoid twisting, align the vertices as shown in the following figure.

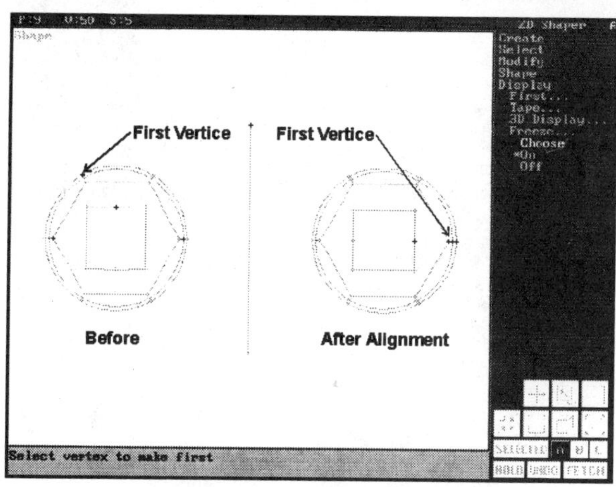

Aligning the first vertices.

RELATED COMMANDS

Display/First/On, Display/First/Off

Create
Select
Modify
Shape
Display
First...
Tape...
3D Display...
Freeze...
Choose
On
Off

Display/First/On

Displays the vertex that was created first in one or more polygons.

Displaying the First Vertex

1. To display the first vertex, select *Display/First/On*. The first vertex turns black, and an asterisk appears next to the command. If the polygon has been selected (red color), the first vertex appears green.

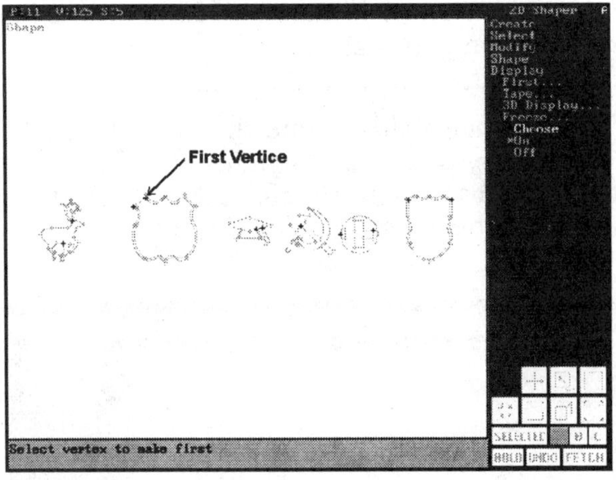

The first vertex appears black, green if the polygon has been selected.

RELATED COMMANDS

Display/First/Choose, Display/First/Off

Display/First/Off

Create
Select
Modify
Shape
Display
First...
Tape...
3D Display...
Freeze...
Choose
On
Off

Turns off the display of all first vertices if they are on.

Turning Off the First Vertex Display

1. The first vertex appear black (green if the polygon has been selected; a selected polygon is red color). If the first vertex display is on, an asterisk appears next to the **ON** command. To turn off the first vertex display, select *Display/First/Off*.

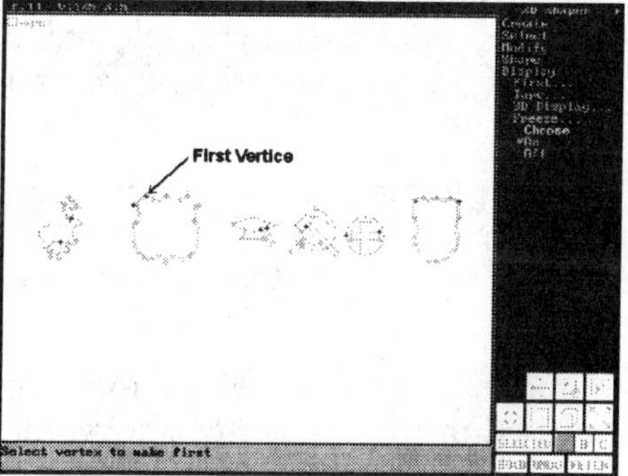

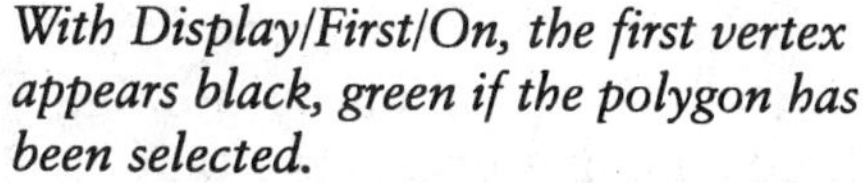

With Display/First/On, the first vertex appears black, green if the polygon has been selected.

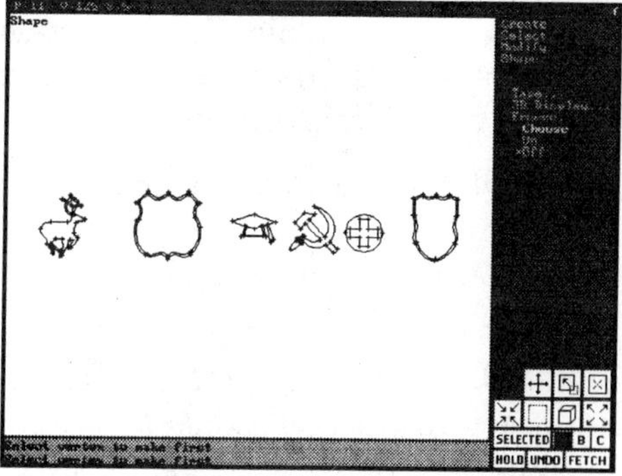

With Display/First/Off, all vertices appear white.

RELATED COMMANDS

Display/First/Choose, Display/First/On

Create
Select
Modify
Shape
Display
First...
Tape...
3D Display...
Freeze...
Move
Find
Show
Hide
Toggle Vsnap

Display/Tape/Move

Moves the tape measure to a new location. The tape is used to measure distances and angles of polygons.

Measuring a Segment

1. Turn the tape display on with *Display/Tape/Show*. The tape appears as a line with a square on one end and a dot on the other. If an asterisk appears next to Show and the tape is still not displayed, select *Display/Tape/Find*.
2. Once the tape is displayed on the screen, click on one end of the tape. This causes the directional arrows to appear, and the end you selected is now attached to the cursor. You can use the Tab key to restrict horizontal and vertical movement.
3. Move the selected end of the tape to the beginning of the location you want to measure. You can make the tape snap to the nearest vertex by selecting *Display/Tape/Vsnap*. Click to place the tape end in its new location.
4. Click on the other end of the tape and move it to the end of the location you want to measure. The length displayed in the status line shows the current length and angle of the tape measure.

NOTE You can move the entire tape to a new location by holding down the Ctrl key when clicking on either end of the tape.

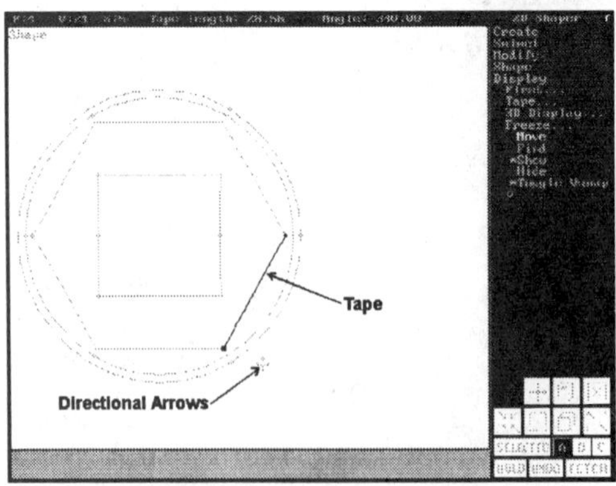

The tape can be used to measure the length and angle of polygons.

RELATED COMMANDS

Display/Tape/Find, Display/Tape/Show, Display/Tape/Hide, Display/Tape/Vsnap

Display/Tape/Find

Create
Select
Modify
Shape
Display
First...
Tape...
3D Display...
Freeze...
Move
Find
Show
Hide
Toggle Vsnap

Turns the Tape Measure icon on and rescales it to 80 percent of the active viewport, centering it within that viewport.

Finding the Tape Measure

1. If you have multiple viewports displayed, select the one you want to use the tape measure in.
2. After selecting *Display/Tape/Find*, the 2D Shaper centers the tape within the active viewport. It is sized to 80 percent of the viewport's length, and resets the angle.

> **NOTE** If you have turned the Tape display on (indicated by an asterisk appearing next to Show in *Display/Tape/Show*) and still do not see the Tape icon, use *Display/Tape/Find*. The Tape icon appears as a line with a square on one end and a dot on the other.

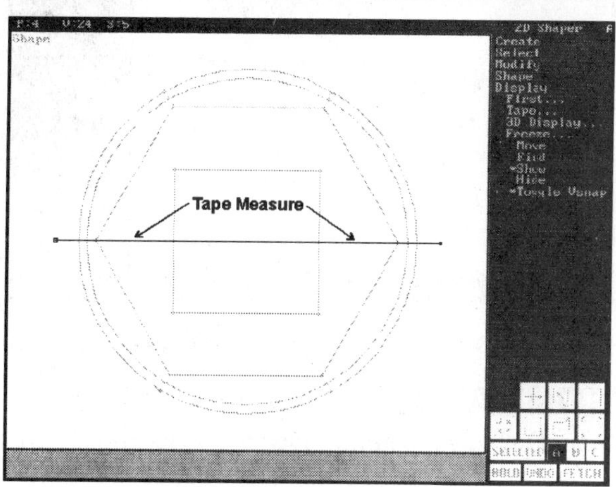

Finding the tape measure.

RELATED COMMANDS

Display/Tape/Move, Display/Tape/Show, Display/Tape/Hide, Display/Tape/Vsnap

Create
Select
Modify
Shape
Display
First...
Tape...
3D Display...
Freeze...
Move
Find
Show
Hide
Toggle Vsnap

Display/Tape/Show

The Tape Measure icon is displayed in the active viewport.

Displaying the Tape Measure

1. Select *Display/Tape/Show.* An asterisk will appear next to the command. The tape appears as a line with a square on one end and a dot on the other.

If you do not see the tape measure icon after turning it on, use *Display/Tape/Find.*

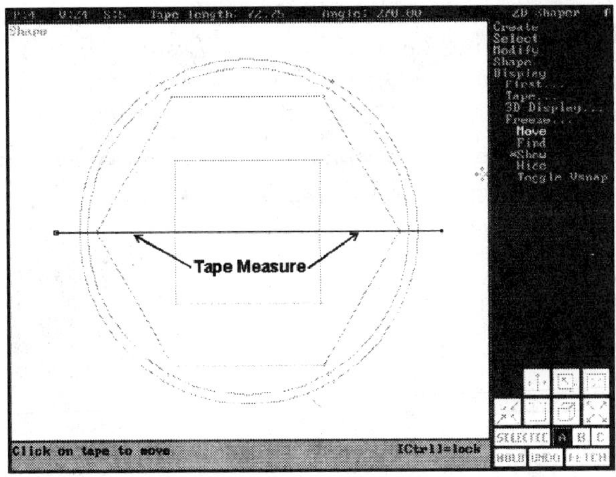

Displaying the Tape Measure icon.

RELATED COMMANDS

Display/Tape/Move, Display/Tape/Find, Display/Tape/Hide, Display/Tape/Vsnap

Display/Tape/Hide

Hides the Tape Measure icon.

Hiding the Tape Measure

1. Select *Display/Tape/Hide*. An asterisk will appear next to the command.

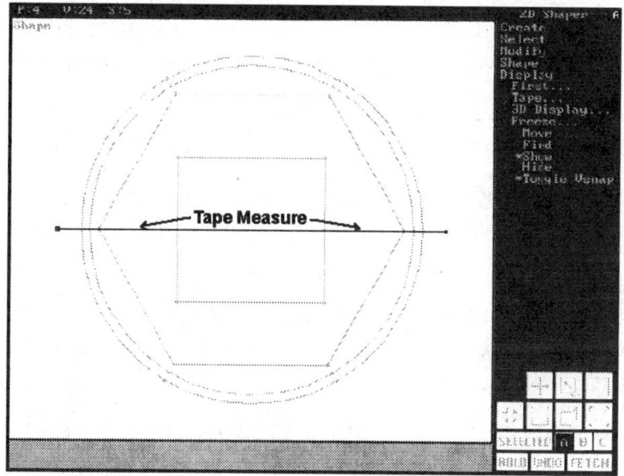

The Tape Measure icon appears as a line with a square on one end and a dot on the other.

RELATED COMMANDS

Display/Tape/Move, Display/Tape/Find, Display/Tape/Show, Display/Tape/Vsnap

Create
Select
Modify
Shape
Display
First...
Tape...
3D Display...
Freeze...
Move
Find
Show
Hide
Toggle Vsnap

Display/Tape/Vsnap

Allows the selected end of the tape measure to snap to the nearest vertex.

Measuring by Snapping to the Nearest Vertex

1. Make sure the tape measure is on and displayed on the screen if not visible. Use *Display/Tape/Find*. This will center the tape within the active viewport, size it to 80 percent of the viewport's length, and reset the angle.
2. Select *Display/Tape/Vsnap* to toggle the vertex snap on. An asterisk will appear next to the command.
3. Select *Display/Tape/Move* and click on one end of the tape. This causes the directional arrows to appear, and the end you selected is now attached to the cursor.
4. Move the selected end of the tape to the beginning of the location you want to measure. The tape will snap to a vertex, provided the vertex is inside the pick box. Click to place the tape end in its new location.
5. Click on the other end of the tape and move it to the end of the location you want to measure. The length displayed in the status line shows the current length and angle of the tape measure.

> **NOTE** You can toggle the Vsnap on and off during the command.

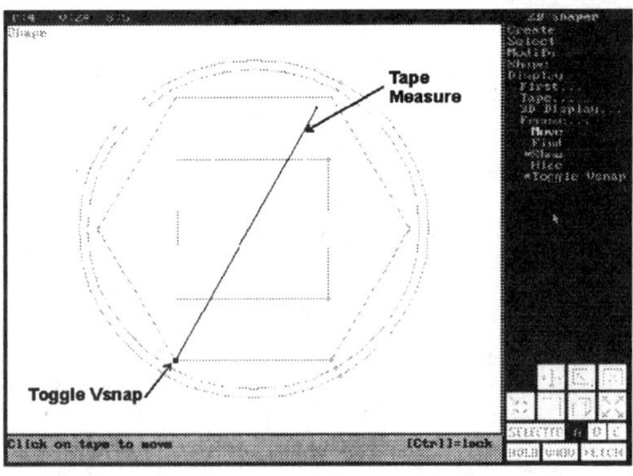

The Vsnap option will snap the selected end of the tape to a vertex.

RELATED COMMANDS

Display/Tape/Move, Display/Tape/Find, Display/Tape/Show, Display/Tape/Hide

Display/3D Display/Choose

Create
Select
Modify
Shape
Display
First...
Tape...
3D Display...
Choose
On
Off

Allows you to select objects from the 3D Editor to display in the 2D Shaper.

Displaying Objects from the 3D Editor

1. In the 3D Editor, display the geometry in the proper viewport.
2. In the 2D Shaper, select *Display/3D Display/Choose*. This invokes the Display Objects dialog box, allowing you to choose the objects you want displayed in the 2D Shaper.
3. The selected 3D objects appear in light gray exactly as they appear in the active 3D Editor viewport.
4. Create your geometry using your 2D Shaper commands. The 3D Mesh display is ignored by the 2D Shaper commands. It has no effect on the polygons created in the 2D Shaper.

If the selected objects from the 3D Editor do not appear on your screen, click several times on the Zoom Out icon.

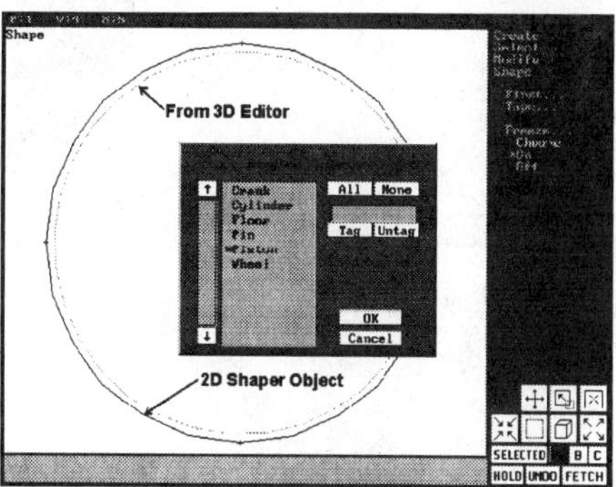

Display Objects dialog box.

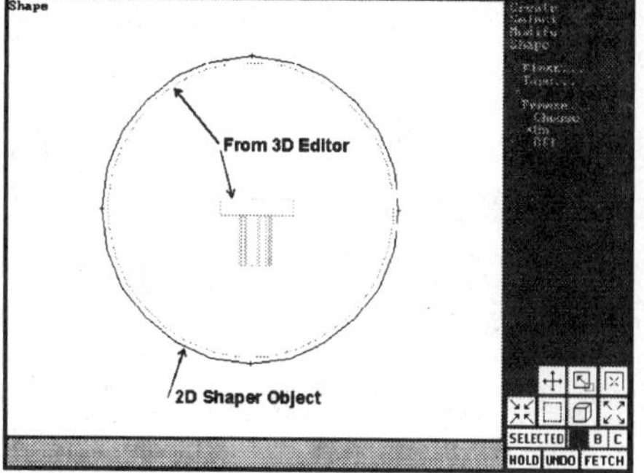

Drawing a sleeve around the piston.

RELATED COMMANDS

Display/3D Display/On, Display/3D Display/Off

Create
Select
Modify
Shape
Display
First...
Tape...
3D Display...
Choose
On
Off

Display/3D Display/On

Displays the selected objects from the 3D Editor.

Displaying Objects from the 3D Editor

1. In the 3D Editor, display the geometry in the proper viewport.
2. In the 2D Shaper, select *Display/3D Display/Choose*. This invokes the Display Objects dialog box, allowing you to choose the objects you want displayed in the 2D Shaper.
3. The selected 3D objects appear in light gray exactly as they appear in the active 3D Editor viewport.
4. Create your geometry using your 2D Shaper commands. The 3D Mesh display is ignored by the 2D Shaper commands. It has no effect on the polygons created in the 2D Shaper.

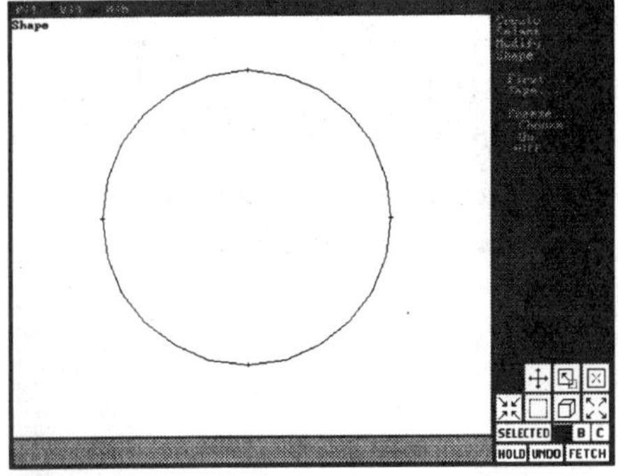

3D Display is off, showing just the piston sleeve.

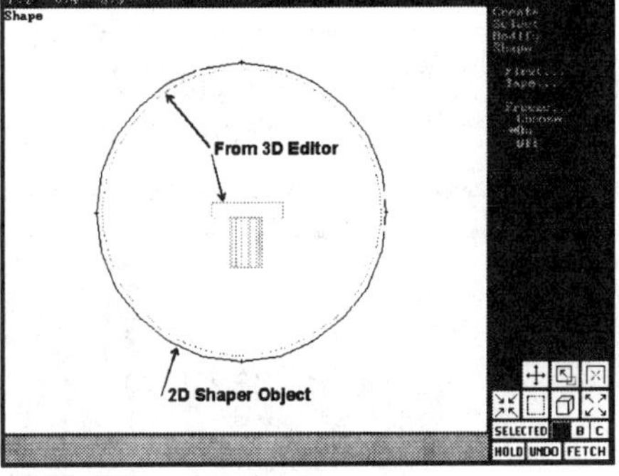

3D Display is on, showing the piston sleeve and piston.

RELATED COMMANDS

Display/3D Display/Choose, Display/3D Display/Off

Display/3D Display/Off

Create
Select
Modify
Shape
Display
First...
Tape...
3D Display...
Choose
On
Off

Hides the selected objects from the 3D Editor.

Hiding Objects from the 3D Editor

1. Selected 3D objects appear in light gray exactly as they appear in the active 3D Editor viewport.
2. To hide the 3D Objects, select *Display/3D Display/Off*.

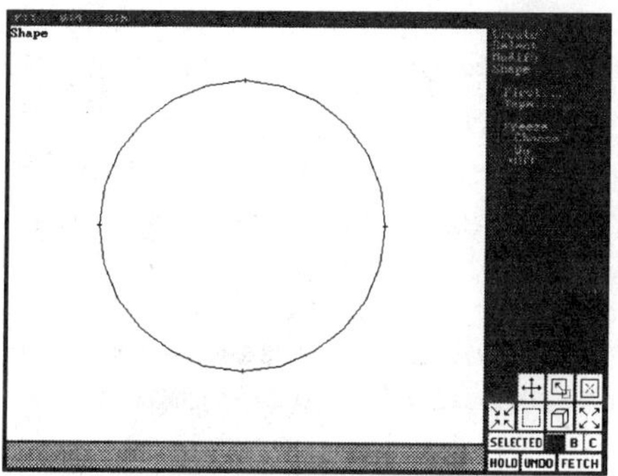

3D Display is off, showing just the piston sleeve.

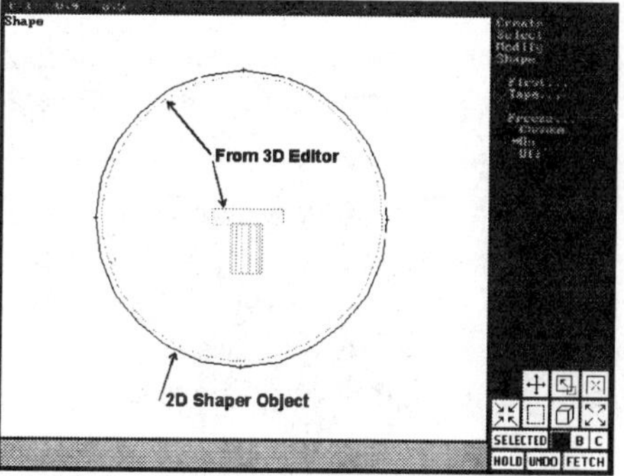

3D Display is on, showing the piston sleeve and piston.

RELATED COMMANDS

Display/3D Display/Choose, Display/3D Display/On

Create
Select
Modify
Shape
Display
First...
Tape...
3D Display..
Freeze....
Polygon
All
None

Display/Freeze/Polygon

Freezes selected polygons so they cannot be modified.

Freezing Selected Polygons

1. To freeze a polygon, select *Display/Freeze/Polygon* and click on it.
2. Frozen polygons appear light gray in color, and are not affected by any Modify commands.
3. To thaw a polygon, select *Display/Freeze/Polygon* and select a frozen polygon, or select *Display/Freeze/None* to thaw all polygons.

NOTE You can also freeze multiple polygons by first creating a selection set. Create a selection set of the polygons you wish to freeze. See *Select/polygon/Quad*, *Select/Polygon/Fence*, and *Select/Polygon/Circle*. Select *Display/Freeze/Polygon* and turn on the **Selected** button in the icon panel. Click anywhere on the screen, and the selected polygons will be frozen.

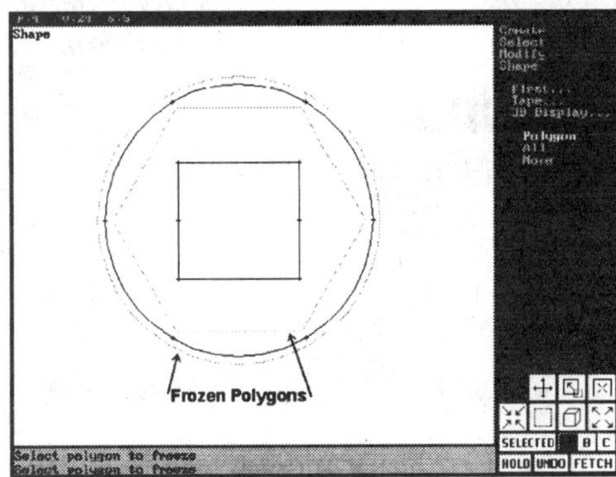

Frozen polygons appear light gray and cannot be altered or modified.

Use *Display/Freeze/Polygon* to trace over existing polygons without inserting additional vertices in the original polygons.

RELATED COMMANDS

Display/Freeze/All, Display/Freeze/None, Select/Polygon/Quad, Select/Polygon/Fence, Select/Polygon/Circle

Display/Freeze/All

Freezes all polygons so they cannot be modified.

Freezing All Polygons

1. To freeze all polygons, select *Display/Freeze/All.*
2. All polygons appear light gray in color, and are not affected by any Modify commands.
3. To thaw a polygon, select *Display/Freeze/Polygon* and select a frozen polygon. Or select *Display/Freeze/None* to thaw all polygons.

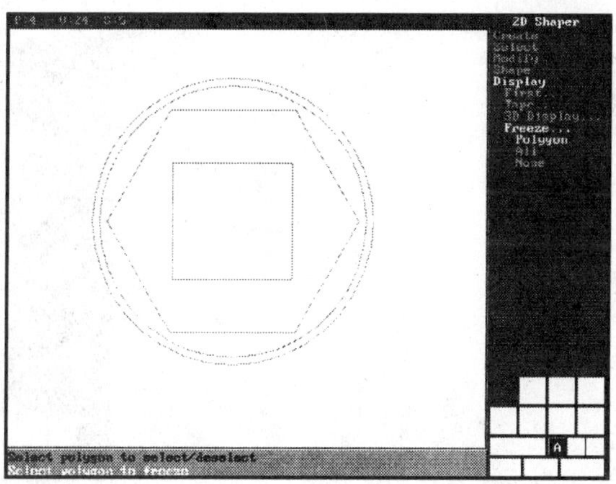

Frozen polygons appear light gray and cannot be modified.

RELATED COMMANDS

Display/Freeze/Polygon, Display/Freeze/None

Create
Select
Modify
Shape
Display
First...
Tape...
3D Display..
Freeze....
Polygon
All
None

Display/Freeze/None

Thaws all frozen polygons.

Thawing Frozen Polygons

1. Frozen polygons appear light gray and cannot be modified or altered.
2. To thaw all polygons, select *Display/Freeze/None*. All polygons revert to their normal color and state and can be modified.
3. To thaw specific polygons, select *Display/Freeze/Polygon* and select a frozen polygon.

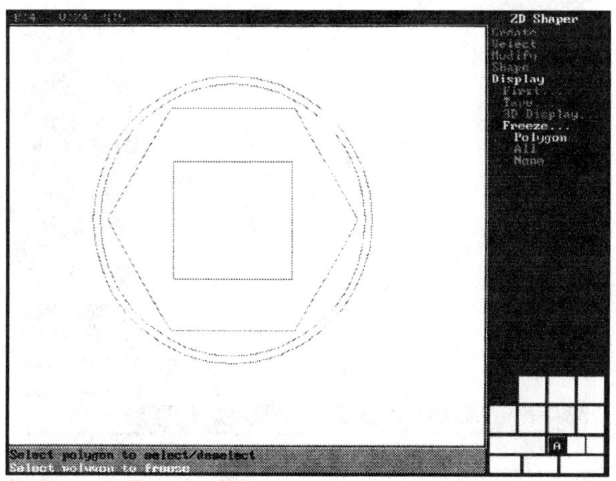

Frozen polygons appear light gray and cannot be altered or modified.

RELATED COMMANDS

Display/Freeze/Polygon, Display/Freeze/All

Shapes/Get/Shaper

Shapes
Path
Deform
3D Display
Objects
Get
Put...
Pick
Move
Rotate
Scale
Compare
Center
Shaper
Disk
Level

Imports a predefined shape, after it is assigned, from the 2D Shaper.

Importing a Shape from the 2D Shaper

1. Create a closed shape in the 2D Shaper.
2. Use the *Shape/Assign* command to tag the shape for export.
3. Switch to the 3D Lofter.
4. Select *Shapes/Get/Shaper*.
5. If the shape is valid, the shape will be displayed in all viewports.
6. If necessary, adjust the size and location of the shape.
7. If different shapes are needed on the path, they can be imported, as long as they have the same number of vertices.
9. Once all shapes have been imported and aligned, use the *Objects/Make* command to create the object.

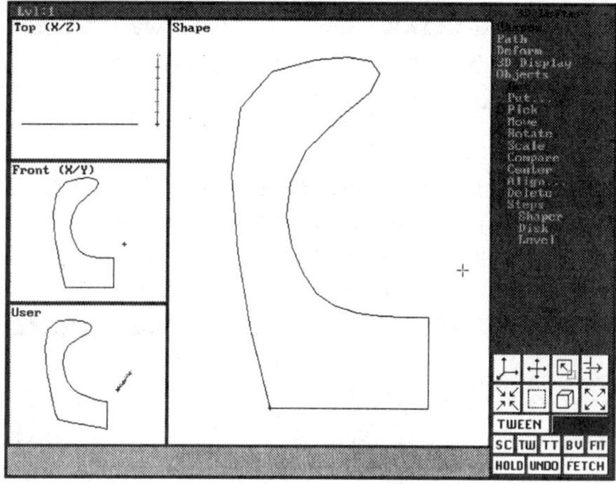

Importing a shape in the 3D Lofter from the 2D Shape.

NOTE To avoid twisted objects, be sure to align the first vertex. See *Display/First* for more information.

RELATED COMMANDS

Shapes/Get/Disk, Shapes/Get/Level, 2D Shaper/Shape/Assign

Shapes
Path
Deform
3D Display
Objects
Get
Put...
Pick
Move
Rotate
Scale
Compare
Center
Shaper
Disk
Level

Shapes/Get/Disk

Imports a predefined shape from a disk.

Importing a Shape from a Disk

1. Create a closed shape in the 2D shaper and save it to disk.
2. Switch to the 3D Lofter.
3. Select *Shapes/Get/Disk.*
4. The Load a 2D Shape dialog box will appear.

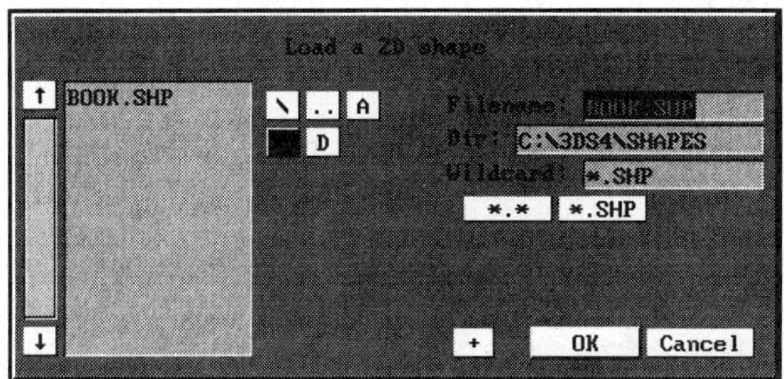

Select the .shp file to import.

5. If the shape is valid, the shape will be displayed in all viewports.

NOTE If different shapes are needed on the path, they can be imported, as long as they have the same number of vertices. It is also important to be sure to align the first vertex using the *Display/First* command to avoid twisted objects.

RELATED COMMANDS

Shapes/Get/Shaper, Shapes/Get/Level

Shapes/Get/Level

Shapes
Path
Deform
3D Display
Objects
Get
Put...
Pick
Move
Rotate
Scale
Compare
Center
Shaper
Disk
Level

Imports a shape on the path from a different level.

Importing a Shape from a Level

1. It is necessary to have a shape imported previously using either *Shape/Get/Shaper* or *Shape/Get/Disk.*
2. Using the [Page Up] and [Page Dn] keys, select the level the shape is to be imported on.
3. Select *Shapes/Get/Level.*
4. Move to a viewport that displays the path. The pick box will appear.
5. Select the vertex or step on the path that contains the shape to be exported to the current level.
6. The shape will be copied to the current level.

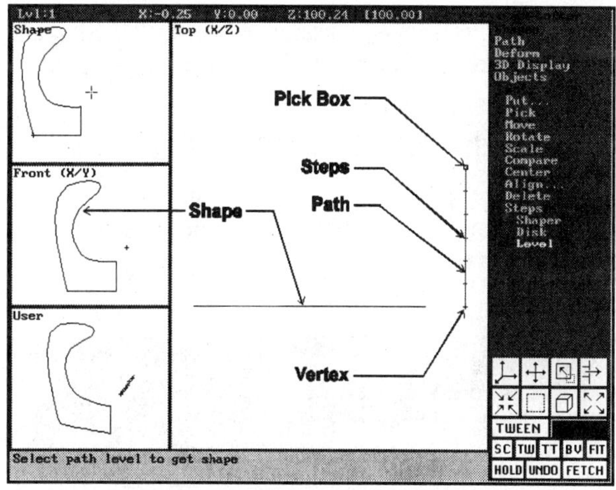

Copying a shape from another level.

RELATED COMMANDS

Shapes/Get/Disk, Shapes/Get/Level, 2D-Shaper/Shape/Assign

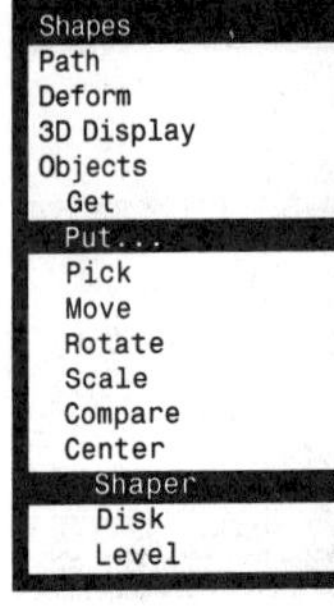

Shapes/Put/Shaper

Exports a shape from the current path level to the 2D Shaper.

Exporting a Shape from the 3D Lofter to the 2D Shaper

1. Using the Page Up and Page Dn keys, select the level that contains the shape to be exported to the 2D Shaper.
2. Now select *Shapes/Put/Shaper*. The current shape will be exported and assigned in the 2D Shaper.
3. You may now switch to the 2D Shaper to edit the shape.
4. If either the Unassign or the Delete option is chosen, a dialog box will be displayed that says the shape has been copied. Click on **Continue** to exit the dialog box.

If a previous shape is assigned in the 2D Shaper, a dialog box will appear as shown below. Choose one of the following options:

Unassign: Unassigns the shape in the 2D Shaper and places the new assigned shape in the 2D Shaper.

Delete: Deletes the shape in the 2D Shaper and replaces it with the shape being exported.

Cancel: Cancels the current operation.

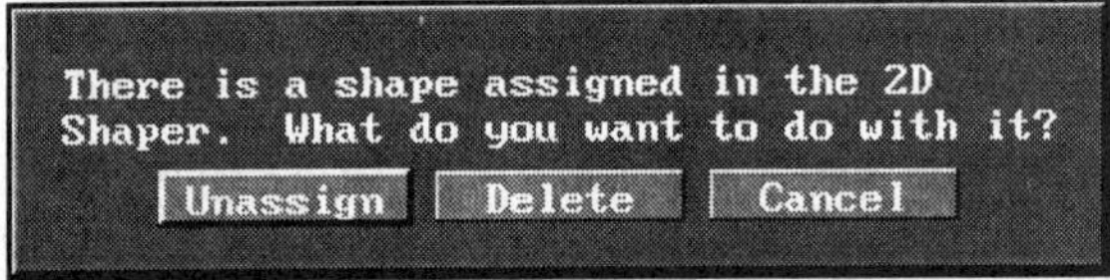

RELATED COMMANDS

Shapes/Put/Disk, Shapes/Put/Level

Shapes/Put/Disk

Shapes
Path
Deform
3D Display
Objects
Get
Put...
Pick
Move
Rotate
Scale
Compare
Center
Shaper
Disk
Level

Exports a shape from the current path level to disk.

Exporting a Shape from the 3D Lofter to a File

1. Using the [Page Up] and [Page Dn] keys, select the level that contains the shape to be exported to a file.
2. Select *Shapes/Put/Disk*. The Save a 2D shape file dialog box appears.

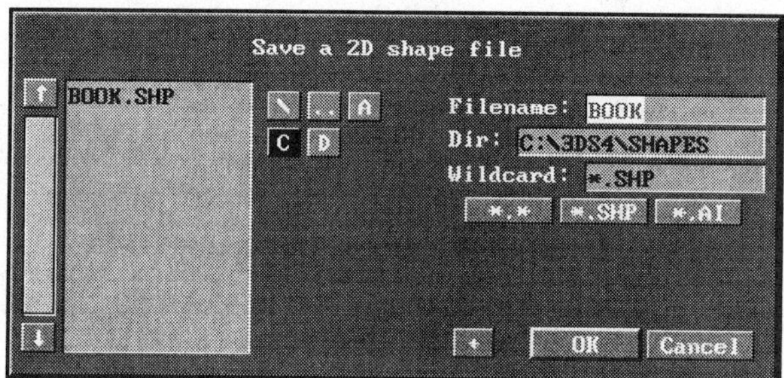

Saving the shape to a disk.

3. Choose either the Shape (*.shp) or Adobe Illustrator (*.ai) file format.
4. Choose the path and filename to save the shape file and click on the **OK** button.
5. If the filename already exists, you will be given the option to overwrite the file.

RELATED COMMANDS

Shapes/Put/Shaper, Shapes/Put/Level

Shapes
Path
Deform
3D Display
Objects
Get
Put...
Pick
Move
Rotate
Scale
Compare
Center
Shaper
Disk
Level

Shapes/Put/Level

Exports a shape from the current path level to another level.

Exporting a Shape from the Current Path Level to Another Level

1. Using the [Page Up] and [Page Dn] keys, select the level that contains the shape to be exported to another level.
2. Select *Shapes/Put/Level.*
3. In any viewport, select the path level the current shape is to be copied to. The path level must be selected by choosing the vertex or one of the steps. If it is not selected properly, the Select a Level on the Path dialog box will appear. Click on **Continue** to try the selection again.
4. If the path level already has a shape, a dialog box will appear asking you if you want to replace the current shape. Click on **Yes** or **No**.

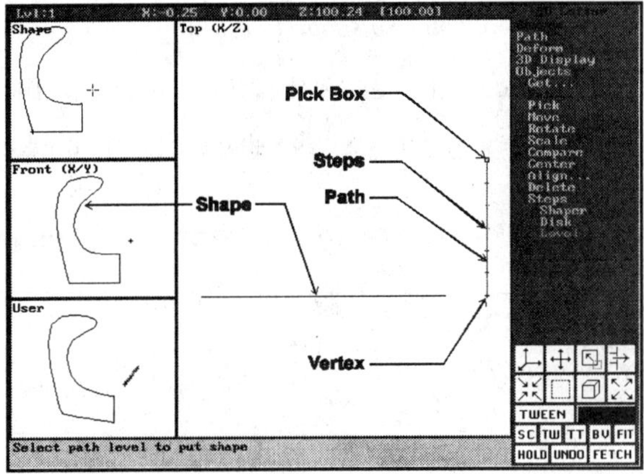

Putting a shape to another level.

RELATED COMMANDS

Shapes/Put/Shaper, Shapes/Put/Disk

Shapes/Pick

Selects a level on the path with the mouse.

Shapes
Path
Deform
3D Display
Objects
  Get
  Put...
  Pick
  Move
  Rotate
  Scale
  Compare
  Center
  Align...
  Delete
  Steps

Using the Mouse to Select a Level on the Path

1. Display a path in a viewport and make that viewport active.
2. Select *Shapes/Pick.*
3. Click on a vertex or a step on the path to make it current. The current level will become highlighted with a white cross hair.

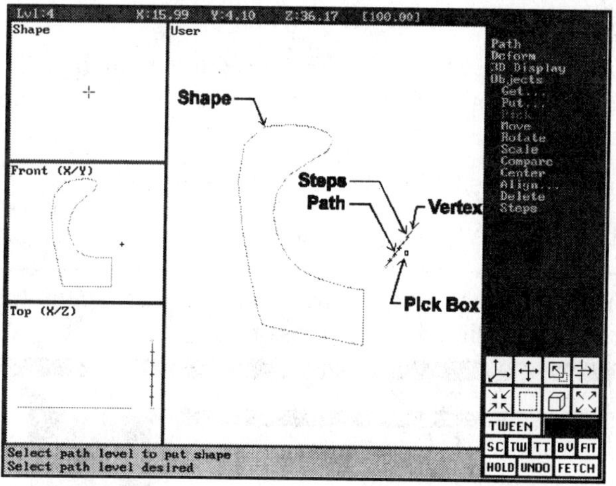

Selecting a level on the path.

The level can also be changed at the keyboard using the Page Dn and Page Up keys.

RELATED COMMAND

Shapes/Put

Shapes
Path
Deform
3D Display
Objects
Get
Put...
Pick
Move
Rotate
Scale
Compare
Center
Align...
Delete
Steps

Shapes/Move

Moves a shape on the current level perpendicular to the path.

Moving the Shape on the Path

1. Make the shape view the active viewport.
2. Use the x and w keys to move to the level where the shape to be moved is located.
3. Select *Shapes/Move* and move the pointer to the shape viewport. The directional cursor will appear in the viewport.
4. Left-click in the shape viewport. The directional cursor will disappear, the shape will dim in color, and the shape on that level will move in relation to your mouse movements.
5. Once the shape is placed, click the left mouse button.
6. To cancel the move, press the right mouse button.

TIP You can constrain the movements of the shape in the vertical and horizontal directions by pressing [Tab].

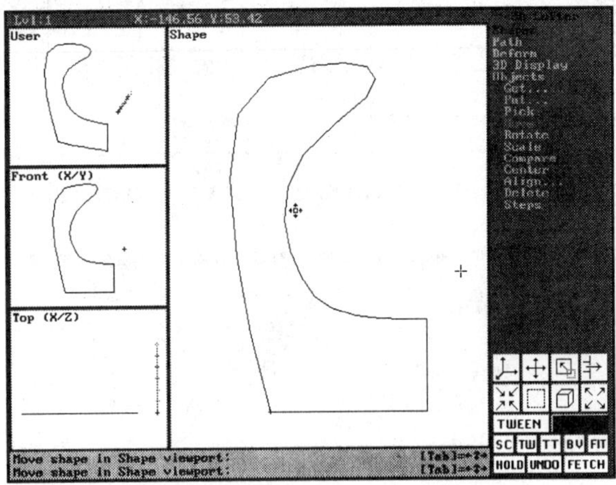

Moving the shape in the 3D Lofter.

RELATED COMMANDS

Shapes/Rotate, Shapes/Scale, Shapes/Compare, Shapes/Center, Shape/Align

Shapes/Rotate

Shapes
Path
Deform
3D Display
Objects
Get
Put...
Pick
Move
Rotate
Scale
Compare
Center
Align...
Delete
Steps

Rotates a shape on the current level perpendicular to the path.

Rotating the Shape on the Path

1. Make the shape view the active viewport.
2. Use the [Page Dn] and [Page Up] keys to move to the level where the shape to be rotated is located.
3. Select *Shapes/Rotate* and move the pointer to the shape viewport. The pick box will appear in the viewport.
4. Select the shape in the shape viewport. The pick box will disappear, the shape will dim in color, and the shape on that level will rotate in relationto your mouse movements.
5. Once the shape is rotated into place, click the left mouse button.
6. To cancel the rotation, press the right mouse button.

TIP You can specify the rotation increment by changing the Angle Snap setting in the Drawing Aids dialog box and pressing [A] to activate Angle Snap.

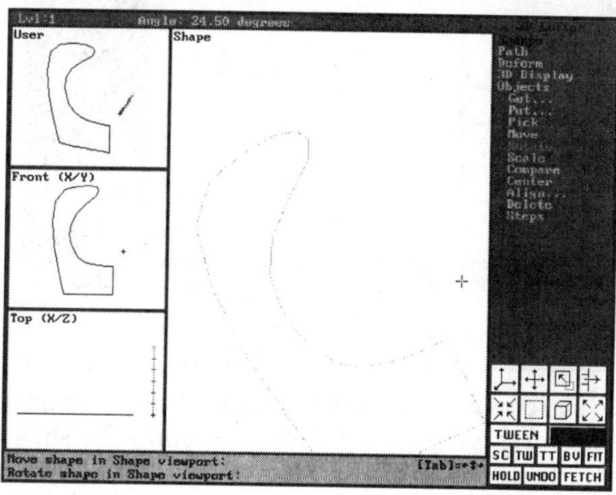

Moving the shape in the 3D Lofter.

RELATED COMMANDS

Shapes/Move, Shapes/Scale, Shapes/Compare, Shapes/Center, Shape/Align, Views-Drawing Aids-Angle Snap

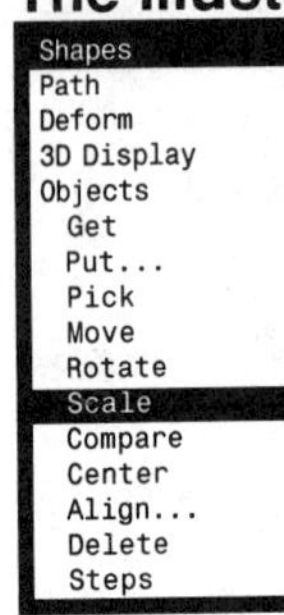

Shapes/Scale

Scales a shape on the current level of the path.

Scaling the Shape on the Path

1. Make the shape view the active viewport.
2. Use the Page Dn and Page Up keys to move to the level where the shape to be rotated is located.
3. Select *Shapes/Scale* and move the pointer to the shape viewport. The directional cursor will appear in the viewport.
4. Left-click in the shape viewport. The directional cursor will disappear, the shape will dim in color, and the shape on that level will be scaled in relation to your mouse movements.
5. Once the shape is scaled properly, click the left mouse button.
6. To cancel the rotation, right-click.

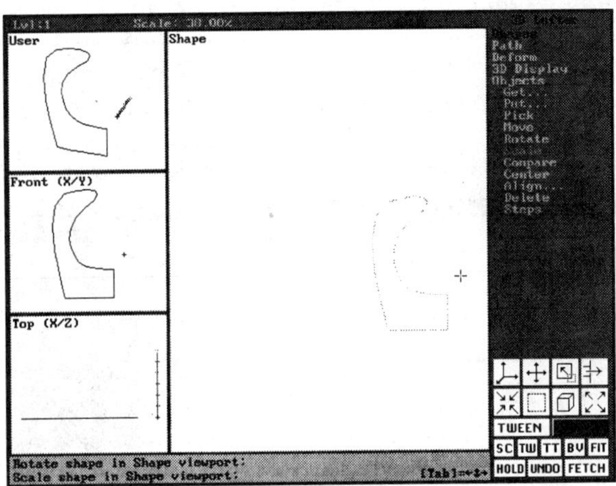

Scaling shapes in the 3D Lofter.

TIP You can change the multidirectional cursor to vertical or horizontal by pressing the Tab key. This will allow the shape to be scaled either vertically or horizontally instead of both ways.

RELATED COMMANDS

Shapes/Move, Shapes/Rotate, Shapes/Compare, Shapes/Center, Shape/Align

Shapes/Compare

Shapes
Path
Deform
3D Display
Objects
  Get
  Put...
  Pick
  Move
  Rotate
  Scale
  Compare
  Center
  Align...
  Delete
  Steps

Displays two or more shapes on a path at the same time in the shape viewport for comparison.

Comparing Two or More Shapes on a Path

1. Make the shape view the active viewport.
2. Use the [Page Dn] and [Page Up] keys to move to the level where the first shape to be compared is located.
3. Select *Shapes/Compare* and move the pointer to a viewport that displays the path. The pick box will appear in the viewport.
4. Click on either a vertex or a step on the path containing the second shape to be compared. The shape on that level will be displayed in yellow and in the shape viewport with the first shape.
5. Repeat step 4 until all shapes to be compared are displayed.

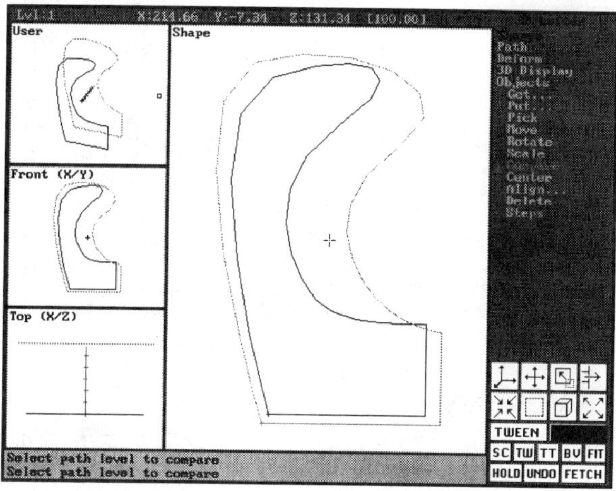

Comparing multiple shapes on different levels in the 3D Lofter.

> **NOTE** This option is useful in aligning the first vertices in the shapes to prepare them for lofting and for adjusting the proportional scale of the multiple shapes without moving back to the 2D Shaper.

RELATED COMMANDS

Shapes/Move, Shapes/Rotate, Shapes/Scale, Shapes/Center, Shape/Align, 2D Shaper/Display/First

Shapes
Path
Deform
3D Display
Objects
Get
Put...
Pick
Move
Rotate
Scale
Compare
Center
Align...
Delete
Steps

Shapes/Center

Centers a shape on the current level about the path.

Centering a Shape on a Path

1. Any viewport can be active.
2. Use the [Page Dn] and [Page Up] keys to move to the level where the shape to be centered is located.
3. Select *Shapes/Center*. The shape will automatically be centered on the path.

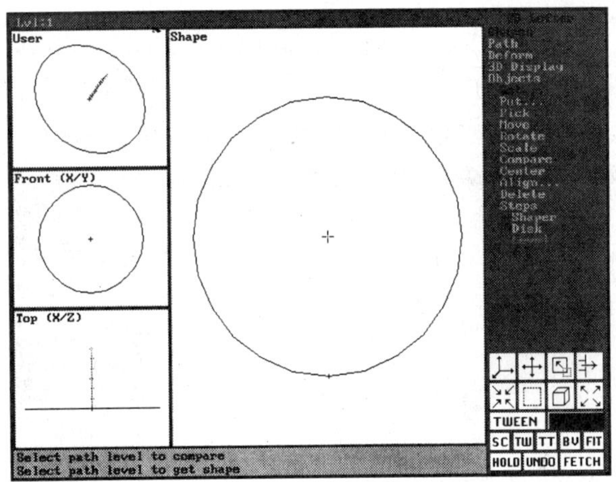

Centering the shape on the path.

RELATED COMMANDS

Shapes/Move, Shapes/Rotate, Shapes/Scale, Shapes/Compare, Shape/Align

Shapes/Align/Left

Shapes
Path
Deform
3D Display
Objects
Get
Put...
Pick
Move
Rotate
Scale
Compare
Center
Align...
Left
Right

This command aligns the left edge of the current shape with the center of a circular path or paths with an identifiable center.

Aligning the Left Edge of a Shape on a Circular Path

1. Any viewport can be active.
2. Use the [Page Dn] and [Page Up] keys to move to the level where the shape to be centered is located.
3. Select *Shapes/Align/Left*. The left edge of the shape will automatically be aligned about the circular path.

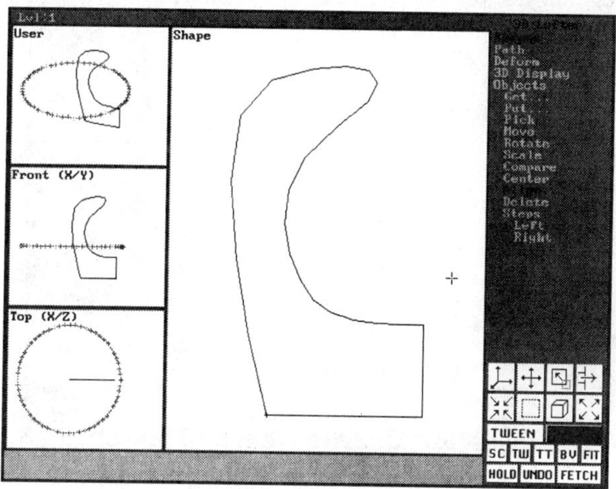

Aligning the shape to the left of the path.

NOTE Though *Shapes/Align/Left* can be used with any shape path, it will only produce predictable results with paths that have an identifiable center (i.e., circular paths, closed paths, arcs, etc.).

RELATED COMMANDS

Shapes/Move, Shapes/Rotate, Shapes/Scale, Shapes/Compare, Shape/Align/Right

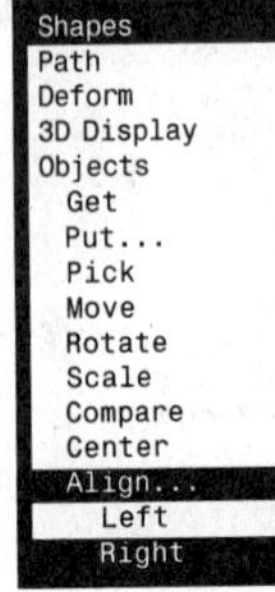

Shapes/Align/Right

This command aligns the right edge of the current shape with the center of a circular path or paths with a identifiable center.

Aligning the Right Edge of a Shape on a Circular Path

1. Any viewport can be active.
2. Use the [Page Dn] and [Page Up] keys to move to the level where the shape to be centered is located.
3. Select *Shapes/Align/Left.* The left edge of the shape will automatically be aligned about the circular path.

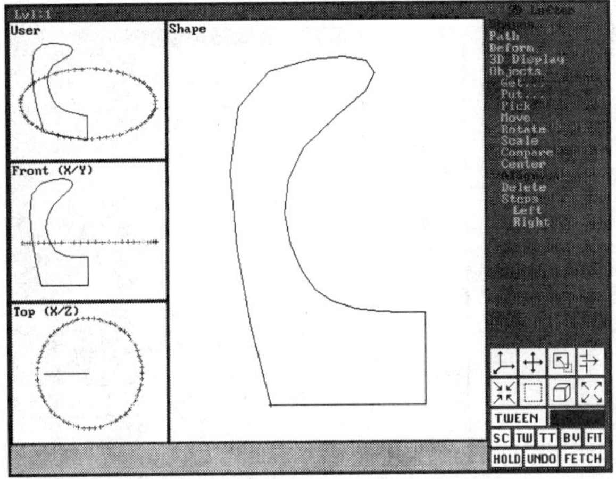

Aligning the shape to the right of the path.

RELATED COMMANDS

Shapes/Move, Shapes/Rotate, Shapes/Scale, Shapes/Compare, Shape/Align/Left, Shape/Delete

Shapes/Delete

Shapes
Path
Deform
3D Display
Objects
Get
Put...
Pick
Move
Rotate
Scale
Compare
Center
Align...
Delete
Steps

Deletes a shape on the current level.

Deleting a Shape on a Path

1. Any viewport can be active.
2. Use the [Page Dn] and [Page Up] keys to move to the level where the shape to be deleted is located.
3. Select *Shapes/Delete.* The dialog box shown below will be displayed.

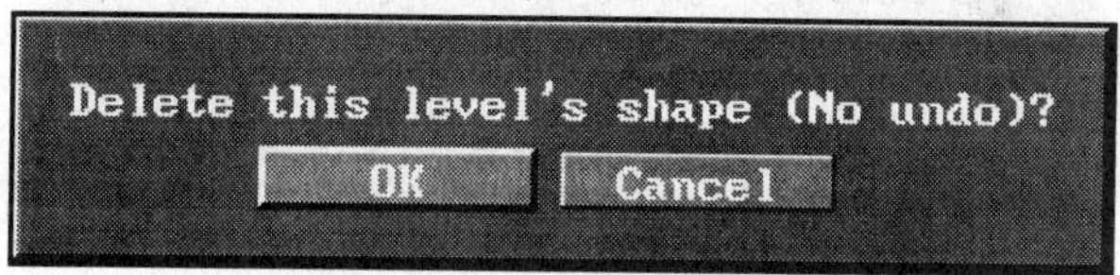

Verifying that the shape is to be deleted.

4. Choose **OK** to delete the shape, **Cancel** to keep the shape.

RELATED COMMAND

2D Shaper/Modify/Polygon/Delete

Shapes
Path
Deform
3D Display
Objects
Get
Put...
Pick
Move
Rotate
Scale
Compare
Center
Align...
Delete
Steps

Shapes/Steps

Sets the number of steps for all shapes to increase shape resolution.

Setting the Number of Steps for all Shapes

1. Select *Shapes/Steps*. The Set Steps dialog box will be displayed as shown below.

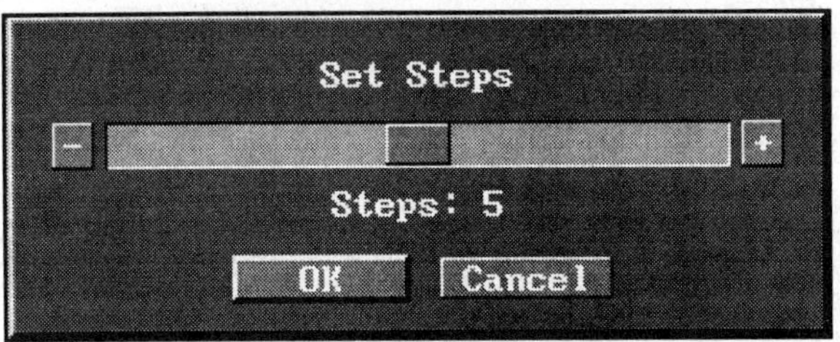

Setting the number of set steps.

2. The range for the steps is 0 to 10.
3. Change the setting by using the following methods. Click the + or - button to change the value in increments of one. Drag the slider to the desired location. Use the pointer and click in the slider area. The slider will automatically jump to that location.
4. To accept the setting click the **OK** button. To cancel the command, click **Cancel**.

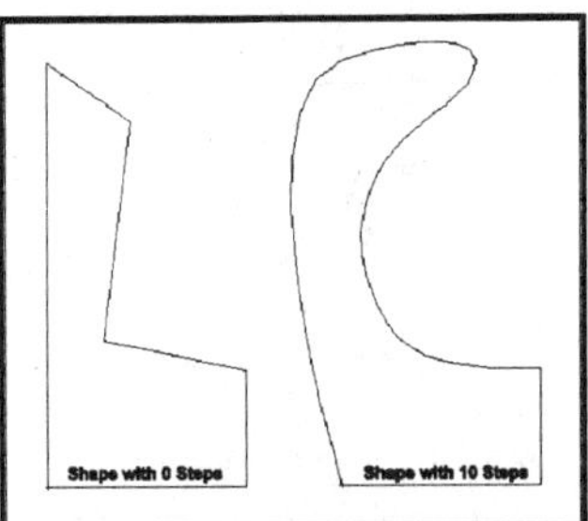

Example of same shape with different step values.

NOTE Increasing the steps also increases the complexity and size of the object being lofted. Be sure to use only the necessary step to conserve memory and storage.

RELATED COMMAND

2D Shaper/Shapes/Steps

Path/Get/Shaper

Shapes
Path
Deform
3D Display
Objects
Get
Put...
Move Vertex
Move Path
Insert Vertex
2D Scale
3D Scale
Skew
Mirror
Shaper
Disk

Imports a predefined path, after it is assigned, from the 2D Shaper.

Importing a Path from the 2D Shaper

1. Create a single polygon in the 2D Shaper.
2. Use the *Shape/Assign* command to tag the shape for export, unless it is the only shape in the 2D Shaper.
3. Switch to the 3D Lofter.
4. Select *Path/Get/Shaper*. The path will be imported on the X/Z plane in the top viewport and displayed in all viewports.
5. If required, change the number of steps using the *Path/Steps* command.
6. Adjust the size and location of the path, if necessary.

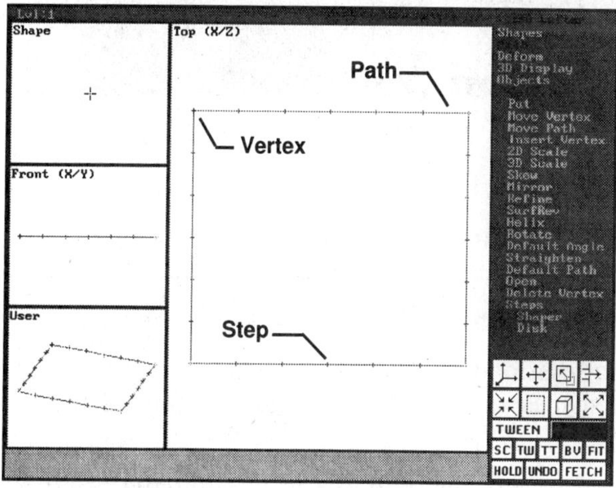

Importing a path from the 2D Shaper

NOTE The path imported will replace the default path created by the 3D Lofter.

RELATED COMMANDS

Path/Get/Disk, Path/Get/Level, 2D-Shaper/Shape/Assign, Path/Steps

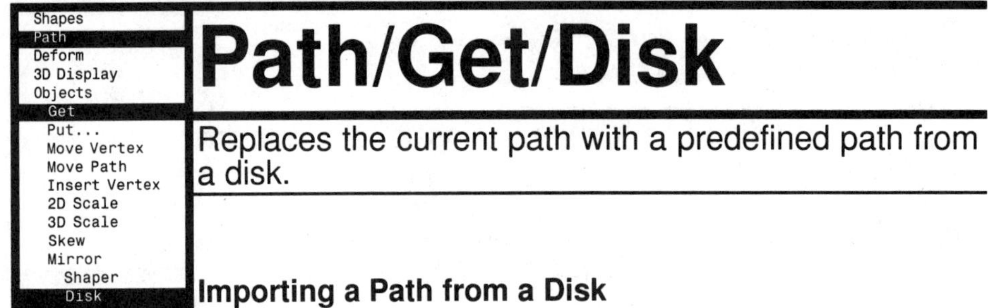

Path/Get/Disk

Replaces the current path with a predefined path from a disk.

Importing a Path from a Disk

1. Select *Path/Get/Disk.*
2. The Load Path from File dialog box will appear.

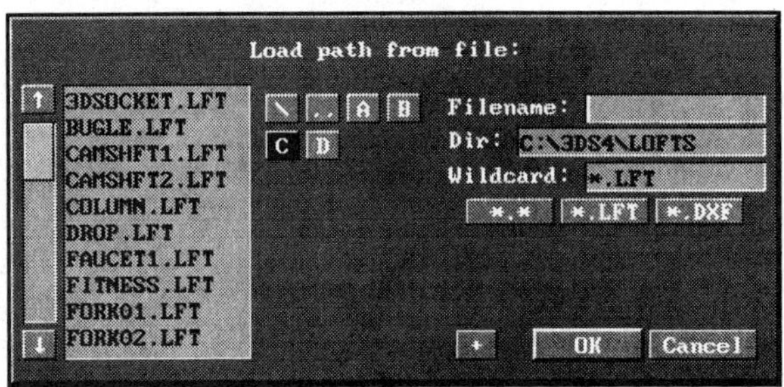

Loading a path from a file.

3. Select the .lft or .dxf file to import.
4. The path will be loaded and displayed in all viewports.

TIP When loading paths, be sure to remember these points:

1. Only the path is loaded from .lft files, not the shapes. If you need to import the shapes as well, use the *Load* command from the File pull-down menu.
2. Be sure there is only one polyline in the .dxf file being imported.

RELATED COMMANDS

Path/Get/Shaper, Path/Get/Level

Path/Put

Shapes
Path
Deform
3D Display
Objects
Get
Put...
Move Vertex
Move Path
Insert Vertex
2D Scale
3D Scale
Skew
Mirror
Refine
SurfRev

Exports a path to the 2D Shaper. If the path is a 3D path, it will be converted into a 2D shape.

Exporting a Path from the 3D Lofter to the 2D Shaper

1. Select *Path/Put*. The current path will then be exported and assigned in the 2D Shaper as a shape.
2. You may now switch to the 2D Shaper to edit the shape.

If a previous shape is assigned in the 2D shaper, a dialog box will appear as shown below. Choose one of the following options.

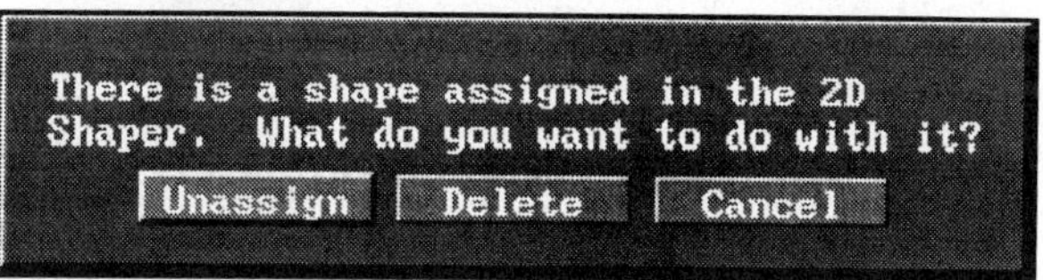

Choose one of the options from the dialog box.

Unassign: Unassigns the shape in the 2D Shaper and places the new assigned shape in the 2D Shaper.
Delete: Deletes the shape in the 2D Shaper and replaces it with the path being exported.
Cancel: Cancels the current operation.

If either the **Unassign** or the **Delete** option is chosen, a dialog box will be displayed that says the shape has been copied. Click on **Continue** to exit the dialog box.

RELATED COMMANDS

Shapes/Put/Disk, Shapes/Put/Level

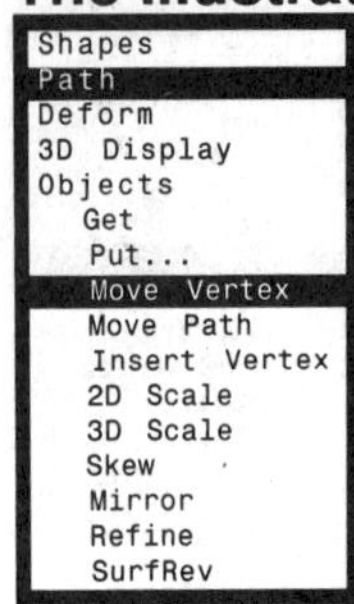

Path/Move Vertex

Moves a vertex on the path and allows the path's spline value to be modified.

Moving a Path Vertex

1. Select *Path/Move Vertex.*
2. Select any viewport other than Shape.
3. Select the vertex to be moved.
4. Use the mouse to select the new location of the vertex.
5. Use the right mouse button to cancel the operation.

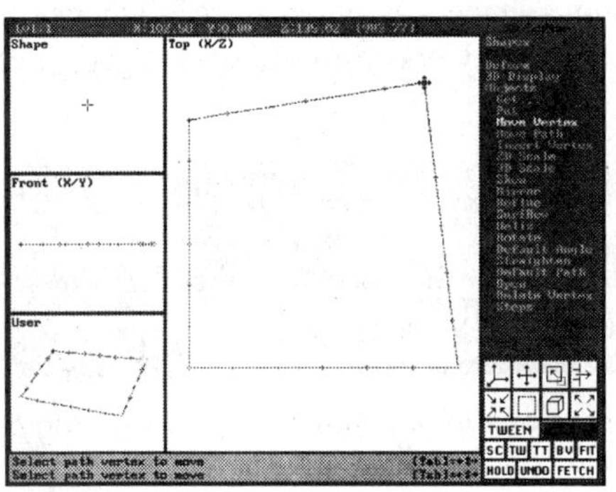

Moving a vertex on the path.

Modifying the Spline Value of the Path.

1. *Select Path/Move Vertex.*
2. Select any viewport other than the Shape.
3. Select the vertex to be moved.
4. Hold and drag on the vertex to be modified.
5. Make adjustments to the spline as necessary.
6. Use the right mouse button to cancel the operation.

TIP The vertex of the path can be moved in three dimensions. This will allow you to create complex 3D shapes such as roller coaster tracks or tunnels.

RELATED COMMANDS

Path/Insert Vertex, 2D Shaper/Modify/Vertex/Adjust

Path/Move Path

Shapes
Path
Deform
3D Display
Objects
Get
Put...
Move Vertex
Move Path
Insert Vertex
2D Scale
3D Scale
Skew
Mirror
Refine
SurfRev

Moves the path in the 3D Lofter in three dimensions.

Moving a Path

1. Select *Path/Move Path.*
2. Select the path. The cursor will change to the multidirectional cursor. Use Tab to constrain the movements vertically or horizontally.
3. Move the path to its new location and click. All viewports will reflect the changes made to the location of the path.
4. Use the right mouse button to cancel the operation.

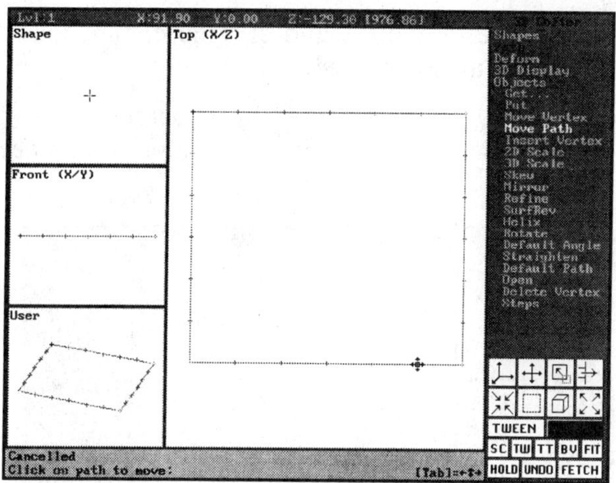

Moving the path.

All shapes will keep their position relative to the path when the path is moved.

RELATED COMMANDS

Path/Move Vertex, Shapes/Move

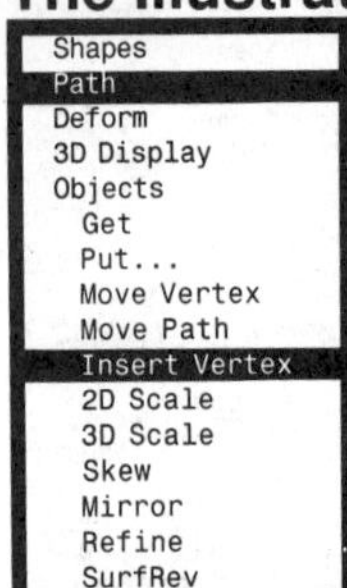

Path/Insert Vertex

Inserts a vertex between the start and end vertices, or after the end vertex.

Inserting a Vertex

1. Select *Path/Insert Vertex.*
2. Activate any viewport other than Shape.
3. Select the point on the path where the new vertex is to be inserted and click. The path changes color and a vertex is attached to the cursor.
4. Click again to place the vertex in the new location or move the cursor to specify a new location for the vertex.
5. Right-click to release the vertex and end the command, otherwise click and continue to add more vertices.
6. The spline value can also be adjusted by selecting the new position and holding down the mouse button. Make adjustments as necessary.
7. Repeat steps 4, 5, and 6 until all vertices have been place.

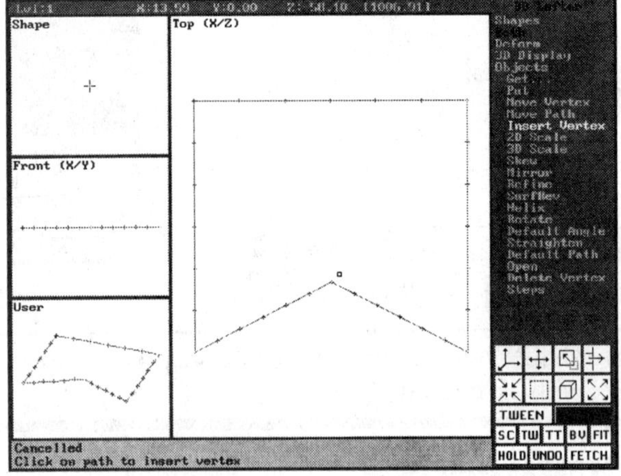

Inserting a vertex on a path.

NOTE As vertices are add, new segments to the path are created. These segments will contain the number of steps specified in the *Path/Steps* command.

RELATED COMMANDS

Path/Move Vertex, 2D Shaper/Modify/Vertex/Adjust

Shapes
Path
Deform
3D Display
Objects
Get
Put...
Move Vertex
Move Path
Insert Vertex
2D Scale
3D Scale
Skew
Mirror
Refine
SurfRev

Path/2D Scale

Scales the path along the plane of the active viewport from its start point.

2D Scaling a Path

1. Select *Path/2D Scale.*
2. Select the path. The cursor will change to the multidirectional cursor. Use [Tab] to constrain the movements vertically or horizontally.
3. The scale will change in relation to the mouse movements. Verify the scale by reading the percentage of scale indicator in the status line.
4. Click to accept the new scale of the path.
5. Use the right mouse button to cancel the operation.

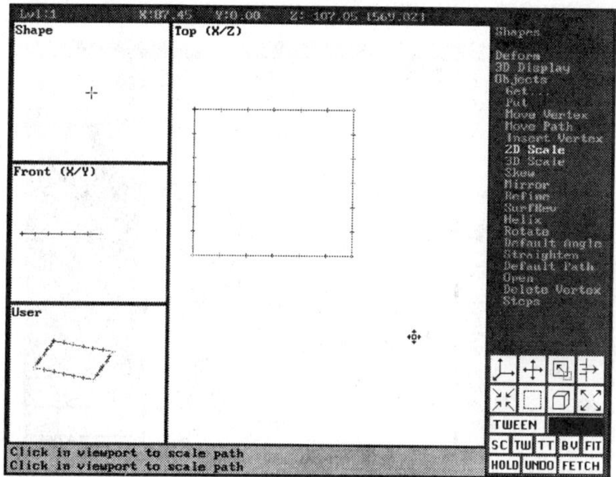

Scaling the path in only two dimensions.

Use this command with paths that are parallel to a 2D plane.

RELATED COMMANDS

Path/Move Vertex, Path/Move Path, Path/3D Scale, Path/Skew

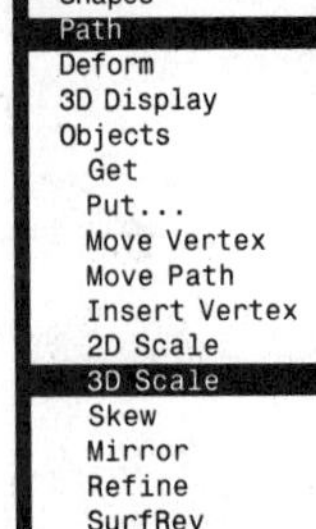

Path/3D Scale

Scales the path in three dimensions about its start point.

3D Scaling a Path

1. Select *Path/3D Scale.*
2. Select the path. The cursor will change to the multidirectional cursor. Use Tab to constrain the movements vertically or horizontally.
3. The scale will change in relation to the mouse movements in all three dimensions. Verify the scale by reading the percentage of scale indicator in the status line.
4. Click to accept the new scale of the path.
5. Use the right mouse button to cancel the operation.

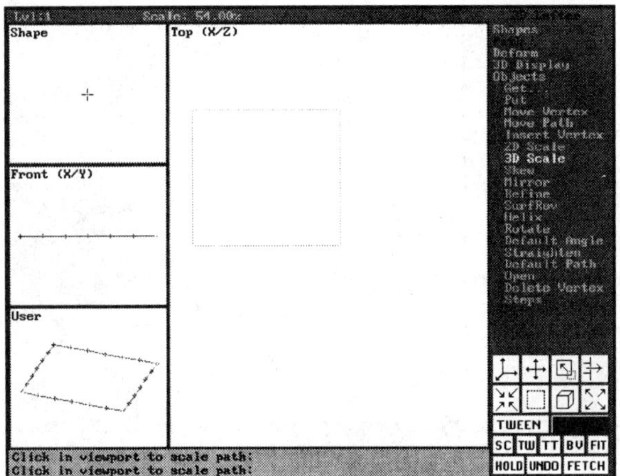

Scaling the path in all three dimensions.

RELATED COMMANDS

Path/Move Vertex, Path/Move Path, Path/2D Scale, Path/Skew

Path/Skew

Shapes
Path
Deform
3D Display
Objects
Get
Put...
Move Vertex
Move Path
Insert Vertex
2D Scale
3D Scale
Skew
Mirror
Refine
SurfRev

Skews a path from its start vertex, parallel to its current viewport plane.

Skewing a Path.

1. Select *Path/Skew.*
2. Select the path. The cursor will change to the multidirectional cursor. Use [Tab] to constrain the movements vertically or horizontally.
3. The skew will change in relation to the mouse movements. Verify the skew in units by reading the offset of the skew indicator in the status line.
4. Click to accept the shape of the path.
5. Use the right mouse button to cancel the operation.

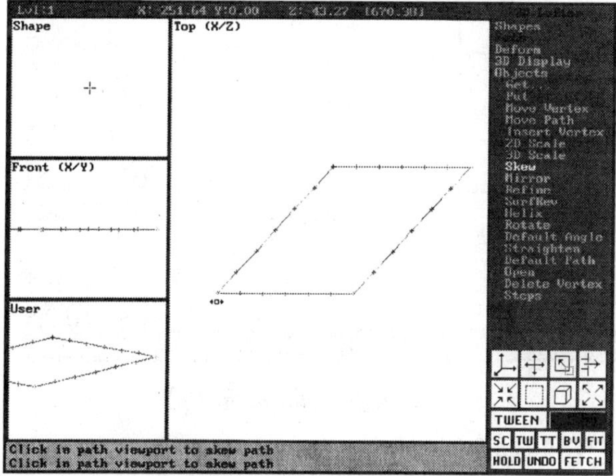

Skewing the path.

RELATED COMMANDS

Path/2D Scale, Path/3D Scale, Path/Mirror

Path/Mirror

Mirrors a path about its start vertex.

Mirroring a Path

1. Select *Path/Mirror.*
2. The cursor will change to the multidirectional cursor. Use [Tab] to constrain the mirror vertically or horizontally or use the multidirectional cursor to mirror the path along both axes.
3. Select the path. The path will now be mirrored.

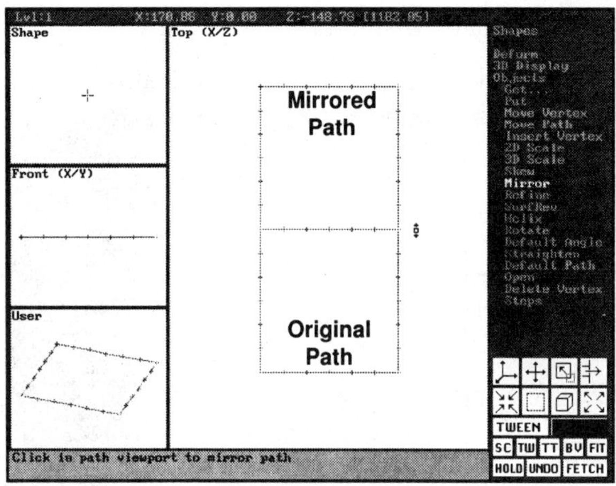

Mirroring the path.

RELATED COMMANDS

Path/2D Scale, Path/3D Scale, Path/Skew

Path/Refine

Shapes
Path
Deform
3D Display
Objects
Get
Put...
Move Vertex
Move Path
Insert Vertex
2D Scale
3D Scale
Skew
Mirror
Refine
SurfRev

Inserts a vertex, or level, on the path without altering its overall shape.

Refining a Path

1. Select *Path/Refine.*
2. Select a point on the path to receive the new vertex. The vertex is inserted and the number of path steps increases between the existing and the new inserted vertex.
3. Use *Path/Move Vertex* to modify its position or spline value.

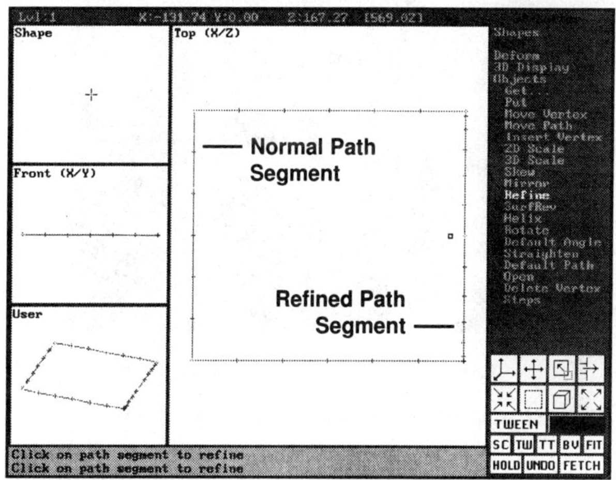

Refining a path without altering its shape.

RELATED COMMANDS

Path/Move Vertex, Path/Insert Vertex

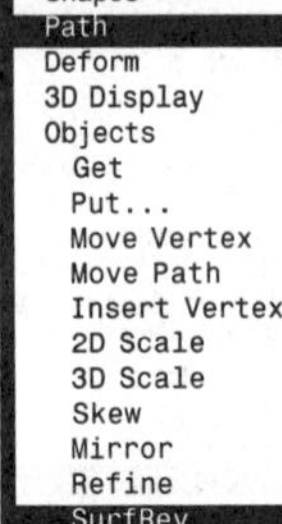

Path/SurfRev

Creates a circular path using the Surface of Revolution dialog box.

Creating a Circular Path Using the Surface of Revolution Dialog Box

1. Select *Path/SurfRev*. The Surface of Revolution dialog box appears as shown below.

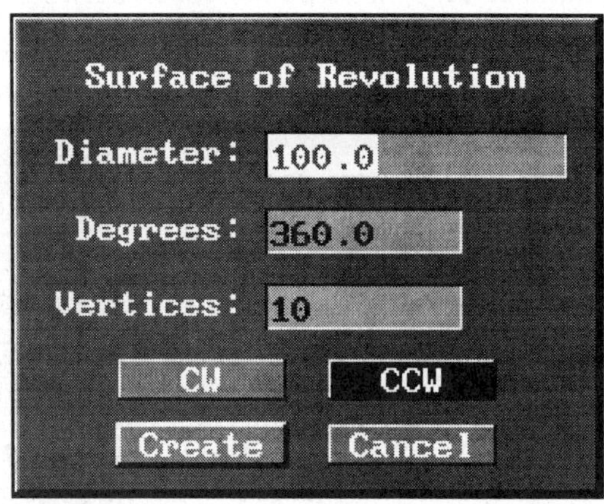

The Surface of Revolution dialog box.

2. Make modifications to the following options:

Diameter: Specify the diameter of the circular path in the units specified in the Unit Setup dialog box.

Degrees: Specify the number of degrees to be included in the circular path. Use any number from 0 to 360.

Vertices: Specify the number of vertices to be included on the circular path.

CW: Specifies whether the circular path is clockwise.

CCW: Specifies whether the circular path is counterclockwise.

Create: Creates the circular path using the options specified above. When the path is created you will be prompted to replace the current path. Select **OK** to accept this option, choose **Cancel** to reject the path.

Cancel: Closes the dialog box without creating the path or saving the settings in the dialog box.

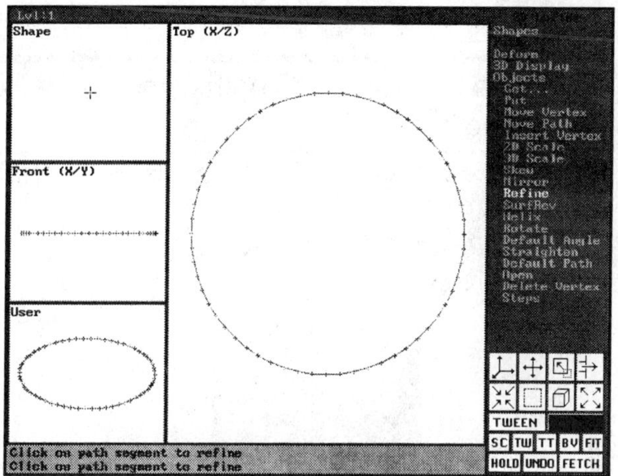

A circular path created using the Surface of Revolution dialog box.

Use the *Shape/Align/Left* or *Shape/Align/Right* to align the shape with the path.

RELATED COMMAND

Path/Helix

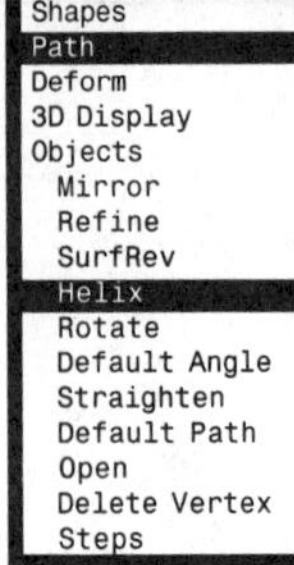

Path/Helix

Creates a helical (spiral) path using the Helix Path Definition dialog box.

Creating a Helical Path using the Helix Path Definition dialog box

1. Select *Path/Helix*. The Helix Path Definition dialog box appears as shown below.

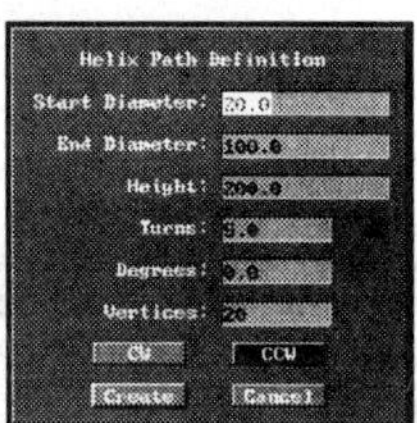

Creating a helical path.

2. Make modifications to the following options:

Start Diameter: Specify the diameter of the (bottom) first turn of the helical path, as shown in the front viewport, in the units specified in the Unit Setup dialog box.

End Diameter: Specify the diameter of the (top) last turn of the helical path.

Height: Specify the height of the helical path.

Turns: Specify the number of turns in the helical path. Not needed if Degrees is specified.

Degrees: Specify the number of degrees to be included on the helical path. Not needed if Turns is specified.

Vertices: Specify the number of vertices to be included on the helical path

CW: Specifies whether the helical path is clockwise.

CCW: Specifies whether the helical path is counterclockwise.

Create: Creates the helical path using the options specified above. When the path is created you will be prompted to replace the current path. Select **OK** to accept this option, choose **Cancel** to reject the path.

Cancel: Closes the dialog box without creating the path or saving the settings in the dialog box.

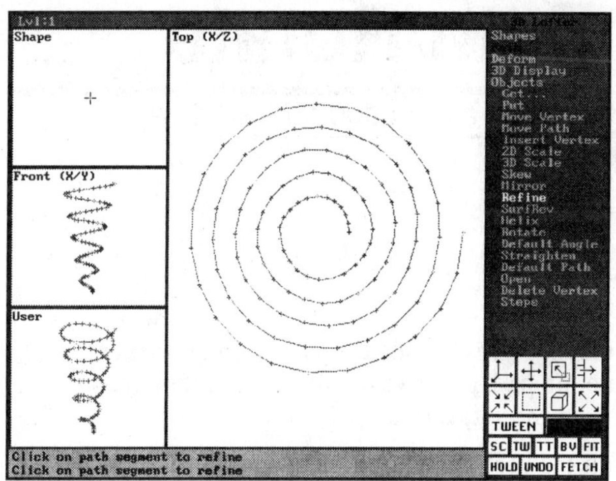

A helical path.

Use the *Path/Center* command to align the shape with the helical path.

RELATED COMMAND

Path/SurfRev

Shapes
Path
Deform
3D Display
Objects
Mirror
Refine
SurfRev
Helix
Rotate
Default Angle
Straighten
Default Path
Open
Delete Vertex
Steps

Path/Rotate

Rotates a path about its start vertex.

Rotating a Path

1. Select *Path/Rotate.*
2. Select the path.
3. Move the mouse right to rotate the path counterclockwise and move the mouse left to rotate the path clockwise. Verify the rotation using the Angle of Rotation display on the status line.
4. To constrain the rotation angle to a specified increment, use the Angle Snap option.
5. Once the path is rotated, click the left mouse button.
6. Use the right mouse button to cancel the operation.

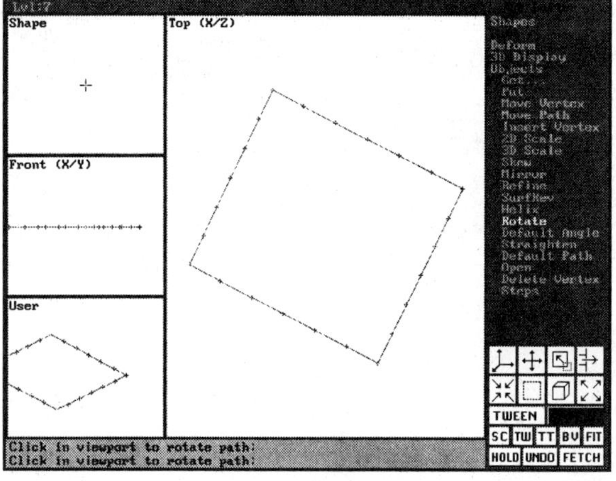

Rotating a path.

The path will rotate about its start point parallel to the active viewport.

RELATED COMMANDS

Path/Move, Path/Mirror, Path/2D Scale, Path/3D Scale, Shapes/Rotate, View-Angle Snap

Path/Default Angle

Restores the original default path angle.

Restoring the Default Path Angle

1. After rotating a path using the *Path/Rotate* command, select *Path/Default Angle*.
2. The dialog box shown below appears if the angle has been changed from the default. Click on **OK** to restore the default path angle or **Cancel** to cancel the command.

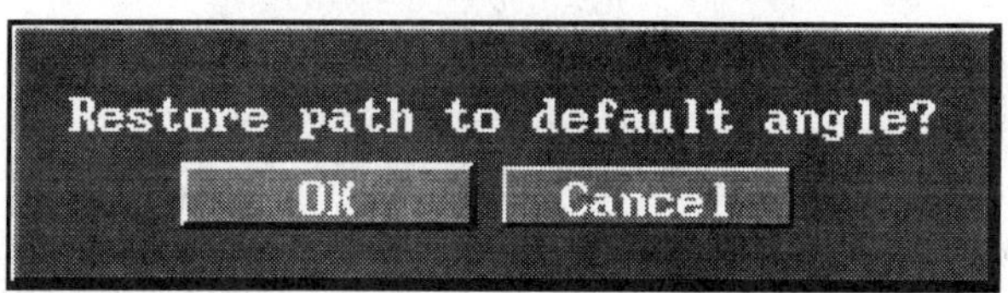

Use this dialog box to restore the default angle.

NOTE The dialog box will not appear if the default angle has not been changed.

RELATED COMMANDS

Path/Move Vertex, Path/Skew, Path/Mirror, Path/Rotate, Path/Straighten

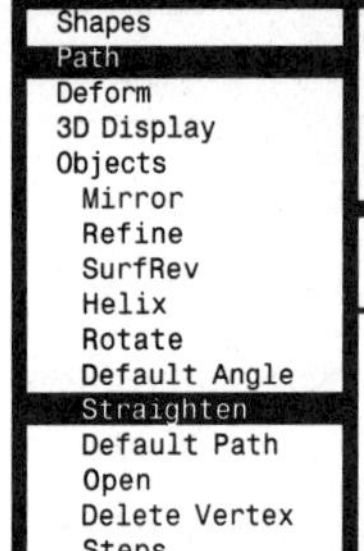

Path/Straighten

Staightens an open path.

Straightening an Open Path

1. Select *Path/Straighten.*
2. The dialog box shown below appears. Click on **OK** to straighten the path or **Cancel** to cancel the command.

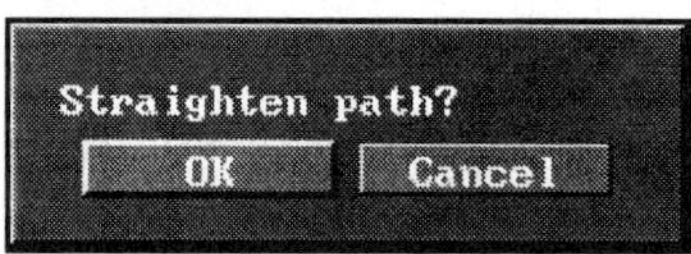

Use the dialog box to verify your selection.

3. If **OK** is chosen, the path will be straightened along the default Z axis.

NOTE A closed path cannot be straightened. If a closed path is chosen to be straightened, the dialog box below is shown. Select **Continue** and modify the path with either the *Path/Open* or the *Path/Delete Vertex* command.

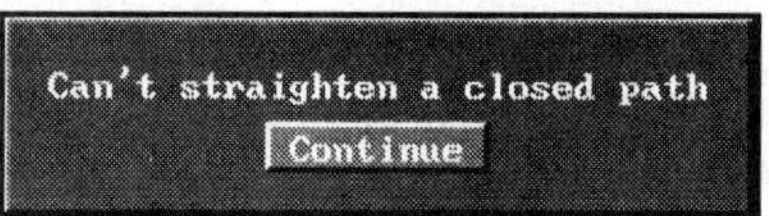

RELATED COMMANDS

Path/Move Vertex, Path/Skew, Path/Mirror, Path/Rotate, Path/Default Angle

Path/Default Path

Shapes
Path
Deform
3D Display
Objects
Mirror
Refine
SurfRev
Helix
Rotate
Default Angle
Straighten
Default Path
Open
Delete Vertex
Steps

Replaces the current path with a single-segment path 100 units long with two vertices and five steps.

Changing the Current Path to the Default Path

1. Select *Path/Default.*
2. The dialog box shown below appears. Click on **OK** to replace the current path with the default path or **Cancel** to cancel the command.

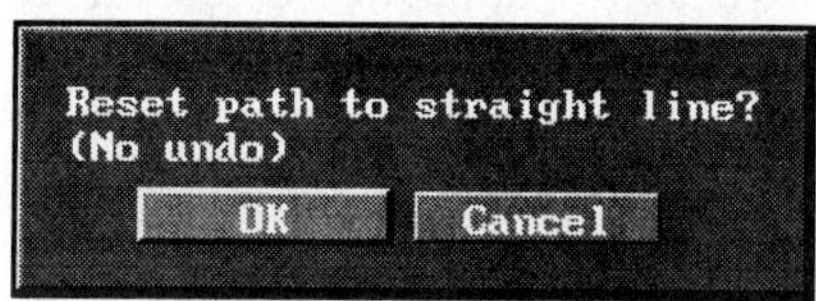

Verifying the default path selection

3. If **OK** is chosen, the current path is replaced with the default path shown below.

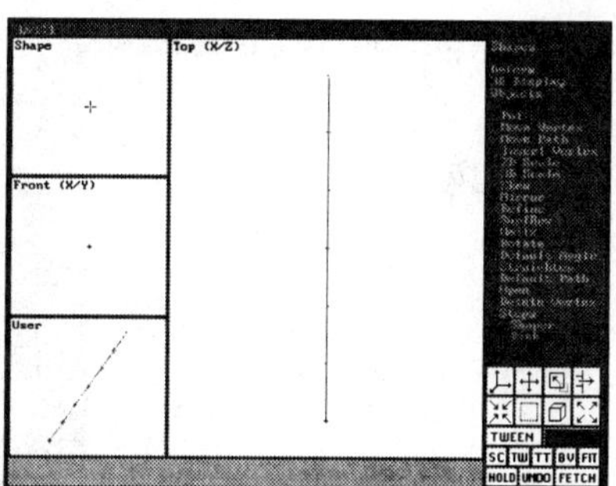

Changing the current path with the default path.

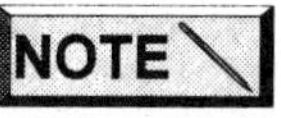

If you want a straight path with all of the shapes intact, use the *Path/Straighten* command.

RELATED COMMANDS

Path/Move Vertex, Path/Skew, Path/Mirror, Path/Rotate, Path/Default Angle, Path/Straighten

Path/Open

Creates an open path from a closed path by deleting a segment.

Creating an Open Path

1. Select *Path/Open*.
2. Click on the segment to be deleted to create the open path.
3. The dialog box shown below appears. Click on **OK** to open the current path or **Cancel** to cancel the command.

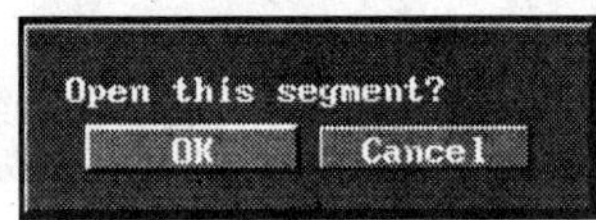

Verifying that the path is to be opened.

4. The path will be opened as shown in the figure below.

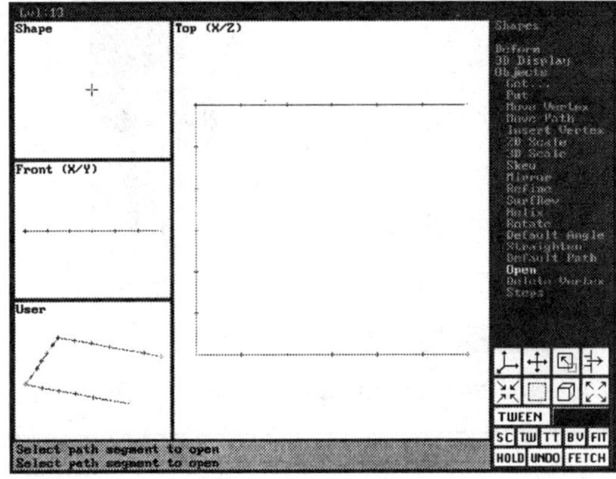

This once-square path, has been opened.

RELATED COMMANDS

Path/Default Angle, Path/Straighten

Path/Delete Vertex

Shapes
Path
Deform
3D Display
Objects
Mirror
Refine
SurfRev
Helix
Rotate
Default Angle
Straighten
Default Path
Open
Delete Vertex
Steps

Deletes a vertex on the path.

Deleting a Vertex on the Path

1. Select *Path/Delete Vertex.*
2. In any viewport, click on the vertex on the path to be deleted.
3. The vertex and any shapes on that level will be deleted.

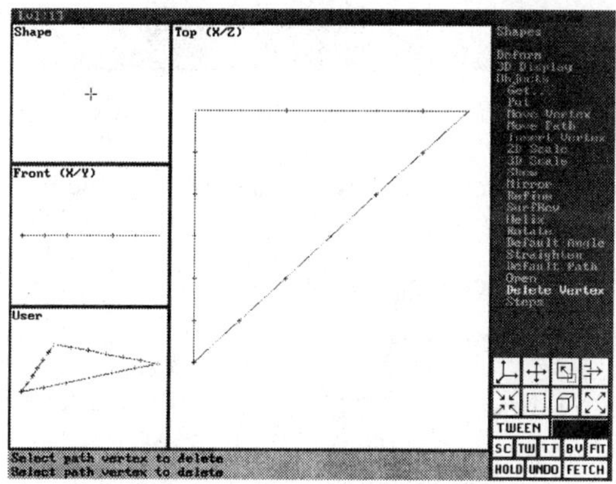

This once square path, has had the lower right vertex deleted.

NOTE If there are only two vertices on the path, a dialog box will be displayed stating that two vertices are need to make a path. Click **Continue** to cancel the command.

RELATED COMMANDS

Path/Default Angle, Path/Straighten

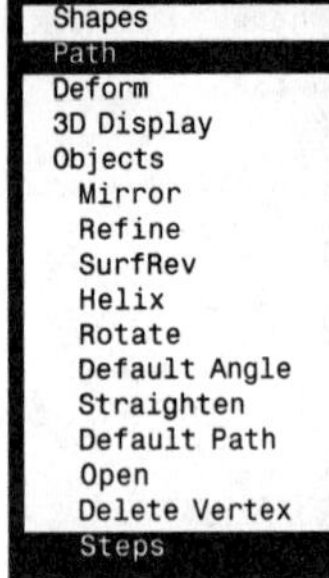

Path/Steps

Sets the number of steps for all shapes to increase shape resolution.

Setting the Number of Steps for all Shapes

1. Select *Path/Steps*. The Set Steps dialog box will be displayed as shown below.

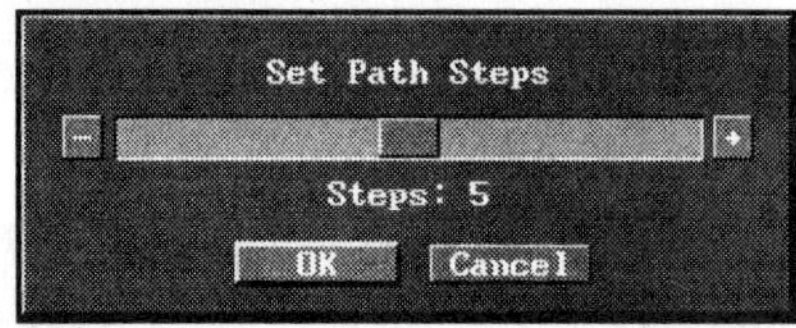

Use the dialog box to change the steps setting.

2. Change the setting by using the following methods. The range for the steps is from 0 to 10.

   Click the + or - buttons to change the value in increments of one.

   Drag the slider to the desired location.

   Use the pointer and click in the slider area. The slider will automatically jump to that location.

3. To accept the setting click the **OK** button. To cancel the command, click **Cancel**.

> **NOTE** Increasing the steps also increases the complexity and size of the object being lofted. Be sure to use only the necessary steps to conserve memory and storage.

RELATED COMMAND

2D Shaper/Shapes/Steps

Deform/Scale/Move

Shapes
Path
Deform
3D Display
Objects
Scale...
Twist...
Teeter...
Move
Insert
Refine
Delete
Limits
Reset
Swap
Symmetry...

Moves a vertex on the blue spline of the scale deformation grid.

Moving a Vertex on the Blue Spline

1. Select *Deform/Scale/Move.* The deformation grid will be displayed.
2. Move the cursor to either the Scale X or Scale Y viewport and click. The multidirectional cursor will appear. Press t until the horizontal cursor appears.
3. Select the vertex on the blue spline to be moved.
4. Move the vertex to its new location and select that point. If needed, the spline value can also be changed.

TIP Use snap to move the vertex in increments of 10 percent.

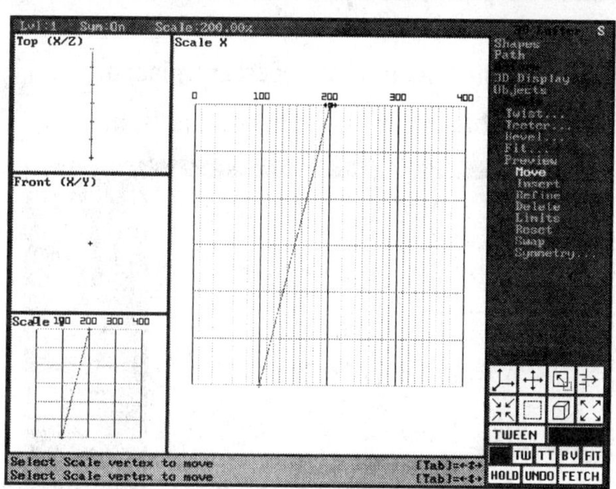

Moving a vertex to adjust the deformation scale.

NOTE Moving a vertex on the blue spline does not change the location of that vertex on the path. It only changes the blue spline's location on the deformation grid, which specifies the percentage of scale for a cross section located at each vertex or step on the path.

RELATED COMMANDS

Deform/Scale/Insert, Deform/Scale/Delete, Deform/Scale/Reset

Shapes
Path
Deform
3D Display
Objects
Scale...
Twist...
Teeter...
Move
Insert
Refine
Delete
Limits
Reset
Swap
Symmetry...

Deform/Scale/Insert

Inserts a vertex on the blue spline of the scale deformation grid.

Inserting a Vertex on the Blue Spline

1. Select *Deform/Scale/Insert.* The deformation grid will be displayed.
2. Move the cursor to either the Scale X or Scale Y viewport and click. The pick box will appear.
3. Move the pick box to the point on the blue spline where a vertex is to be added and select that point. A new vertex will be added. At this point the spline value can also be adjusted.

> **NOTE** Inserting a vertex on the blue spline does not insert a vertex on the path. It only adds a vertex to the blue spline on the deformation grid, which specifies the percentage of scale for a cross section located at each vertex or step on the path.

4. Move the cursor to place the new vertex. If no new position is needed, right-click to complete the operation.
5. Continue steps 3-4 until all new vertices are placed.
6. When you have completed this command, right-click.

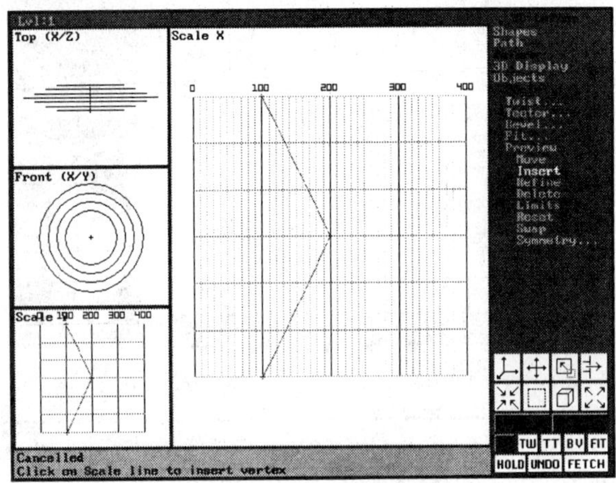

Inserting a vertex to adjust the deformation scale

RELATED COMMANDS

Deform/Scale/Move, Deform/Scale/Delete, Deform/Scale/Reset

Deform/Scale/Refine

Shapes
Path
Deform
3D Display
Objects
Scale...
Twist...
Teeter...
Move
Insert
Refine
Delete
Limits
Reset
Swap
Symmetry...

Inserts a vertex on the blue spline of the scale deformation grid without effecting its curvature.

Refining the Blue Spline

1. Select *Deform/Scale/Refine*. The deformation grid will be displayed.
2. Move the cursor to either the Scale X or Scale Y viewport and click. The pick box will appear.
3. Move the pick box to the point on the blue spline where a vertex is to be added and select that point.

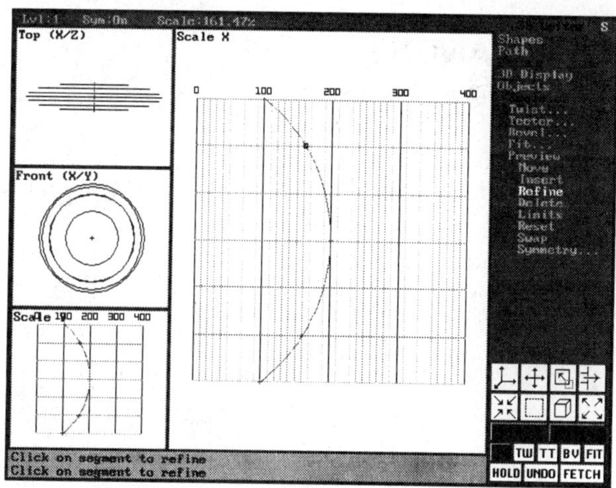

Refining the deformation blue spline.

RELATED COMMANDS

Deform/Scale/Insert, Deform/Scale/Delete

Shapes
Path
Deform
3D Display
Objects
Scale...
Twist...
Teeter...
Move
Insert
Refine
Delete
Limits
Reset
Swap
Symmetry...

Deform/Scale/Delete

Deletes any vertex other than the two end vertices on the blue spline of the scale deformation grid.

Deleting a Vertex on the Blue Spline

1. Select *Deform/Scale/Delete.* The deformation grid will be displayed.
2. Move the cursor to either the Scale X or Scale Y viewport and click. The pick box will appear.
3. Select the vertex on the blue spline to be deleted. That vertex will be deleted.

RELATED COMMANDS

Deform/Scale/Insert, Deform/Scale/Refine

Deform/Scale/Limits

Shapes
Path
Deform
3D Display
Objects
Scale...
Twist...
Teeter...
Move
Insert
Refine
Delete
Limits
Reset
Swap
Symmetry...

Changes the percent scale displayed on the deformation grid.

Changing the Percent Scale Display on the Deformation Grid

1. Select *Deform/Scale/Limits*. The "Scale Deformation Limit" dialog box appears as shown below.

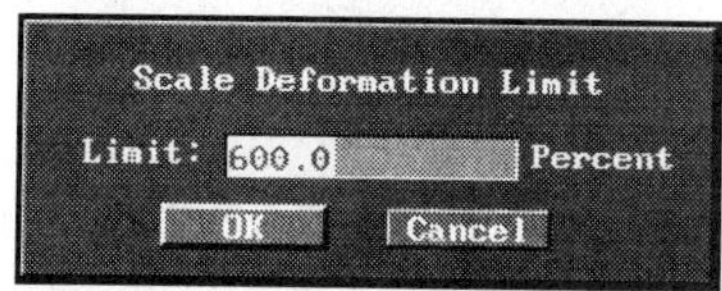

Changing the scale deformation grid limits.

2. Change the default value of 400.0 to change the limit.
3. Select **OK** to accept the changes or choose **Cancel** to cancel the selection.
4. If **OK** is selected, the new scale limits will be displayed in the Scale X and Scale Y viewports.

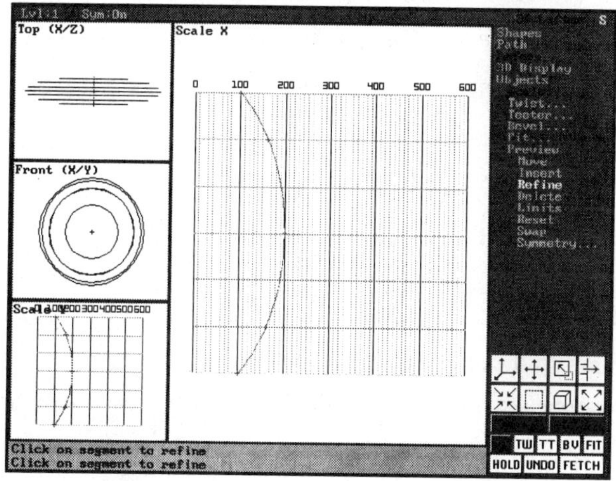

Changing the deformation grid limits.

RELATED COMMAND

Deform/Scale/Reset

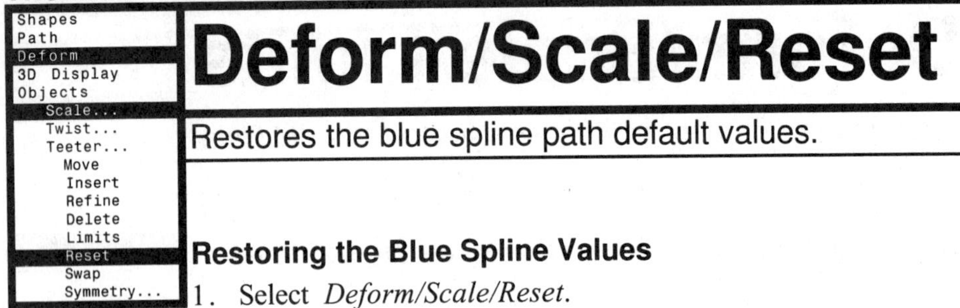

Deform/Scale/Reset

Restores the blue spline path default values.

Restoring the Blue Spline Values

1. Select *Deform/Scale/Reset.*
2. If symmetry is on, the following dialog box will appear.

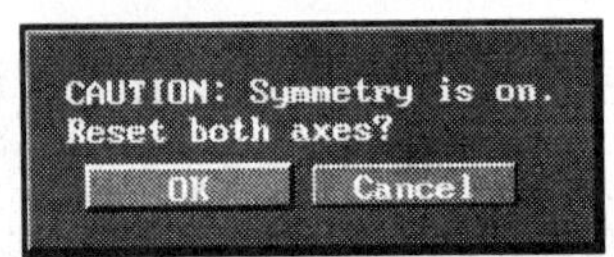

Use this dialog box to verify changes.

3. Select **OK** to reset both axes, choose **Cancel** to cancel the command.
4. If symmetry is off, the following dialog box will appear.

Use this dialog box to verify changes.

5. Make a selection from the list below.

X: Resets the X-axis grid.

Y: Resets the Y-axis grid.

Both: Resets both the X and Y-axis grids.

Cancel: Cancel the command.

This command will not change the deformation grid limits.

RELATED COMMANDS

Deform/Scale/Insert, Deform/Scale/Delete, Deform/Scale/Refine, Deform/Scale/Symmetry

Deform/Scale/Swap

Shapes
Path
Deform
3D Display
Objects
Scale...
Twist...
Teeter...
Move
Insert
Refine
Delete
Limits
Reset
Swap
Symmetry...

Swaps the blue spline values between the X and Y-axis grid.

Swapping X and Y-axis grid values

1. Select *Deform/Scale/Swap*. The X and Y axis values will be swapped.

This command works only if Symmetry is turned off.

RELATED COMMANDS

Deform/Scale/Symmetry/Off

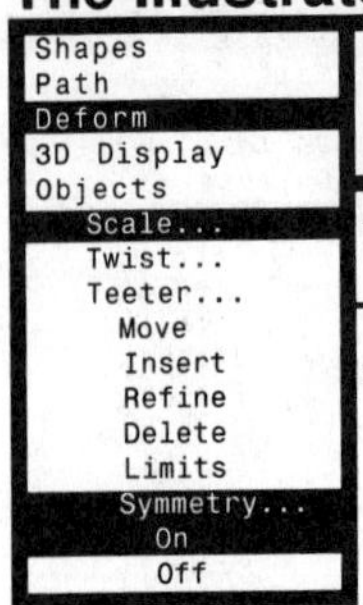

Deform/Scale/Symmetry/On

Turns Symmetry On.

Turning Symmetry On

1. Select *Deform/Scale/Symmetry/On.* Symmetry is now activated and *Sym:On* appears in the status line.
2. Any changes made to the blue spline will now be applied to the both axes.

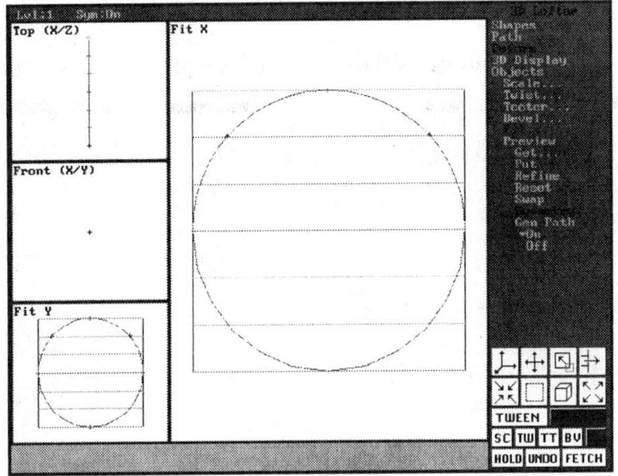

Turning Symmetry On

RELATED COMMANDS

Deform/Scale/Symmetry/Off

Shapes
Path
Deform
3D Display
Objects
Scale...
Twist...
Teeter...
Move
Insert
Refine
Delete
Limits
Symmetry...
On
Off

Deform/Scale/Symmetry/Off

Turns Symmetry Off.

Turning Symmetry Off

1. Select *Deform/Scale/Symmetry/Off.* Symmetry is now deactivated and *Sym:Off* appears in the status line.
2. Changes to the blue spline must now be made independently.

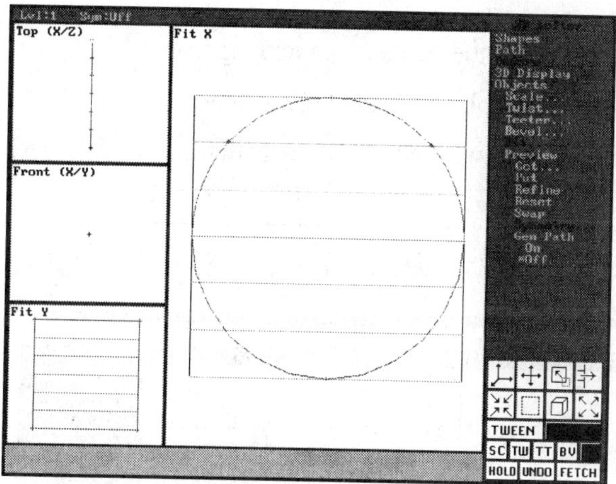

Turning Symmetry Off

RELATED COMMANDS

Deform/Scale/Symmetry/Off

Shapes
Path
Deform
3D Display
Objects
Scale...
Twist...
Teeter...
Bevel...
Fit...
Move
Insert
Refine
Delete
Limits
Reset

Deform/Twist/Move

Moves a vertex on the blue spline of the Twist deformation grid.

Moving a Vertex on the Blue Spline

1. Select *Deform/Twist/Move*. The deformation grid will be displayed.
2. Move the cursor to the Twist viewport and click. The multidirectional cursor will appear. Press [Tab] until the horizontal cursor appears.
3. Select the vertex on the blue spline to be moved.
4. Move the vertex to its new location and select that point. If needed, the spline value can also be changed.

Use snap to move the vertex in increments of 10 units.

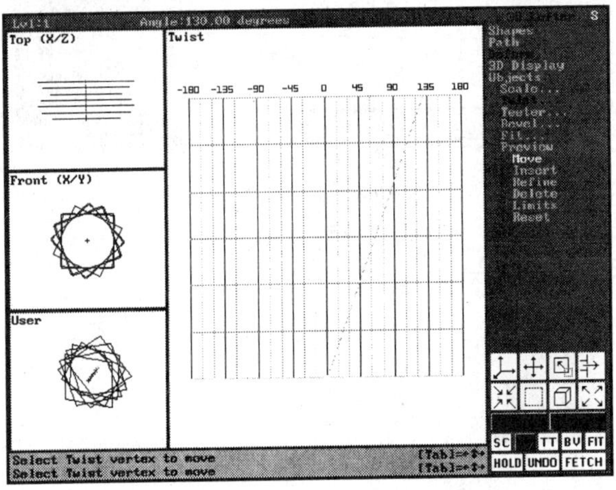

Moving the blue spline on the twist deformation grid.

NOTE Moving a vertex on the blue spline does not change the location of that vertex on the path. It only changes the blue spline's location on the deformation grid, which specifies the angle of twist for a cross section located at each vertex or step on the path.

RELATED COMMANDS

Deform/Twist/Insert, Deform/Twist/Delete, Deform/Twist/Reset

Deform/Twist/Insert

Shapes
Path
Deform
3D Display
Objects
Scale...
Twist...
Teeter...
Bevel...
Fit...
Move
Insert
Refine
Delete
Limits
Reset

Inserts a vertex on the blue spline of the Twist deformation grid.

Inserting a Vertex on the Blue Spline

1. Select *Deform/Twist/Insert.* The deformation grid will be displayed.
2. Move the cursor to the Twist viewport and click. The pick box will appear.
3. Move the pick box to the point on the blue spline where a vertex is to be added and select that point. A new vertex will be added. At this point the spline value also can be adjusted.
4. Move the cursor to place the new vertex. If no new position is needed, right-click to complete the operation.
5. Continue steps 3and 4 until all new vertices are placed or right-click to cancel the command.

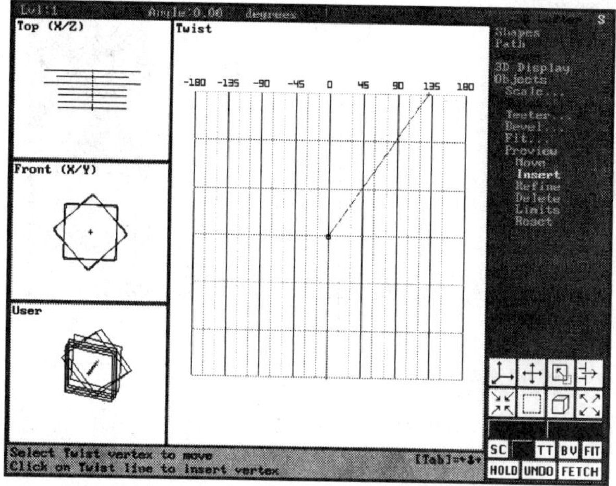

Inserting a vertex on the blue spline of the twist deformation grid.

NOTE Inserting a vertex on the blue spline does not insert a vertex on the path. It only adds a vertex to the blue spline on the deformation grid, which specifies the degree of twist for a cross section located at each vertex or step on the path.

RELATED COMMANDS

Deform/Twist/Move, Deform/Twist/Delete, Deform/Twist/Reset

Deform/Twist/Refine

Inserts a vertex on the blue spline of the Twist deformation grid without affecting its curvature.

Refining the Blue Spline

1. Select *Deform/Twist/Refine.* The deformation grid will be displayed.
2. Move the cursor to the Twist viewport and click. The pick box will appear.
3. Move the pick box to the point on the blue spline where a vertex is to be added and select that point.

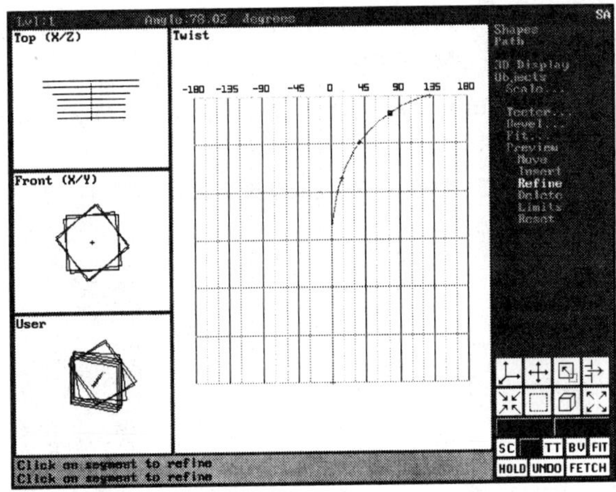

Refining the blue spline.

RELATED COMMANDS

Deform/Twist/Insert, Deform/Twist/Delete

Deform/Twist/Delete

Shapes
Path
Deform
3D Display
Objects
Scale...
Twist...
Teeter...
Bevel...
Fit...
Move
Insert
Refine
Delete
Limits
Reset

Deletes any vertex other than the two end vertices on the blue spline of the Twist deformation grid.

Deleting a Vertex on the Blue Spline

1. Select *Deform/Twist/Delete*. The deformation grid will be displayed.
2. Move the cursor to the Twist viewport and click. The pick box will appear.
3. Select the vertex on the blue spline to be deleted. That vertex will be deleted.

RELATED COMMANDS

Deform/Twist/Insert, Deform/Twist/Refine

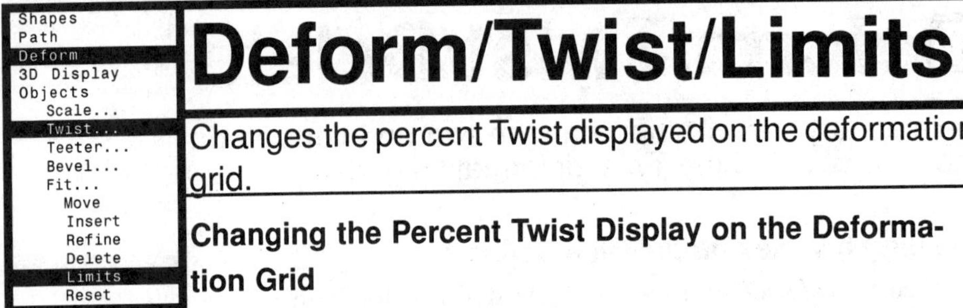

Deform/Twist/Limits

Changes the percent Twist displayed on the deformation grid.

Changing the Percent Twist Display on the Deformation Grid

1. Select *Deform/Twist/Limits*. The Twist Deformation Limit dialog box appears as shown below.

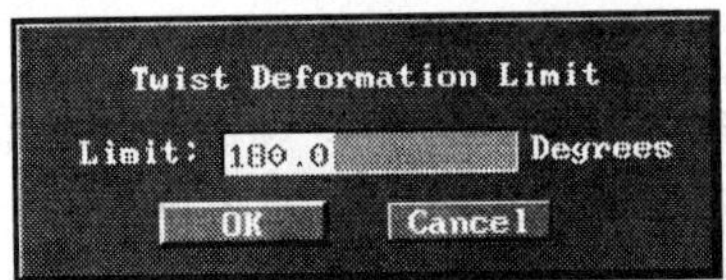

Change the limits using the Twist Deformation Limit dialog box.

2. Change the default value of 180.0 to change the limit.
3. Select **OK** to accept the changes or choose **Cancel** to cancel the selection.
4. If **OK** is selected, the new twist limits will be displayed in the Twist viewport.

Keeping the limits as small as possible allows for easier adjustments of smaller increments of percentages.

RELATED COMMAND

Deform/Scale/Limits

Deform/Twist/Reset

Restores the blue spline path default values.

Restoring the Blue Spline Values

1. Select *Deform/Twist/Reset.* The following dialog box will be displayed.

Verifying the reset selection

2. Select **OK** to reset the blue spline; choose **Cancel** to cancel the command.

This command will not change the deformation grid limits.

RELATED COMMANDS

Deform/Twist/Insert, Deform/Twist/Delete, Deform/Twist/Refine

Shapes
Path
Deform
3D Display
Objects
Teeter...
Bevel...
Fit...
Move
Insert
Refine
Delete
Limits
Reset
Swap
Symmetry...

Deform/Teeter/Move

Moves a vertex on the blue spline of the Teeter deformation grid.

Moving a Vertex on the Blue Spline

1. Select *Deform/Teeter/Move.* The deformation grid will be displayed.
2. Move the cursor to either the Teeter X or Teeter Y viewport and click. The multidirectional cursor will appear. Press Tab until the horizontal cursor appears.
3. Select the vertex on the blue spline to be moved.
4. Move the vertex to its new location and select that point. If needed, the spline value can also be changed.

TIP Use snap to move the vertex in increments of 10 degrees.

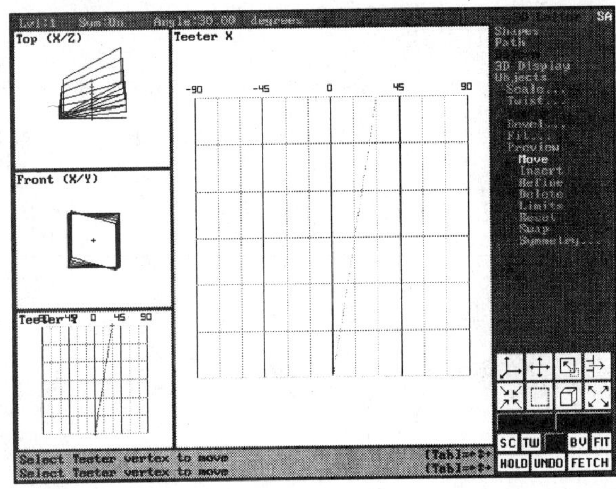

Moving the blue spline on the Teeter deformation grid.

NOTE Moving a vertex on the blue spline does not change the location of that vertex on the path. It only changes the blue spline's location on the deformation grid, which specifies the percentage of teeter for a cross section located at each vertex or step on the path.

RELATED COMMANDS

Deform/Teeter/Insert, Deform/Teeter/Delete, Deform/Teeter/Reset

Deform/Teeter/Insert

Shapes
Path
Deform
3D Display
Objects
Scale...
Twist...
Teeter...
Bevel...
Fit...
Move
Insert
Refine
Delete
Limits
Reset

Inserts a vertex on the blue spline of the Teeter deformation grid.

Inserting a Vertex on the Blue Spline

1. Select *Deform/Teeter/Insert.* The deformation grid will be displayed.
2. Move the cursor to either the Teeter X or Teeter Y viewport and click. The multidirectional cursor will appear. Press [Tab] until the horizontal cursor appears.
3. Move the pick box to the point on the blue spline where a vertex is to be added and select that point. A new vertex will be added. At this point the spline value also can be adjusted.
4. Move the cursor to place the new vertex. If no new position is needed, right-click to complete the operation.
5. Continue steps 3 and 4 until all new vertices are placed or right-click to cancel the command.

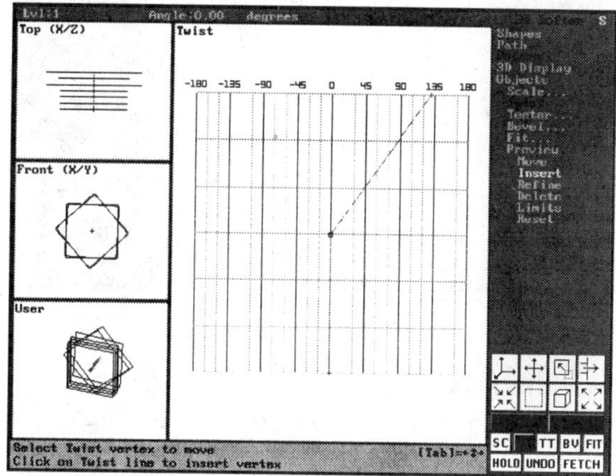

Inserting a vertex on the blue spline of the Teeter deformation grid.

NOTE Inserting a vertex on the blue spline does not insert a vertex on the path. It only adds a vertex to the blue spline on the deformation grid, which specifies the degree of twist for a cross section located at each vertex or step on the path.

RELATED COMMANDS

Deform/Teeter/Move, Deform/Teeter/Delete, Deform/Teeter/Reset

Shapes
Path
Deform
3D Display
Objects
Teeter...
Bevel...
Fit...
Move
Insert
Refine
Delete
Limits
Reset
Swap
Symmetry...

Deform/Teeter/Refine

Inserts a vertex on the blue spline of the Twist deformation grid without affecting its curvature.

Refining the Blue Spline

1. Select *Deform/Teeter/Refine.* The deformation grid will be displayed.
2. Move the cursor to either the Teeter X or Teeter Y viewport and click. The pick box will appear.
3. Move the pick box to the point on the blue spline where a vertex is to be added and select that point.

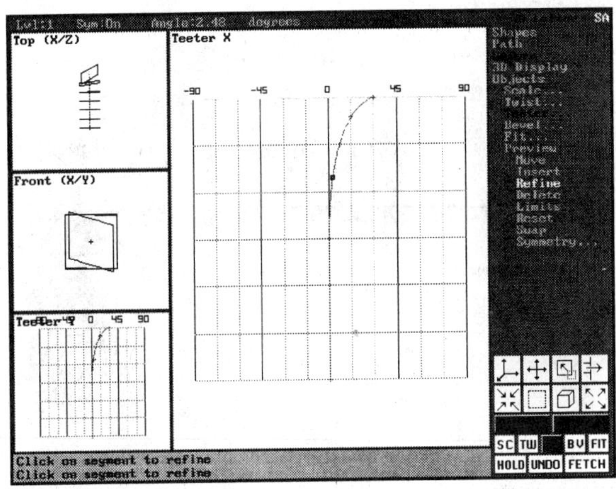

Refining the blue spline.

RELATED COMMANDS

Deform/Teeter/Insert, Deform/Teeter/Delete

Deform/Teeter/Delete

Shapes
Path
Deform
3D Display
Objects
Teeter...
Bevel...
Fit...
Move
Insert
Refine
Delete
Limits
Reset
Swap
Symmetry...

Deletes any vertex other than the two end vertices on the blue spline of the Teeter deformation grid.

Deleting a Vertex on the Blue Spline

1. Select *Deform/Teeter/Delete.* The deformation grid will be displayed.
2. Move the cursor to either the Teeter X or Teeter Y viewport and click. The pick box will appear.
3. Select the vertex on the blue spline to be deleted. That vertex will be deleted.

RELATED COMMANDS

Deform/Teeter/Insert, Deform/Teeter/Refine

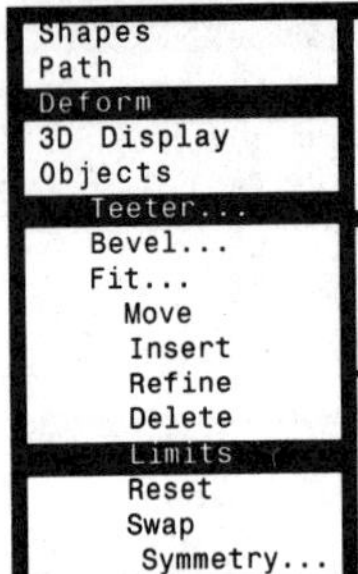

Deform/Teeter/Limits

Changes the percent Teeter displayed on the deformation grid.

Changing the Percent Teeter Display on the Deformation Grid

1. Select *Deform/Teeter/Limits*. The Teeter Deformation Limit dialog box appears as shown below.

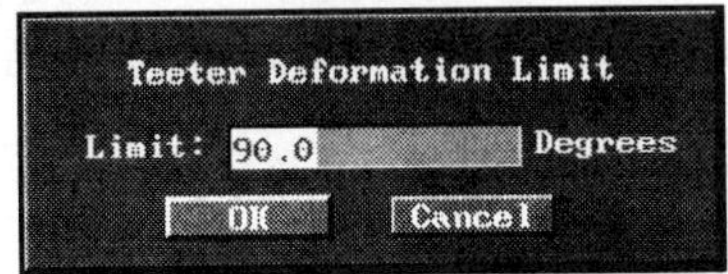

Change the limits using the Twist Deformation Limit dialog box.

2. Change the default value of 180.0 to change the limit.
3. Select **OK** to accept the changes or choose **Cancel** to cancel the selection.
4. If **OK** is selected, the new Teeter limits will be displayed in the Twist viewport.

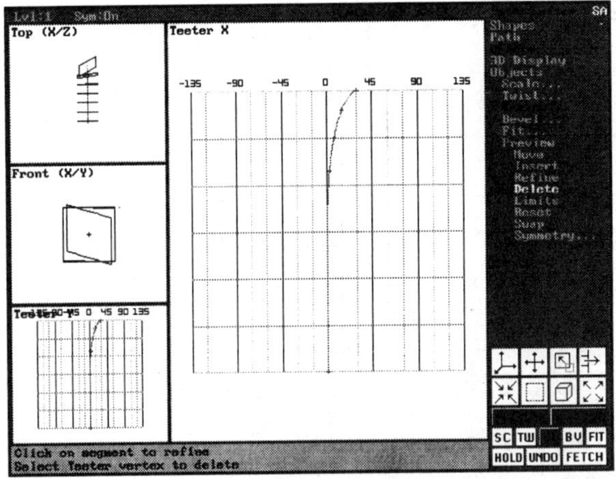

The limits on the teeter deformation grid have been modified.

Keeping the limits as small as possible allows for easier adjustments of smaller increments of percentages.

RELATED COMMAND

Deform/Scale/Limits

Deform/Teeter/Reset

Shapes
Path
Deform
3D Display
Objects
Teeter...
Bevel...
Fit...
Move
Insert
Refine
Delete
Limits
Reset
Swap
Symmetry...

Restores the blue spline path default values.

Restoring the Blue Spline Values

1. If Symmetry is on, the following dialog box will appear.

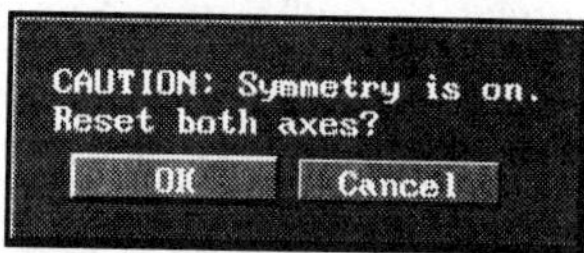

Verifying the reset procedure.

2. Select **OK** to reset both axes; choose **Cancel** to cancel the command.
3. If Symmetry is off, the following dialog box will appear.

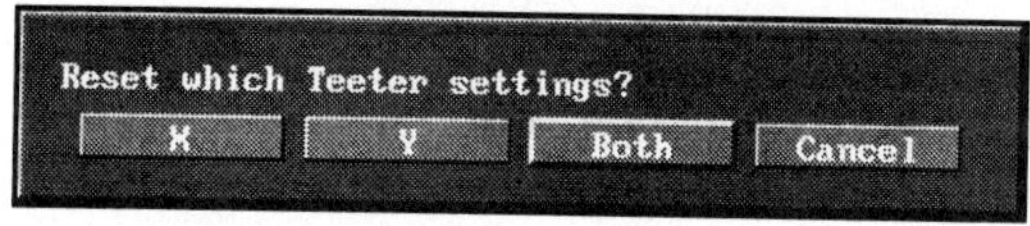

Selecting the teeter setting to reset.

4. Select from the list below.

X: Resets the X-axis grid.

Y: Resets the Y-axis grid.

Both: Resets both the X and Y-axis grids.

Cancel: Cancels the command.

This command will not change the deformation grid limits.

RELATED COMMANDS

Deform/Teeter/Insert, Deform/Teeter/Delete, Deform/Teeter/Refine, Deform/Teeter/Symmetry

Shapes
Path
Deform
3D Display
Objects
Teeter...
Bevel...
Fit...
Move
Insert
Refine
Delete
Limits
Reset
Swap
Symmetry...

Deform/Teeter/Swap

Swaps the blue spline values between the X and Y-axis grid.

Swapping X and Y-axis Grid Values

1. Select *Deform/Teeter/Swap*.
2. The X and Y axis values will be swapped.

This command works only if Symmetry is turned off.

RELATED COMMAND

Deform/Teeter/Symmetry/Off

Shapes
Path
Deform
3D Display
Objects
Teeter...
Bevel...
Fit...
Refine
Delete
Limits
Reset
Swap
Symmetry...
On
Off

Deform/Teeter/Symmetry/On

Turns Symmetry On.

Turning Symmetry On

1. Select *Deform/Scale/Symmetry/On*. Symmetry is now activated and *Sym:On* appears in the status line.

2. Any changes made to the blue spline will now be applied to the both axes.

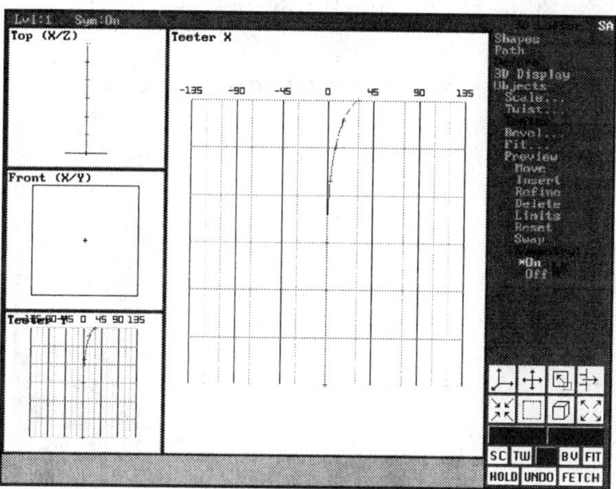

Turning Symmetry On

RELATED COMMANDS

Deform/Teeter/Symmetry/Off

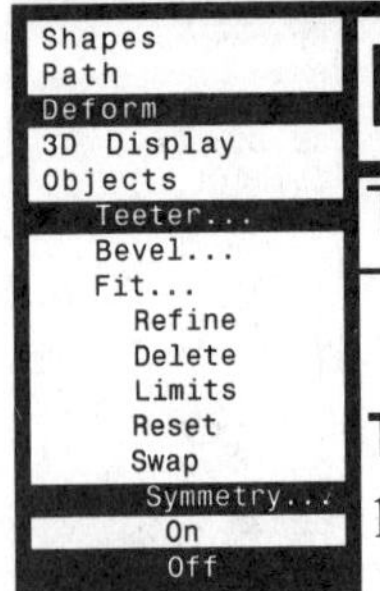

Deform/Teeter/Symmetry/Off

Turns Symmetry off.

Turning Symmetry Off

1. Select *Deform/Scale/Symmetry/Off*. Symmetry is now deactivated and *Sym:Off* appears in the status line.
2. Changes to the blue spline must now be made independently.

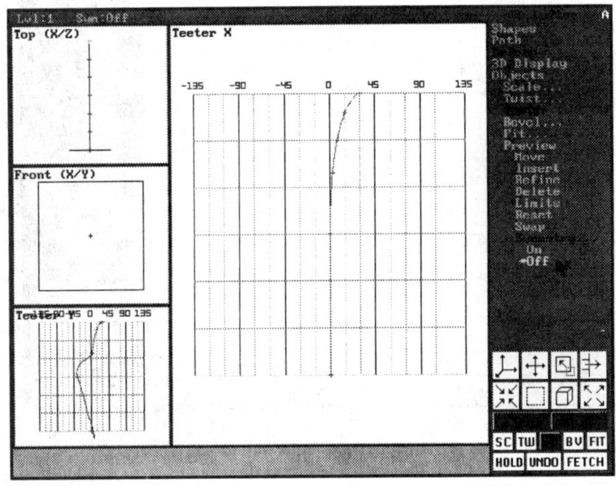

Turning symmetry off

RELATED COMMAND

Deform/Scale/Symmetry/Off

Deform/Bevel/Move

Shapes
Path
Deform
3D Display
Objects
Scale...
Twist...
Teeter...
Bevel...
Fit...
Move
Insert
Refine
Delete
Limits
Reset

Moves a vertex on the blue spline of the Bevel deformation grid.

Moving a Vertex on the Blue Spline

1. Select *Deform/Bevel/Move.* The deformation grid will be displayed.
2. Move the cursor to the Bevel viewport and click. The multidirectional cursor will appear. Press [Tab] until the horizontal cursor appears.
3. Select the vertex on the blue spline to be moved.
4. Move the vertex to its new location and select that point. If needed, the spline value can also be changed.

TIP Use snap to move the vertex in increments of 10 units.

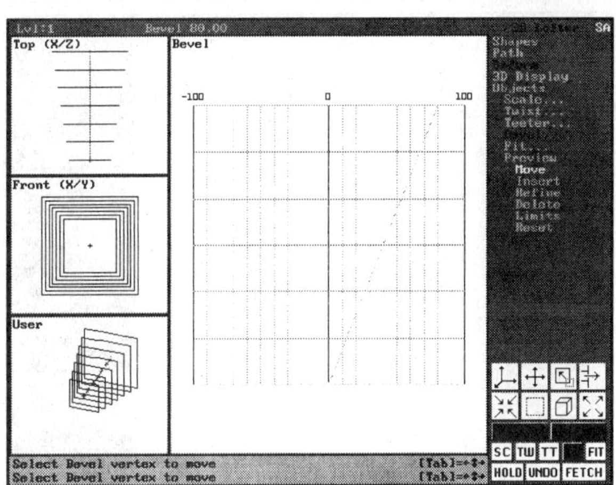

Moving the blue spline on the Bevel deformation grid.

NOTE Moving a vertex on the blue spline does not change the location of that vertex on the path. It only changes the blue spline's location on the deformation grid, which specifies the angle of twist for a cross section located at each vertex or step on the path.

RELATED COMMANDS

Deform/Bevel/Insert, Deform/Bevel/Delete, Deform/Bevel/Reset

Shapes
Path
Deform
3D Display
Objects
Scale...
Twist...
Teeter...
Bevel...
Fit...
Move
Insert
Refine
Delete
Limits
Reset

Deform/Bevel/Insert

Inserts a vertex on the blue spline of the Bevel deformation grid.

Inserting a Vertex on the Blue Spline

1. Select *Deform/Bevel/Insert.* The deformation grid will be displayed.
2. Move the cursor to the Bevel viewport and click. The pick box will appear.
3. Move the pick box to the point on the blue spline where a vertex is to be added and select that point. A new vertex will be added. At this point the spline value also can be adjusted.
4. Move the cursor to place the new vertex. If no new position is needed, right-click to complete the operation.
5. Continue steps 3 and 4 until all new vertices are placed or right-click to cancel the command.

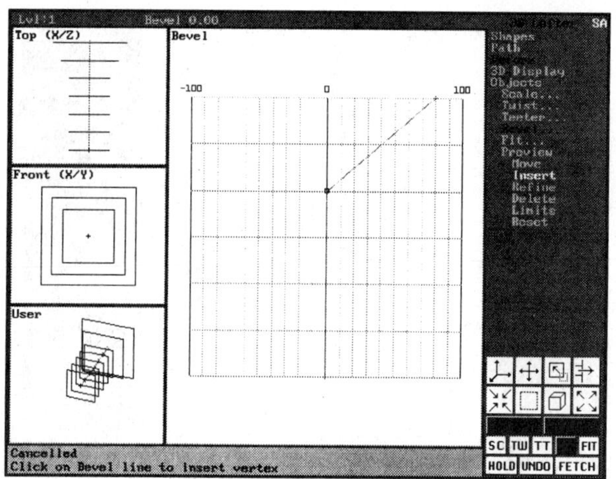

Inserting a vertex on the blue spline of the bevel deformation grid.

NOTE Inserting a vertex on the blue spline does not insert a vertex on the path. It only adds a vertex to the blue spline on the deformation grid, which specifies the degree of twist for a cross section located at each vertex or step on the path.

RELATED COMMANDS

Deform/Bevel/Move, Deform/Bevel/Delete, Deform/Bevel/Reset

Deform/Bevel/Refine

Shapes
Path
Deform
3D Display
Objects
Scale...
Twist...
Teeter...
Bevel...
Fit...
Move
Insert
Refine
Delete
Limits
Reset

Inserts a vertex on the blue spline of the Bevel deformation grid without affecting its curvature.

Refining the Blue Spline

1. Select *Deform/Bevel/Refine.* The deformation grid will be displayed.
2. Move the cursor to the Bevel viewport and click. The pick box will appear.
3. Move the pick box to the point on the blue spline where a vertex is to be added and select that point.

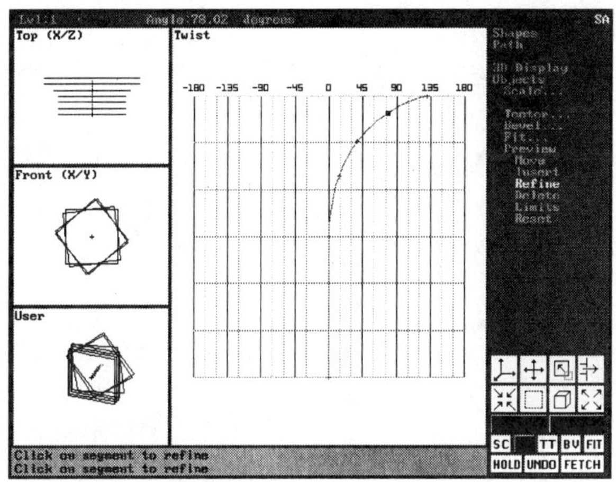

Refining the blue spline.

RELATED COMMANDS

Deform/Bevel/Insert, Deform/Bevel/Delete

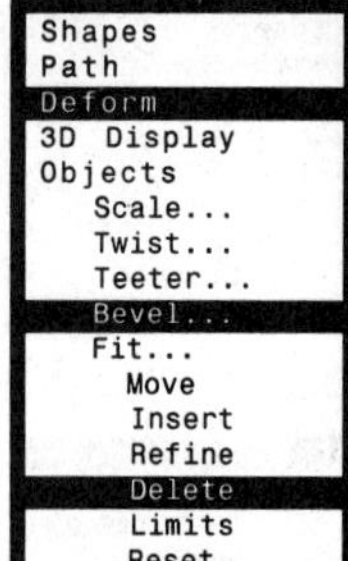

Deform/Bevel/Delete

Deletes any vertex other than the two end vertices on the blue spline of the Bevel deformation grid.

Deleting a Vertex on the Blue Spline

1. Select *Deform/Bevel/Delete.* The deformation grid will be displayed.
2. Move the cursor to the Bevel viewport and click. The pick box will appear.
3. Select the vertex on the blue spline to be deleted. That vertex will be deleted.

RELATED COMMANDS

Deform/Bevel/Insert, Deform/Bevel/Refine

Deform/Bevel/Limits

Changes the percent bevel displayed on the deformation grid.

Changing the Percent Bevel Display on the Deformation Grid

1. Select *Deform/Bevel/Limits*. The Bevel Deformation Limit dialog box appears as shown below.

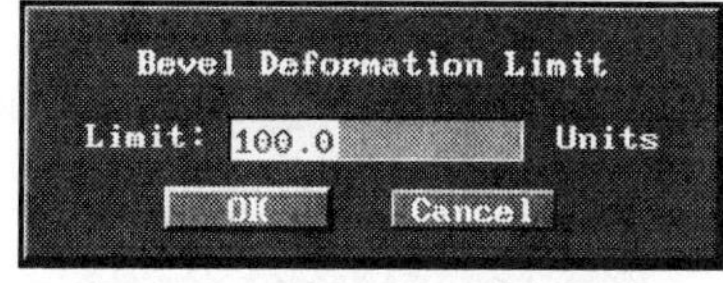

Change the limits using the Bevel Deformation Limit dialog box.

2. Change the default value of 100.0 to change the limit.
3. Select **OK** to accept the changes or choose **Cancel** to cancel the selection.
4. If **OK** is selected, the new twist limits will be displayed in the Bevel viewport.

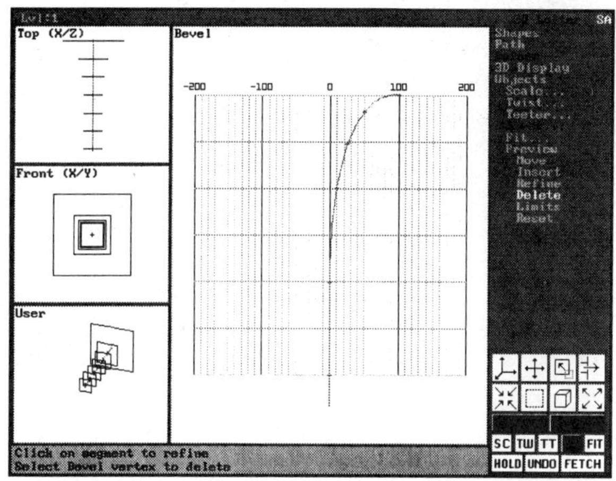

Viewing the changes made to the Bevel deformation limits.

Keeping the limits as small as possible allows for easier adjustments of smaller increments of percentages.

RELATED COMMAND

Deform/Bevel/Limits

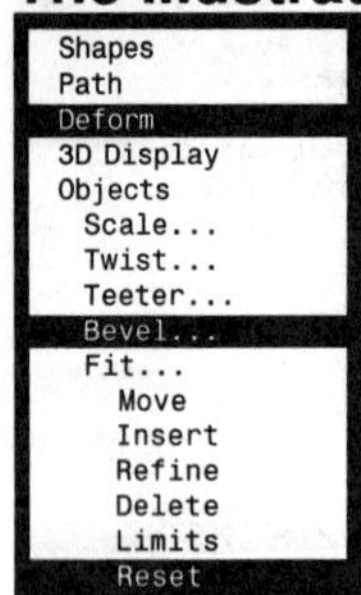

Deform/Bevel/Reset

Restores the blue spline path default values.

Restoring the Blue Spline Values

1. Select *Deform/Bevel/Reset*. The following dialog box will be displayed.

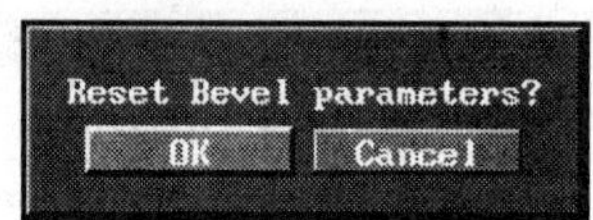

Verifying the reset selection

2. Select **OK** to reset the blue spline; choose **Cancel** to cancel the command.

This command will not change the deformation grid limits.

RELATED COMMANDS

Deform/Bevel/Insert, Deform/Bevel/Delete, Deform/Bevel/Refine

Deform/Fit/Get/Shaper

Shapes
Path
Deform
3D Display
Objects
Scale...
Twist...
Teeter...
Bevel...
Fit...
Preview
Get...
Put
Refine
Shaper
Disk

Imports a predefined shape from the 2D Shaper.

Importing a Shape from the 2D Shaper

1. Create a closed shape in the 2D Shaper.
2. Use *Shape/Assign* to tag the shape for export unless it is the only shape in the 2D Shaper.
3. Switch to the 3D Lofter.
4. Select *Deform/Fit/Get/Shaper*.
5. If the shape is valid, the shape will be displayed in the Fit X and Fit Y viewports.
6. If the shape is invalid, one of the four following message dialog boxes will appear as shown below.

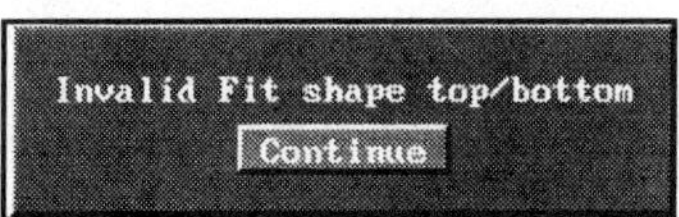

*Click **Continue** to correct the invalid fit shape.*

*Click **Continue** to correct the self intersecting shape.*

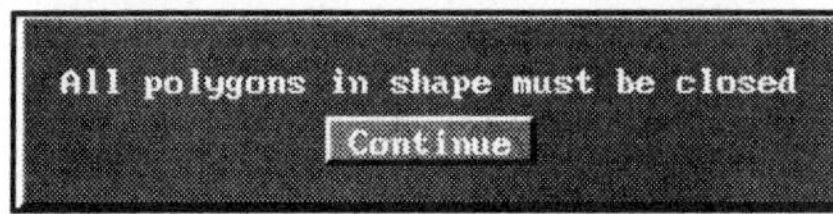

*Click **Continue** to close the open shape.*

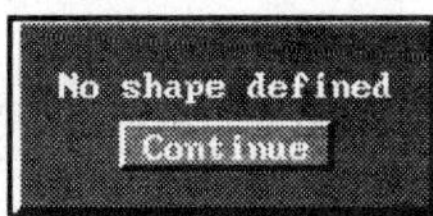

*Click **Continue** to return to the 2D Shaper and assign a shape.*

7. If an error does occur, make the necessary correction and repeat step 4.

> **NOTE** Be sure to assign the shape if there is more than one shape present in the 2D Shaper. If the shape is the only shape in the 2D Shaper, you do not have to assign that shape.

RELATED COMMANDS

Deform/Fit/Get/Disk, Shapes/Get/Shaper

Deform/Fit/Get/Disk

Shapes
Path
Deform
3D Display
Objects
Scale...
Twist...
Teeter...
Bevel...
Fit...
Preview
Get...
Put
Refine
Shaper
Disk

Imports a predefined shape from a disk to either active fit (X or Y) viewport.

Importing a Shape from a Disk

1. Create a closed shape in the 2D Shaper and save it.
2. Switch to the 3D Lofter.
3. Activate the Fit X or Fit Y viewport.
4. Select *Deform/Fit/Get/Disk.*
5. The Load a 2D Shape dialog box will appear.
6. Select the .shp file to import.
7. If the shape is valid, it will be displayed in all viewports.
8. If the shape is invalid, one of the message dialog boxes shown below will appear.
9. If an error does occur, make the necessary correction and repeat step 4.

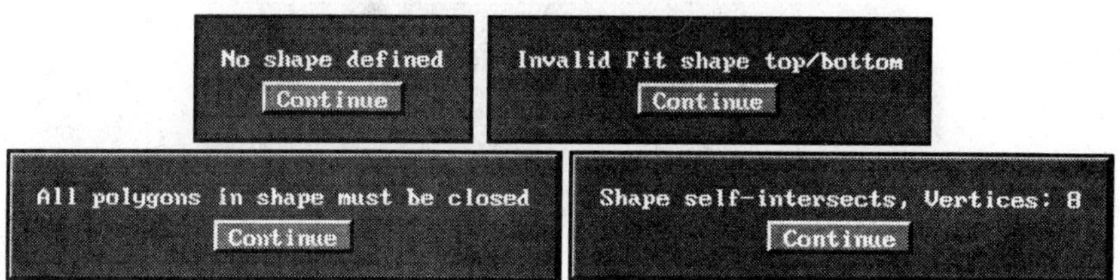

Ensure that a shape is valid or one of these dialog boxes will be displayed.

RELATED COMMANDS

Deform/Fit/Get/Shaper, Shapes/Get/Disk

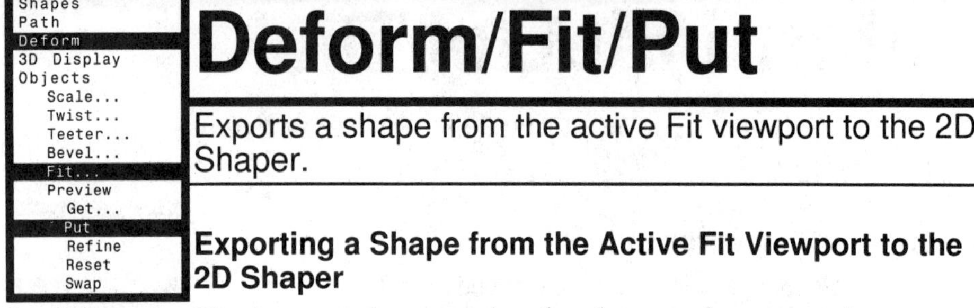

Deform/Fit/Put

Exports a shape from the active Fit viewport to the 2D Shaper.

Exporting a Shape from the Active Fit Viewport to the 2D Shaper

1. Select the Fit viewport that contains the shape to be exported.
2. Now select *Deform/Fit/Put.* The current shape will be exported and assigned in the 2D Shaper and the dialog box shown below will be displayed.

This dialog box will verify that the shape has been exported.

3. You may now switch to the 2D Shaper to edit the shape.

If a previous shape is assigned, a dialog box will appear as shown below. Choose one of the following options.

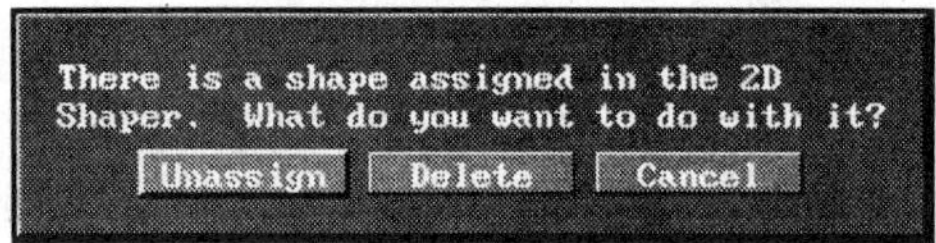

Unassign: Unassigns the shape in the 2D shaper and places the new assigned shape in the 2D Shaper.

Delete: Deletes the shape in the 2D shaper and replaces it with the shape being exported.

Cancel: Cancels the current operation.

If either **Unassign** or **Delete** is chosen, a dialog box will be displayed that says the shape has been copied. Click on **Continue** to exit the dialog box.

RELATED COMMANDS

Shapes/Put/Shaper, Shapes/Put/Disk, Shapes/Put/Level

Deform/Fit/Refine

Shapes
Path
Deform
3D Display
Objects
Scale...
Twist...
Teeter...
Bevel ...
Fit...
Preview
Get...
Put
Refine
Reset
Swap

Inserts a vertex on the fit shape of the active Fit viewport.

Refining the Fit Shape

1. Select *Deform/Fit/Refine*. The deformation grid will be displayed.
2. Move the cursor to the Fit X or Fit Y viewport and click. The pick box will appear.
3. Move the pick box to the point on the Fit shape where a vertex is to be added and select that point.

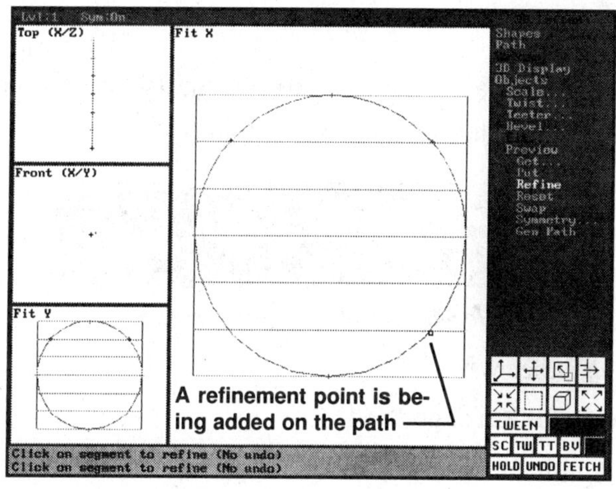

Refining the circular path.

RELATED COMMANDS

Deform/Bevel/Refine, Deform/Scale/Refine, Deform/Teeter/Refine, Deform/Twist/Refine

Deform/Fit/Reset

Removes the Fit shape in the Fit X and/or Fit Y viewport.

Removing a Fit Shape

1. Select *Deform/Fit/Reset.*

2. If Symmetry is on, the following dialog box will appear.

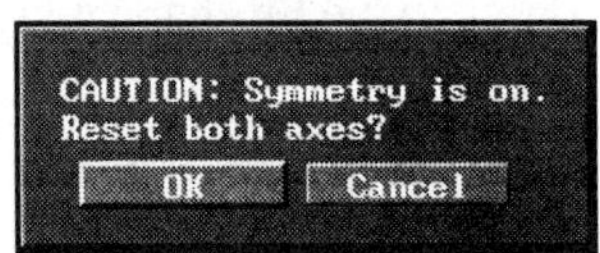

Verifying the reset procedure.

3. Select **OK** to reset both axes; choose **Cancel** to cancel the command.

4. If symmetry is off, the following dialog box will appear.

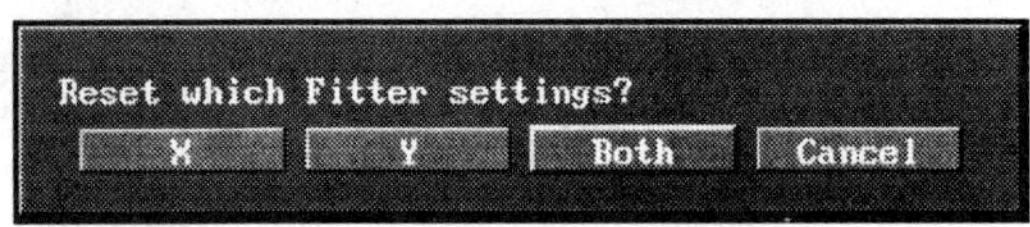

Selecting the Teeter setting to reset.

5. Select from the list below.

   X: Resets the X-axis grid.

   Y: Resets the Y-axis grid.

   Both: Resets both the X and Y-axis grids.

   Cancel: Cancels the command.

RELATED COMMANDS

Deform/Teeter/Insert, Deform/Teeter/Delete, Deform/Teeter/Refine, Deform/Teeter/Symmetry

Deform/Fit/Swap

Swaps the fit shapes found in the Fit X and Fit Y viewports.

Shapes
Path
Deform
3D Display
Objects
Scale...
Twist...
Teeter...
Bevel...
Fit...
Preview
Get...
Put
Refine
Reset
Swap

Swapping Fit Shapes in the Fit X and Fit Y Viewports

1. Select *Deform/Fit/Swap.*
2. The fit shapes in the Fit X and Fit Y viewports will be swapped.

NOTE This command works only if Symmetry is turned off.

RELATED COMMAND

Deform/Teeter/Symmetry/Off

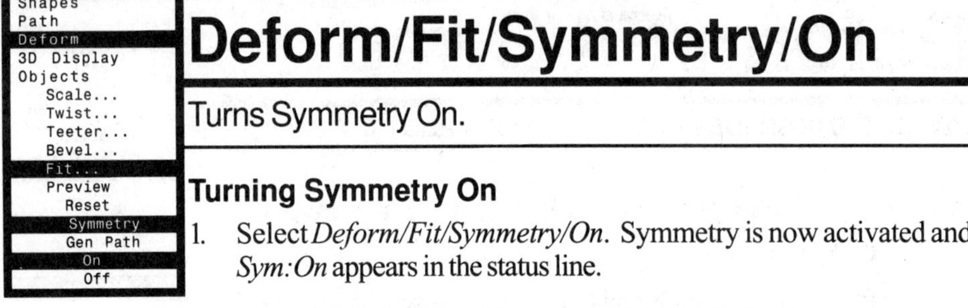

Deform/Fit/Symmetry/On

Turns Symmetry On.

Turning Symmetry On

1. Select *Deform/Fit/Symmetry/On*. Symmetry is now activated and *Sym:On* appears in the status line.
2. Any changes made to the blue spline will now be applied to the both axes.

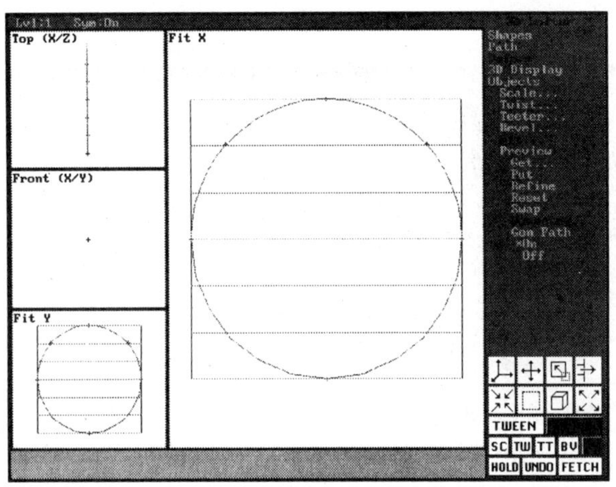

Turning Symmetry On

RELATED COMMAND

Deform/Fit/Symmetry/Off

Deform/Fit/Symmetry/Off

Turns Symmetry Off.

Shapes
Path
Deform
3D Display
Objects
Scale...
Twist...
Teeter...
Bevel...
Fit...
Preview
Reset
Symmetry
Gen Path
On
Off

Turning Symmetry Off

1. Select *Deform/Fit/Symmetry/Off.* Symmetry is now deactivated and *Sym:Off* appears in the status line.
2. Changes to the blue spline must now be made independently.

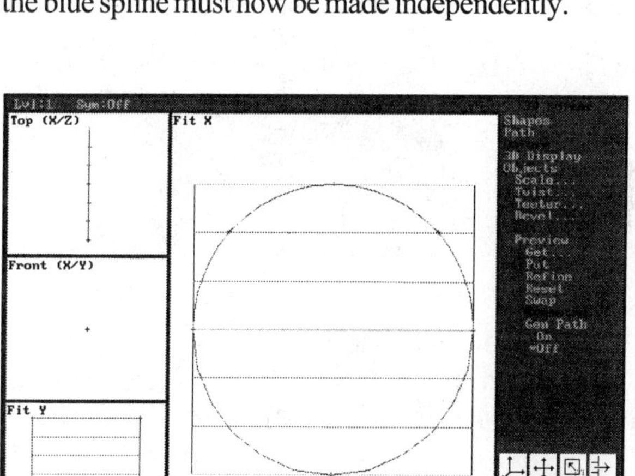

Turning Symmetry Off

RELATED COMMAND

Deform/Fit/Symmetry/Off

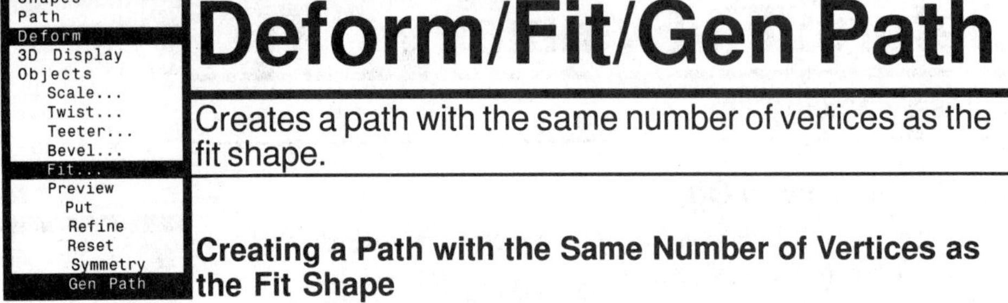

Deform/Fit/Gen Path

Creates a path with the same number of vertices as the fit shape.

Creating a Path with the Same Number of Vertices as the Fit Shape

1. Ensure that there is a fit shape in both the Fit X and Fit Y viewports.

2. Select *Deform/Fit/Gen Path*. The following dialog box will appear.

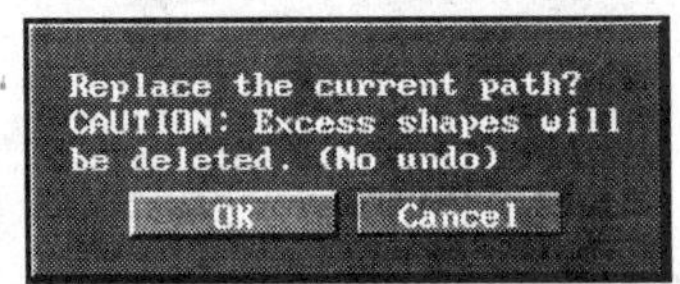

Use this dialog box to verify the selection.

3. Click on **OK** to accept the modifications to the default path. Modifications will be made based on the Y axis of both the Fit X and Fit Y shapes as shown below. The length of the path is based on the length of the first shape that was imported.

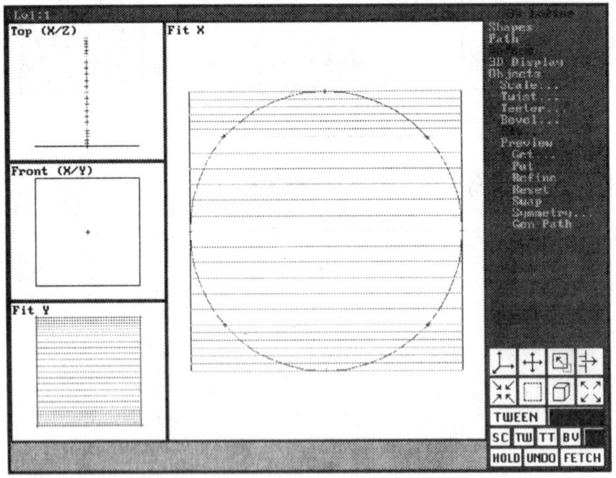

This path has been generated to fit the shape.

RELATED COMMANDS

Path/Insert Vertex, Path/Default Path

Deform/Preview

Creates a preview of the model in the viewports.

Creating a Preview

1. Create all necessary shapes and fit shapes.

2. Select *Deform/Preview*. The Preview Controls dialog box appears

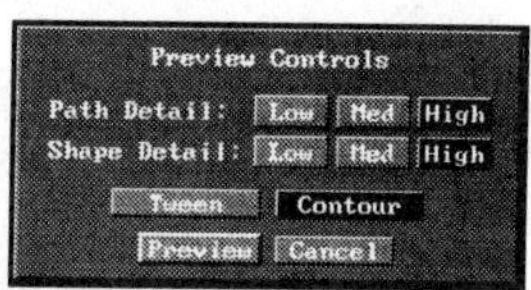

Select the level of detail for the preview.

3. Use the settings described below to control the complexity of the model.

Path Detail

Low: Previews with no path steps
Med: Previews with 50 percent of the path steps
High: Previews with all path steps

Shape Detail

Low: Previews with no shape steps
Med: Previews with 50 percent of the shape steps
High: Previews with all shape steps

Tween: When activated, Tween places a cross section on all path levels. When deactivated, Tween only previews the levels with shapes and the path vertices.

Contour: When activated, Contour will loft shapes perpendicular to the path. When deactivated, Contour will loft shapes parallel to the X/Y plane.

Preview: Displays a preview of the model with the above settings.

Cancel: Cancels the preview command.

> **TIP** Increasing complexity increases memory requirements for the model as well as affecting rendering performance. In many cases it will not yield a better rendering.

RELATED COMMANDS

Objects/Preview, Objects/Make

Shapes
Path
Deform
3D Display
Objects
Choose
On
Off
Const...
Tape...
Speed...

3D Display/Choose

Select the objects to be displayed when 3D display is on.

Choosing Objects to Be Displayed

1. Select *3D Display/Choose.* The "View 3D Objects" dialog box shown below appears.

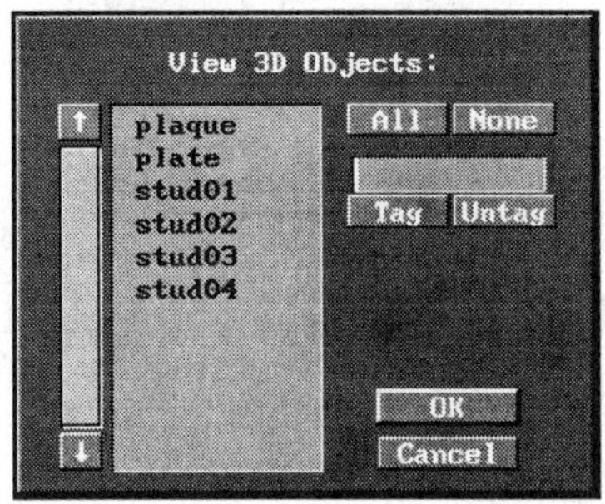

Select the objects to be displayed.

2. Select the objects to be displayed or choose one of the following options.

   All: Selects all objects listed in the dialog box.

   None: Deselects all objects listed in the dialog box.

   Cancel: Cancel the command and close the dialog box.

   OK: Accept the selections and close the dialog box.

3. Select *3D Display/On* to view the objects in the viewports.

TIP It is often quicker, in large multiple selections, to click the all button and then select singularly the objects not to be included in the 3D Display.

RELATED COMMANDS

3D Display/On, 3D Display/Off

3D Display/On

Displays selected objects located in the 3D Editor in the orthographic and user viewports in the 3D Lofter.

Turning 3D Display On

1. Select the objects to be displayed using the *3D Display/Choose* command.
2. Select *3D Display/On*. The objects selected will appear in all 3D Lofter orthographic and user viewports and an asterisk will appear next to the command.

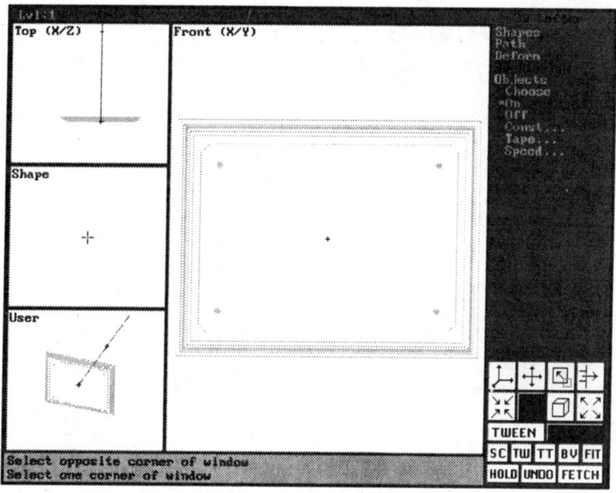

View an object from the 3D Editor in the 3D Lofter.

TIP This command is useful to reference shape, size, and appearance visually in an existing object for the new object being created in the lofter.

RELATED COMMANDS

3D Display/Choose, 3D Display/Off

Shapes
Path
Deform
3D Display
Objects
Choose
On
Off
Const...
Tape...
Speed...

3D Display/Off

Turns off the display of selected objects located in the 3D Editor in the orthographic and user viewports in the 3D Lofter.

Turning 3D Display Off

1. Ensure that previously displayed objects are in the viewports.
2. Select *3D Display/Off.* All 3D Editor objects are removed from the 3D Lofter orthographic and user viewports and an asterisk appears next to the command.

RELATED COMMANDS

3D Display/Choose, 3D Display/On

3D Display/Const/Place

Shapes
Path
Deform
3D Display
Objects
Choose
On
Off
Const...
Tape...
Speed...
Place
Show
Hide
Home

Changes the location of the construction planes.

Placing the Construction Plane

1. Select *3D Display/Const/Place.*
2. Activate an orthographic viewport where the construction plane is to be moved.
3. Select a point in the viewport to represent the intersection of the two planes being placed. Black cross hairs will appear in all orthographic viewports representing the intersection of the two planes displayed in the appropriate viewport. **Example**: In the top viewport, the X (horizontal) and Z (vertical) plane intersection is displayed.

NOTE This command effects both the 3D Lofter and the 3D Editor construction planes.

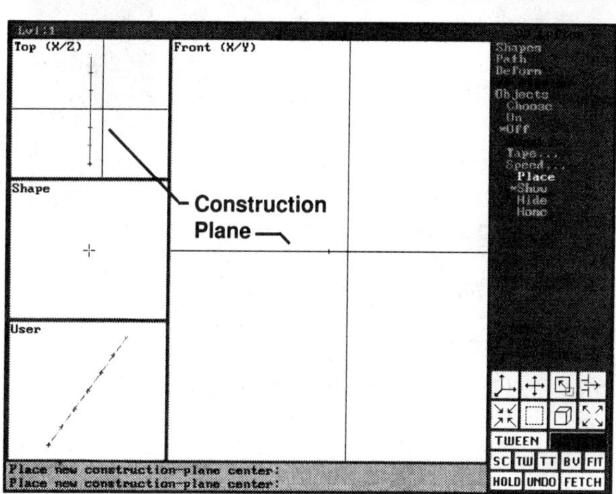

Viewing the construction plane.

TIP This command assists in the correct placement of paths and mesh objects being created in the 3D Lofter in relation to other existing mesh objects.

RELATED COMMANDS

3D Display/Const/Show, 3D Display/Const/Hide, 3D Display/Const/Home

Shapes
Path
Deform
3D Display
Objects
Choose
On
Off
Const...
Tape...
Speed...
Place
Show
Hide
Home

3D Display/Const/Show

Displays the construction plane in the 3D Lofter orthographic viewports.

Displaying the Construction Planes

1. Use *3D Display/Const/Place* to set the location of the construction plane if necessary.

2. Select *3D Display/Const/Show*. The construction plan crosshairs appear in all orthographic viewports in the 3D Lofter and an asterisk appears next to the command.

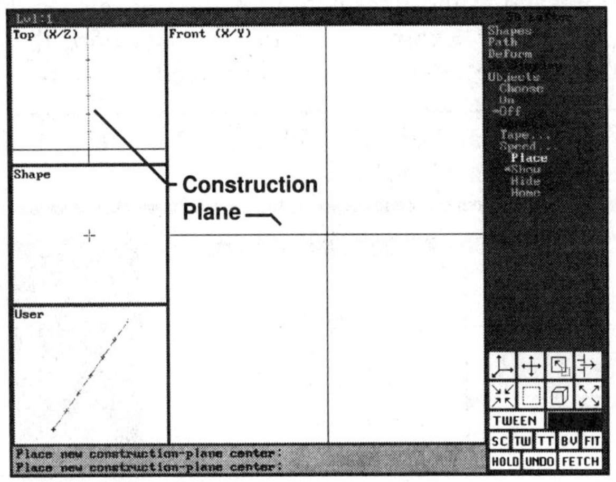

Viewing the construction plane.

RELATED COMMANDS

3D Display/Const/Place, 3D Display/Const/Hide, 3D Display/Const/Home

3D Display/Const/Hide

Shapes
Path
Deform
3D Display
Objects
Choose
On
Off
Const...
Tape...
Speed...
Place
Show
Hide
Home

Hides the construction plane in the 3D Lofter orthographic viewports.

Hiding the Construction Planes

1. Ensure that the construction planes are displayed using *3D Display/Const/Show* or that they are placed by using *3D Display/Const/Place* command.
2. Select *3D Display/Const/Hide*. The construction plane crosshairs disappear in all orthographic viewports in the 3D Lofter and an asterisk appears next to the command.

RELATED COMMANDS

3D Display/Const/Place, 3D Display/Const/Show, 3D Display/Const/Home

Shapes
Path
Deform
3D Display
Objects
Choose
On
Off
Const...
Tape...
Speed...
Place
Show
Hide
Home

3D Display/Const/Home

Moves the construction plane back to its default (home) position at coordinates 0,0,0.

Moving the Construction Planes to their Default Positions

1. Ensure that the construction planes were moved previously from their default location using *3D Display/Const/Place*.

2. Select *3D Display/Const/Home*. The construction plan cross hairs return to their default position.

RELATED COMMANDS

3D Display/Const/Place, 3D Display/Const/Show, 3D Display/Const/Hide

3D Display/Tape/Move

Shapes
Path
Deform
3D Display
Objects
Choose
On
Off
Const...
Tape...
Speed...
Move
Find
Show
Hide
Toggle Vsnap

Adjusts or moves the tape measure icon.

Adjusting the Tape Measure Icon

1. Ensure that the tape measure icon is displayed in an orthographic viewport using the *3D Display/Tape/Show* command.
2. Select *3D Display/Tape/Move.*
3. Select the orthographic viewport where the tape measure icon is to be adjusted.
4. Select either end of the tape measure icon.
5. Move the selected end of the tape measure icon to its new location and select that point. The tape length and angle are displayed in the status line.
6. Make further adjustments to both ends as necessary.

TIP If exact measurement of objects are needed, use *3D Display/Tape/Toggle VSnap* command.

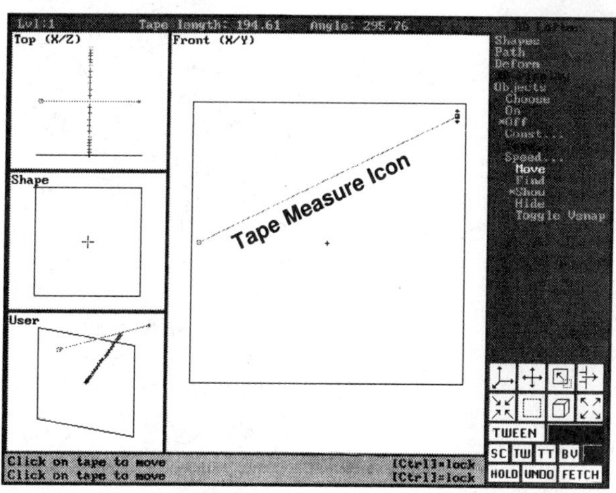

Use the tape measure to measure distances.

TIP Use the [Tab] key to constrain movements in the horizontal or vertical direction.

Moving the Tape Measure Icon

1. Ensure that the tape measure icon is displayed in an orthographic viewport using the *3D Display/Tape/Show* command.
2. Select *3D Display/Tape/Move.*
3. Select the orthographic viewport where the Tape Measure icon is to be moved.
4. Hold the Ctrl key and select either end of the Tape Measure icon. A white copy of the icon will appear connected to the cursor and a green reference icon will remain at its beginning location.
5. Move the tape measure icon to its new location. The tape length and angle are displayed in the status line.
6. Make further adjustments as necessary.

If you cannot find the Tape Measure icon, use the *3D Display/Tape/Find* command.

RELATED COMMANDS

3D Display/Tape/Find, 3D Display/Tape/Show, 3D Display/Tape/Hide, 3D Display/Tape/Toggle VSnap

3D Display/Tape/Find

Shapes
Path
Deform
3D Display
Objects
Choose
On
Off
Const...
Tape...
Speed...
Move
Find
Show
Hide
Toggle Vsnap

Adjusts the tape measure icon in the active viewport so that it may be located easily.

Finding the Tape Measure Icon

1. Select an orthographic or user viewport.
2. Select *3D Display/Tape/Find.* The tape measure icon will be scaled to 80 percent of the active viewport. It will also be centered within that viewport and reset to its default angle of 270 degrees. The tape length and angle are displayed in the status line.

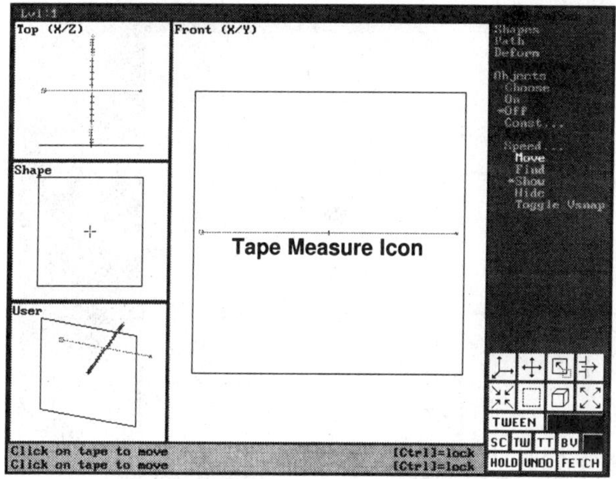

Finding the tape measure icon.

RELATED COMMANDS

3D Display/Tape/Show, 3D Display/Tape/Hide

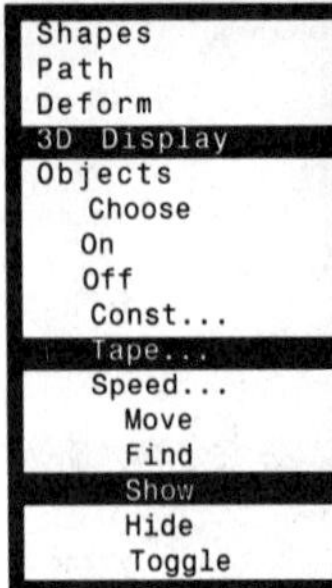

3D Display/Tape/Show

Displays the Tape Measure icon.

Displaying the Tape Measure Icon

1. Select *3D Display/Tape/Show*. The Tape Measure icon will be displayed in all orthographic and user viewports at its previously defined location and direction. An asterisk will appear next to the command. The tape length and angle are also displayed in the status line.
2. Use *3D Display/Tape/Move* to adjust the tape measure icon.

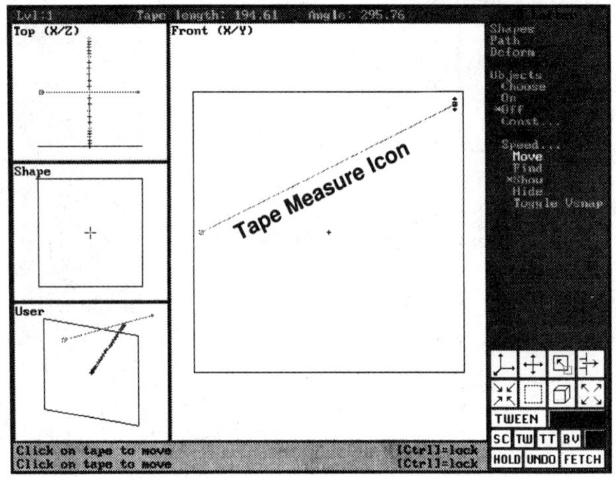

Showing the tape measure in the 3D Lofter.

Use the *3D Display/Tape/Find* command if the Tape Measure icon cannot be seen after using this command.

RELATED COMMANDS

3D Display/Tape/Move, 3D Display/Tape/Find, 3D Display/Tape/Hide

3D Display/Tape/Hide

Hides the tape measure icon.

Shapes
Path
Deform
3D Display
Objects
Choose
On
Off
Const...
Tape...
Speed...
Move
Find
Show
Hide
Toggle Vsnap

Hiding the Tape Measure Icon

1. Ensure that the tape measure icon has been displayed previously using either *3D Display/Tape/Show* or *3D Display/Tape/Find*.
2. Select *3D Display/Tape/Hide*. The tape measure icon will disappear from the orthographic and user viewports and an asterisk will appear next to the command.

RELATED COMMANDS

3D Display/Tape/Find, 3D Display/Tape/Show

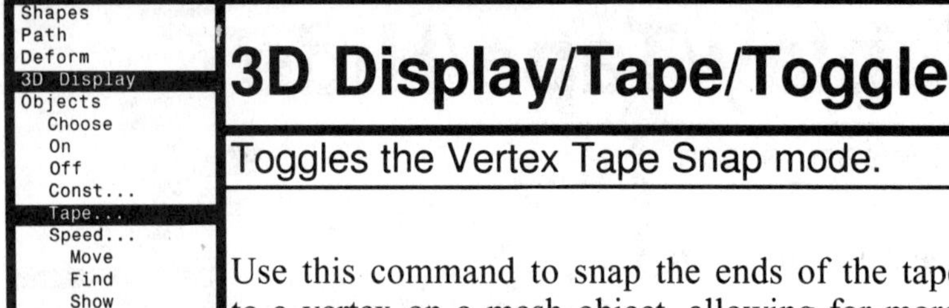

3D Display/Tape/Toggle VSnap

Toggles the Vertex Tape Snap mode.

Use this command to snap the ends of the tape measure icon to a vertex on a mesh object, allowing for more accurate measurement of a line.

Turning on Vertex Tape Snap mode

1. Select *3D Display/Tape/Toggle VSnap*. An Asterisk appears next to the command.

2. Use *3D Display/Tape/Move* to snap the ends of the tape measure icon to any vertex on a line, face, or path.

> **NOTE** For the end of the tape measure icon to snap to a vertex, the vertex must be in the pick box when the location of the end of the tape measure icon is selected.

RELATED COMMANDS

3D Display/Tape/Find, 3D Display/Tape/Show

3D Display/Speed/Fastdraw

Shapes
Path
Deform
3D Display
Objects
Choose
On
Off
Const...
Tape...
Speed...
Fastdraw
FullDraw
Set Fast

Turns on Fastdraw and displays mesh objects with a reduced number of faces to speed redraw times.

Turning on Fastdraw

1. Ensure that *3D Display/On* is selected and that mesh objects can be seen in the orthographic viewports.
2. Use *3D Display/Speed/Set Fast* to specify the number of faces that will be used to represent mesh objects.
3. Select *3D Display/Speed/Fastdraw*. An asterisk will appear next to the command and the mesh objects will be displayed with a reduced number of faces.
4. Use the *3D Display/Speed/Fulldraw* command to display the mesh objects with all faces.

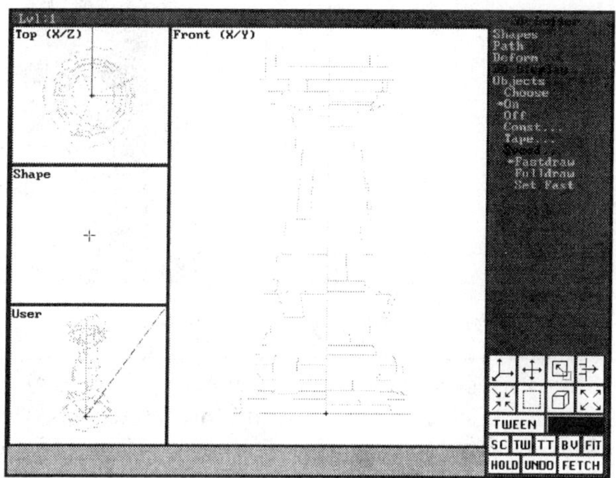

Using fastdraw to view an object.

NOTE Using this command can speed up redraws significantly on complicated mesh objects with slower systems. It is not necessary to use this command if simple to moderate size mesh objects are being displayed on medium to fast systems.

RELATED COMMANDS

3D Display/Speed/Fulldraw, 3D Display/Speed/Set Fast

```
Shapes
Path
Deform
3D Display
Objects
  Choose
  On
  Off
  Const...
  Tape...
  Speed...
    Fastdraw
    FullDraw
    Set Fast
```

3D Display/Speed/Fulldraw

Turns on Fulldraw and displays mesh objects all faces.

Turning On Fulldraw

1. Ensure that *3D Display/On* is selected and that mesh objects can be seen in the orthographic viewports.
2. Select *3D Display/Speed/Fulldraw*. An asterisk will appear next to the command and the mesh objects will be displayed with all faces.

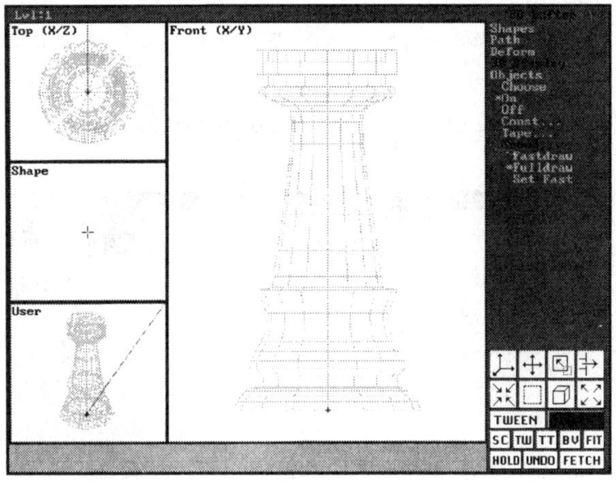

Using fulldraw to view an object.

Using this command can slowdown redraws significantly on complicated mesh object with slower systems.

RELATED COMMANDS

3D Display/Speed/Fastdraw, 3D Display/Speed/Set Fast

3D Display/Speed/Set Fast

Shapes
Path
Deform
3D Display
Objects
Choose
On
Off
Const...
Tape...
Speed...
Fastdraw
FullDraw
Set Fast

Specifies the number of faces used to represent a mesh object.

Changing the Number of Faces for Mesh Objects

1. Select *3D Display/Speed/Set Fast.* The "Set Fastdraw Speed" dialog box appears as shown below.

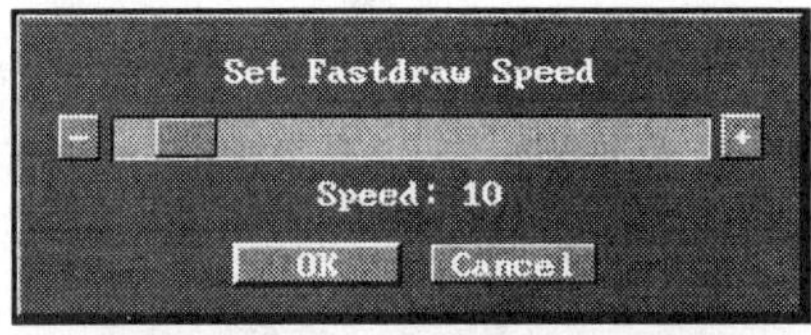

Use this dialog box to change the set fast attributes.

2. Move the slider up or down to specify the number of faces. The range is from 2 to 100. A setting of 2 displays every other face and a setting of 100 displays every 100th face.
3. Click on **OK** to accept the setting or **Cancel** to cancel the command.
4. If **OK** was selected, use *3D Display/Speed/Fastdraw* to display the mesh object with the new settings.

> **NOTE** Be careful not to specify too high a setting. If the setting is higher than the number of faces in the mesh object, that object will not be seen. If multiple objects are displayed, it is important to make the setting small enough for the object with the fewest number of faces.

RELATED COMMANDS

3D Display/Speed/Fastdraw, 3D Display/Speed/Fulldraw

Shapes
Path
Deform
3D Display
Objects
Make
Preview

Objects/Make

Creates a mesh object in the 3D Editor with the current 3D Lofter settings.

Creating a Mesh Object

1. Adjust all 3D Lofter settings needed to create the mesh object.

2. Select *Objects/Make.* The Object Lofting Controls dialog box appears as shown below.

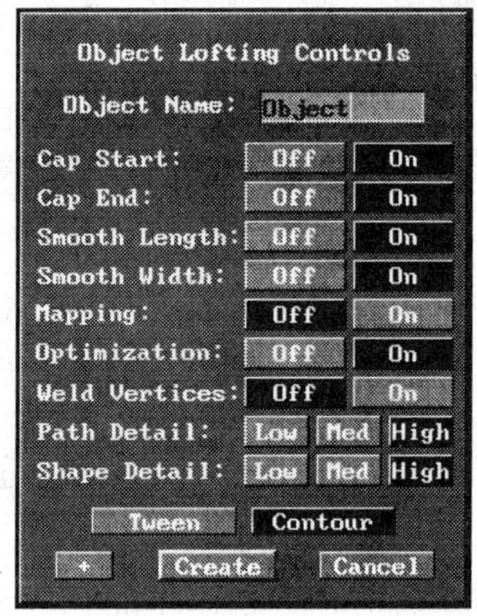

Select the options needed to make the object.

3. Make selections in the dialog box as described below.

Object Name: Enter a unique name for the mesh object to be created. This name can have from one to ten letters and a default name is provided.

Cap Start: Specifies whether the start of a mesh object is capped. If the start is capped, a face will be created to close the start of the object.

Cap End: Specifies whether the end of a mesh object is capped. If the end is capped, a face will be created to close the end of the object.

Smooth Length: Specifies whether smooth shading is applied along the length edges of the mesh object. If this setting is **OFF**, the object will appear faceted along the length edges.

Smooth Width: Specifies whether smooth shading is applied along the width edges of the mesh object. If this setting is **OFF**, the object will appear faceted along the width edges.

Mapping: Specifies whether mapping coordinates are applied along the length and perimeter of the mesh object. When this setting is on, selecting the **Create** or **+** button will display the Mapping Coordinate Repeat Values dialog box as shown below. Make the selections in the dialog box as described below.

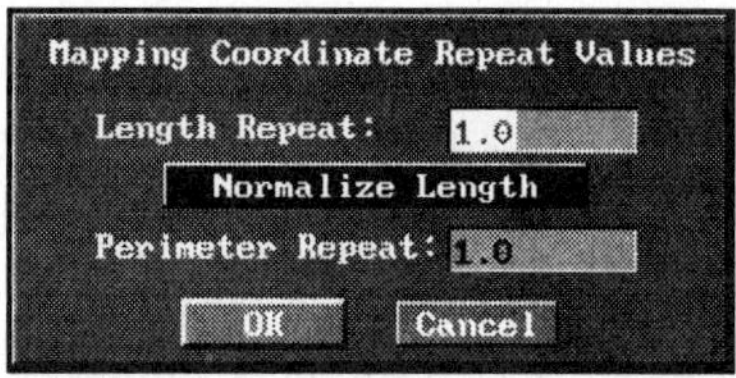

Use this dialog box to adjust mapping coordinates.

Length Repeat: Specifies the number of times a material pattern is repeated along the length of the mesh object.

Normalize Length: Specifies whether the number of path vertices affects the material pattern. If selected, the material pattern will be applied down the length of the mesh object. If the option is not chosen, the mapped pattern is distorted based on the spacing between the steps on the path.

Perimeter Repeat: Specifies the number of times a material pattern is repeated around the perimeter of the mesh object.

Optimization: Specifies whether optimization is on or off. If optimization is on, all steps along the lofting path are ignored and a less complex mesh object is created. If optimization is off, all steps along the lofting path are used to create a complex mesh object.

Weld Vertices: Specifies whether core vertices are removed when the mesh object is created. If weld vertices is on, all vertices within the Weld-Threshold parameter in the *Systems Options* command will be joined into a single vertex. If weld vertices is off, this option is ignored. Generally, this option is only used when creating SurfRev mesh objects.

Path Detail: Tween must be onto use this option. Alters the step settings on the path before creating the mesh object. Make the selection from the list below.

Low: Uses no path steps.

Med: Uses half of the path steps.

High: Uses all of the path steps.

Shape Detail: Tween must be **On** to use this option. Alters the step settings on the shape before creating the mesh object. Make the selection from the following list.

Low: Uses no shape steps.

Med: Uses half of the shape steps.

High: Uses all of the shape steps.

Tween: When Tween is selected, a shape is place on all path steps on the mesh object being created. If this option is not selected, only steps with shapes will be considered in the lofting process.

Contour: When Contour is selected, all shapes along the path will be lofted perpendicular to the path. If this option is not selected, all shapes will be lofted parallel to the X/Y plane.

+: Use this option to accept the next incremental name for the object.

Create: Creates the loft in the 3D Editor using all options previously selected.

Cancel: Cancels the command and closes the dialog box.

> **NOTE** All options in the Object Lofting Controls dialog box effect the complexity of the mesh object being created. Be careful to choose only the necessary options. Extremely complex mesh objects may not render any better than less complex models.

RELATED COMMAND

Object/Preview

Object/Preview

Creates a preview of the model in the viewports.

Creating a Preview

1. Create all necessary shapes and fit shapes.
2. Select *Deform/Preview.* The Preview Controls dialog box appears as shown below.

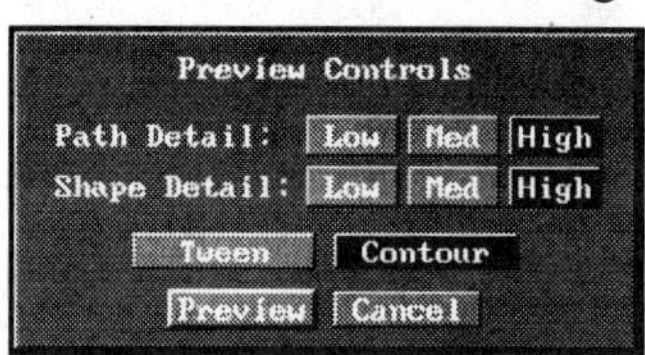

Select the options needed to preview the object.

3. Use the settings described below to control the complexity of the model.

Path Detail

Low: Previews with no path steps

Med: Previews with 50 percent of the path steps

High: Previews with all path steps

Shape Detail

Low: Previews with no shape steps

Med: Previews with 50 percent of the shape steps

High: Previews with all shape steps

Tween: When activated, Tween places a cross section on all path levels. When deactivated, Tween only previews the levels with shapes and the path vertices.

Contour: When activated, Contour lofts shapes perpendicular to the path. When deactivated, Contour will loft shapes parallel to the X/Y plane.

Preview: Displays a preview of the model with the above settings.

Cancel: Cancels the preview command.

TIP Increasing complexity increases the memory requirements for the model as well as for rendering performance. In many cases it does not yield a better rendering. Make models only as complex as necessary.

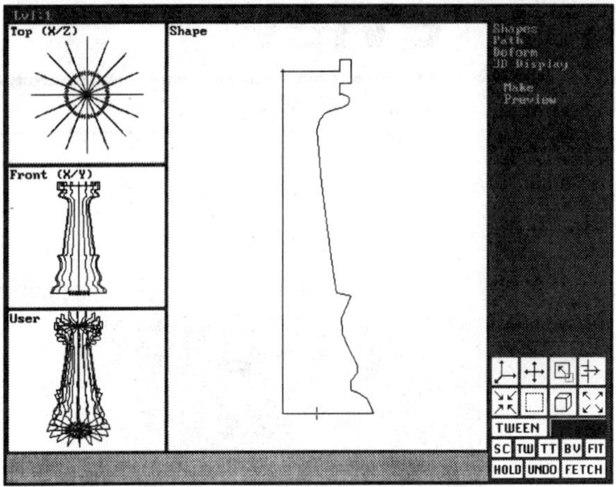

Viewing a preview of an object.

RELATED COMMAND

Objects/Make

Create/Box

Create
Box
LSphere...
GSphere...
Hemisphere...
Cylinder...
Tube...
Torus...
Cone...
Vertex
Face...
Element...
Object...
Faceted
Smoothed
Values

Creates a 3D, six-sided box by specifying the width, height, and length. You can also create a cube with equal sides.

Creating a Box

1. In the active viewport (except a camera or spotlight viewport), click to place one corner of the box.

To create a cube with equal sides, hold down the Ctrl key when selecting the first point.

2. Define two dimensions of the box by moving the mouse diagonally. The status line displays the current width and height. Click to set the correct size, or right-click to cancel the operation

You can also enter the dimensions of the box at the keyboard. This must be done prior to clicking the first corner.

3. To define the length of the box, click in any viewport. Draw a line representing the length of the box. The length is displayed in the status bar.
4. When the line is the correct length, click to create the box. The box is created on the near side of the construction plane if created in an orthographic viewport, or placed on the near side of the the User plane if created in the User viewport.
5. In the Name for new object: dialog box, assign the box a unique name.

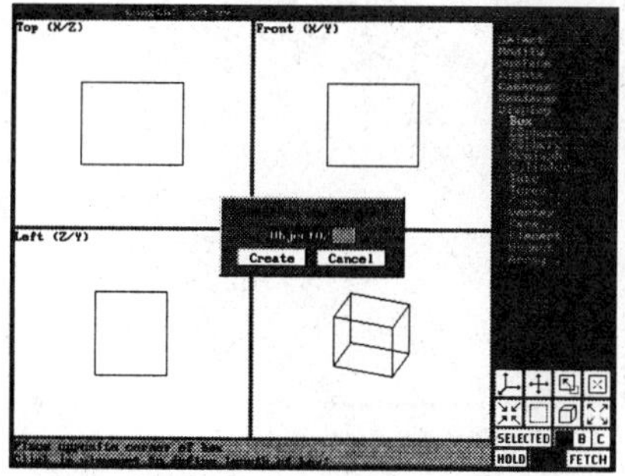

Creating a box and assigning it a name.

RELATED COMMAND

Views–Drawing Aids, Display/Const, Display/User View

Create
Box
LSphere...
GSphere...
Hemisphere...
Cylinder...
Tube...
Torus...
Cone...
Vertex
Face...
Element...
Object...
Faceted
Smoothed
Values

Create/LSphere/Faceted

Creates a faceted 3D sphere. The number of segments is specified with *Create/LSphere/Values*.

Creating a Faceted LSphere

1. Set the number of segments you want the LSphere to contain with *Create/LSphere/Values*.
2. In the active viewport (except a camera or spotlight viewport), click to place the center of the LSphere. The sphere is placed at the center of the construction plane if created in an orthographic viewport, or placed at the center of the the User plane if created in the User viewport.
3. As you move the mouse away from the center, the LSphere is drawn. Moving the mouse in a circle will rotate the LSphere. See *Views–Drawing Aids, Views–Use Snap, Views–Use Grid,* and *Views–Angle Snap*.
4. When the LSphere is the correct size, click to create it, or right-click to cancel.
5. In the Name for new object: dialog box, assign the LSphere a unique name.

TIP If you are creating a sphere to interact with other geometry (such as with *Create/Object/Boolean*), the LSphere is the best choice because it can be separated easily along an even plane. Select *Create/LSphere/Smooth* if you want the finished object to have a smooth rendered image.

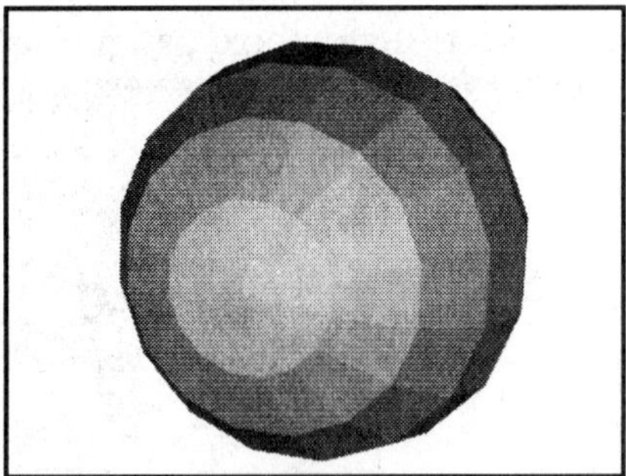

A faceted LSphere has distinct edges between its faces.

RELATED COMMANDS

Create/LSphere/Smoothed, Create/LSphere/Values, Views-Drawing Aids, Views–Use Snap, Views–Use Grid, Views–Angle Snap, Display/Const, Display/User View

Create/LSphere/Smoothed

Create
Box
LSphere...
GSphere...
Hemisphere...
Cylinder...
Tube...
Torus...
Cone...
Vertex
Face...
Element...
Object...
Faceted
Smoothed
Values

Creates a smoothed 3D sphere. The number of segments is specified with *Create/LSphere/Values.*

Creating a Smoothed LSphere

1. Set the number of segments you want the LSphere to contain with *Create/LSphere/Values.*
2. In the active viewport (except a camera or spotlight viewport), click to place the center of the Lsphere. The LSphere is placed at the center of the construction plane if created in an orthographic viewport, or placed at the center of the the User plane if created in the User viewport.
3. As you move the mouse away from the center, the LSphere is drawn. Moving the mouse in a circle will rotate the Lsphere. See *Views–Drawing Aids, Views–Use Snap, Views–Use Grid,* and *Views–Angle Snap.*
4. When the LSphere is the correct size, click to create it, or right-click to cancel.
5. In the Name for new object: dialog box, assign the LSphere a unique name.

TIP If you are creating a sphere to interact with other geometry (such as with *Create/Object/Boolean*), the LSphere is the best choice because it can be separated easily along an even plane. Select *Create/lSphere/Faceted* if you want the finished object to have distinct edges between its faces.

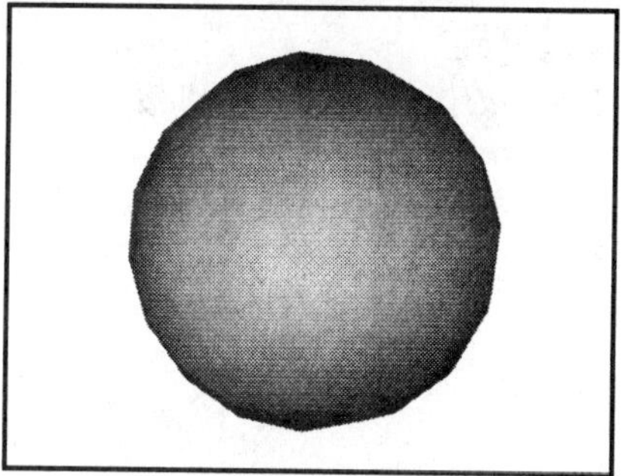

A smoothed LSphere appears polished.

RELATED COMMANDS

Create/LSphere/Faceted, Create/LSphere/Values, Views-Drawing Aids, Views–Use Snap, Views–Use Grid, Views–Angle Snap, Display/Const, Display/User View

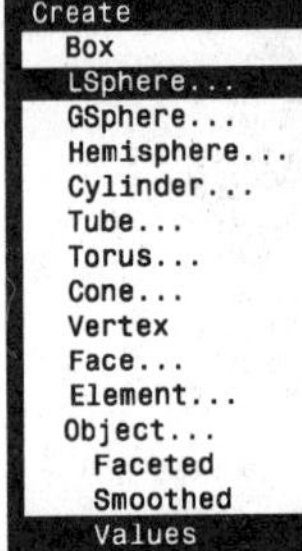

Create/LSphere/Values

Specifies the number of longitudinal segments in an LSphere.

Specifying the Longitudinal Segments

1. Select *Create/LSphere/Values* before creating a LSphere. In the Set Lat-Long Sphere Segments dialog box, set the number of longitudinal segments. The default setting is 16. Valid range is from 4 to 100.
2. Set the type of LSphere you want to create from the menu, either smooth or faceted. The following illustrations show how the number of longitudinal segments affects smoothed and faceted LSpheres.

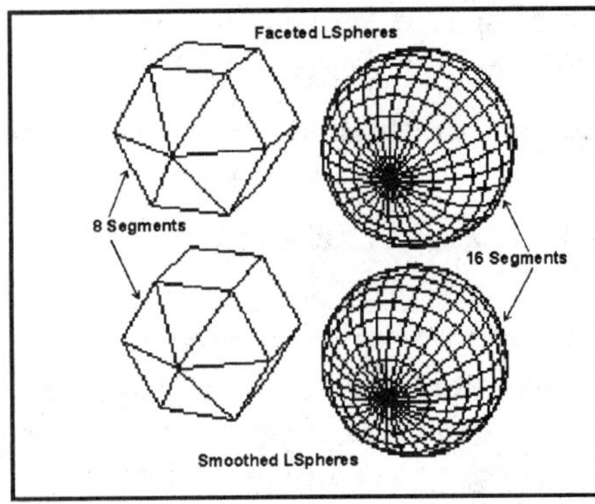

Wireframe smoothed and faceted LSpheres with different segment values.

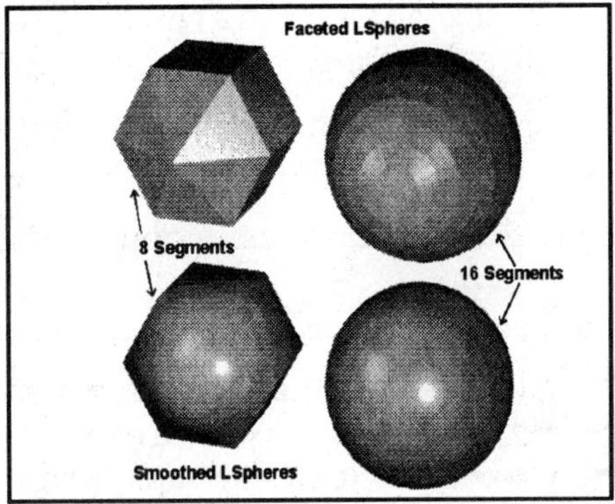

Rendered smoothed and faceted LSpheres with different segment values.

RELATED COMMANDS

Create/LSphere/Faceted, Create/LSphere/Smoothed

Create/GSphere/Faceted

Create
Box
LSphere...
GSphere...
Hemisphere...
Cylinder...
Tube...
Torus...
Cone...
Vertex
Face...
Element...
Object...
Faceted
Smoothed
Values

Creates a facteted 3D sphere constructed of triangles. The number of faces is specified with *Create/GSphere/ Values*.

Creating a Faceted GSphere

1. Set the number of segments you want the GSphere to contain with *Create/GSphere/Values*.
2. In the active viewport (except a camera or spotlight viewport), click to place the center of the Gsphere. The GSphere is placed at the center of the construction plane if created in an orthographic viewport, or placed at the center of the the User plane if created in the User viewport.
3. As you move the mouse away from the center, the GSphere is drawn. Moving the mouse in a circle will rotate the GSphere. See *Views–Drawing Aids, Views–Use Snap, Views–Use Grid,* and *Views–Angle Snap*.
4. When the GSphere is the correct size, click to create it, or right-click to cancel.
5. In the Name for new object: dialog box, assign the GSphere a unique name.

TIP GSpheres are best for deforming and manipulating, because none of the faces is coplanar and each can be manipulated. Select *Create/GSphere/Smooth* if you want the rendered object to have a smooth appearance.

A faceted GSphere has distinct edges between its faces.

RELATED COMMANDS

Create/GSphere/Smoothed, Create/GSphere/Values, Views–Drawing Aids, Views–Use Snap, Views–Use Grid, Views–Angle Snap, Display/Const, Display/User View

Create
Box
LSphere...
GSphere...
Hemisphere...
Cylinder...
Tube...
Torus...
Cone...
Vertex
Face...
Element...
Object...
Faceted
Smoothed
Values

Create/GSphere/Smoothed

Creates a smoothed 3D sphere consisting of triangles. The number of segments is specified with *Create/GSphere/Values*.

Creating a Smoothed GSphere

1. Set the number of segments you want the GSphere to contain with *Create/GSphere/Values*.
2. In the active viewport (except a camera or spotlight viewport), click to place the center of the GSphere. The GSphere is placed at the center of the construction plane if created in an orthographic viewport, or placed at the center of the the User plane if created in the User viewport.
3. As you move the mouse away from the center, the GSphere is drawn. Moving the mouse in a circle will rotate the GSphere. See *Views–Drawing Aids, Views–Use Snap, Views-Use Grid,* and *Views–Angle Snap*.
4. When the GSphere is the correct size, click to create it, or right-click to cancel.
5. In the Name for new object: dialog box, assign the GSphere a unique name.

TIP GSpheres are best for deforming and manipulating, because none of the faces is coplanar and each can be manipulated. Select *Create/GSphere/Faceted* if you want the rendered image to have distinct edges.

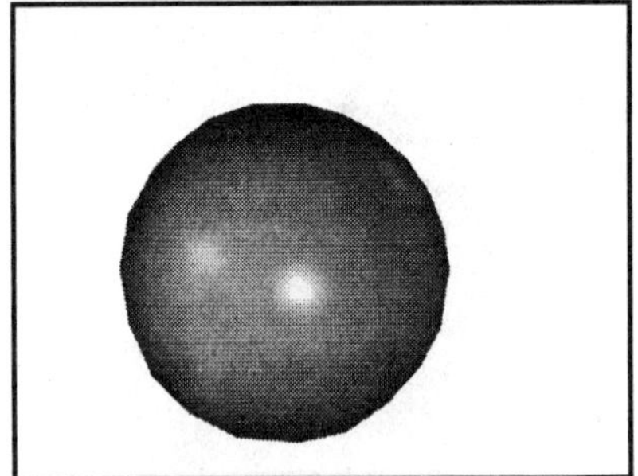

A smoothed GSphere appears polished.

RELATED COMMANDS

Create/GSphere/Smoothed, Create/GSphere/Values, Views–Drawing Aids, Views–Use Snap, Views–Use Grid, Views-Angle Snap, Display/Const, Display/User View

Create/GSphere/Values

Create
Box
LSphere...
GSphere...
Hemisphere...
Cylinder...
Tube...
Torus...
Cone...
Vertex
Face...
Element...
Object...
Faceted
Smoothed
Values

Specifies the number of faces in a GSphere.

Specifying the Number of Faces

1. Select *Create/GSphere/Values* before creating a GSphere. In the Geodesic Sphere Faces dialog box, set the number of faces. The default setting is 256. Valid range is from 4 to 10,000.
2. Set the type of GLSphere you want to create, either smooth or faceted. The following illustrations show how the number of faces affects smoothed and faceted Gspheres.

NOTE Although the Values dialog box asks you to set the Geodesic Sphere Faces, a GSphere is not the same as a geodesic dome. GSpheres are made from isosceles triangles, which can vary in size a great deal. Geodesic domes are made from equilateral triangles, which are all very close in size. Do not confuse a GSphere with a geodesic dome.

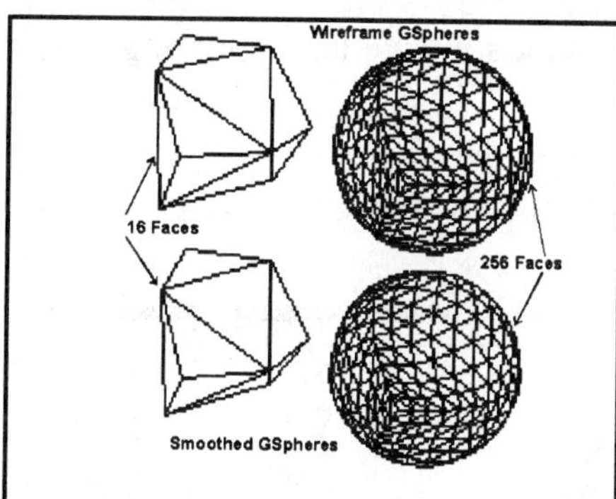

Wireframe smoothed and faceted GSpheres with different face values.

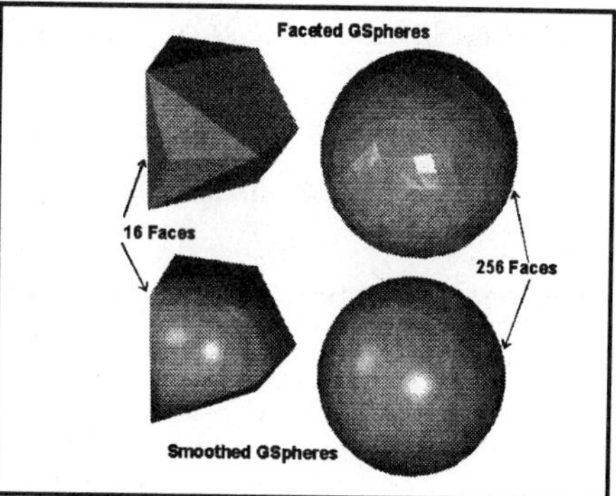

Rendered smoothed and faceted GSpheres with different face values.

RELATED COMMANDS

Create/GSphere/Faceted, Create/GSphere/Smoothed

Create
Box
LSphere...
GSphere...
Hemisphere...
Cylinder...
Tube...
Torus...
Cone...
Vertex
Face...
Element...
Object...
Faceted
Smoothed
Values

Create/Hemisphere/Faceted

Creates a faceted 3D hemisphere, or dome. The number of segments is specified with *Create/Hemisphere/Values*.

Creating a Faceted Hemisphere

1. Set the number of segments you want the hemisphere to contain with *Create/Hemisphere/Values*.
2. In the active viewport (except a camera or spotlight viewport), click to place the center of the hemisphere. The hemisphere is placed on the near side of the near side of the construction plane if created in an orthographic viewport, or placed on the near side of the the User plane if created in the User viewport.
3. As you move the mouse away from the center, the hemisphere is drawn. Moving the mouse in a circle will rotate the hemisphere. See *Views–Drawing Aids, Views–Use Snap, Views–Use Grid,* and *Views–Angle Snap*.
4. When the hemisphere is the correct size, click to create it, or right-click to cancel.
5. In the Name for new object: dialog box, assign the hemisphere a unique name.

A hemisphere is half of an LSphere. See *Create/LSphere/Faceted.*

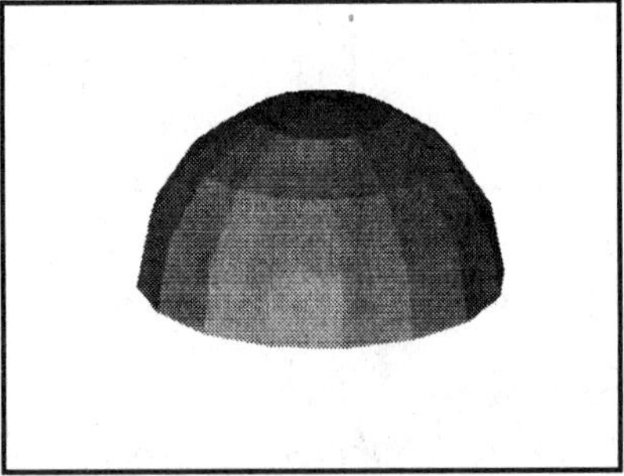

A faceted hemisphere has distinct edges between its faces.

RELATED COMMANDS

Create/LSphere/Faceted, Create/Hemisphere/Smoothed Create/Hemisphere/Values, Views-Drawing Aids, Views–Use Snap, Views–Use Grid, Views–Angle Snap, Display/Const, Display/User View

Create/Hemisphere/Smoothed

Create
Box
LSphere...
GSphere...
Hemisphere...
Cylinder...
Tube...
Torus...
Cone...
Vertex
Face...
Element...
Object...
Faceted
Smoothed
Values

Creates a smoothed 3D hemisphere. The number of segments is specified with *Create/Hemisphere/Values*.

Creating a Smoothed Hemisphere

1. Set the number of segments you want the hemisphere to contain with *Create/Hemisphere/Values*.
2. In the active viewport (except a camera or spotlight viewport), click to place the center of the hemisphere. The hemisphere is placed on the near side of the construction plane if created in an orthographic viewport, or placed on the near side of the the User plane if created in the User viewport.
3. As you move the mouse away from the center, the hemisphere is drawn. Moving the mouse in a circle will rotate the hemisphere. See *Views–Drawing Aids, Views–Use Snap, Views–Use Grid,* and *Views–Angle Snap*.
4. When the hemisphere is the correct size, click to create it, or right-click to cancel.
5. In the Name for new object: dialog box, assign the hemisphere a unique name.

NOTE A hemisphere is half of an LSphere. See *Create/LSphere/Smoothed.*

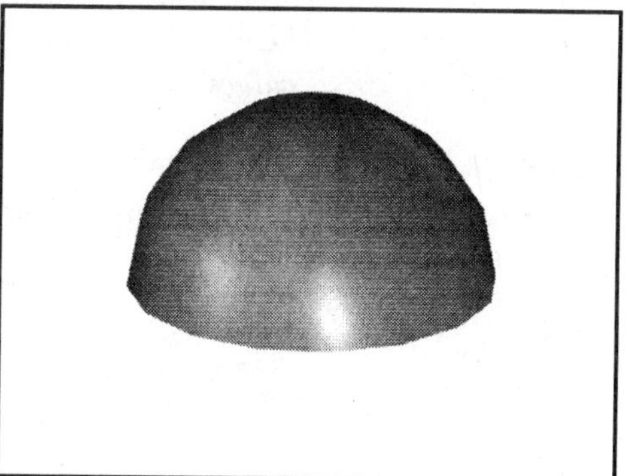

A smoothed hemisphere appears polished.

RELATED COMMANDS

Create/LSphere/Smoothed, Create/Hemisphere/Faceted, Create/Hemisphere/Values, Views-Drawing Aids, Views–Use Snap, Views–Use Grid, Views–Angle Snap, Display/Const, Display/User View

Create
Box
LSphere...
GSphere...
Hemisphere...
Cylinder...
Tube...
Torus...
Cone...
Vertex
Face...
Element...
Object...
Faceted
Smoothed
Values

Create/Hemisphere/Values

Specifies the number of longitudinal segments in a hemisphere.

Specifying the Longitudinal Segments

1. Select *Create/LSphere/Values* before creating a hemisphere. In the Set Hemisphere Segments dialog box, set the number of longitudinal segments. The default setting is 16. Valid range is from 4 to 100.

2. Set the type of hemisphere you want to create, either smooth or faceted. The following illustrations show how the number of longitudinal segments affects smoothed and faceted hemispheres.

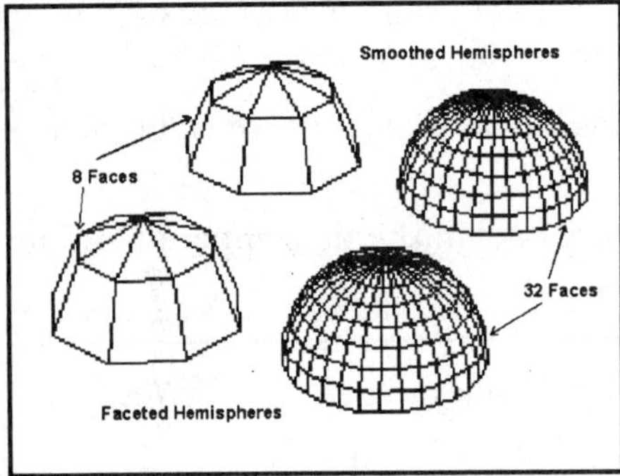

Wireframe smoothed and faceted hemispheres with different segment values.

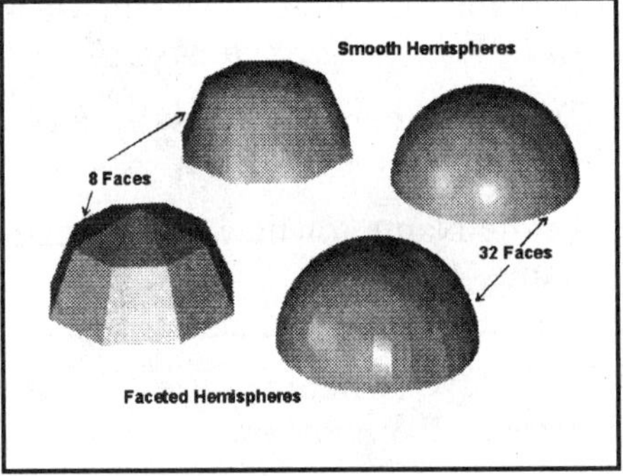

Rendered smoothed and faceted hemispheres with different segment values.

RELATED COMMANDS

Create/Hemisphere/Faceted, Create/Hemisphere/Smoothed

Create/Cylinder/Faceted

Create
Box
LSphere...
GSphere...
Hemisphere...
Cylinder...
Tube...
Torus...
Cone...
Vertex
Face...
Element...
Object...
Faceted
Smoothed
Values

Creates a faceted cylinder, consisting of two end polygons with connecting segments.

Creating a Segmented Cylinder

1. Select *Create/Cylinder/Values* to set the number of sides and segments.
2. In the active viewport (except a camera or spotlight viewport), click to place the center of an equal-sided polygon. The base of the cylinder is placed on the near side of the construction plane if created in an orthographic viewport, or placed on the near side of the the User plane if created in the User viewport.
3. As you move the mouse away from the center, an equal-sided polygon is drawn. Moving the mouse in a circle will rotate the polygon. See *Views–Drawing Aids, Views–Use Snap, Views–Use Grid,* and *Views–Angle Snap.*
4. When the polygon is the correct size, click. The polygon disappears.
5. To define the length of the cylinder, click in any viewport. Define the cylinder's length by moving the mouse, which draws a line representing the cylinder's length.
6. When the cylinder is the correct length, click to create it.
7. In the Name for new object: dialog box, assign the cylinder a unique name.

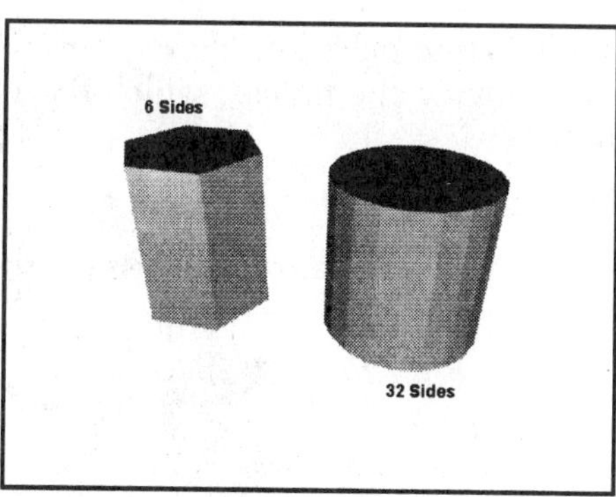

Faceted cylinders have distinct edges between their faces.

RELATED COMMANDS

Create/Cylinder/Value, Create/Cylinder/Smoothed, Views-Drawing Aids, Views–Use Snap, Views–Use Grid, Views–Angle Snap, Display/Const, Display/User View

Create
Box
LSphere...
GSphere...
Hemisphere...
Cylinder...
Tube...
Torus...
Cone...
Vertex
Face...
Element...
Object...
Faceted
Smoothed
Values

Create/Cylinder/Smoothed

Creates a smoothed cylinder, consisting of two end polygons with connecting segments.

Creating a Smoothed Cylinder

1. Select *Create/Cylinder/Value* to set the number of sides and segments.

> **TIP** When creating a smoothed cylinder, set the side value according to how you will view the completed cylinder. If the ends cannot be seen, use a minimum number of sides. The figure below shows a six-sided cylinder and a 30-sided cylinder. Although the profiles of their edges are different, they render very similarly.

2. In the active viewport (except a camera or spotlight viewport), click to place the center of an equal-sided polygon. The base of the cylinder is placed on the near side of the construction plane if created in an orthographic viewport, or placed on the near side of the the User plane if created in the User viewport.
3. As you move the mouse away from the center, an equal sided polygon is drawn. Moving the mouse in a circle will rotate the polygon. See *Views–Drawing Aids, Views–Use Snap, Views–Use Grid,* and *Views-Angle Snap*.
4. When the polygon is the correct size, click. The polygon disappears.
5. To define the length of the cylinder, click in any viewport. Define the cylinder's length by moving the mouse, which draws a line representing the cylinder's length.
6. When the cylinder is the correct length, click to create it.
7. In the Name for new object: dialog box, assign the cylinder a unique name.

Creating smoothed cylinders.

RELATED COMMANDS

Create/Cylinder/Value, Create/Cylinder/Faceted, Views–Drawing Aids, Views–Use Snap, Views–Use Grid, Views-Angle Snap, Display/Const, Display/User View

Create/Cylinder/Values

Create
Box
LSphere...
GSphere...
Hemisphere...
Cylinder...
Tube...
Torus...
Cone...
Vertex
Face...
Element...
Object...
Faceted
Smoothed
Values

Adjusts the sides and segments of smoothed and segmented cylinders.

Adjusting the Sides and Segments of Cylinders

1. When you select *Create/Cylinder/Values* the Set Cylinder Values dialog box appears.
2. Specify the number of sides from 3 to 100. The side of the cylinder is the flat surface running along the length. The default number is 6.
3. Specify the number of segments from 1 to 100. The segment of the cylinder is the area between the two cross sections.
4. Set the type of cylinder you want to create, either smooth or faceted. The following illustrations show how the number of faces and segments affects smoothed and faceted cylinders.

TIP Unless you are creating a cylinder with the intention of bending it, it should be created with only one segment to save faces. Segments only affect the rendering quality of the cylinder if you deform or bend it.

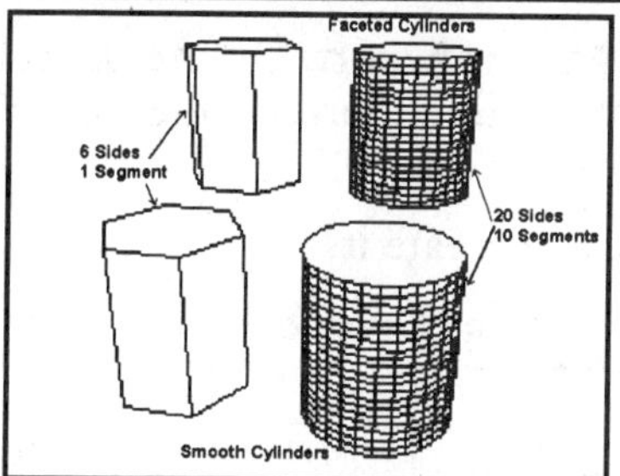

Wireframe smoothed and faceted cylinders with different side and segment values.

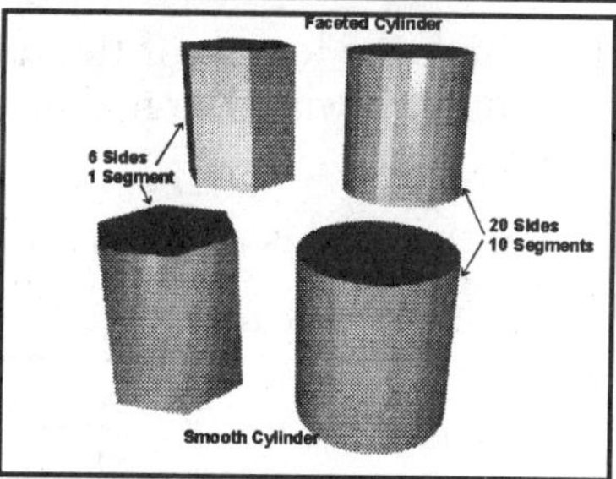

Rendered smoothed and faceted cylinders with different side and segment values.

TIP The number of sides determines the overall smoothness of the cylinder. If you need extremely smooth cylinders for high–resolution images, you can loft circles that contain more than 100 sides (the maximum value for cylinder segments).

RELATED COMMANDS

Create/Cylinder/Smoothed, Create/Cylinder/Faceted

Create
Box
LSphere...
GSphere...
Hemisphere...
Cylinder...
Tube...
Torus...
Cone...
Vertex
Face...
Element...
Object...
Faceted
Smoothed
Values

Create/Tube/Faceted

Creates a faceted tube. It consists of two end polygons with connecting segments. The two end polygons are defined by specifying the inner and outer diameters of the tube.

Creating a Segmented Tube

1. Select *Create/Tube/Values* to set the number of sides and segments.
2. In the active viewport (except a camera or spotlight viewport), click to place the center of the first equal-sided polygon. The base of the tube is placed on the near side of the construction plane if created in an orthographic viewport, or placed on the near side of the User plane if created in the User viewport.
3. As you move the mouse away from the center, an equal-sided polygon is drawn. Moving the mouse in a circle will rotate the polygon. See *Views–Drawing Aids, Views–Use Snap, Views–Use Grid,* and *Views–Angle Snap*.
4. When the polygon is the correct size, click.
5. Move the mouse to set the diameter of the second polygon. It can be larger or smaller than the first. After clicking to set the diameter, the polygon disappears.
6. To define the length of the tube, click in any viewport. Define the tube's length by moving the mouse, which draws a line representing the tube's length.
7. When the tube is the correct length, click to create it.
8. In the Name for new object: dialog box, assign the tube a unique name.

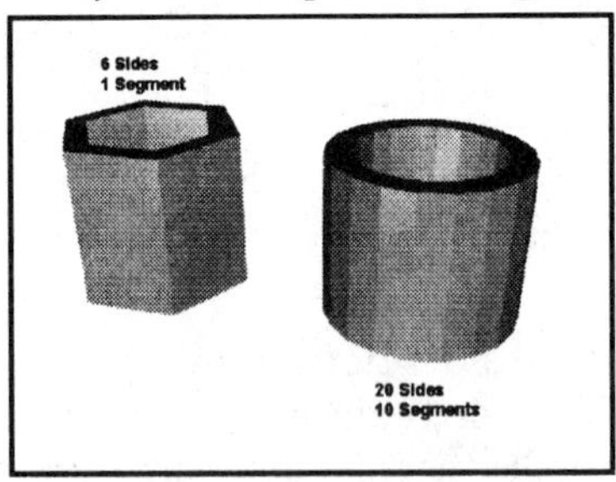

Creating faceted tubes.

RELATED COMMANDS

Create/Tube/Value, Create/Tube/Smoothed, Views-Drawing Aids, Views–Use Snap, Views–Use Grid, Views–Angle Snap, Display/Const, Display/User View

Create/Tube/Smoothed

Create
Box
LSphere...
GSphere...
Hemisphere...
Cylinder...
Tube...
Torus...
Cone...
Vertex
Face...
Element...
Object...
Faceted
Smoothed
Values

Creates a smoothed tube. It consists of two end polygons with connecting segments. The two end polygons are defined by specifying the inner and outer diameters of the tube.

Creating a Smoothed Tube

1. Select *Create/Tube/Value* to set the number of sides and segments.
2. In the active viewport (except a camera or spotlight viewport), click to place the center of the first equal-sided polygon. The base of the tube is placed on the near side of the construction plane if created in an orthographic viewport, or placed on the near side of the User plane if created in the User viewport.
3. As you move the mouse away from the center, an equal-sided polygon is drawn. Moving the mouse in a circle will rotate the polygon. See *Views–Drawing Aids, Views–Use Snap, Views–Use Grid,* and *Views–Angle Snap*.
4. When the polygon is the correct size, click.
5. Move the mouse to set the diameter of the second polygon. It can be larger or smaller than the first. After clicking to set the diameter, the polygon disappears.
6. To define the length of the tube, click in any viewport. Define the tube's length by moving the mouse, which draws a line representing the tube's length.
7. When the tube is the correct length, click to create it.
8. In the Name for new object: dialog box, assign the tube a unique name.

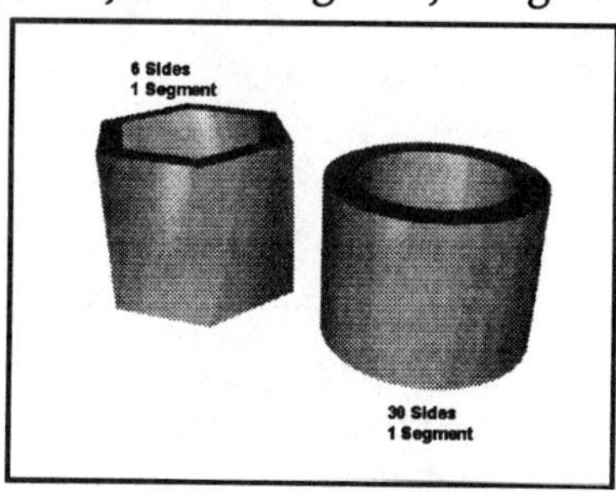

Creating smoothed tubes.

RELATED COMMANDS

Create/Tube/Values, Create/Tube/Faceted, Views–Drawing Aids, Views–Use Snap, Views–Use Grid, Views–Angle Snap, Display/Const, Display/User View

Create
Box
LSphere...
GSphere...
Hemisphere...
Cylinder...
Tube...
Torus...
Cone...
Vertex
Face...
Element...
Object...
Faceted
Smoothed
Values

Create/Tube/Values

Adjusts the sides and segments of smoothed and segmented tubes.

Adjusting the Sides and Segments of Tubes

1. When you select *Create/Tube/Values* the Set Tube Values dialog box appears.
2. Specify the number of sides from 3 to 100. The side of the tube is the flat surface running along the length. The default number is 6.
3. Specify the number of segments from 1 to 100. The segment of the cylinder is the area between the two cross sections.
4. Set the type of tube you want to create from the menu, either smooth or faceted. The following illustrations show how the number of faces and segments affects smoothed and faceted tubes.

TIP Unless you are creating a tube with the intention of bending it, it should be created with only one segment to save faces. Segments only affect the rendering quality of the tube if you deform or bend it.

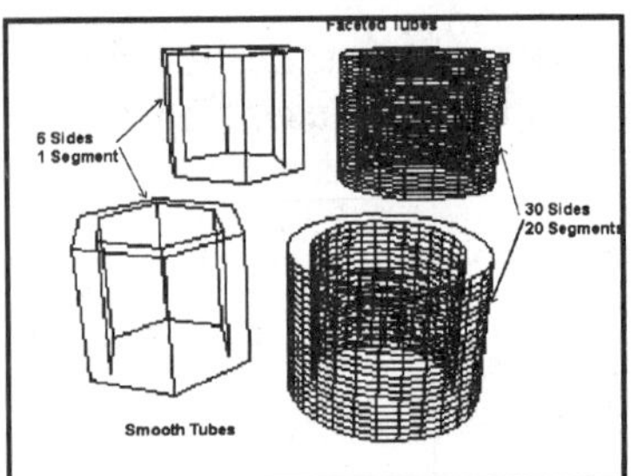

Wireframe smoothed and faceted tubes with different side and segment values.

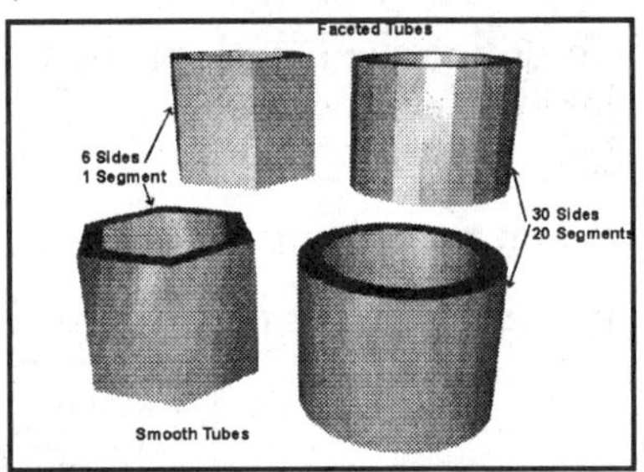

Rendered smoothed and faceted tubes with different side and segment values.

TIP The number of sides determines the overall smoothness of the tube. If you need extremely smooth tubes for high resolution images, you can loft circles that contain more than 100 sides (the maximum value for cylinder segments).

RELATED COMMANDS

Create/Tube/Smoothed, Create/Tube/Faceted

Create/Torus/Faceted

Create
Box
LSphere...
GSphere...
Hemisphere...
Cylinder...
Tube...
Torus...
Cone...
Vertex
Face...
Element...
Object...
Faceted
Smoothed
Values

Creates a faceted 3D doughnut shape, called a torus.

Creating a Faceted Torus

1. Select *Create/Torus/Values* to set the number of sides and segments.
2. In the active viewport (except a camera or spotlight viewport), click to place the center of the first equal sided polygon. The torus is placed on the center of the construction plane if created in an orthographic viewport, or placed on the center of the User plane if created in the User viewport.
3. As you move the mouse away from the center, an equal sided polygon is drawn. Moving the mouse in a circle will rotate the polygon. This will be the inner diameter of the torus. See *Views–Drawing Aids, Views–Use Snap, Views–Use Grid,* and *Views–Angle Snap*.
4. When the polygon is the correct size, click.
5. Move the mouse to set the diameter of the second concentric polygon. This polygon will be the outer diameter of the torus.
6. Click to set the diameter of the second polygon, or right-click to cancel.
7. In the Name for new object: dialog box, assign the torus a unique name.

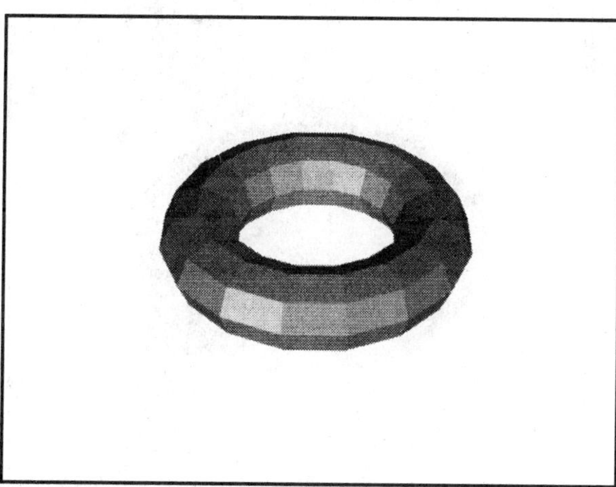

Creating a faceted torus.

RELATED COMMANDS

Create/Torus/Value, Create/Torus/Smoothed, Views–Drawing Aids, Views–Use Snap, Views–Use Grid, Views–Angle Snap, Display/Const, Display/User View

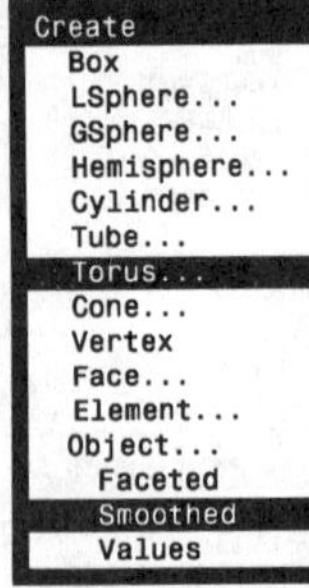

Create/Torus/Smoothed

Creates a smoothed 3D doughnut shape, called a torus.

Creating a Smoothed Torus

1. Select *Create/Torus/Value* to set the number of sides and segments.
2. In the active viewport (except a camera or spotlight viewport), click to place the center of the first equal-sided polygon. The torus is placed on the center of the construction plane if created in an orthographic viewport, or placed on the center of the User plane if created in the User viewport.
3. As you move the mouse away from the center, an equal-sided polygon is drawn. Moving the mouse in a circle will rotate the polygon. This will be the inner diameter of the torus. See *Views–Drawing Aids, Views–Use Snap, Views–Use Grid,* and *Views–Angle Snap*.
4. When the polygon is the correct size, click.
5. Move the mouse to set the diameter of the second concentric polygon. This polygon will be the outer diameter of the torus.
6. Click to set the diameter of the second polygon, or right-click to cancel.
7. In the Name for new object: dialog box, assign the torus a unique name.

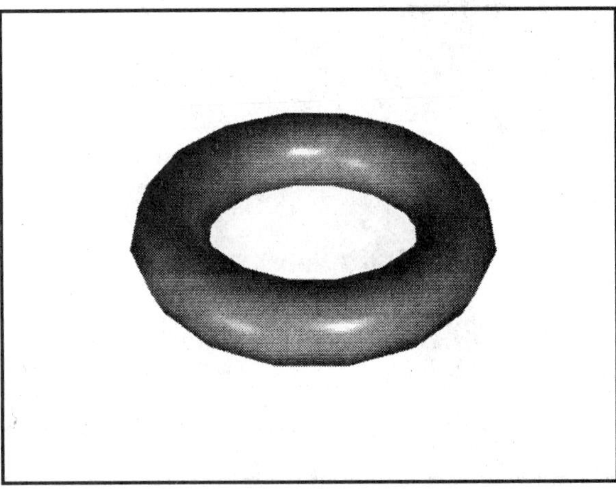

Creating a smoothed torus.

RELATED COMMANDS

Create/Torus/Values, Create/Torus/Faceted, Views–Drawing Aids, Views–Use Snap, Views–Use Grid, Views-Angle Snap, Display/Const, Display/User View

Create/Torus/Values

Create
Box
LSphere...
GSphere...
Hemisphere...
Cylinder...
Tube...
Torus...
Cone...
Vertex
Face...
Element...
Object...
Faceted
Smoothed
Values

Adjusts the sides and segments of a smoothed and segmented torus.

Adjusting the Sides and Segments of a Torus

1. When you select *Create/Torus/Values* the Set Torus Values dialog box appears.
2. Specify the number of sides from 3 to 100. The sides of the torus are the facets of its cross section. The default number is 8.
3. Specify the number of segments from 1 to 100. The segment of the torus is the areas between the cross sections that are arranged in a radical fashion about the circumference.
4. Set the type of torus you want to create from the menu, either smooth or faceted. The following illustrations show how the number of faces and segments affects a smoothed and faceted torus.

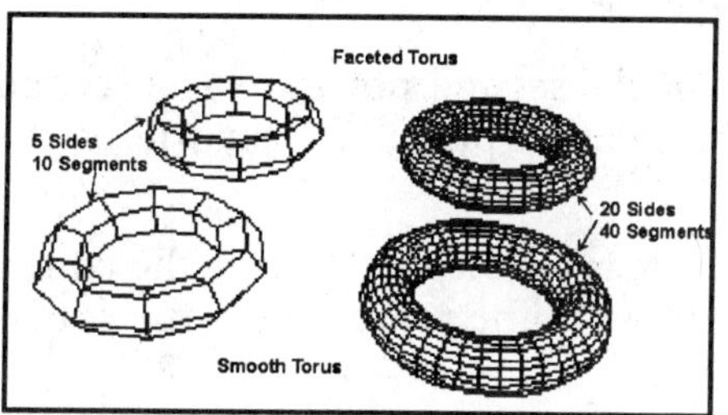

Wireframe smoothed and faceted torus with different side and segment values.

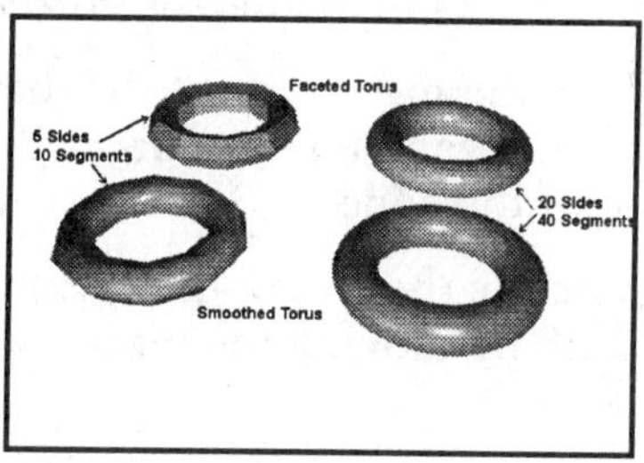

Rendered smoothed and faceted torus with different side and segment values.

RELATED COMMANDS

Create/Torus/Smoothed, Create/Torus/Faceted

Create
Box
LSphere...
GSphere...
Hemisphere...
Cylinder...
Tube...
Torus...
Cone...
Vertex
Face...
Element...
Object...
Faceted
Smoothed
Values

Create/Cone/Faceted

Creates a 3D faceted cone. You have the option of making the end polygons the same or different diameters.

Creating a Faceted Cone

1. Select *Create/Cone/Values* to set the number of sides and segments.
2. In the active viewport (except a camera or spotlight viewport), click to place the center of the first equal-sided polygon. The cone is placed on the near side of the construction plane if created in an orthographic viewport, or placed on the near side of the User plane if created in the User viewport.
3. As you move the mouse away from the center, an equal-sided polygon is drawn. Moving the mouse in a circle will rotate the polygon. See *Views–Drawing Aids, Views–Use Snap, Views–Use Grid,* and *Views–Angle Snap*.
4. When the polygon is the correct size, click.
5. Move the mouse to set the diameter of the second polygon. The second polygon can be larger or smaller than the first polygon. This will be the top of the cone.
6. To define the length of the cone, click in any viewport. Define the cone's length by moving the mouse, which draws a line representing the cone's length.
7. When the cone is the correct length, click to create it and assign the cone a unique name in the Name for new object: dialog box.

> **NOTE** You cannot create a cone that sharpens to a single point. If you create the cone with a radius of 0, it will still contain a small, flat, circular tip.

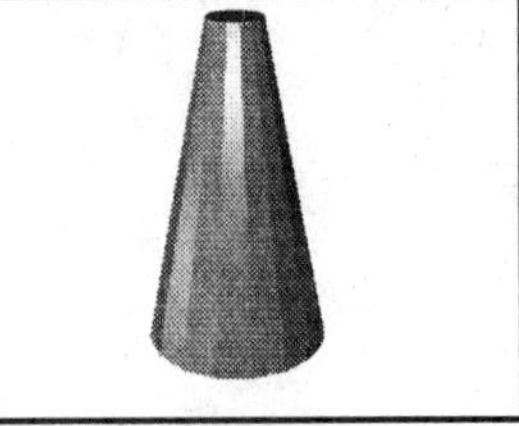

Creating a faceted cone.

RELATED COMMANDS

Create/Cone/Value, Create/Cone/Smoothed, Views–Drawing Aids, Views–Use Snap, Views–Use Grid, Views–Angle Snap, Display/Const, Display/User View

Create
Box
LSphere...
GSphere...
Hemisphere...
Cylinder...
Tube...
Torus...
Cone...
Vertex
Face...
Element...
Object...
Faceted
Smoothed
Values

Create/Cone/Smoothed

Creates a 3D smoothed cone. You have the option of making the end polygons the same or different diameters.

Creating a Smoothed Cone

1. Select *Create/Cone/Values* to set the number of sides and segments.
2. In the active viewport (except a camera or spotlight viewport), click to place the center of the first equal-sided polygon. The cone is placed on the near side of the construction plane if created in an orthographic viewport, or placed on the near side of the User plane if created in the User viewport.
3. As you move the mouse away from the center, an equal-sided polygon is drawn. Moving the mouse in a circle will rotate the polygon. See *Views–Drawing Aids, Views–Use Snap, Views–Use Grid* and *Views–Angle Snap*.
4. When the polygon is the correct size, click.
5. Move the mouse to set the diameter of the second polygon. The second polygon can be larger or smaller than the first polygon. This will be top of the cone.
6. To define the length of the cone, click in any viewport. Define the cone's length by moving the mouse, which draws a line representing the cone's length.
7. When the cone is the correct length, click to create it and assign the cone a unique name in the Name for new object: dialog box.

> **NOTE** You cannot create a cone that sharpens to a single point. If you create the cone with a radius of 0, it will still contain a small, flat, circular tip.

Creating a smoothed cone.

RELATED COMMANDS

Create/Cone/Value, Create/Cone/Smoothed, Views-Drawing Aids, Views–Use Snap, Views–Use Grid, Views–Angle Snap, Display/Const, Display/User View

Create
Box
LSphere...
GSphere...
Hemisphere...
Cylinder...
Tube...
Torus...
Cone...
Vertex
Face...
Element...
Object...
Faceted
Smoothed
Values

Create/Cone/Values

Adjusts the sides and segments of smoothed and segmented cones.

Adjusting the Sides and Segments of a Cone

1. When you select *Create/Cone/Values* the Set Cone Values dialog box appears.
2. Specify the number of sides from 3 to 100. The side of the cone is the space between the longitudinal segments that run along the length of the cone. The default number is 16.
3. Specify the number of segments from 1 to 100. The segment of the cone is the area between the two cross sections. Because the default number of segments of a cone is 1, a default cone contains only a top and bottom polygon.
4. Set the type of cone you want to create, either smooth or faceted from the menu. The following illustrations show how the number of faces and segments affects smoothed and faceted cones.

NOTE Because a cone is not spherical, the higher the segment and face values are set, the smoother the cone will render.

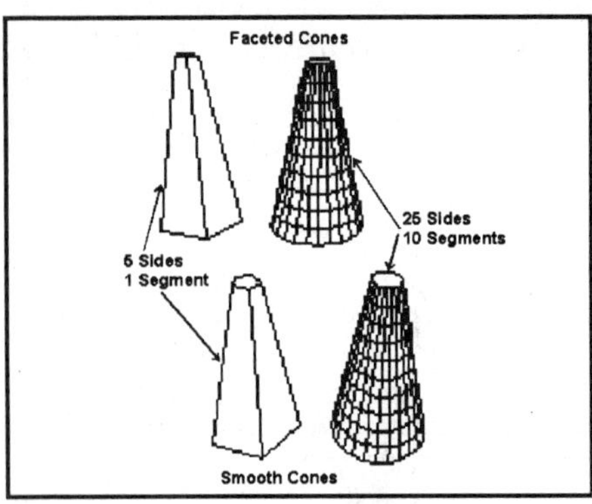

Wireframe smoothed and faceted cones with different side and segment values.

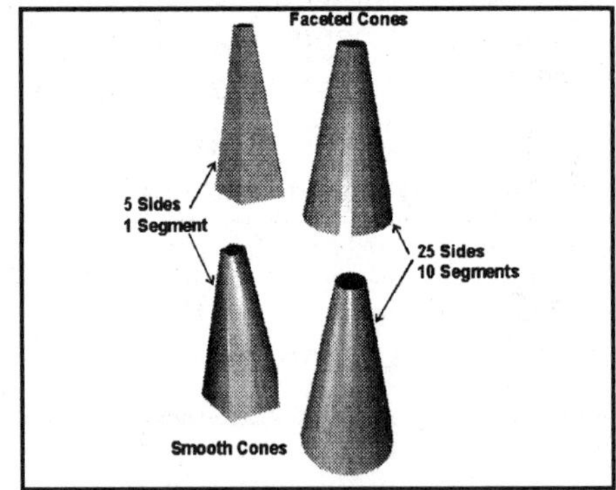

Rendered smoothed and faceted cones with different side and segment values.

RELATED COMMANDS

Create/Cone/Smoothed, Create/Cone/Faceted

Create/Vertex

Create
Hemisphere...
Cylinder...
Tube...
Torus...
Cone...
Vertex
Face...
Element...
Object...
Array...
Build
Copy
Extrude
Detach
Tessellate

Allows you to add one or more vertices to an existing object.

Adding Vertices to an Existing Object

1. Select *Create/Vertex* and click on the object you want to add the vertex to.
2. After selecting the object to add the vertex to, the cursor changes to a crosshair. Place the crosshair where you want the vertex and click.
3. When you are through adding vertices, either select another command, or right-click and select another object to add vertices to.

NOTE Adding vertices to an existing object is done primarily for one reason: to build faces upon. They never define a mesh by themselves, and cannot be rendered independently. To build faces from the vertices, see *Create/Face/Build*

TIP In the standard display mode, vertices appear as small dots about the size of a pixel on the screen. If you are having trouble seeing the vertices, switch the display mode to *Display/Geometry/Vert Ticks*.

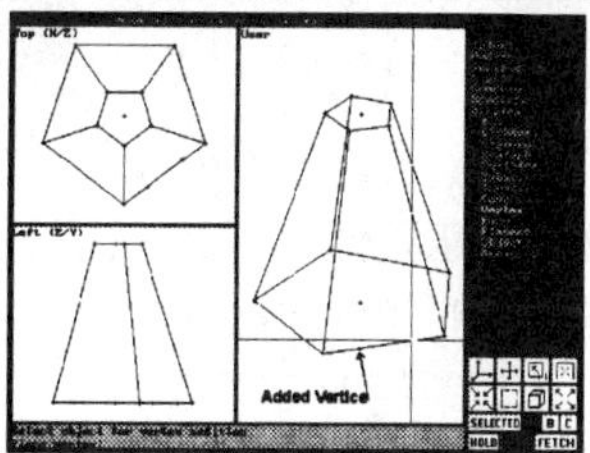

Creating a vertex on an existing object.

NOTE If you are having difficulty placing the vertices in the correct location, try turning on the construction planes with *Display/Const/Show*. Vertices are created on the current construction plane, meaning that if you create a vertice in the Top (X/Z) viewport, the vertices are placed on the XZ plane.

RELATED COMMANDS

Display/Geometry/Vert Ticks, Display/Const/Show

Create
Hemisphere...
Cylinder...
Tube...
Torus...
Cone...
Vertex
Face...
Element...
Object...
Array...
Build
Copy
Extrude
Detach
Tessellate

Create/Face/Build

Creates a new face by connecting three existing vertices of the same object.

Building a Face from Three Existing Vertices

1. Select *Create/Face/Build* and click on the first vertex. As you move the mouse a blue line will appear on the screen.
2. Click on the second vertex. All vertices must exist in the same object. Moving the mouse will cause a blue triangle to appear between the two selected vertices and the cursor.
3. Click on the third vertex to create the face.

TIP When building new faces, it is necessary to select the vertices on the object. In the standard display mode, vertices appear as small dots about the size of a pixel on the screen. If you are having trouble seeing the vertices, switch the display mode to *Display/Geometry/Vert Ticks*.

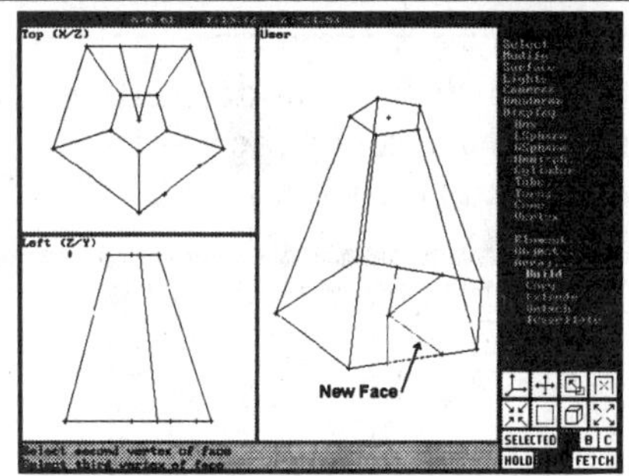

Building a face from three existing vertices.

NOTE The order in which you select the vertices when creating the face is very important. Connecting the vertices in a counterclockwise manner creates the face with the normal facing you. Connecting the vertices in a clockwise manner orients the normal away from you. If the face does not appear when rendering, the face normal is on the side facing away from you. See *2-Sided* in the *Materials Editor*, *Surface/Normals/Face Flip*, and *Render/Render View*.

RELATED COMMANDS

Create/Object/Attach, Display/Geometry/Vert Ticks, Surface/Normals/Face Flip, Render/Render View, 2-Sided in the Materials Editor

Create/Face/Copy

Create
Hemisphere...
Cylinder...
Tube...
Torus...
Cone...
Vertex
Face...
Element...
Object...
Array...
Build
Copy
Extrude
Detach
Tessellate

Copies one or more faces of an existing object and creates a *new* object.

Copying an Existing Face

1. Select one or more faces. See *Select/Face/Single, Select/Face/Quad, Select/Face/Fence,* and *Select/Face/Circle.*
2. After selecting multiple faces, a white bounding box appears, which is attatched to the cursor. When picking a single face, first click on a vertex. Next, click on the face to make the bounding box appear.
3. Move the box using the directional cursors. You can cycle through the cursors using the [Tab] key. When you have moved the bounding box to the desired location, click.
4. 3D Studio prompts you for a unique name, because the copied face or faces are now an independent object.

TIP To make it easier to see and select a face, you can display all of the geometry with *Display/Geometry/All Lines.*

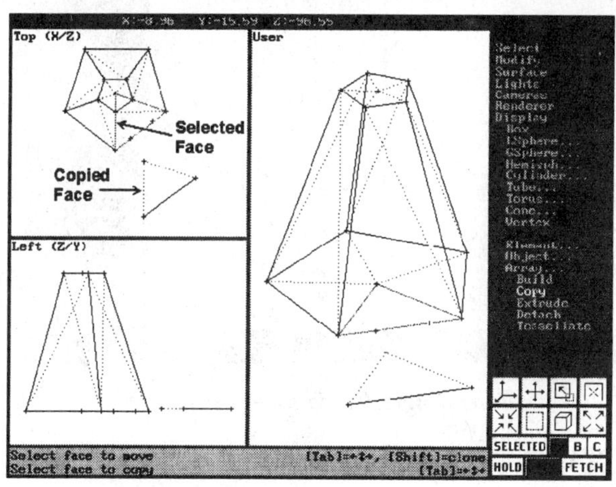

Copying a face from an existing object.

RELATED COMMANDS

Display/Geometry/All Lines, Select/Face/Single, Select/Face/Quad, Select/Face/Fence, Select/Face/Circle

Create
Hemisphere...
Cylinder...
Tube...
Torus...
Cone...
Vertex
Face...
Element...
Object...
Array...
Build
Copy
Extrude
Detach
Tessellate

Create/Face/Extrude

Extrudes one or more faces from an existing object. A face can be extruded either in or out.

Copying an Existing Face

1. Select one or more faces. See *Select/Face/Single, Select/Face/Quad, Select/Face/Fence,* and *Select/Face/Circle.*
2. Draw a line in any viewport to define the length of the extrusion. The length is displayed in the status bar at the top of the screen.
3. After drawing the line, select the direction (either **In** or **Out,** which is based on the direction of the normals) you want the face or faces to be extruded.

To make it easier to see and select a face, you can display all of the geometry with *Display/Geometry/All Lines.*

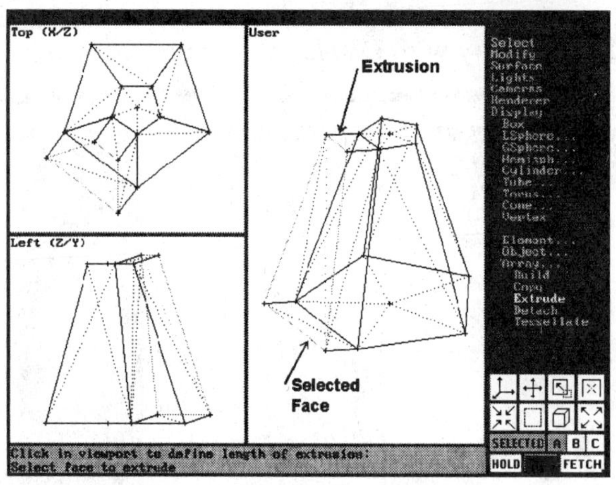

Extruding selected faces outward.

RELATED COMMANDS

Display/Geometry/All Lines, Select/Face/Single, Select/Face/Quad, Select/Face/Fence, Select/Face/Circle

Create/Face/Detach

Create
Hemisphere...
Cylinder...
Tube...
Torus...
Cone...
Vertex
Face...
Element...
Object...
Array...
Build
Copy
Extrude
Detach
Tessellate

Detaches one or more faces from an existing object, creating a new object. It can also be used to combine selected faces or objects into a single object.

Detaching Existing Face(s)

1. Select one or more faces you want to detach. See *Select/Face/Single, Select/Face/Quad, Select/Face/Fence,* and *Select/Face/Circle*.
2. After selecting one or more faces, the Detach selected faces? alert box appears. Select OK to detach the selected faces.
3. 3D Studio prompts you for a unique name, because the detached face or faces are now an independent object. If the detached face is moved to new position, a hole is left in the original object.

NOTE When faces are detached, 3D Studio creates duplicate vertices and leaves the original vertices intact. The total number of faces in the object remains the same, but the number of vertices increases. The detached faces still look like part of the original object.

To make it easier to see and select a face, you can display all of the geometry with *Display/Geometry/All Lines*.

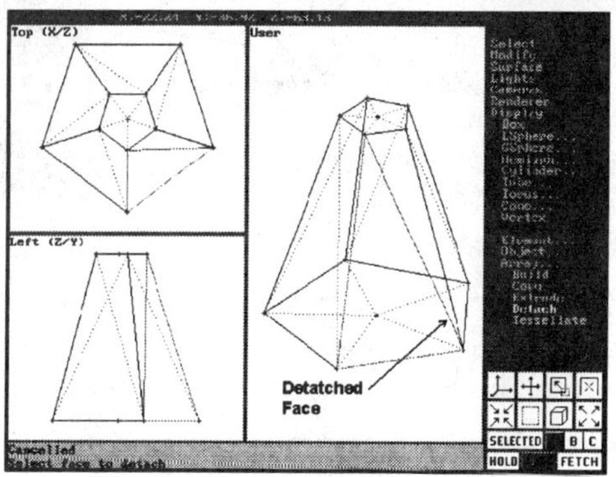

Detatching a selected face.

RELATED COMMANDS

Display/Geometry/All Lines, Select/Face/Single, Select/Face/Quad, Select/Face/Fence, Select/Face/Circle

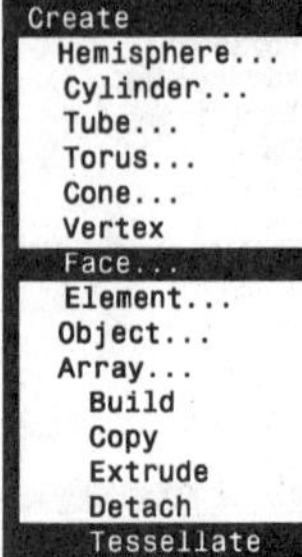

Create/Face/Tessellate

Subdivides one or more faces of an existing object. This is done by adding a vertex to the center of each selected face and drawing three connecting lines from the new vertex to the three original vertices.

Tessellating an Existing Object

1. Select one or more faces you want to tesselate. See *Select/Face/Single, Select/Face/Quad, Select/face/Fence,* and *Select/Face/Circle.*
2. After selecting the faces you want to tesselate, an alert box appears. Select **OK** to tesselate the selected face(s).

You can use *Create/Face/Tesselate* to increase the complexity of an object that requires more faces for detailed editing.

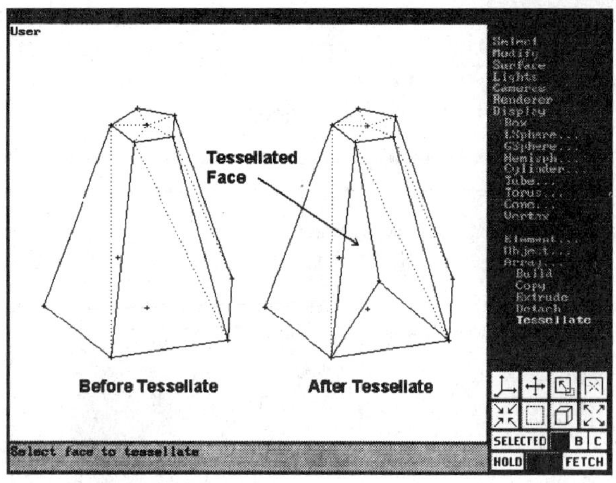

You can use tesselate to increase the complexity of object.

To make it easier to see and select a face, you can display all of the geometry with *Display/Geometry/All Lines.*

RELATED COMMANDS

Display/Geometry/All Lines, Select/Face/Single, Select/Face/Quad, Select/Face/Fence, Select/Face/Circle

Create/Element/Copy

Create
GSphere
Hemisphere...
Cylinder...
Tube...
Torus...
Cone...
Vertex
Face...
Element...
Object...
Array...
Copy
Detach
Tessellate
Explode

Copies an element of an existing object, creating a new object.

Copying an Element

1. Select the element you want to copy. After selecting the element, a white bounding box attatches to the cursor.
2. Move the bounding box to the new location, using the directional cursors. You can cycle through the directional cursors by pressing the [Tab] key.
3. After placing the element, click the left mouse button. The element you selected to copy is now an independent object, and must be assigned a unique name.

NOTE An *object* is a mesh object, a collection of one or more vertices that has a netlike appearance. An *element* can be thought of as a subset of an object that can be used as a potential building block. It can be broken off, modified, cloned, reattatched, or used in a Boolean operation. See *Create/Element/Detach* and *Create/Object/Attach*.

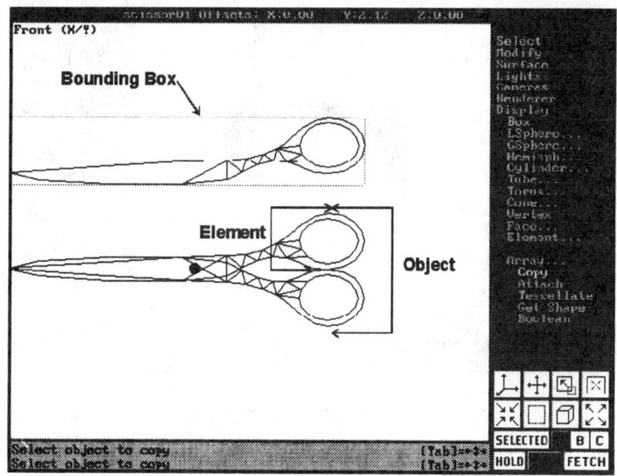

Copying an element of an existing object.

RELATED COMMANDS

Create/Element/Detach, Create/Object/Attach

Create
GSphere
Hemisphere...
Cylinder...
Tube...
Torus...
Cone...
Vertex
Face...
Element...
Object...
Array...
Copy
Detach
Tessellate
Explode

Create/Element/Detach

Detatches an element from an existing object, creating a new object.

Detaching an Element

1. Select the element you want to detach.
2. When the Detach Element alert box appears, select **OK** to detach the selected element.
3. The detatched element has now become an independent object. Assign it a unique name, and click on **Create**.

> **NOTE** An *object* is a mesh object, a collection of one or more vertices that has a netlike appearance. An *element* can be thought of as a subset of an object that can be used as a potential building block. It can be broken off, modified, cloned, reattatched, or used in a Boolean operation. See *Create/Element/Detach* and *Create/Object/Attach*.

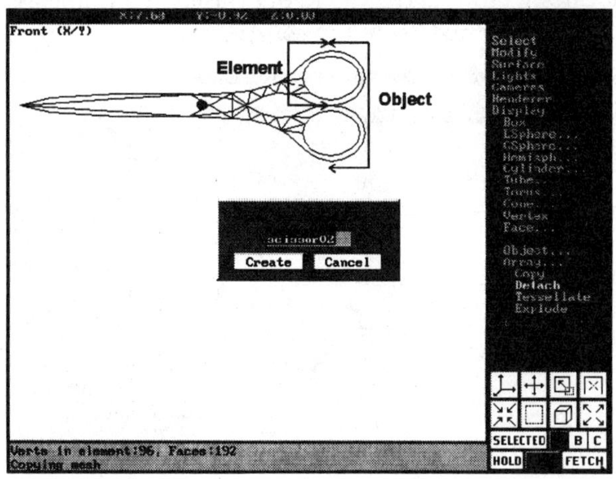

Detatching an element.

RELATED COMMAND

Create/Object/Attach

Create/Element/Tessellate

Create
GSphere
Hemisphere...
Cylinder...
Tube...
Torus...
Cone...
Vertex
Face...
Element...
Object...
Array...
Copy
Detach
Tessellate
Explode

Subdivides the faces of a selected element. This is done by adding a vertex to the center of each face in the selected element and drawing three connecting lines from the new vertex to the three original vertices in each face.

Tessellating an Element

1. Select the element you want to tessellate.
2. In the Tessellate Element alert box, select **OK**.

> **NOTE** An *object* is a mesh object, a collection of one or more vertices that has a netlike appearance. An *element* can be thought of as a subset of an object that can be used as a potential building block. It can be broken off, modified, cloned, reattatched, or used in a Boolean operation. See *Create/Element/Detach* and *Create/Object/Attach*.

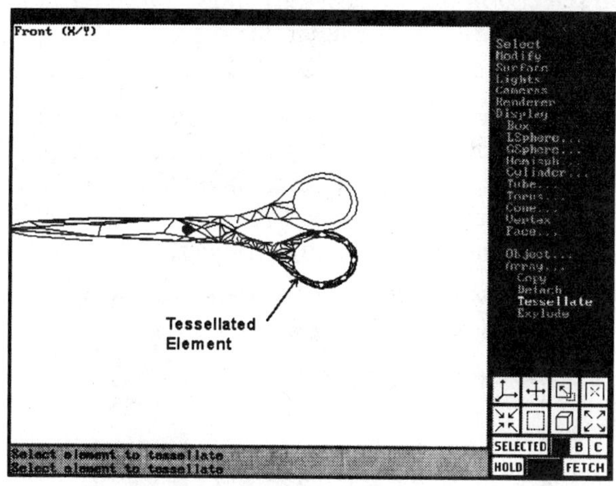

You can use tesselate to increase the complexity of an element.

RELATED COMMANDS

Create/Element/Detach, Create/Object/Attach

Create
GSphere
Hemisphere...
Cylinder...
Tube...
Torus...
Cone...
Vertex
Face...
Element...
Object...
Array...
Copy
Detach
Tessellate
Explode

Create/Element/Explode

Explodes an object into multiple elements. This is based on the angles of the object's edges.

Exploding an Object

1. Select the object to explode.
2. In the Explode Object dialog box, set the Edge angle in the Angle threshold box and select Elements or Objects.

   Angle threshold. This angle determines what edges will be separated. The separated edges will become part of another element or object. For example, if this is set to 24 degrees, all edges between faces where the normals have an included angle greater than 24 degrees will be broken off and become part of a separate element or object. if you set the angle to 0, all triangular faces will become separate objects or elements.

   Explode into. If you select **elements,** all faces surrounded by edge angles greater than the Angle Threshold will become separate elements of the selected object. If you select **objects,** all faces surrounded by edge angles greater than the Angle Threshold will become separate objects.

> **NOTE** You can restore all of the exploded objects to a single object by first creating a selection set of all the exploded objects. See *Select/Object/Single, Select/Object/Quad, Select/Object/Fence,* and *Select/Object/Circle*. After creating the selection set, use *Create/Face/Detach* to combine the selected objects into a single object.

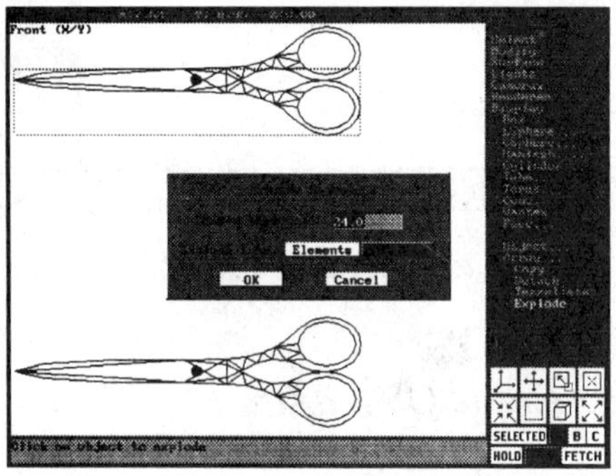

Exploding an object.

RELATED COMMAND

Create/Face/Detach

Create/Object/Copy

Create
Hemisphere...
Cylinder...
Tube...
Torus...
Cone...
Vertex
Face...
Element...
Object...
Array...
Copy
Attach
Tessellate
Get Shape
Boolean

Copies one or more existing objects, creating a new object.

Creating a Copy of a Single Object

1. Select a single object.
2. After selecting a single object, a white bounding box appears enclosing the object. Move the box to the desired location and click. You can use the directional cursors to move the bounding box. Use the Tab key to cycle through the three directional cursors.
3. In the Name for new object: dialog box, give the copied object a new unique name.

Creating a Copy of Multiple Objects

1. Create a selection set of multiple objects using *Select/Object/Single, Select/Object/Quad, Select/Object/Fence,* or *Select/Object/Circle.*
2. After selecting multiple objects, a white bounding box appears enclosing the objects. Move the box to the desired location and click. You can use the directional cursors to move the bounding box. Use the Tab key to cycle through the three directional cursors.
3. After moving the bounding box, the Copy objects to: alert box appears.

   Single. Creates a single new object. All copies of the selected objects are its elements. The Name for new object: dialog box appears, prompting for a new unique name for the object.

   Multilple. Creates individual copies of each of the selected objects. A Name for new object: dialog box appears for *each* object in the selection set.

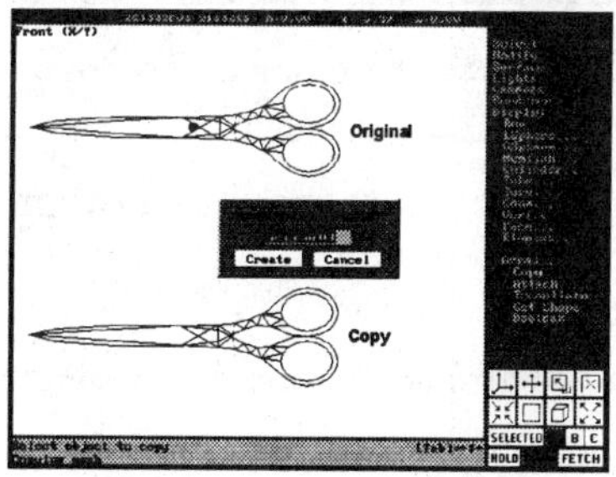

Copying a single object.

RELATED COMMANDS

Create/Element/Detach, Create/Object/Attach

Create
Hemisphere...
Cylinder...
Tube...
Torus...
Cone...
Vertex
Face...
Element...
Object...
Array...
Copy
Attach
Tessellate
Get Shape
Boolean

Create/Object/Attach

Attaches two objects together. Each object can contain one or multiple elements.

Attaching Objects

1. Select the first object to attach. The name of the object is displayed in the prompt line at the bottom of the screen.
2. Select the second object. The first object is attatched to the second, making it an element of the latter.

> **NOTE** When attaching objects, the first object selected becomes an element of the second object. The name of the second object is maintained, and the name of the first object is deleted.

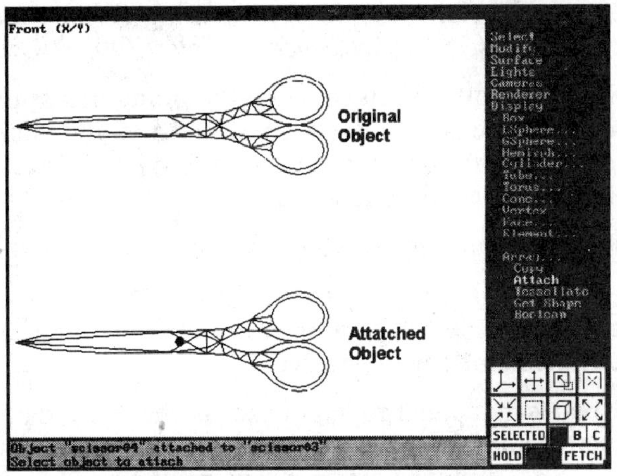

The effect of attaching one object to another.

> **NOTE** When one object is attached to another, the first object is deleted from the 3D Scene and Keyframer because it becomes an element of the second object.

RELATED COMMAND

Create/Element/Detach

Create/Object/Tessellate

Create
Hemisphere...
Cylinder...
Tube...
Torus...
Cone...
Vertex
Face...
Element...
Object...
Array...
Copy
Attach
Tessellate
Get Shape
Boolean

Subdivides the faces of one or more selected objects.

Tessellating an Object

1. Select the objects you want to tessellate.
2. In the Tessellate Controls alert box, you have two choices for tessellating the faces, and can adjust the tension along the edges of each face.

   Face-Center. A vertex is added to the center of each face in the selected object and three connected lines are drawn from the new vertex to the three original vertices in each face.

   Edge. A vertice is inserted in the middle of each edge, and three lines are drawn connecting those vertices. As a result of selecting Edge, four faces are created out of one face.

   Edge Tension. A negative value pulls the vertices inward, resulting in a concave effect. A positive value pulls the vertices outward, resulting in a rounded effect.
3. After selecting the face tessellation method and adjusting the tension, select **OK**.

> **TIP** You can use *Create/Object/Tesselate* to increase the complexity of an object that requires more faces for detailed editing. If, however, you want to do detailed editing of only a portion of the object, tessellate selected faces with *Create/Face/Tessellate*. This will keep object complexity to a minimum.

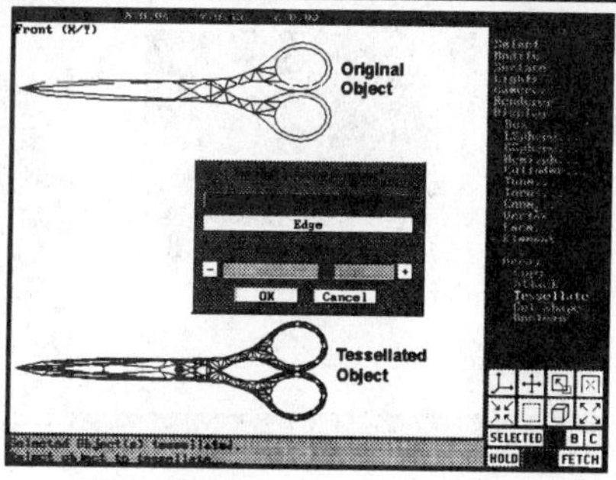

Tessellating a single object.

RELATED COMMANDS

Create/Face/Tessellate, Create/Object/Tessellate

Create
Hemisphere...
Cylinder...
Tube...
Torus...
Cone...
Vertex
Face...
Element...
Object...
Array...
Copy
Attach
Tessellate
Get Shape
Boolean

Create/Object/Get Shape

Brings closed shapes that exist in the 2D Shaper directly into the 3D Editor.

Importing 2D Shapes

1. Create a closed polygon and assign it as a shape in the 2D Shaper. See *Shape/Assign* in the 2D Shaper. If no shape is assigned, all polygons are used.

2. In the 3D Editor, select *Create/Object/Get Shape*. The Shape Control dialog box appears with the following options:

   Object Name. Assign the object a new, unique name.

   Current Step Setting. Displays the current step value of the shape you are importing. This can be changed in the 2D Shaper under *Shapes/Steps*.

   Shape Detail. Corresponds to the number of vertices per segment as shown in the Current Step Setting. The High Option creates all of the vertices in the current Step setting, **Medium Option** creates half of them, and **Low Option** ignores steps, connecting only the defined vertices.

   Cap Shape. If Cap Shape is turned off, only vertices are imported into the 3D Editor.

3. After setting the options in the Shape Creation Control dialog box and selecting OK, the 2D mesh object is placed coplaner to the current viewport in the 3D Editor.

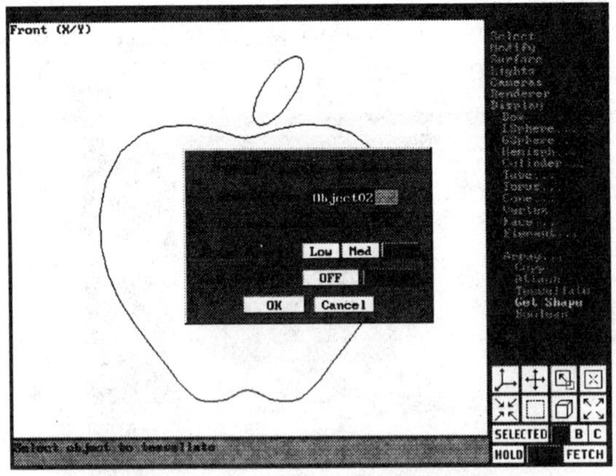

Importing an object from the 2D Shaper.

RELATED COMMAND

Shape/Assign

Create
Hemisphere...
Cylinder...
Tube...
Torus...
Cone...
Vertex
Face...
Element...
Object...
Array...
Copy
Attach
Tessellate
Get Shape
Boolean

Create/Object/Boolean

Combines two objects by performing a Boolean (union, subtraction, intersection) operation. The first object is altered and the second object is deleted.

Types of Boolean Operations

Union
The two selected objects are combined by removing the segments in the overlapping portions.
Subtraction
The overlapping portion of the second object is subtracted from the first object. The remainder of the second object is deleted.
Intersection
Only the overlapping portion of the two objects is retained.

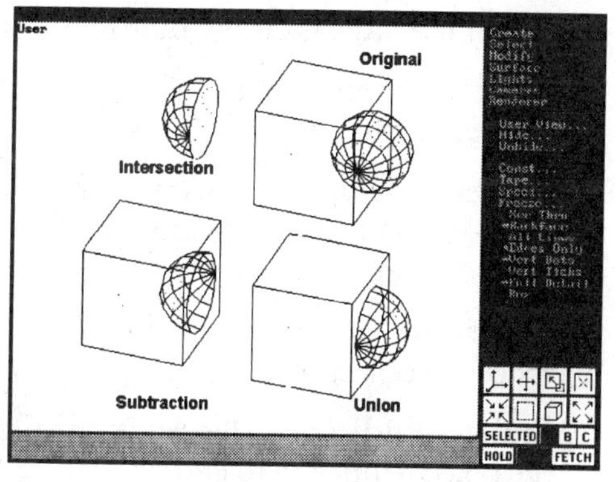

Boolean operations.

Performing a Boolean Operation

1. Select the first object to alter.
2. Select the second object. The Boolean Operation dialog box appears.
3. Select the Boolean operation to perform. You are also given the following options:

   Weld Elements: Determines whether the vertices of the faces from the second object that remain after the Boolean operation are welded to the first object.

   Hold: Clicking on will store the current geometry in the Hold buffer. Clicking on the **Hold** button will allow you to restore you original geometry after performing a Boolean operation by using the **Fetch** (Ctrl F) button.
4. After setting the appropriate options, click on **OK** to perform the Boolean operation.

RELATED COMMAND

Create/Boolean in the 2D Shaper for performing Boolean operations on 2D shapes.

Create
GSphere
Hemisphere...
Cylinder...
Tube...
Torus...
Cone...
Vertex
Face...
Element...
Object...
Array...
Linear
Radial
Move
Rotate

Create/Array/Linear

Creates a straight-line array of single or multiple objects

Creating a Linear Array

1. Select *Create/Array/Linear*, then click in any orthographic or User viewport that you want to create the array in.
2. When the unidirectional cursor appears, press the [Tab] key until the cursor points in the direction you want the array to be created in.
3. Click on the object you want to array. To array multiple objects, first create a selection set. See *Select/Object/Single, Select/Object/Quad, Select/Object/Fence,* or *Select/Object/Circle*.
4. When the Linear Array dialog box appears, set the following options:

   Total number in array: The total number of objects that will be copied, *including* the original.

   Object Spacing: The distance between the centers or ends of the object. This depends on the setting of the Center-to-Center button and the End-to-End button.

   Center–to–Center: The value set in the Object Spacing box will be used to space the object from center to center.

   End–to–End: The value set in the Object Spacing box will be used to space the object from end to end.

   Array Length: Specifies the overall length of the array.

   Calculate: The values in the Linear Array box depend on each other. You can enter any two values and select the Calculate button to calculate the third button. For example, if you know you want to array 10 objects with a spacing of 20, enter these values in the appropriate box and select Calculate. The Array Length will be calculated.
5. After setting the values in the Linear Array dialog box, select OK. The specified number of objects is created, using the information supplied in the Linear Array dialog box.

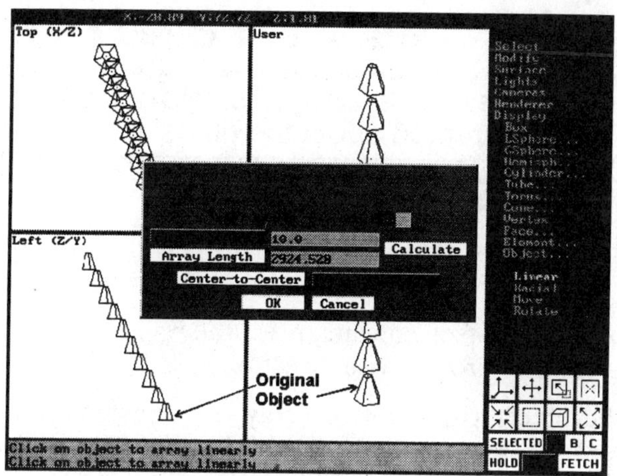

Creating a linear array.

RELATED COMMANDS

Create/Array/Radial, Create/Array/Move, Create/Array/Rotate

Create
GSphere
Hemisphere...
Cylinder...
Tube...
Torus...
Cone...
Vertex
Face...
Element...
Object...
Array...
Linear
Radial
Move
Rotate

Create/Array/Radial

Creates a circular array of single or multiple objects. The array is created about the global or local axis.

Creating a Radial Array

1. Select *Create/Array/Radial*, then click in any orthographic or User viewport that you want to create the array in.
2. When the rotation cursor appears, press the Tab key to switch between a clockwise and counterclockwise direction.
3. Click on the object you want to array. To array multiple objects, first create a selection set. See *Select/Object/Single, Select/Object/Quad, Select/Object/Fence,* or *Select/Object/Circle*.
4. When the Radial Array dialog box appears, set the following options:

   Total number in array: The total number of objects that will be copied, *including* the original.

   Degrees: The distance between the centers of the objects, in degrees.

   Arc Length: Overall length of the arc.

   Calculate: Either the **Arc Length** or **Degrees** button may be active at one time. Selecting **Calculate** will update the value for the button that is not active.

   Rotate Objects: Each object is rotated to match the rotation of the array.
5. After setting the values in the Radial Array dialog box, select **OK**. The specified number of objects is created, using the information supplied in the Radial Array dialog box.

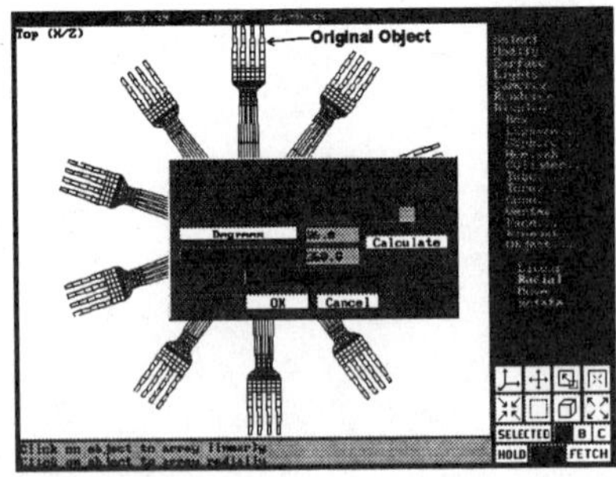

Creating a circular array, with the objects rotated.

RELATED COMMANDS

Create/Array/Linear, Create/Array/Move, Create/Array/Rotate, Modify/Axis/Place, Local Axis icon

Create/Array/Move

Create
GSphere
Hemisphere...
Cylinder...
Tube...
Torus...
Cone...
Vertex
Face...
Element...
Object...
Array...
Linear
Radial
Move
Rotate

Creates an array of single or multiple objects based on an offset created with the mouse.

Creating a Linear Array with Move

1. Select *Create/Array/Move*, then click in any orthographic or User viewport that you want to create the array in.
2. When the unidirectional cursor appears, press the [Tab] key until the cursor points in the direction you want the array to be created in. Selecting the Free Move cursor will allow you to create an array at an angle.
3. Click on the object you want to array. To array multiple objects, first create a selection set. See *Select/Object/Single, Select/Object/Quad, Select/Object/Fence,* or *Select/Object/Circle.*
4. Move the object a specified distance and angle from the original object and click. To move the object a specified distance, use the Snap and Grid functions. See *Views–Drawing Aids, Views–Use Snap,* and *Views–Use Grid.*
5. Enter the total number of objects to be arrayed in the dialog box, including the original, and click on **OK**.

TIP Unlike the *Create/Array/Linear* command, you can create angled arrays with *Create/Array/Move*.

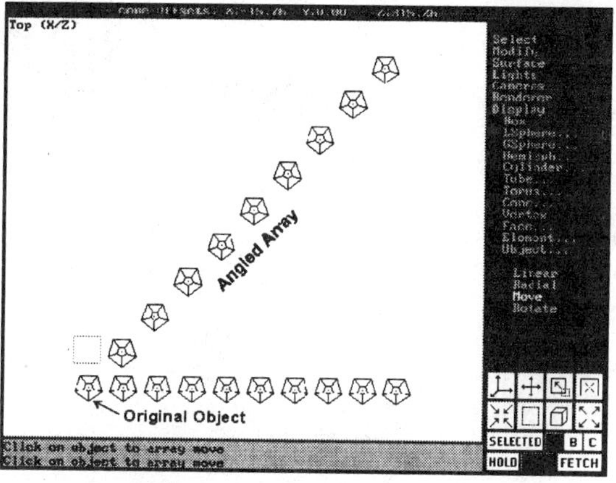

Creating a linear array with move.

RELATED COMMANDS

Create/Array/Linear, Create/Array/Radial, Create/Array/Rotate

Create
GSphere
Hemisphere...
Cylinder...
Tube...
Torus...
Cone...
Vertex
Face...
Element...
Object...
Array...
Linear
Radial
Move
Rotate

Create/Array/Rotate

Creates a circular array of single or multiple objects. The degree of rotation is specified with the mouse.

Creating a Circular Array with Rotate

1. Select *Create/Array/Rotate*, then click on the object you want to array. To array multiple objects, first create a selection set. See *Select/Object/Single, Select/Object/Quad, Select/Object/Fence,* or *Select/Object/Circle*.
2. Rotate the object a specified angle. The object can be rotated about the local axis or global axis. See *Local Axis icon* and *Views-Angle Snap*.
3. Enter the total number of objects to be arrayed in the dialog box, including the original, and click on **OK**.

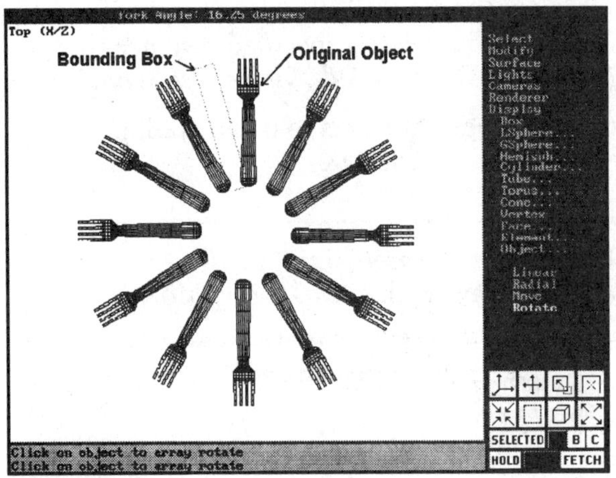

Creating a circular array with the rotate option.

RELATED COMMANDS

Create/Array/Linear, Create/Array/Radial, Create/Array/Move, Modify/Axis/Place, Local Axis icon, Views–Angle Snap

Select/Vertex/Single

Create
Select
Modify
Surface
Lights
Vertex...
Face...
Element
Object...
All
None
Invert
Single
Quad
Fence
Circle

Assigns individual vertices to a selection set.

Creating a Selection Set of Individual Vertices

1. Activate an icon letter (A, B, or C) at the bottom of the screen. All selected vertices will be assigned to the letter highlighted.
2. Click on each vertex you want added to the selection set. Selected vertices appear in red.
3. Clicking on selected (red) vertices will remove them from the selection set.

> **TIP** By default, vertices are displayed on the screen as a dot about the size of a pixel. To make the vertices easier to select, display the vertices as tick marks instead of dots by selecting *Display/Geometry/Vert Ticks.*

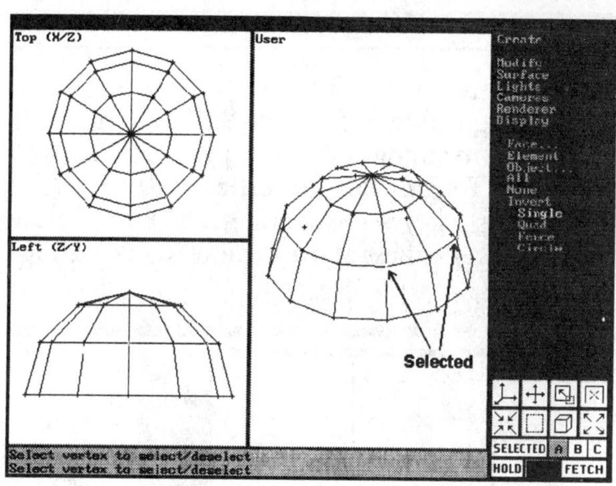

Selecting single vertices.

RELATED COMMANDS

Display/Geometry/Vert Ticks, Select/Vertex/Quad, Select/Vertex/Fence, Select/Vertex/Circle

Create
Select
Modify
Surface
Lights
Vertex...
Face...
Element
Object...
All
None
Invert
Single
Quad
Fence
Circle

Select/Vertex/Quad

Assigns vertices to a selection set by defining a box around the vertices.

Creating a Selection Set with Quad

1. Activate an icon letter (A, B, or C) at the bottom of the screen. All selected vertices will be assigned to the letter highlighted.
2. Define a box around the vertices by clicking to place one corner of the box.
3. Move the mouse diagonally to enclose the vertices, then click to set the opposite corner. All vertices within the box are selected. Selected vertices appear in red.

TIP By default, vertices are displayed on the screen as a dot about the size of a pixel. To make the vertices easier to select, display the vertices as tick marks instead of dots by selecting *Display/Geometry/Vert Ticks*.

NOTE Deselecting vertices with the Quad option is affected by the Region-Toggle option. See *Info–System Options*. By default, Region Toggle is set to **ON**, meaning vertices switch states each time you select them. If you turn Region Toggle **OFF**, no vertices will be deselected. You can, however, hold down the Alt key while defining the Quad. This will deselect all vertices within the Quad, regardless of the Region Toggle setting.

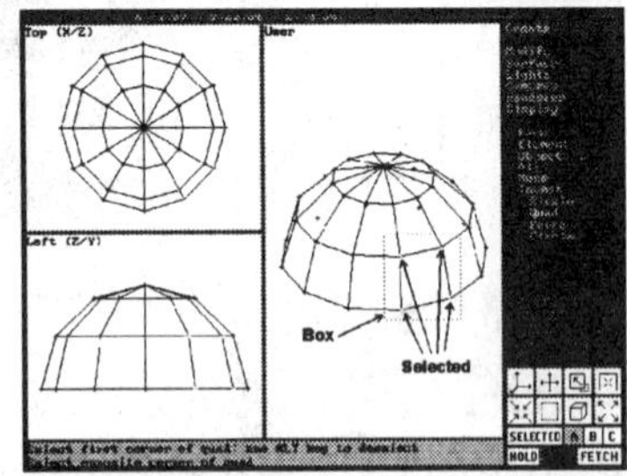

Selecting vertices with a box.

RELATED COMMANDS

Display/Geometry/Vert Ticks, Select/Vertex/Single, Select/Vertex/Fence, Select/Vertex/Circle

Select/Vertex/Fence

Create
Select
Modify
Surface
Lights
Vertex...
Face...
Element
Object...
All
None
Invert
Single
Quad
Fence
Circle

Assigns vertices to a selection set by defining a box around the vertices.

Creating a Selection Set with Fence

1. Activate an icon letter (A, B, or C) at the bottom of the screen. All selected vertices will be assigned to the letter highlighted.
2. Define a polygon around the vertices. Begin by clicking to set a point. Click the mouse to create a segment, then click to set a second point.
3. Continue setting points and creating segments until all vertices you want selected are enclosed within the polygon.
4. Close the polygon and complete the selection set by either clicking at the first point in the polygon or pressing the **Spacebar**. All vertices within the polygon are selected. Selected vertices appear in red.

> **NOTE** When deselecting vertices, the Fence option is affected by the Region-Toggle option. See *Info–System Options*. Region Toggle is set to **On** by default, meaning vertices switch states each time you select them. If you turn region toggle **Off**, no vertices will be deselected. Holding down the Alt key while defining the Fence will deselect all vertices within the polygon regardless of the Region Toggle setting.

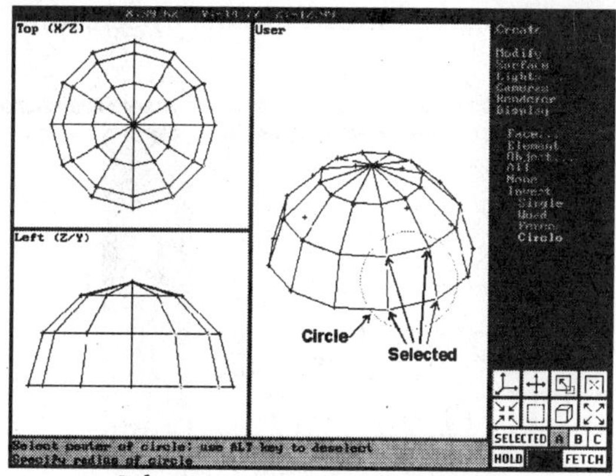

Selecting vertices with a fence.

RELATED COMMANDS

Display/Geometry/Vert Ticks, Select/Vertex/Single, Select/Vertex/Quad, Select/Vertex/Circle

Create
Select
Modify
Surface
Lights
Vertex...
Face...
Element
Object...
All
None
Invert
Single
Quad
Fence
Circle

Select/Vertex/Circle

Assigns vertices to a selection set by defining a circle around the vertices.

Creating a Selection Set with Circle

1. Activate an icon letter (A, B, or C) at the bottom of the screen. All selected vertices will be assigned to the letter highlighted.
2. Define a circle around the vertices by first clicking to set the center of the circle.
3. Move the mouse to define the diameter of the circle. All vertices within the circle are selected. Selected vertices appear in red.

NOTE The Circle option is affected by the Region-Toggle option. See *Info–System Options*. By default, Region Toggle is set to **ON**, meaning vertices switch states each time you select them. If you turn region toggle **OFF**, no vertices will be deselected. Holding down the [Alt] key while defining the circle will deselect all vertices within the circle, regardless of the Region Toggle setting.

TIP By default, vertices are displayed on the screen as a dot about the size of a pixel. To make the vertices easier to select, display the vertices as tick marks instead of dots by selecting *Display/Geometry/Vert Ticks*.

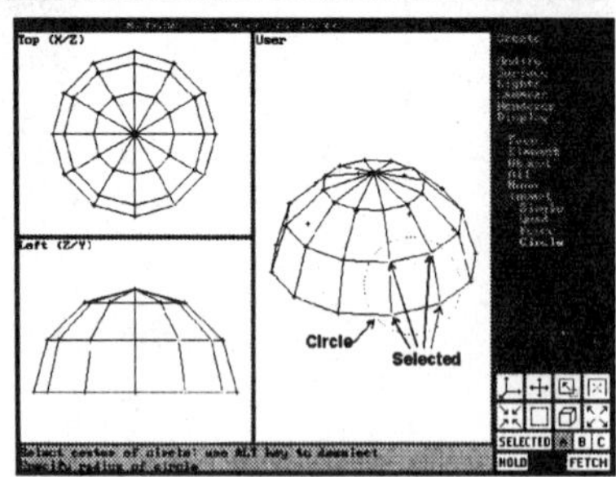

Selecting vertices with a circle.

RELATED COMMANDS

Display/Geometry/Vert Ticks, Select/Vertex/Single, Select/Vertex/Quad, Select/Vertex/Fence

Select/Face...

Create
Select
Modify
Vertex..
Face...
Element
Object...
All
None
Invert
Single
Quad
Fence
Circle
Window
Crossing

Assigns individual and selected faces to a selection set.

Creating a Selection Set of Faces

1. Activate an icon letter (A, B, or C) at the bottom of the screen. All selected faces will be assigned to the letter highlighted.

TIP A face in a mesh object appears as a triangular polygon with three vertices. To see the faces in a mesh select *Display/Geometry/Full Detail* and *Display/Geometry/All Lines.*

2. Choose a face selection method. See *Select/Face/Single, Select/Face/Quad, Select/Face/Fence,* or *Select/Face/Circle.* Selected faces appear in red.

NOTE Selection with the *Select/Face/Quad, Select/Face/Fence,* or *Select/Face/Circle* options are affected by the Window and Crossing options. Only one option may be active at a time. When the Window mode is active, only faces *totally enclosed* within the defined region are included in the selection set. When the Crossing mode is active, all faces *crossing, touching,* or *enclosed by* the defined region are included in the selection set. See *Select/Face/Window* and *Select/Face/Crossing.*

NOTE All of the Select/Face... options are affected by the Region-Toggle switch. See *Info–System Options.* Region Toggle is set to **ON** by default, meaning faces switch states each time you select them. If you turn region toggle to **OFF**, no faces will be deselected. Holding down the [Alt] key while selecting faces will deselect the affected faces regardless of the Region Toggle setting.

RELATED COMMANDS

Select/Face/Single, Select/Face/Quad, Select/Face/Fence, Select/Face/Circle, Select/Face/Window, Select/Face/Crossing

Create
Select
Modify
Vertex..
Face...
Element
Object...
All
None
Invert
Single
Quad
Fence
Circle
Window
Crossing

Select/Face/Single

Assigns individual faces to a selection set.

Creating a Selection Set of Individual Faces

1. Activate an icon letter (A, B, or C) at the bottom of the screen. All selected faces will be assigned to the letter highlighted.
2. Click on a vertex and move the mouse. As you move the mouse, all faces that share that vertex are highlighted in blue, one at a time. When the face you want is highlighted in blue, click to select it. Selected faces appear in red.
3. Clicking on selected (red) faces will remove them from the selection set.

> **TIP** A face in a mesh object appears as a triangular polygon with three vertices. To see the faces in a mesh select *Display/Geometry/Full Detail* and *Display/Geometry/All Lines.* For more information on selecting faces and assinging them to a selection set, see *Select/Face...*

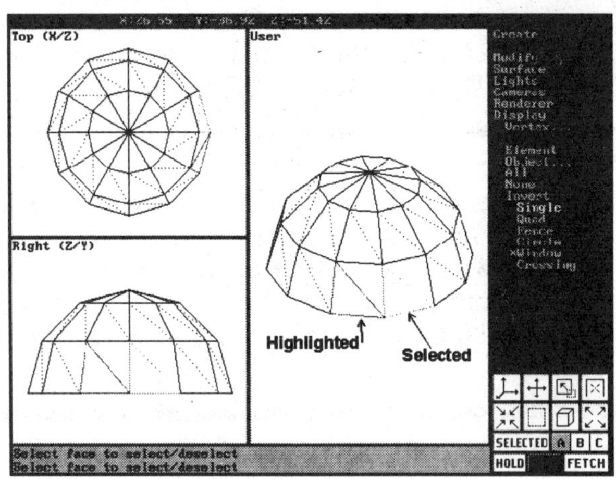

Selecting single faces.

RELATED COMMANDS

Select/Face..., Select/Face/Quad, Select/Face/Fence, Select/Face/Circle

Select/Face/Quad

Create
Select
Modify
Vertex..
Face...
Element
Object...
All
None
Invert
Single
Quad
Fence
Circle
Window
Crossing

Assigns faces to a selection set by defining a box around the faces.

Creating a Selection Set with Quad

1. Activate an icon letter (A, B, or C) at the bottom of the screen. All selected faces will be assigned to the letter highlighted.
2. Define a box around the faces by clicking to place one corner of the box.

> **NOTE** Selection with the Quad option is affected by the Window and Crossing options. Only one option may be active at a time. When the Window mode is active, only faces *totally enclosed* within the defined region are included in the selection set. When the Crossing mode is active, all faces *crossing, touching* or *enclosed by* the defined region are included in the selection set. See *Select/Face/Window* and *Select/Face/Crossing*. For more information on selecting faces and assinging them to a selection set, see *Select/Face...*

3. Move the mouse diagonally to enclose the faces, then click to set the opposite corner. With the Window mode active, all faces within the box are selected. Selected faces appear in red.

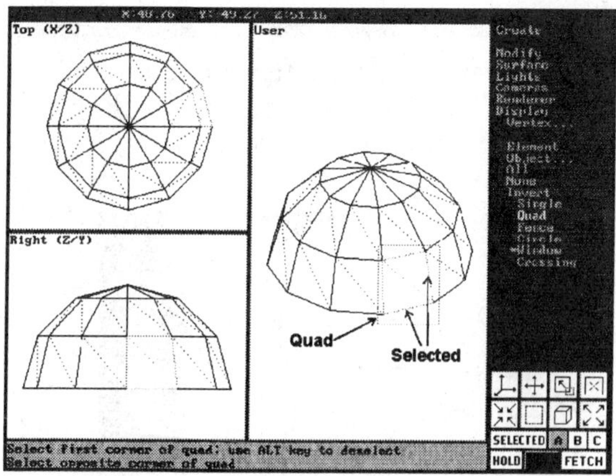

Selecting faces with the Quad–Window option.

RELATED COMMANDS

Select/Face..., Select/Face/Single, Select/Face/Fence, Select/Face/Circle, Select/Face/Window, Select/Face/Crossing

Create
Select
Modify
Vertex..
Face...
Element
Object...
All
None
Invert
Single
Quad
Fence
Circle
Window
Crossing

Select/Face/Fence

Assigns faces to a selection set by defining a polygon around the faces.

Creating a Selection Set with Fence

1. Activate an icon letter (A, B, or C) at the bottom of the screen. All selected faces will be assigned to the letter highlighted.
2. Define a polygon around the faces you want to select. Begin by clicking to set a point. Click the mouse to create a segment, then click to set a second point.
3. Continue setting points and creating segments until all faces you want selected are enclosed within the polygon.

> **NOTE** Selection with the Fence option is affected by the Window and Crossing options. Only one option may be active at a time. When the Window mode is active, only faces *totally enclosed* within the defined region are included in the selection set. When the Crossing mode is active, all faces *crossing, touching* or *enclosed by* the defined region are included in the selection set. See *Select/Face/Window* and *Select/Face/Crossing*. For more information on selecting faces and assinging them to a selection set, see *Select/Face...*

4. Close the polygon created with the fence and complete the selection set by clicking at the first point in the fence or pressing the **Spacebar.** With the Window mode active, all objects within the fence are selected. Selected objects appear in red.

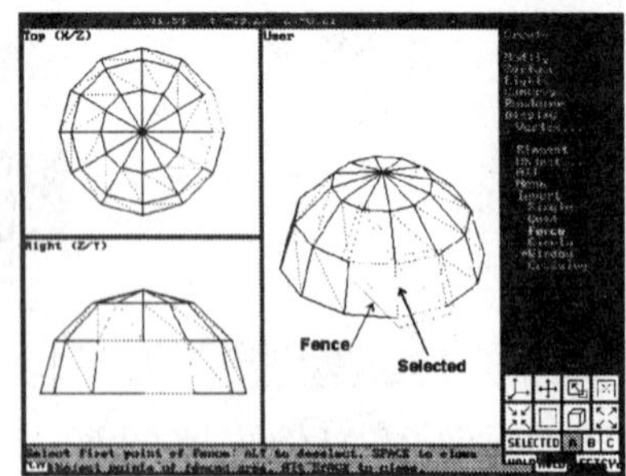

Selecting faces with the Fence–Window option.

RELATED COMMANDS

Select/Face..., Select/Face/Single, Select/Face/Quad, Select/Face/Circle, Select/Face/Window, Select/Face/Crossing

Select/Face/Circle

Create
Select
Modify
Vertex..
Face...
Element
Object...
All
None
Invert
Single
Quad
Fence
Circle
Window
Crossing

Assigns faces to a selection set by defining a circle around the faces.

Creating a Selection Set with Circle

1. Activate an icon letter (A, B, or C) at the bottom of the screen. All selected faces will be assigned to whichever letter is highlighted.
2. Define a circle around the faces by first clicking to set the center of the circle.

NOTE Selection with the Circle option is affected by the Window and Crossing options. Only one option may be active at a time. When the Window mode is active, only faces *totally enclosed* within the defined region are included in the selection set. When the Crossing mode is active, all faces *crossing, touching,* or *enclosed by* the defined region are included in the selection set. See *Select/Face/Window* and *Select/Face/Crossing.* For more information on selecting faces and assinging them to a selection set, see *Select/Face...*

3. Move the mouse to define the diameter of the circle. With the Window mode active, all faces within the circle are selected. Selected faces appear in red.

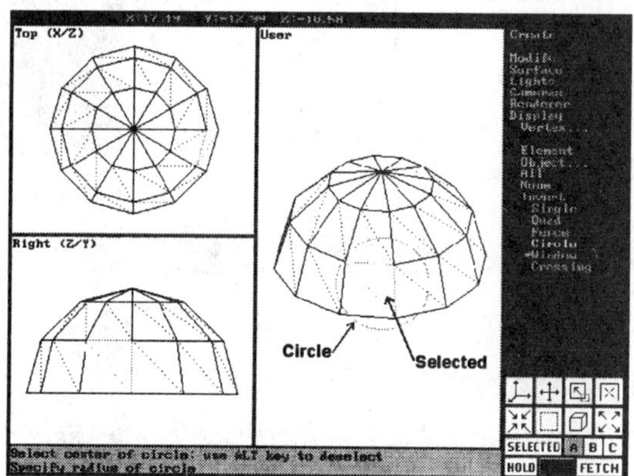

Selecting Faces with the Circle–Window option.

RELATED COMMANDS

Select/Face..., Select/Face/Single, Select/Face/Quad, Select/Face/Fence, Select/Face/Window, Select/Face/Crossing

Create
Select
Modify
Vertex..
Face...
Element
Object...
All
None
Invert
Single
Quad
Fence
Circle
Window
Crossing

Select/Face/Window

Affects regional selection by selecting only those faces that are totally enclosed within the defined region.

Using the Window Option

1. Used in combination with the *Select/Face/Quad, Select/Face/Fence,* and *Select/Face/Circle* commands.
2. When the Window mode is active, all three vertices of a face must be *totally enclosed* within the region defined by any of the previous commands to be included in the selection set.

TIP A face in a mesh object appears as a triangular polygon with three vertices. To see the faces in a mesh select *Display/Geometry/Full Detail* and *Display/Geometry/All Lines.* For more information on selecting faces and assinging them to a selection set, see *Select/Face...*

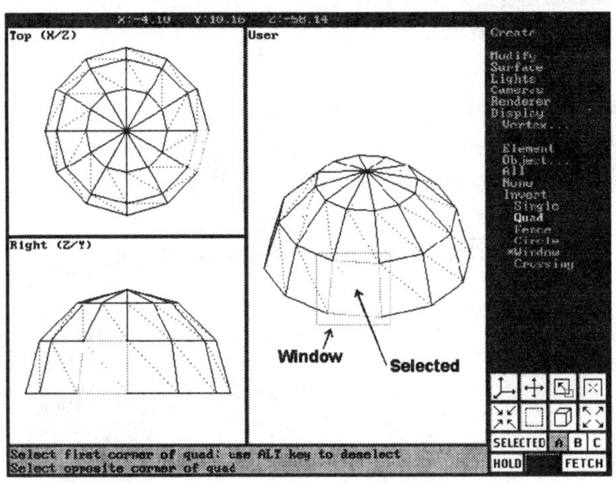

Selecting faces with the Quad–Window option.

RELATED COMMANDS

Select/Face/Single, Select/Face/Quad, Select/Face/Fence, Select/Face/Circle, Select/Face/Crossing

Select/Face/Crossing

Create
Select
Modify
Vertex..
Face...
Element
Object...
All
None
Invert
Single
Quad
Fence
Circle
Window
Crossing

Affects regional selection by selecting faces that touch, cross, or are enclosed by the defined region.

Using the Crossing Option

1. Used in combination with the *Select/Polygon/Quad, Select/Polygon/Fence,* and *Select/Polygon/Circle* commands.
2. When the Crossing mode is active, all faces *touching, crossing,* or *inside* the region defined by any of the previous commands are included in the selection set. Any face with a vertex falling within the crossing region is selected. Note that a single vertex can be connected to as many as six or more faces.

> **TIP** A face in a mesh object appears as a triangular polygon with three vertices. To see the faces in a mesh select *Display/Geometry/Full Detail* and *Display/Geometry/All Lines.* For more information on selecting faces and assinging them to a selection set, see *Select/Face...*

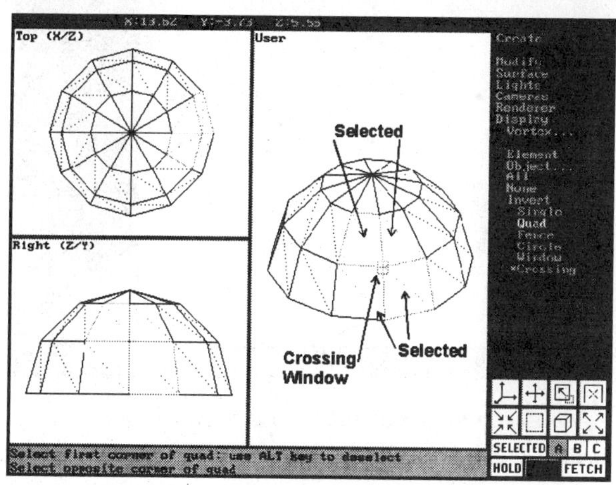

Selecting a polygon with the Quad–Crossing option.

RELATED COMMANDS

Select/Face/Single, Select/Face/Quad, Select/Face/Fence, Select/Face/Circle, Select/Face/Window

Create
Select
Modify
Surface
Lignts
Cameras
Renderer
Display
Vertex..
Face...
Element
Object...
All
None
Invert

Select/Element

Assigns a single element to a selection set.

Selecting an Element

1. Activate an icon letter (A, B, or C) at the bottom of the screen. All selected elements will be assigned to the letter highlighted.
2. Click on the element you want. The selected element will turn red.

> **NOTE** An *object* is a mesh object, a collection of one or more vertices that has a netlike appearance. An *element* can be thought of as a subset of an object that can be used as a potential building block. It can be broken off, modified, cloned, reattached, or used in a Boolean operation. See *Create/Object/Attach* and *Create/Element/Detach.*

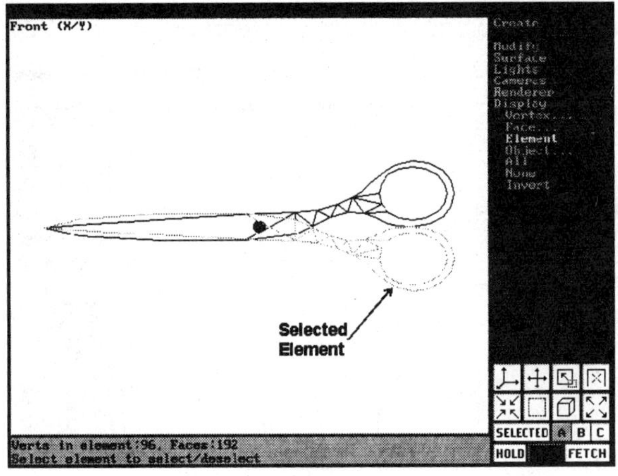

Assigning an element to a selection set.

> **NOTE** Although you can assign more than one element to a selection set, you cannot use any element command (*Modify/Element/Move, Modify/Element/Rotate,* etc.) with the **Selected** button.

RELATED COMMANDS

Create/Object/Attach, Create/Element/Detach

Select/Object...

Create
Select
Modify
Element
Object...
All
None
Invert
Single
Quad
Fence
Circle
Window
Crossing
By Name
By Color

Assigns individual and selected objects to a selection set.

Creating a Selection Set of Objects

1. Activate an icon letter (A, B, or C) at the bottom of the screen. All selected objects will be assigned to the letter highlighted.

NOTE Selection with the *Select/Object/Quad, Select/Object/Fence,* or *Select/Object/Circle* options is affected by the Window and Crossing options. Only one option can be active at a time. When the Window mode is active, only objects *totally enclosed* within the defined region are included in the selection set. When the Crossing mode is active, all objects *crossing, touching,* or *enclosed by* the defined region are included in the selection set. See *Select/Object/Window* and *Select/Object/Crossing.*

2. Choose an object selection method. See *Select/Object/Single, Select/Object/Quad, Select/Object/Fence,* or *Select/Object/Circle.* Selected objects appear in red.

NOTE An *object* is a mesh object, a collection of one or more vertices that has a netlike appearance. An *element* can be thought of as a subset of an object that can be used as a potential building block. It can be broken off, modified, cloned, reattached, or used in a Boolean operation. See *Create/Object/Attach* and *Create/Element/Detach.*

NOTE All of the *Select/Object...* options are affected by the Region-Toggle switch. See *Info-System Options.* Region Toggle is set to **ON** by default, meaning objects switch states each time you select them. If you turn region toggle to **OFF**, no objects will be deselected. Holding down the Alt key while selecting objects will deselect the affected objects regardless of the Region Toggle setting.

RELATED COMMANDS

Select/Object/Single, Select/Object/Quad, Select/Object/Fence,Select/Object/Circle,Select/Object/Window, Select/Object/Crossing

Create
Select
Modify
Element
Object...
All
None
Invert
Single
Quad
Fence
Circle
Window
Crossing
By Name
By Color

Select/Object/Single

Assigns individual objects to a selection set.

Creating a Selection Set of Individual Objects

1. Activate an icon letter (A, B, or C) at the bottom of the screen. All selected objects will be assigned to the letter highlighted.
2. Click on each object you want added to the selection set. Selected objects appear in red.
3. Clicking on selected (red) objects will remove them from the selection set.

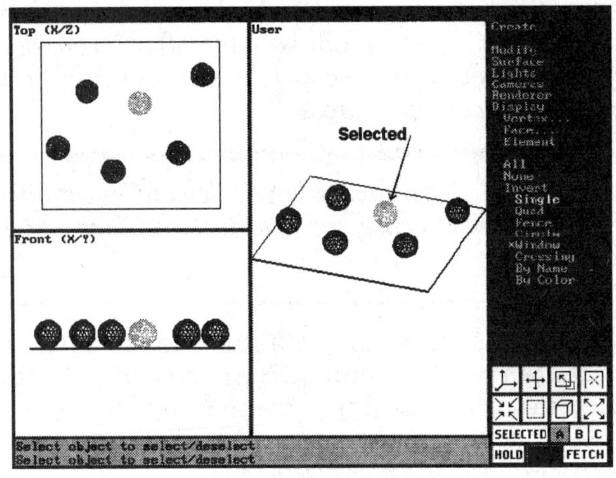

Selecting single objects.

RELATED COMMANDS

Select/Object..., Select/Object/Quad, Select/Object/Fence, Select/Object/Circle, Select/Object/By Name, Select/Object/By Color

Select/Object/Quad

Create
Select
Modify
Element
Object...
All
None
Invert
Single
Quad
Fence
Circle
Window
Crossing
By Name
By Color

Assigns objects to a selection set by defining a box around the objects.

Creating a Selection Set with Quad

1. Activate an icon letter (A, B, or C) at the bottom of the screen. All selected objects will be assigned to the letter highlighted.
2. Define a box around the objects by clicking to place one corner of the box.

> **NOTE** Selection with the *Select/Object/Quad* option is affected by the Window and Crossing options. Only one option may be active at a time. When the Window mode is active, only objects *totally enclosed* within the defined region are included in the selection set. When the Crossing mode is active, all objects *crossing, touching,* or *enclosed by* the defined region are included in the selection set. See *Select/Object/Window* and *Select/Object/Crossing*.

3. Move the mouse diagonally to enclose the objects, then click to set the opposite corner. With the Window mode active, all objects within the box are selected. Selected objects appear in red.

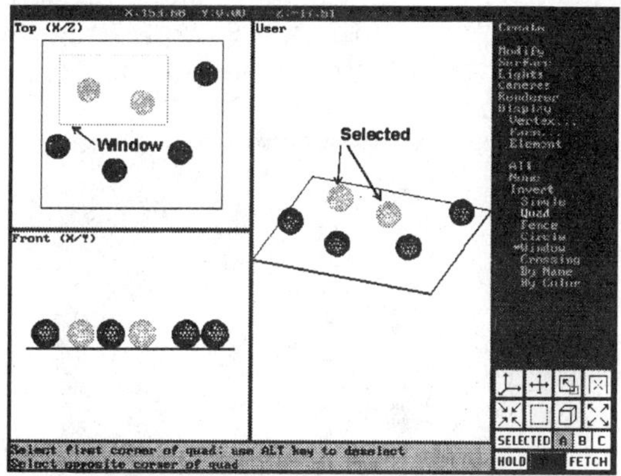

Selecting objects with the Quad–Window option.

RELATED COMMANDS

Select/Object..., Select/Object/Single, Select/Object/Fence, Select/Object/Circle, Select/Object/Window, Select/Object/Crossing, Select/Object/By Name, Select/Object/By Color

Create
Select
Modify
Element
Object...
All
None
Invert
Single
Quad
Fence
Circle
Window
Crossing
By Name
By Color

Select/Object/Fence

Assigns objects to a selection set by defining a polygon around the objects.

Creating a Selection Set with Fence

1. Activate an icon letter (A, B, or C) at the bottom of the screen. All selected objects will be assigned to the letter highlighted.
2. Define a polygon around the objects you want to select. Begin by clicking to set a point. Click the mouse to create a segment, then click to set a second point.
3. Continue setting points and creating segments until all objects you want selected are enclosed within the polygon.

> **NOTE** Selection with the *Select/Object/Quad* option is affected by the Window and Crossing options. Only one option may be active at a time. When the Window mode is active, only objects *totally enclosed* within the defined region are included in the selection set. When the Crossing mode is active, all objects *crossing, touching,* or *enclosed by* the defined region are included in the selection set. See *Select/Object/Window* and *Select/Object/Crossing.*

4. Close the polygon created with the fence and complete the selection set by clicking at the first point in the fence or pressing the **Spacebar**. With the Window mode active, all objects within the fence are selected. Selected objects appear in red.

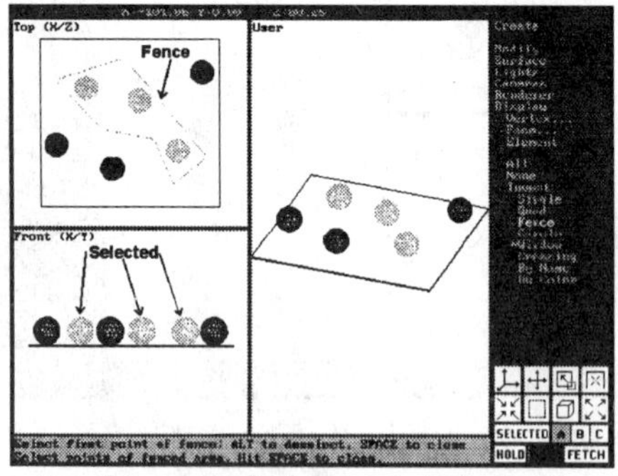

Selecting objects with the Fence–Window option.

RELATED COMMANDS

Select/Object..., Select/Object/Single, Select/Object/Quad, Select/Object/Circle, Select/Object/Window, Select/Object/Crossing

Select/Object/Circle

Create
Select
Modify
Element
Object...
All
None
Invert
Single
Quad
Fence
Circle
Window
Crossing
By Name
By Color

Assigns objects to a selection set by defining a circle around the objects.

Creating a Selection Set with Circle

1. Activate an icon letter (A, B, or C) at the bottom of the screen. All selected objects will be assigned to the letter highlighted.
2. Define a circle around the objects by first clicking to set the center of the circle.

> **NOTE** Selection with the *Select/Object/Quad* option is affected by the Window and Crossing options. Only one option may be active at a time. When the Window mode is active, only objects *totally enclosed* within the defined region are included in the selection set. When the Crossing mode is active, all objects *crossing, touching,* or *enclosed by* the defined region are included in the selection set. See *Select/Object/Window* and *Select/Object/Crossing*.

3. Move the mouse to define the diameter of the circle. With the Window mode active, all objects within the circle are selected. selected objects appear in red.

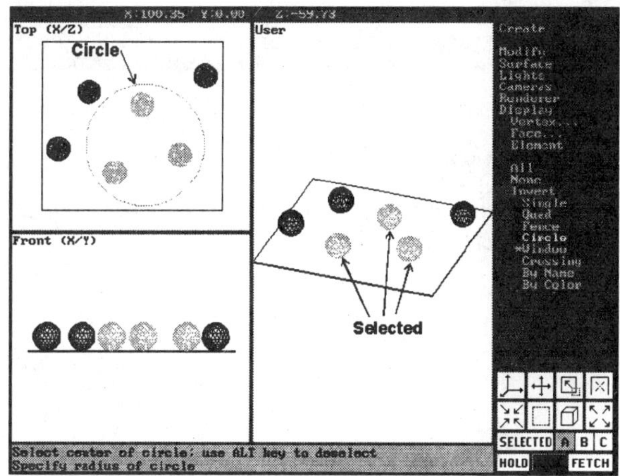

Selecting objects with the Circle–Window option.

RELATED COMMANDS

Select/Object..., Select/Object/Single, Select/Object/Quad, Select/Object/Fence, Select/Object/Window, Select/Object/Crossing

Create
Select
Modify
Element
Object...
All
None
Invert
Single
Quad
Fence
Circle
Window
Crossing
By Name
By Color

Select/Object/Window

Affects regional selection by selecting only those objects that are totally enclosed within the defined region.

Using the Window Option

1. Used in combination with the *Select/Object/Quad, Select/Object/Fence,* and *Select/Object/Circle* commands.
2. When window mode is active, all objects *totally enclosed* within the region defined by any of the previous commands are included in the selection set.

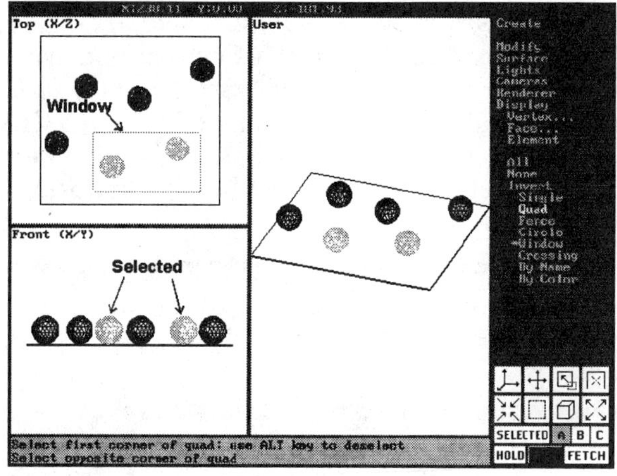

Selecting a object with the Quad–Window option.

RELATED COMMANDS

Select/Object..., Select/Object/Single, Select/Object/Quad, Select/Object/Fence, Select/Object/Circle, Select/Object/Crossing

Select/Object/Crossing

Create
Select
Modify
Element
Object...
All
None
Invert
Single
Quad
Fence
Circle
Window
Crossing
By Name
By Color

Affects regional selection by selecting objects that touch, cross or are enclosed by the defined region.

Using the Crossing Option

1. Used in combination with the *Select/Object/Quad, Select/Object/Fence,* and *Select/Object/Circle* commands.
2. When Crossing is active, all objects touching, crossing or inside the region defined by any of the previous commands are included in the selection set.

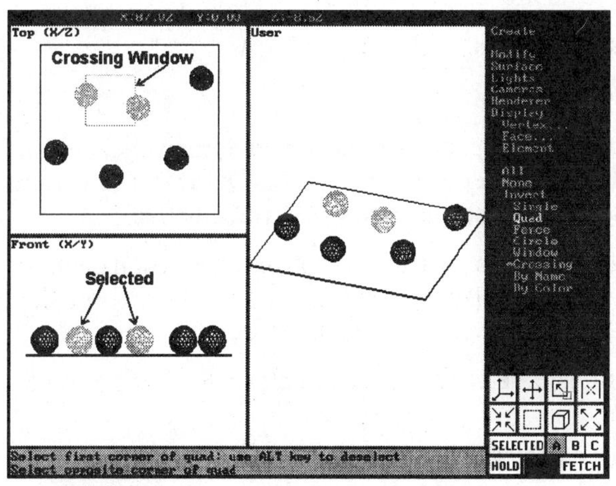

Selecting a object with the Quad–Crossing option.

RELATED COMMANDS

Select/Object..., Select/Object/Single, Select/Object/Quad, Select/Object/Fence, Select/Object/Circle, Select/Object/Window

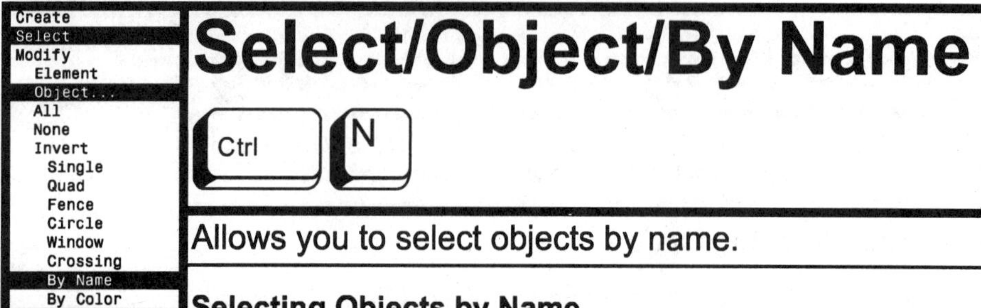

Select/Object/By Name

Allows you to select objects by name.

Selecting Objects by Name

1. Selecting *Select/Object/By Name* invokes the Select Objects By Name dialog box. All currently displayed objects are listed in the dialog box.
2. Tag the objects you want to select by clicking on them with the mouse. Selected objects are tagged with an asterisk.

   All. Selects all objects.

   None. Deselects all objects.

   Tag. Enter a wild card pattern in the text box, then click on **UnTag** to *select* the objects. Wild card patterns are the same as DOS asterisk (*) and question mark (?) patterns, except that the names are case sensitive.

   Untag. Enter a wild card pattern in the text box, then click on **Tag** to *deselect* the objects. Wild card patterns are the same as DOS asterisk (*) and question mark (?) patterns, except that the names are case- sensitive.
3. After tagging the desired objects, click on **OK**. The selected objects will turn red.

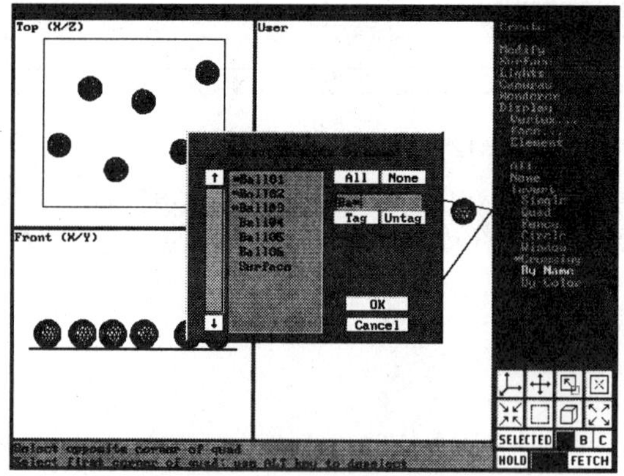

Selecting objects by name.

RELATED COMMANDS

Select/Objects..., Select/Object/Single, Select/Object/Quad, Select/Object/Fence, Select/Object/Circle, Select/Object/Window, Select/Object/Crossing, Select/Object/By Color

Select/Object/By Color

Create
Select
Modify
Element
Object...
All
None
Invert
Single
Quad
Fence
Circle
Window
Crossing
By Name
By Color

Used with the *Modify/Object/Change Color* command, allows you to select all objects that have the same color.

Selecting Objects by Color

1. To select objects by color, it is advantageous to have objects with different colors. If all objects are the same color, using *Select/Object/By Color* will select all objects. See *Modify/Object/Change Color* and the **Create Color** button.
2. To select all objects with the same color, select an object. All other objects with the same color are selected. If any objects are already in the selection set, they are removed.

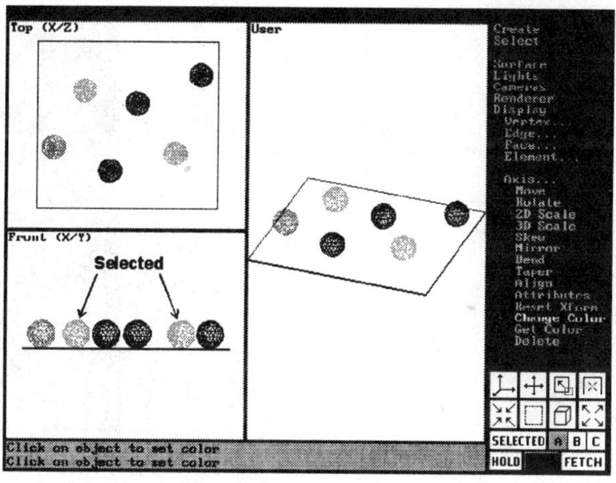

Selecting objects by color.

RELATED COMMANDS

Select/Objects..., Select/Object/Single, Select/Object/Quad, Select/Object/Fence, Select/Object/Circle, Select/Object/Window, Select/Object/Crossing, Select/Object/By Name

Select/All

All objects are assigned to the current selection set.

Using the All Option

1. When you use the *Select/All* option, all objects in the 3D Editor turn red, indicating they are selected.

NOTE The current state of all selected objects is ignored when using *Select/All*. Any previously selected items do not toggle to an unselected state. If there are any objects in an active selection set, that set is replaced by a new selection set containing all polygons.

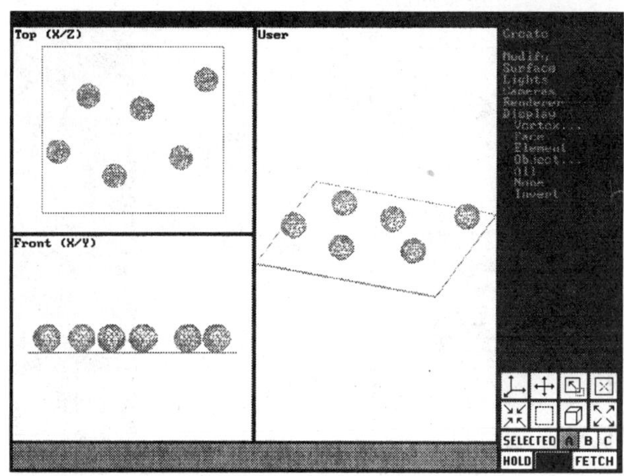

Selecting all polygons.

RELATED COMMANDS

Select/None, Select/Invert

Create
Select
Modify
Surface
Lights
Cameras
Renderer
Display
Vertex..
Face...
Element
Object...
All
None
Invert

Select/None

Any previously selected objects are deselected.

Using the None Option

1. When you use *Select/None*, all objects in the 3D Editor turn white, indicating they are not selected.

NOTE The current state of all selected objects is ignored when using *Select/None*. Any previously selected items do not toggle to an unselected state. If there are any objects in an active selection set, the set is replaced by a new selection set containing all polygons.

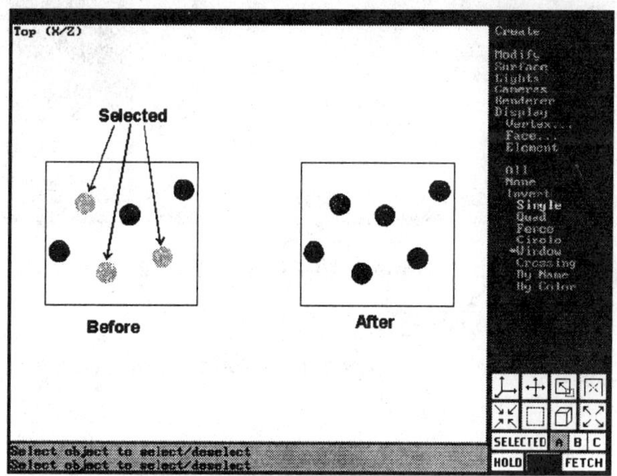

The Select/None option.

RELATED COMMANDS

Select/All, Select/Invert

Create
Select
Modify
Surface
Lignts
Cameras
Renderer
Display
Vertex..
Face...
Element
Object...
All
None
Invert

Select/Invert

The selection state of all displayed objects is reversed, with selected objects becoming unselected and vice versa.

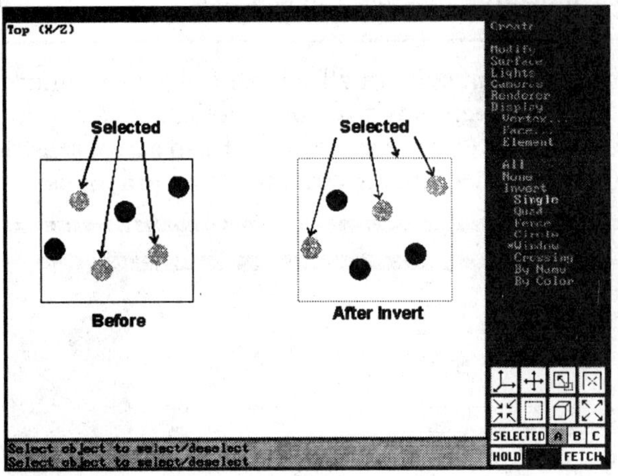

Inverting selected objects.

RELATED COMMANDS

Select/Polygon/Single, Select/Polygon/Quad, Select/Polygon/Fence, Select/Polygon/Circle

Modify/Vertex...

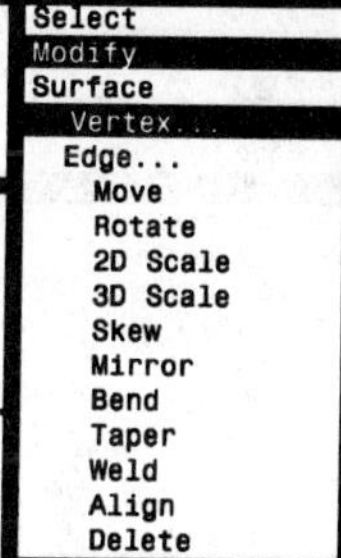

The following key combinations can be used in the majority of the Modify/Vertex commands to help in selecting vertices.

Ctrl

Holding down the **Ctrl** key while selecting vertices will add them to the current selection set. See also *Select/Vertex/Single*.

Pressing the **Alt** and **W** keys while in the command enters the Quad-Window selection mode. Cross-hairs appear on the screen, allowing you to define a selection set box and add vertices to the selection set. See also *Select/Vertex/Quad.*

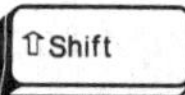

Holding down the **Shift** key when selecting vertices creates a clone of a single or a selection set of vertices. The resulting vertices become a separate object without faces.

RELATED COMMANDS

Modify/Vertex/Move, Modify/Vertex/Rotate, Modify/Vertex/2D Scale, Modify/Vertex/3D Scale, Modify/Vertex/Skew, Modify/Vertex/Mirror, Modify/Vertex/Bend, Modify/Vertex/Taper

Select
Modify
Surface
Vertex...
Edge...
Move
Rotate
2D Scale
3D Scale
Skew
Mirror
Bend
Taper
Weld
Align
Delete

Modify/Vertex/Move

Moves single or multiple vertices in a mesh object.

How to Move a Vertex

1. Press the **Hold** button (Ctrl H) to store the current state of your geometry, viewport configuration, and selection set.
2. Select the vertex you want to move. You can select more than one vertex by pressing special keys when selecting the vertices. See *Modify/Vertex....* You can also create a selection set of vertices. See *Select/Vertex/Single*, *Select/Vertex/Quad, Select/Vertex/Fence,* and *Select/Vertex/Circle*.
3. As you move the mouse, the selected vertices will move. If you are moving a single vertex, its connecting edges are displayed as you move it. If you are moving a selection set of vertices, a boundary box is displayed. You can use the Tab key to control horizontal and vertical movement.
4. Click to place the vertex. If the results are not what you wanted, press the **Fetch** button (Ctrl F) to restore the original geometry and configuration.

TIP By default, vertices are displayed on the screen as a dot about the size of a pixel. To make the vertices easier to select, display the vertices as tick marks instead of dots by selecting *Display/Geometry/Vert Ticks*.

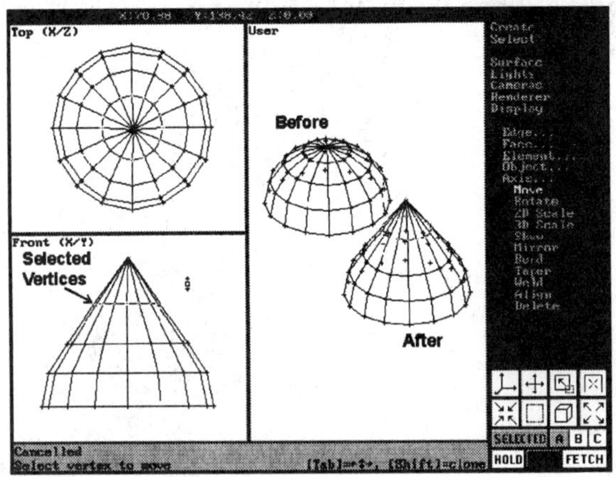

Moving a selection set of vertices.

RELATED COMMANDS

Modify/Vertex..., Select/Vertex/Quad, Select/Vertex/Fence, Select/Vertex/Circle, Views–Use Snap, Views–Use Grid

Modify/Vertex/Rotate

Select
Modify
Surface
Vertex...
Edge...
Move
Rotate
2D Scale
3D Scale
Skew
Mirror
Bend
Taper
Weld
Align
Delete

Rotates one or multiple vertices around the local or global axis.

Rotating a Vertex

1. Press the **Hold** button (Ctrl H) to store the current state of your geometry, viewport configuration, and selection set.
2. Select the vertex you want to rotate. You can select more than one vertex by pressing special keys when selecting the vertices. See *Modify/Vertex....* You can also create a selection set of vertices. See *Select/Vertex/Single, Select/Vertex/Quad, Select/Vertex/Fence,* and *Select/Vertex/Circle.*
3. As you move the mouse, the selected vertices are rotated about the active axis. See *Modify/Axis/Show* and the Local Axis icon.
4. Click to place the vertex. If the results are not what you wanted, press the **Fetch** button (Ctrl F) to restore the original geometry and configuration.

> **TIP** By default, vertices are displayed on the screen as a dot about the size of a pixel. To make the vertices easier to select, display the vertices as tick marks instead of dots by selecting *Display/Geometry/Vert Ticks.*

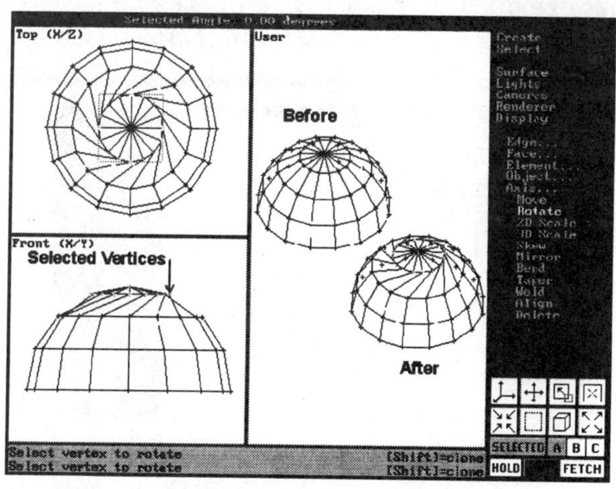

Rotating selected vertices.

RELATED COMMANDS

Modify/Vertex..., Select/Vertex/Quad, Select/Vertex/Fence, Select/Vertex/Circle, Views–Use Snap, Views–Use Grid, Modify/Axis/Show

Select
Modify
Surface
Vertex...
Edge...
Move
Rotate
2D Scale
3D Scale
Skew
Mirror
Bend
Taper
Weld
Align
Delete

Modify/Vertex/2D Scale

Scales the distance between one or multiple vertices. You can also scale the distance between one or multiple vertices to or from the local or global axis. This is done along the plane of the active viewport.

2D Scaling Vertices

1. Press the **Hold** button (Ctrl H) to store the current state of your geometry, viewport configuration, and selection set.
2. Select the vertex you want to 2D Scale. You can select more than one vertex by pressing special keys when selecting the vertices. See *Modify/Vertex....* You can also create a selection set of vertices. See *Select/Vertex/Single, Select/Vertex/Quad, Select/Vertex/Fence,* and *Select/Vertex/Circle.*
3. As you move the mouse, the distance between the vertices and the active axis increases or decreases. See *Modify/Axis/Show, Local Axis* icon. You can use the Tab key to control horizontal and vertical scaling.
4. Click to place the vertex. If the results are not what you wanted, press the **Fetch** button (Ctrl F) to restore the original geometry and configuration.

TIP By default, vertices are displayed on the screen as a dot about the size of a pixel. To make the vertices easier to select, display the vertices as tick marks instead of dots by selecting *Display/Geometry/Vert Ticks.*

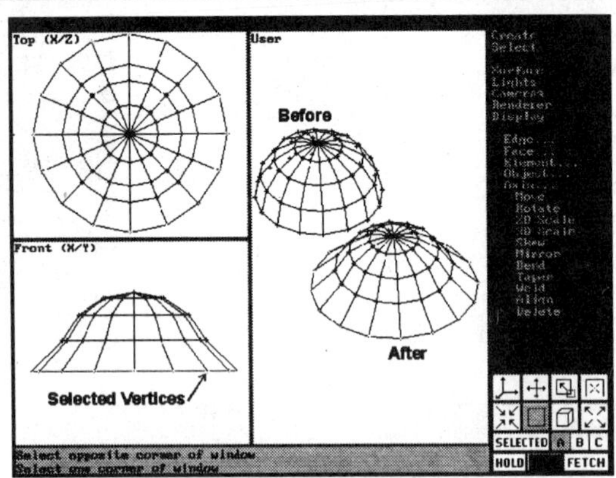

Scaling multiple vertices along the plane of the Top viewport.

RELATED COMMANDS

Modify/Vertex..., Modify/Vertex/3D Scale, Select/Vertex/Quad, Select/Vertex/Fence, Select/Vertex/Circle, Views–Use Snap, Views–Use Grid, Modify/Axis/Show

Select
Modify
Surface
Vertex...
Edge...
Move
Rotate
2D Scale
3D Scale
Skew
Mirror
Bend
Taper
Weld
Align
Delete

Modify/Vertex/3D Scale

Scales the distance between one or multiple vertices to or from the local or global axis. The distance is scaled along the X, Y, and Z axis equally.

3D Scaling Vertices

1. Press the **Hold** button (Ctrl H) to store the current state of your geometry, viewport configuration, and selection set.
2. Select the vertex you want to 3D Scale. You can select more than one vertex by pressing special keys when selecting the vertices. See *Modify/Vertex....* You can also create a selection set of vertices. See *Select/Vertex/Single, Select/Vertex/Quad, Select/Vertex/Fence,* and *Select/Vertex/Circle.*
3. As you move the mouse, the distance between the vertices and the active axis increases or decreases equally along the X, Y, and Z axis. See *Modify/Axis/Show, Local Axis* icon.
4. Click to place the vertex. If the results are not what you wanted, press the **Fetch** button (Ctrl F) to restore the original geometry and configuration.

TIP By default, vertices are displayed on the screen as a dot about the size of a pixel. To make the vertices easier to select, display the vertices as tick marks instead of dots by selecting *Display/Geometry/Vert Ticks.*

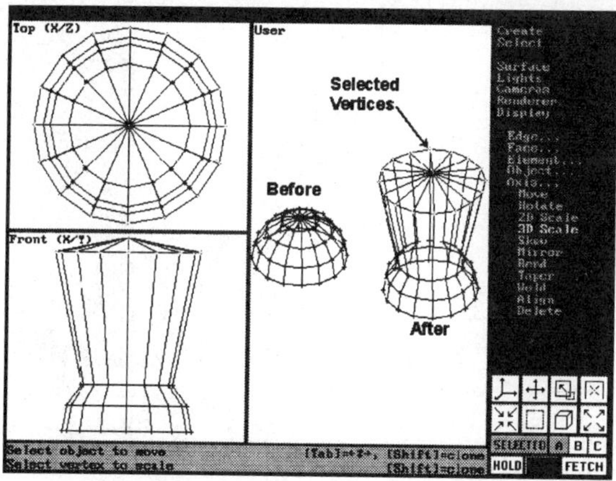

Scaling multiple vertices in three dimensions.

RELATED COMMANDS

Modify/Vertex..., Modify/Vertex/2D Scale, Select/Vertex/Quad, Select/Vertex/Fence, Select/Vertex/Circle, Views–Use Snap, Views–Use Grid, Modify/Axis/Show

Select
Modify
Surface
Vertex...
Edge...
Move
Rotate
2D Scale
3D Scale
Skew
Mirror
Bend
Taper
Weld
Align
Delete

Modify/Vertex/Skew

One or more selected vertices are adjusted on a plane parallel to the global or local axis.

Skewing Selected Vertices

1. Press the Hold button (Ctrl H) to store the current state of your geometry, viewport configuration, and selection set.
2. Select the vertex you want to skew. You can select more than one vertex by pressing special keys when selecting the vertices. See *Modify/Vertex....* You can also create a selection set of vertices. See *Select/Vertex/Single, Select/Vertex/Quad, Select/Vertex/Fence,* and *Select/Vertex/Circle*.
3. As you move the mouse, the white boundary box indicates the distortion. This is done on a plane parallel to the local or global axis. See *Modify/Axis/Show,* Local Axis icon. You can skew horizontally or vertically by pressing the (Tab) key.
4. Click to place the vertex. If the results are not what you wanted, press the **Fetch** button (Ctrl F) to restore the original geometry and configuration.

> **TIP** By default, vertices are displayed on the screen as a dot about the size of a pixel. To make the vertices easier to select, display the vertices as tick marks instead of dots by selecting *Display/Geometry/Vert Ticks*.

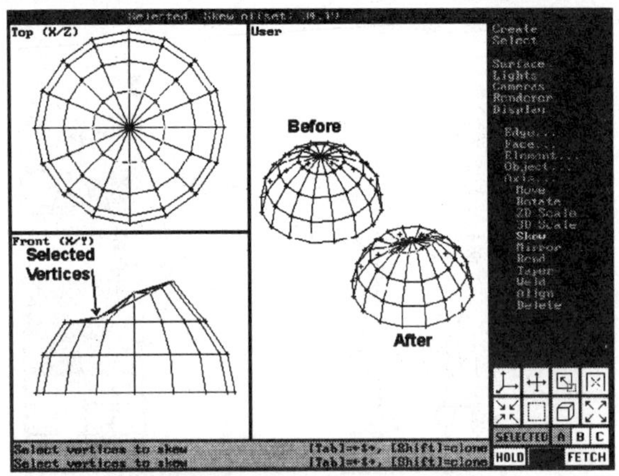

Skewing selected vertices vertically in a plane parallel to the Front viewport.

RELATED COMMANDS

Modify/Vertex..., Select/Vertex/Quad, Select/Vertex/Fence, Select/Vertex/Circle, Views–Use Snap, Views–Use Grid, Modify/Axis/Show

Modify/Vertex/Mirror

Select
Modify
Surface
Vertex...
Edge...
Move
Rotate
2D Scale
3D Scale
Skew
Mirror
Bend
Taper
Weld
Align
Delete

Mirrors and copies the selected vertices. This is based on the location of the cursor and the distance between the cursor and the original vertices.

Mirroring Selected Vertices

1. Press the **Hold** button (Ctrl H) to store the current state of your geometry, viewport configuration, and selection set.
2. Select the vertex you want to mirror. You can select more than one vertex by pressing special keys when selecting the vertices. See *Modify/Vertex....* You can also create a selection set of vertices. See *Select/Vertex/Single, Select/Vertex/Quad, Select/Vertex/Fence,* and *Select/Vertex/Circle.*
3. As you move the mouse, the white boundary box indicates the vertices that will be mirrored. This is done on a plane parallel to the selected viewport. You can use the Tab key to cycle through different mirror axes.
4. Click to place the vertex. The selected vertices are mirrored about a plane halfway between the original vertices and the placed vertices. To leave the original vertices in place and create a mirrored copy, hold down the Shift key when you click to place the vertex. If the results are not what you wanted, press the **Fetch** button (Ctrl F) to restore the original geometry and configuration.

TIP By default, vertices are displayed on the screen as a dot about the size of a pixel. To make the vertices easier to select, display the vertices as tick marks instead of dots by selecting *Display/Geometry/Vert Ticks.*

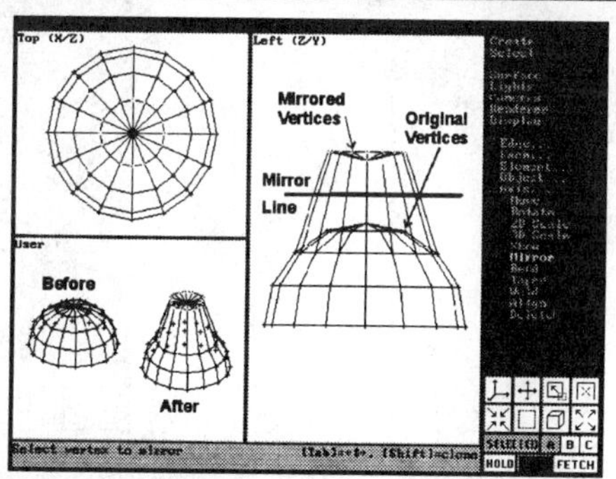

Mirroring selected vertices along the vertical axis.

RELATED COMMANDS

Modify/Vertex..., Select/Vertex/Quad, Select/Vertex/Fence, Select/Vertex/Circle, Views–Use Snap, Views–Use Grid, Modify/Axis/Show

Select
Modify
Surface
Vertex...
Edge...
Move
Rotate
2D Scale
3D Scale
Skew
Mirror
Bend
Taper
Weld
Align
Delete

Modify/Vertex/Bend

Bends selected vertices about the plane in the active viewport.

Bending Selected Vertices

1. Press the **Hold** button (Ctrl H) to store the current state of your geometry, viewport configuration, and selection set.
2. Because you cannot bend single vertices, first create a selection set of vertices. You can select more than one vertex by pressing special keys when selecting the vertices. See *Modify/Vertex....* You can also create a selection set of vertices. See *Select/Vertex/Quad, Select/Vertex/Fence,* and *Select/Vertex/Circle*.
3. As you move the mouse, the white boundary box indicates the vertices that will be bent. This is done on a plane parallel to the selected viewport. At least two of the selected vertices must lie on a plane parallel to the active viewport. You can use the Tab key to cycle through different unidirectional cursors.
4. A gradually increasing rotation is applied to the selected vertices, beginning at the base of the bend. Click to place the vertex. If the results are not what you wanted, press the **Fetch** button (Ctrl F) to restore the original geometry and configuration.

TIP By default, vertices are displayed on the screen as a dot about the size of a pixel. To make the vertices easier to select, display the vertices as tick marks instead of dots by selecting *Display/Geometry/Vert Ticks*.

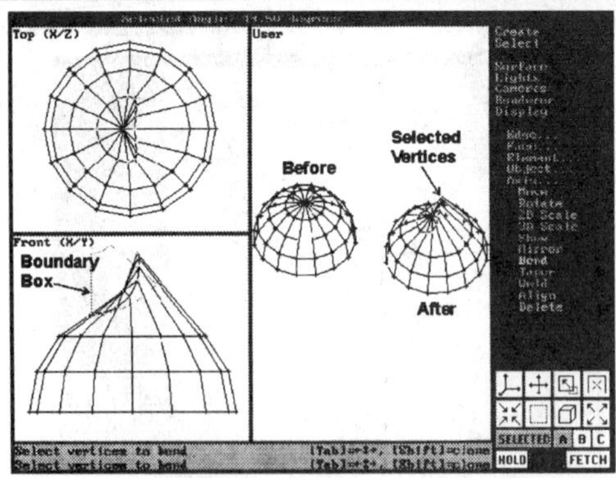

Bending selected vertices to the right side in the Front viewport.

RELATED COMMANDS

Modify/Vertex..., Select/Vertex/Quad, Select/Vertex/Fence, Select/Vertex/Circle, Views–Use Snap, Views–Use Grid, Modify/Axis/Show

Modify/Vertex/Taper

Select
Modify
Surface
Vertex...
Edge...
Move
Rotate
2D Scale
3D Scale
Skew
Mirror
Bend
Taper
Weld
Align
Delete

Tapers selected vertices, resulting in a widening or narrowing of the object. The taper is done in relation to the global or local axis.

Tapering Selected Vertices

1. Press the **Hold** button (Ctrl H) to store the current state of your geometry, viewport configuration, and selection set.
2. Because you cannot taper single vertices, first create a selection set of vertices. You can select more than one vertex by pressing special keys when selecting the vertices. See *Modify/Vertex...*. You can also create a selection set of vertices. See *Select/Vertex/Quad, Select/Vertex/Fence,* and *Select/Vertex/Circle.*
3. As you move the mouse, the white boundary box indicates the vertices that will be bent. This is done on a plane parallel to the selected viewport about the local or global axis. See *Modify/Axis/Show,* Local Axis icon. You can use the Tab key to cycle through different unidirectional cursors, which allow you select the side of the vertex group to taper.
4. When your object has the desired taper, click to place the vertex. If the results are not what you wanted, press the **Fetch** button (Ctrl F) to restore the original geometry and configuration.

TIP By default, vertices are displayed on the screen as a dot about the size of a pixel. To make the vertices easier to select, display the vertices as tick marks instead of dots by selecting *Display/Geometry/Vert Ticks.*

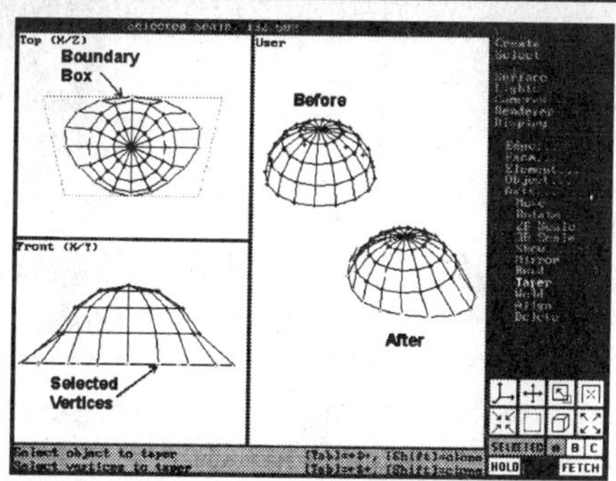

Tapering selected vertices about the global axis in the Top view.

RELATED COMMANDS

Modify/Vertex..., Select/Vertex/Quad, Select/Vertex/Fence, Select/Vertex/Circle, Views–Use Snap, Views–Use Grid, Modify/Axis/Show

Select
Modify
Surface
Vertex...
Edge...
Move
Rotate
2D Scale
3D Scale
Skew
Mirror
Bend
Taper
Weld
Align
Delete

Modify/Vertex/Weld

Welds two vertices together.

Welding Two Vertices Together

1. Select the first vertex.
2. As you move the mouse, the first vertex and its connecting lines move. Locate the mouse over the second vertex and click.
3. At the Weld this vertex? box, click **OK** to weld the vertices together.

> **TIP** You can use *Modify/Vertex/Weld* to eliminate seams where two vertices intersect. Seams often will appear when rendering an object that has intersecting vertices that have not been welded.

> **NOTE** When welding two vertices together, both vertices must be part of the same object. To weld two vertices from separate objects, first attach the objects. The objects will then be combined, and are elements of the same object. See *Create/Object/Attach*.

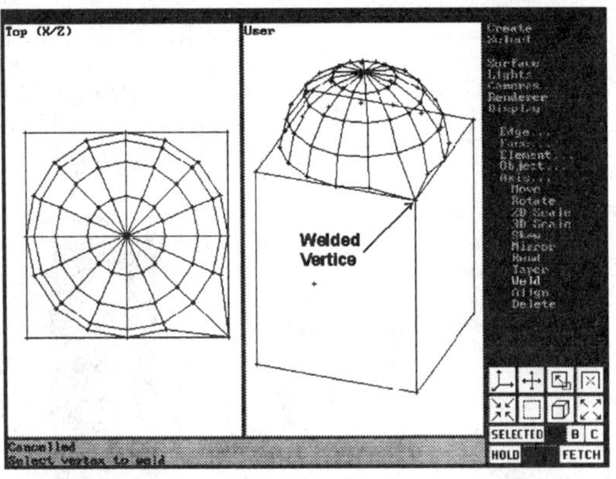

Welding vertices together in the same object.

> **TIP** By default, vertices are displayed on the screen as a dot about the size of a pixel. To make the vertices easier to select, display the vertices as tick marks instead of dots by selecting *Display/Geometry/Vert Ticks*.

RELATED COMMANDS

Create/Object/Attach, Display/Geometry/Vert Ticks

Select
Modify
Surface
Vertex...
Edge...
Move
Rotate
2D Scale
3D Scale
Skew
Mirror
Bend
Taper
Weld
Align
Delete

Modify/Vertex/Align

Aligns one or selected vertices to the construction plane of the active viewport.

Aligning Selected Vertices

1. Press the **Hold** button (Ctrl H) to store the current state of your geometry, viewport configuration, and selection set.
2. Select the vertex you want to align. You can select more than one vertex by pressing special keys when selecting the vertices. See *Modify/Vertex....* You can also create a selection set of vertices. See *Select/Vertex/Quad, Select/Vertex/Fence,* and *Select/Vertex/Circle*.
3. When you click the mouse in the active viewport, the selected vertices are aligned with the construction plane that is parallel to the active viewport. If the results are not what you wanted, press the **Fetch** button (Ctrl F) to restore the original geometry and configuration.

TIP: To change the construction planes, see *Display/Const./Place*. To modify the user plane, see *Display/User View/Align*.

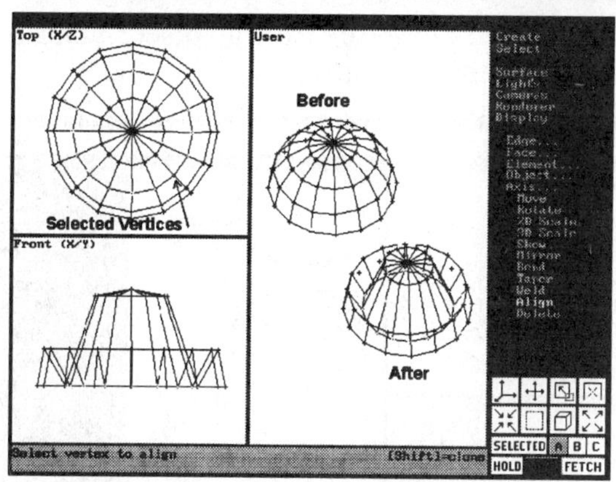

Aligning selected vertices in the Top view.

TIP: By default, vertices are displayed on the screen as a dot about the size of a pixel. To make the vertices easier to select, display the vertices as tick marks instead of dots by selecting *Display/Geometry/Vert Ticks*.

RELATED COMMANDS

Display/Const./Place, Display/User View/Align

Select
Modify
Surface
Vertex...
Edge...
Move
Rotate
2D Scale
3D Scale
Skew
Mirror
Bend
Taper
Weld
Align
Delete

Modify/Vertex/Delete

Deletes single or selected vertices.

Deleting Selected Vertices

1. Press the **Hold** button (Ctrl H) to store the current state of your geometry, viewport configuration, and selection set.
2. Select the vertex you want to delete. You can select more than one vertex by pressing special keys when selecting the vertices. See *Modify/Vertex....* You can also create a selection set of vertices. See *Select/Vertex/Quad, Select/Vertex/Fence,* and *Select/Vertex/Circle.*
3. Click in any viewport. At the Delete Vertices? box, select **OK** to delete the selected vertices. If the results are not what you wanted, press the **Fetch** button (Ctrl F) to restore the original geometry and configuration.

TIP By default, vertices are displayed on the screen as a dot about the size of a pixel. To make the vertices easier to select, display the vertices as tick marks instead of dots by selecting *Display/Geometry/Vert Ticks.*

When you delete a vertex from an object, you also delete all faces connected to that vertex.

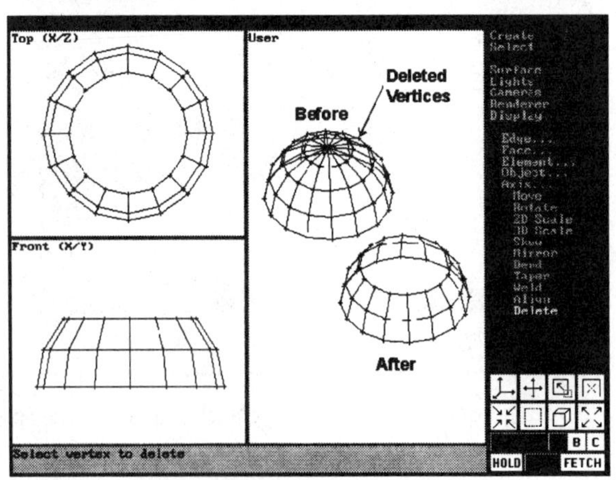

Deleting selected vertices.

RELATED COMMAND

Modify/Vertex...

Modify/Edge/Divide

Create
Select
Modify
Surface
Vertex...
Edge...
Face...
Element...
Object...
Axis...
Divide
Turn
Visible
Invisible
AutoEdge
Delete

Divides an edge of an object into two.

Dividing an Edge

1. Display all of the edges on the object by selecting *Display/ Geometry/All Lines.*
2. Select the edge to divide. As a result, the selected edge is divided in two. A vertex is placed at the center of the selected edge, and that vertex is connected to the opposite vertices of both faces.

NOTE An edge is the side of a face; it is formed by two vertices. You can display edges by selecting *Display/Geometry/All Lines*. If your geometry looks cluttered after displaying all lines, select *Display/Geometry/ Backface* to remove the hidden lines.

TIP Use *Modify/Edge/Divide* to increase the complexity of an object. This can be useful if you need to do detailed editing of an object.

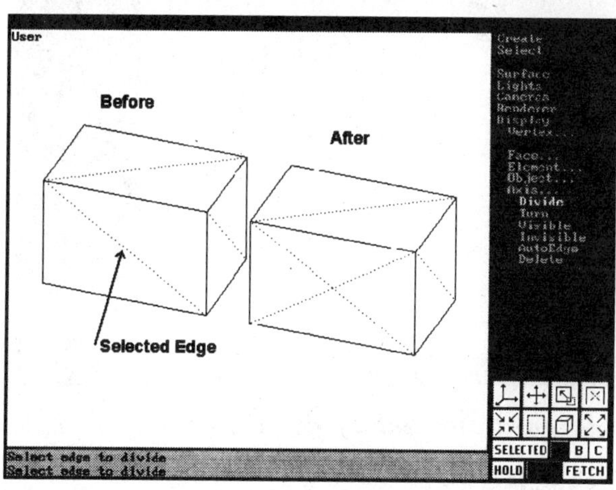

Dividing an edge increases the complexity of an object.

RELATED COMMANDS

Display/Geometry/All Lines, Create/Face/Tessellate

Create
Select
Modify
Surface
Vertex...
Edge...
Face...
Element...
Object...
Axis...
Divide
Turn
Visible
Invisible
AutoEdge
Delete

Modify/Edge/Turn

Turns the direction of an edge shared by two faces.

Turning an Edge

1. Display all of the edges on the object by selecting *Display/ Geometry/All Lines.* Press the **Hold** button (Ctrl H) to store the current state of your geometry and viewport configuration.
2. Click on the edge you want to turn.
3. If the results are not what you wanted, press the **Fetch** button (Ctrl F) to restore the original geometry and configuration.

> **NOTE** An edge is the side of a face; it is formed by two vertices. You can display edges by selecting *Display/Geometry/All Lines*. If your geometry looks cluttered after displaying all lines, select *Display/Geometry/ Backface* to remove the hidden lines.

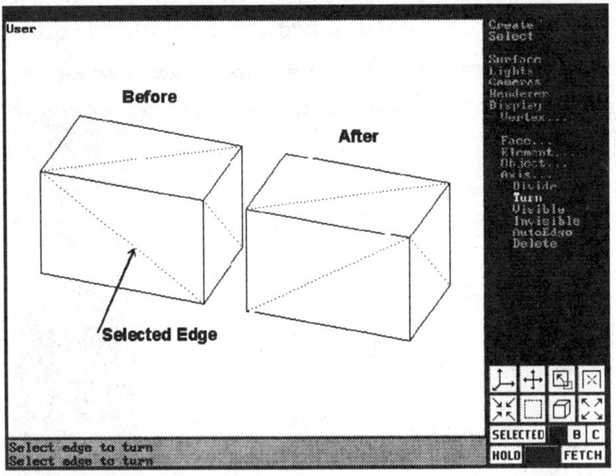

Turning an edge reorients the direction of the selected edge.

RELATED COMMAND

Display/Geometry/All Lines

Modify/Edge/Visible

Create
Select
Modify
Surface
Vertex...
Edge...
Face...
Element...
Object...
Axis...
Divide
Turn
Visible
Invisible
AutoEdge
Delete

Changes a dotted construction line defining an edge into a solid line.

Making an Edge Visible

1. Display all of the edges on the object by selecting *Display/Geometry/All Lines.*
2. Select the edge construction line you want to change into a solid-edge line.
3. To display solid edge-lines only, select *Display/Geometry/Edges Only*. All construction lines you made visible still appear as solid edge lines.

NOTE An edge is the side of a face; it is formed by two vertices. You can display edges by selecting *Display/Geometry/All Lines*. If your geometry looks cluttered after displaying all lines, select *Display/Geometry/Backface* to remove the hidden lines.

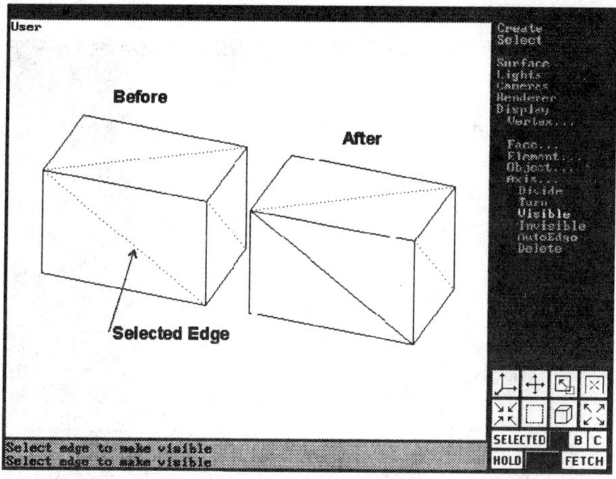

Making an edge visible changes a dotted construction line into a solid–edge line.

RELATED COMMANDS

Display/Geometry/All Lines, Modify/Edge/Invisible

Create
Select
Modify
Surface
Vertex...
Edge...
Face...
Element...
Object...
Axis...
Divide
Turn
Visible
Invisible
AutoEdge
Delete

Display/Edge/Invisible

Changes a solid line defining an edge into a dotted construction line.

Making an Edge Invisible

1. Display all of the edges on the object by selecting *Display/Geometry/All Lines.*
2. Select the solid line defining an edge line you want to change into a dotted construction line.
3. To display solid-edge lines only, select *Display/Geometry/Edges Only*. All solid lines defining an edge that you made invisible will no longer appear.

> **NOTE** An edge is the side of a face; it is formed by two vertices. You can display edges by selecting *Display/Geometry/All Lines*. If your geometry looks cluttered after displaying all lines, select *Display/Geometry/Backface* to remove the hidden lines.

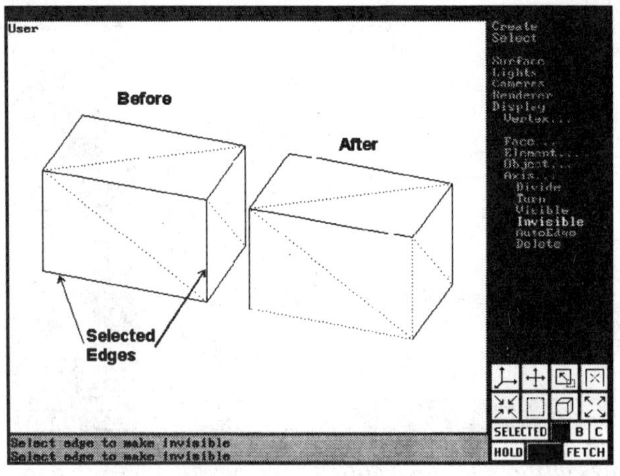

Making an edge invisible changes a solid line defining an edge into a dotted construction line.

RELATED COMMANDS

Display/Geometry/All Lines, Modify/Edge/Visible

Modify/Edge/AutoEdge

Create
Select
Modify
Surface
Vertex...
Edge...
Face...
Element...
Object...
Axis...
Divide
Turn
Visible
Invisible
AutoEdge
Delete

Changes the visibility of an object's edges based on the angle between the normals of the adjacent faces.

Changing the Visibility of an Object's Edges

1. Display all of the edges on the object by selecting *Display/Geometry/All Lines.* Press the **Hold** button (Ctrl H) to store the current state of your geometry and viewport configuration.
2. Choose *Modify/Edge/AutoEdge* and select the object.
3. In the Auto Edge dialog box, enter the angle. All edges between adjacent faces where the angle between the face normals are below the entered angle will become construction lines.
4. If the results are not what you wanted, press the **Fetch** button (Ctrl F) to restore the original geometry and configuration.

> **NOTE** An edge is the side of a face; it is formed by two vertices. You can display edges by selecting *Display/Geometry/All Lines*. If your geometry looks cluttered after displaying all lines, select *Display/Geometry/Backface* to remove the hidden lines.

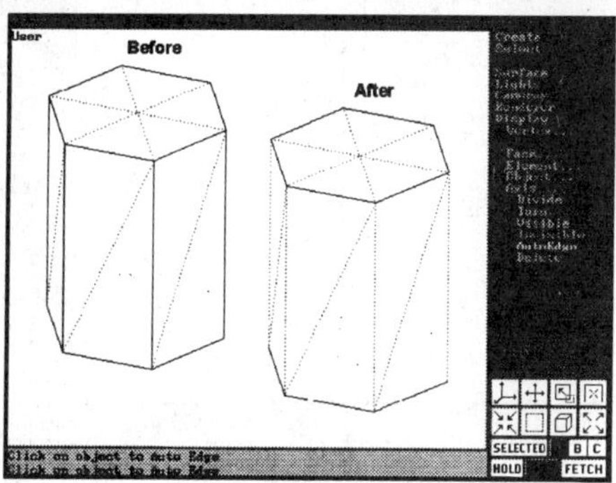

Using AutoEdge on an object with an angle of 70 degrees.

> **NOTE** This command is very useful if you are using a material with wire attributes, because only visible edges with wire surfaces will appear in the rendering.

RELATED COMMANDS

Display/Geometry/All Lines, Modify/Edge/Visible, Modify/Edge/Invisible

Create
Select
Modify
Surface
Vertex...
Edge...
Face...
Element...
Object...
Axis...
Divide
Turn
Visible
Invisible
AutoEdge
Delete

Modify/Edge/Delete

Deletes an edge or construction line from an object.

Deleting an Edge

1. Display all of the edges on the object by selecting *Display/Geometry/All Lines.* Press the **Hold** button (Ctrl H) to store the current state of your geometry and viewport configuration.
2. Select the edge or construction line you want to delete. In response to the Delete this edge? prompt, select **OK.**
3. As a result all faces sharing the selected edge are deleted. If the results are not what you wanted, press the **Fetch** button (Ctrl F) to restore the original geometry and configuration.

When you delete an edge or construction line from the object, all faces sharing that edge are also deleted.

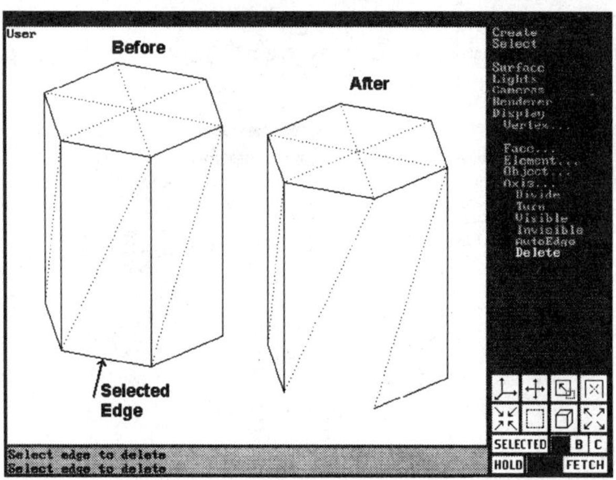

Deleting an edge deletes all faces sharing that edge.

RELATED COMMAND

Display/Geometry/All Lines

Modify/Face...

Select
Modify
Surface
Face...
Element...
Move
Rotate
2D Scale
3D Scale
Skew
Mirror
Bend
Taper
Collapse
Align
Delete

The following key combinations can be used in the majority of the Modify/Face commands to help in selecting faces.

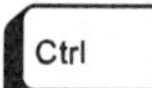

Holding down the **Ctrl** key while selecting faces will add them to the current selection set. See *Select/Face/Single*.

Pressing the **Alt** and **W** keys while in the command enters the Quad-Window selection mode. Cross-hairs appear on the screen, allowing you to define a selection set box and add faces to the selection set. See *Select/Face/Quad.*

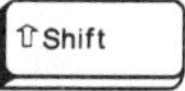

Holding down the **Shift** key when selecting faces creates a clone of a single or a selection set of faces. The resulting faces become a separate object.

By default, all faces of an object are not displayed. To display all faces of an object, select *Display/Geometry/All Lines*.

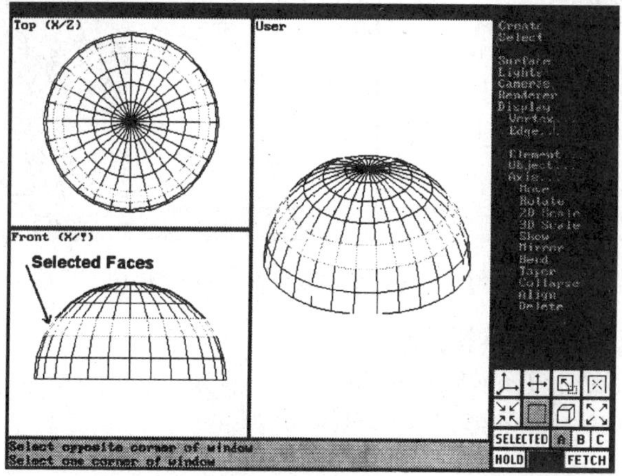

Several different key combinations can be used to create a selection set of faces.

RELATED COMMANDS

Select/Face/Single, Select/Face/Quad, Select/Face/Fence, Select/Face/Circle

Select
Modify
Surface
Face...
Element...
Move
Rotate
2D Scale
3D Scale
Skew
Mirror
Bend
Taper
Collapse
Align
Delete

Modify/Face/Move

Moves single or multiple faces in a mesh object.

How to Move a Face

1. Press the **Hold** button (Ctrl H) to store the current state of your geometry, viewport configuration, and selection set.
2. Select the face you want to move. You can select more than one face by pressing special keys when selecting the vertices. See *Modify/Face....* You can also create a selection set of faces. See *Select/Face/Single*, *Select/Face/Quad*, *Select/Face/Fence*, and *Select/Face/Circle*.
3. As you move the mouse, the selected faces will move. As you move the single or multiple faces, a boundary box represents it position. You can use the Tab key to control horizontal and vertical movement.
4. Click to place the face. If the results are not what you wanted, press the **Fetch** button (Ctrl F) to restore the original geometry and configuration.

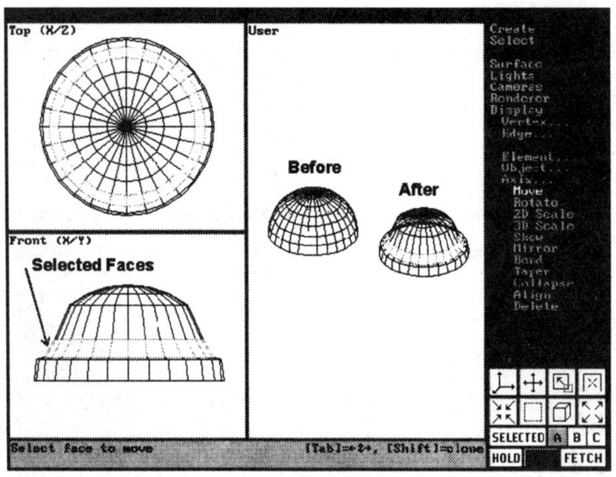

Moving a selection set of faces vertically.

RELATED COMMANDS

Modify/Face..., Select/Face/Single, Select/Face/Quad, Select/Face/Fence, Select/Face/Circle, Views–Use Snap, Views–Use Grid

Modify/Face/Rotate

Select
Modify
Surface
Face...
Element...
Move
Rotate
2D Scale
3D Scale
Skew
Mirror
Bend
Taper
Collapse
Align
Delete

Rotates one or multiple faces around the local or global axis.

Rotating a Face

1. Press the **Hold** button (Ctrl H) to store the current state of your geometry, viewport configuration, and selection set.
2. Select the face you want to rotate. You can select more than one face by pressing special keys when selecting the faces. See *Modify/Face....* You can also create a selection set of faces. See *Select/Face/Single*, *Select/Face/Quad*, *Select/Face/Fence,* and *Select/Face/Circle.*
3. As you move the mouse, the selected faces are rotated about the active axis. See *Modify/Axis/Show* and the Local Axis icon.
4. Click to place the face. If the results are not what you wanted, press the **Fetch** button (Ctrl F)to restore the original geometry and configuration.

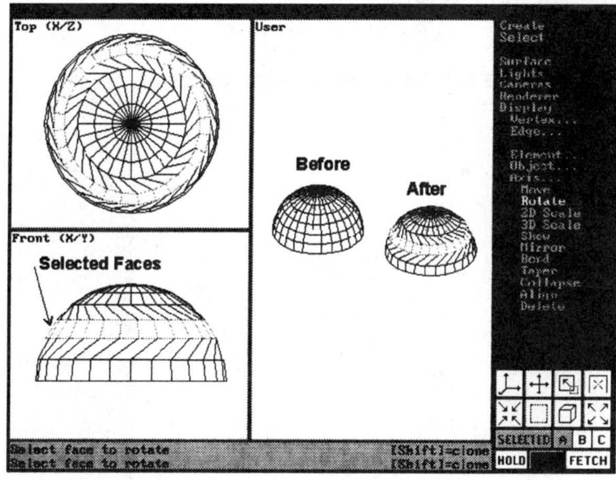

Rotating selected faces about the global axis.

RELATED COMMANDS

Modify/Face..., Select/Face/Single, Select/Face/Quad, Select/Face/Fence, Select/Face/Circle, Views–Use Snap, Views–Use Grid, Modify/Axis/Show, Local Axis icon

Select
Modify
Surface
Face...
Element...
Move
Rotate
2D Scale
3D Scale
Skew
Mirror
Bend
Taper
Collapse
Align
Delete

Modify/Face/2D Scale

Scales one or multiple faces to or from the local or global axis. This is done along the plane of the active viewport.

2D Scaling Faces

1. Press the **Hold** button (Ctrl H) to store the current state of your geometry, viewport configuration, and selection set.
2. Select the face you want to 2D Scale. You can select more than one vertex by pressing special keys when selecting the faces. See *Modify/Face....* You can also create a selection set of faces. See *Select/Face/Single, Select/Face/Quad, Select/Face/Fence,* and *Select/Face/Circle.*
3. As you move the mouse, the distance between the faces and the active axes increases or decreases. See *Modify/Axis/Show,* Local Axis icon. You can use the Tab key to control horizontal and vertical scaling.
4. Click to place the face. If the results are not what you wanted, press the **Fetch** button (Ctrl F) to restore the original geometry and configuration.

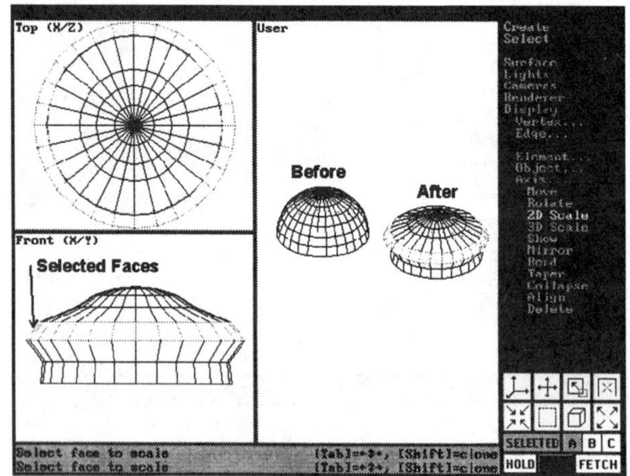

Scaling multiple faces along the plane of the Top viewport.

RELATED COMMANDS

Modify/Face..., Modify/Face/3D Scale, Select/Face/Single, Select/Face/Quad, select/Face/Fence, Select/Face/Circle, Views–Use Snap, Views–Use Grid, Modify/Axis/Show

Modify/Face/3D Scale

Select
Modify
Surface
Face...
Element...
Move
Rotate
2D Scale
3D Scale
Skew
Mirror
Bend
Taper
Collapse
Align
Delete

Scales one or multiple faces to or from the local or global axis. The faces are scaled along the X, Y, and Z axis equally.

3D Scaling Faces

1. Press the **Hold** button (Ctrl H) to store the current state of your geometry, viewport configuration, and selection set.
2. Select the face you want to 3D Scale. You can select more than one face by pressing special keys when selecting the faces. See *Modify/Face....* You can also create a selection set of faces. See *Select/Face/Single, Select/Face/Quad, Select/Face/Fence,* and *Select/Face/Circle.*
3. As you move the mouse, the distance between the faces and the active axes increases or decreases equally along the X, Y, and Z axis. See *Modify/Axis/Show,* Local Axis icon.
4. Click to place the face. If the results are not what you wanted, press the **Fetch** button (Ctrl F) to restore the original geometry and configuration.

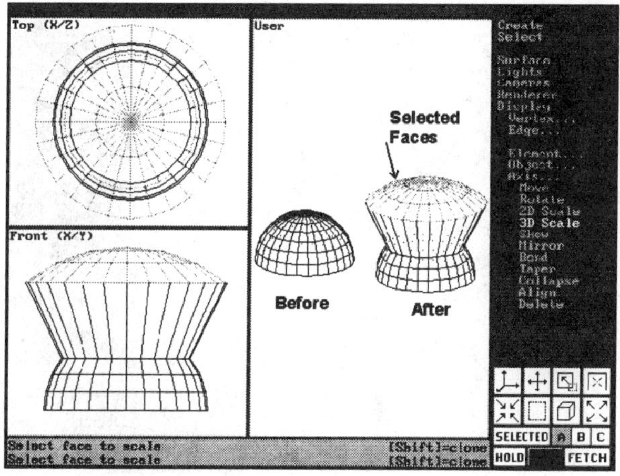

Scaling multiple faces in three dimensions about the global axis.

RELATED COMMANDS

Modify/Face/2D Scale, Modify/Face..., Select/Face/Single, Select/Face/Quad, Select/Face/Fence, Select/Face/Circle, Views–Use Snap, Views–Use Grid, Modify/Axis/Show

Select
Modify
Surface
Face...
Element...
Move
Rotate
2D Scale
3D Scale
Skew
Mirror
Bend
Taper
Collapse
Align
Delete

Modify/Face/Skew

One or more selected faces are adjusted on a plane parallel to the global or local axis.

Skewing Selected Faces

1. Press the **Hold** button (Ctrl H) to store the current state of your geometry, viewport configuration, and selection set.
2. Select the face you want to skew. You can select more than one face by pressing special keys when selecting the faces. See *Modify/Face....* You can also create a selection set of faces. See *Select/Face/Single, Select/Face/Quad, Select/Face/Fence,* and *Select/Face/Circle.*
3. As you move the mouse, the white boundary box indicates the distortion. This is done on a plane parallel to the local or global axis. See *Modify/Axis/Show,* Local Axis icon. You can skew horizontally or vertically by pressing the Tab key.
4. Click to place the face. If the results are not what you wanted, press the **Fetch** button (Ctrl F) to restore the original geometry and configuration.

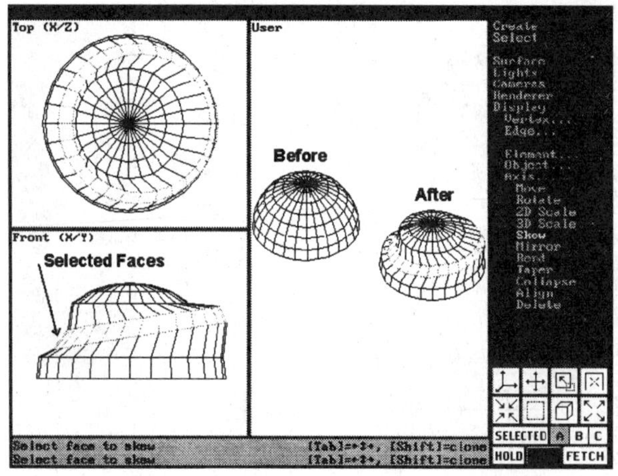

Skewing selected faces horizontally and vertically in a plane parallel to the Front viewport.

RELATED COMMANDS

Modify/Face..., Select/Face/Single, Select/Face/Quad, Select/Face/Fence, Select/Face/Circle, Views–Use Snap, Views–Use Grid, Modify/axis/Show, Local Axis

Modify/Face/Mirror

Select
Modify
Surface
Face...
Element...
Move
Rotate
2D Scale
3D Scale
Skew
Mirror
Bend
Taper
Collapse
Align
Delete

Mirrors and copies the selected faces. This is based on the location of the cursor and the distance between the cursor and the original faces.

Mirroring Selected Faces

1. Press the **Hold** button (Ctrl H) to store the current state of your geometry, viewport configuration, and selection set.
2. Select the face you want to mirror. You can select more than one vertice by pressing special keys when selecting the faces. See *Modify/Face...*. You can also create a selection set of faces. See *Select/Face/Single, Select/Face/Quad, Select/Face/Fence,* and *Select/Face/Circle*.
3. As you move the mouse, the white boundary box indicates the faces that will be mirrored. This is done on a plane parallel to the selected viewport. You can use the Tab key to cycle through different mirror axes.
4. Click to place the face. If you want to copy the faces, hold down the Shift key when you click to place the face. The selected faces are mirrored about a plane halfway between the original faces and the placed faces. If the results are not what you wanted, press the **Fetch** button (Ctrl F)to restore the original geometry and configuration.

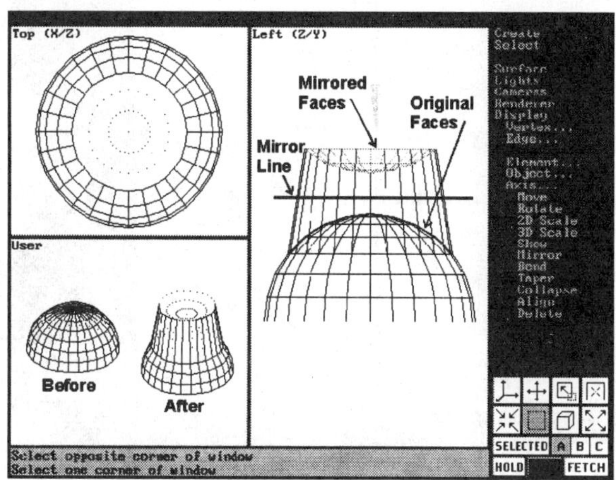

Mirroring selected faces along the vertical axis.

RELATED COMMANDS

Modify/Face..., Select/Face/Single, Select/Face/Quad, Select/Face/Fence, Select/Face/Circle, Views–Use Snap, Views–Use Grid, Modify/Axis/Show

Select
Modify
Surface
Face...
Element...
Move
Rotate
2D Scale
3D Scale
Skew
Mirror
Bend
Taper
Collapse
Align
Delete

Modify/Face/Bend

Bends selected faces about the plane in the active viewport.

Bending Selected Faces

1. Press the **Hold** button (Ctrl H) to store the current state of your geometry, viewport configuration, and selection set.
2. Since you cannot bend single faces, first create a selection set of faces. You can select more than one face by pressing special keys when selecting the faces. See *Modify/Face....* You can also create a selection set of faces. See *Select/Face/Single, Select/Face/Quad, Select/Face/Fence,* and *Select/Face/Circle.*
3. As you move the mouse, the white boundary box indicates the faces that will be bent. This is done on a plane parallel to the selected viewport. At least two of the selected faces must lie on a plane parallel to the active viewport. You can use the Tab key to cycle through different unidirectional cursors.
4. A gradually increasing rotation is applied to the selected faces, beginning at the base of the bend. Click to place the face. If the results are not what you wanted, press the **Fetch** button (Ctrl F)to restore the original geometry and configuration.

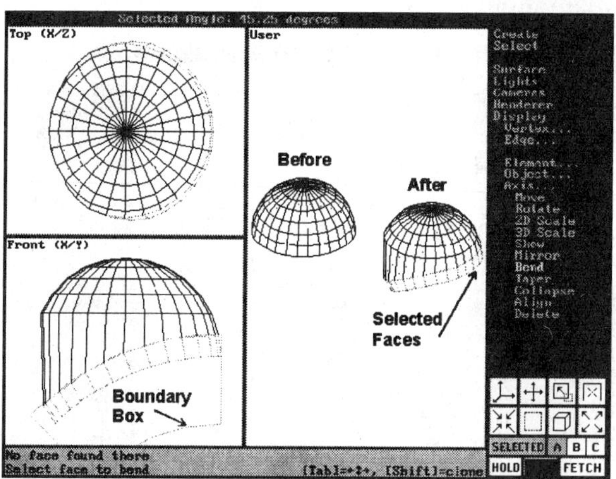

Bending selected faces to the right side in the Front viewport.

RELATED COMMANDS

Modify/Face..., Select/Face/Quad, Select/Face/Fence, Select/Face/Circle, Views–Use Snap, Views–Use Grid, Modify/Axis/Show

Modify/Face/Taper

Select
Modify
Surface
Face...
Element...
Move
Rotate
2D Scale
3D Scale
Skew
Mirror
Bend
Taper
Collapse
Align
Delete

Tapers selected faces, resulting in a widening or narrowing of the object. The taper is done in relation to the global or local axis.

Tapering Selected Faces

1. Press the **Hold** button (Ctrl H) to store the current state of your geometry, viewport configuration, and selection set.
2. Because you cannot taper single faces, first create a selection set of faces. You can select more than one face by pressing special keys when selecting the faces. See *Modify/Face....* You can also create a selection set of faces. See *Select/Face/Single, Select/Face/Quad, Select/Face/Fence,* and *Select/Face/Circle.*
3. As you move the mouse, the white boundary box indicates the faces that will be bent. This is done on a plane parallel to the selected viewport about the local or global axis. See *Modify/Axis/Show,* Local Axis icon. You can use the Tab key to cycle through different unidirectional cursor which allows you select the side of the Face group to taper.
4. When your object has the desired taper, click to place the face. If the results are not what you wanted, press the **Fetch** button (Ctrl F) to restore the original geometry and configuration.

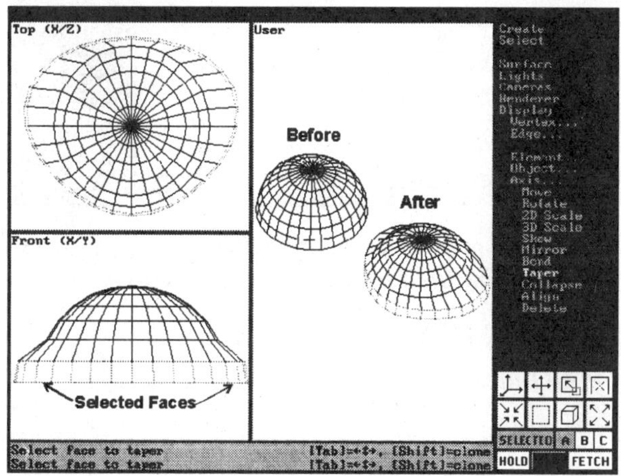

Tapering selected faces about the global axis in the Top view.

RELATED COMMANDS

Modify/Face..., Select/Face/Single, Select/Face/Quad, Select/Face/Fence, Select/Face/Circle, Views–Use Snap, Views–Use Grid, Modify/Axis/Show

Modify/Face/Collapse

Collapses a selected face to a single vertex point.

Collapsing a Face

1. Press the **Hold** button (Ctrl H) to store the current state of your geometry, viewport configuration, and selection set.
2. Select the face you want to collapse.
3. In response to the Collapse this face? prompt, select **OK.**
4. The selected face is deleted, and a vertex is inserted at the center of the selected face. Adjacent connecting faces are connected to the new vertex. If the results are not what you wanted, press the **Fetch** button (Ctrl F) to restore the original geometry and configuration.

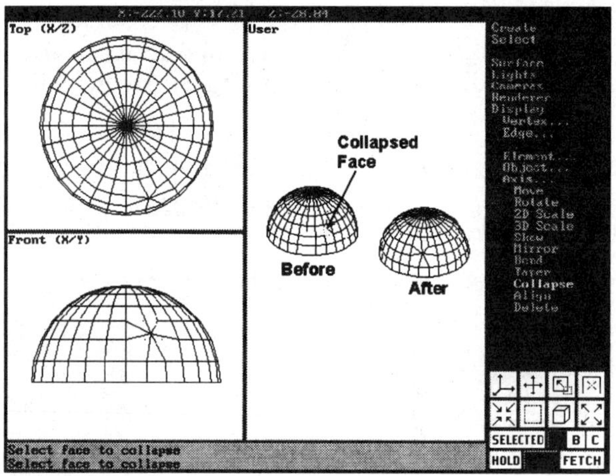

Collapsing a face deletes it and replaces it with a vertex, connecting the adjacent faces to the new vertex.

RELATED COMMAND

Display/Geometry/All Lines

Modify/Face/Align

Select
Modify
Surface
Face...
Element...
Move
Rotate
2D Scale
3D Scale
Skew
Mirror
Bend
Taper
Collapse
Align
Delete

Aligns a selected face to the construction plane of the active viewport.

Aligning a Face

1. Press the **Hold** button (Ctrl H) to store the current state of your geometry, viewport configuration, and selection set.
2. Select the face you want to align.
3. Select one of the following options from the Align method: selection box:

   Facing Toward: Aligns the selected face so the face normal is toward you.

   Facing Away: Aligns the selected face so the face normal is away from you.
4. When you click the mouse in the active viewport, the selected face is aligned with the construction plane that is parallel to the active viewport. If the results are not what you wanted, press the **Fetch** button (Ctrl F) to restore the original geometry and configuration.

NOTE Using *Modify/Face/Align* moves the selected face and its three vertices only, leaving the rest of the geometry in place. In addition, selecting **Facing Away** flips the face over and tangles its vertices.

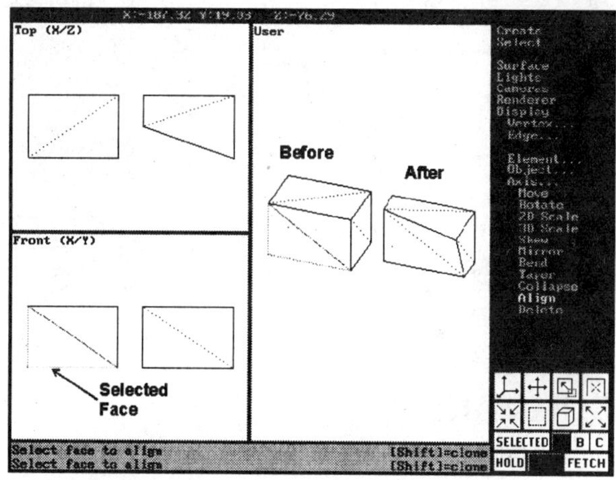

Aligning a selected face in the front viewport.

RELATED COMMANDS

Display/Const/Show, Display/Const/Place

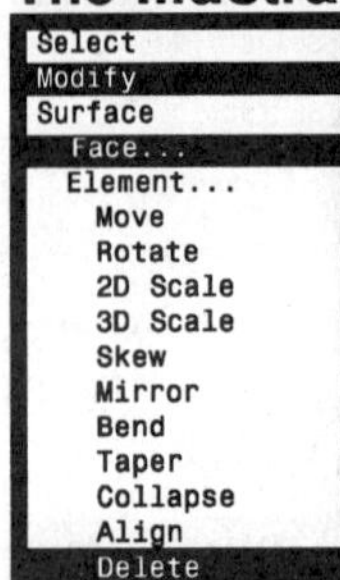

Modify/Face/Delete

Deletes single or selected faces.

Deleting Selected Faces

1. Press the **Hold** button (Ctrl H) to store the current state of your geometry, viewport configuration, and selection set.
2. Select the face you want to delete. You can select more than one face by pressing special keys when selecting the vertices. See *Modify/Face....* You can also create a selection set of vertices. See *Select/Face/Single, Select/Face/Quad, Select/Face/Fence,* and *Select/Face/Circle.*
3. Click in any viewport. At the Delete Faces? box, select **OK** to delete the selected faces. If the deletion results in single vertices that are not attached to anything, the Delete isolated vertices box will appear. Select **Yes** to delete both the selected faces and vertices. Select **No** to delete only the faces.
4. If the results are not what you wanted, press the **Fetch** button (Ctrl F) to restore the original geometry and configuration.

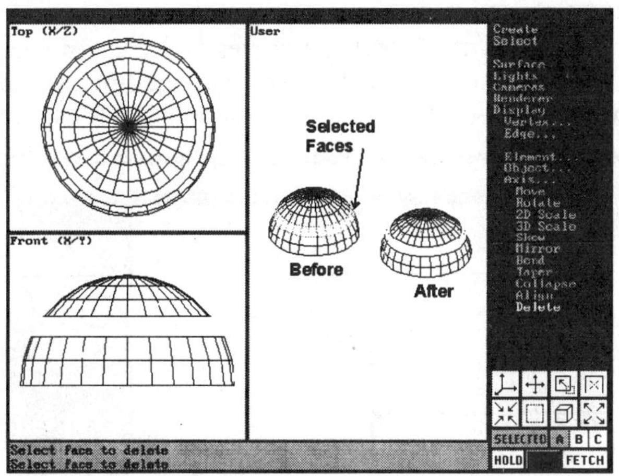

Deleting selected faces.

RELATED COMMANDS

Modify/Face..., Select/Face/Single, Select/Face/Quad, Select/Face/Fence, Select/Face/Circle

Modify/Element...

Select
Modify
Surface
Face...
Element...
Object...
Move
Rotate
2D Scale
3D Scale
Skew
Mirror
Bend
Taper
Align
Delete

An element is one of two or more individual mesh objects that are grouped together into one large object.

Object
A collection of one or more vertices and faces that form a net-like appearance.

Element
An individual mesh object that, when grouped together, forms an object. An element can be thought of as a subset of an object. See also *Create/Element/Detach* and *Create/Object/Attach*.

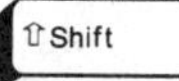

Cloning Elements
When using any of the *Modify/Elements* commands (except *Modify/Element/Delete*), holding down the **Shift** key before selecting it will create a clone or copy of the element. When an element is cloned, it becomes a separate object, and must be assigned a unique name.

Elements can only be modified one at a time. While a selection set may contain several elements, you can only modify one at a time.

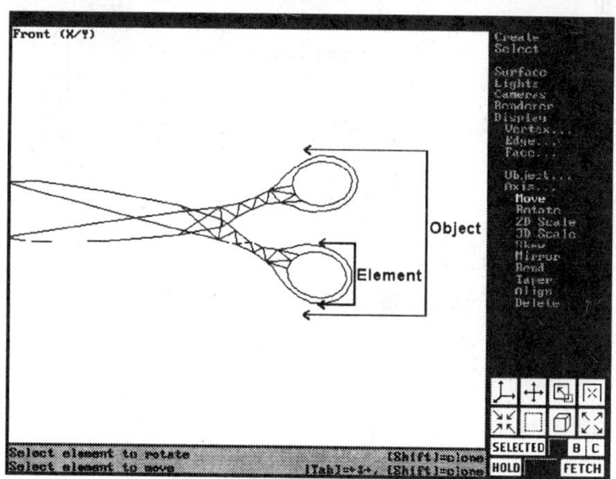

An element is one or more meshed objects grouped together into an object.

RELATED COMMANDS

Create/Element/Detach, Create/Object/Attach

Select
Modify
Surface
Face...
Element...
Object...
Move
Rotate
2D Scale
3D Scale
Skew
Mirror
Bend
Taper
Align
Delete

Modify/Element/Move

Moves a single element in a mesh object.

How to Move an Element

1. Select the element you want to move. You can only select one element to move at a time. Holding down the Shift key before selecting the element will create a clone or copy of the element.
2. After selecting the element, a white bounding box appears. As you move the mouse, the bounding box will move. You can use the Tab key to control horizontal and vertical movement.
3. Click to place the element, or right-click to cancel the operation.

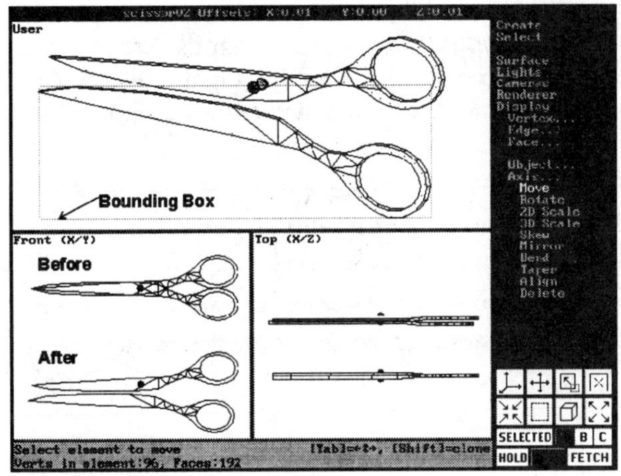

Moving an element.

RELATED COMMANDS

Modify/Element..., Views–Use Snap, Views–Use Grid

Modify/Element/Rotate

Select
Modify
Surface
Face...
Element...
Object...
Move
Rotate
2D Scale
3D Scale
Skew
Mirror
Bend
Taper
Align
Delete

Rotates an element around the local or global axis.

Rotating an Element

1. Select the element you want to rotate. You can only select one element to rotate at a time. Holding down the [Shift] key before selecting the element will create a clone or copy of the element.
2. After selecting the element, a white bounding box appears. As you move the mouse, the bounding box is rotated about the active axis. See *Modify/Axis/Show* and the Local Axis icon.
3. Click to place the element, or right click to cancel the operation.

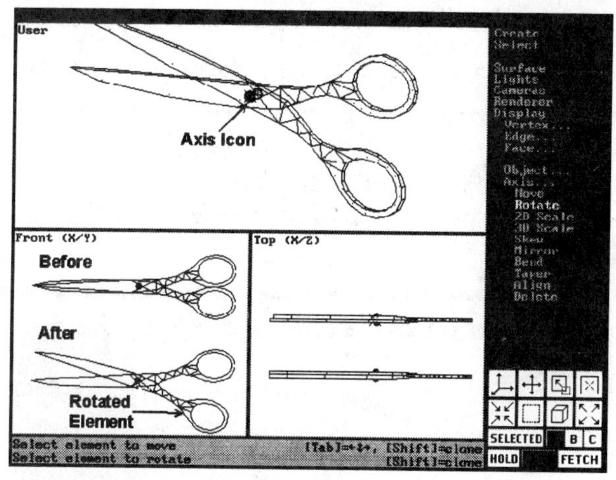

Rotating an element about the global axis.

RELATED COMMANDS

Modify/Element, Views–Use Snap, Views–Use Grid, Modify/Axis/Show

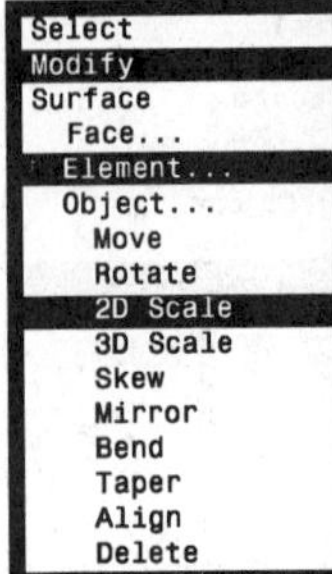

Modify/Element/2D Scale

Scales a single element to or from the local or global axis. This is done along the plane of the active viewport.

2D Scaling of an Element

1. Select the element you want to 2D Scale. You can only select one element to scale at a time. Holding down the Shift key before selecting the element will create a clone or copy of the element.
2. After selecting the element, a white bounding box appears. As you move the mouse, the element is increased or decreased in size. The element is scaled according to the cursor you use. You can use the Tab key to control horizontal, vertical, and overall scaling. The element is scaled according to the axis of the active viewport. See *Modify/Axis/Show* and the Local Axis icon.
3. Click to place the scaled element, or right-click to cancel the operation.

> **NOTE** Using *Modify/Element/2D Scale* scales the element along the plane of the active viewport. It does not maintain the proportion of the element. To maintain the proportion of the element when scaling, use *Modify/Element/3D Scale.*

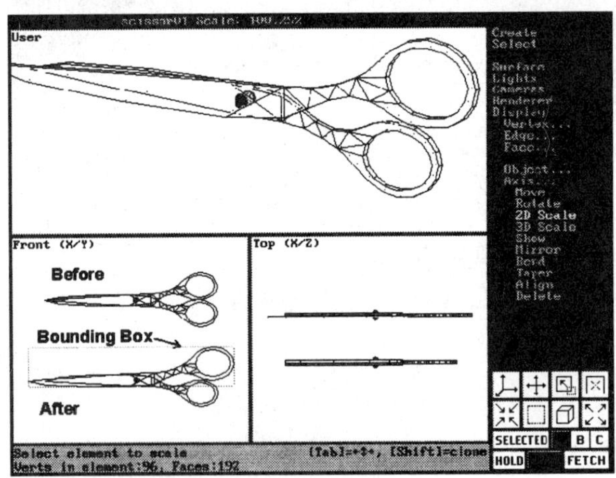

Scaling an element unidirectionally about the local axis in the Front viewport.

RELATED COMMANDS

Modify/Element..., Modify/Element/3D Scale, Views–Use Snap, Views–Use Grid, Modify/Axis/Show

Modify/Element/3D Scale

Select
Modify
Surface
Face...
Element...
Object...
Move
Rotate
2D Scale
3D Scale
Skew
Mirror
Bend
Taper
Align
Delete

Scales a single element to or from the local or global axis. The element is scaled along the X, Y, and Z axis equally.

3D Scaling an Element

1. Select the element you want to 3D Scale. You can only select one element to scale at a time. Holding down the [Shift] key before selecting the element will create a clone or copy of the element.
2. After selecting the element, a white bounding box appears. As you move the mouse, the element is increased or decreased in size equally along the X, Y, and Z axis about the global or local axis. See *Modify/Axis/Show,* Local Axis icon.
3. Click to place the element or right-click to cancel the operation.

Unlike *Modify/Element/2D Scale*, using 3D Scale maintains the proportion of the element.

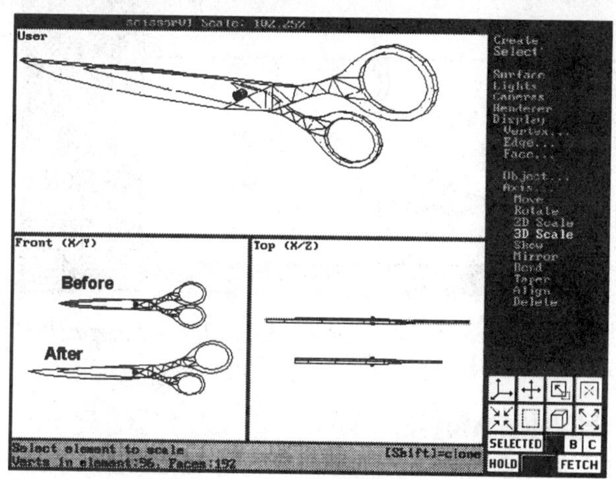

Scaling an element proportionally about the global axis.

RELATED COMMANDS

Modify/Element, Modify/Element/2D Scale, Views–Use Snap, Views–Use Grid, Modify/Axis/Show

Select
Modify
Surface
Face...
Element...
Object...
Move
Rotate
2D Scale
3D Scale
Skew
Mirror
Bend
Taper
Align
Delete

Modify/Element/Skew

A selected element is adjusted on a plane parallel to the global or local axis.

Skewing a Selected Element

1. Select the element you want to skew. You can only select one element to skew at a time. Holding down the [Shift] key before selecting the element will create a clone or copy of the element.
2. After selecting the element, a white bounding box appears. As you move the mouse, the element is skewed either horizontally or vertically. You can change skew directions by pressing the [Tab] key. The skewing is done on a plane parallel to the global or local axis. See *Modify/Axis/Show,* Local Axis icon.
3. Click to place the element or right-click to cancel the operation.

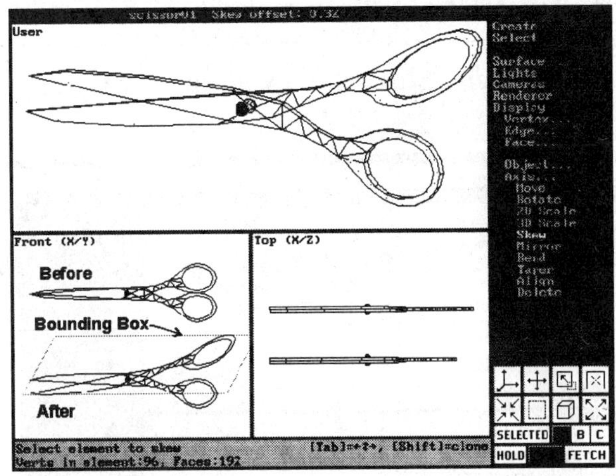

Skewing a selected element horizontally and vertically in a plane parallel to the Front viewport.

RELATED COMMANDS

Modify/Element..., Views–Use Snap, Views–Use Grid, Modify/Axis/Show

Modify/Element/Mirror

Select
Modify
Surface
Face...
Element...
Object...
Move
Rotate
2D Scale
3D Scale
Skew
Mirror
Bend
Taper
Align
Delete

Mirrors and optionally copies the selected element. This is based on the location of the cursor and the distance between the cursor and the original element.

Mirroring a Selected Element

1. Select the element you want to mirror. You can only select one element to mirror at a time. Holding down the Shift key before selecting the element will create a clone or copy of the element.
2. As you move the mouse, the white boundary box indicates the element that will be mirrored. This is done on a plane parallel to the selected viewport. You can use the Tab key to cycle through different mirror axes.
3. Click to place the element or right-click to cancel the operation. The selected element is mirrored about a plane halfway between the original element and the placed element.

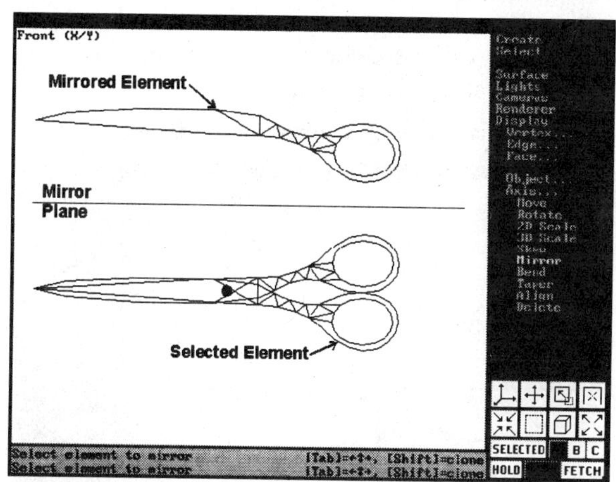

Mirroring and cloning (with the Shift) a selected element along the vertical axis.

RELATED COMMANDS

Modify/Element..., Views–Use Snap, Views–Use Grid

Select
Modify
Surface
Face...
Element...
Object...
Move
Rotate
2D Scale
3D Scale
Skew
Mirror
Bend
Taper
Align
Delete

Modify/Element/Bend

Bends a selected element about the plane in the active viewport.

Bending a Selected Element

1. Select the element you want to bend. Holding down the [Shift] key before selecting the element will create a clone or copy of the element.
2. As you move the mouse, the white boundary box indicates the element that will be bent. This is done on a plane parallel to the selected viewport. You can use the [Tab] key to cycle through different unidirectional cursors.
3. A gradually increasing rotation is applied to the selected element, beginning at the base of the bend. Click to place the element or right–click to cancel the operation.

TIP To achieve a smooth bend, the object must have enough geometry to allow a gradual application of the bend. In the 3D Lofter, increase the step value and use Tween when you make the object. In the 3D Editor, increase the Values parameter before creating the object.

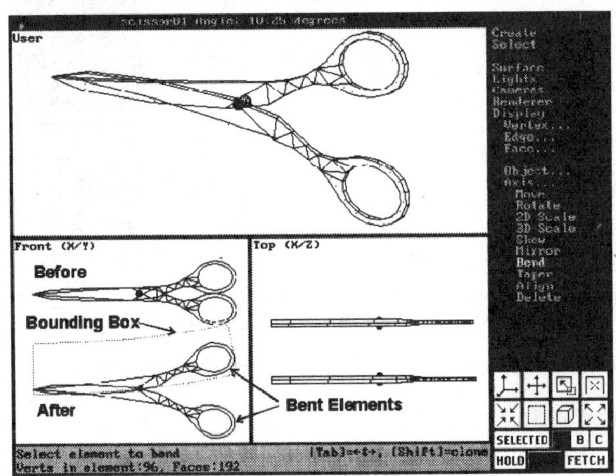

Bending two elements to the top and bottom in the Front viewport.

RELATED COMMANDS

Modify/Element..., Views–Use Snap, Views–Use Grid

Modify/Element/Taper

Select
Modify
Surface
Face...
Element...
Object...
Move
Rotate
2D Scale
3D Scale
Skew
Mirror
Bend
Taper
Align
Delete

Tapers a selected element, resulting in a widening or narrowing of the element. The taper is done in relation to the global or local axis.

Tapering a Selected Element

1. Select the element you want to taper. Holding down the [Shift] key before selecting the element will create a clone or copy of the element.
2. As you move the mouse, the white boundary box indicates the element that will be tapered. This is done on a plane parallel to the selected viewport about the local or global axis. See *Modify/Axis/Show,* Local Axis icon. You can use the [Tab] key to cycle through different unidirectional cursor which allows you select the side of the element that will be tapered.
3. When your element has the desired taper, click to place it or right- click to cancel the operation.

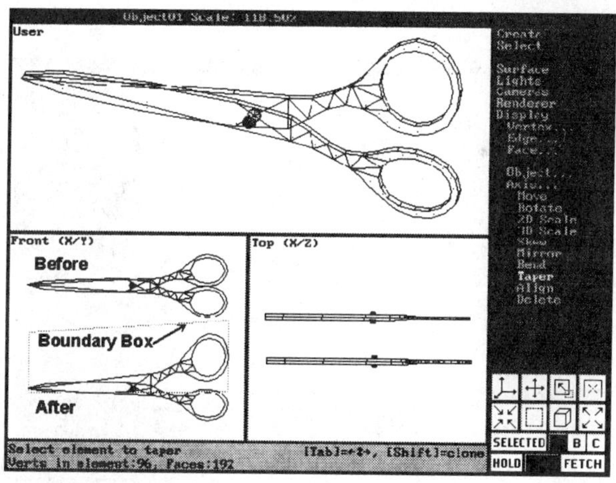

Tapering a selected element about the global axis in the Front view.

RELATED COMMANDS

Modify/Element, Views–Use Snap, Views–Use Grid, Modify/Axis/Show

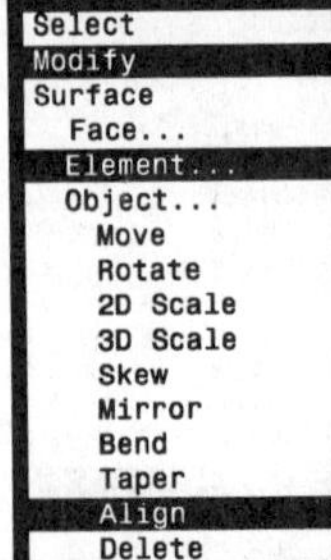

Modify/Element/Align

Aligns a selected face of an element so it is coplanar to the plane of the active viewport.

Aligning an Element

1. Press the **Hold** button (Ctrl H) to store the current state of your geometry, viewport configuration, and selection set.
2. Select a face in the element you want to align.
3. Select one of the following options from the Align method: selection box:

   Facing Toward: Aligns the selected face so the *face normal* is toward you.

   Facing Away: Aligns the selected face so the *face normal* is away from you.
4. When you click the mouse in the active viewport, the selected face is aligned with the construction plane that is parallel to the active viewport. The rest of the element is also moved, based on the alignment of the selected face. If the results are not what you wanted, press the **Fetch** button (Ctrl F) to restore the original geometry and configuration.

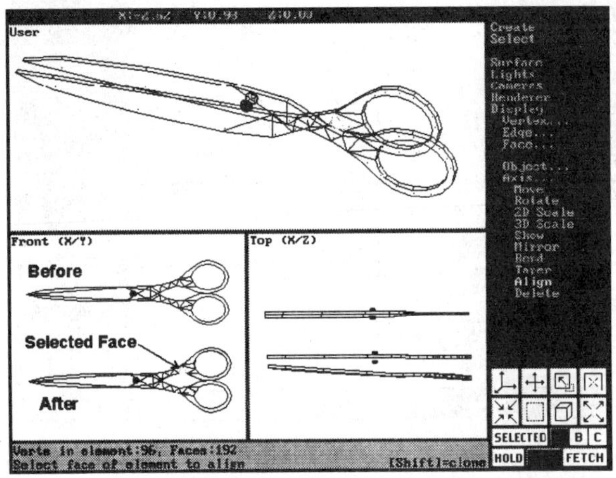

Aligning a selected face of an element to the front viewport.

RELATED COMMANDS

Modify/Element..., Modify/Face/Align

Modify/Element/Delete

Deletes a selected element.

Deleting a Selected Element

1. Press the **Hold** button (Ctrl H) to store the current state of your geometry, viewport configuration, and selection set.
2. Select the element you want to delete.
3. At the Delete Element? box, select **OK** to delete the selected element.
4. If the results are not what you wanted, press the **Fetch** button (Ctrl F) to restore the original geometry and configuration.

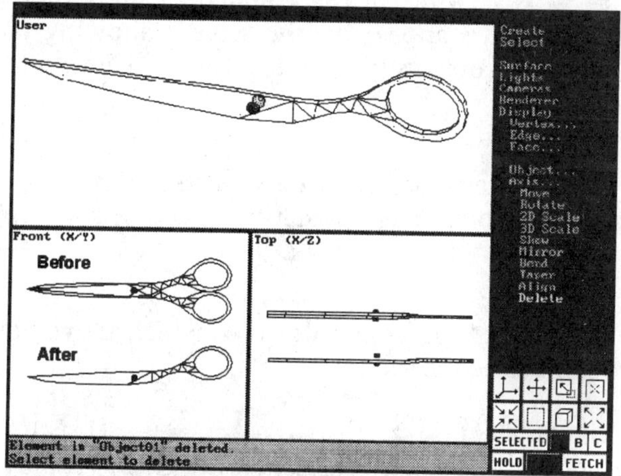

Deleting a selected element.

RELATED COMMAND

Modify/Element

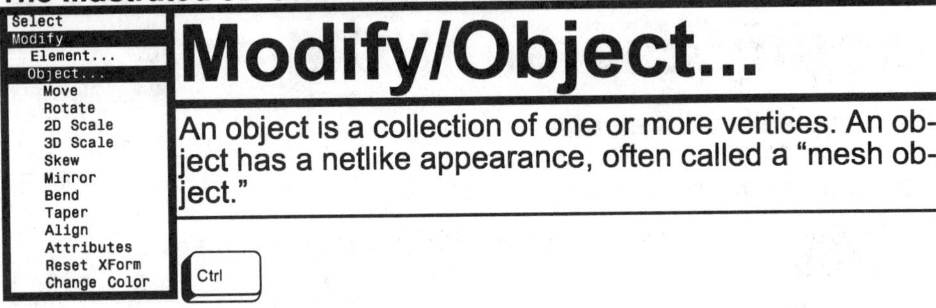

Modify/Object...

An object is a collection of one or more vertices. An object has a netlike appearance, often called a "mesh object."

Ctrl

Holding down the **Ctrl** key while selecting objects will add them to the current selection set. See *Select/Object/Single*.

Alt W

Pressing the **Alt+W** keys while in the command enters the Quad-Window selection mode. Crosshairs appear on the screen, allowing you to define a selection set box and add objects to the selection set. See *Select/Object/Quad.*

⇧Shift

Holding down the **Shift** key when selecting objects creates a clone or copy of a single or a selection set of objects. The resulting objects become a separate object.

Ctrl N

Accesses the Select Objects by Name dialog box, which allows you to add or remove objects from the selection set.

RELATED COMMANDS

Modify/Element, Select/Object/Single, Select/Object/Quad

Select
Modify
Element...
Object...
Axis...
Move
Rotate
2D Scale
3D Scale
Skew
Mirror
Bend
Taper
Align
Attributes
Reset XForm

Modify/Object/Move

Moves or copies single or multiple objects.

How to Move an Object

1. Select the object you want to move. Holding down the Shift key before selecting the object will create a cloned copy of the object. You can select more than one object by pressing special keys when selecting the vertices. See *Modify/Object....* You can also create a selection set of objects. See *Select/Object/Single, Select/Object/Quad, Select/Object/Fence,* and *Select/Object/Circle.*
2. As you move the mouse, the selected objects will move. As you move the single or multiple objects, a boundary box represents its position. You can use the Tab key to control horizontal and vertical movement.
3. Click to place the object, or right-click to cancel the command.

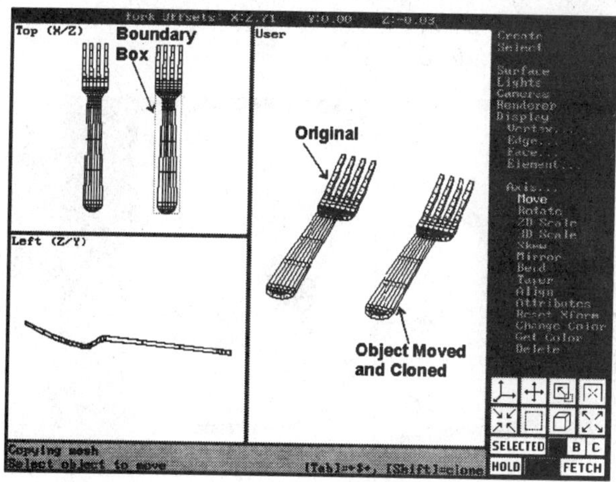

Moving and creating a clone (hold down the Shift key when selecting the object) of an object.

RELATED COMMANDS

Modify/Object..., Select/Object/Single, Select/Object/Quad, Select/Object/Fence, Select/Object/Circle, Views–Use Snap, Views–Use Grid

Select
Modify
Element...
Object...
Move
Rotate
2D Scale
3D Scale
Skew
Mirror
Bend
Taper
Align
Attributes
Reset XForm
Change Color

Modify/Object/Rotate

Rotates single or multiple objects around the local or global axis.

Rotating an Object

1. Press the **Hold** button (Ctrl H) to store the current state of your geometry, viewport configuration, and selection set.
2. Select the object you want to rotate. Holding down the Shift key before selecting the object will create a clone or copy of the object. You can select more than one object by pressing special keys when selecting the objects. See *Modify/Object....* You can also create a selection set of objects. See *Select/Object/Single, Select/Object/Quad, Select/Object/Fence,* and *Select/Object/Circle.*
3. As you move the mouse, the selected objects are rotated about the active axis. See *Modify/Axis/Show* and the Local Axis icon.
4. Click to place the object, or right-click to cancel the operation. If the results are not what you wanted, press the **Fetch** button (Ctrl F) to restore the original geometry and configuration.

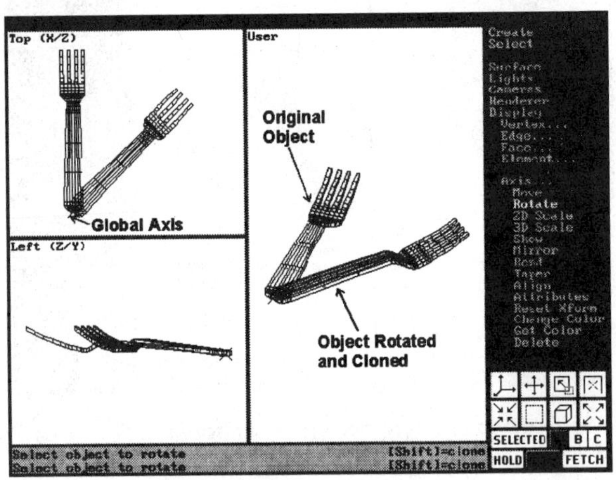

Rotating and cloning (hold down the Shift key when selecting the object) an object about the global axis.

RELATED COMMANDS

Modify/Object..., Select/Object/Single, Select/Object/Quad, Select/Object/Fence, Select/Object/Circle, Views–Use Snap, Views–Use Grid, Modify/Axis/Show, Local Axis icon

Modify/Object/2D Scale

Select
Modify
Element...
Object...
Move
Rotate
2D Scale
3D Scale
Skew
Mirror
Bend
Taper
Align
Attributes
Reset XForm
Change Color

Scales one or multiple objects to or from the local or global axis. This is done along the plane of the active viewport.

2D Scaling Objects

1. Press the **Hold** button ([Ctrl][H]) to store the current state of your geometry, viewport configuration, and selection set.
2. Select the object you want to 2D Scale. Holding down the [Shift] key before selecting the object will create a clone or copy of the object. You can select more than one object by pressing special keys when selecting the objects. See *Modify/Object....* You can also create a selection set of objects. See *Select/Object/Single, Select/Object/Quad, Select/Object/Fence,* and *Select/Object/Circle.*
3. As you move the mouse, the respective scale between the objects and the active axis increases or decreases. See *Modify/Axis/Show,* Local Axis icon. You can use the [Tab] key to control horizontal, vertical, and unidirectional scaling.
4. Click to place the object. If the results are not what you wanted, press the **Fetch** button ([Ctrl][F]) to restore the original geometry and configuration.

NOTE Using *Modify/Object/2D* Scale scales the object along the plane of the active viewport. It does not maintain the proportion of the object. To maintain the proportion of the object when scaling, use *Modify/Object/3D Scale.*

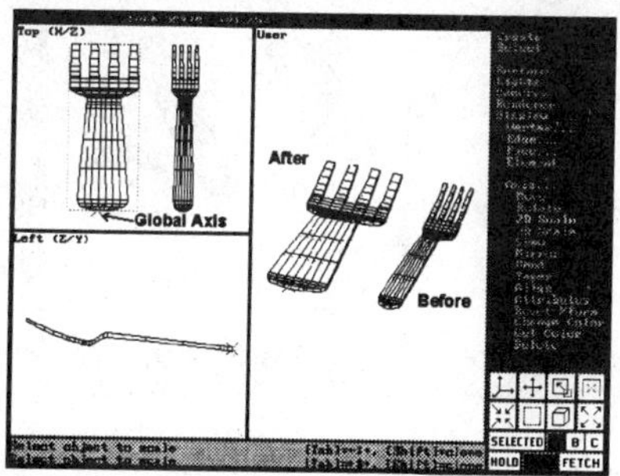

Scaling an object horizontally with the global axis along the plane of the Top viewport.

RELATED COMMANDS

Modify/Object/3D Scale, Modify/Object..., Select/Object/Single, Select/Object/Quad, Select/Object/Fence, Select/Object/Circle, Views–Use Snap, Views–Use Grid, Modify/Axis/Show

Select
Modify
Element...
Object...
Move
Rotate
2D Scale
3D Scale
Skew
Mirror
Bend
Taper
Align
Attributes
Reset XForm
Change Color

Modify/Object/3D Scale

Scales one or multiple objects to or from the local or global axis. The objects are scaled along the X, Y, and Z axis equally.

3D Scaling Objects

1. Press the **Hold** button (Ctrl H) to store the current state of your geometry, viewport configuration, and selection set.
2. Select the object you want to 3D Scale. Holding down the Shift key before selecting the object will create a clone or copy of the object. You can select more than one object by pressing special keys when selecting the objects. See *Modify/Object....* You can also create a selection set of objects. See *Select/Object/Single, Select/Object/Quad, Select/Object/Fence,* and *Select/Object/Circle*.
3. As you move the mouse, the scale between the objects and the active axis increases or decreases equally along the X, Y, and Z axis. See *Modify/Axis/Show,* Local Axis icon.
4. Click to place the object. If the results are not what you wanted, press the **Fetch** button (Ctrl F) to restore the original geometry and configuration.

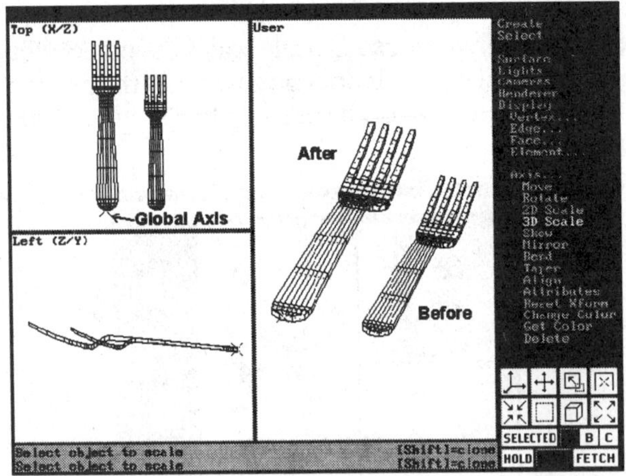

Scaling an object in three dimensions about the global axis.

RELATED COMMANDS

Modify/Object/2D Scale, Modify/Object..., Select/Object/Single, Select/Object/Quad, Select/Object/Fence, Select/Object/Circle, Views–Use Snap, Views–Use Grid, Modify/Axis/Show

Modify/Object/Skew

Select
Modify
Element...
Object...
Move
Rotate
2D Scale
3D Scale
Skew
Mirror
Bend
Taper
Align
Attributes
Reset XForm
Change Color

One or more selected objects are adjusted on a plane parallel with the global or local axis.

Skewing Selected Objects

1. Press the **Hold** button (Ctrl H) to store the current state of your geometry, viewport configuration, and selection set.
2. Select the object you want to skew. Holding down the Shift key before selecting the object will create a clone or copy of the object. You can select more than one object by pressing special keys when selecting the objects. See *Modify/Object....* You can also create a selection set of objects. See *Select/Object/Single, Select/Object/Quad, Select/Object/Fence,* and *Select/Object/Circle.*
3. As you move the mouse, the white boundary box indicates the distortion. This is done on a plane parallel to the local or global axis. See *Modify/Axis/Show,* Local Axis icon. You can skew horizontally or vertically by pressing the Tab key.
4. Click to place the object or right-click to cancel the operation. If the results are not what you wanted, press the **Fetch** button (Ctrl F) to restore the original geometry and configuration.

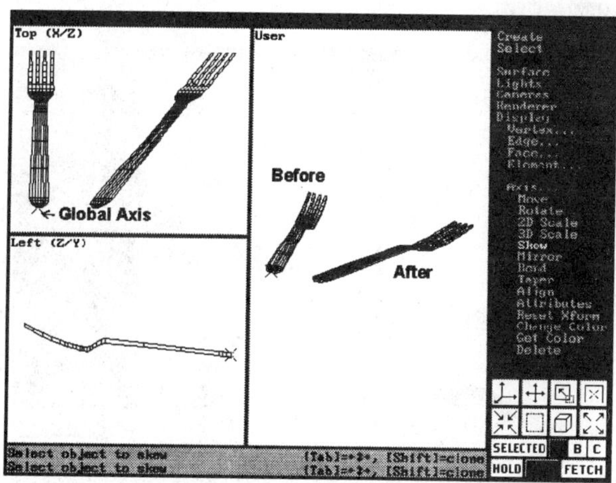

Skewing an object horizontally in a plane parallel to the Top viewport.

RELATED COMMANDS

Modify/Object..., Select/Object/Single, Select/Object/Quad, Select/Object/Fence, Select/Object/Circle, Views–Use Snap, Views–Use Grid, Modify/Axis/Show

Select
Modify
Element...
Object...
Move
Rotate
2D Scale
3D Scale
Skew
Mirror
Bend
Taper
Align
Attributes
Reset XForm
Change Color

Modify/Object/Mirror

Mirrors and/or copies the selected objects. This is based upon the location of the cursor and the distance between the cursor and the original objects.

Mirroring Selected Objects

1. Press the **Hold** button (Ctrl H) to store the current state of your geometry, viewport configuration, and selection set.
2. Select the object you want to mirror. Holding down the Shift key before selecting the object will create a clone or copy of the object. You can select more than one object by pressing special keys when selecting the objects. See *Modify/Object....* You can also create a selection set of objects. See *Select/Object/Single, Select/Object/Quad, Select/Object/Fence,* and *Select/Object/Circle.*
3. As you move the mouse, the white boundary box indicates the objects that will be mirrored. This is done on a plane parallel to the selected viewport. You can use the Tab key to cycle through different mirror axis.
4. Click to place the object. The selected objects are mirrored about a plane halfway between the original objects and the placed objects. If the results are not what you wanted, press the **Fetch** button (Ctrl F)to restore the original geometry and configuration.

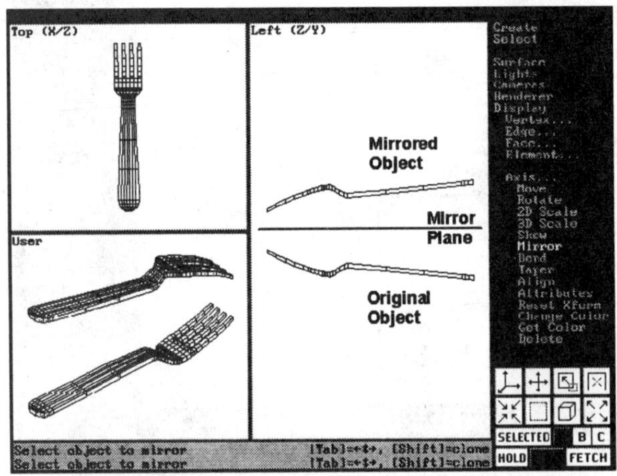

Mirroring a selected object along the vertical axis.

RELATED COMMANDS

Modify/Object..., *Select/Object/Single, Select/Object/Quad, Select/Object/Fence, Select/Object/Circle, Views–Use Snap, Views–Use Grid, Modify/Axis/Show*

Modify/Object/Bend

Select
Modify
Element...
Object...
Move
Rotate
2D Scale
3D Scale
Skew
Mirror
Bend
Taper
Align
Attributes
Reset XForm
Change Color

Bends selected objects about the plane in the active viewport.

Bending Selected Objects

1. Press the **Hold** button (Ctrl H) to store the current state of your geometry, viewport configuration, and selection set.
2. Select the object you want to mirror. Holding down the Shift key before selecting the object will create a clone or copy of the object. You can select more than one object by pressing special keys when selecting the objects. See *Modify/Object....* You can also create a selection set of objects. See *Select/Object/Single, Select/Object/Quad, Select/Object/Fence,* and *Select/Object/Circle.*
3. As you move the mouse, the white boundary box indicates how the object will be bent. This is done on a plane parallel to the selected viewport. You can use the Tab key to cycle through different unidirectional cursors.
4. A gradually increasing rotation is applied to the selected object, beginning at the base of the bend. Click to place the object. If the results are not what you wanted, press the **Fetch** button (Ctrl F) to restore the original geometry and configuration.

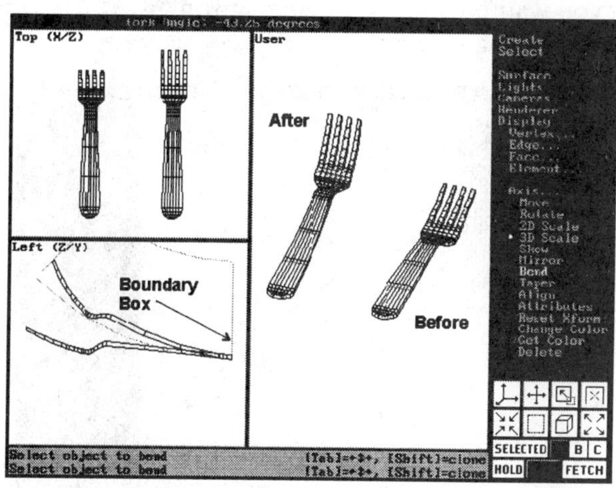

Bending a selected object upward in the Left viewport.

RELATED COMMANDS

Modify/Object..., *Select/Object/Single, Select/Object/Quad, Select/Object/Fence, Select/Object/Circle, Views–Use Snap, Views–Use Grid*

Select
Modify
Element...
Object...
Move
Rotate
2D Scale
3D Scale
Skew
Mirror
Bend
Taper
Align
Attributes
Reset XForm
Change Color

Modify/Object/Taper

Tapers selected objects, resulting in a widening or narrowing of the object. The taper is done in relation to the global or local axis.

Tapering Selected Objects

1. Press the **Hold** button ([Ctrl][H]) to store the current state of your geometry, viewport configuration, and selection set.
2. Select the object you want to taper. Holding down the [Shift] key before selecting the object will create a clone or copy of the object. You can select more than one object by pressing special keys when selecting the objects. See *Modify/Object....* You can also create a selection set of objects. See *Select/Object/Single, Select/Object/Quad, Select/Object/Fence,* and *Select/Object/Circle.*
3. As you move the mouse, the white boundary box indicates how the object will be tapered. This is done on a plane parallel to the selected viewport about the local or global axis. See *Modify/Axis/Show,* Local Axis icon. You can use the [Tab] key to cycle through different unidirectional cursor which allows you select the side of the object to taper.
4. When your object has the desired taper, click to place the object. If the results are not what you wanted, press the **Fetch** button ([Ctrl][F]) to restore the original geometry and configuration.

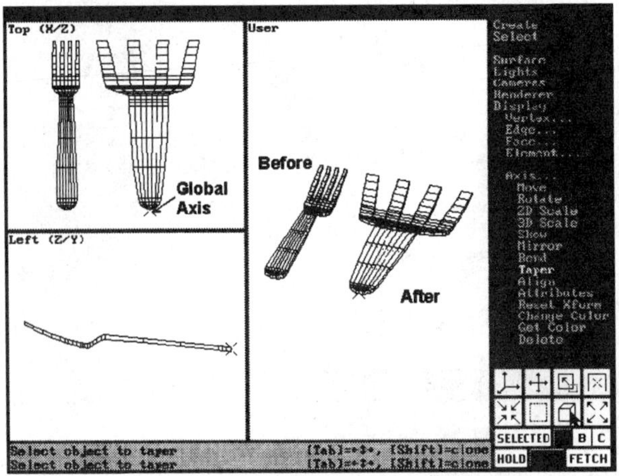

Tapering an object about the global axis in the Top view.

RELATED COMMANDS

Modify/Object..., *Select/Object/Single, Select/Object/Quad, Select/Object/Fence, Select/Object/Circle, Views–Use Snap, Views–Use Grid, Modify/Axis/Show*

Select
Modify
Element...
Object...
Move
Rotate
2D Scale
3D Scale
Skew
Mirror
Bend
Taper
Align
Attributes
Reset XForm
Change Color

Modify/Object/Align

Aligns a selected face of an object so that it is coplanar to the plane of the active viewport.

Aligning an Object

1. Press the **Hold** button (Ctrl H) to store the current state of your geometry, viewport configuration, and selection set.
2. Select a face in the object you want to align.
3. Select one of the following options from the Align method: selection box:

   Facing Toward: Aligns the selected face so the face normal is toward you.

   Facing Away: Aligns the selected face so the face normal is away from you.
4. When you click the mouse in the active viewport, the selected face is aligned with the construction plane that is parallel to the active viewport. The rest of the object is also moved, based upon the alignment of the selected face. If the results are not what you wanted, press the **Fetch** button (Ctrl F) to restore the original geometry and configuration.

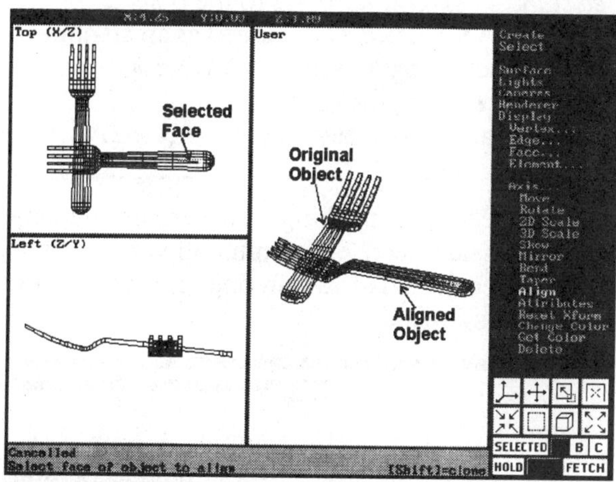

Aligning a selected face of an object to the Top viewport.

RELATED COMMANDS

Modify/Object..., Modify/Face/Align

Select
Modify
Element...
Object...
Move
Rotate
2D Scale
3D Scale
Skew
Mirror
Bend
Taper
Align
Attributes
Reset XForm
Change Color

Modify/Object/Attributes

Allows you to alter various attributes of a selected object.

Altering an Object's Attributes

Selecting an object in any viewport accesses the Object Attributes dialog box with the following options:

Old name: Displays the current name of the selected object.
New name: Enter a new unique name to rename the object.
Vertices: Displays the number of vertices in the selected object.
Faces: Displays the number of faces in the selected object.
Matte Object: If active, the object will be invisible when rendering but will block any geometry behind it. However, it will not block the background.
Cast Shadows: Active by default, meaning the object will cast shadows on other objects.
Receive Shadows: Active by default, meaning the object will receive shadows cast by other objects.
External Process Name: Accesses the AXP Selector dialog box, allowing you to assign an *animated stand-in external process* to the object.
On/Off: If turned on, the AXP process is assigned as an attribute of the object.
Settings: Used to change the settings of selected AXP programs. The AXP program must be assigned prior to selecting the object.
Load/Save: Lets you save and reload settings for selected AXP programs.

> **TIP** You can speed up rendering by accessing the Object Attributes dialog box and selectively turning off various attributes. Turning off Cast Shadows and Receive Shadows on objects whose shadows are never seen will increase rendering speed.

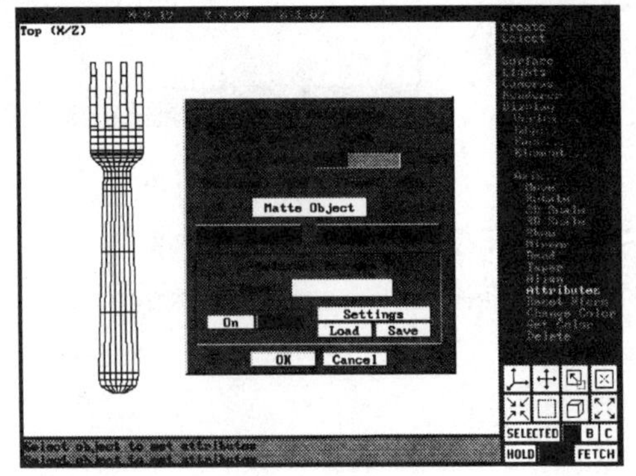

Various attributes of an object can be modified with the Object Attributes dialog box.

RELATED COMMAND

None

Modify/Object/Reset XForm

Select
Modify
Element...
Object...
Move
Rotate
2D Scale
3D Scale
Skew
Mirror
Bend
Taper
Align
Attributes
Reset XForm
Change Color

Resets the orientation of the local axis of a selected object with the world coordinate system.

Resetting the Local Axis of an Object

1. Select the object you want to realign.
2. At the Reset transform of Object(s) box, select OK. The object's bounding box is now realigned square to the world axis. The object itself is not affected when realigning the bounding box.

> **NOTE** When an object is created, a bounding box is also created that encloses the object. As the object is rotated and modified, the bounding box no longer relates to the world axis. The *Modify/Object/Reset XForm* command can be used to realign the sides of the bounding box so they correspond to the world axis.

> **TIP** The *Modify/Object/Reset XForm* command can be used to coordinate the Local Axis of an object with the world coordinates used by the Keyframer. See *Hierarchy/Object Pivot* in the Keyframer.

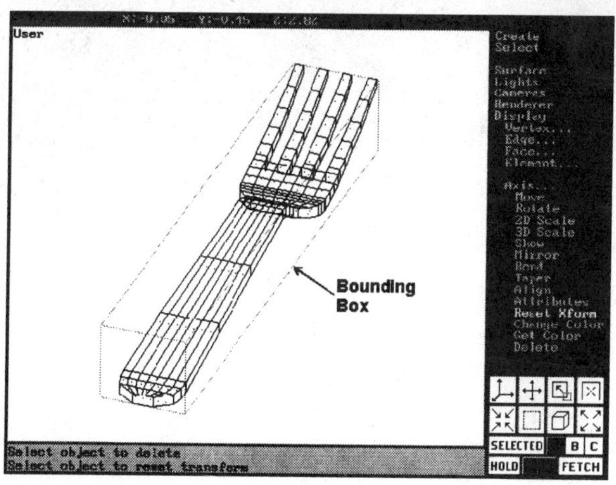

An object's bounding box is fixed when the object is created.

RELATED COMMAND

Hierarchy/Object Pivot in the Keyframer

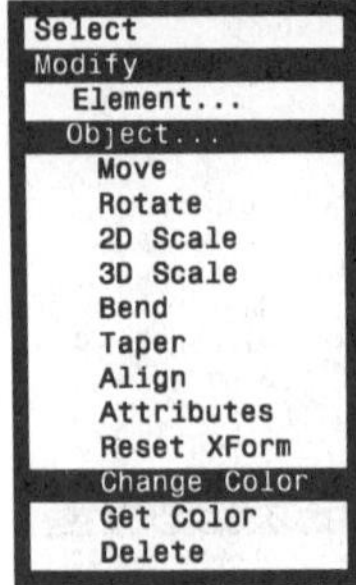

Modify/Object/Change Color

Allows you to change the display color of a selected object.

Changing an Object's Color

1. Select *Modify/Object/Change Color* and click on the object. You can also create a selection set of objects to change the color of. See *Select/Object/Single, Select/Object/Quad, Select/Object/Fence,* and *Select/Object/Circle.*
2. In the Recolor Object dialog box, select the color you want the object(s) to be, and click on **OK**.
3. The object is now redisplayed in the selected color.

The Recolor Object dialog box will display a solid white box if your display is not set up to show 256 colors.

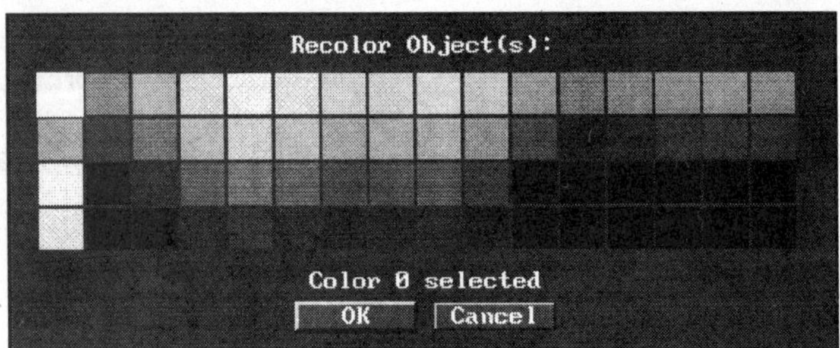

The Recolor Object dialog box can be used to change the color of an existing object.

RELATED COMMAND

Select/Object/By Color

Modify/Object/Get Color

Select
Modify
Element...
Object...
Move
Rotate
2D Scale
3D Scale
Bend
Taper
Align
Attributes
Reset XForm
Change Color
Get Color
Delete

Changes either the create color or active color to a color selected from an object.

Getting an Object's Color

1. Select *Modify/Object/Get Color* and click on the object you want to get the color from.
2. The Place color into: dialog box appears, asking you where you want the color placed.

   Create Color: The color of the selected object is placed in the color swatch between the **Hold** and **Fetch** buttons. Any subsequent objects created will have this color.

   Active Color: Sets the active color in the Recolor Object(s) dialog box. See *Modify/Object/Change Color*. This will allow you to easily assign other objects the same color by simply selecting in the Recolor Object dialog box.

   Cancel: Cancels the command.

NOTE The create color is color used when new objects are created. It appears in the color swatch between the **Hold** and **Fetch** buttons. The active color is the color outlined in white in the Recolor Object(s) dialog box.

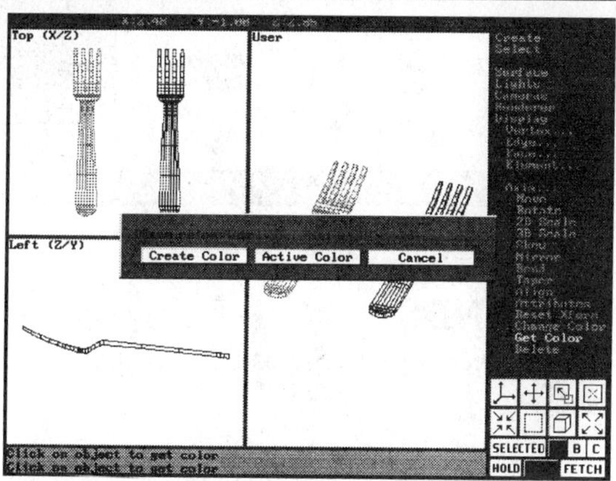

Using the Get Color option allows you to assign a color from a selected object as the active color or the create color.

RELATED COMMAND

Select/Object/By Color

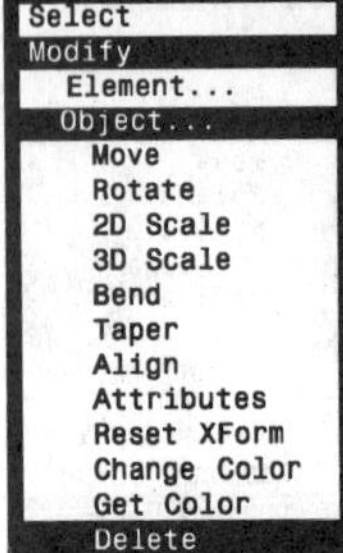

Modify/Object/Delete

Deletes single or selected objects.

Deleting Selected Objects

1. Press the **Hold** button (Ctrl H) to store the current state of your geometry, viewport configuration, and selection set.
2. Select the object you want to delete. You can select more than one object by pressing special keys when selecting the vertices. See *Modify/Object....* You can also create a selection set of vertices. See *Select/Object/Single, Select/Object/Quad, Select/Object/Fence,* and *Select/Object/Circle.*
3. Click in any viewport. At the Delete Object(s)? box, select **OK** to delete the selected object.
4. If the results are not what you wanted, press the **Fetch** button (Ctrl F) to restore the original geometry and configuration.

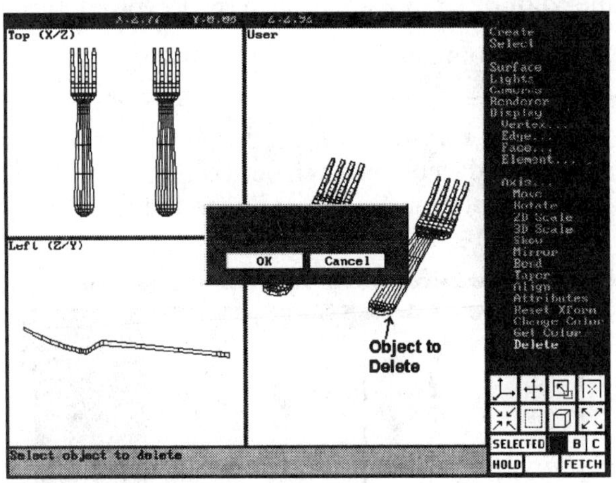

Deleting a selected object.

RELATED COMMANDS

Modify/Object..., Select/Object/Single, Select/Object/Quad, Select/Object/Fence, Select/Object/Circle.

Create
Select
Modify
Surface
Lights
Vertex...
Edge...
Face...
Element...
Object...
Axis...
Place
Align...
Show
Hide
Home

Modify/Axis/Place

Repositions the global axis.

Moving the Global Axis

1. To move the global axis, place the cursor at the desired location and click. To properly locate the axis in 3D space you need to pick points in two viewports. The axis will appear as a small black X.

If you do not want the axis displayed, you can turn it off with the *Modify/Axis/Hide* command.

You can also position the global axis by entering coordinates directly at the keyboard.

By default, the global axis is centered at 0X,0Y,0Z origin of 3D Space. You can display the axis in its current location with *Modify/Axis/Show.*

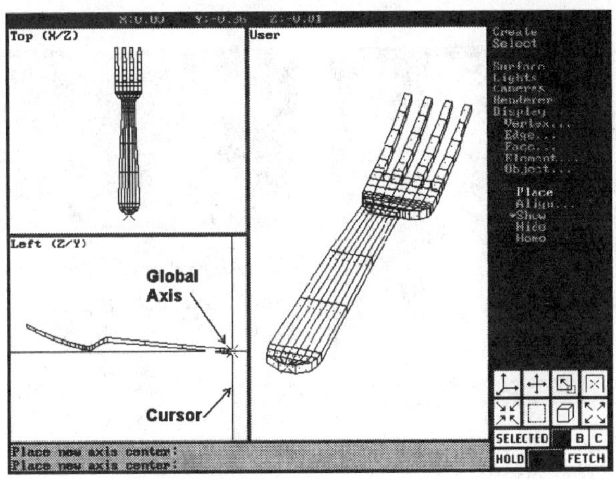

Placing the global axis.

RELATED COMMANDS

Modify/Axis/Hide, Modify/Axis/Show, Modify/Axis/Home

Create
Select
Modify
Surface
Lights
Vertex...
Edge...
Face...
Element...
Object...
Axis...
Place
Align...
Vertex
Element
Object

Modify/Axis/Align/Vertex

Aligns the global axis to a single or multiple vertices.

Aligning the Global Axis to a Single Vertex

1. Select the vertex you want to align the global axis to.
2. The axis will appear as a small black X on the selected vertex.

Aligning the Global Axis to Multiple Vertices

1. Create a selection set of vertices that you want to align the axis to. See *Select/Vertex/Quad, Select/Vertex/Fence,* and *Select/Vertex/Circle.*
2. Choose the *Modify/Axis/Align/Vertex* command, then click on the **Selected** button. Click in any viewport, and the Alignment Options dialog box will be displayed.
3. Select the type of alignment you want. The alignment is performed on a 2D plane represented by the current viewport. To place the axis in the center of a 3D group of vertices, perform the alignment in two different viewports.

TIP By default, vertices are displayed on the screen as a dot about the size of a pixel. To make the vertices easier to select, display the vertices as tick marks instead of dots by selecting *Display/Geometry/Vert Ticks.*

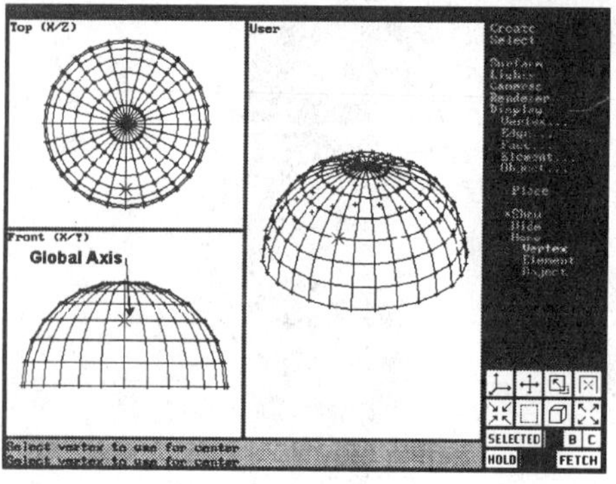

To align the global axis to a single vertex, select the vertex.

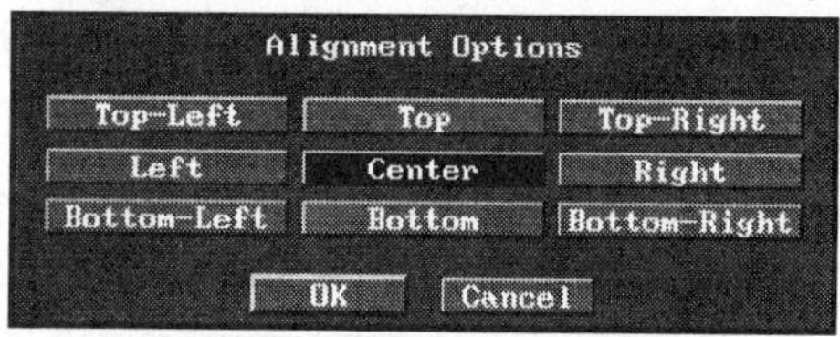

The Alignment Options dialog box allows you to select the type of desired alignment on a selection set of vertices.

RELATED COMMANDS

Modify/Axis/Hide, Modify/Axis/Show, Modify/Axis/Align/Element, Modify/Axis/Align/Object

Create
Select
Modify
Surface
Lights
Vertex...
Edge...
Face...
Element...
Object...
Axis...
Place
Align...
Vertex
Element
Object

Modify/Axis/Align/Element

Aligns the global axis to a selected element.

Aligning the Global Axis to a Selected Element

1. Select the object you want to align the axis to.
2. After selecting the element, the Alignment Options dialog box appears. Select the type of alignment. You can align the axis to the center, corners, or sides of a 2D bounding box surrounding the selected element.

> **TIP** To place the axis in the center of a 3D element, perform the alignment in two different viewports.

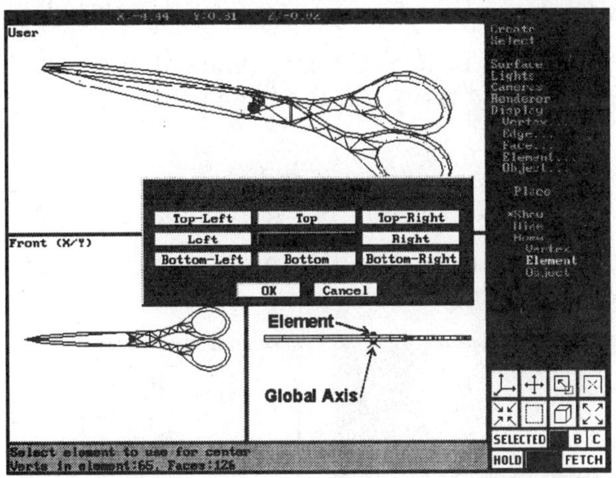

Aligning the global axis in the center of an element.

RELATED COMMANDS

Modify/Axis/Hide, Modify/Axis/Show, Modify/Axis/Align/Vertex, Modify/Axis/Align/Object

Modify/Axis/Align/Object

Aligns the global axis to single or multiple objects.

Aligning the Global Axis to a Single Object

1. Select the object you want to align the global axis to.
2. After selecting the object, the Alignment Options dialog box appears. Select the type of alignment. You can align the axis to the center, corners, or sides of a 2D bounding box surrounding the selected object.
3. The axis will appear as a small black X.

Aligning the Global Axis to Multiple Objects

1. Create a selection set of objects that you want to align the axis to. See *Select/Object/Quad, Select/Object/Fence,* and *Select/Object/Circle.*
2. Choose the *Modify/Axis/Align/Object* command, then click on the **Selected** button. Click in any viewport, and the Alignment Options dialog box will be displayed.
3. Select the type of alignment you want. You can align the axis to the center, corners, or sides of a 2D bounding box surrounding all of the selected objects.
4. To place the axis in the center of a 3D group of objects, perform the alignment again in a different orthogonal viewport.

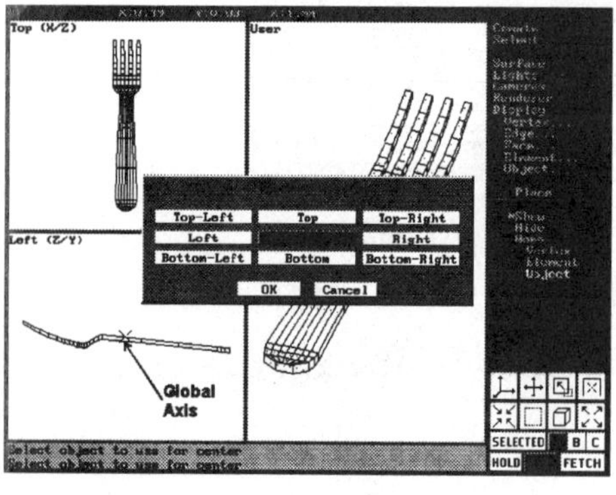

Aligning the global axis in the center of a selected object.

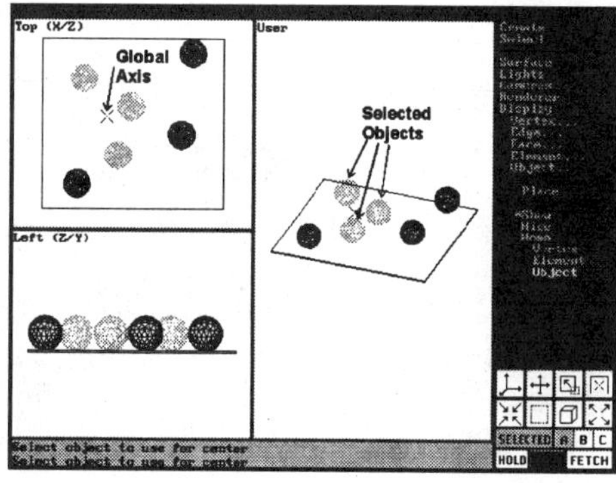

Aligning the global axis in the center of a group of objects.

RELATED COMMANDS

Modify/Axis/Hide, Modify/Axis/Show, Modify/Axis/Align/Vertex, Modify/Axis/Align/Element

Modify/Axis/Show

Create
Select
Modify
Surface
Lights
Vertex...
Edge...
Face...
Element...
Object...
Axis...
Place
Align...
Show
Hide
Home

Displays the global axis.

Displaying the Global Axis

1. To display the global axis, select *Modify/Axis/Show.*

NOTE After selecting *Modify/Axis/Show,* an asterisk appears next to the command. If you still do not see the global axis, click on the Zoom Out icon.

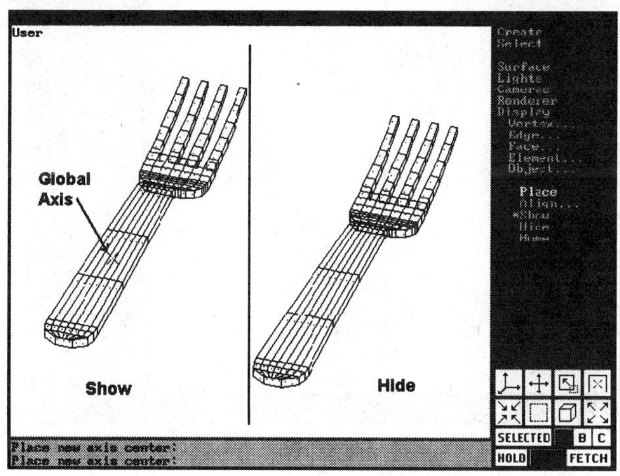

The global axis appears as a small black X.

RELATED COMMANDS

Modify/Axis/Place, Modify/Axis/Home Modify/Axis/Hide

Create
Select
Modify
Surface
Lights
Vertex...
Edge...
Face...
Element...
Object...
Axis...
Place
Align...
Show
Hide
Home

Modify/Axis/Hide

Hides the global axis if it is currently displayed.

Hiding the Global Axis

1. To hide the global axis, select *Modify/Axis/Hide*.

NOTE Hiding the global axis has no effect on any command that uses it.

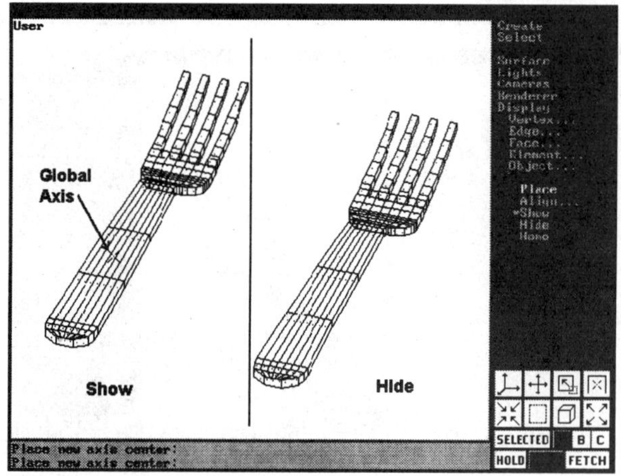

Hiding the global axis.

RELATED COMMANDS

Modify/Axis/Place, Modify/Axis/Show, Modify/Axis/Home

Modify/Axis/Home

Create
Select
Modify
Surface
Lights
Vertex...
Edge...
Face...
Element...
Object...
Axis...
Place
Align...
Show
Hide
Home

Resets the global axis to the 0X, 0Y, 0X location, the origin of 3D Editor space.

Sending the Global Axis Home

1. To reset the global axis to the default location of 0X, 0Y, 0Z, select *Modify/Axis/Home*.

> **NOTE** If the global axis does not appear as a small black X in the drawing area, first check wheter there is an asterisk before the *Modify/Axis/Show* command. This indicates whether the axis is currently displayed. If it still is not visible on the screen, click on the Zoom Out icon until it becomes visible.

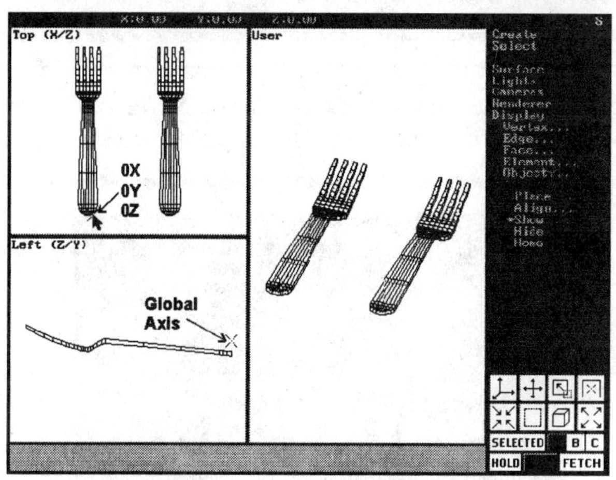

Resetting the global axis to its default position.

RELATED COMMANDS

Modify/Axis/Place, Modify/Axis/Show, Modify/Axis/Hide

Modify
Surface
Lights
Cameras
Material...
Smoothing...
Normals...
Mapping...
Choose
Acquire
Show
Rename
Get Library
Make Library
Assign...
Box...

Surface/Material/Choose

Selects a material from the current material library.

Choosing a Material

1. Click on *Surface/Material/Choose* to access the Material Selector dialog box. The dialog box lists all materials in the current materials library.
2. Select the desired material. For a complete explanation of all codes regarding the materials, see *Material–Get Material* in the Materials editor.

You can change the material library with *Surface/Material/Get Library.* You can change the material library with *Surface/Material/Get Library.*

NOTE

Selecting the **Default** button on the Material Selector dialog box will use the default white Phong plastic material.

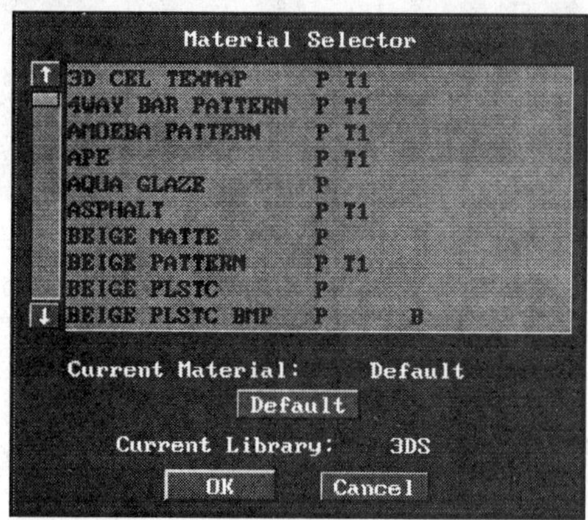

The Material Selector dialog box is used to select the current material.

RELATED COMMANDS

Surface/Material/Assign, Surface/Material/Get Library

Surface/Material/Acquire

Modify
Surface
Lights
Cameras
Material...
Smoothing...
Normals...
Mapping...
Choose
Acquire
Show
Rename
Get Library
Make Library
Assign...
Box...

Obtains a material assigned to an existing object and allows you to use that material as the current material.

Acquiring a Material

1. Choose *Surface/Material/Acquire*, then select an object in any viewport to display the Material Selector dialog box.
2. The Material Selector dialog box lists all materials assigned to the selected object. Depending on the object selected, more than one material may be displayed.
3. Click on the name of a material that you want to be the current material. The name of the selected material will appear following the Current Material: label.
4. After selecting the material, click on **OK**. You can now use *Surface/Material/Assign* to use the selected material on other objects.

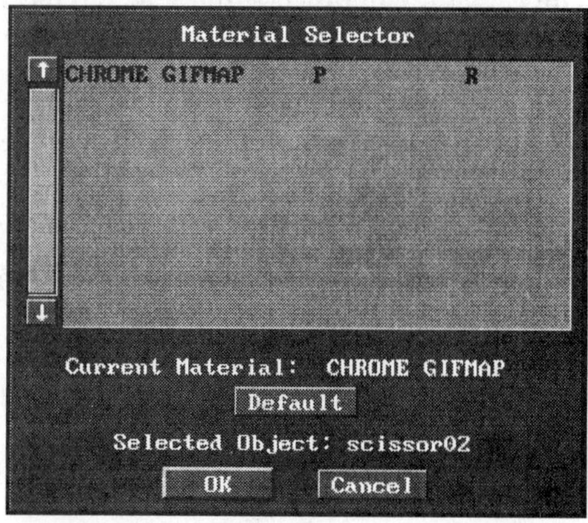

Use Surface/Material/Acquire to obtain a material assigned to an existing object.

RELATED COMMAND

Surface/Material/Assign

```
Modify
Surface
Lights
Cameras
  Material...
  Smoothing...
  Normals...
  Mapping...
    Choose
    Acquire
    Show
    Rename
    Get Library
    Make Library
    Assign...
    Box...
```

Surface/Material/Show

Shows all materials assigned to objects in the scene.

Showing All Materials in the Scene

1. Select *Surface/Material/Show* to access the Show Materials dialog box.
2. The Show Materials dialog box lists all material assigned to faces in the current scene.

Selecting Faces by Material

1. Selecting Faces by Material will add geometry to the current selection set. To clear the selection set, first use *Select/None* before selecting faces by material.
2. To select a face by material, first access the Show Materials dialog box by selecting *Surface/Material/Show*.
3. In the Show Materials dialog box, click on one or more materials. After clicking on a material, an asterisk will precede the selected names. Alternately click on **All** to select all materials, or **None** to deselect all materials.
4. After selecting the desired materials, click on **OK**. All faces that contain the selected materials turn red, indicating they are part of the current selection set. See *Select/Face/Single*.

TIP You can use *Selecting Faces by Material* to assign new material to faces previously assigned a material.

1. Use *Select/None* to clear the selection set.
2. Use *Surface/Material/Show* to select the faces assigned the old material.
3. Use *Surface/Material/Choose* and select the new material you want to assign to the selected faces.
4. Use *Surface/Material/Assign/Face*, clicking on the **Selected** button to assign the new material to the selected faces.

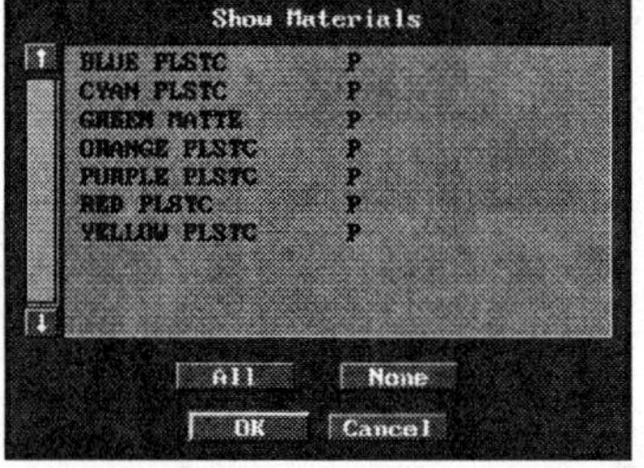

The Show Materials dialog box lists all materials used in the current scene.

RELATED COMMANDS

Surface/Material/Choose, Surface/Material/Assign/Face

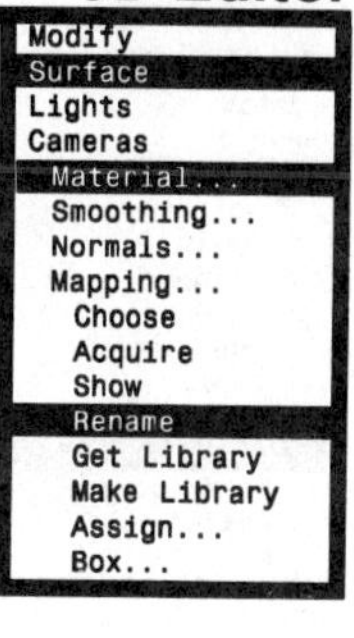

Surface/Material/Rename

Allows you to rename any material in the current scene.

Renaming a Material

1. Select *Surface/Material/Rename* to access the Rename Material dialog box. The dialog box lists all materials currently used in the scene.
2. Select the material you want to rename, and click on **OK**.
3. When the second Rename Material dialog box appears, enter the new name in the edit field, and click on **Rename**.

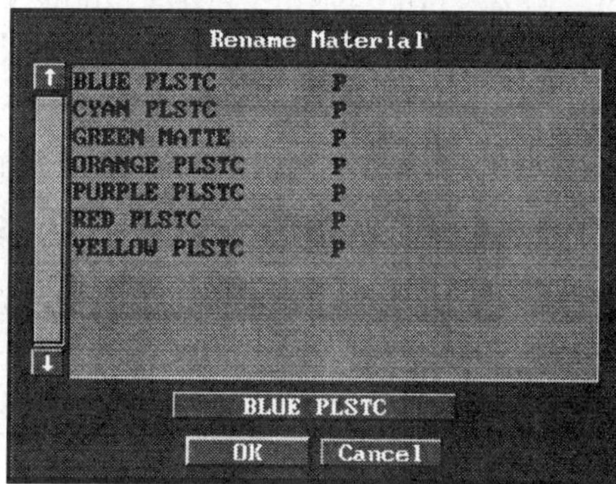

To rename a material, first select the material you want to rename.

Rename Material
Current name: BLUE PLSTC
New name: BLUE PLSTC
Rename
Cancel

Enter the new name in the edit field to rename the selected material.

RELATED COMMAND

Surface/Material/Show

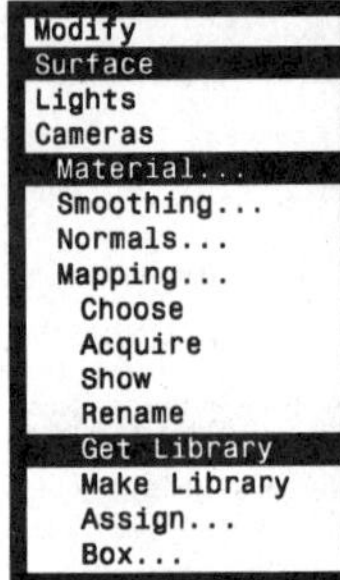

Surface/Material/Get Library

Selects and loads a new materials library, replacing the current materials library in memory.

Selecting a New Materials Library

1. Select *Surface/Material/Get Library* to access the Select a material library to load dialog box.
2. Change to the appropriate drive and directory, and load the new materials library. Library files have an **.mli* file extension.

Loading a new materials library does not have any effect on the materials already assigned to objects in the current scene.

TIP

Each material in the scene must have a unique name. If you have two materials in the scene with the same name, rename the new material in the Materials Editor. See *Current Material* in the Materials Editor. To globally replace all old materials in the scene with the new material, use *Surface/Material/Assign/Update*.

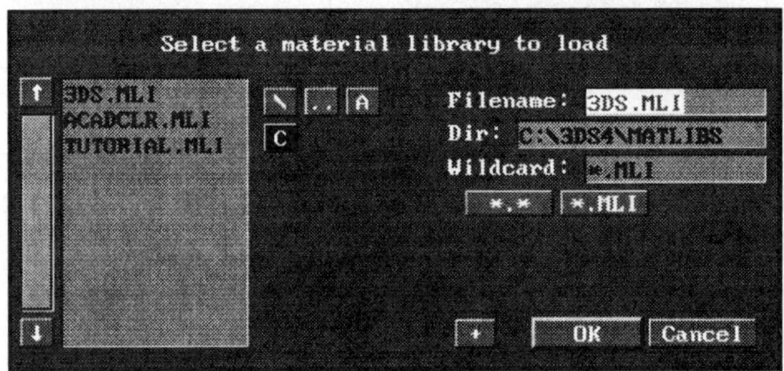

Loading a new materials library does not have any effect on materials used in the current scene.

RELATED COMMAND

Surface/Material/Make Library

Surface/Material/Make Library

Modify
Surface
Lights
Cameras
Material...
Smoothing...
Normals...
Mapping...
Choose
Acquire
Show
Rename
Get Library
Make Library
Assign...
Box...

Saves a new materials library with all materials assigned to geometry in the current scene.

Making a New Materials Library

1. Select *Surface/Material/Make Library* to access the Select a material library to save dialog box.
2. Change to the appropriate drive and directory and enter the name of the new materials library. Click on **OK** to create the new library.

> **TIP** Because a new materials library only contains material definitions from the current model, you can save these material definitions as the basis for creating new custom material libraries. See *Library–Merge Library* in the Materials Editor.

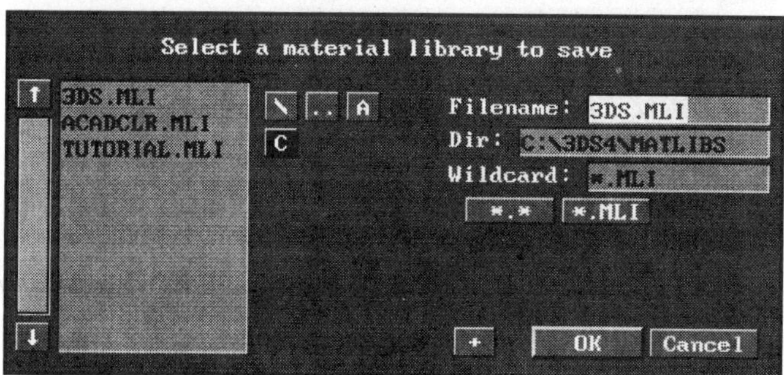

To save a new materials library, enter the new filename.
Note that the filename in the file selector defaults to the last materials library loaded.

RELATED COMMANDS

Library–Merge Library, Library–Save Library, Library–Delete Library all in the Materials Editor.

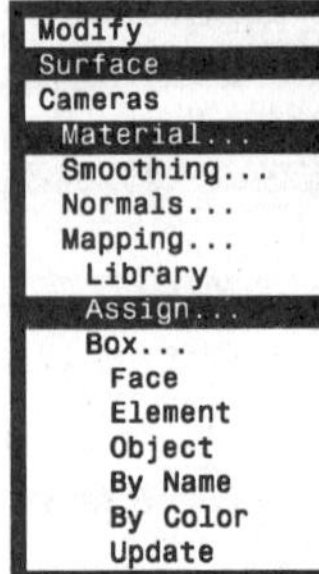

Surface/Material/Assign...

Assigns the current material to faces, elements, or objects.

Assigning a Material to a Face, Element, or Object

1. Select the material to assign to the object. See *Surface/Material/Choose* and *Surface/Material/Acquire*.
2. Selecting *Surface/Material/Assign* displays a list of subcommands, allowing you to assign the material to faces, elements, or objects.

NOTE When using any of the Assign commands, it is possible to assign a material that has the same name as an already assigned material but has different properties. When this happens, 3D Studio displays a Caution box.

The Caution box is displayed if you attempt to assign a new material to the scene that already is using the same material name.

Caution Box Options

Update: Assigns the *new* material to the selected geometry.

Use Mesh: Assigns the *previous* material to the selected geometry.

Cancel: Cancels the new materials assignment.

TIP To keep the original material assignments and use the new material, go to the Materials Editor and display the new material. Click on the material name in the box after Current Material: and rename the material with a unique name.

RELATED COMMANDS

Surface/Assign/Face, Surface/Assign/Element, Surface/Assign/Object, Surface/Assign/By Name, Surface/Assign/By Color

Surface/Material/Assign/Face

Modify
Surface
Cameras
Material...
Smoothing...
Normals...
Mapping...
Library
Assign...
Box...
Face
Element
Object
By Name
By Color
Update

Assigns the current material to single or multiple faces.

Assigning a Material to a Single Face

1. Select the material you want to assign to the face with *Surface/Material/Choose* or *Surface/Material/Acquire.*
2. Select *Surface/Material/Assign/Face* and select the face you want to assign the material to. You can create a selection set of faces by holding down the [Ctrl] key when clicking on a face.
3. Click on **OK** to assign the material.

Assigning a Material to Multiple Faces

1. Select the material you want to assign to the faces with *Surface/Material/Choose* or *Surface/Material/Acquire.*
2. Create a selection set of faces. See *Select/Face/Single, Select/Face/Quad, Select/Face/Fence,* and *Select/Face/Circle.*
3. Select Surface/Material/Assign/Face and click on the **Selected** button.
4. Click in any viewport, and click on **OK** to assign the material.

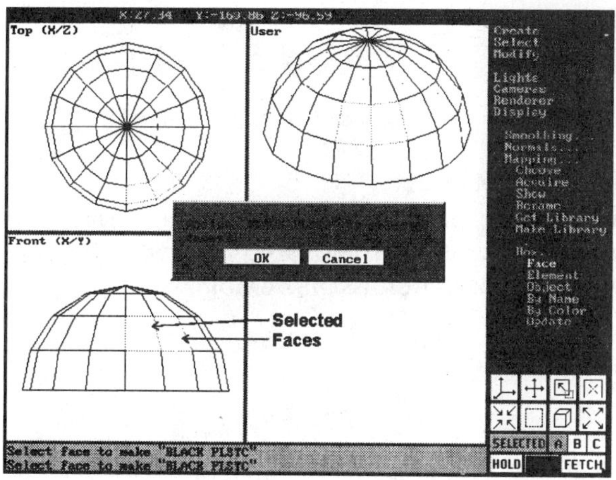

Assigning a material to selected faces.

RELATED COMMANDS

Surface/Material/Assign..., Surface/Material/Choose, Surface/Material/Acquire, Surface/Material/Assign/Element, Surface/Material/Assign/Object, Surface/Material/Assign/By Name, Surface/Material/Assign/By Color

Modify
Surface
Cameras
Material...
Smoothing...
Normals...
Mapping...
Library
Assign...
Box...
Face
Element
Object
By Name
By Color
Update

Surface/Material/Assign/Element

Assigns the current material to a selected element.

Assigning a Material to a Selected Element

1. Select the material you want to assign to the element with *Surface/Material/Choose* or *Surface/Material/Acquire*.
2. Click on the element you want to assign the material to.
3. Click on **OK** to assign the material to the element.

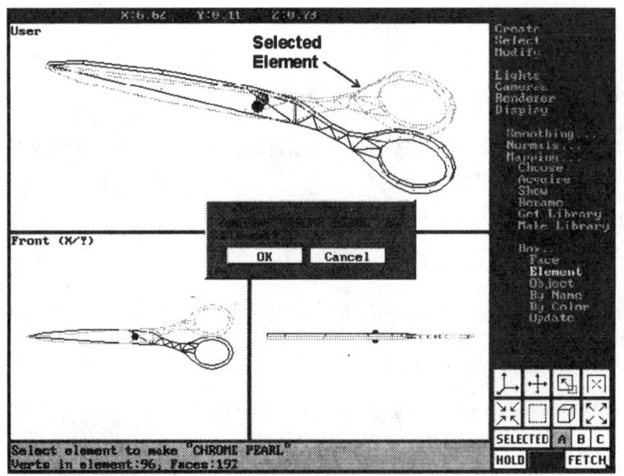

Assigning a material to a selected element.

RELATED COMMANDS

Surface/Material/Assign..., Surface/Material/Choose, Surface/Material/Acquire, Surface/Material/Assign/Face, Surface/Material/Assign/Object, Surface/Material/Assign/By Name, Surface/Material/Assign/By Color

Surface/Material/Assign/Object

Modify
Surface
Cameras
Material...
Smoothing...
Normals...
Mapping...
Library
Assign...
Box...
Face
Element
Object
By Name
By Color
Update

Assigns the current material to single or multiple objects.

Assigning a Material to a Single Object

1. Select the material you want to assign to the object with *Surface/Material/Choose* or *Surface/Material/Acquire*.
2. Select *Surface/Material/Assign/Object* and select the object you want to assign the material to. You can create a selection set of objects by holding down the Ctrl key when clicking on an object.
3. Click on **OK** to assign the material.

Assigning a Material to Multiple Objects

1. Select the material you want to assign to the objects with *Surface/Material/Choose* or *Surface/Material/Acquire*.
2. Create a selection set of objects. See *Select/Object/Single*, *Select/Object/Quad*, *Select/Object/Fence*, and *Select/Object/Circle*.
3. Select *Surface/Material/Assign/Object* and click on the **Selected** button.
4. Click in any viewport, and click on **OK** to assign the material.

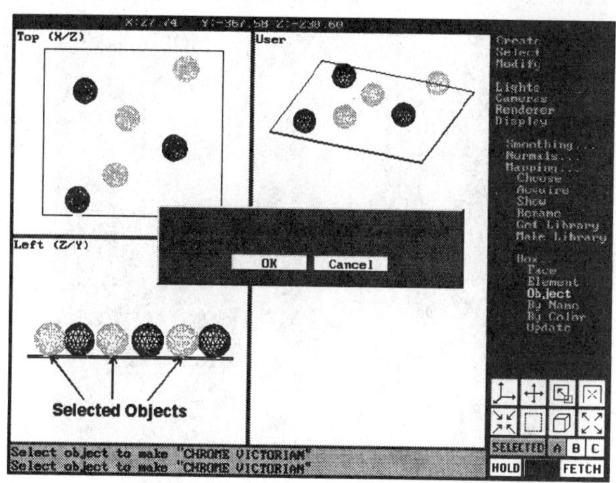

Assigning a material to selected objects.

RELATED COMMANDS

Surface/Material/Assign..., Surface/Material/Choose, Surface/Material/Acquire, Surface/Material/Assign/Face, Surface/Material/Assign/Element, Surface/Material/Assign/By Name, Surface/Material/Assign/By Color

Modify
Surface
Cameras
Material...
Smoothing...
Normals...
Mapping...
Library
Assign...
Box...
Face
Element
Object
By Name
By Color
Update

Surface/Material/Assign/By Name

Assigns the current material to objects selected by name.

Assigning Material to Objects Selected by Name

1. Select the material you want to assign to the objects with *Surface/Material/Choose* or *Surface/Material/Acquire.*
2. Selecting *Surface/Material/Assign/By Name* accesses a dialog box listing all displayed objects in the scene by name.
3. Tagging the objects causes an asterisk to appear next to the name. Tagged objects will have the current material assigned to them. You also have the following options:

   All: Tags all names in the list.

   None: Untags all names in the list.

   Tag: Tags multiple names. Begin by entering the name in the text box above the button. You can use wild cards to tag several names. For example, entering **B*** in the text box will tag all names beginning with the letter B.

   Untag: Untags multiple names. As with **Tag,** you can use wild cards.
4. Click on **OK** to assign the current material to all tagged objects.

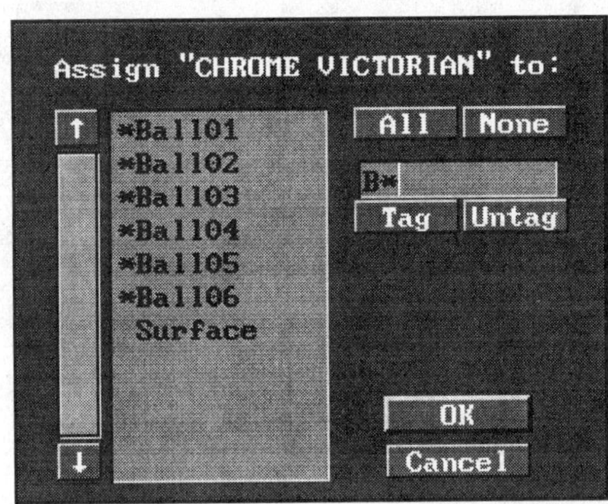

Assigning the current material to objects by name, using the wild card option.

RELATED COMMANDS

Surface/Material/Assign..., Surface/Material/Choose, Surface/Material/Acquire, Surface/Material/Assign/Face, Surface/Material/Assign/Element, Surface/Material/Assign/Object, Surface/Material/Assign/By Color

Surface/Material/Assign/By Color

Assigns the current material to objects selected by color.

Modify
Surface
Cameras
Material...
Smoothing...
Normals...
Mapping...
Library
Assign...
Box...
Face
Element
Object
By Name
By Color
Update

Assigning Material to Objects Selected by Color

1. To assign material to objects by color, you first must have objects with assigned colors. See *Modify/Object/Change Color.*
2. Select the material you want to assign to the objects with *Surface/Material/Choose* or *Surface/Material/Acquire.*
3. Select *Surface/Material/Assign/By Color.*
4. Selecting an object with a defined color will assign the current material to all other objects with the same color.
5. Click on **OK** to assign the current material to all objects with the same color.

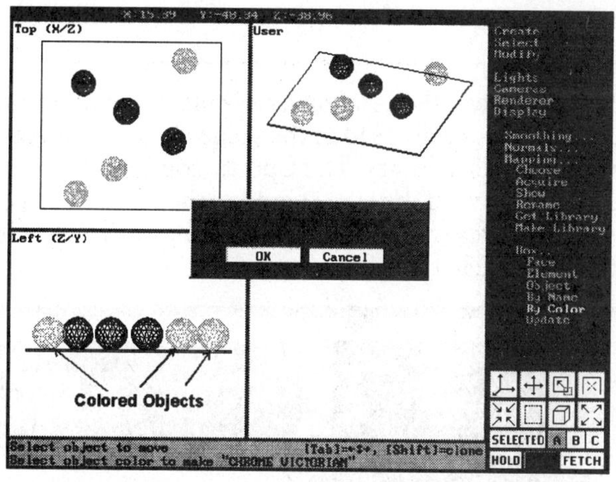

Assigning the current material to all objects with the same color.

RELATED COMMANDS

Surface/Material/Assign..., Surface/Material/Choose, Surface/Material/Acquire, Surface/Material/Assign/Face, Surface/Material/Assign/Element, Surface/Material/Assign/Object, Surface/Material/Assign/By Name

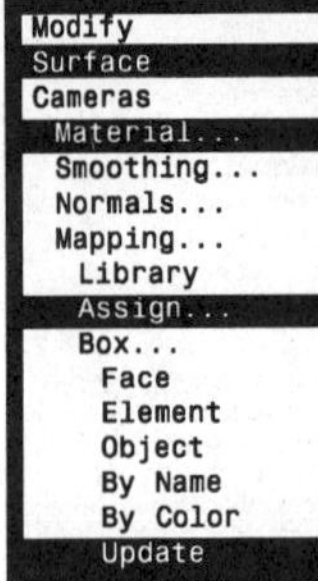

Surface/Material/Assign/Update

Updates all materials in the scene with materials in the current library.

Updating All Materials

1. Select the materials library you want to use with *Surface/Material/Get Library*.
2. Selecting *Surface/Material/Assign/Update* will display a warning box, giving you the option of continuing. Select **OK** to update all materials.
3. If all material names in the scene are the same as material names in the current library, an information box is displayed saying, All materials updated.
4. If not all material names in the scene are the same as material names in the current library, an information box will be displayed informing how many materials were updated.

NOTE Although each material in a *scene* must have a unique name, you can have materials used in the scene with the same name as materials in the materials library. The Update command will update all currently assigned materials with the same name as those materials in the current library. It is possible, however, to have a material in the library with a different property than the material in the scene.

This operation will update all materials in the scene with those in the library.
Are you sure you want to continue?
OK Cancel

The warning box giving you the option of updating all materials in the current scene.

Updated 0 of 7 materials in mesh
Continue

The information box displaying how many materials were updated.

RELATED COMMANDS

Surface/Material/Select, Surface/Material/Get Library

Surface/Material/Box/Assign

Modify
Surface
Cameras
Material...
Smoothing...
Normals...
Mapping...
Show
Rename
Get Library
Make Library
Assign...
Box...
Assign
Modify
Acquire

Allows you to assign six different materials to single or multiple objects.

Assigning Materials to an Object with a Box

1. Select *Surface/Material/Box/Assign* and select an object.
2. In the Assign Box Materials dialog box, select each of the six buttons to assign a material to the specified side. Each time you select a button, a material selector box appears allowing you to select a material.
3. Select **OK**. When the object is rendered, each of the six materials appears on the faces whose normals are facing the specified side.

NOTE: This is a special form of material assignment that can apply six different materials to different sides of an object, based on the bounding box of an object. You do not need mapping coordinates, because they are ignored by the box assignment.

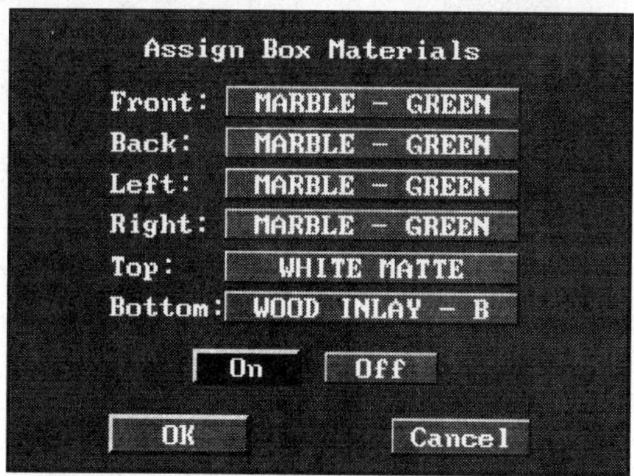

Assigning six materials to the bounding box of an object.

Assigning materials with a box is a convenient way of assigning materials to boxlike objects, such as rooms or buildings.

RELATED COMMANDS

Surface/Material/Box/Modify, Surface/Material/Box/Acquire

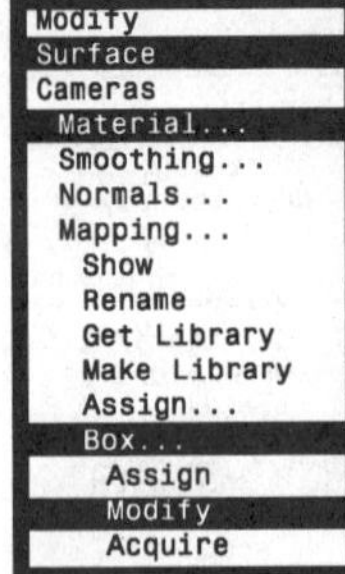

Surface/Material/Box/Modify

Edits materials assigned with the *Surface/Material/Box/Assign* command.

Editing Box Materials Assigned to an Object

1. To modify box materials, they first must have been assigned to the object with *Surface/Material/Box/Assign*.
2. Select *Surface/Material/Box/Modify* and select the object.
3. Select any of the six buttons to change the material, then select **OK**.

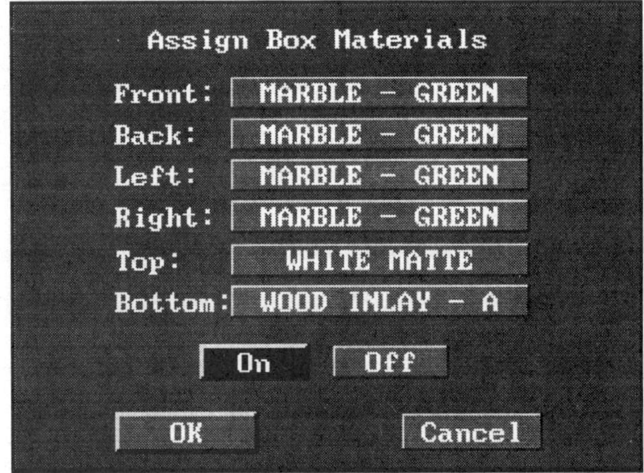

Modifying materials assigned to an object with Surface/Material/Box/Assign.

RELATED COMMANDS

Surface/Material/Box/Assign, Surface/Material/Box/Acquire

Surface/Material/Box/Acquire

Modify
Surface
Cameras
Material...
Smoothing...
Normals...
Mapping...
Show
Rename
Get Library
Make Library
Assign...
Box...
Modify
Assign
Acquire

Acquires the six box materials assigned to an object with *Surface/Material/Box/Assign*.

Copying Box Materials from One Object to Another

1. Select *Surface/Material/Box/Acquire* and click on the object that contains the desired box material.
2. Select *Surface/Material/Box/Assign* and select the object you want to assign the box materials to.
3. In the Assign Box Materials dialog box, click **OK**, or select any material to change it.

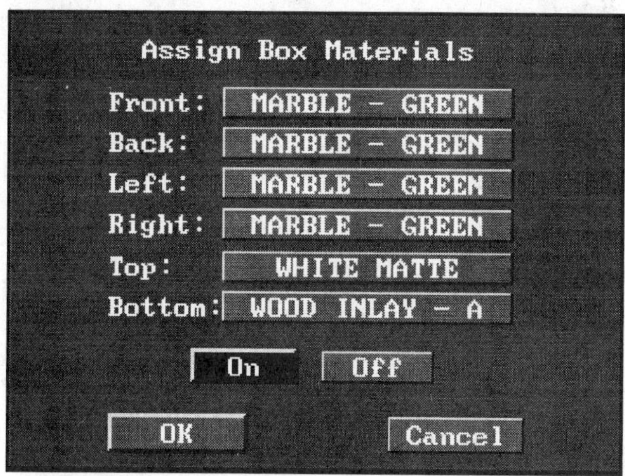

Copying box materials from one object to another.

RELATED COMMAND

Surface/Material/Box/Assign

Create
Select
Modify
Surface
Lights
Cameras
Material...
Smoothing...
Normals...
Mapping...
Group
Acquire
Show
Face...
Element...
Object...

Surface/Smoothing...

Used to define which parts of an object are rendered as smooth-shaded surfaces and which are rendered as faceted surfaces.

Understanding Smoothing

1. When arcs, circles, and splines are created in 3D Studio, they are approximated with segments, which in turn are made up of faces. The more segments and faces an object has, the smoother the curve.
2. As the segments and faces of an object increase, so does the complexity of the model. As the model becomes more complex, the screen redraws become slower, rendering time increases, and disk storage space for the model increases.
3. To maintain speed and efficiency in modeling, 3D Studio uses the concept of *smoothing*. Smoothing can create the illusion of roundness by assigning smoothing groups at the face, element, and object levels. Although the object does not change appearance in the 3D Editor when smoothed, it can be rendered as if the geometry were actually spherical.

NOTE By default, 3D Studio assigns a smoothing group to every face in an object when it is created.

TIP Smoothing does not affect an object's geometry, only the way it is rendered. The roundness of a curve's perimeter is determined by the number of faces it has when it was created. When creating a model, you need to balance the number of faces in the object with the amount of detail needed. Balancing the number of faces in an object, combined with effective smoothing properties, can create realistic images as well as efficient models.

Applying smoothing alternately to every other row of faces.

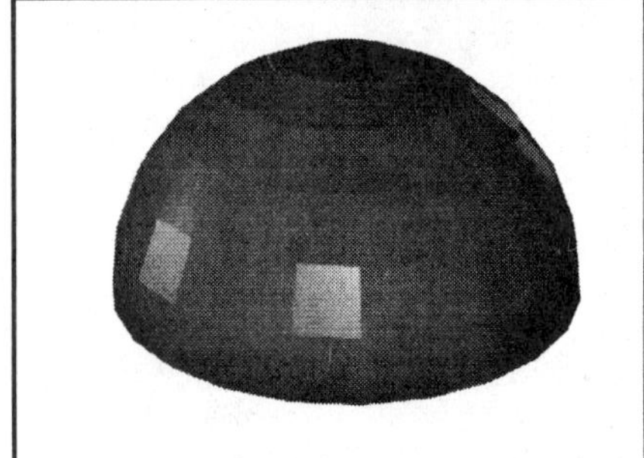

RELATED COMMAND

Surface/Smoothing/Show

Surface/Smoothing/Group

Used with the *Surface/Smoothing/.../Assign* commands to specify the current smoothing group.

Assigning a Smoothing Group

1. Selecting *Surface/Smoothing/Group* accesses the Smoothing Group Selector dialog box. Click on a smoothing group number to select it, then select OK.
2. Select the face, element, or object you want to apply a smoothing group to. See *Surface/Smoothing/Face...*, *Surface/Smoothing/Element...*, and *Surface/Smoothing/Object....*

> **TIP** A good modeling technique is to use one smoothing group for all rounded objects. Use the other 31 groups for specific smoothing occurrences.

The Smoothing Group Selector dialog box is used to assign smoothing groups to selected faces, elements, or objects.

RELATED COMMANDS

Surface/Smoothing..., Surface/Smoothing/Face, Surface/Smoothing/Element, Surface/Smoothing/Object

Create
Select
Modify
Surface
Lights
Cameras
Material...
Smoothing...
Normals...
Mapping...
Group
Acquire
Show
Face...
Element...
Object...

Surface/Smoothing/Acquire

Displays the smoothing group or groups assigned to a specific face.

Acquiring a Smoothing Group

1. Select *Surface/Smoothing/Acquire* and select a single face in the object. To select a face, first click on a vertex attatched to the face. The second click will choose the face.
2. The Acquire smoothing group dialog box appears, displaying all smoothing groups assigned to that face.
3. Highlight the smoothing group you wish to acquire, and select **OK.** That smoothing group is now the current smoothing group.

TIP After acquiring the smoothing group from a face, you can assign it using *Surface/Smoothing/Face/Assign*, *Surface/Smoothing/Element/Assign*, *Surface/Smoothing/Object/Assign.*

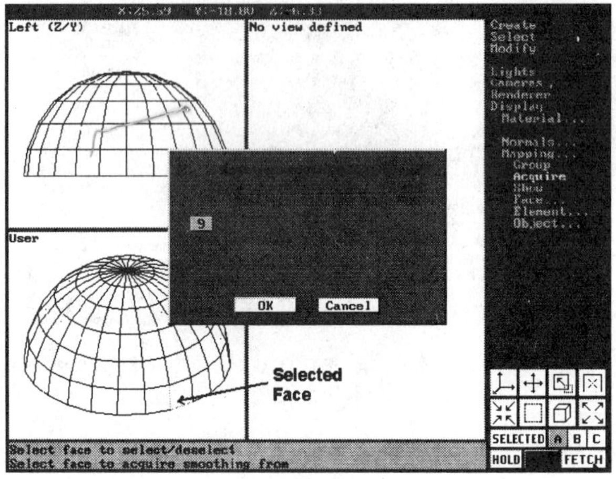

Acquiring a smoothing group from a face.

RELATED COMMANDS

Surface/Smoothing, Surface/Smoothing/Face/Assign, Surface/Smoothing/Element/Assign, Surface/Smoothing/Object/Assign

Surface/Smoothing/Show

Create
Select
Modify
Surface
Lights
Cameras
Material...
Smoothing...
Normals...
Mapping...
Group
Acquire
Show
Face...
Element...
Object...

Highlights faces that are assigned to a specific smoothing group.

Showing Faces Assigned to a Smoothing Group

1. If you currently have any objects selected (selected objects appear red), choose *Select/None*.
2. Select *Surface/Smoothing/Show* to access the Show Smoothing Groups dialog box. A numbered button appears for each smoothing group used in the current scene.
3. Click on a number to select it, then click **OK**.
4. The faces that have the assigned smoothing group appear in red as part of a selection set.

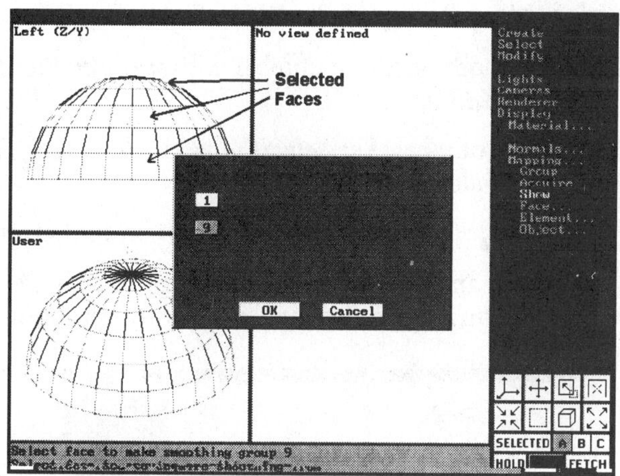

Faces assigned to a specific smoothing group appear as part of a selection set.

RELATED COMMAND

Surface/Smoothing...

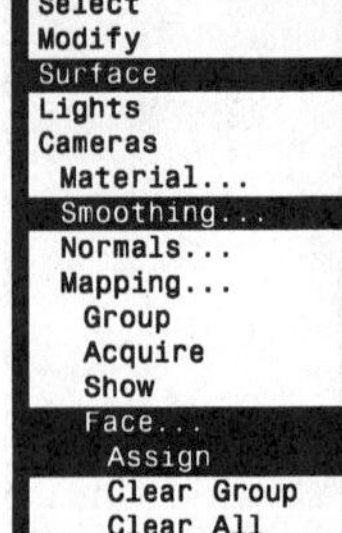

Surface/Smoothing/Face/Assign

Assigns the current smoothing group number to single or multiple faces.

Assigning a Smoothing Group to a Single Face

1. Define the current smoothing group number with *Surface/Smoothing/Group* or *Surface/Smoothing/Acquire.*
2. Select *Surface/Smoothing/Face/Assign* and click on a face. To select a face, first click on a vertex attatched to the face. The second click will choose the face.
3. You can create a selection set of faces by holding down the Ctrl key when selecting faces. The selected face is assigned the current smoothing group number.

Assigning a Smoothing Group to Multiple Faces

1. Define the current smoothing group number with *Surface/Smoothing/Group* or *Surface/Smoothing/Acquire.*
2. Create a selection set of faces. See *Select/Face/Single*, *Select/Face/Quad, Select/Face/Fence,* and *Select/Face/Circle.*
3. Choose *Surface/Smoothing/Face/Assign* and click on the **Selected** button.
4. Click in any viewport, and the current smoothing group is assigned to the selected faces. This information is displayed in the prompt line at the bottom of the screen.

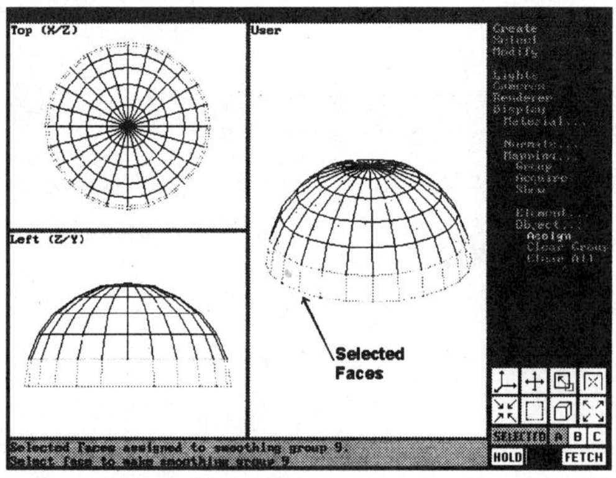

Assigning a smoothing group to a selection set of faces.

RELATED COMMANDS

Surface/Smoothing..., Surface/Smoothing/Element/Assign, Surface/Smoothing/Object/Assign

Surface/Smoothing/Face/Clear Group

Modify
Surface
Lights
Material...
Smoothing...
Normals...
Mapping...
Group
Acquire
Show
Face...
Element..
Object...
Assign
Clear Group
Clear All

Removes the current smoothing group from single or multiple faces.

Removing a Smoothing Group from a Single Face

1. Define the current smoothing group number with *Surface/Smoothing/Group* or *Surface/Smoothing/Acquire.*
2. Select *Surface/Smoothing/Face/Clear Group* and click on a face. To select a face, first click on a vertex attatched to the face. The second click will choose the face.
3. You can create a selection set of faces by holding down the [Ctrl] key when selecting faces. The current smoothing group number is removed from selected face.

Removing a Smoothing Group from Multiple Faces

1. Define the current smoothing group number with *Surface/Smoothing/Group* or *Surface/Smoothing/Acquire.*
2. Create a selection set of faces. See *Select/Face/Single*, *Select/Face/Quad*, *Select/Face/Fence,* and *Select/Face/Circle.*
3. Choose *Surface/Smoothing/Face/Clear Group* and click on the **Selected** button.
4. Click in any viewport, and the current smoothing group is cleared from the selected faces. This information is displayed in the prompt line at the bottom of the screen.

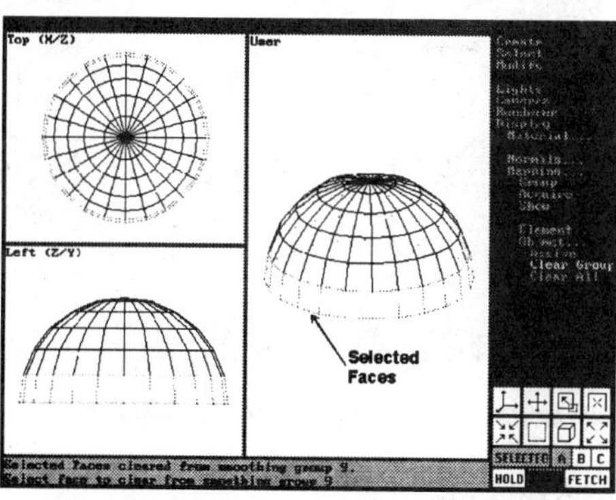

Clearing a smoothing group from a selection set of faces.

RELATED COMMANDS

Surface/Smoothing..., Surface/Smoothing/Element/Clear Group, Surface/Smoothing/Object/Clear Group

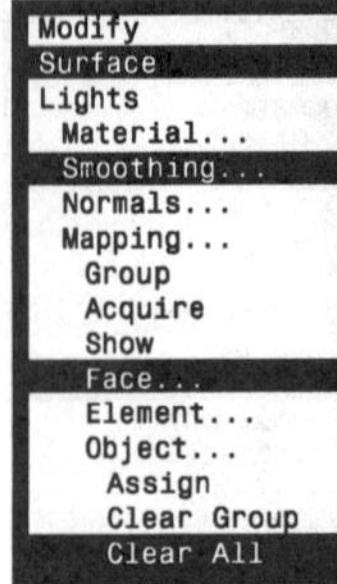

Surface/Smoothing/Face/Clear All

Clears all smoothing group numbers from single or multiple faces.

Removing all Smoothing Groups from a Single Face

1. Select *Surface/Smoothing/Face/Clear All* and click on a face. To select a face, first click on a vertex attatched to the face. The second click will choose the face.
2. You can create a selection set of faces by holding down the Ctrl key when selecting faces. All smoothing groups are removed from the selected face.

Removing all Smoothing Groups from Multiple Faces

1. Create a selection set of faces. See *Select/Face/Single*, *Select/Face/Quad*, *Select/Face/Fence,* and *Select/Face/Circle.*
2. Choose *Surface/Smoothing/Face/Clear All* and click on the **Selected** button.
3. Click in any viewport, and the current smoothing group is cleared from the selected faces. This information is displayed in the prompt line at the bottom of the screen.

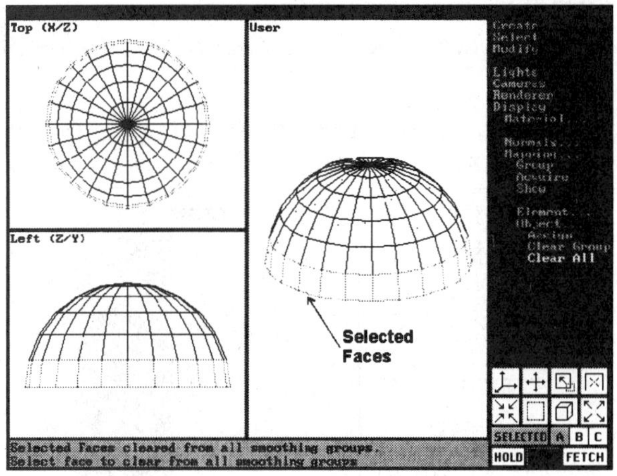

Clearing all smoothing groups from a selection set of faces.

RELATED COMMANDS

Surface/Smoothing..., Surface/Smoothing/Element/Clear Group, Surface/Smoothing/Object/Clear Group

Modify
Surface
Lights
Material...
Smoothing...
Normals...
Group
Acquire
Show
Face...
Element...
Object...
Assign
Clear Group
Clear All
Auto Smooth

Surface/Smoothing/Element/Assign

Assigns the current smoothing group number to an element.

Assigning a Smoothing Group to an Element

1. Define the current smoothing group number with *Surface/Smoothing/Group* or *Surface/Smoothing/Acquire*.
2. Select *Surface/Smoothing/Element/Assign* and click on an element. The selected element is assigned the current smoothing group number.

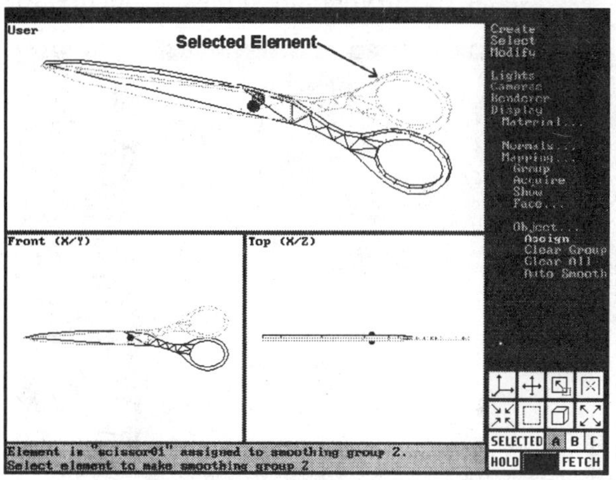

Assigning a smoothing group to an element.

RELATED COMMANDS

Surface/Smoothing, Surface/Smoothing/Face/Assign, Surface/Smoothing/Object/Assign

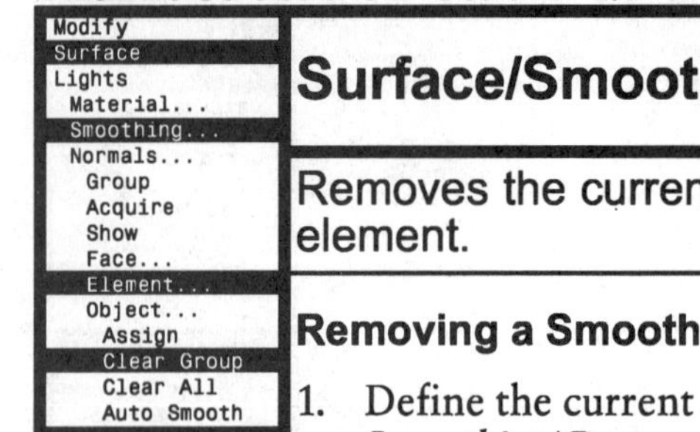

Surface/Smoothing/Element/Clear Group

Removes the current smoothing group from a selected element.

Removing a Smoothing Group from a Selected Element

1. Define the current smoothing group number with *Surface/Smoothing/Group* or *Surface/Smoothing/Acquire.*
2. Select *Surface/Smoothing/Face/Clear Group* and click on an element. The current smoothing group number is removed from the selected element. This information is displayed in the prompt line at the bottom of the screen.

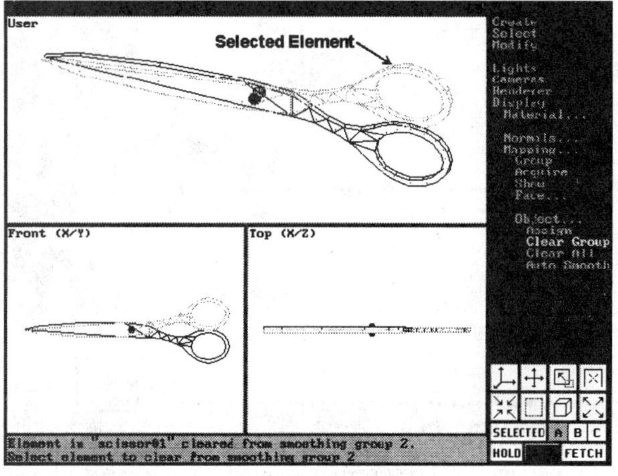

Clearing a smoothing group from a selected element.

RELATED COMMANDS

Surface/Smoothing, Surface/Smoothing/Element/Clear Group, Surface/Smoothing/Object/Clear Group

Modify
Surface
Lights
Material...
Smoothing...
Normals...
Group
Acquire
Show
Face...
Element...
Object...
Assign
Clear Group
Clear All
Auto Smooth

Surface/Smoothing/Element/Clear All

Clears all smoothing group numbers from a selected element.

Removing all Smoothing Groups from a Selected Element

1. Select *Surface/Smoothing/Element/Clear All* and click on an element.
2. All smoothing groups are removed from the selected element.

> **TIP** By default, 3D Studio assigns a smoothing group to every face in an object when it is created. If you are going to do custom smoothing, use *Surface/Smoothing/Element/Clear All* to remove all smoothing groups from the element before assigning your own smoothing.

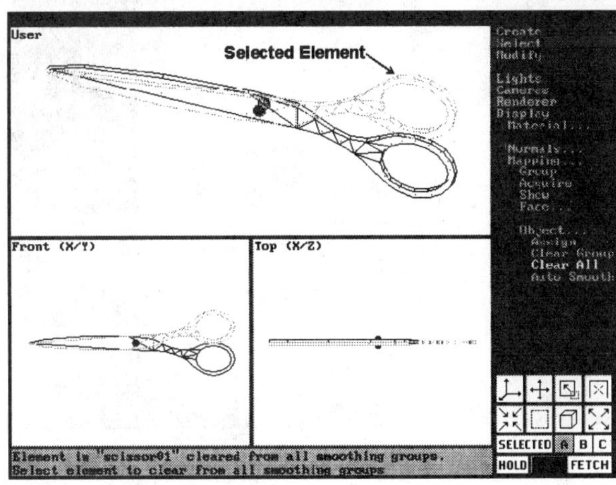

Clearing all smoothing groups from a selected element.

RELATED COMMANDS

Surface/Smoothing..., Surface/Smoothing/face/Clear Group, Surface/Smoothing/Object/Clear Group

Modify
Surface
Lights
Material...
Smoothing...
Normals...
Group
Acquire
Show
Face...
Element...
Object...
Assign
Clear Group
Clear All
Auto Smooth

Surface/Smoothing/Element/AutoSmooth

Assigns smoothing groups to an element's faces based on their angle to one another.

AutoSmoothing an Element

1. Select an element, then select *Surface/Smoothing/Element/AutoSmooth*.
2. In the Auto Smooth dialog box, enter the edge angle above which you do not want any smoothing. For examples on how the edge angle affects AutoSmoothing, see *Surface/Smoothing/Object/Auto Smooth*.

AutoSmooth is useful only if the element has varying angles.

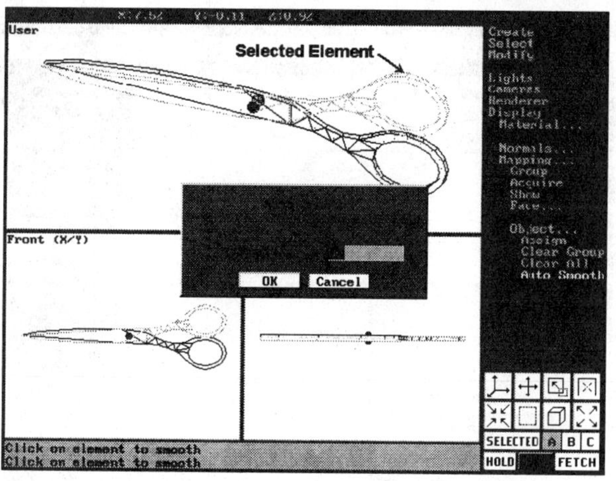

Setting AutoSmooth to 30 degrees for a selected element.

RELATED COMMANDS

Surface/Smoothing..., Surface/Smoothing/Object/Auto Smooth

Surface/Smoothing/Object/Assign

Modify
Surface
Lights
Material...
Smoothing...
Normals...
Group
Acquire
Show
Face...
Element...
Object...
Assign
Clear Group
Clear All
Auto Smooth

Assigns the current smoothing group number to single or multiple objects.

Assigning a Smoothing Group to a Single Object

1. Define the current smoothing group number with *Surface/Smoothing/Group* or *Surface/Smoothing/Acquire*.
2. Select *Surface/Smoothing/Object/Assign* and click on an object. You can create a selection set of objects by holding down the Ctrl key when selecting objects. The selected object is assigned the current smoothing group number.

Assigning a Smoothing Group to Multiple Objects

1. Define the current smoothing group number with *Surface/Smoothing/Group* or *Surface/Smoothing/Acquire.*
2. Create a selection set of objects. See *Select/Object/Single*, *Select/Object/Quad, Select/Object/Fence,* and *Select/Object/Circle.*
3. Choose *Surface/Smoothing/Object/Assign* and click on the **Selected** button.
4. Click in any viewport, and the current smoothing group is assigned to the selected objects. This information is displayed in the prompt line at the bottom of the screen.

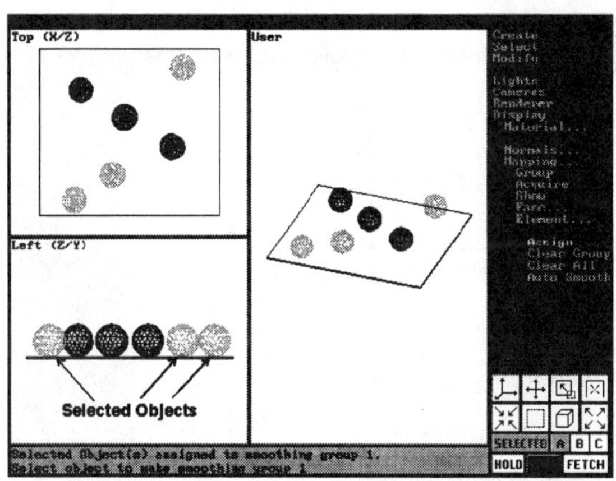

Assigning a smoothing group to a selection set of objects.

RELATED COMMANDS

Surface/Smoothing..., Surface/Smoothing/Face/Assign, Surface/Smoothing/Element/Assign

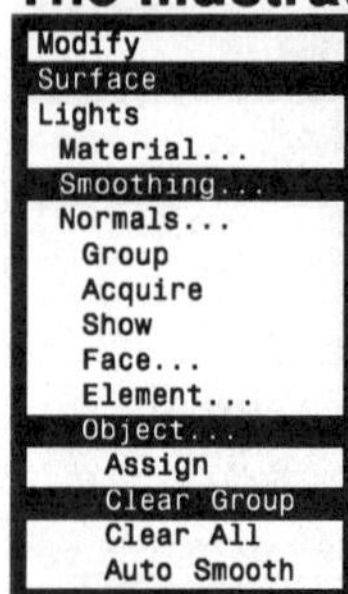

Surface/Smoothing/Object/Clear Group

Removes the current smoothing group from single or multiple objects.

Removing a Smoothing Group from a Single Object

1. Define the current smoothing group number with *Surface/Smoothing/Group* or *Surface/Smoothing/Acquire.*
2. Select *Surface/Smoothing/Object/Clear Group* and click on an object. You can create a selection set of objects by holding down the [Ctrl] key when selecting objects. The current smoothing group number is removed from selected object.

Removing a Smoothing Group from Multiple Objects

1. Define the current smoothing group number with *Surface/Smoothing/Group* or *Surface/Smoothing/Acquire.*
2. Create a selection set of objects. See *Select/Object/Single*, *Select/Object/Quad*, *Select/Object/Fence*, and *Select/Object/Circle*.
3. Choose *Surface/Smoothing/Object/Clear Group* and click on the **Selected** button.
4. Click in any viewport, and the current smoothing group is cleared from the selected objects. This information is displayed in the prompt line at the bottom of the screen.

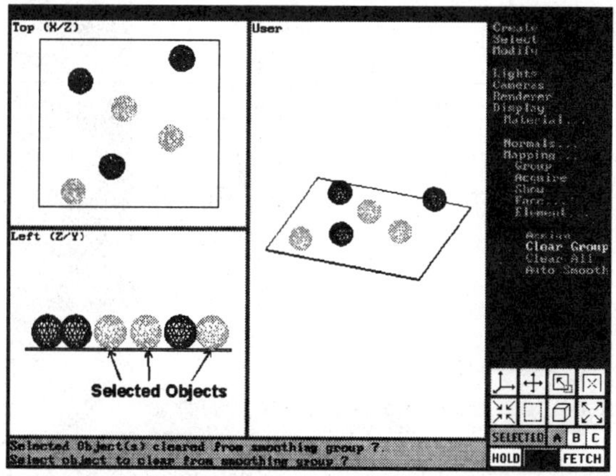

Clearing a smoothing group from a selection set of objects.

RELATED COMMANDS

Surface/Smoothing, Surface/Smoothing/Face/Clear Group, Surface/Smoothing/Element/Clear Group

Surface/Smoothing/Object/Clear All

Modify
Surface
Lights
Material...
Smoothing...
Normals...
Group
Acquire
Show
Face...
Element...
Object...
Assign
Clear Group
Clear All
Auto Smooth

Clears all smoothing group numbers from single or multiple objects.

Removing All Smoothing Groups from a Single Object

1. Select *Surface/Smoothing/Face/Clear All* and click on an object. You can create a selection set of objects by holding down the Ctrl key when selecting objects. All smoothing groups are removed from the selected object.

Removing All Smoothing Groups from Multiple Objects

1. Create a selection set of objects. See *Select/Object/Single*, *Select/Object/Quad*, *Select/Object/Fence*, and *Select/Object/Circle*.
2. Choose *Surface/Smoothing/Object/Clear All* and click on the **Selected** button.
3. Click in any viewport, and the selected objects are cleared from all smoothing groups. This information is displayed in the prompt line at the bottom of the screen.

TIP By default, 3D Studio assigns a smoothing group to every face in an object when it is created. If you are going to do custom smoothing, use *Surface/Smoothing/Element/Clear All* to remove all smoothing groups from the element before assigning your own smoothing.

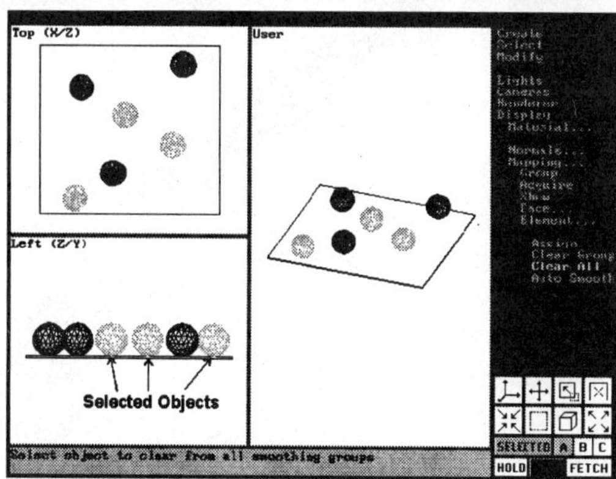

Clearing all smoothing groups from a selection set of objects.

RELATED COMMANDS

Surface/Smoothing..., Surface/Smoothing/Element/Clear All, Surface/Smoothing/Face/Clear All

Modify
Surface
Lights
Material...
Smoothing...
Normals...
Group
Acquire
Show
Face...
Element...
Object...
Assign
Clear Group
Clear All
Auto Smooth

Surface/Smoothing/Object/AutoSmooth

Automatically assigns smoothing groups to a single object's or multiple objects' faces based on their angle to one another.

AutoSmoothing an Object

1. Select an object.
2. In the Auto Smooth dialog box, enter the edge angle above which you do not want any smoothing.

AutoSmoothing Multiple Objects

1. Create a selection set of objects. See *Select/Object/Single*, *Select/Object/Quad*, *Select/Object/Fence*, and *Select/Object/Circle*.
2. Choose *Surface/Smoothing/Object/AutoSmooth* and click on the **Selected** button.
3. In the Auto Smooth dialog box, enter the edge angle above which you do not want any smoothing.

> **NOTE** AutoSmooth is useful only if the element has varying angles.

No smoothing.

AutoSmooth set to 15 degrees.

AutoSmooth set to 90 degrees.

RELATED COMMANDS

Surface/Smoothing..., Surface/Smoothing/Element/Auto Smooth

Surface/Normals/Face Flip

Create
Select
Modify
Surface
Lights
Cameras
Renderer
Display
Material...
Smoothing...
Normals...
Mapping...
Face Flip
Element Flip
Object Flip
Object Unify

Flips the direction of the surface normals on single or multiple faces.

Flipping the Normals of Selected Faces

1. Create a selection set of the faces you want to flip the normals of. See *Select/Face/Single*, *Select/Face/Quad*, *Select/Face/Fence*, and *Select/Face/Circle*.
2. Select *Surface/Normals/Face Flip*. If multiple faces were selected, click on the **Selected** button.
3. After clicking in any viewport, select **OK** in the Flip normals of Faces? box.

NOTE All faces in 3D Studio are created one-sided, with the front being the side with the surface normal. When rendering, the back side of the face is invisible to the renderer.

TIP When a face appears to be missing when rendering an object, you have three options:

1. Use *Surface/Normals/Face Flip* to reverse the normals of the missing face or faces.
2. Activate the Force 2-Sided option in the Render Still Image dialog box. This is accessed by selecting *Render/Render View*. This will render both sides of all faces in the scene, consequently increasing rendering time.
3. Apply two sided materials to the geometry. This can be done in the Materials Editor under *2-Sided*.

Flipping the normals of selected faces.

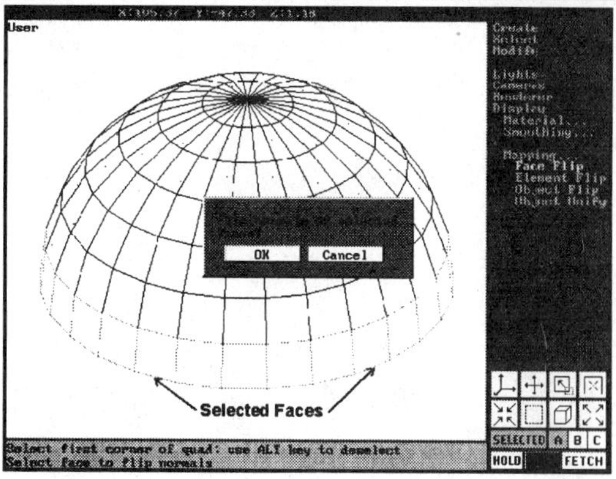

RELATED COMMANDS

Surface/Normals/Element Flip, *Surface/Normals/ Object Flip*

Create
Select
Modify
Surface
Lights
Cameras
Renderer
Display
Material...
Smoothing...
Normals...
Mapping...
Face Flip
Element Flip
Object Flip
Object Unify

Surface/Normals/Element Flip

Flips the direction of the surface normals on a selected element

Flipping the Normals of an Element

1. Select *Surface/Normals/Element Flip* and click on the element.
2. After selecting the element, select **OK** in the Flip normals of Element? box.

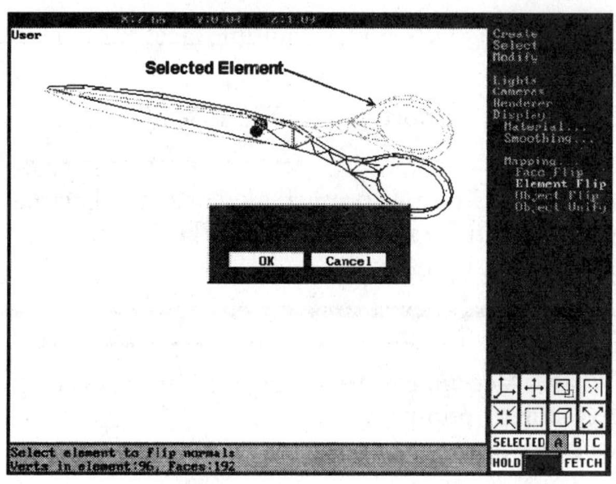

Flipping the normals of a selected element.

RELATED COMMANDS

Surface/Normals/Face Flip, Surface/Normals/Object Flip

Surface/Normals/Object Flip

Create
Select
Modify
Surface
Lights
Cameras
Renderer
Display
Material...
Smoothing...
Normals...
Mapping...
Face Flip
Element Flip
Object Flip
Object Unify

Flips the direction of the surface normals on single or multiple objects.

Flipping the Normals of Selected Objects

1. Create a selection set of the objects you want to flip the normals of. See *Select/Face/Single*, *Select/Object/Quad*, *Select/Object/Fence*, and *Select/Object/Circle*. Alternately, select a single object.
2. Select *Surface/Normals/Object Flip*. If multiple objects were selected, click on the **Selected** button.
3. After clicking in any viewport, select **OK** in the Flip normals of Object(s)? box.

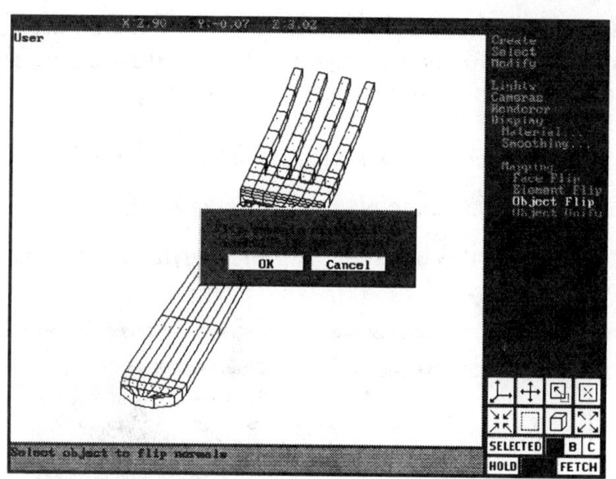

Flipping the normals of an object.

RELATED COMMANDS

Surface/Normals/Face Flip, *Surface/Normals/Element Flip*

Create
Select
Modify
Surface
Lights
Cameras
Renderer
Display
Material...
Smoothing...
Normals...
Mapping...
Face Flip
Element Flip
Object Flip
Object Unify

Surface/Normals/Object Unify

Flips the normals of an object so they all point in the same direction.

Unifying an Object

1. Create a selection set of the objects you want to unify. See *Select/Object/Single*, *Select/Object/Quad*, *Select/Object/Fence*, and *Select/Object/Circle*. Alternately, select a single object.
2. Select *Surface/Normals/Object Unify*. If multiple objects were selected, click on the **Selected** button.
3. After clicking in any viewport, select **OK** in the Unify normals of Object(s)? box.

> **TIP** Importing **.dxf* or **.flm* files into 3D Studio occasionally results in surface normals facing in different directions. To correct this and make the objects render properly do the following:
>
> 1. Weld all of the vertices together with *Modify/Vertex/Weld*.
> 2. Unify the object with *Surface/Normals/Object Unify*.
> 3. Render the object. If it is invisible, flip the normals with *Surface/Normals/Object Flip*.

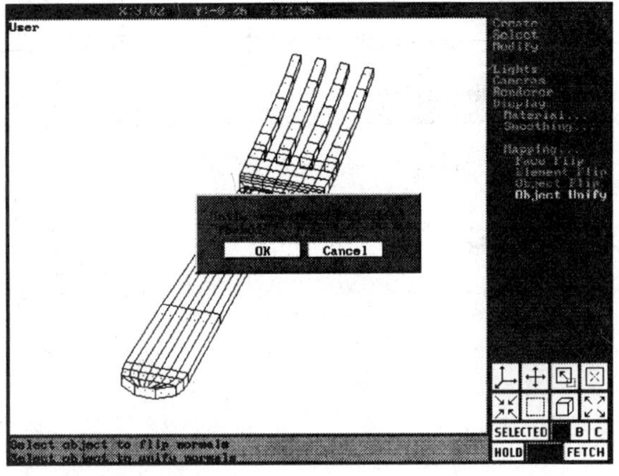

Unifying the normals of an object.

RELATED COMMANDS

Modify/Vertex/Weld, Surface/Normals/Object Flip

Surface/Mapping...

Modify
Surface
Lights
Cameras
Material...
Smoothing...
Normals...
Mapping...
Type
Adjust...
Apply Obj.
Apply Elem.
Remove
Planar
Cylindrical
Spherical

Used to define how mapped materials are applied to elements and objects.

Methods of Applying Mapping Coordinates

1. **Object Creation.** When creating objects in the 3D Lofter, turn on the **Mapping** button in the Object Lofting Controls dialog box. See *Objects/Make* in the 3D Lofter.
2. **Face-mapped Materials.** Activate the **Face Map** button in the Materials Editor. This will map a material bitmap to every facet of the object. Using a face-mapped material does not require mapping coordinates on an object.
3. **Square Objects.** On square objects you can apply multiple materials to all six sides of an object. See *Surface/Material/Box.*
4. **Directly Applying Mapping Coordinates.** Directly apply mapping coordinates to an object; see below.

> **NOTE** Any material using a texture, opacity, bump, specular, shininess, or self-illumination material requires mapping coordinates applied to the object. Without the mapping coordinates, the bitmapped material will not appear on the object. Some objects, however, have mapping coordinats applied automatically during the lofting process. See *Material–Get Material* in the Materials Editor for an explanation of materials that need mapping coordinates.

Directly Applying Mapping Coordinates

Complete the following steps to directly apply mapping coordinates to an object,

1. Select the type of mapping projection you want; planar, cylindrical, or spherical. See *Surface/Mapping/Type/Planar*, *Surface/Mapping/Type/Cylindrical*, and *Surface/Mapping/Type/Spherical.*
2. Modify the position, rotation, scaling, and tiling of the map to fit the object. See the commands under *Surface/Mapping/Adjust.*
3. Apply the adjusted map to the object or element. See *Surface/Mapping/Apply Obj.* and *Surface/Mapping/Apply Elem.*

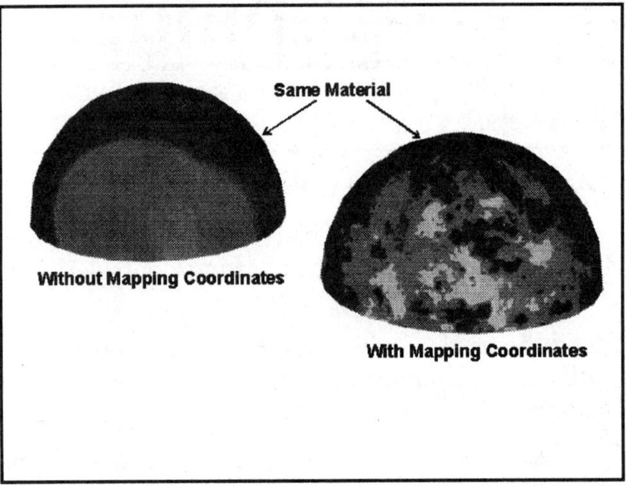

A material requiring mapping coordinates does not render properly.

NOTE Once you have applied mapping coordinates to an object or element, you can assign different materials to the object without having to reapply the coordinates.

RELATED COMMANDS

Objects/Make in the 3D Lofter, Surface/Material/Box, Face Map button in the Materials Editor

Modify
Surface
Lights
Cameras
Material...
Smoothing...
Normals...
Mapping...
Type...
Adjust...
Apply Obj.
Apply Elem.
Remove
Planar
Cylindrical
Spherical

Surface/Mapping/Type/Planar

Sets a planar mapping projection type.

Setting a Planar Mapping Projection

1. Select *Surface/Mapping/Type/Planar*. An asterisk appears beside the command.
2. The planar icon appears in all viewports.
3. The small vertical line indicates the top of the icon, with the dark line always to the right side. If you cannot see the icon, try *Surface/Mapping/Adjust/Find*.

A planar projection keeps the map flat and projects it infinitely *through* the object.

TIP

Because the planar map is projected indefinitely through the object, it does not matter how close the icon is to the mesh. The size of the icon and its angle do matter, however.

Icon Size. To keep your material undistorted, you need to keep the icon in the same proportions as the material. See *Surface/Mapping/Adjust/Scale* to size the icon.

Icon Angle. Planar maps are meant to be applied square to a mesh's face. This can cause streaks along the sides of the object. To avoid streaking, try one of the following:

1. Rotate the planar map at a 45 degree angle in both of the viewports that show the icon from the edge. See *Surface/Mapping/Adjust/Rotate*.
2. Detach the sides of the object and apply separate mapping coordinates. See *Create/Face/Detach*.
3. Create the material using the *Face–Map* option in the Materials editor. This will apply the map to every facet of the object. Using a face-mapped material does not require mapping coordinates.

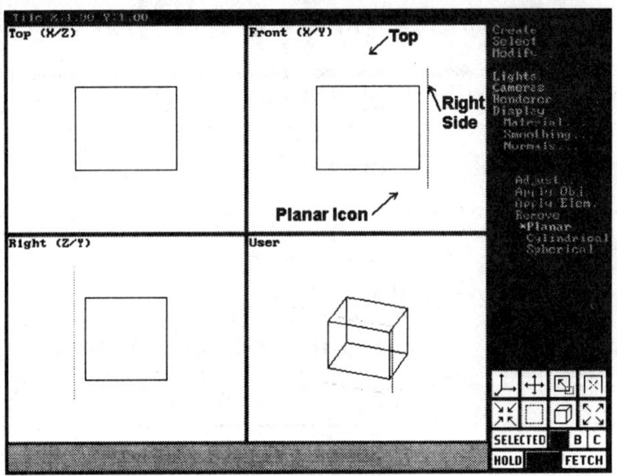

The planar mapping projection keeps the map flat and projects it infinitely through the object.

RELATED COMMANDS

Surface/Mapping..., Surface/Mapping/Adjust/Scale, Surface/Mapping/Adjust/Rotate

Modify
Surface
Lights
Cameras
Material...
Smoothing...
Normals...
Mapping...
Type...
Adjust...
Apply Obj.
Apply Elem.
Remove
Planar
Cylindrical
Spherical

Surface/Mapping/Type/Cylindrical

Sets a cylindrical mapping projection type.

Setting a Planar Mapping Projection

1. Select *Surface/Mapping/Type/Cylindrical*. An asterisk appears beside the command.
2. The cylindrical icon appears in all viewports.
3. The small vertical line indicates the top of the icon. The dark line indicates the back of the icon. This line also represents the seam where the two sides of the map will meet. If you cannot see the icon, try *Surface/Mapping/Adjust/Find*.

NOTE A cylindrical map is projected from the center point outward to infinity. Because of this the diameter of the map is not important, only the location of its center. See *Surface/Mapping/Adjust/Align* and *Surface/Mapping/Adjust/Center*.

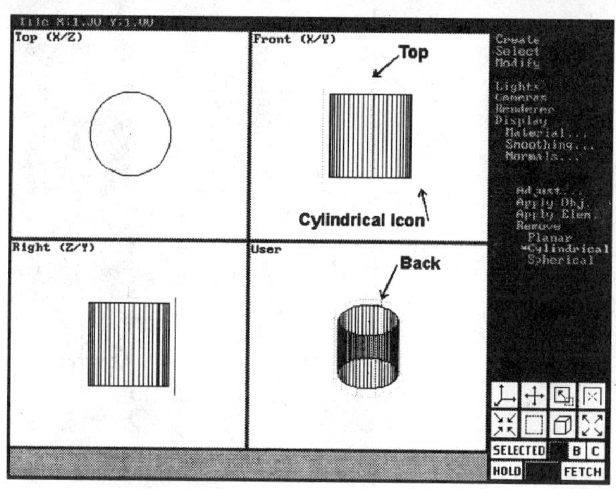

A cylindrical mapping projection curves the map into a cylinder and wraps it around the object.

RELATED COMMANDS

Surface/Mapping..., Surface/Mapping/Adjust/Align, Surface/Mapping/Adjust/Center

Modify
Surface
Lights
Cameras
Material...
Smoothing...
Normals...
Mapping...
Type...
Adjust...
Apply Obj.
Apply Elem.
Remove
Planar
Cylindrical
Spherical

Surface/Mapping/Type/Spherical

Sets a spherical mapping projection type.

Setting a Planar Mapping Projection

1. Select *Surface/Mapping/Type/Spherical*. An asterisk appears beside the command.
2. The spherical icon appears in all viewports. The small vertical line indicates the top of the icon. The dark line indicates the seam where the left and right edges of the map meet. If you cannot see the icon, try *Surface/Mapping/Adjust/Find.*

NOTE A spherical map begins by stretching the map vertically about the object from the top pole to the bottom pole. The map is then wrapped horizontally, starting at the seam and going all around.

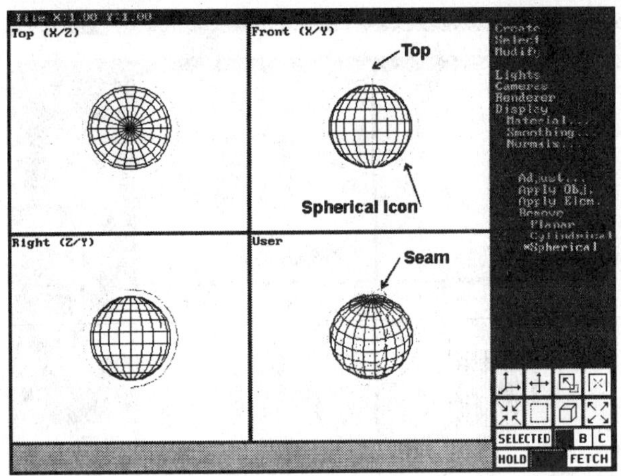

The spherical map mapping projection curves the map into a sphere and wraps it around the object.

RELATED COMMANDS

Surface/Mapping..., Surface/Mapping/Adjust/Align, Surface/Mapping/Adjust/Center

Surface/Mapping/Adjust/Find

Modify
Surface
Normals...
Mapping...
Adjust...
Apply Obj.
Find
Move
Rotate
Scale
Region Fit
Bitmap Fit
View Align
Face Align
Center
Tile

Locates an icon that is not visible on the screen. The icon is scaled to three-quarters of the current viewport while maintaining its aspect ratio and rotation angle.

Finding the Icon

1. After selecting a mapping type (with *Surface/Mapping/Type/Planar, Surface/Mapping/Type/Cylindrical,* or *Surface/Mapping/Type/Spherical)* if the icon is not visible, select *Surface/Mapping/Adjust/Find.*
2. Click **OK** in the Rescale map icon to viewport? box.
3. The icon is scaled to approximately three-quarters of the active viewport. The aspect ratio and rotation angles remain the same.

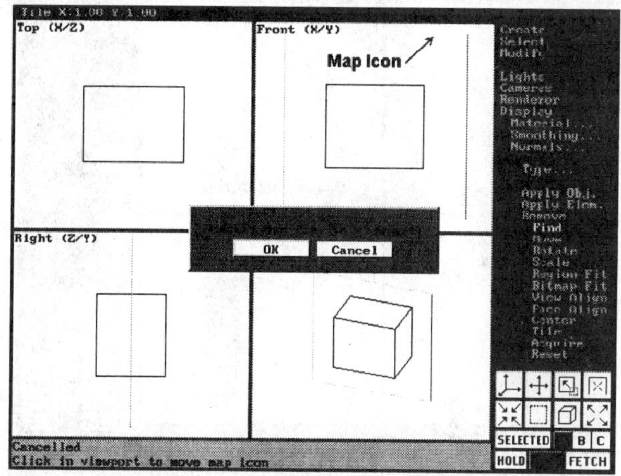

Use Surface/Mapping/Adjust/Find if the mapping icon is not visible.

RELATED COMMANDS

Surface/Mapping..., Surface/Mapping/Adjust/Move, Surface/Mapping/Adjust/Scale

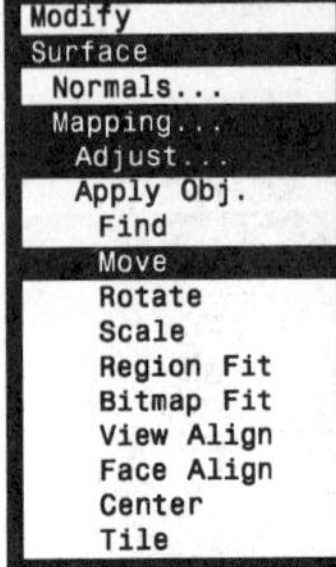

Surface/Mapping/Adjust/Move

Repositions the mapping icon in the current viewport.

Moving the Mapping Icon

1. Select a mapping type (with *Surface/Mapping/Type/Planar, Surface/Mapping/Type/Cylindrical,* or *Surface/Mapping/Type/Spherical)* to display the appropriate mapping icon on the screen.
2. Select *Surface/Mapping/Adjust/Move* and click anywhere in any noncamera or nonspotlight viewport.
3. Moving the mouse moves the mapping icon parallel to the plane of the selected viewport. Use the [Tab] key to cycle through horizontal and vertical movement.
4. Click to set the new mapping icon position.

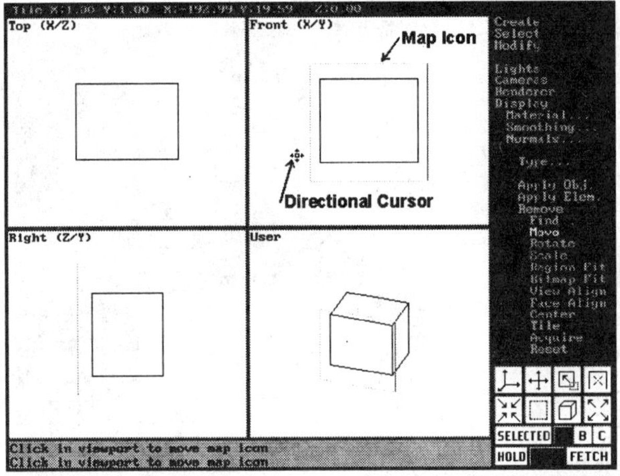

Use Surface/Mapping/Adjust/Move to adjust the position of the mapping icon.

RELATED COMMANDS

Surface/Mapping..., Surface/Mapping/Adjust/Move, Surface/Mapping/Adjust/Center, Views–Drawing Aids

Surface/Mapping/Adjust/Rotate

Modify
Surface
Normals...
Mapping...
Adjust...
Apply Obj.
Find
Move
Rotate
Scale
Region Fit
Bitmap Fit
View Align
Face Align
Center
Tile

Rotates the mapping icon about its center.

Rotating the Mapping Icon

1. Select a mapping type (with *Surface/Mapping/Type/Planar, Surface/Mapping/Type/Cylindrical,* or *Surface/Mapping/Type/Spherical)* to display the appropriate mapping icon on the screen.
2. Select *Surface/Mapping/Adjust/Rotate* and click anywhere in any noncamera or nonspotlight viewport.
3. Moving the mouse sideways causes the icon to rotate left or right about its center. The status line at the top of the screen displays the amount of rotation. To rotate the icon along a different axis, make a different viewport active.
4. Click to set the new mapping icon position.

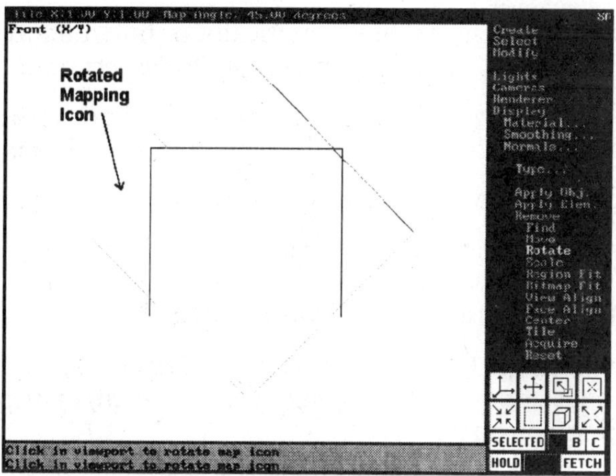

Moving the mouse sideways rotates the mapping icon about its center.

To rotate the icon a specific amount, use the angle snap. See *Views–Use Snap* and *Views–Drawing Aids.*

RELATED COMMANDS

Surface/Mapping..., Surface/Mapping/Adjust/Find, Views–Use Snap, Views–Drawing Aids.

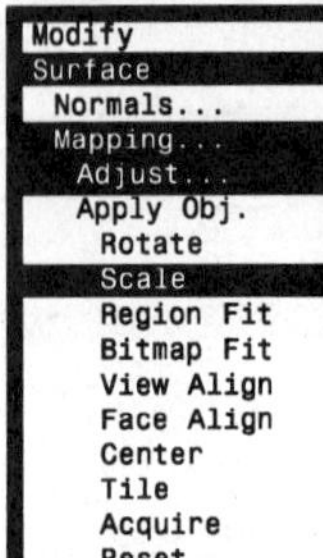

Surface/Mapping/Adjust/Scale

Adjusts the size or aspect ration of the mapping icon. You can scale the icon about its center or size the icon to the exact extents of the object.

Scaling the Mapping Icon About its Center

1. Select a mapping type (with *Surface/Mappingype/Planar, Surface/Mapping/Type/Cylindrical,* or *Surface/Mapping/Type/Spherical)* to display the appropriate mapping icon on the screen.
2. Select *Surface/Mapping/Adjust/Scale* and click anywhere in any noncamera or nonspotlight viewport.
3. Moving the mouse scales the mapping icon about its center. Use the Tab key to specify the direction of the scale. Scaling the icon has the following effect on the mapping icons:

   Planar. Can be scaled horizontally, vertically, or horizontally and vertically. Scaling the icon in one direction only changes the aspect ratio of the mapping.

   Cylindrical. Can be scaled horizontally and vertically, or vertically only. Scaling the icon vertically only changes the aspect ration of the mapping.

   Spherical. Can only be scaled in both directions.
4. Click to set the new mapping icon size.

Scaling the Mapping Icon to the Exact Object Extents

1. Select a mapping type (with *Surface/Mapping/Type/Planar, Surface/Mapping/Type/Cylindrical,* or *Surface/Mapping/Type/Spherical)* to display the appropriate mapping icon on the screen.
2. Use the Tab key to specify the direction of the scale.
3. Hold down the Alt key and select the object.
4. The mapping icon is centered on the object and scaled in the direction of the arrow cursors to match the extents of the object.

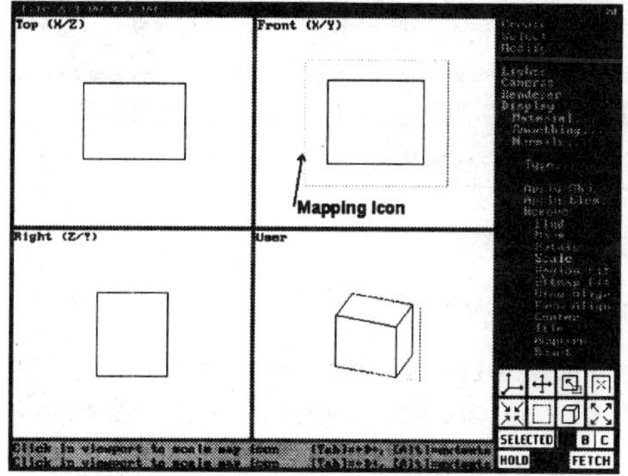

The mapping icon before scaling.

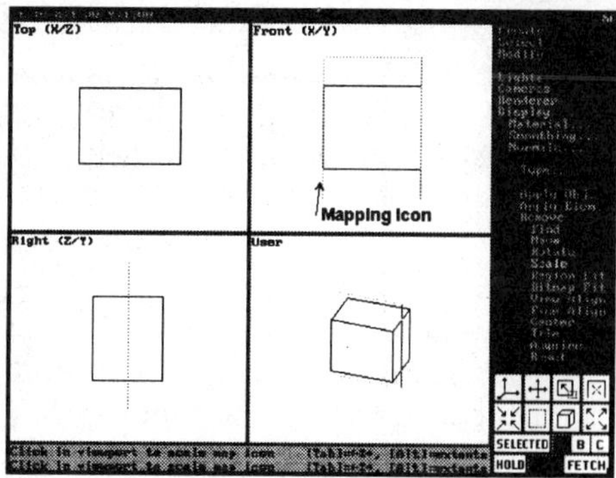

The mapping icon after scaling horizontally to match the extents of the object.

RELATED COMMANDS

Surface/Mapping..., Surface/Mapping/Adjust/Region Fit

Modify
Surface
Normals...
Mapping...
Adjust...
Apply Obj.
Rotate
Scale
Region Fit
Bitmap Fit
View Align
Face Align
Center
Tile
Acquire
Reset

Surface/Mapping/Adjust/Region Fit

Draws a planar mapping icon in a nonperspective viewport by defining a quadrilateral.

Drawing a Planar Mapping Icon

1. Select *Surface/Mapping/Adjust/Region Fit*.
2. Click in any noncamera or nonspotlight viewport to set the upper left corner of the icon. Pressing and holding the [Ctrl] key before setting the first corner will constrain the quadrilateral to a square.
3. Drag the mouse diagonally to create a quadrilateral that defines the size and aspect ratio of the map.
4. Click to set the new map.

TIP Using the Snap and Grid functions allows you to fit the map size to actual drawing units. See *Views–Drawing Aids*, *Views–Use Snap*, and *Views-Use Grid*.

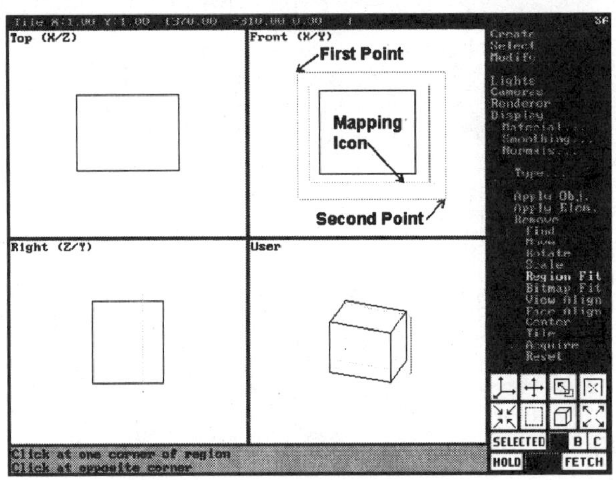

Drawing a planar mapping icon by defining a quadrilateral.

RELATED COMMANDS

Surface/Mapping..., Surface/Mapping/Adjust/Scale

Surface/Mapping/Adjust/Bitmap Fit

Modify
Surface
Normals...
Mapping...
Adjust...
Apply Obj.
Rotate
Scale
Region Fit
Bitmap Fit
View Align
Face Align
Center
Tile
Acquire
Reset

Proportions a planar mapping icon to a selected bitmap.

Proportioning a Planar Icon to a Selected Bitmap

1. Select *Surface/Mapping/Adjust/Bitmap Fit* to access the Select bitmap for aspect ratio fit dialog box.
2. Select the bitmap file you are going to assign to the object and click **OK**. The planar icon is proportioned instantly and accurately to the same aspect rario as the selected bitmap.

TIP To scale the planar icon and maintain the aspect ratio, use *Surface/Mapping/Adjust/Scale* and adjust the horizontal and vertical scaling at the same time.

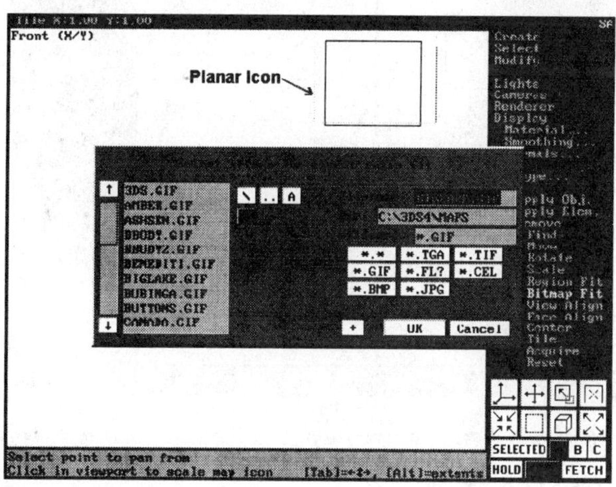

Proportioning a planar icon to a selected bitmap.

RELATED COMMANDS

Surface/Mapping..., Surface/Mapping/Adjust/Scale

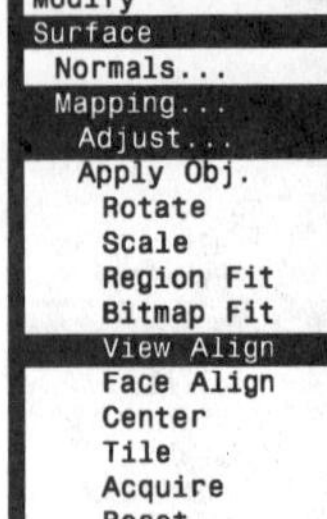

Surface/Mapping/Adjust/View Align

Quickly orients the mapping icon to a selected viewport. The icon is rotated about the center, so the position or scale of the icon is not affected.

Aligning the Mapping Icon to a View

1. Select a mapping type (with *Surface/Mapping/Type/Planar, Surface/Mapping/Type/Cylindrical,* or *Surface/Mappingl/Type/Spherical)* to display the appropriate mapping icon on the screen.
2. Select *Surface/Mapping/Adjust/View Align* and click anywhere in any noncamera or nonspotlight viewport. The mapping icon is now aligned with the viewport.

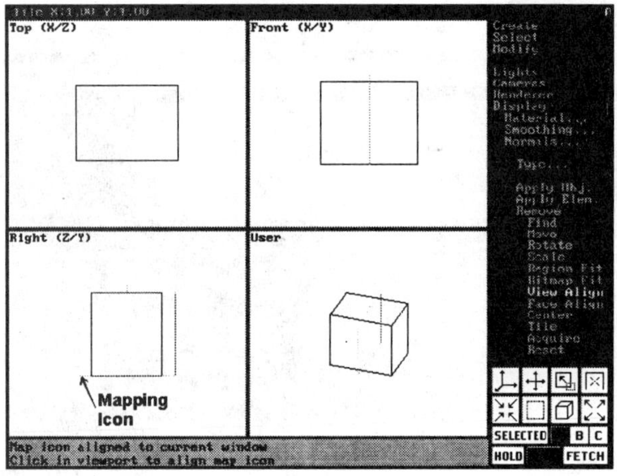

Using View Align to align the planar icon to the Right view.

RELATED COMMAND

Surface/Mapping...

Surface/Mapping/Adjust/Face Align

Modify
Surface
Normals...
Mapping...
Adjust...
Apply Obj.
Rotate
Scale
Region Fit
Bitmap Fit
View Align
Face Align
Center
Tile
Acquire
Reset

Rotates the current mapping icon to be parallel with a selected face. The icon is rotated in place and does not actually move to the face.

Aligning a Mapping Icon to a Face

1. Select a mapping type (with *Surface/Mapping/Type/Planar, Surface/Mapping/Type/Cylindrical,* or *Surface/Mapping/Type/Spherical)* to display the appropriate mapping icon on the screen.
2. Select a face that you want to align the mapping icon to. See *Select/Face/Single*.
3. Select *Surface/Mapping/Adjust/Face Align*. The front of the map icon is rotated so that it faces the same direction as the face normal. The position or scale of the map icon is not affected.

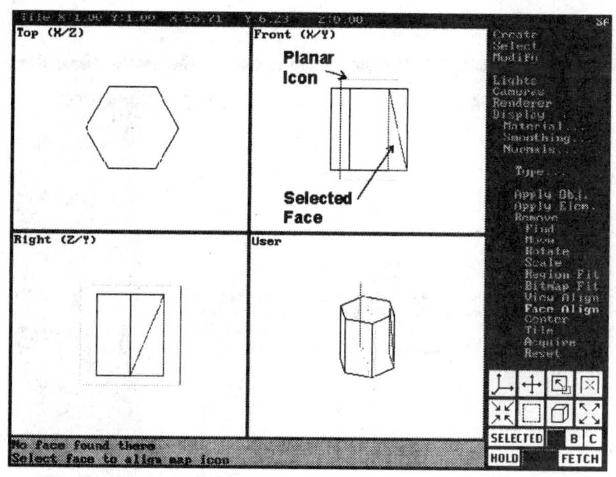

Aligning the Planar mapping icon with a face.

RELATED COMMAND

Surface/Mapping...

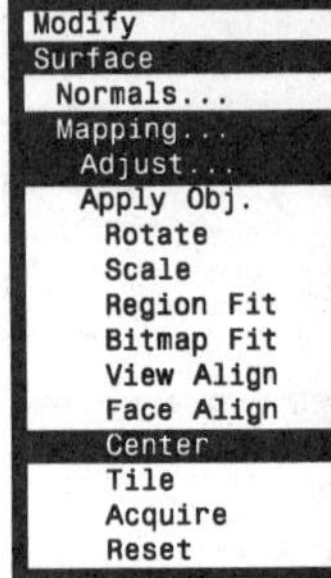

Surface/Mapping/Adjust/Center

Centers the current mapping icon about the local axis of a selected object.

Centering a Mapping Icon on a Selected Object

1. Select a mapping type (with *Surface/Mapping/Type/Planar, Surface/Mapping/Type/Cylindrical,* or *Surface/Mapping/Type/Spherical)* to display the appropriate mapping icon on the screen.
2. Select the object you want to center the mapping icon on.
3. Select *Surface/Mapping/Adjust/Center.* Clicking **OK** to the Center map icon on object prompt will center the mapping icon on the three-dimensional center of the object's bounding box.

Use *Surface/Mapping/Adjust/Center* to properly locate spherical or cylindrical mapping on objects.

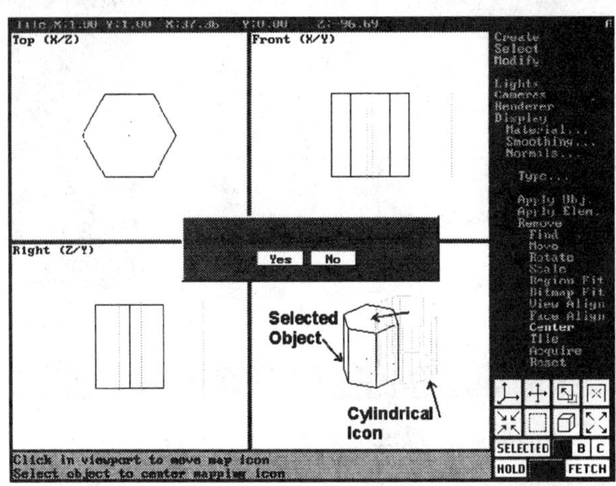

Centering a Cylindrical mapping icon on a cylinder.

RELATED COMMAND

Surface/Mapping...

Surface/Mapping/Adjust/Tile

Modify
Surface
Normals...
Mapping...
Adjust...
Apply Obj.
Rotate
Scale
Region Fit
Bitmap Fit
View Align
Face Align
Center
Tile
Acquire
Reset

Controls horizontal and vertical repeat values within the area of the map icon.

Adjusting the Repeat Values for a Map

1. Select a mapping type (with *Surface/Mapping/Type/Planar, Surface/Mapping/Type/Cylindrical*, or *Surface/Mapping/Type/Spherical)* to display the appropriate mapping icon on the screen.
2. Selecting *Surface/Mapping/Adjust/Tile* accesses the Map Tiling Setup dialog box.
3. Enter the number of times you want the map repeated horizontally in the X Repeat field.
4. Enter the number of times you want the map repeated vertically in the Y Repeat field.
5. Click on **OK** to accept the repeat values.

> **TIP** The effect of changing the Tile settings is equivalent to scaling the map icon. For example, an X repeat of 8 is the equivalent of scaling the icon to 50 percent along the X axis. See *Surface/Mapping/Adjust/Scale*.

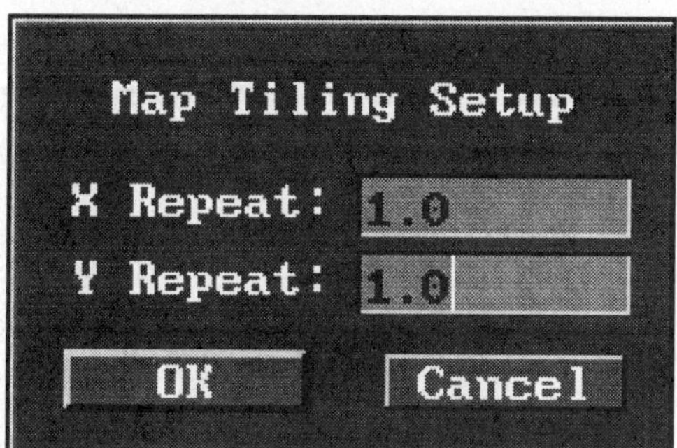

Tiling the map will repeat the map horizontally and vertically.

RELATED COMMANDS

Materials/Mapping, Surface/Mapping/Adjust/Scale

Modify
Surface
Normals...
Mapping...
Adjust...
Apply Obj.
Rotate
Scale
Region Fit
Bitmap Fit
View Align
Face Align
Center
Tile
Acquire
Reset

Surface/Mapping/Adjust/Acquire

Obtains the mapping icon from a selected object.

Acquiring a Mapping Icon

1. To acquire a mapping icon from an object, it first must have been assigned with *Surface/Mapping/Apply Obj*.
2. Select *Surface/Mapping/Adjust/Acquire* and click on the object you want to acquire the mapping icon from.
3. Click **OK** at the acquire map icon from object dialog box. The mapping icon will appear as it was originally assigned to the object.

NOTE When you scale, move, or rotate an object, the map icon is not updated or changed. If you want to be able to adjust or acquire mapping icons accurately later, make sure you update them if you modify the object.

TIP Since mapping coordinates are very important and can be time-consuming to create, use *Surface/Mapping/Adjust/Acquire* to re-adjust mapping coordinates that have already been assigned and to copy their settings to other objects.

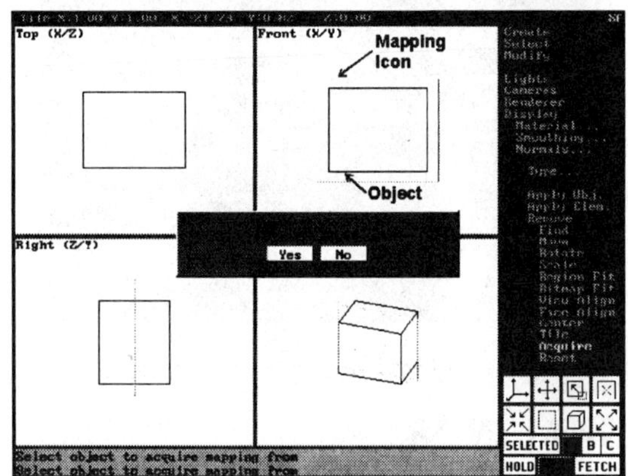

Acquiring a mapping icon is very useful to readjust a map that has already been assigned.

RELATED COMMAND

Surface/Mapping...

Surface/Mapping/Adjust/Reset

Modify
Surface
Normals...
Mapping...
Adjust...
Apply Obj.
Rotate
Scale
Region Fit
Bitmap Fit
View Align
Face Align
Center
Tile
Acquire
Reset

Returns the mapping icon to its default square proportion. The position or scale of the mapping icon is not changed.

Resetting the Mapping Icon

1. To reset a mapping icon, you first must have a mapping icon displayed. See *Surface/Mapping/Type/Planar, Surface/Mapping/Type/Cylindrical,* or *Surface/Mapping/Type/Spherical* to display the appropriate mapping icon on the screen.
2. Select *Surface/Mapping/Adjust/Reset* and click on the mapping icon you want to reset. You are given the following options:

   Aspect Ratio: Resets only the aspect ratio to its default 1:1 ratio.

   Rotation: Resets only the rotation angle.

   Both: Resets the aspect ratio and rotation angle.

   Cancel: Cancels the command and does not change the selected mapping icon.
3. After selecting the appropriate Reset option, the mapping icon is adjusted accordingly.

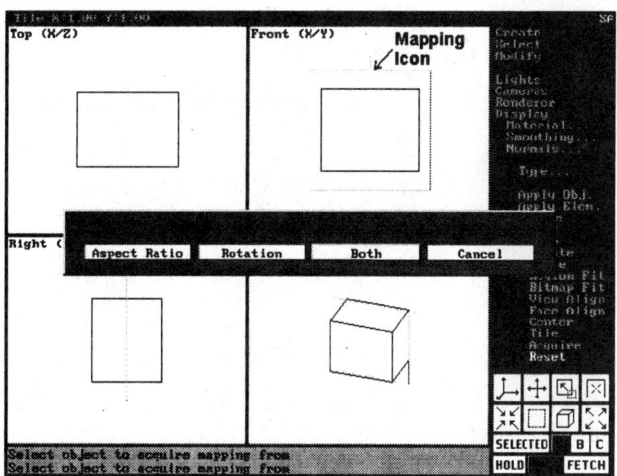

Resetting the mapping icon to its default aspect ratio and rotation.

RELATED COMMAND

Surface/Mapping...

Create
Select
Modify
Surface
Lights
Cameras
Renderer
Material...
Smoothing...
Normals...
Mapping...
Type...
Adjust...
Apply Obj.
Apply Elem.
Remove

Surface/Mapping/Apply Obj.

Applies the current mapping icon to single or multiple objects.

Applying a Mapping Icon to a Single Object

1. Select a mapping type (with *Surface/Mapping/Type/Planar, Surface/Mapping/Type/Cylindrical,* or *Surface/Mapping/Type/Spherical*) to display the appropriate mapping icon on the screen.
2. Select one or several of the *Surface/Mapping/Adjust...* commands to adjust the map to the object.
3. Select *Surface/Mapping/Apply Obj.* and click on the object you want to apply the map to.
4. Select **OK** in the Apply mapping coordinates to selected objects box.
5. The map is assigned to the selected object. You can adjust the map later with *Surface/Mapping/Adjust/Acquire.*

Applying a Mapping Icon to Multiple Objects

1. Select a mapping type (with *Surface/Mapping/Type/Planar, Surface/Mapping/Type/Cylindrical,* or *Surface/Mapping/Type/Spherical*) to display the appropriate mapping icon on the screen.
2. Select one or several of the *Surface/Mapping/Adjust...* commands to adjust the map to the object.
3. Create a selection set of objects you want to apply the mapping icon to. See *Select/Object/Quad, Select/Object/Fence,* and *Select/Object/Circle.*
4. Select *Surface/Mapping/Apply Obj.*, click on the **Selected** button, and click anywhere on the active viewport.
5. Select **OK** in the Apply mapping coordinates to "selected objects" box.
6. The same mapping icon is assigned to all selected objects. You can adjust the map later on each individual object with *Surface/Mapping/Adjust/Acquire.*

Applying a spherical map to selected objects.

RELATED COMMANDS

Surface/Mapping..., Surface/Mapping/Adjust/Acquire

Surface/Mapping/Apply Elem.

Create
Select
Modify
Surface
Lights
Cameras
Renderer
Material...
Smoothing...
Normals...
Mapping...
Type...
Adjust...
Apply Obj.
Apply Elem.
Remove

Applies the current mapping icon to a selected element.

Applying a Mapping Icon to a Selected Element

1. Select a mapping type (with *Surface/Mapping/Type/Planar, Surface/Mapping/Type/Cylindrical,* or *Surface/Mapping/Type/Spherical*) to display the appropriate mapping icon on the screen.
2. Select one or several of the *Surface/Mapping/Adjust...* commands to adjust the map to the element.
3. Select *Surface/Mapping/Apply Elem.* and click on the element you want to apply the map to.
4. Select **OK** in the Apply mapping coordinates to this element? box.
5. The map is assigned to the selected element.

NOTE You cannot readjust or copy mapping coordinates with *Surface/Mapping/Adjust/Acquire* commands that have been applied to separate elements.

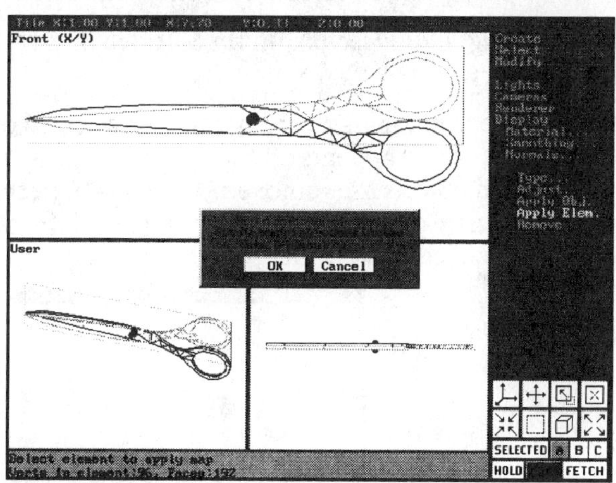

Applying a planar map to a selected element.

RELATED COMMANDS

Surface/Mapping..., Surface/Mapping/Apply Obj.

Create
Select
Modify
Surface
Lights
Cameras
Renderer
Material...
Smoothing...
Normals...
Mapping...
Type...
Adjust...
Apply Obj.
Apply Elem.
Remove

Surface/Mapping/Remove

Removes all mapping coordinates from single and multiple objects.

Removing Mapping Coordinates from a Single Object

1. To remove a mapping coordinate from an object, it first must have been assigned mapping coordinates.
2. Select *Surface/Mapping/Adjust/Remove* and click on the object you want to remove the mapping coordinates from.
3. Click **OK** at the Remove mapping coordinates from selected objects dialog box. Although the mapping icon will still appear on the screen, all mapping coordinates assigned to the object are removed. You can check this by selecting *Surface/Mapping/Adjust/Acquire* and clicking on the object you just removed the mapping coordinates from.

Removing Mapping Coordinates from Multiple Objects

1. To remove mapping coordinates from multiple objects, they first must have been assigned mapping coordinates.
2. Create a selection set of objects you want to remove the mapping coordinate from. See *Select/Object/Quad, Select/Object/Fence,* and *Select/Object/Circle*.
3. Select *Surface/Mapping/Remove*, click on the **Selected** button, and click anywhere on the active viewport.
4. Select **OK** in the Remove mapping coordinates from selected objects box. Although the mapping icon still appears on the screen, all mapping coordinates assigned to all selected objects are removed. You can check this by selecting *Surface/Mapping/Adjust/Acquire* and clicking on one of the objects you just removed the mapping coordinates from.

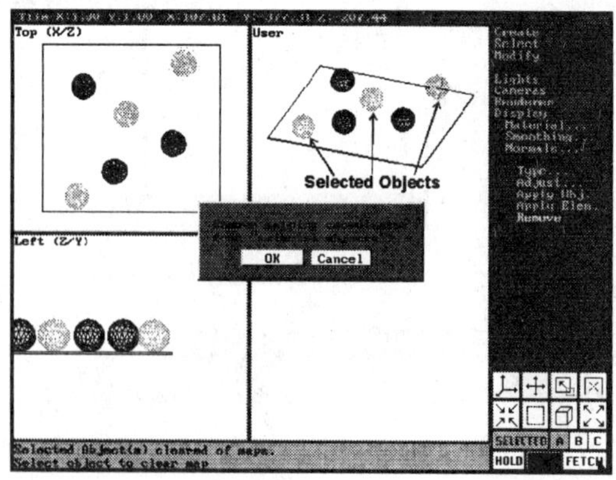

Removing all mapping coordinates from multiple objects.

RELATED COMMAND

Surface/Mapping...

Lights/Ambient

Modify
Surface
Lights
Cameras
Renderer
Display
Ambient
Omni...
Spot...
Create
Move
Place Hilite
Adjust
Ranges
Delete

Adjusts the color of ambient light within a scene.

Ambient light has no source or direction and casts no shadows or highlights. If no other light is present in a scene, all rendered objects will appear without definition and will be rendered as silhouettes.

Changing the Ambient Color Light

1. Select *Lights/Ambient.* The Ambient Light Definition dialog box shown below appears.

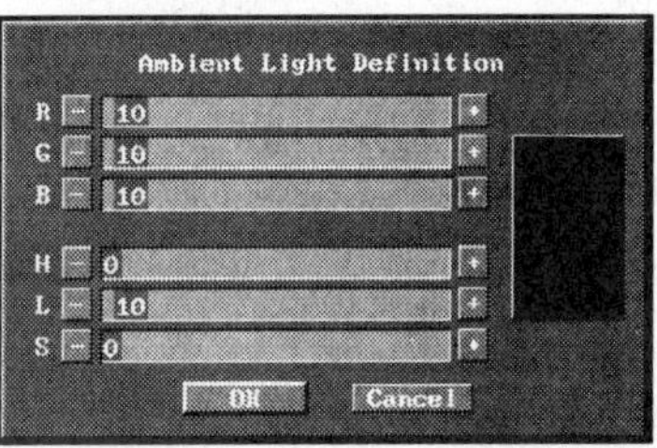

Adjust the ambient light with this dialog box.

2. Make adjustments to the dialog box sliders. Click the **+** button to increase a value and click **-** to decrease a value. All changes to ambient light are displayed in the color box on the right of the dialog box. All dialog box controls are described below.

   R: Adjusts the Red value.

   G: Adjusts the Green value.

   B: Adjusts the Blue value.

   H: Adjusts the Hue (color) value.

   L: Adjusts the Luminance (brightness) value.

   S: Adjusts the Saturation (purity) value.

   OK: Accepts the settings and closes the dialog box.

   Cancel: Cancels the settings and closes the dialog box.

Rarely will ambient lighting be the only light used in a scene. Use it to increase contrast by decreasing ambient settings.

RELATED COMMANDS

Lights/Omni/Create, Lights/Spotlight/Create

Lights/Omni/Create

Creates an Omni light for use in the 3D Editor and the Keyframer.

Omni lights are similar to light bulbs in that light radiates from the source in all directions.

Creating an Omni Light

1. Activate an orthographic or user viewport to receive the Omni light.
2. Select *Lights/Omni/Create.*
3. Click in the active viewport at the location for the light. The Light Definition dialog box appears.

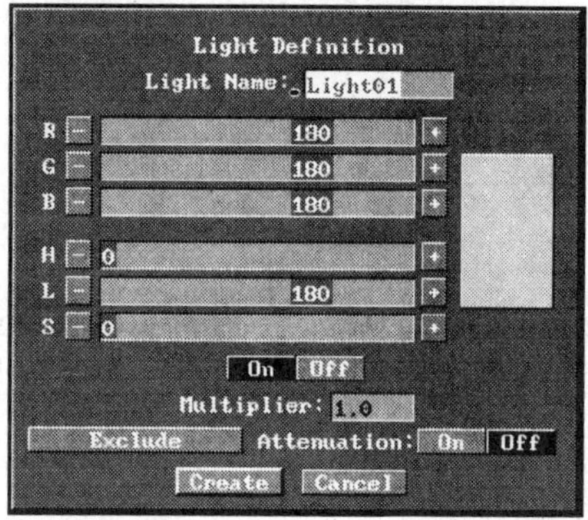

Use this dialog box to create an Omni light.

4. Give the Light a unique name in the **Light Name:** input box.
5. Make adjustments to the dialog box sliders. Click the **+** button to increase a value and click **-** to decrease a value. All changes to Omni light are displayed in the color box on the right of the dialog box. All dialog box controls and settings are described below.

   R: Adjusts the Red value.

   G: Adjusts the Green value.

   B: Adjusts the Blue value.

   H: Adjusts the Hue (color) value.

   L: Adjusts the Luminance (brightness) value.

   S: Adjusts the Saturation (purity) value.

   On: Turns the Omni light on. When the light is on, it appears yellow in the 3D Editor or Keyframer.

Off: Turns the Omni light off. When the light is off, it appears black in the 3D Editor or Keyframer.

Multiplier: Amplifies the amount of light. A setting of 2 will double the light value. A setting of -2 will halve the light value. The effective range is from -10 to 10.

Exclude: Used to exclude objects that are receiving light from this particular Omni light. Once this option is selected, the Object Selection dialog box appears. Select those objects to be excluded and click on the **OK** button. The button will appear red if one or more objects have been selected to be excluded.

Attenuation: Determines whether the Omni light's intensity drops off to a value of zero over a predefined range. **On** turns on Attenuation and **Off** turns off Attenuation.

Create: Creates the Omni light with the above settings and closes the dialog box. The Omni light icon [*] will now appear in the active viewport.

Cancel: Cancels the command and closes the dialog box.

Omni lights do not cast shadows. If you wish to create shadows use Spotlights instead.

RELATED COMMANDS

Lights/Ambient, Lights/Omni/Create, Lights/Omni/Move, Lights/Omni/Adjust, Lights/Spot/Create

Modify
Surface
Lights
Cameras
Renderer
Display
Ambient
Omni...
Spot...
Create
Move
Place Hilite
Adjust
Ranges
Delete

Lights/Omni/Move

Changes the location of an Omni light or allows you to create a clone of an existing light at a new location.

Moving an Omni Light

1. Ensure that an Omni light has been created previously using *Lights/Omni/Create.*
2. Select *Lights/Omni/Move.*
3. Select the orthographic or user viewport that contains the Omni light to be moved.
4. Click on the light.
5. Move the light to its new location and click to place or right-click to cancel.

Cloning an Omni Light

1. Ensure that an Omni light has been created previously using *Lights/Omni/Create.*
2. Select *Lights/Omni/Move.*
3. Select the orthographic or user viewport that contains the Omni light to be moved.
4. Hold the [Shift] and click on the light.
5. Move the new cloned light to its new location and click to place or right-click to cancel.

To constrain the movement of the Omni light vertically or horizontally by use [Tab] and activate the directional cursors.

RELATED COMMANDS

Lights/Omni/Create, Light/Omni/Place Hilite, Lights/Spot/Move

Lights/Omni/Place Hilite

Modify
Surface
Lights
Cameras
Renderer
Display
  Ambient
  Omni...
  Spot...
    Create
    Move
    Place Hilite
    Adjust
    Ranges
    Delete

Moves a previously created Omni light to a new location that will create a highlight at a specified location on an object.

Placing a Highlight on an Object

1. Ensure that the object to receive the highlight has been created and that an Omni light has been created previously.
2. Select *Lights/Omni/Place Hilite.*
3. Click in the viewport that is best suited for selecting the highlight location.
4. Click at the location of the object to receive the highlight.
5. Click on the Omni light that is to cast the highlight. The Omni light will be moved to the new location.
6. To verify that the highlight has been placed properly, render that viewport.

RELATED COMMANDS

Lights/Omni/Create, Lights/Spot/Move

Modify
Surface
Lights
Cameras
Renderer
Display
Ambient
Omni...
Spot...
Create
Move
Place Hilite
Adjust
Ranges
Delete

Lights/Omni/Adjust

Changes the values of previously created Omni lights.

Adjusting an Omni Light

1. Ensure that an Omni light has been created using *Lights/Omni/Create.*
2. Select *Lights/Omni/Adjust.*
3. Click in the viewport that contains the Omni light to be adjusted.
4. Click on the Omni light to be adjusted. The Light Definition dialog box appears.

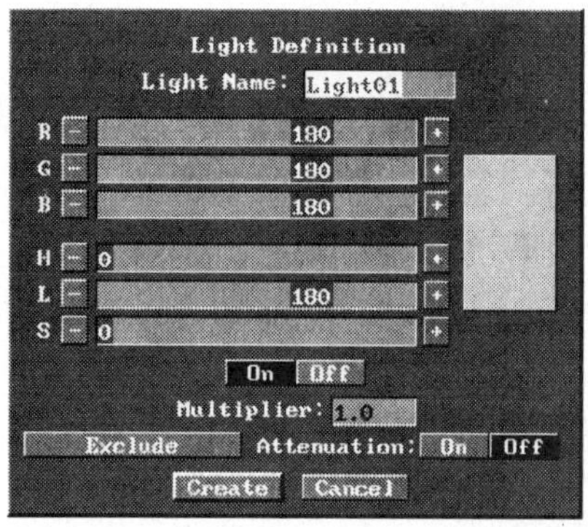

Use this dialog box to create an Omni light.

5. Make adjustments to the dialog box sliders. Click the + button to increase a value and click – to decrease a value. All changes to Omni light are displayed in the color box on the right of the dialog box. All dialog box controls and settings are described below.

   Light Name: Adjusts the name of the light.

   R: Adjusts the Red value.

   G: Adjusts the Green value.

   B: Adjusts the Blue value.

   H: Adjusts the Hue (color) value.

   L: Adjusts the Luminance (brightness) value.

   S: Adjusts the Saturation (purity) value.

   On: Turns the Omni light on. When the light is on, it appears yellow in the 3D Editor or Keyframer.

   Off: Turns the Omni light off. When the light is off, it appears black in the 3D Editor or Keyframer.

Multiplier: Amplifies the amount of light. A setting of 2 will double the light value. A setting of -2 will halve the light value. The effective range is from -10 to 10.

Exclude: Used to exclude objects that are receiving light from this particular Omni light. Once this option is selected, the Object Selection dialog box appears. Select those objects to be excluded and click on the **OK** button. The button will appear red if one or more objects have been selected to be excluded.

Attenuation: Determines whether the Omni light's intensity drops off to a value of zero over a predefined range. **On** turns on Attenuation and **Off** turns off Attenuation.

OK: Adjusts the Omni light with the above settings and closes the dialog box.

Cancel: Cancels the command and closes the dialog box.

RELATED COMMAND

Lights/Omni/Create

Modify
Surface
Lights
Cameras
Renderer
Display
Ambient
Omni...
Spot...
Create
Move
Place Hilite
Adjust
Ranges
Delete

Lights/Omni/Ranges

Adjusts the range of attenuation for a previously created Omni light.

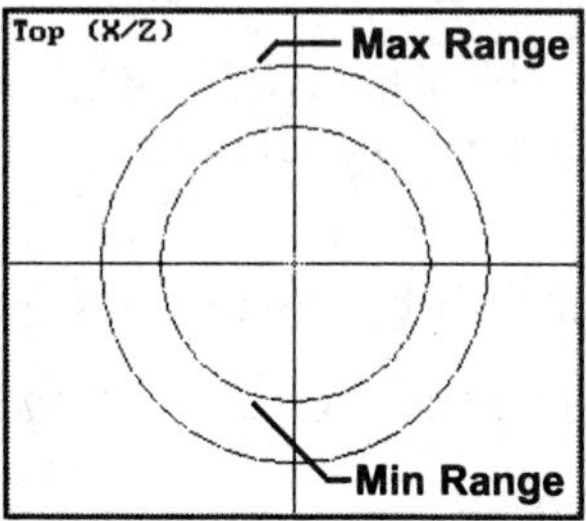

Setting the Attenuation Range

1. Ensure that an Omni light has been created previously using *Lights/Create/Omni* and that the Attenuation**:** option has been set to **On**.
2. Select *Lights/Omni/Ranges*.
3. Select the orthographic or user viewport that contains the Omni light.
4. Click on the Omni light.
5. Move the mouse to change the size of one of two concentric circles and click. Adjusting the outer circle will set the maximum range that the Omni light can cast light. The inner circle would then be the point where the light begins to drop off (attenuate).
6. Move the mouse again to size the second circle and click to finish the command. Right-click to cancel the command.
7. Repeat steps 2 through 6 in another orthographic viewport to adjust the range in all three dimensions.

RELATED COMMAND

Lights/Omni/Create

Lights/Omni/Delete

Deletes a previously created Omni light.

Deleting an Omni Light

1. Ensure that an Omni light has been previously created using *Lights/Omni/Create*.
2. Select *Lights/Omni/Delete*.
3. Click on the Omni light to delete in any viewport. The Omni light will be deleted from the scene.

RELATED COMMANDS

Lights/Omni/Create, Lights/Spot/Delete

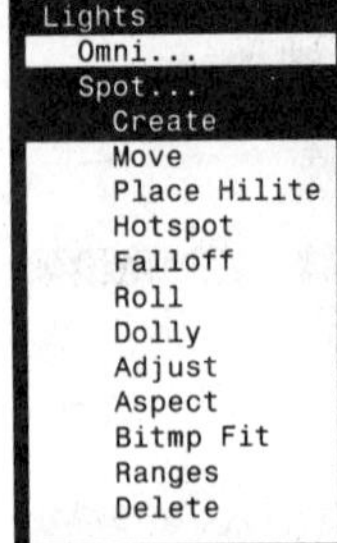

Lights/Spot/Create

Creates a Spotlight and target for use in both the 3D Editor and Keyframer.

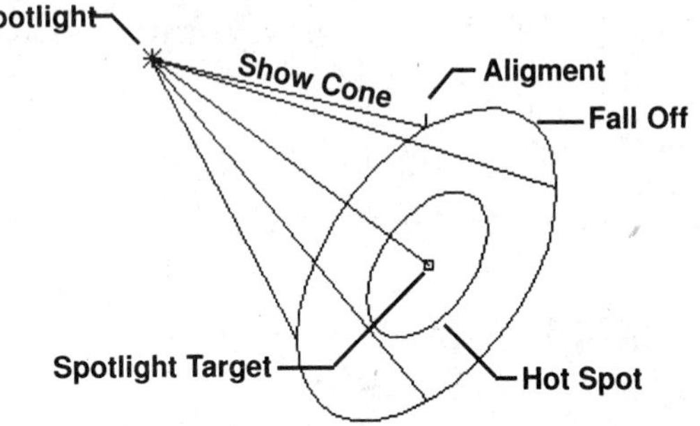

Creating a Spotlight

1. Activate an orthographic or user viewport that is to receive the Spotlight.
2. Select *Lights/Spot/Create*.
3. Click in the active viewport at the location for the spotlight.
4. Move the mouse and click to select the location for the spotlight target. The Spotlight Definition dialog box appears as shown below.

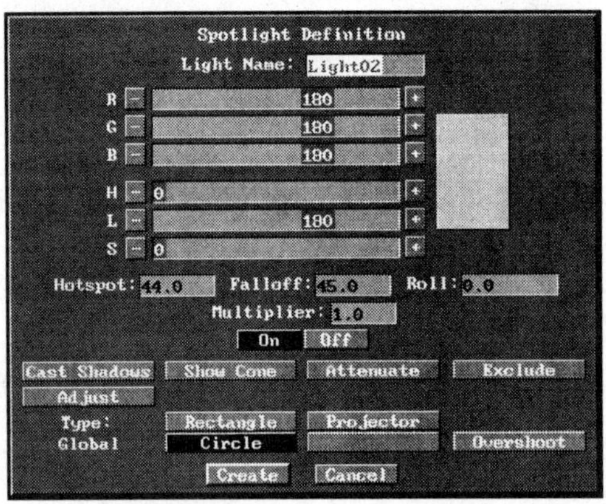

Use this dialog box to adjust the spotlight.

5. Give the spotlight a unique name in the Light Name: input box.
6. Make adjustments to the dialog box sliders. Click the + button to increase a value and click – to decrease a value. All changes to spotlight are displayed in the color box on the right of the dialog box. All dialog box controls and settings are described below.

   R: Adjusts the Red value.

G: Adjusts the Green value.

B: Adjusts the Blue value.

H: Adjusts the Hue (color) value.

L: Adjusts the Luminance (brightness) value.

S: Adjusts the Saturation (purity) value.

Hotspot: Adjusts the value for the hotspot. The hotspot is the angular width of the beam of light thrown. The value range is 1 degree (narrow beam) to 174.5 degrees (wide beam). This value can be changed visually using *Lights/Spot/Hotspot.*

Falloff: Adjusts the value for the falloff. The falloff is the angular width of the falloff of light to darkness. The value range is 1 to 175 degrees. This value can be changed visually using *Lights/Spot/Falloff.*

Roll: Adjusts the rotation of the spotlight about the center of the falloff area. The value range is -180 (counterclockwise) to 180 (clockwise) degrees.

Multiplier: Adjusts the power of the light. The effective value range is -10 (low power) to 10 (high power).

On: Turns the Spotlight on. When the light is on, it appears yellow in the 3D Editor or Keyframer.

Off: Turns the Spotlight off. When the light is off, it appears black in the 3D Editor or Keyframer.

Cast Shadows: Turns on or off the Spotlight's ability to cast shadows. If this option is on, the button will be red. The shadows will be cast only on metal or phong materials surfaces.

Adjust: Displays the Local Shadow Control dialog box shown below. Adjust the controls as described below.

Map bias: Adjusts the shadow map toward or away from the shadow-casting object(s). The value range is any positive number.

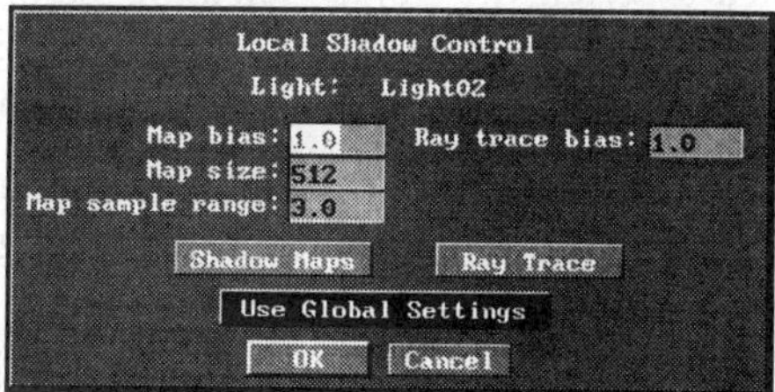

The Shadow Control dialog box.

Map Size: Adjusts the size of shadow maps. The value range is 10 to 4,096 pixels^2. Increasing this value from the default 512 will take up more memory and may not produce more realistic shadows.

Map Sample Range: Adjusts the sharpness of the edge of a shadow map. The value range is 1 (sharp edges) to 5 (softer edges). Values higher than 5 will have unpredictable results.

Ray Trace Bias: Adjusts the ray trace map toward or away from the shadow-casting object(s) The value range is any positive number.

Shadow Maps: Selects the shadow maps method of producing shadows from the Spotlight using the map settings described above. When this selection is chosen, the button is red.

Ray Trace: Selects the ray trace method of producing shadows from the spotlight using the Ray Trace Bias setting describe above. When this selection is chosen, the button is red.

Use Global Settings: Selects whether to use the above shadow settings **(OFF)** or to use the setting specified with the *Renderer/Setup/Shadows* command **(ON)**.

OK: Accepts the above settings and returns to the Spotlight Definition dialog box.

Cancel: Cancels the above settings and returns to the Spotlight Definition dialog box.

Type: Automatically displays whether **Local** or **Global** shadow-casting methods are used.

Show Cone: Turns show cone on and off. The show cone visually displays the hotspot and falloff of the spotlight either with concentric circles or with rectangles, depending on which option is chosen. A short yellow line is displayed at the edge of the show cone which represents the top alignment of a projector map.

Attenuate: Turns attenuation on or off. If attenuate is on, the light gradually decreases in intensity between the hotspot and falloff. If this option is off, the hotspot and falloff are ignored.

Exclude: Excludes objects that are receiving light from this particular spotlight. Once this option is selected, the Object Selection dialog box appears. Select those objects to be excluded and click on the **OK** button. The button will appear red if one or more objects have been selected to be excluded.

Rectangle/Circle: Click on this button to cycle through both of these options. Choosing **Circle**, selects a circular spotlight. Choosing **Rectangle**, selects a rectangular spotlight.

Projector: Selects a bitmap to be projected by the spotlight. Once this option is turned on, select the blank button below. A dialog box will appear. Use this dialog box to select the bitmap to be projected.

Overshoot: Gives the spotlight the characteristics of an Omni light. Light is projected in all directions but all shadows and image projection settings remain intact.

Create: Creates the spotlight with the above settings and closes the dialog box

Cancel: Cancels the command and closes the dialog box.

Using a Spotlight Viewport.

1. Use the spotlight viewport to allow for more accurate placement of projectors, hotspots, and falloffs.
2. Ensure that a spotlight has been created using the *Lights/Spot/Create* command.
3. Click on the viewport to receive the spotlight view and type ⇧Shift $4. If there is only one spotlight in the scene, the viewport will change to that a view looking down the axis of the spotlight. If there is more than one spotlight, the Spotlight Selector dialog box will appear.
4. Select the Spotlight to create the view and click on **OK**. Click **Cancel** to cancel the command.

RELATED COMMANDS

Lights/Omni/Create, Lights/Spot/Adjust

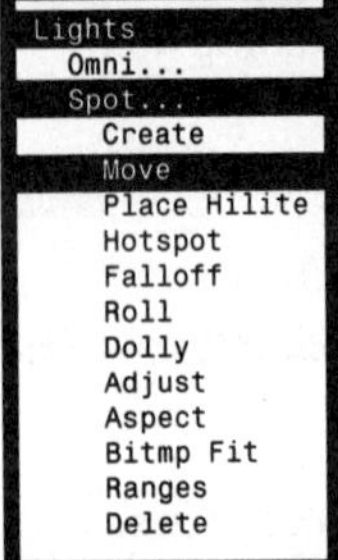

Lights/Spot/Move

Changes the location of a Spotlight or allows you to create a clone of an existing light at a new location.

Moving a Spotlight

1. Ensure that a Spotlight has been created previously using *Lights/Spot/Create.*
2. Select *Lights/Spot/Move.*
3. Select the orthographic or user viewport that contains the Spotlight to be moved.
4. Click on the light or the target. To move both at the same time, hold the Ctrl key before clicking on the light.
5. Move the light, target, or both to the new location and click to place or right-click to cancel.

Cloning a Spotlight

1. Ensure that a Spotlight has been created previously using *Lights/Spot/Create.*
2. Select *Lights/Spot/Move.*
3. Select the orthographic or user viewport that contains the Spotlight to be moved.
4. Hold the Shift key and click on the light.
5. Move the new cloned light to its new location and click to place or right-click to cancel.

To constrain the movement of the Spotlight vertically or horizontally use Tab and activate the directional cursors.

RELATED COMMANDS

Lights/Omni/Create, Lights/Omni/Move, Light/Spot/Place Hilite

Lights/Spot/Place Hilite

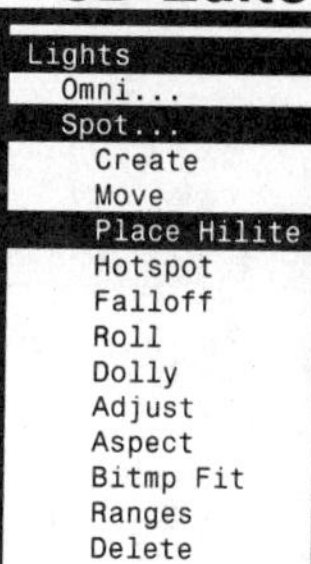

Moves a previously created Spotlight to a new location that will create a highlight at a specified location on an object.

Placing a Highlight on an Object

1. Ensure that the object to receive the highlight has been created and that a Spotlight has been created previously.
2. Select *Lights/Spot/Place Hilite.*
3. Click in the viewport that is best suited for selecting the highlight location.
4. Click at the location of the object to receive the highlight.
5. Click on the Spotlight that is to cast the highlight. The Spotlight will be moved to the new location.
6. To verify that the highlight has been placed properly, render that viewport.

RELATED COMMANDS

Lights/Spot/Create, Lights/Spot/Move

Lights/Spot/Hotspot

Changes the size of the hotspot on a previously created Spotlight .

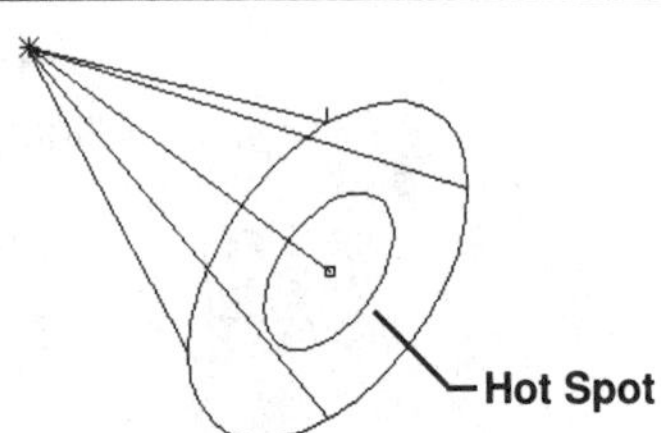

Modifying a Spotlight Hotspot

1. Ensure that a Spotlight has been created previously using *Lights/Spot/Create*.
2. Select *Lights/Spot/Hotspot*.
3. Click in the viewport that contains the Spotlight with the hotspot to be adjusted.
4. Click on the Spotlight asterisk (*). The Spotlight cone appears, which represents the hotspot and falloff. The hotspot is the inner circle or rectangle. The angle of the hotspot is displayed on the status line.
5. Move the mouse sideways to adjust the angle of the hotspot. The angle of the hotspot can be no more than 0.5 degrees less than the falloff.
6. Once the hotspot is modified to its new angle, click to accept the changes, or right-click to cancel the command.

To allow for more accurate adjustment of the angle, turn angle snap on by pressing [A].

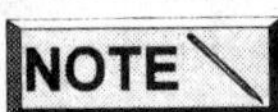

This command can also be used to clone a Spotlight. To clone a Spotlight, hold [Shift] and complete step 4 above.

Use the Spotlight view to adjust the hotspot and falloff. Click in a viewport and press [Shift][$ 4].

RELATED COMMANDS

Lights/Spot/Create, Lights/Spot/Falloff

Lights/Spot/Falloff

Lights
Omni...
Spot...
Create
Move
Place Hilite
Hotspot
Falloff
Roll
Dolly
Adjust
Aspect
Bitmp Fit
Ranges
Delete

Changes the size of the falloff on a previously created Spotlight.

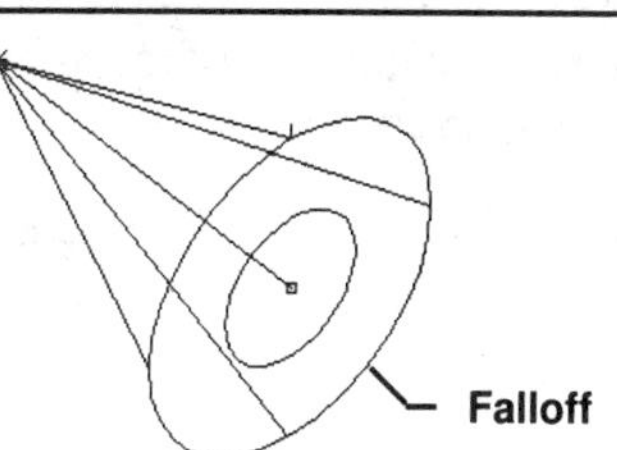

Modifying a Spotlight Falloff

1. Ensure that a Spotlight has been created previously using *Lights/Spot/Create*.
2. Select *Lights/Spot/Falloff*.
3. Click in the viewport that contains the Spotlight with the falloff to be adjusted.
4. Click on the Spotlight asterisk (*). The Spotlight cone appears, which represents the hotspot and falloff. The falloff is the outer circle or rectangle. The angle of the falloff is displayed on the status line.
5. Move the mouse sideways to adjust the angle of the falloff. The angle can be no more than 0.5 degrees greater than the hotspot.
6. Once the falloff is modified to its new angle, click to accept the changes, or right-click to cancel the command.

TIP To allow for more accurate adjustment of the angle, turn angle snap on by pressing A.

NOTE This command can also be used to clone a Spotlight. To clone a Spotlight, hold Shift and complete step 4 above.

TIP Use the Spotlight view to adjust the hotspot and falloff. Click in a viewport and press Shift $4.

RELATED COMMANDS

Lights/Spot/Create, Lights/Spot/Hotspot

Lights
Omni...
Spot...
Create
Move
Place Hilite
Hotspot
Falloff
Roll
Dolly
Adjust
Aspect
Bitmp Fit
Ranges
Delete

Lights/Spot/Roll

Adjusts the roll of a Spotlight by rotating it clockwise or counterclockwise.

Use roll to adjust the location of rectangular spotlights and to assist in proper rotation of projection maps.

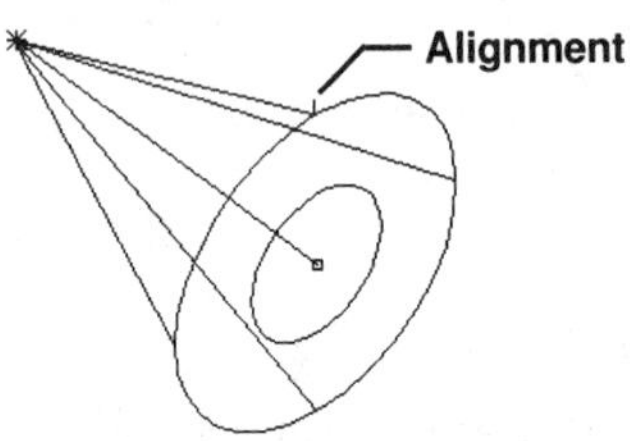

Adjusting the Roll of a Spotlight

1. Ensure that a Spotlight has been created previously using *Lights/Spot/Create*.
2. Select *Lights/Spot/Roll*.
3. Click in the viewport that contains the Spotlight.
4. Click on the Spotlight asterisk (*). The Spotlight cone appears and the roll angle appears in the status line.
5. Move the mouse sideways to adjust the roll of the Spotlight.
6. Once the roll is modified, click to accept the changes, or right-click to cancel the command.

To allow for more accurate adjustment of the angle, turn angle snap on by pressing [A].

This command can also be used to clone a Spotlight. To clone a Spotlight, hold [Shift] and complete step 4 above.

Use the Spotlight view to adjust the Roll. Click in a viewport and press [Shift] [$ 4].

RELATED COMMANDS

Lights/Spot/Create, Camera/Roll

Lights/Spot/Dolly

Lights
Omni...
Spot...
Create
Move
Place Hilite
Hotspot
Falloff
Roll
Dolly
Adjust
Aspect
Bitmp Fit
Ranges
Delete

Adjusts the Spotlight toward or away from its target location.

Dolly the Spotlight

1. Ensure that a Spotlight has been created previously using *Lights/ Spot/Create.*
2. Select *Lights/Spot/Dolly*.
3. Click in the viewport that contains the Spotlight.
4. Click on the Spotlight asterisk (*).
5. Move the mouse sideways to dolly the Spotlight.
6. Click to accept the changes, or right-click to cancel the command.

This command can also be used to clone a Spotlight. To clone a Spotlight, hold [Shift] and complete step 4 above.

Use the Spotlight view to adjust the Dolly. Click in a viewport and press [Shift] [4].

RELATED COMMANDS

Lights/Spot/Create, Camera/Dolly

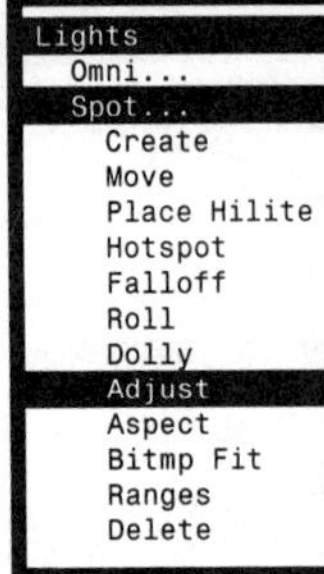

Lights/Spot/Adjust

Changes the settings of a predefined Spotlight using the same Spotlight Definition dialog box as the *Light/Spot/Create* command.

See *Light/Spot/Create* for details on all settings in the Spotlight Definition dialog box.

Adjusting Spotlight Settings

1. Ensure that a Spotlight has been created previously using *Lights/Spot/Create*.
2. Select *Lights/Spot/Adjust*.
3. Click in the viewport that contains the Spotlight.
4. Click on the Spotlight or target icon. The Spotlight Definition dialog box appears.
5. Make adjustments as necessary.

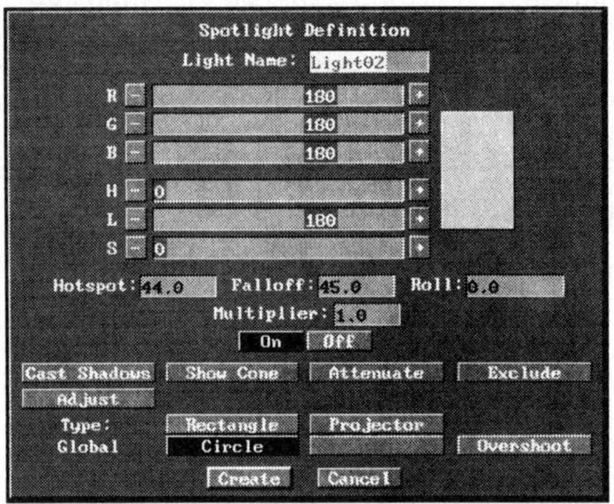

Use this dialog box to adjust the spotlight.

6. Click **OK** to accept the changes or click **Cancel** to exit the command without using the new settings.

RELATED COMMAND

Lights/Spot/Create

Lights/Spot/Aspect

Adjusts the aspect ratio of rectangular spotlights without changing the hotspot or falloff settings.

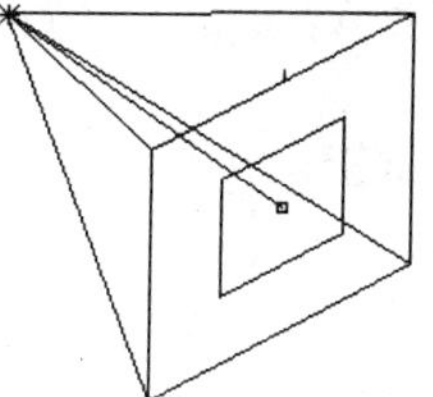

Rectangular Spotlight

Adjusting the Aspect Ratio

1. Ensure that a Spotlight has been created previously using *Lights/Spot/Create*.
2. Select *Lights/Spot/Adjust*.
3. Click in the viewport that contains the Spotlight.
4. Click on the rectangular Spotlight or target icon in an orthographic or user viewport.
5. Move the mouse sideways to adjust the aspect. The status line displays the aspect ratio. Values less than 1 create a rectangle that is wider than it is tall. Values greater than 1 create a rectangle that is taller than it is wide.
6. Click to accept the changes, or right-click to cancel the command.

NOTE This command can also be used to clone a Spotlight. To clone a Spotlight, hold [Shift] and complete setup 4 above.

RELATED COMMAND

Lights/Spot/Create

Lights/Spot/Bitmap Fit

Modifies the aspect ratio of a rectangular Spotlight to match that of a bitmap.

Modifying the Aspect Ratio of a Spotlight Using a Bitmap

1. Ensure that a Spotlight has been created previously using *Lights/Spot/Create.*
2. Select *Lights/Spot/Bitmap Fit.*
3. Click in the viewport that contains the Spotlight.
4. Click on the Spotlight icon (*) in an orthographic or user viewport. The File Selector dialog box appears.
5. Select the bitmap to be used. The falloff is adjusted to match the selected map.

This command generally is used to match the aspect ratio with a bitmap that is being projected by the Spotlight.

RELATED COMMAND

Lights/Spot/Create

Lights/Spot/Ranges

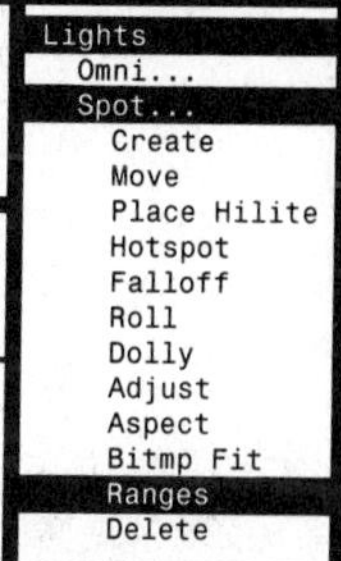

Determines the start and end ranges of an attenuated Spotlight .

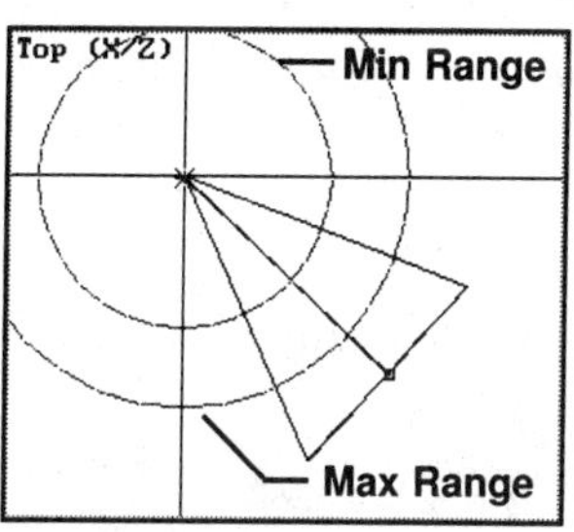

Adjusting the Range of a Spotlight

1. Ensure that a Spotlight has been created previously using *Lights/Spot/Create.*
2. Select *Lights/Spot/Ranges.*
3. Click in the viewport that contains the Spotlight.
4. Click on the Spotlight icon (*) in an orthographic or user viewport.
5. Move the mouse to alter one of the circle or rectangles. If the inner circle is being modified, the start range is being modified or the point where light begins to drop off. If the outer circle is being modified, the end range is being modified or the maximum range the light will spread. Click to set the range.
6. Now move the mouse to alter the other circle or rectangle. Click to set the range or right-click to cancel the command.
7. Click in another orthographic viewport and repeat steps 2 through 6 to ensure that the light is adjusted in all three dimensions.

RELATED COMMANDS

Lights/Spot/Create, Lights/Spot/Hotspot, Lights/Spot/Falloff

Lights/Spot/Delete

Deletes a previously created Spotlight .

Deleting an Spotlight

1. Ensure that a Spotlight has been previously created using *Lights/Spot/Create*.
2. Select *Lights/Spot/Delete*.
3. Click on the Spotlight to delete in any viewport. The Spotlight will be deleted from the scene.

RELATED COMMANDS

Lights/Spot/Create, Lights/Omni/Delete

Cameras/Create

Creates a camera.

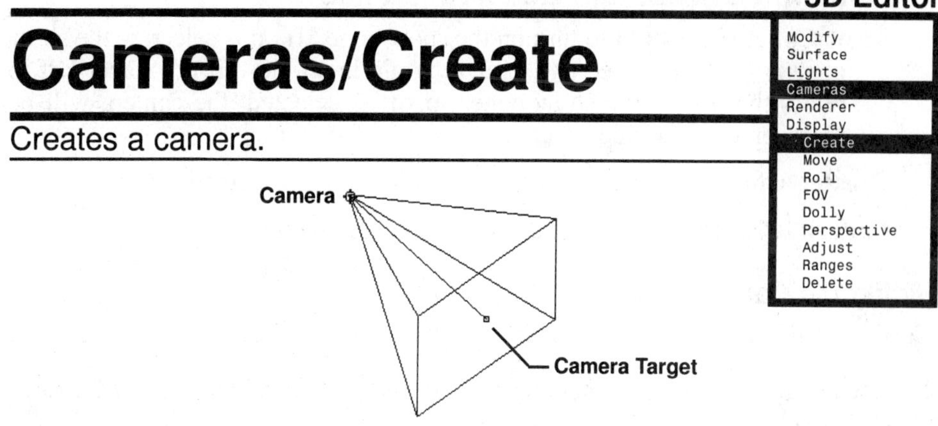

Creating a Camera

1. Activate an orthographic viewport to place the camera.
2. Select *Cameras/Create.*
3. In the active viewport, select the location of the camera.
4. Select the location of the camera target. The Camera Definition dialog box appears.

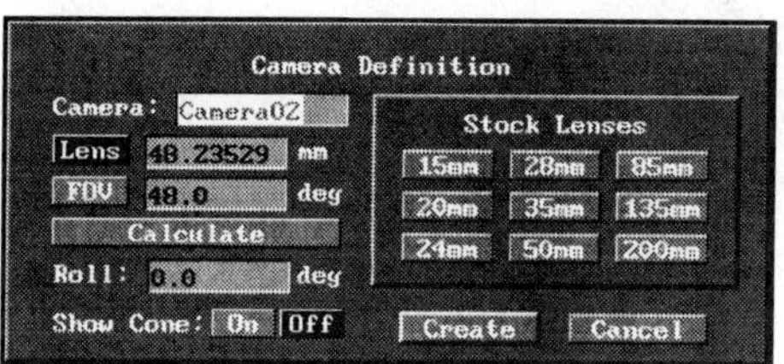

Make adjustments to the Camera with this dialog box.

5. Make settings to the camera using the following options.

   Camera: Give the camera a unique name. It can be up to 10 characters long.

   Lens: Enter a lens in millimeters (mm) or select a lens size from the Stock Lens. The range of camera sizes is 9.857142mm (wide angle) to 10,000,000mm (narrow angle).

   FOV: Enter the camera's Field of View. Field of View is expressed in angles. The range for these angles are 0.00025 degrees to 175 degrees. To determine the corresponding Lens, click on **Calculate**.

   Roll: Used to roll the camera from -180 to 180 degrees. Positive values rotate the camera clockwise; negative values rotate the camera counterclockwise.

Show Cone: Select **On** to turn on the show cone. If on is selected, the show cone will be displayed as a cyan pyramid in all viewports. Select **Off** to reject the use of the show cone. If off is selected, the camera will be represented by a blue line.

Create: Creates a camera in all viewports with the selected settings.

Cancel: Cancels the command and exits the dialog box.

Hiding the Camera Icon(s)

1. Ensure that a camera has been created using *Camera/Create*.
2. Use [Alt] [C] to hide the camera icon(s). Press [Alt] [C] again to display the camera icon(s).

Using a Camera Viewport.

1. Click in any viewport.
2. Use [C] to change the viewport to a camera viewport. If there are multiple cameras, a dialog box will be displayed listing the names of all cameras. Select the camera view to be displayed in the active viewport and click on **OK**.
3. Multiple camera viewports can be created by repeating steps 1 and 2 in another viewport.

RELATED COMMANDS

Cameras/Move, Cameras/Roll, Cameras/FOV

Cameras/Move

Modify
Surface
Lights
Cameras
Renderer
Display
Create
Move
Roll
FOV
Dolly
Perspective
Adjust
Ranges
Delete

Moves a created previously camera or camera target or creates a clone of the camera.

Moving a Camera or Camera Target

1. Ensure that a camera has been created previously using *Cameras/Create.*
2. Select *Cameras/Move.*
3. Click in the orthographic viewport where the camera is to be moved.
4. Select either the camera or the target. The camera or the target is displayed in gray, while the original position is displayed in blue.
5. Move the camera or target to its new location and click to set or right-click to cancel the command.

Cloning a Camera

1. Ensure that a camera has been created previously using *Cameras/Create.*
2. Select *Cameras/Move.*
3. Click in the orthographic viewport where the camera is to be cloned.
4. Hold down [Shift]. Select either the camera or the target.
5. Move the cloned camera to its new position and click or right-click to cancel the command.

Moving the Camera and Target Simultaneously

1. Ensure that a camera has been created previously using *Cameras/Create.*
2. Select *Cameras/Move.*
3. Click in the orthographic viewport where the camera is to be moved.
4. Hold down [Ctrl]. Select either the camera or the target.
5. Move the camera to its new position and click to accept the changes or right-click to cancel the command.

RELATED COMMANDS

Cameras/Create, Cameras/Roll

Modify
Surface
Lights
Cameras
Renderer
Display
Create
Move
Roll
FOV
Dolly
Perspective
Adjust
Ranges
Delete

Cameras/Roll

Adjusts the roll of a camera by rotating it clockwise or counterclockwise.

Adjusting the Roll of a Camera

1. Ensure that a camera has been created previously using *Cameras/Create.*
2. Select *Cameras/Roll.*
3. Click in the viewport that contains the camera.
4. Click on the camera or target. The camera field of view appears in white and the roll angle appears in the status line.
5. Move the mouse sideways to adjust the roll of the camera.
6. Once the roll is modified, click to accept the changes, or right-click to cancel the command.

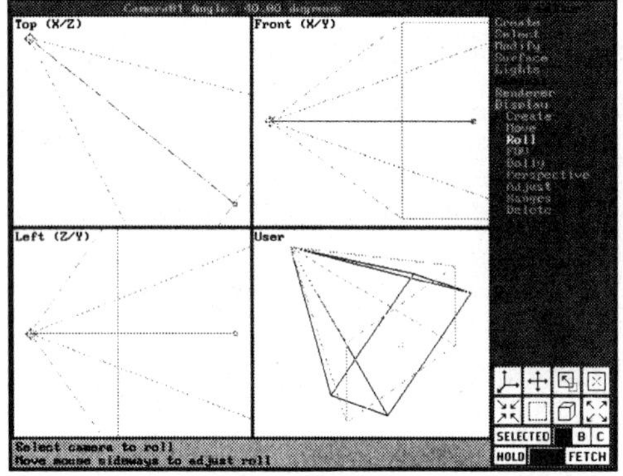

Adjusting the Roll of a Camera.

TIP To allow for more accurate adjustment of the angle, turn angle snap on by pressing [A].

NOTE This command can also be used to clone a Camera. To clone a Camera, hold [Shift] and complete setup 4 above.

TIP Use the camera view to adjust the Roll. Click in a viewport and press [C].

RELATED COMMANDS

Cameras/Create, Lights/Spot/Roll

Cameras/FOV

Modify
Surface
Lights
Cameras
Renderer
Display
Create
Move
Roll
FOV
Dolly
Perspective
Adjust
Ranges
Delete

Adjusts the field of view (FOV) for a created previously camera.

Adjusting the FOV of a Camera

1. Ensure that a camera has been created previously using *Cameras/Create.*
2. Select *Cameras/FOV.*
3. Click in any orthographic viewport.
4. Select the camera or target whose FOV is to be modified. If the Show Cone is on, the original field of view is displayed in cyan and any new changes are displayed in white. If the Show Cone is off, the changes for the FOV are displayed in white and no reference to the prior FOV is displayed. The FOV is displayed in the status line.
5. Move the mouse sideways to adjust the FOV.
6. Click to accept the new FOV settings or right-click to cancel the command.

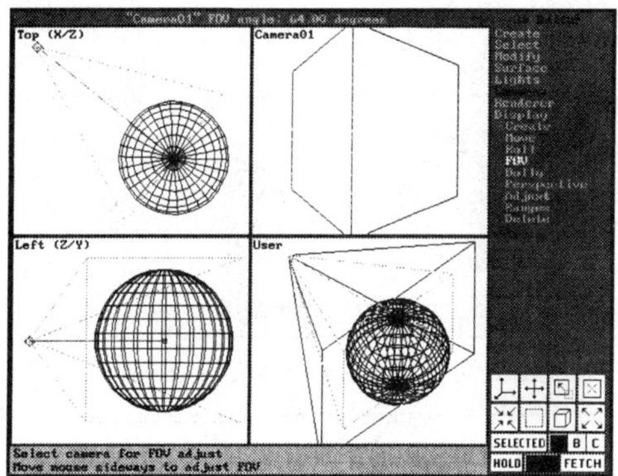

Adjusting the Field of View of a Camera.

RELATED COMMAND

Cameras/Create

Modify
Surface
Lights
Cameras
Renderer
Display
  Create
  Move
  Roll
  FOV
  Dolly
  Perspective
  Adjust
  Ranges
  Delete

Cameras/Dolly

Adjusts the camera toward or away from its target location.

Dolly the Camera

1. Ensure that a camera has been created previously using *Cameras/Create.*
2. Select *Cameras/Dolly.*
3. Click in the viewport that contains the camera.
4. Click on the camera.
5. Move the mouse sideways to dolly the camera.
6. Click to accept the changes, or right-click to cancel the command.

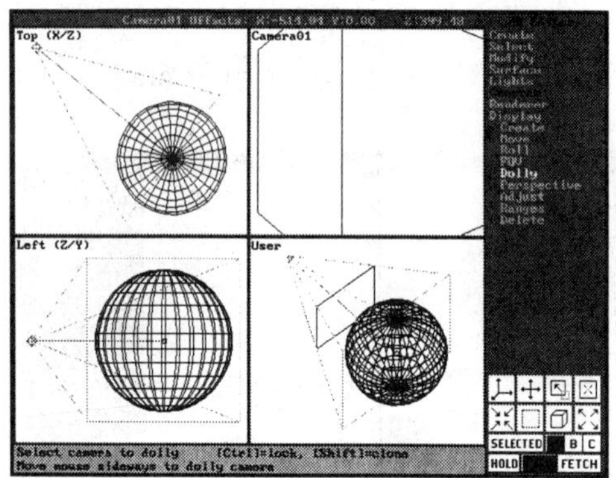

Adjusting the Dolly of a Camera.

NOTE This command can also be used to clone a Camera. To clone a Camera, hold [Shift] and complete setup 4 above.

TIP Use the camera view to adjust the Roll. Click in a viewport and press [C].

RELATED COMMANDS

Cameras/Create, Lights/Spot/Dolly

Cameras/Perspective

Modify
Surface
Lights
Cameras
Renderer
Display
Create
Move
Roll
FOV
Dolly
Perspective
Adjust
Ranges
Delete

Adjusts the FOV and dollies the camera to adjust the perspective of a camera composition.

Changing the Camera Perspective

1. Ensure that a camera has been created previously using *Cameras/Create.*
2. Select *Cameras/Perspective.*
3. Click in the orthographic viewport that contains the camera.
4. Click on the camera.
5. Move the mouse sideways to adjust the perspective. As the camera is moved, the FOV remains unchanged.
6. Click to accept the changes, or right-click to cancel the command.

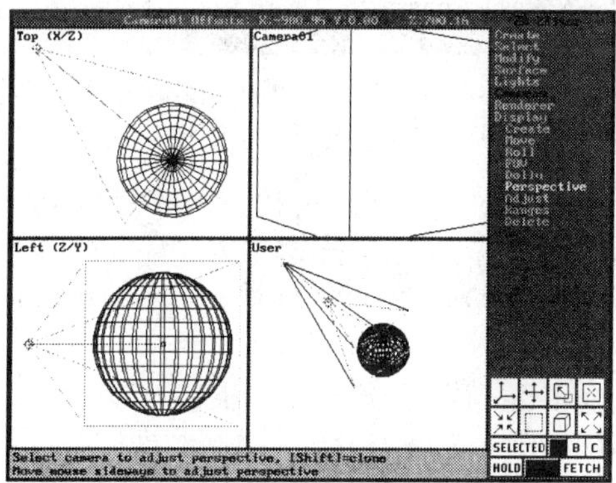

Adjusting the Dolly of a Camera.

This command is useful to match the perspective of a scene with that of a bitmap being used as a background.

RELATED COMMANDS

Cameras/Create, Cameras/Dolly, Cameras/FOV

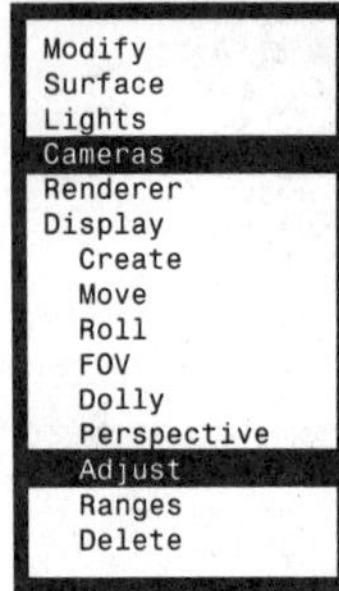

Cameras/Adjust

Adjusts the values of a created previously camera.

Changing the Camera Perspective

1. Ensure that a camera has been created previously using *Cameras/Create.*
2. Select *Cameras/Adjust.*
3. Click in the viewport that contains the camera to be adjusted.
4. Click on the camera to be adjusted. The Camera Definition dialog box appears.

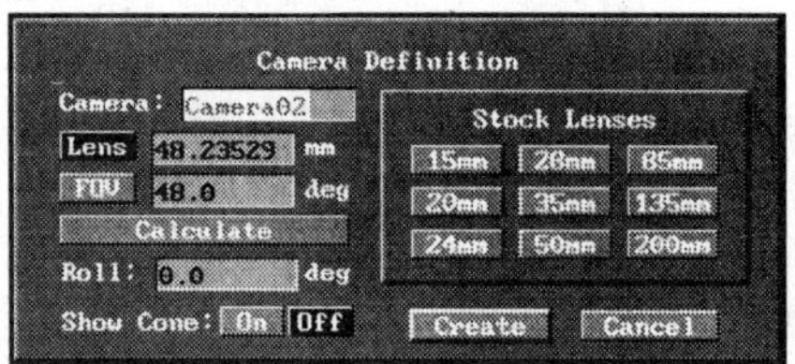

Adust the Camera with this dialog box.

5. Make settings to the camera using the following options.

Camera: Give the camera a unique name. It can be up to 10 characters long.

Lens: Enter a lens in millimeters (mm) or select a lens size from Stock Lenses. The range of camera sizes is 9.857142mm (wide angle) to 10,000,000mm (narrow angle).

FOV: Enter the camera's Field of View. Field of View is expressed in angles. The range for these angles is 0.00025 degrees to 175 degrees. To determine the corresponding Lens, click on the **Calculate** button.

Roll: Used to roll the camera from -180 to 180 degrees. Positive values rotate the camera clockwise; negative values rotate the camera counterclockwise.

Show Cone: Select **On** to turn on the show cone. If **On** is selected, the show cone will be displayed as a cyan pyramid in all viewports. Select **Off** reject the use of the show cone. If **Off** is selected, the camera will be represented by a blue line.

Create: Creates a camera in all viewports with the selected settings.

Cancel: Cancels the command and exits the dialog box.

RELATED COMMANDS

Camera/Create, Cameras/Move, Cameras/Roll, Cameras/FOV

Cameras/Ranges

Modify
Surface
Lights
Cameras
Renderer
Display
Create
Move
Roll
FOV
Dolly
Perspective
Adjust
Ranges
Delete

Adjusts the near and far range limits for fog and atmosphere effects.

Adjusting the Camera Range Limits

1. Ensure that a camera has been created previously.
2. Select *Cameras/Ranges*.
3. Select the camera, not the target. The current ranges are displayed around the camera as red concentric circles.
4. Move the mouse to change the size of the first range.
5. Click to set the range.
6. Move the mouse again to change the size of the second range. The two circles will appear as shown in the figure below.
7. Click to set the range or right-click to cancel the command.

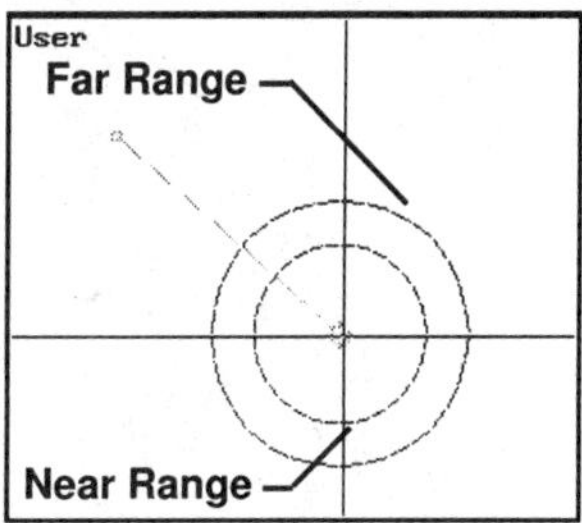

Setting the Near and Far ranges of a Camera.

The circle closest to the camera represents the near range, the circle farther away represents the far range.

RELATED COMMAND

Renderer/Setup/Atmosphere

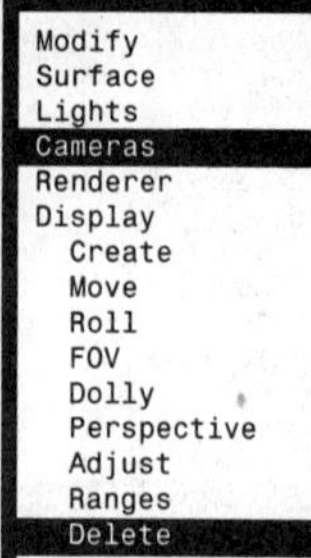

Cameras/Delete

Deletes a created previously camera in the Keyframer and the 3D Editor.

Deleting a Camera

1. Ensure that a camera has been created previously using *Camera/Create.*
2. Select *Camera/Delete.*
3. Click on the camera to delete in any viewport. The camera is deleted from the scene.

RELATED COMMAND

Cameras/Omni/Create, Cameras/Spot/Delete

Renderer/Render View

Renderer
Render View
Render Region
Render Blowup
Render Object
Render Last
Setup...
Atmosphere
Background
Configure
Options
Shadows
Make .CUB
View
Image
Flic

Renders an active viewport.

Rendering an Active Viewport

1. Select *Renderer/Render View.*
2. Click in any viewport to render. The Render Still Image dialog box appears.

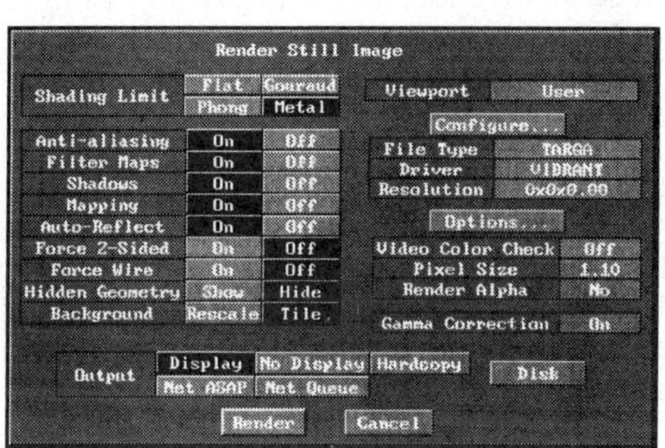

Configure the renderer with this dialog box.

3. Configure the renderer using the following options.

Shading Limit: Select the shading method used in the rendering.

Flat: Renders each face as a single solid color; useful for quick renderings where very little detail is needed.

Gouraud: Renders each face as a color gradient; useful for checking light placement and scene composition. No materials, textures, shades, or shadows are displayed.

Phong: Renders each pixel individually using its given surface properties. Phong is required for shading, shadows, bump mapping, transparency, and reflections.

Metal: Renders each pixel and applies a rendering technique that gives each object a metallic look. Metal is required for shading, shadows, bump maps, transparency, and reflections.

Antialiasing: Select **On** to prevent "jaggies" in curved lines and diagonal lines. Select **Off** only to speed up "check" renderings.

Filter Maps: Select **On** to filter mapped materials. Select **Off** when background objects need to appear sharp and defined.

Shadows: Select **On** to cast shadows from spotlights in a scene. Select **Off** if no shadows are needed and to decrease rendering time.

Mapping: Select **On** to use material maps. Select **Off** to ignore map materials and decrease rendering time.

Auto-Reflect: Select **On** to use reflection maps. Select **Off** to ignore reflection maps and decrease rendering time.

Forced 2-sided: Select **On** to render both sides of the faces in a scene. This is useful if objects do not have their faces properly "normalized" or the inside of an object needs to be rendered as well as the outside. Select **Off** to ignore two-sided faces and to dramatically reduce the amount of rendering time.

Force Wire: Select **On** to render all surfaces using a single pixel-width wire attribute. Select **Off** to render all surfaces normally.

Hidden Geometry: Select **Show** to render hidden objects as well as visible objects. Use this option to ensure that automatic reflection maps are created. Select **Hide** to render only the objects that are not hidden.

Background: Select **Rescale** to change modify the background bitmap resolution to match that of the rendering resolution. Select **Tile** to keep the existing bitmap resolution, but to repeat the bitmap if its resolution is smaller than that of the rendering resolution.

Configure: Displays the Device Configuration dialog box. See *Renderer/Setup/Configure* for more information.

Options: Displays the Render Options dialog box. See *Renderer/Setup/Option* for more information.

Output: Determines the output of the Renderer.

Display: Renders to the screen.

No Display: Selects the **Null** display driver.

Hard Copy: Renders to a configured hardcopy device.

Net ASAP: Places the rendering as the number one priority in a network rendering configuration.

Net Queue: Places the rendering as the lowest priority in the network rendering configuration.

Disk: Renders to a file. When this option is selected and the **Render** button is selected, a file selector will be displayed. Choose the name and location of the file and click on **OK**. The Renderer will proceed.

4. Select **Render** to start the rendering process or **Cancel** to cancel the command and close the dialog box.

5. If **Render** is selected, the Rendering in Progress... dialog box appears as shown below. The rendering progress bar gives a visual indication of how much time is left for the rendering and the rest of the dialog box is devoted to displaying what options were chosen for the rendering. Use the spacebar to toggle between this dialog box

and the image being rendered.

6. To cancel the rendering, press [Esc] or right-click.
7. Once the rendering is completed it will be displayed on screen. Press [Esc] or right-click to return to the viewport display.

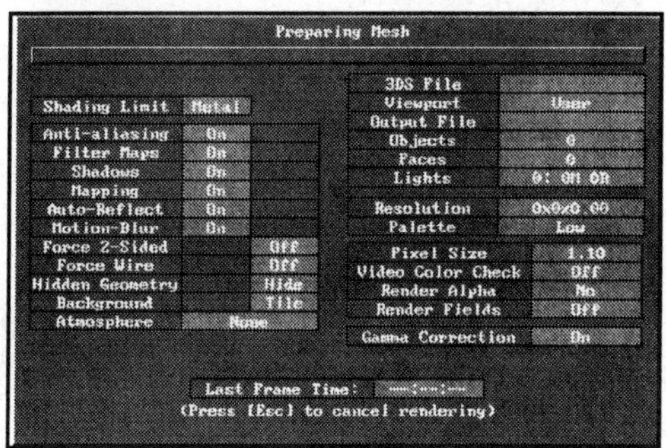

The rendering status is displayed.

RELATED COMMANDS

Renderer/Render Last, Renderer/Setup/Configure

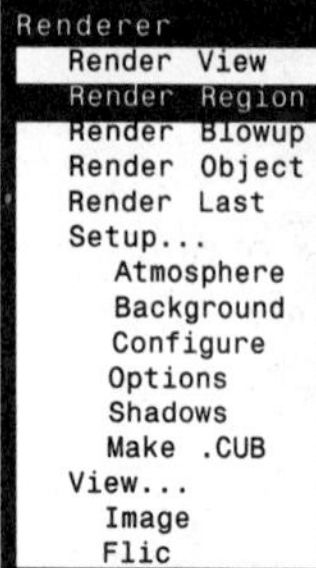

Render/Render Region

Renders a selected region of the active viewport.

Rendering a Region

1. Activate the viewport that contains the region to be rendered.
2. Select *Render/Render Region.*
3. In the active viewport, click to specify the beginning corner of the region. Move the mouse diagonally to the opposite corner of the region and click as shown in the figure below. The Render Still Image dialog box appears.
4. Repeat the steps of the *Renderer/Render View* command. Only the selected region will be rendered as shown below.
5. Use Esc to cancel the rendering.

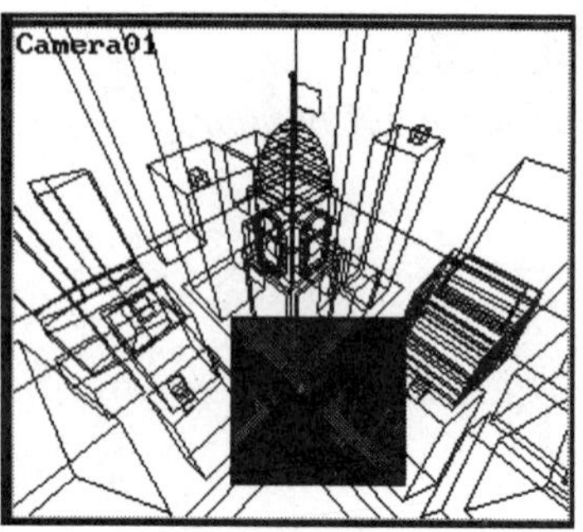

Rendering a Region.

TIP To compare this region with a previous rendered view, set the CLEAR-BUFFER setting in the *3ds.set* file to NO using a text editor. Use *Renderer/Render View* to render a scene. Make any adjustments to an object within the region to be compared. Select *Renderer/Render Region*. Because the previous rendering will not be cleared from the frame buffer, the new region will be placed directly on top of the old region in the previous rendering and allow a comparison.

RELATED COMMANDS

Renderer/Render View, Renderer/Render Blowup

Renderer/Render Blowup

```
Renderer
  Render View
  Render Region
  Render Blowup
  Render Object
  Render Last
  Setup...
    Atmosphere
    Background
    Configure
    Options
    Shadows
    Make .CUB
  View...
    Image
    Flic
```

Renders a region and then scales the region to match that of the rendering resolution.

Rendering a Blowup

1. Activate the viewport that contains the region to be rendered.
2. Select *Render/Render Blowup.*
3. In the active viewport, click to specify the beginning corner of the region, move the mouse diagonally to the opposite corner of the region, and click as shown in the figure below. The Render Still Image dialog box appears.
4. Repeat the steps of *Renderer/Render View.* Note that the Configure button in the Render Still Image dialog box is not accessible. The selected region will be rendered to match the resolution of the rendering device as shown below.
5. Use [Esc] or right-click to cancel the rendering.

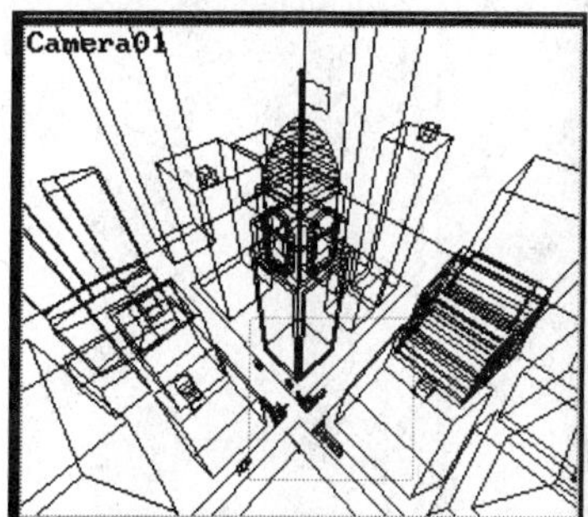

Region is specified.

The rendered region.

RELATED COMMANDS

Render/Render View, Renderer/Render Region

Renderer
- Render View
- Render Region
- Render Blowup
- Render Object
- Render Last
- Setup...
  - Atmosphere
  - Background
  - Configure
  - Options
  - Shadows
  - Make .CUB
- View...
  - Image
  - Flic

Renderer/Render Object

Renders a single object in a scene.

Rendering a Single Object

1. Create an object in the 3D Editor.
2. Activate the viewport that contains the object to be rendered.
3. Select *Render/Render Object.*
4. In the active viewport, click on the object to be rendered. The Render Still Image dialog box appears.
5. Repeat the steps of the *Renderer/Render View* command. Only the selected object will be rendered as shown below.
6. Use Esc or right-click to cancel the rendering.

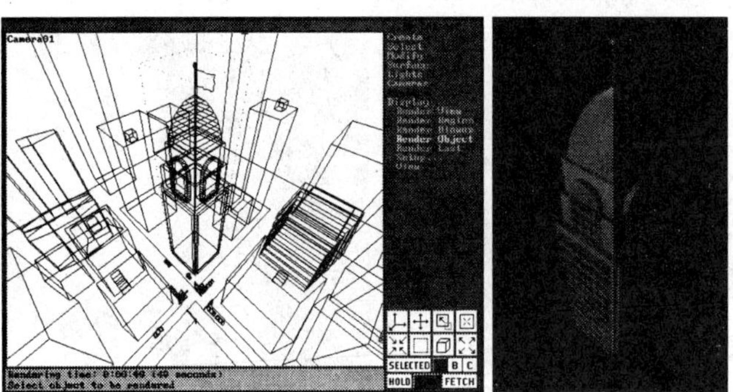

Rendering a single object in a scene

Use this command to quickly view the changes to an object such as geometry modifications and light placement.

RELATED COMMAND

Renderer/Render View

Renderer/Render Last

```
Renderer
  Render View
  Render Region
  Render Blowup
  Render Object
  Render Last
  Setup...
    Atmosphere
    Background
    Configure
    Options
    Shadows
    Make .CUB
  View...
    Image
    Flic
```

Repeats the last rendering command using all previous settings.

Using Render Last

1. Ensure that a rendering was created previously using *Render View*, *Render Region*, *Render Blowup*, or *Render Object*.
2. Make necessary changes to the scene.
3. Select *Renderer/Render Last*. No dialog box is displayed and the rendering is immediately started using all previous rendering configurations.
4. Use [Esc] or right-click to cancel the rendering.

> **TIP** Use this command to compare changes made to the scene without excess keystrokes or command selections.

RELATED COMMANDS

Renderer/Render View, Renderer/Render Region, Renderer/Render Blowup, Renderer/Render Object.

Renderer
Render View
Render Region
Render Blowup
Render Object
Render Last
Setup...
Atmosphere
Background
Configure
Options
Shadows
Make .CUB
View...
Image
Flic

Renderer/Setup/Atmosphere

Modifies the Atmosphere settings.

Modifying Atmosphere Settings

1. Select *Renderer/Setup/Atmosphere.* The Atmosphere Definition dialog box appears as shown below.

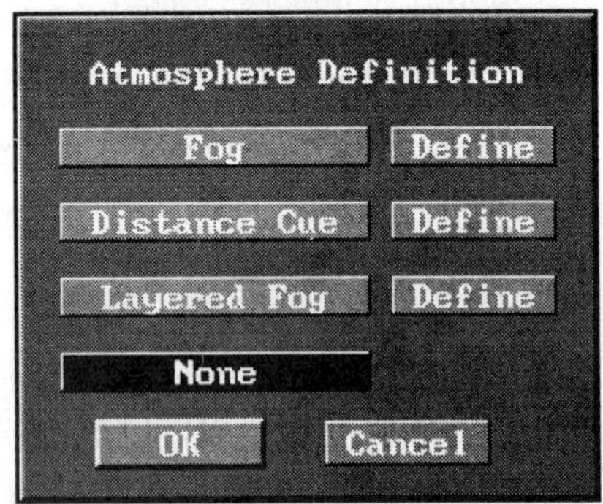

Control Atmospheric settings with this dialog box.

2. Select the options from the list below.

   Fog: Fades the colors of the objects to another color (default is white) to simulate a fog effect in a camera viewport.

   Distance Cue: Fades the colors of the objects to black in a camera viewport.

   Layered Fog: Creates a layer of fog that is independent from the camera viewport and can be placed based on world coordinates.

   None: Deselects all atmosphere effects.

   Define: Selects the define button to the right of an effect to modify that effect's settings.

   OK: Accepts the settings and closes the dialog box.

   Cancel: Cancels the command and closes the dialog box.

3. Render the scene to see the new effects.

Modify the Fog Definition

1. Select *Renderer/Setup/Atmosphere.* The Atmosphere Definition dialog box appears.

2. Select **Fog**.

3. Click on the *Define* button next to fog. The Fog Definition dialog box appears as shown below. Make changes to the settings as explained below. Use the color sliders to establish fog color.

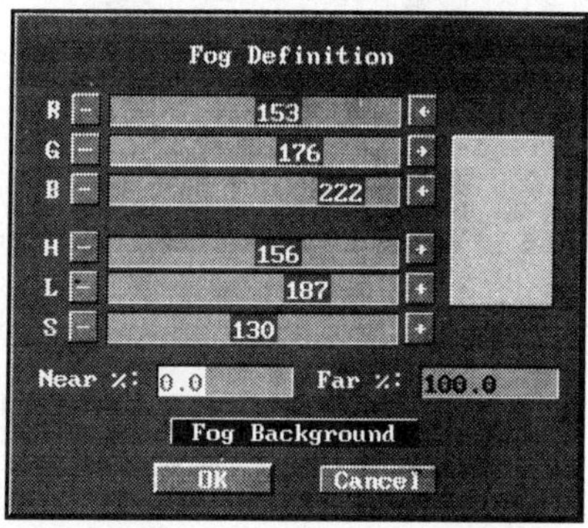

Use this dialog box to control the fog attributes.

R: Changes the red color value of the fog.

G: Changes the green color value of the fog.

B: Changes the blue color value of the fog.

H: Changes the hue value of the fog.

L: Changes the luminance value of the fog.

S: Changes the saturation value of the fog.

Near %: Specifies the percentage that the color value will affect the objects near the front of the scene. 0% would yield no effect while 100% would change the color of all objects to the selected color

Far %: Specifies the percentage that the color value will effect the objects in the rear of the scene.

Fog Background: Changes the background to match the color value of the Far % value.

OK: Accepts the settings and closes the dialog box.

Cancel: Cancels the command and closes the dialog box.

4. Render the scene to see the fog effect applied.

Modifying the Distance Cue

1. Select *Renderer/Setup/Atmosphere.* The Atmosphere Definition dialog box appears.
2. Select *Distance Cue.*
3. Click on the **Define** button next to distance cue. The Distance-Cueing dialog box appears as shown below. Make changes to the settings as explained below.

Near %: Specifies the percentage that the objects near the front of the scene will dim: 0% yields no effect while 100% dims the object to black.

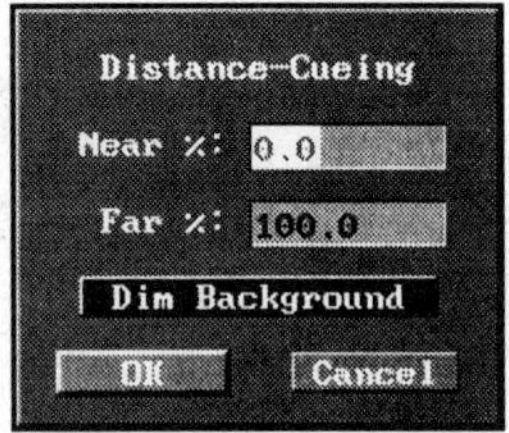

The Distance-Cueing dialog box.

Far %: Specifies the percentage that the objects to the rear of the scene will dim.

Dim Background: Changes the background to match the dim value of the Far % value.

OK: Accepts the settings and closes the dialog box.

Cancel: Cancels the command and closes the dialog box.

4. Render the scene to see the fog effect applied.

Modifying the Layered Fog

1. Select *Renderer/Setup/Atmosphere*. The Atmosphere Definition dialog box appears.
2. Select *Layered Fog*.
3. Click on the *Define* button next to distance cue. The Layered Fog Definition dialog box appears as shown below. Make changes to the settings as explained below.

   R: Changes the red color value of the fog.

   G: Changes the green color value of the fog.

   B: Changes the blue color value of the fog.

   H: Changes the hue value of the fog.

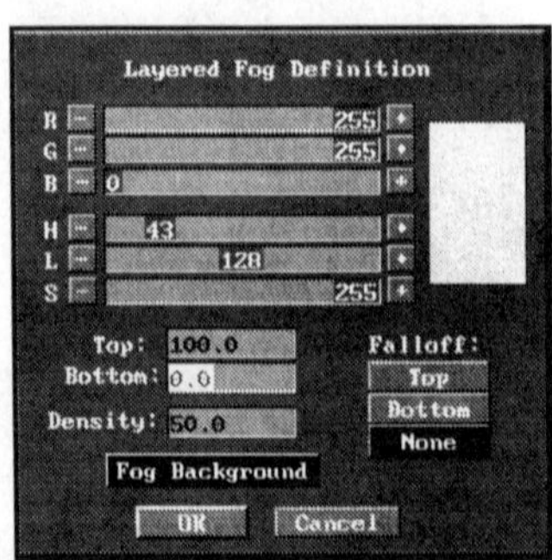

Use this dialog box to control the Layered Fog attributes.

L: Changes the luminance value of the fog.

S: Changes the saturation value of the fog.

Top: Sets the top altitude, in world coordinates, of the layer of fog.

Bottom: Sets the bottom altitude, in world coordinates, of the layer of fog.

Density: Specifies the opacity of the layer of fog: 100% yields a layer of fog that is completely opaque whereas 50% yields a layer of fog that is half as opaque.

Falloff:

Top: When selected, the density of the fog at the top altitude drops to 0%.

Bottom: When selected, the density of the fog at the bottom altitude would drop to 0%.

None: When selected, will produce a layer of fog with the same density from top to bottom altitudes.

Fog Background: Changes the background to match the values set in the Layered Fog Definition dialog box.

OK: Accepts the settings and closes the dialog box.

Cancel: Cancels the command and closes the dialog box.

4. Render the scene to see the fog effect applied.

RELATED COMMAND

Renderer/Setup/Background

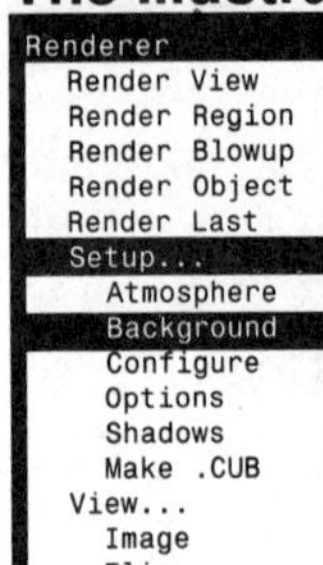

Renderer/Setup/Background

Defines the background of a scene using a solid color, a gradient, or a bitmap.

Setting up a Background

1. Select *Renderer/Setup/Background.* The Background Method dialog box appears as shown below.

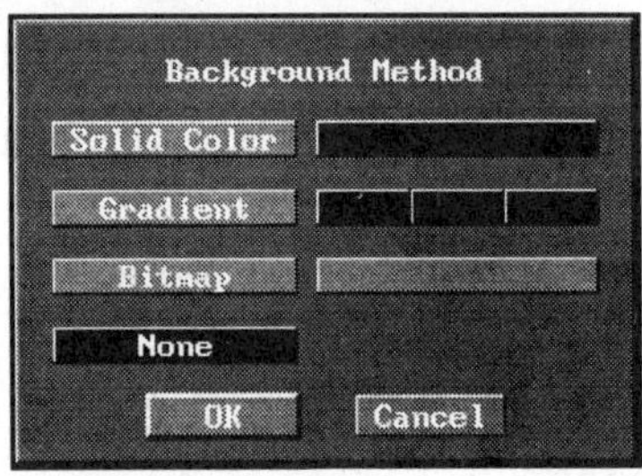

The Background Method dialog box.

2. Select the options from the list below.

   Solid Color: Changes the color of the background.

   Gradient: Sets a gradient color pattern for the background.

   Bitmap: Selects a bitmap to be used as the background.

   None: Deselects all backgrounds.

   OK: Accepts the settings and closes the dialog box.

   Cancel: Cancels the command and closes the dialog box.

3. Render the scene to see the new effects.

Modifying a Solid Background

1. Select *Renderer/Setup/Background.* The Background Method dialog box appears.

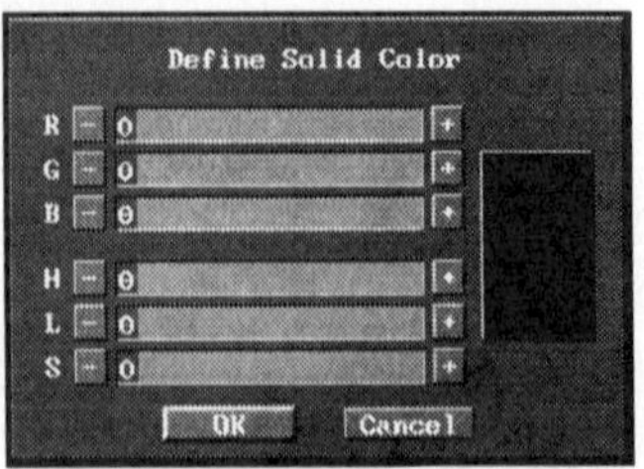

Select the Background Color with this dialog box.

2. Select *Solid Color.*
3. Click on the color swatch to the right of the *Solid Color* button. The Define Solid Color dialog box appears as shown below. Make changes to the settings below.

   R: Changes the red color value of the fog.

   G: Changes the green color value of the fog.

   B: Changes the blue color value of the fog.

   H: Changes the hue value of the fog.

   L: Changes the luminance value of the fog.

   S: Changes the saturation value of the fog.

   OK: Accepts the settings and closes the dialog box.

   Cancel: Cancels the command and closes the dialog box.
4. Render the scene to see the background effect applied.

Modifying a Gradient Background

1. Select *Renderer/Setup/Background.* The Background Method dialog box appears.
2. Select *Gradient.* The Define Gradient Colors dialog box appears.
3. Click on the gradient swatch to the right of the *Gradient* button. The Define Gradient Colors dialog box appears as shown below.

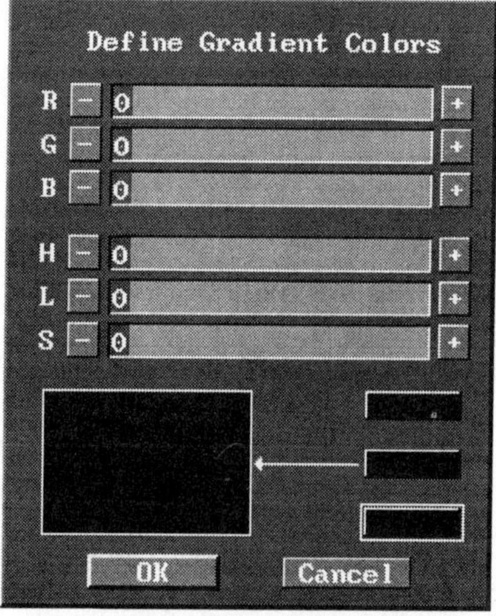

Defining a Gradient Background.

4. Select the top, middle, or bottom swatch at the bottom right of the dialog box.
5. Make changes to the gradient color by selecting the swatch and then changing the color sliders. The changes will be shown in the background preview window at the bottom left of the dialog box.
6. Repeat step 5 for the two remaining gradient colors if necessary.
7. Select **OK** to accept the values and close the dialog box. Select **Cancel** to cancel the command and close the dialog box.
8. Render the scene to see the background effect applied.

Selecting a Bitmap Background

1. Select *Renderer/Setup/Background.* The Background Method dialog box appears.
2. Select *Bitmap.*
3. Select the button to the right of the *Bitmap* button. A file selector dialog box appears.
4. Select the bitmap file to used as a background. The Background Method dialog box reappears with the name of the bitmap file on the button.
5. Render the scene to see the bitmap background.

NOTE When rendering, if the bitmap resolution does not match the rendering resolution, a warning will be displayed and you will be offered the option of scaling the background to match the rendering resolution.

RELATED COMMAND

Renderer/Render View

Renderer/Setup/Configure

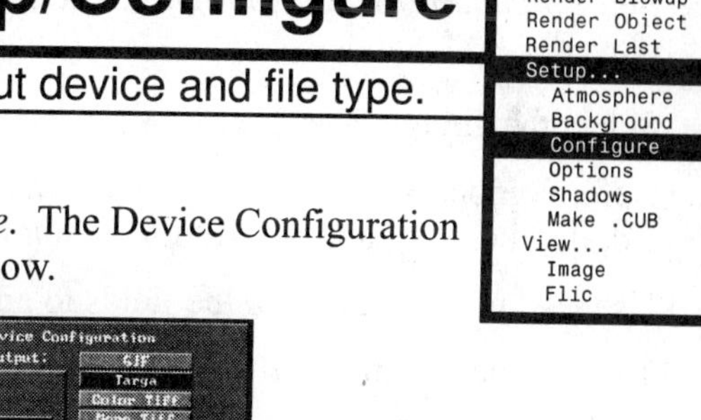

Configures the Renderer output device and file type.

Configuring the Renderer

1. Select *Renderer/Setup/Configure.* The Device Configuration dialog box appears as shown below.

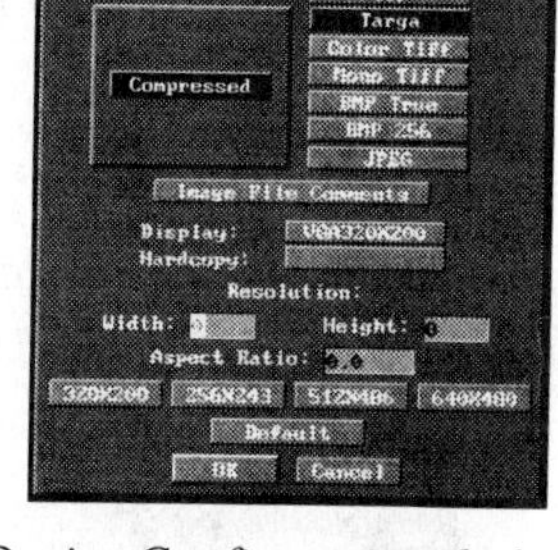

The Device Configuration dialog box.

2. Make changes as outlined in the sections below.
3. Render the scene to verify the changes.

Configuring the Rendering File Output

1. Select *Renderer/Setup/Configure.* The Device Configuration dialog box is displayed.
2. Make a selection from the **File Output:** options as shown below.

   Compressed: Compresses the renderer output file.

   Gif: Creates a Graphics Interchange Format (.gif) file.

   Targa: Creates a Targa (.tga) file.

   Color Tiff: Creates a color Tagged Image File Format (.tif) file.

   Mono Tiff: Creates a monochrome Tagged Image File Format (.tif) file.

   BMP True: Creates a Microsoft® Windows™ truecolor bitmap (.bmp) file.

   BMP 256: Creates a Microsoft® Windows™ 256- color bitmap (.bmp) file.

   JPEG: Creates a Joint Photographic Experts Group (.jpg) file.
3. Click **OK** to accept the selection.

Adding Comments to a Targa File

1. Select *Renderer/Setup/Configure*. The Device Configuration dialog box is displayed.
2. Select the **Image File Comments** button.
3. Before rendering using *Renderer/Render View* or any other render command, a dialog box will appear. Add the comments in the dialog box.
4. Use [Tab] to cycle through the fields to add comments.
5. To view the comments after the rendering has been completed, select *File-File Info*.

Changing the Rendering Device

1. Select *Renderer/Setup/Configure*. The Device Configuration dialog box is displayed.

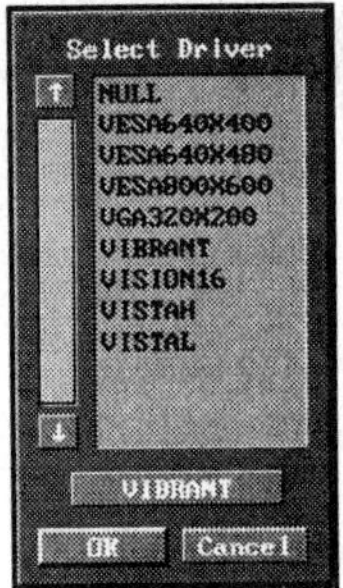

Selecting a rendering driver.

2. Select the button to the right of **Display:**. The Select Driver dialog box appears as shown below.
3. Select the display device from the list below. The selection will appear in the selection box.

   NULL: Turns off output to the screen. Use this option when rendering to a file that has a resolution larger than that of the display. Using the NULL setting decreases rendering times.

   VESA: Renders to the VESA display driver.

   VGA320X200: Renders to the VGA320X200 Variable Graphics Array (VGA) driver.

   VIBRANT: Renders to the VIBRANT driver.

   VISION16: Renders to the Vision Technologies Vision 16 frame grabber.

   VISTAH: Renders to the Truevision Vista high- resolution (756x486) frame buffer.

VISTAL: Renders to the Truevision Vista low- resolution (512x468) frame buffer.

4. Click **OK** to accept the selection. The dialog box will be closed and the display device will be shown on the button.

Changing the Hardcopy Device

1. Select *Renderer/Setup/Configure.* The Device Configuration dialog box is displayed.
2. Select the button to the right of **Hardcopy:**.
3. Select the hardcopy device from the list. The selection will appear in the selection box.
4. Click **OK** to accept the selection. The dialog box will be closed and the display device will be shown on the button.

Changing the Resolution of a Rendering

1. Select *Renderer/Setup/Configure.* The Device Configuration dialog box is displayed.
2. Make the appropriate **Resolution:** settings from the list below.

   Width: Specifies the resolution width of the rendering.

   Height: Specifies the resolution height of the rendering.

   Aspect Ratio: Specifies the aspect ratio for the rendering, which corrects such problems as circles being rendered as ovals.

   320x200: Automatically sets the resolution and aspect ratio for standard VGA devices.

   512x400: Automatically sets the resolution and aspect ratio for Targa devices.

   640x400: Automatically sets the resolution and aspect ratio for VGA.

   600x480: Automatically sets the resolution and aspect ratio for extended mode VGA.

   Default: Changes the resolution and aspect ratio to its default values.
3. Click **OK** to accept the selection.

RELATED COMMANDS

Renderer/Render View, Renderer/Setup/Options

Renderer
Render View
Render Region
Render Blowup
Render Object
Render Last
Setup...
Atmosphere
Background
Configure
Options
Shadows
Make.CUB
View...
Image
Flic

Renderer/Setup/Options

Modifies the systems parameters available for rendering.

Modifying Rendering System Parameters

1. Select *Renderer/Setup/Options*. The Render Options dialog box is displayed as shown below.

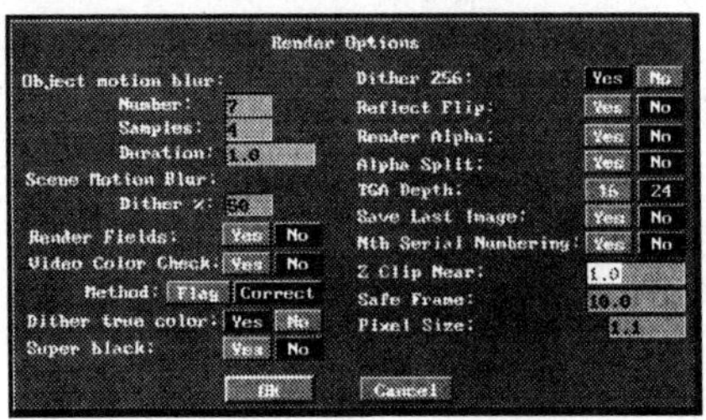

This busy dialog box is not as complicated as it appears.

2. Make the appropriate changes to the parameters listed below.

Object motion blur: Blurs an object when rendered to give it the appearance of movement. Before setting these parameters, ensure that an object has been selected for motion blur with the *Object/Motion Blur* command in the Keyframer.

Number: Sets the number of times that the object will be duplicated to produce the blur effect.

Samples: Dithers the motion-blur copies that were specified with the *Number:* setting. The value should be less than or equal to the *Number:* setting.

Duration: Sets the spacing between the original object and its motion blue copies. This determines the amount of time that the "shutter" is open during the frame.

Scene Motion Blur: Applies motion blur to the whole scene.

Dither %: Sets the percentage of dither to be used.

Render Field: Renders to video fields on videotape as opposed to frames in a file.

Video Color Check: Verifies that the color value for pixels is within the safe limits for NTSC and PAL video formats using one of the two methods listed below.

Video Color Check: Verifies that the color value for pixels is within the safe limits for NTSC and PAL video formats using one of the two methods listed below.

Method:

Flag: Any pixels that fall out of the limits are rendered in black. This allows you to see the incorrect pixels.

Correct: Automatically reduces the pixel to a safe color level.

Dither true color: Performs color and alpha calculation in 64-bit mode before transferring the information to 24- or 32- bit output files.

Super Black: Sets the deepest black in the scene to the SUPER-BLACK parameter in the *3ds.set* file.

Dither-256: Used only with 256 color VGA, this option dithers colors to smooth out color transitions.

Reflect-Flip: When set to Yes, reflection maps are flipped.

Render-Alpha: Renders Targa files at 32-bits which increases definition of objects for use with Video Post.

Alpha-Spit: Saves the additional information provided by Render-Alpha as a separate file. A rendering with a filename *rocket.tga* has its alpha information saved in a file with the filename *a_rocket.tga*.

TGA Depth:

16: Creates 16-bit dithered Targa files.

24: Creates 24-bit Targa files.

Save-Last-Image: Determines whether the last rendering is temporarily saved to disk so that it may be viewed using *Renderer/View/Last* or saved using *Render/View/Save Last.*

Nth Serial Numbering: Selects numbering of successive Targa rendering files.

Z-Clip-Near: Specifies the clipping plane distance from the camera. The value will be determined based on the given units. Change the clipping plane to a value larger than 1 to see inside an object after it is rendered.

Safe Frame: Sets the amount, in percentages, outside the screen for the safe frame. The range of the values is 0 through 100.

Pixel Size: Changes the pixel size from 1.0 to 1.5. A larger value smooths object edges for use in broadcast quality renderings.

Renderer
Render View
Render Region
Render Blowup
Render Object
Render Last
Setup...
Atmosphere
Background
Configure
Options
Shadows
Make .CUB
View...
Image
Flic

Renderer/Setup/Shadows

Modifies the values of the shadows parameters.

Modifying Shadow Parameters

1. Select *Renderer/Setup/Shadows.* The Global Shadow Control dialog box appears as shown below.

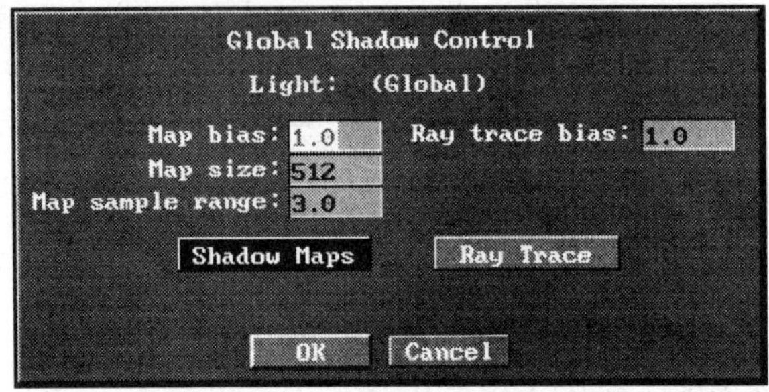

The Global Shadow Control dialog box.

2. Make the appropriate changes to the parameters listed below.

Map bias: Adjusts the shadow map toward or away from the shadow-casting object(s). The value range is any positive number.

Map size: Adjusts the size of shadow maps. The value range is 10 to 4,096 pixels^2. Increasing this value from the default 512 will take up more memory and may not produce more realistic shadows.

Map sample range: Adjusts the sharpness of the edge of a shadow map. The value range is 1 (sharp edges) to 5 (softer edges). Values higher than 5 will yield unpredictable results.

Ray trace bias: Adjusts the ray trace map either toward or away from the shadow-casting object(s) The value range is any positive number.

Shadow Maps: Selects the shadow maps method of producing shadows from the spotlight using the map settings described above. When this selection is chosen, the button is red.

Ray Trace: Selects the ray trace method of producing shadows from the spotlight using the Ray Trace Bias setting describe above. When this selection is chosen, the button is red.

Use Global Settings: Selects whether to use the above shadow settings (Off) or the setting specified with *Renderer/Setup/Shadows* (On).

OK: Accepts the above settings and returns to the Spotlight Definition dialog box.

Cancel: Cancels the above settings and returns to the Spotlight Definition dialog box.

3. Render the scene to see the adjustments.

RELATED COMMAND

Lights/Spot/Adjust

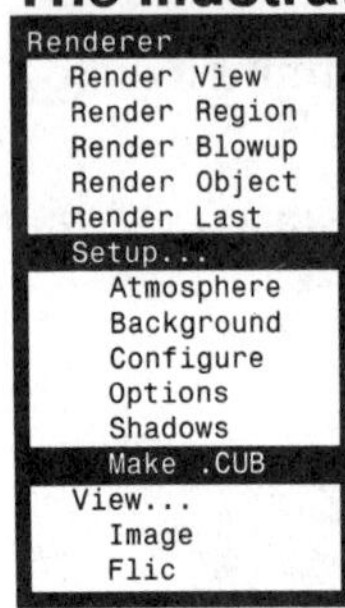

Renderer/Setup/Make .CUB

Creates six Targa files that make up the cubic environment map from the center of a selected object. It also creates an ASCII file that list the names of the six Targa files that can be assigned as a material later.

Making a Cubic Environment Map (*.cub*) File

1. Select *Renderer/Setup/Make .CUB.*

2. Click on an object in the active viewport that contains the center of the cubic reflection map. The Generate Cubic Environment Map dialog box appears as shown below.

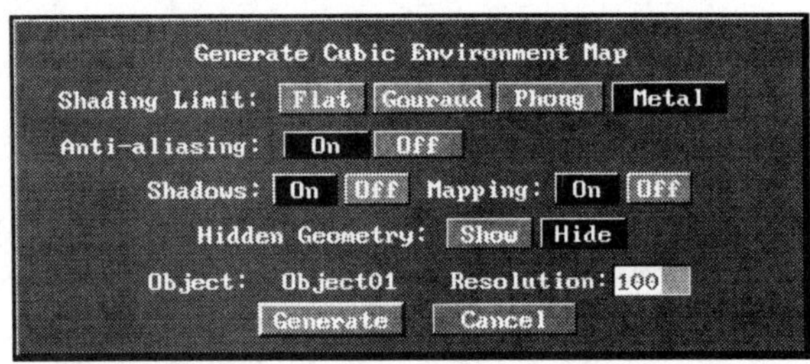

Use this dialog box to create Cubic Reflection Maps.

3. Make the appropriate changes to the parameters listed below.

Shading Limit:

Flat: Renders each face as a single solid color; useful for quick renderings where very little detail is needed.

Gouraud: Renders each face as a color gradient; useful for checking light placement and scene composition. No materials, textures, shades, or shadows are displayed.

Phong: Renders each pixel individually using its given surface properties. Phong is required for shading, shadows, bump mapping, transparency, and reflections.

Metal: Renders each pixel and applies a rendering technique that gives each object a metallic look. Metal is required for shading, shadows, bump maps, transparency, and reflections.

Antialiasing: Select **On** to prevent "jaggies" in curved lines and diagonal lines in the renderings. Select **Off** only to speed up renderings.

Shadows: Select **On** to cast shadows from Spotlights in a scene. Select **Off** if no shadows are needed and to decrease rendering time.

Mapping: Select **On** to use material maps in the reflections. Select **Off** to ignore map materials and decrease rendering time.

Hidden Geometry: Select **Show** to render hidden objects as well as visible objects. Use this option to ensure that automatic reflection maps are created. Select **Hide** to render only the objects that are not hidden.

Object: Displays the name of the object selected.

Resolution: Sets the size in pixels of the cubic reflection map. Because this is a cubic reflection map, a value of 200 creates a file with a resolution of 200 x 200.

4. After setting the parameters, select **Generate**. A file selector will appear.
5. Enter a six-character filename and location for the *.cub* file and click **OK**. The Rendering in Progress dialog box appears and the six files are rendered to disk. They will not appear on the screen. The .cub ASCII file is also created.
6. The six files are named using the six characters provided and then ended with the appropriate view descriptions as shown below.

rocketbk.tga	Back
rocketdn.tga	Bottom (Down)
rocketft.tga	Front
rocketlf.tga	Left
rocketrt.tga	Right
rocketup.tga	Top (Up)

Using the *.cub* File as a Reflection Map

1. Activate the Materials Editor.
2. Select the reflection map button for a material. A file selector will appear.
3. Select the *.cub* file as the reflection map and click on **OK**.
4. The *.cub* file will appear on the reflection map button.
5. Render the scene.

RELATED COMMAND

Renderer/Render View

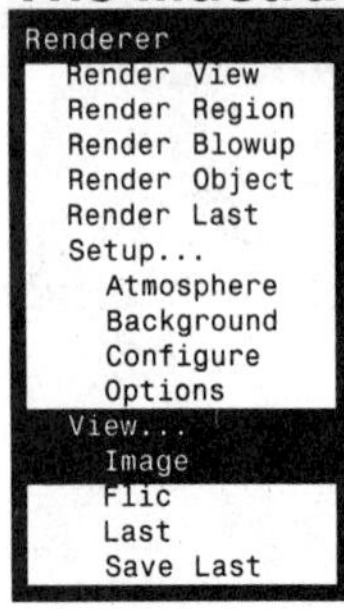

Renderer/View/Image

Displays a previously created bitmap file on the screen.

Displaying an Image on the Screen

1. Select *Renderer/View/Image*. A file selector appears.
2. Select the bitmap file to be viewed and click on **OK**.
3. If the bitmap file resolution matches or is lower than the screen display resolution, it will be displayed on the screen.
4. If the bitmap resolution is greater than the screen resolution the dialog box shown below will be displayed.

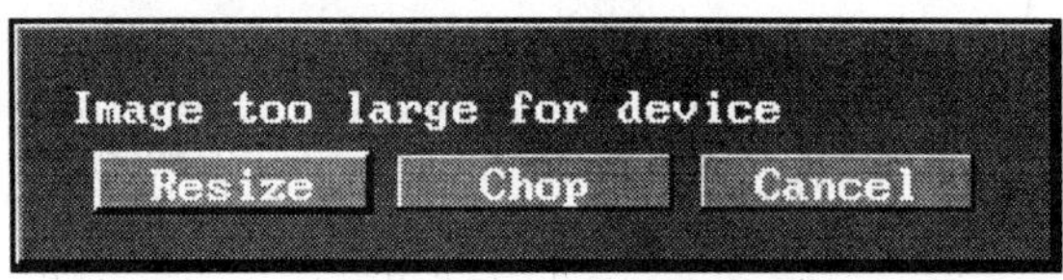

Make the proper selection for this warning dialog box.

5. Select **Chop** to display only the upper left corner of the image.
6. Select **Resize** to modify the resolution of the image to match that of the display device resolution.
7. If the image is not within the map path, the dialog box below is displayed. This is just a reminder that to use the image in a scene, it must be in the map path. Use the *Info-Configure* pull-down menu to add this path.

Heed this warning or the bitmap cannot be used.

8. Press [Esc] or right-click to return to the viewport display.

RELATED COMMANDS

Info-Configure, Program-Image Browser, Renderer/View/Flic, Renderer/View/Last

Renderer/View/Flic

Displays a previously created animation on the screen.

Renderer
Render View
Render Region
Render Blowup
Render Object
Render Last
Setup...
Atmosphere
Background
Configure
Options
View...
Image
Flic
Last
Save Last

Displaying and Animation

1. Select *Renderer/View/Flic.* A file selector appears.
2. Select the animation file to be viewed and click on **OK**. The animation will be played on the screen.
3. Use the following keys to control the animation.

[→] Increases playback speed.

[←] Decreases playback speed.

[↑] Return to default speed (20 fps).

[↓] Pause/resume playback.

[→][ ] Frame by frame (during pause only).

[Esc] Exit playback and return to viewport display.

TIP To view VGA animations without loading 3D Studio, use the *DOS* program *AAPLAY.EXE* , which is found in the 3DS4 sub-directory or *AAWIN.EXE* for Windows.

RELATED COMMAND

Renderer/View/Image

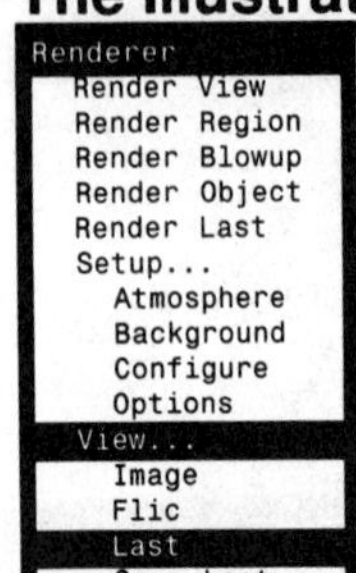

Renderer/View/Last

Displays the last rendered image.

Displaying the Last Rendered Image

1. Ensure that the Save-Last-Image parameter is set to Yes in the Render Options dialog box displayed using *Renderer/Setup/ Options*.
2. Select *Renderer/View/Last*. The last rendering will be displayed on the current configured display device.
3. Press [Esc] or right-click to return to the viewport display.

RELATED COMMAND

Renderer/View/Flic

Renderer/View/Save Last

Renderer
Render View
Render Region
Render Blowup
Render Object
Render Last
Setup...
Atmosphere
Background
Configure
Options
View...
Image
Flic
Last
Save Last

Saves the last rendered image to a specified filename and location.

Saving the Last Rendered Image

1. Ensure that the Save-Last-Image parameter is set to Yes in the Render Options dialog box displayed using *Renderer/Setup/Options*.
2. Select *Renderer/View/Save Last*. A file selector will be displayed.
3. Enter a filename and location for the image file. Choose a file output format and select **OK**. The image file will be saved.

RELATED COMMAND

Renderer/View/Last

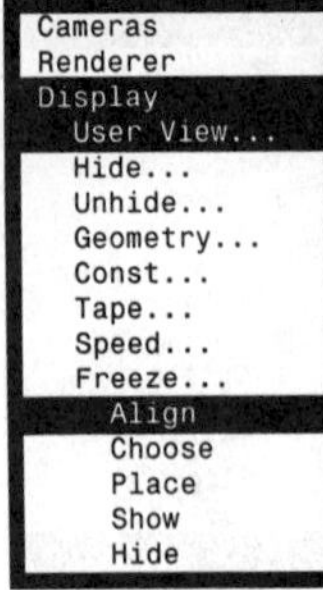

Display/User View/Align

Aligns the user plane in a user viewport to a predefined plane of a face on an object.

Aligning a User Plane in an Active User Viewport.

1. Ensure that an object has been created that includes a face with which to align the user plane.
2. Ensure that a user view is displayed showing the object that contains the face with which to align the user plane.
3. Select *Display/User View/Align.*
4. Activate the user viewport that contains the face with which to align the user plane.
5. Select a vertex on the plane. A face will be highlighted in blue as shown in the figure below.
6. Move the mouse. All faces that contain the selected vertex will be highlighted individually.
7. Select the face. The user view will now be parallel with the plane.
8. To view the alignment in any orthographic view, select *Display/User View/Show.*

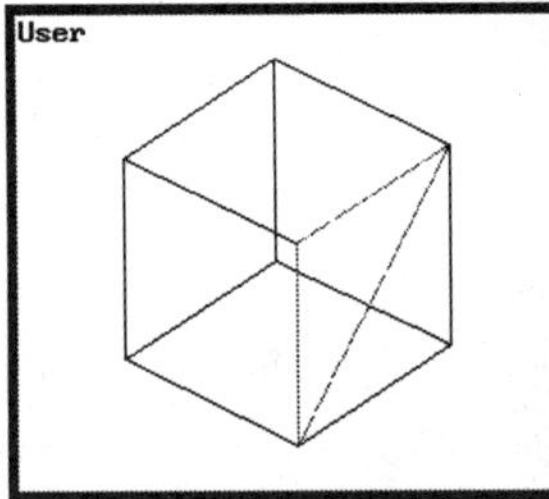

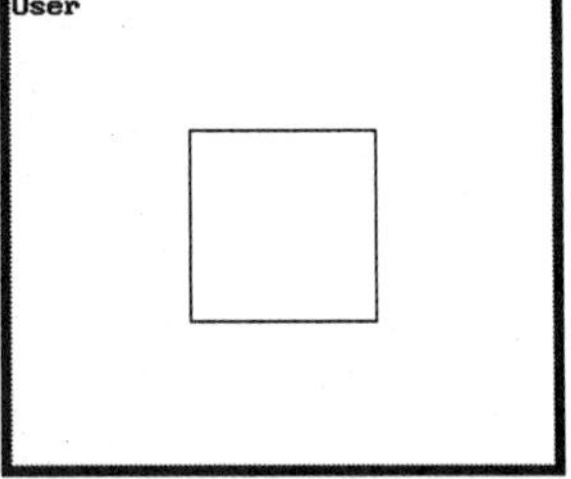

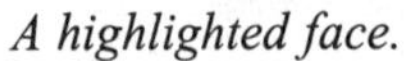
A highlighted face.

View Aligned with the face.

RELATED COMMANDS

Display/User View/Choose, Display/User View/Show, Display/User View/Hide, Modify/Object/Align

Cameras
Renderer
Display
User View...
Hide...
Unhide...
Geometry...
Const...
Tape...
Speed...
Freeze...
Align
Choose
Place
Show
Hide

Display/User View/Choose

Adjusts the orthographic viewports to display the user plane selected in a specific user viewport.

Choosing a User Plane to be Displayed

1. Ensure that a user plane has been defined using *Display/User View/Align.*

2. Select *Display/User View/Choose.* The user view is displayed as a plane, represented by a cyan line, in all orthographic viewports. The user viewport title changes from white to cyan and an asterisk is placed next to *Display/User View/Show.*

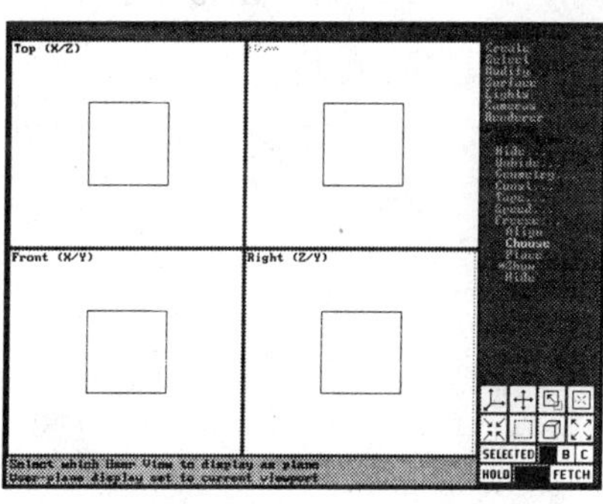

Displaying the User View as a plane.

RELATED COMMANDS

Display/User View/Align, Display/User View/Show, Display/User View/Hide

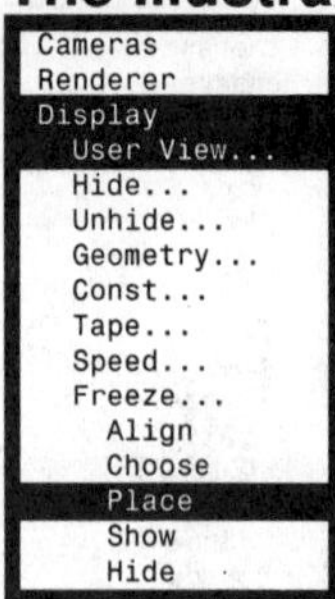

Display/User View/Place

Moves the user plane to a new location by moving its center point.

Placing the User Plane

1. Ensure that a user plane has been defined using *Display/User View/Align.*
2. Select *Display/User View/Place.*
3. Activate a viewport to move the user plane.
4. Select a new location for the center point of the user plane. The user plane, represented by a cyan line, will be relocated to the new position.

RELATED COMMANDS

Display/User View/Align, Display/User View/Show, Display/User View/Hide

Display/User View/Show

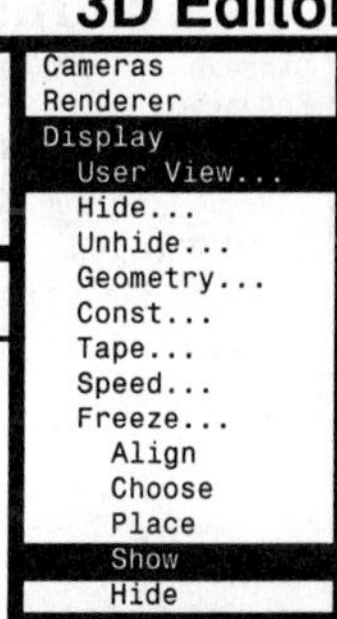

Displays the user plane.

Displaying the User Plane

1. Ensure that a user plane has been defined using *Display/User View/Align.*
2. Select *Display/User View/Show.* An asterisk appears next to the command and the user viewport title changes from white to cyan.

RELATED COMMANDS

Display/User View/Align, Display/User View/Hide

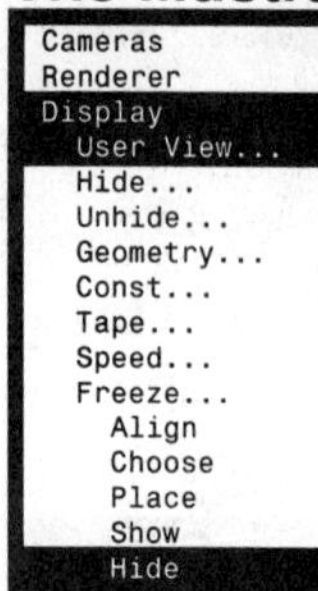

Display/User View/Hide

Hides the user plane.

Hiding the User Plane

1. Ensure that a user plane has been defined using *Display/User View/Align* and that it is displayed using *Display/User View/Show*.
2. Select *Display/User View/Hide*. An asterisk appears next to the command and the user viewport title changes from cyan to white.

RELATED COMMANDS

Display/User View/Align, Display/User View/Hide

Display/Hide/Face

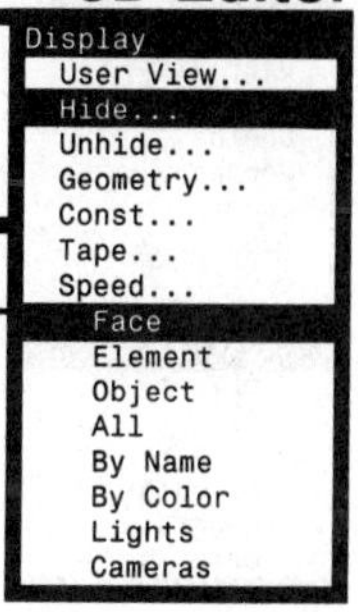

Display
User View...
Hide...
Unhide...
Geometry...
Const...
Tape...
Speed...
Face
Element
Object
All
By Name
By Color
Lights
Cameras

Hides one or more faces in all viewports.

Hiding a Face

1. Ensure that an object or face has been created previously.
2. Select *Display/Hide/Face.*
3. In any viewport, select a vertex on the plane. A face will be highlighted in blue.
4. Move the mouse. All faces that contain the selected vertex will be highlighted individually.
5. Move the mouse until the face to be hidden is highlighted.
6. Select the face. That face will be hidden in all viewports.
7. To redisplay the hidden face, select *Display/Unhide/All.*

RELATED COMMAND

Display/Unhide/Face

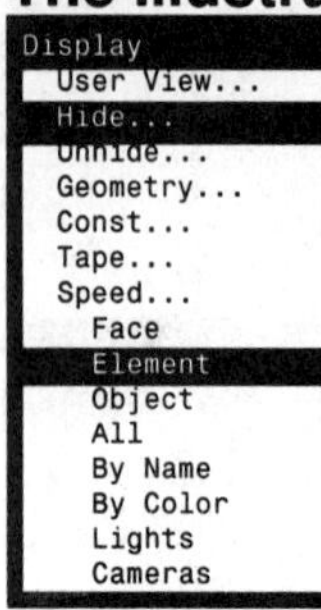

Display/Hide/Element

Hides an element in all viewports.

Hiding an Element

1. Ensure that an element has been created previously.
2. Select *Display/Hide/Element.*
3. In any viewport, select the element to be hidden. That element will be hidden in all viewports.
4. To redisplay the hidden element, select *Display/Unhide/Object* or *Display/Unhide/All.*

An element is an object that has been grouped within another object.

RELATED COMMAND

Display/Unhide/Object

Display/Hide/Object

Display
User View...
Hide...
Unhide...
Geometry...
Const...
Tape...
Speed...
Face
Element
Object
All
By Name
By Color
Lights
Cameras

Hides an object in all viewports.

Hiding an Object

1. Ensure that an object has been created previously.
2. Select *Display/Hide/Object.*
3. In any viewport, select the object to be hidden. That object will be hidden in all viewports.
4. To redisplay the hidden object, select *Display/Unhide/By Name*, *Display/Unhide/By Color,* or *Display/Unhide/All.*

RELATED COMMAND

Display/Unhide/Object

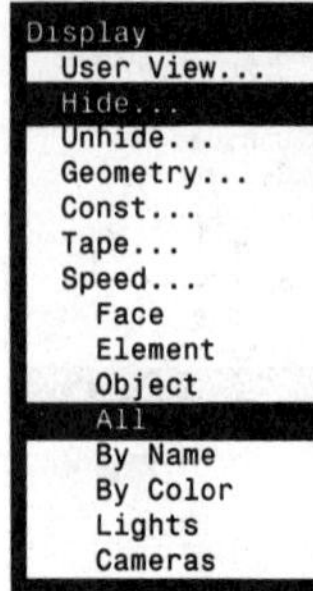

Display/Hide/All

Hides all geometry in all viewports.

Hiding all Objects

1. Ensure that geometry has been created previously.
2. Select *Display/Hide/All.* All geometry is hidden in all viewports.
3. To redisplay the hidden element, select *Display/Unhide/All.*

RELATED COMMAND

Display/Unhide/All

Display/Hide/By Name

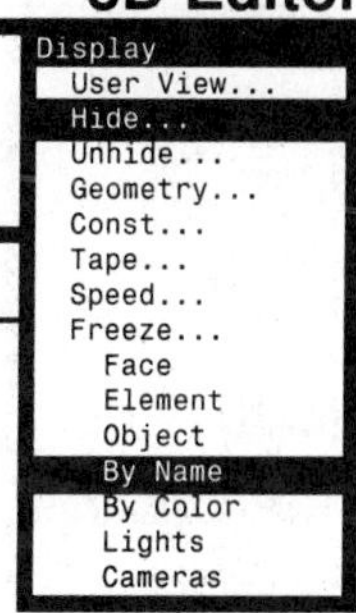

Hides objects by selecting their names.

Hiding an Object by Selecting Its Name.

1. Ensure that an object has been created previously.
2. Select *Display/Hide/By Name.* The Hide Objects: dialog box appears as shown below.

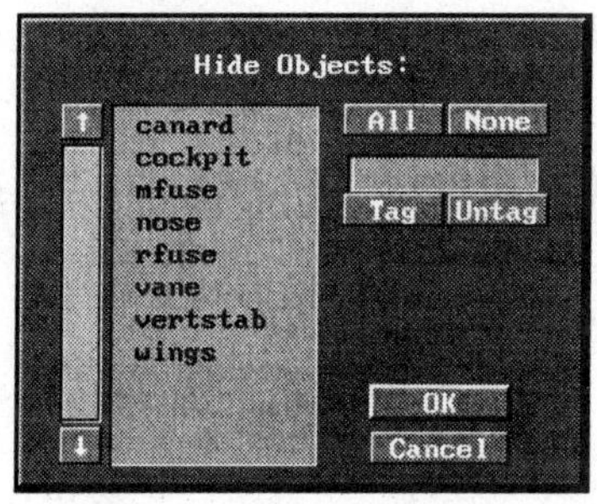

Select the name of the object to hide.

3. Select the object(s) in the dialog box to be hidden or use the following options.
4. **All**—Selects all the objects in the list.
5. **None**—Deselects all objects in the list.
6. **Tag**—Place the wild card pattern in the text box above this button. Click on the tag button. All objects that match the wild card are selected.
7. **Untag**—Place the wild card pattern in the text box above this button. Click on the untag button. All objects that match the wild card are deselected.
8. Select **OK** to accept the selection and close the dialog box. The objects selected will be hidden in all viewports.
9. Select **Cancel** to cancel the command and exit the dialog box.

RELATED COMMAND

Display/Unhide/By Name

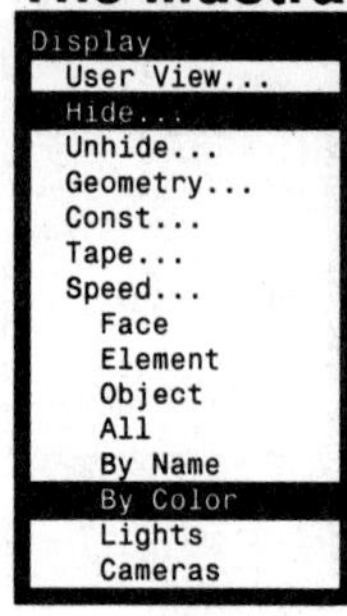

Display/Hide/By Color

Hides all objects with the same color, in all viewports.

Hiding Objects with the Same Color.

1. Ensure that an object has been created previously.
2. Select *Display/Hide/Color*.
3. In any viewport, select the object to be hidden. That object will be hidden in all viewports as will any other objects that are the same color.
4. To redisplay the hidden objects, select *Display/Unhide/By Color*.

RELATED COMMANDS

Display/Unhide/By Color, Modify/Object/Change Color

Display/Hide/Lights

```
Display
  User View...
  Hide...
  Unhide...
  Geometry...
  Const...
  Tape...
  Speed...
  Freeze...
    Face
    Element
    Object
    All
    By Name
    Lights
    Cameras
```

Hides all light icons in all viewports.

Hiding Light Icons

1. Ensure that lights have been created previously.
2. Select *Display/Hide/Lights.* All light icons are hidden in all viewports.
3. To redisplay the light icon, select *Display/Unhide/Lights.*

Hiding the light icon does not turn the light off. Use *Lights/Omni/Adjust* or *Lights/Spot/Adjust* to turn off lights.

RELATED COMMAND

Display/Unhide/Lights

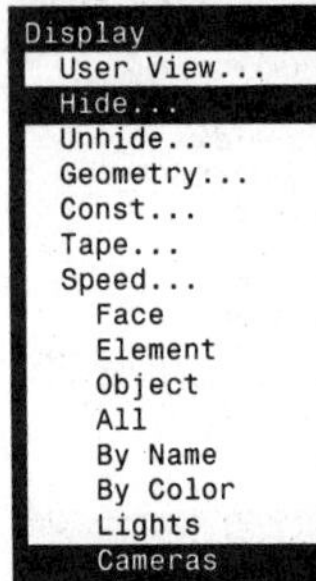

Display/Hide/Cameras

Hides all camera icons in all viewports.

Hiding Camera Icons

1. Ensure that a camera has been created previously.
2. Select *Display/Hide/Camera.* All camera icons are hidden in all viewports.
3. To redisplay the camera icon, select *Display/Unhide/Camera.*

Hiding the camera icon does not disable the camera. The camera view can still be seen in a viewport or used for rendering.

RELATED COMMAND

Display/Unhide/Cameras

Display/Unhide/Element

Display
User View...
Hide...
Unhide...
Geometry...
Const...
Tape...
Speed...
Freeze...
Element
Object
All
By Name
By Color
Lights
Cameras

Displays hidden portions of an element in all viewports.

Unhiding an Element Portion

1. Ensure that a portion of an element has been hidden previously.
2. Select *Display/Unhide/Element.*
3. In any viewport, select a vertex that lies on the visible portion of a partially hidden element. That element will be redisplayed in all viewports.

Unhiding all of an Element

1. Ensure that an element has been hidden previously.
2. Select *Display/Unhide/Object.*
3. Select the object that contains the element. The object and all of its elements will be redisplayed.

NOTE An element is an object that has been grouped within another object.

RELATED COMMAND

Display/Hide/Element

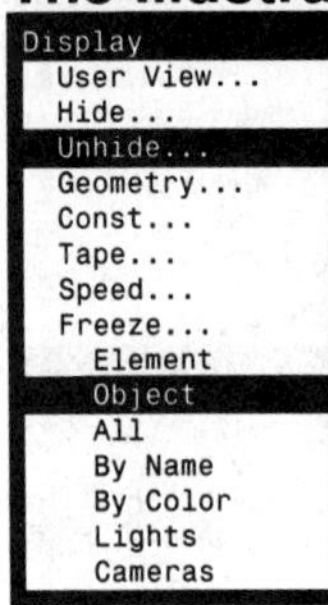

Display/Unhide/Object

Redisplays an object that is partially hidden in all viewports.

Unhiding a Portion of an Object

1. Ensure that a portion of an object has been hidden previously.
2. Select *Display/Unhide/Object*.
3. In any viewport, select a vertex that lies on the visible portion of a partially hidden object. That object will be redisplayed in all viewports.

To unhide a totally hidden object, use *Display/Unhide/By Name*, *Display/Unhide/By Color*, or *Display/Unhide/All*.

RELATED COMMAND

Display/Hide/Object

Display/Unhide/All

Redisplays all hidden geometry in all viewports.

Display
User View...
Hide...
Unhide...
Geometry...
Const...
Tape...
Speed...
Freeze...
Element
Object
All
By Name
By Color
Lights
Cameras

Unhiding All Objects

1. Ensure that geometry has been hidden previously.
2. Select *Display/Unhide/All.* All geometry is redisplayed in all viewports.

RELATED COMMAND

Display/Hide/All

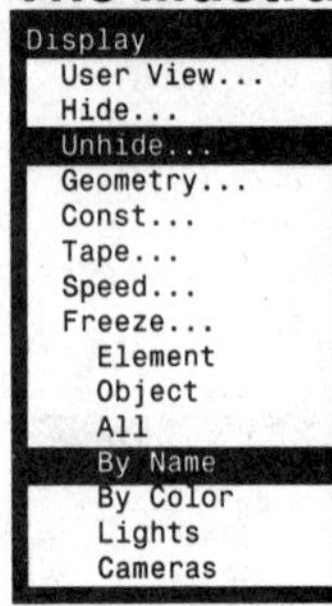

Display/Unhide/By Name

Redisplays all hidden geometry by selecting its name.

Unhiding an Object by Selecting Its Name.

1. Ensure that an object has been hidden previously.
2. Select *Display/Unhide/By Name.* The Unhide Objects: dialog box appears as shown below.

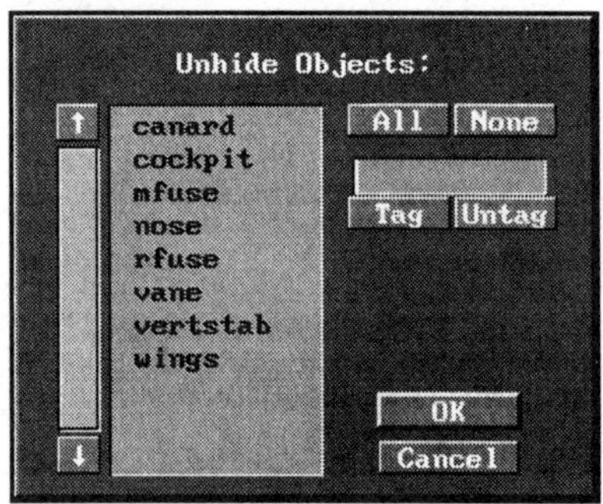

Select the name of the object to Unhide.

3. Select the object(s) in the dialog box to be redisplayed or use the following options.
4. **All**—Selects all the objects in the list.
5. **None**—Deselects all objects in the list.
6. **Tag**—Place the wild card pattern in the text box above this button. Click on the tag button. All objects that match the wild card are selected.
7. **Untag**—Place the wild card pattern in the text box above this button. Click on the untag button. All objects that match the wild card are deselected.
8. Select **OK** to accept the selection and close the dialog box. The objects selected will be redisplayed in all viewports.
9. Select **Cancel** to cancel the command and exit the dialog box.

RELATED COMMAND

Display/Hide/By Name

Display/Unhide/By Color

Display
User View...
Hide...
Unhide...
Geometry...
Const...
Tape...
Speed...
Freeze...
Element
Object
All
By Name
By Color
Lights
Cameras

Redisplays all objects previously hidden with the same color, in all viewports.

Unhiding Objects with the Same Color

1. Ensure that geometry has been created previously.
2. Select *Display/Unhide/By Color*. The Unhide Objects: object palette dialog box appears.
3. Select the color that matches the color of the object(s) to be redisplayed.
4. Select **OK** to accept the selection and close the dialog box. All objects that match the color selected will be redisplayed in all viewports.
5. Select **Cancel** to cancel the command and exit the dialog box.

RELATED COMMANDS

Display/Hide/By Color, Modify/Object/Change Color

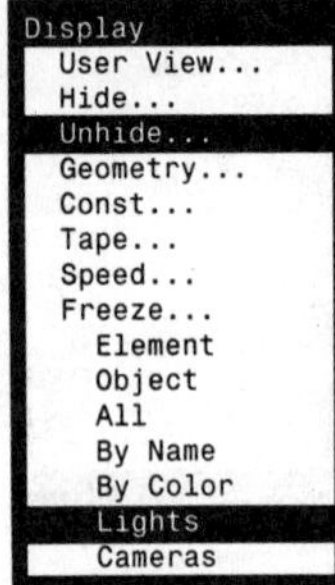

Display/Unhide/Lights

Redisplays all light icons in all viewports.

Unhiding all Light Icons

1. Ensure that lights have been hidden previously.
2. Select *Display/Unhide/Lights*. All light icons are redisplayed in all viewports.

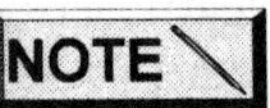

Unhiding the light icon does not turn the light on. Use *Lights/Omni/Adjust* or *Lights/Spot/Adjust* to turn on lights.

RELATED COMMAND

Display/Hide/Lights

Display
User View...
Hide...
Unhide...
Geometry...
Const...
Tape...
Speed...
Freeze...
Element
Object
All
By Name
By Color
Lights
Cameras

Display/Unhide/Cameras

Redisplays all camera icons in all viewports.

Unhiding all Camera Icons

1. Ensure that a camera icon has been hidden previously.
2. Select *Display/Unhide/Camera.* All camera icons are redisplayed in all viewports.

RELATED COMMAND

Display/Hide/Cameras

Display
User View...
Hide...
Unhide...
Geometry...
Const...
Tape...
Speed...
See Thru
Backface
All Lines
Edges Only
Vert Dots
Vert Ticks
Full Detail
Box

Display/Geometry/See Thru

Displays all edges of all geometry in all viewports.

Displaying the Edges of All Geometry

1. Ensure that geometry has been created previously.

2. Select *Display/Geometry/See Thru*. All geometry will be displayed in the viewports with all backfaces on.

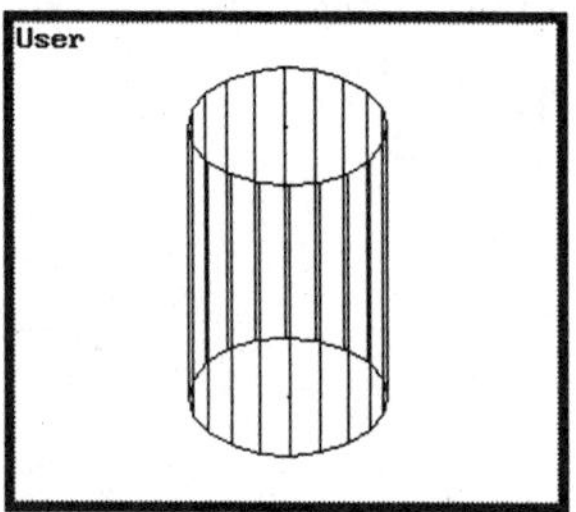

Using Geometry See Thru.

TIP Use *Display/Geometry/All Lines* and *Display/Geometry/Edges Only* to modify the amount of geometry to be displayed and decrease regeneration time.

RELATED COMMANDS

Display/Geometry/Backface, Display/Geometry/See Thru

Display/Geometry/Backface

Display
User View...
Hide...
Unhide...
Geometry...
Const...
Tape...
Speed...
See Thru
Backface
All Lines
Edges Only
Vert Dots
Vert Ticks
Full Detail
Box

Displays all faces that are facing the viewport. Hides all faces that are facing away from the viewport (backfaces).

Hiding the Backface of Geometry

1. Ensure that geometry has been created previously.
2. Select *Display/Geometry/Backface.* All backfaces will be turned off as shown in the figure below.

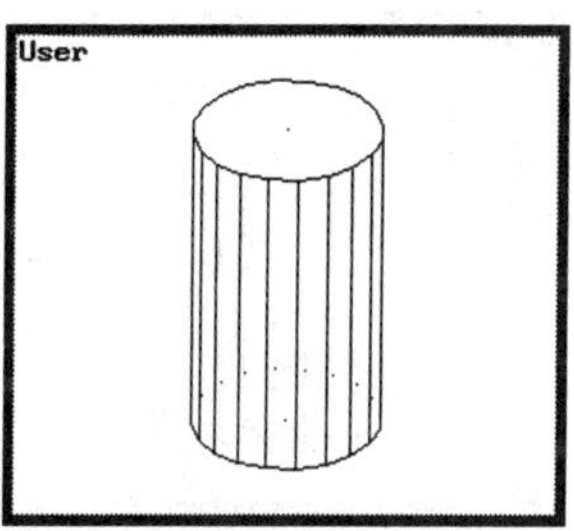

Using Geometry Backface.

TIP Use *Display/Geometry/All Lines* and *Display/Geometry/Edges Only* to modify the amount of geometry to be displayed and decrease regeneration time.

RELATED COMMANDS

Display/Geometry/See Thru, Display/Geometry/See Thru

Display
User View...
Hide...
Unhide...
Geometry...
Const...
Tape...
Speed...
See Thru
Backface
All Lines
Edges Only
Vert Dots
Vert Ticks
Full Detail
Box

Display/Geometry/All Lines

Displays edges and construction lines on the objects in the viewports.

Displaying All Lines on an Object

1. Ensure that geometry has been created previously.
2. Select *Display/Geometry/All Lines*. The edges and the construction lines that form an object are displayed.

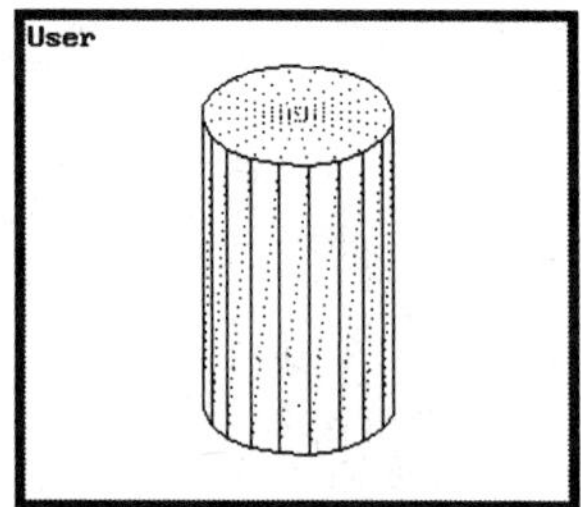

Using Geometry All Lines.

TIP This command causes many excessive lines to be displayed and increases regeneration times. Use *Display/Geometry/Edges Only* to decrease regeneration time.

RELATED COMMAND

Display/Geometry/Edges Only

Display/Geometry/Edges Only

Display
User View...
Hide...
Unhide...
Geometry...
Const...
Tape...
Speed...
See Thru
Backface
All Lines
Edges Only
Vert Dots
Vert Ticks
Full Detail
Box

Displays only the edges of the objects in the viewports.

Displaying Only Edges of an Object

1. Ensure that geometry has been created previously.
2. Select *Display/Geometry/Edges Only*. Only the edges that form an object are displayed.

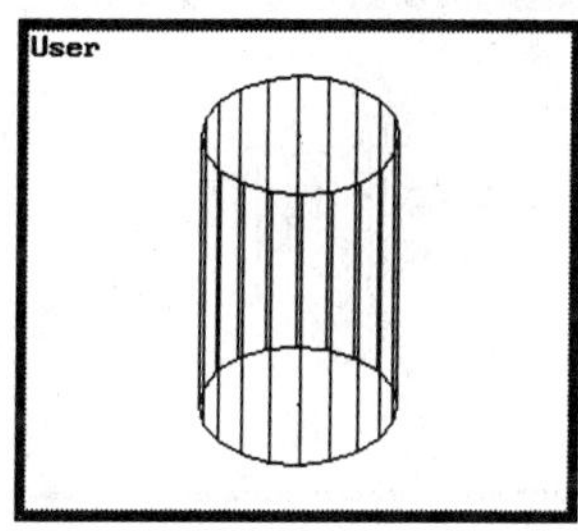

Using Geometry Edges Only.

RELATED COMMAND

Display/Geometry/All Lines

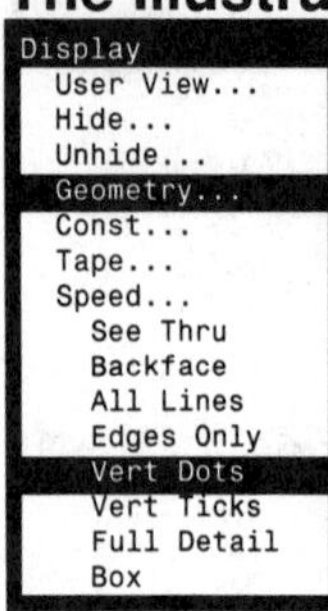

Display/Geometry/Vert Dots

Displays vertices as single dots or pixels.

Displaying Vertices as a Single Pixel

1. Ensure that geometry has been created previously.
2. Select *Display/Geometry/Vert Dots.* All vertices are displayed as single pixels.

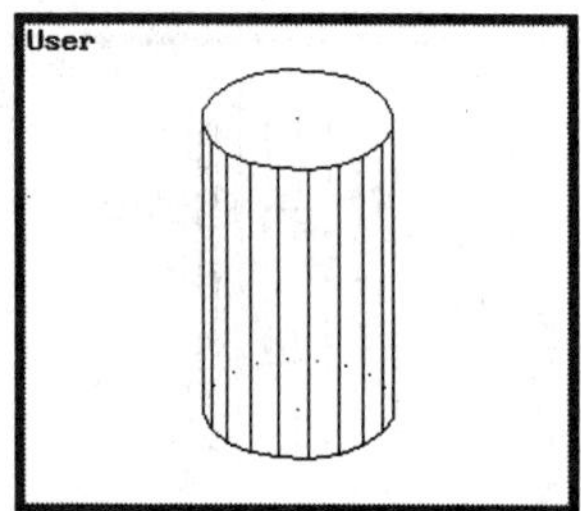

Using Geometry Vertical Dots.

TIP Using this option reduces regeneration time but does not allow for clear visibility of selected vertices. Use *Display/Geometry/Vert Ticks* when working with multiple selections of vertices.

RELATED COMMAND

Display/Geometry/Vert Ticks

Display/Geometry/Vert Ticks

Display
User View...
Hide...
Unhide...
Geometry...
Const...
Tape...
Speed...
See Thru
Backface
All Lines
Edges Only
Vert Dots
Vert Ticks
Full Detail
Box

Displays vertices as tick marks (+).

Displaying Vertices as Tick Marks

1. Ensure that geometry has been created previously.
2. Select *Display/Geometry/Vert Ticks*. All vertices are displayed as tick marks.

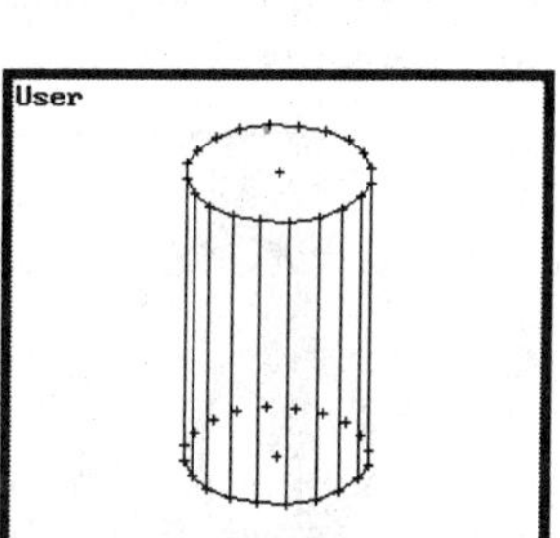

Using Geometry Vertical Ticks.

TIP Using this option increases regeneration time but allows clear visibility of selected vertices. Use *Display/Geometry/Vert Dots* to decrease regeneration time.

RELATED COMMAND

Display/Geometry/Vert Dots

Display/Geometry/Full Detail

Displays geometry with all vertices, edges, faces, and elements.

Displaying Geometry in Full Detail

1. Ensure that geometry has been created previously.
2. Select *Display/Geometry/Full Detail.* The objects are displayed with vertices, edges, faces, and all elements.

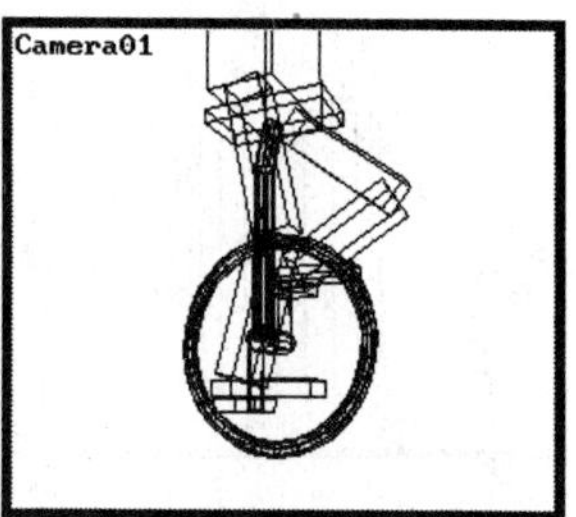

Using Geometry Full Detail.

RELATED COMMANDS

Display/Geometry/Box, Display/Speed

Display/Geometry/Box

Display
User View...
Hide...
Unhide...
Geometry...
Const...
Tape...
Speed...
See Thru
Backface
All Lines
Edges Only
Vert Dots
Vert Ticks
Full Detail
Box

Displays geometry in box mode.

Displaying Geometry in Box Mode.

1. Ensure that geometry has been created previously and is being displayed with vertices, edges, or faces.
2. Select *Display/Geometry/Box*. The objects are displayed in box mode.

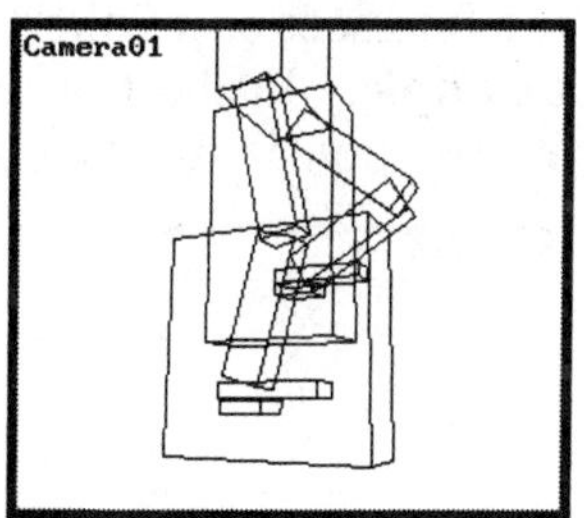

Using Box mode to display geometry.

NOTE The box represents the bounding box of the object. If the object is rendered it will not be rendered as a box.

TIP Using this mode dramatically decreases regeneration time but does not allow for vertices' adjustment or modification. Use this command for tasks that do not require the display of vertices, such as camera/light placement, arranging objects in a scene, or viewport configuration.

RELATED COMMANDS

Display/Geometry/Full Detail, Display/Speed

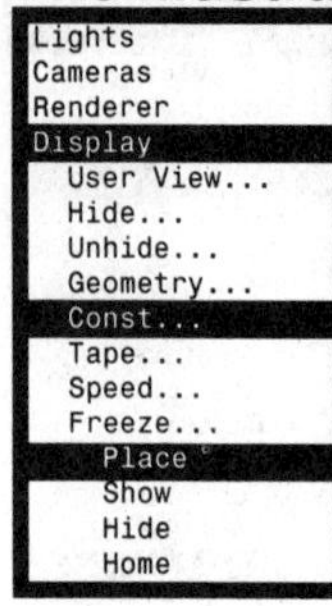

Display/Const/Place

Changes the location of the construction planes.

Placing the Construction Plane

1. Select *Display/Const/Place.*
2. Activate an orthographic viewport where the construction plane is to be moved.
3. Select a point in the viewport to represent the intersection of the two planes being placed. Black crosshairs will appear in all orthographic viewports representing the intersection of the two planes displayed in the appropriate viewport. **Example**: In the top viewport, the X (horizontal) and Z (vertical) plane intersection is displayed.

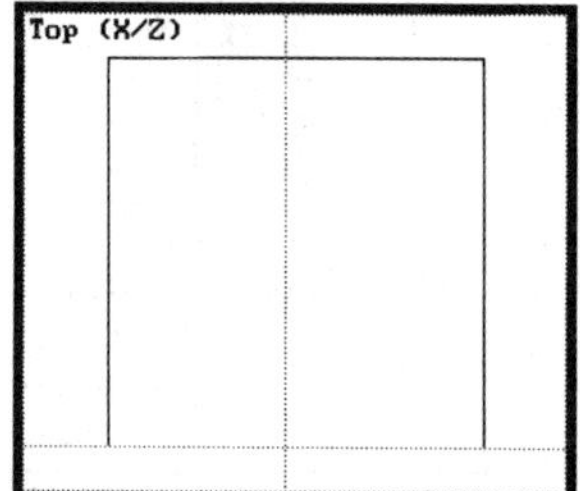

Placing the Construction Plane.

This command affects the 3D Editor and the 3D Lofter construction planes.

RELATED COMMANDS

Display/Const/Show, Display/Const/Hide, Display/Const/Home

Display/Const/Show

Lights
Cameras
Renderer
Display
User View...
Hide...
Unhide...
Geometry...
Const...
Tape...
Speed...
Freeze...
Place
Show
Hide
Home

Displays the construction plane in the orthographic viewports.

Displaying the Construction Planes

1. Use *Display/Const/Place* to set the location of the construction plane if necessary.

2. Select *Display/Const/Show*. The construction plane crosshairs appear in all orthographic viewports and an asterisk appears next to the command.

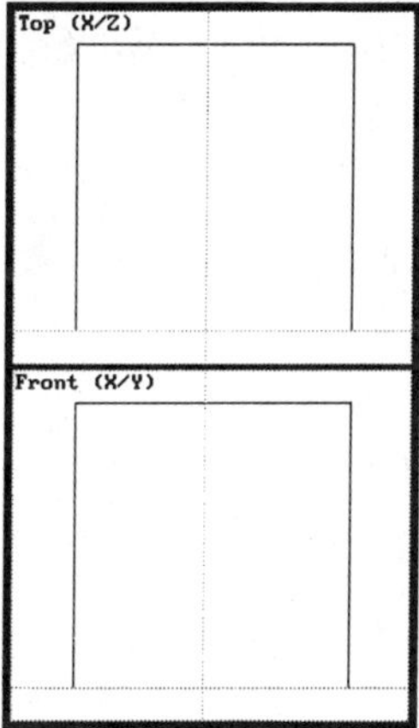

Displaying the Construction Plane.

RELATED COMMANDS

Display/Const/Place, Display/Const/Hide, Display/Const/Home

Lights
Cameras
Renderer
Display
User View...
Hide...
Unhide...
Geometry...
Const...
Tape...
Speed...
Freeze...
Place
Show
Hide
Home

Display/Const/Hide

Hides the construction plane in the orthographic viewports.

Hiding the Construction Planes

1. Ensure that the construction planes are displayed using *Display/Const/Show* or that they are placed by using *Display/Const/Place*.
2. Select *Display/Const/Hide*. The construction plane crosshairs disappear in all orthographic viewports and an asterisk appears next to the command.

RELATED COMMANDS

Display/Const/Place, Display/Const/Show, Display/Const/Home

Display/Const/Home

Lights
Cameras
Renderer
Display
User View...
Hide...
Unhide...
Geometry...
Const...
Tape...
Speed...
Freeze...
Place
Show
Hide
Home

Moves the construction plane back to its default (home) position at coordinates (0,0,0).

Moving the Construction Planes to Their Default Positions

1. Ensure that the construction planes were moved previously from their default location using *Display/Const/Place*.

2. Select *Display/Const/Home*. The construction planes crosshairs return to their default position.

RELATED COMMANDS

Display/Const/Place, Display/Const/Show, Display/Const/Hide

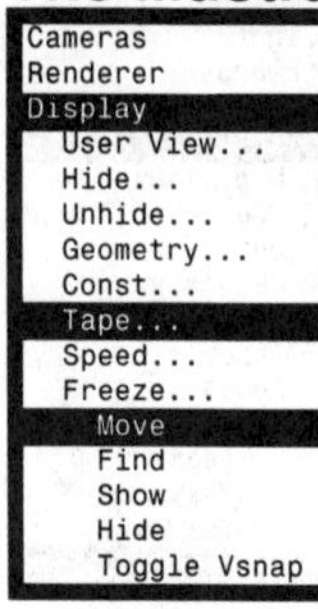

Display/Tape/Move

Adjusts or moves the Tape Measure icon.

Adjusting the Tape Measure Icon

1. Ensure that the Tape Measure icon is displayed in an orthographic viewport using *Display/Tape/Show*.
2. Select *Display/Tape/Move*.
3. Select the orthographic viewport where the Tape Measure icon is to be adjusted.
4. Select either end of the Tape Measure icon.
5. Move the selected end of the Tape Measure icon to its new location and select that point. The tape length and angle are displayed in the status line.
6. Make further adjustments to both ends as necessary.

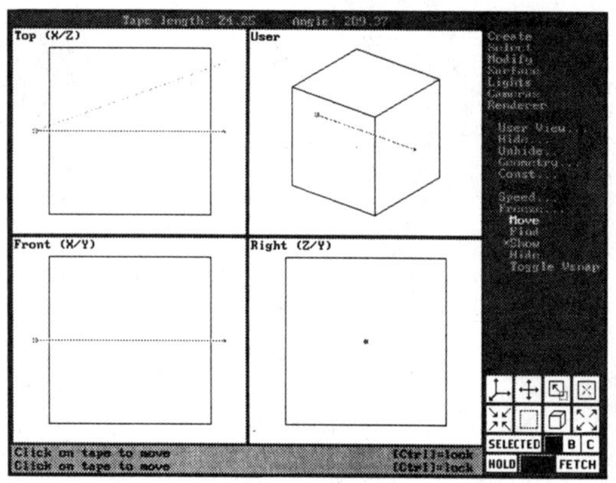

Moving the Tape to measure distance.

If exact measurement of objects is needed, use *Display/Tape/Toggle VSnap*.

TIP

Use [Tab] to constrain movements in the horizontal or vertical direction.

Moving the Tape Measure Icon

1. Ensure that the Tape Measure icon is displayed in an orthographic viewport using *Display/Tape/Show*.
2. Select *Display/Tape/Move*.
3. Select the orthographic viewport where the tape measure icon is to be moved.

4. Hold down Ctrl and select either end of the tape measure icon. A white copy of the icon will appear connected to the cursor and a green reference icon will remain at its beginning location.

5. Move the tape measure icon to its new location. The tape length and angle are displayed in the status line.

6. Make further adjustments as necessary.

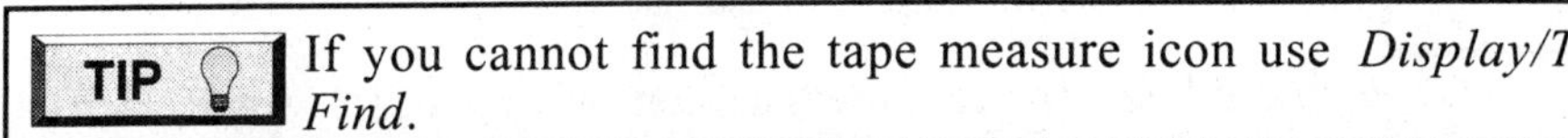

TIP: If you cannot find the tape measure icon use *Display/Tape/Find.*

RELATED COMMANDS

Display/Tape/Find, Display/Tape/Show, Display/Tape/Hide, Display/Tape/Toggle VSnap

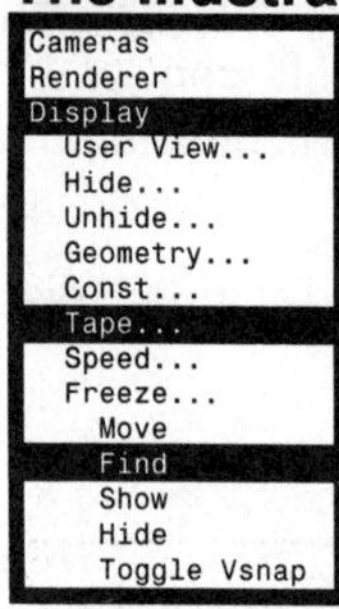

Display/Tape/Find

Adjusts the Tape Measure icon in the active viewport so that it may be located easily.

Finding the Tape Measure Icon

1. Select an orthographic or user viewport.
2. Select *Display/Tape/Find*. The Tape Measure icon will be scaled to 80 percent of the active viewport. It will also be centered within that viewport and reset to its default angle of 270 degrees. The tape length and angle are displayed in the status line.

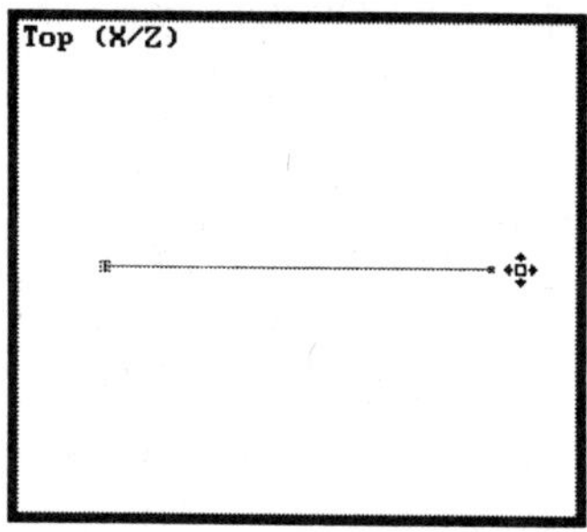

Use this command to locate the Tape Measure icon.

RELATED COMMANDS

Display/Tape/Show, Display/Tape/Hide

Display/Tape/Show

Cameras
Renderer
Display
User View...
Hide...
Unhide...
Geometry...
Const...
Tape...
Speed...
Freeze...
Move
Find
Show
Hide
Toggle Vsnap

Displays the Tape Measure icon.

Displaying the Tape Measure Icon

1. Select *Display/Tape/Show*. The Tape Measure icon will be displayed in all orthographic and user viewports at its previously defined location and direction. An asterisk will appear next to the command. The tape length and angle are also displayed in the status line.

2. Use the *Display/Tape/Move* command to adjust the Tape Measure icon.

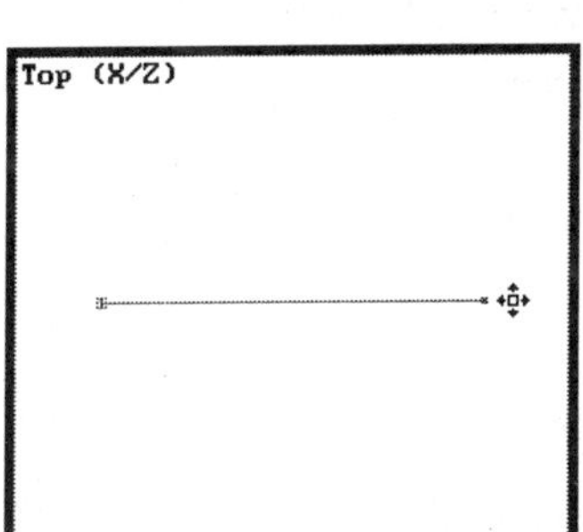

Use this command to show the Tape Measure icon.

Use *Display/Tape/Find* if the Tape Measure icon cannot be seen after using this command.

RELATED COMMANDS

Display/Tape/Move, Display/Tape/Find, Display/Tape/Hide

```
Cameras
Renderer
Display
  User View...
  Hide...
  Unhide...
  Geometry...
  Const...
  Tape...
  Speed...
  Freeze...
    Move
    Find
    Show
    Hide
    Toggle Vsnap
```

Display/Tape/Hide

Hides the Tape Measure icon.

Hiding the Tape Measure Icon

1. Ensure that the Tape Measure icon has been displayed previously using either *Display/Tape/Show* or *Display/Tape/Find*.
2. Select *Display/Tape/Hide*. The Tape Measure icon will disappear from the orthographic and user viewports and an asterisk will appear next to the command.

RELATED COMMANDS

Display/Tape/Find, Display/Tape/Show

Display/Tape/Toggle VSnap

Cameras
Renderer
Display
User View...
Hide...
Unhide...
Geometry...
Const...
Tape...
Speed...
Freeze...
Move
Find
Show
Hide
Toggle Vsnap

Toggles the Vertex Tape Snap mode.

Use this command to snap the ends of the Tape Measure icon to a vertex on a mesh object, allowing for more accurate measurement of a line.

Turning on Vertex Tape Snap Mode

1. Select *Display/Tape/Toggle VSnap*. An asterisk will appear next to the command.

2. Use *Display/Tape/Move* to snap the ends of the Tape Measure icon to any vertex on a line, face, or path.

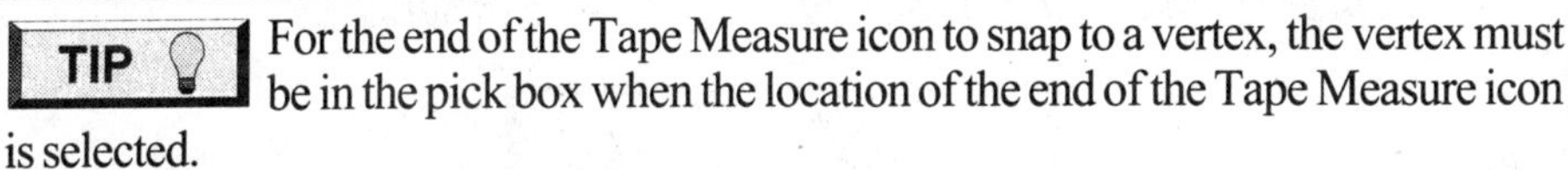

TIP: For the end of the Tape Measure icon to snap to a vertex, the vertex must be in the pick box when the location of the end of the Tape Measure icon is selected.

RELATED COMMANDS

Display/Tape/Find, Display/Tape/Show

Cameras
Renderer
Display
User View...
Hide...
Unhide...
Geometry...
Const...
Tape...
Speed...
Fastdraw
Fulldraw
Set Fast
By Name
By Color
Object

Display/Speed/Fastdraw

Turns on Fastdraw and displays mesh objects with a reduced number of faces to speed redraw times.

Turning on Fastdraw

1. Ensure that geometry has been created previously.
2. Use *Display/Speed/Set Fast* to specify the number of faces that will be used to represent mesh objects.
3. Select *Display/Speed/Fastdraw*. An asterisk will appear next to the command and the mesh objects will be displayed with a reduced number of faces.
4. Use *Display/Speed/Fulldraw* to display the mesh objects with all faces.

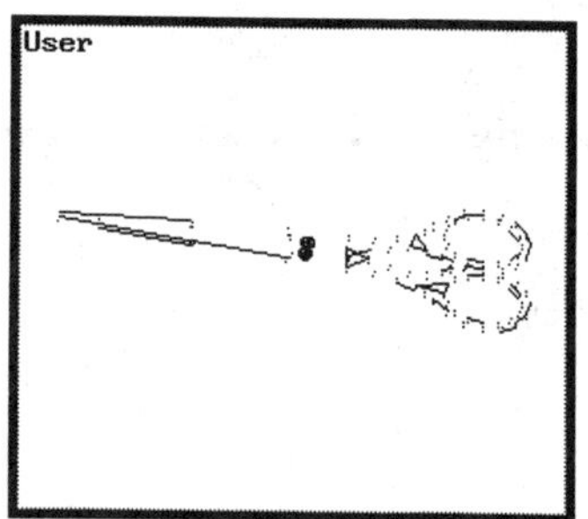

Displaying geometry using Fastdraw.

NOTE Using this command can decrease regeneration times significantly on complicated mesh objects with slower systems. It is not necessary to use this command if simple to moderate-size mesh objects are being displayed on medium to fast systems.

RELATED COMMANDS

Display/Speed/Fulldraw, Display/Speed/Set Fast

Display/Speed/Fulldraw

Cameras
Renderer
Display
User View...
Hide...
Unhide...
Geometry...
Const...
Tape...
Speed...
Fastdraw
Fulldraw
Set Fast
By Name
By Color
Object

Displays all faces on mesh objects.

Turning On Fulldraw

1. Ensure that geometry has been created previously.

2. Select *Display/Speed/Fulldraw*. An asterisk will appear next to the command and the mesh objects will be displayed with all faces.

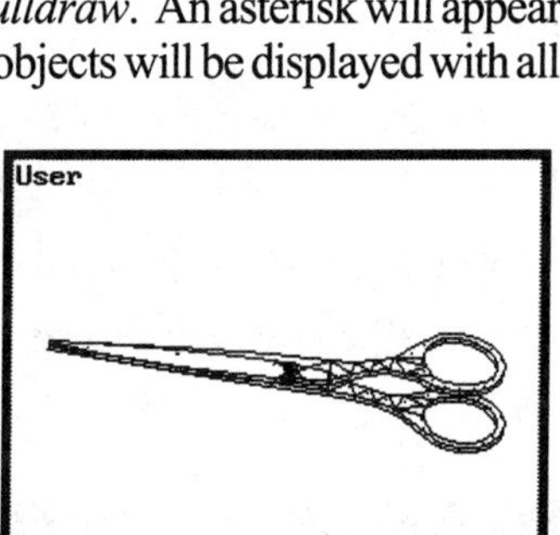

Displaying geometry using Fulldraw.

NOTE Using this command can increase regeneration significantly times on complicated mesh object with slower systems.

RELATED COMMANDS

Display/Speed/Fastdraw, Display/Speed/Set Fast

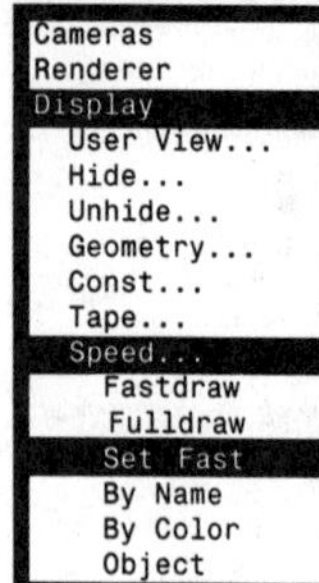

Display/Speed/Set Fast

Specifies the number of faces used to represent a mesh object.

Changing the Number of Faces for Mesh Objects

1. Select *Display/Speed/Set Fast.* The Set Fastdraw Speed dialog box appears as shown below.
2. Move the slider side to side to specify the number of faces. The range is 2 to 100. A setting of 2 displays every other face and a setting of 100 displays every 100th face.
3. Click on **OK** to accept the setting or **Cancel** to cancel the command.
4. If **OK** was selected, use *Display/Speed/Fastdraw* to display the mesh object with the new settings.

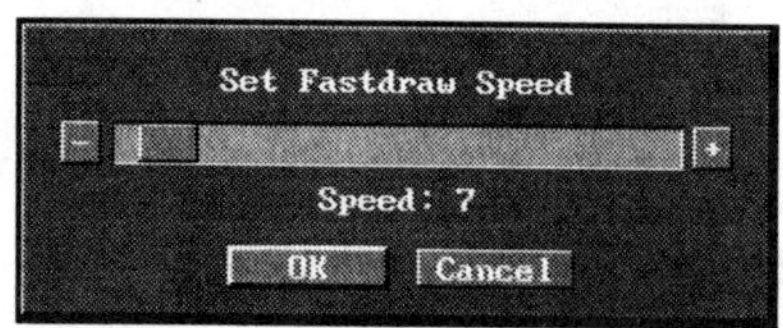

Use this dialog box to control the level of detail.

NOTE Be careful not to specify too high a setting. If the setting is higher than the number of faces in the mesh object, the object will not be seen. If multiple objects are displayed, it is important to make the setting small enough for the object with fewest faces.

RELATED COMMANDS

Display/Speed/Fastdraw, Display/Speed/Fulldraw

Cameras
Renderer
Display
User View...
Hide...
Unhide...
Geometry...
Const...
Tape...
Speed...
Fastdraw
Fulldraw
Set Fast
By Name
By Color
Object

Display/Speed/By Name

Assigns Fastdraw mode to individual objects.

Assigning Fastdraw Mode to Individual Object

1. Ensure that geometry has been created previously.
2. Select *Display/Speed/By Name*. The Select Fastdraw Objects dialog box appears.
3. Select the object(s) in the dialog box or use the following options.

   All—Selects all objects in the list.

   None—Deselects all objects in the list.

   Tag—Place the wild card pattern in the text box above this button. Click on the **Tag** button. All objects that match the wild card are selected.

   Untag—Place the wild card pattern in the text box above this button. Click on the **Untag** button. All objects that match the wild card are deselected.
4. Select **OK** to accept the selection and close the dialog box. The objects selected are redisplayed in all viewports in Fastdraw mode.
5. Select **Cancel** to cancel the command and exit the dialog box.

RELATED COMMAND

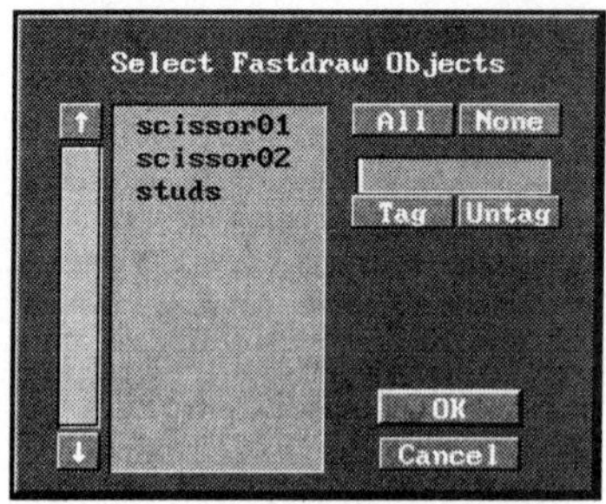

Select the object to Fastdraw.

NOTE The *Display/Speed/Fastdraw* setting overrides this command.

Display/Speed/Fastdraw

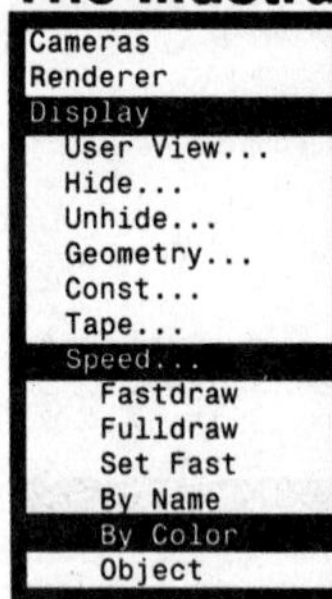

Display/Speed/By Color

Assigns Fastdraw mode to objects with the same color.

Assigning Fastdraw Mode to Objects with the Same Color

1. Ensure that geometry has been created previously.
2. Select *Display/Speed/By Color.*
3. In any viewport, select the object to receive Fastdraw mode. That object will be redisplayed in Fastdraw mode as will all other objects that are the same color.

RELATED COMMAND

Display/Speed/Fast Draw

Display/Speed/Object

Cameras
Renderer
Display
User View...
Hide...
Unhide...
Geometry...
Const...
Tape...
Speed...
Fastdraw
Fulldraw
Set Fast
By Name
By Color
Object

Assigns Fastdraw mode to a single object.

Assigning Fastdraw Mode to an Object

1. Ensure that an object has been created previously.
2. Select *Display/Speed/Object.*
3. In any viewport, select the object. That object will be redisplayed in Fastdraw mode.
4. Repeating steps 2 and 3 will toggle Fastdraw mode for the object.

The *Display/Speed/Fastdraw* setting overrides this command.

RELATED COMMAND

Display/Speed/Fastdraw

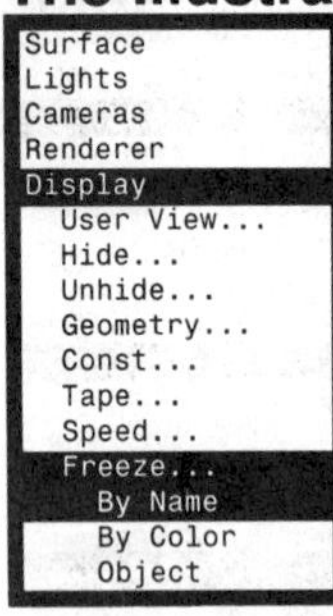

Display/Freeze/By Name

Freezes individual objects.

Freezing Individual Objects

1. Ensure that geometry has been created previously.
2. Select *Display/Freeze/By Name.* The Freeze Objects dialog box appears.
3. Select the object(s) in the dialog box or use the following options.

   All—Selects all objects in the list.

   None—Deselects all objects in the list.

   Tag—Place the wild card pattern in the text box above this button. Click on the **Tag** button. All objects that match the wild card are selected.

   Untag—Place the wild card pattern in the text box above this button. Click on the **Untag** button. All objects that match the wild card are deselected.
4. Select **OK** to accept the selection and close the dialog box. The objects selected will be displayed in all viewports in gray. When frozen, the objects cannot be modified, but they can be rendered.
5. Select **Cancel** to cancel the command and exit the dialog box.

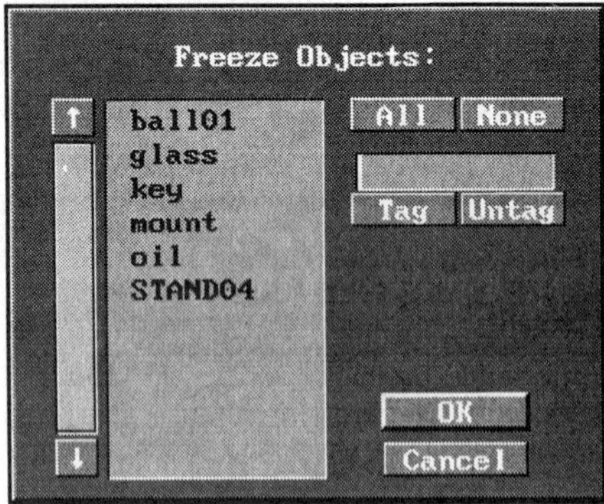

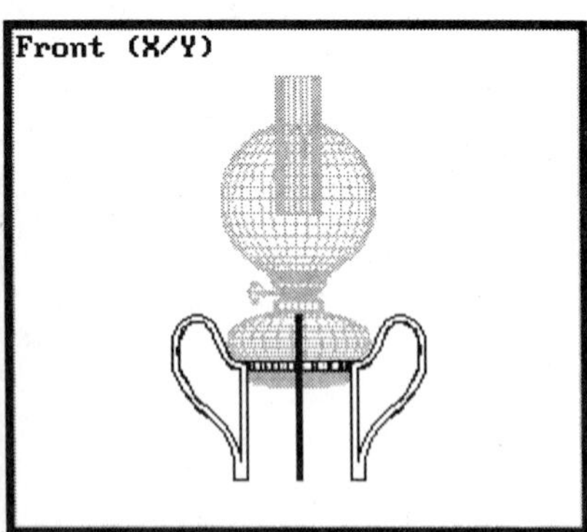

Selecting objects by name to Freeze.

RELATED COMMANDS

Display/Freeze/By Color, Display/Freeze/Object

Display/Freeze/By Color

Freezes objects with the same color.

Freezing objects with the Same Color

1. Ensure that geometry has been created previously.
2. Select *Display/Freeze/By Color*.
3. In any viewport, select an object to freeze. That object will be frozen as will all other objects that are the same color.

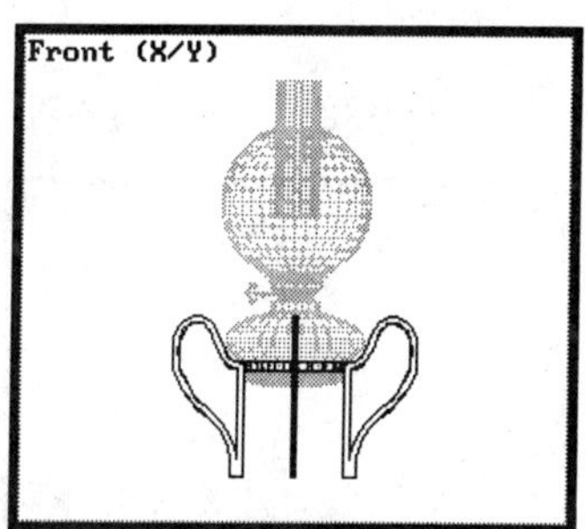

Selecting objects to Freeze by color.

RELATED COMMANDS

Display/Freeze/By Name, Display/Freeze/Object

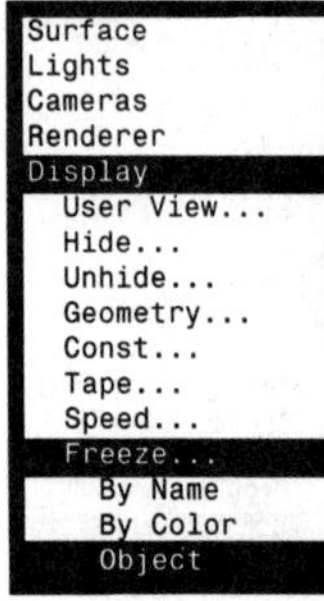

Display/Freeze/Object

Freezes a single object.

Freezing a Single Object

1. Ensure that an object has been created previously.
2. Select *Display/Freeze/Object.*
3. In any viewport, select the object to be frozen. That object will be displayed in gray as shown below. When frozen, the objects cannot be modified, but they can be rendered.
4. Repeating steps 2 and 3 will toggle the freezing of an object.

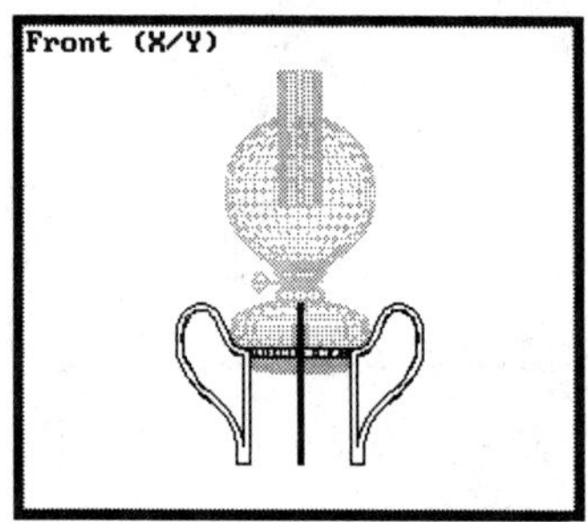

Selecting objects to Freeze.

RELATED COMMANDS

Display/Freeze/By Color, Display/Freeze/By Name

Hierarchy/Link

Hierarchy
Object
Lights
Cameras
Paths
Link
Unlink
Link Info
Place Pivot
Object Pivot
Center Pivot
Create Dummy
Dup Links
Dup Branches
Inherit Links
Show Tree

Creates an invisible connection between two components by linking them as child and parent.

Linking Two Components by Selecting Them

1. Select *Hierarchy/Link* and select the child object.
2. Select the parent object. With the two objects linked, anything that happens to the parent object also happens to the child object. To display the link, see *Hierarchy/Show Tree*.

Linking Two Objects by Name

1. When specifying links, it is often difficult to select the correct object. To make selection easier, use the Select Objects by Name function.
2. Select *Hierarchy/Link*, and when prompted to select the child object, press the [H] key. A dialog box appears, listing all of the objects in the scene. To select one or more child objects, click on them. An asterisk appears next to selected objects. Notice you can also enter text and use wild cards in the text box above the **Tag** and **Untag** options.
3. When prompted for the parent object, again press the [H] key to access another dialog box. Click on the object you want to make the parent object. To display the link, see *Hierarchy/Show Tree*.

> **NOTE** When two objects are linked together as child and parent, anything that happens to the parent also happens to the child. However, nothing that happens to the child has any effect on the parent.

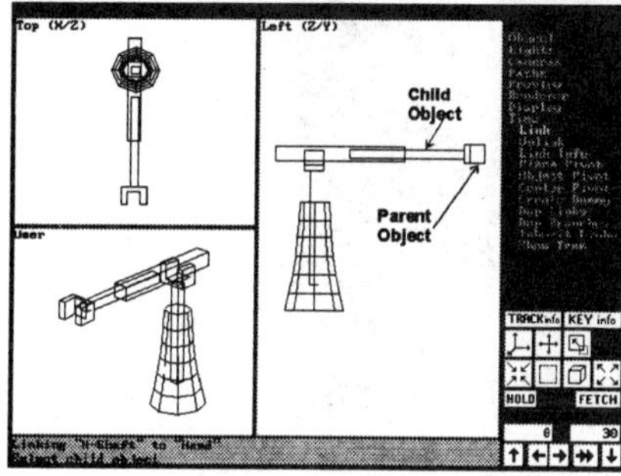

Linking the H-Shaft to the Hand.

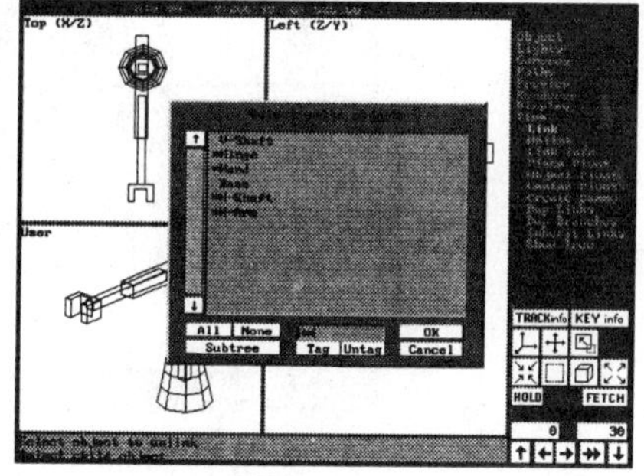

The [H] key accesses a dialog box, allowing you to select child and parent objects by name.

RELATED COMMANDS

Hierarchy/Show Tree, Hierarchy/Unlink

Hierarchy
Object
Lights
Cameras
Paths
Link
Unlink
Link Info
Place Pivot
Object Pivot
Center Pivot
Create Dummy
Dup Links
Dup Branches
Inherit Links
Show Tree

Hierarchy/Unlink

Severs the link between a child and its parent.

Unlinking a Child and Parent by Selection

1. Select *Hierarchy/Unlink.*
2. Select the child component to unlink it. The prompt lines at the bottom of the screen indicate the object has been unlinked. If you are unsure of the linking between the objects, use *Hierarchy/Show Tree.*

Unlinking a Child and Parent by Name

1. Select *Hierarchy/Unlink.*
2. When prompted to select the object to unlink, press the [H] key to display the names of linked objects.
3. Use *Hierarchy/Show Tree* if you want to confirm that the objects are no longer linked.

NOTE Objects are either linked or unlinked throughout the entire animation. If you unlink objects at any time during an animation, they become unlinked in all other frames.

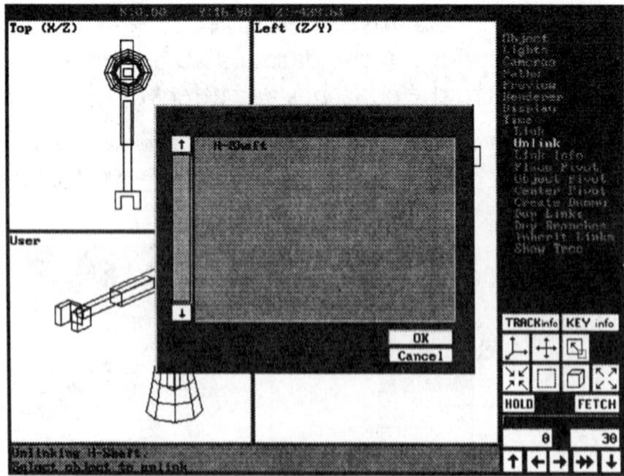

Using a dialog box to unlink objects by name.

RELATED COMMANDS

Hierarchy/Link, Hierarchy/Show Tree

Hierarchy
Object
Lights
Cameras
Paths
Link
Unlink
Link Info
Place Pivot
Object Pivot
Center Pivot
Create Dummy
Dup Links
Dup Branches
Inherit Links
Show Tree

Hierarchy/Link Info

Controls the linking of a child to its parent on any axis of Rotate or Scale changes.

Releasing the Linkage of a Child to Its Parent

1. Select *Hierarchy/Link Info* and click on a child to display the Define Link Type dialog box. You can also press the [H] key to select the child object by name.
2. The six buttons under Rotate and Scale control the influence the parent object has over the child.

   Rotate: When the X, Y, and Z buttons are red (selected), the child will inherit the rotation from the parent.

   Scale: When selected (red), the child will inherit the appropriate scale transformations from the parent.
3. Select the appropriate buttons to enable (red) or disable (gray) specific inheritances or transformations from the parent.

NOTE In the figure below, the H-Shaft (child) is linked to the Hand (parent). In this example of the robot arm, the hand would rotate around the X, Y, and Z axis to simulate the movement of the hand. As the hand rotates, however, you would not want the H-Shaft to rotate. For this example you would select *Hierarchy/Link Info* and choose the H-Shaft (child). In the Define Link Type dialog box, deselect the X, Y, and Z buttons under Rotate. Now when the Hand is rotated about any axis, the H-Shaft will not be rotated.

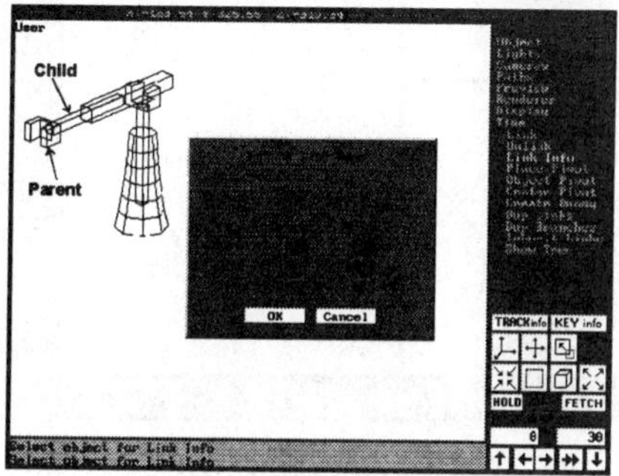

Use the Define Link Type dialog box to enable or disable inheritance from a parent object along a specific axis.

RELATED COMMANDS

Hierarchy/Link, Hierarchy/Show Tree

Hierarchy
Object
Lights
Cameras
Paths
Link
Unlink
Link Info
Place Pivot
Object Pivot
Center Pivot
Create Dummy
Dup Links
Dup Branches
Inherit Links
Show Tree

Hierarchy/Place Pivot

Displays a small X on the screen indicating the object's current pivot point. You can reposition the pivot point by picking new points on the screen.

Placing an Object's Pivot Point

1. Select *Hierarchy/Place Pivot* and select the object you want to adjust the pivot point of. You can also press the H key to select the object by name.
2. A small X appears on the screen, indicating where the object's current pivot point is located.
3. Locate a new pivot point for the object with the screen crosshairs. Note that you must make at least two picks in different viewports to locate the pivot point in all three axes.
4. When the pivot point is at the correct location, press the Esc key or right-click.

NOTE The pivot point is the point around which the object is rotated or scaled. Although Pivot Point is under the Hierarchy menu, it can be used with all objects, not just those that are linked.

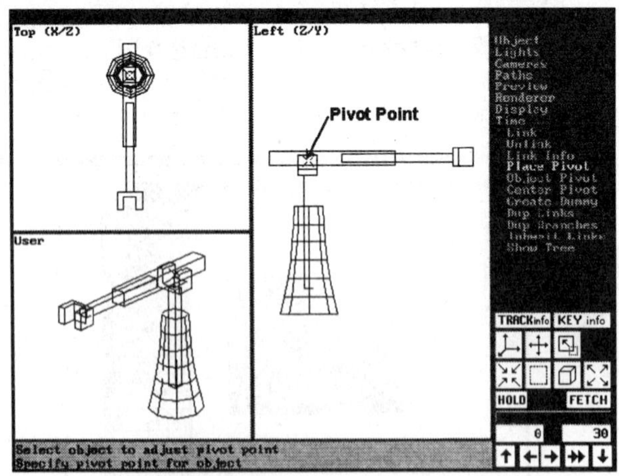

Placing a new pivot point.

RELATED COMMANDS

Hierarchy/Object Pivot, Hierarchy/Center Pivot

Hierarchy
Object
Lights
Cameras
Paths
Link
Unlink
Link Info
Place Pivot
Object Pivot
Center Pivot
Create Dummy
Dup Links
Dup Branches
Inherit Links
Show Tree

Hierarchy/Object Pivot

Temporarily hides all objects in the scene except for the selected object and its parent, allowing you to set its pivot point.

Placing an Object's Pivot Point

1. Select *Hierarchy/Object Pivot* and select the object you want to adjust the pivot point of. You can also press the [H] key to select the object by name.
2. All objects are temporarily hidden on the screen except for the selected object and its parent. A small X appears on the screen, indicating where the object's current pivot point is located.
3. Locate a new pivot point for the object with the screen crosshairs. Note that you must make at least two picks in different viewports to locate the pivot point in all three axis.
4. When the pivot point is at the correct location, press the [Esc] key or right-click.

> **NOTE** The pivot point is the point around which the object is rotated or scaled. Although Object Pivot is under the Hierarchy menu, it can be used with all objects, not just those that are linked.

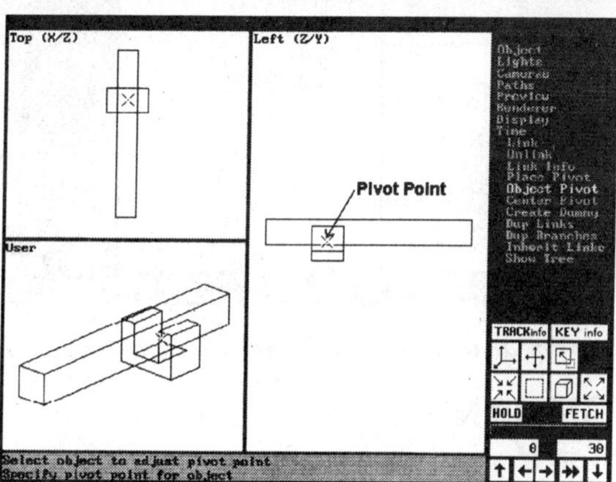

Hierarchy/Object Pivot hides all objects except the selected object and its parent, allowing you to place a new pivot point.

RELATED COMMANDS

Hierarchy/Place Pivot, Hierarchy/Center Pivot

Hierarchy
Object
Lights
Cameras
Paths
Link
Unlink
Link Info
Place Pivot
Object Pivot
Center Pivot
Create Dummy
Dup Links
Dup Branches
Inherit Links
Show Tree

Hierarchy/Center Pivot

Realigns the pivot point within the bounding box of the object.

Placing an Object's Pivot Point at Its Default Location

1. Select *Hierarchy/Center Pivot* and select the object you want to center the pivot point of. You can also press the H key to select the object by name.
2. To display the location of the pivot point, select *Hierarchy/Place Pivot* and select the object. A small X appears on the screen, indicating the object's default pivot point.

NOTE The pivot point is the point around which the object is rotated or scaled. Although Object Pivot is under the Hierarchy menu, it can be used with all objects, not just those that are linked.

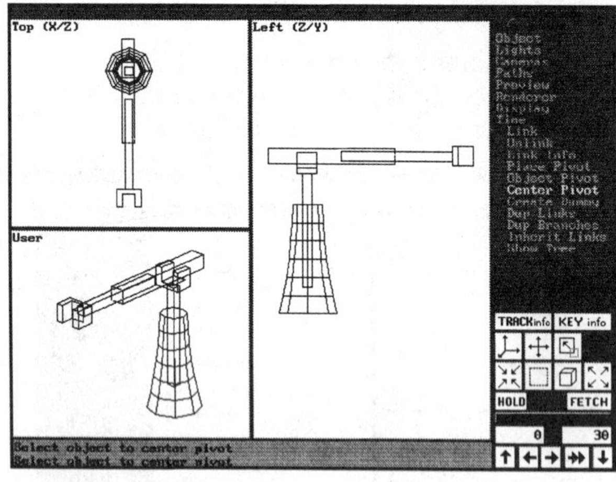

Realigning an object's pivot point to its default location.

RELATED COMMANDS

Hierarchy/Place Pivot, Hierarchy/Object Pivot

Hierarchy
Object
Lights
Cameras
Paths
Link
Unlink
Link Info
Place Pivot
Object Pivot
Center Pivot
Create Dummy
Dup Links
Dup Branches
Inherit Links
Show Tree

Hierarchy/Create Dummy

Creates an invisible, nonrendering object that can be linked to other objects.

Creating a Dummy Object

1. Select *Hierarchy/Create Dummy* and click to set the center of the dummy object.
2. Move the mouse to define the size of the dummy object. Right-click to create the dummy object.
3. Enter a unique name for the dummy object, or click on **Create** to accept the default name.

> **TIP** Use dummy objects to break complex animations down into simpler ones. By linking several objects to the dummy object, it is easier to change the path of the dummy object than to change the path of all the other linked objects separately.

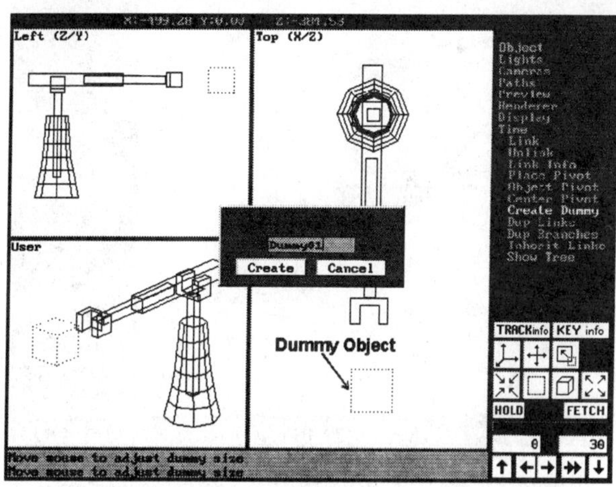

Dummy objects are invisible, nonrendering objects that can be linked to other objects.

RELATED COMMAND

Hierarchy/Link

Hierarchy
Object
Lights
Cameras
Paths
Link
Unlink
Link Info
Place Pivot
Object Pivot
Center Pivot
Create Dummy
Dup Links
Dup Branches
Inherit Links
Show Tree

Hierarchy/Dup Links

Copies the last item in the tree structure of a selected object. The new object is connected to the tree structure using the same information that connected the selected object to its parent.

Duplicating the Last Object on an Object's Tree Structure

1. Before creating a duplicate link, you must have at least two objects linked together in a hierarchical tree. See *Hierarchy/Link* and *Hierarchy/Show Tree.*
2. Select *Hierarchical/Dup Links* and click on any object. Because the objects are all in the same chain, it doesn't matter what object you select.
3. A new object is created, inheriting the link between the previous object and its parent. This link includes any distance offset, scale change, and rotational change.
4. You can click on the object again to create additional duplicate links.

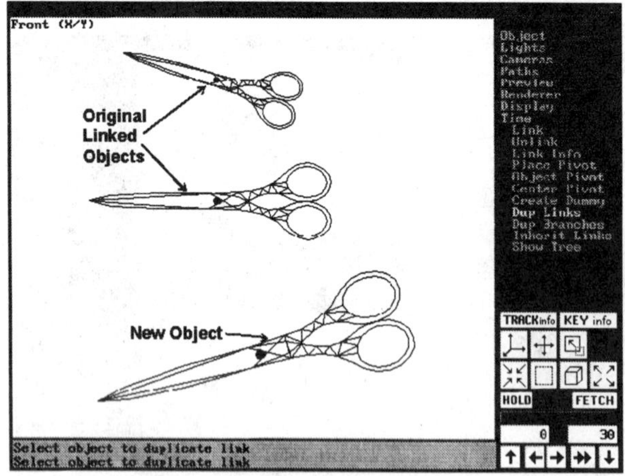

A new object is created, inheriting the relative link between the previous object and its parent.

RELATED COMMANDS

Hierarchy/Link, Hierarchy/Show Tree, Hierarchy/Dup Branches

Hierarchy/Dup Branches

Hierarchy
Object
Lights
Cameras
Paths
Link
Unlink
Link Info
Place Pivot
Object Pivot
Center Pivot
Create Dummy
Dup Links
Dup Branches
Inherit Links
Show Tree

Creates additional objects by examining all child objects linked to a parent object. For each child object connected to the parent, a new object is connected to the tree structure using the same information that connected the selected object to its parent

Duplicating All Objects on an Object's Tree Structure

1. Before creating multiple duplicate links, you should have at least three objects linked together in a hierarchical tree. See *Hierarchy/Link* and *Hierarchy/Show Tree*.
2. Select *Hierarchical/Dup Branches* and click on an object. With this command, the object selected will affect duplicated objects.

   Selecting the Parent Object: A new object is added to every end branch object in the tree. The branching relationship between the end object and parent object is also duplicated.

   Selecting an End Object: A new object is only added to the end of the selected object, using the branching relationship between the selected object and its parent.
3. You can click on the object again to create additional duplicate links.

> **NOTE** This command is similar to the *Hierarchy/Dup Links* command except that *all* links coming out of the parent object are duplicated on the child object.

Multiple new objects are created, inheriting the relative link between the previous object and its parent.

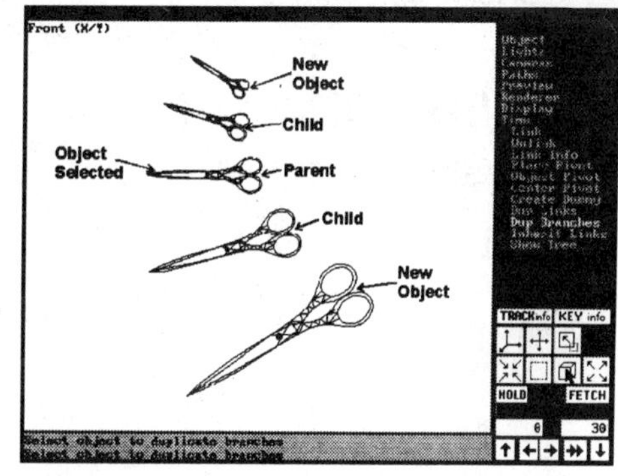

RELATED COMMANDS

Hierarchy/Link, Hierarchy/Show Tree, Hierarchy/Dup Links

Hierarchy
Object
Lights
Cameras
Paths
Link
Unlink
Link Info
Place Pivot
Object Pivot
Center Pivot
Create Dummy
Dup Links
Dup Branches
Inherit Links
Show Tree

Hierarchy/Inherit Links

Link information is passed along the hierarchical tree to objects already linked together.

Inheriting Links to Objects Linked Together

1. Before inheriting links, you should have at least three objects linked together in a hierarchical tree. See *Hierarchy/Link* and *Hierarchy/Show Tree*.
2. Select *Hierarchical/Inherit Links* and click on the parent object.
3. All remaining objects inherit the link information between the parent and first child object.

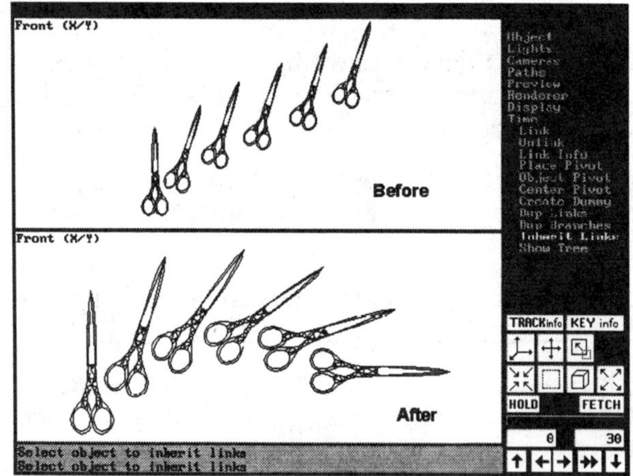

All remaining objects inherit the link information between the parent object and the first child object.

RELATED COMMANDS

Hierarchy/Link, Hierarchy/Show Tree, Hierarchy/Inherit Links

Hierarchy/Show Tree

Hierarchy
Object
Lights
Cameras
Paths
Link
Unlink
Link Info
Place Pivot
Object Pivot
Center Pivot
Create Dummy
Dup Links
Dup Branches
Inherit Links
Show Tree

Displays the hierarchical list of all components. Child objects are indented beneath their parent.

Displaying the Object Attachment Tree

1. Selecting *Hierarchy/Show Tree* accesses the Object Attachment Tree dialog box.
2. Each object that also exists in the 3D Editor has an asterisk beside it.
3. All dummy objects, lights, cameras, and instance objects have no asterisk.
4. Child objects are indented beneath their parent.

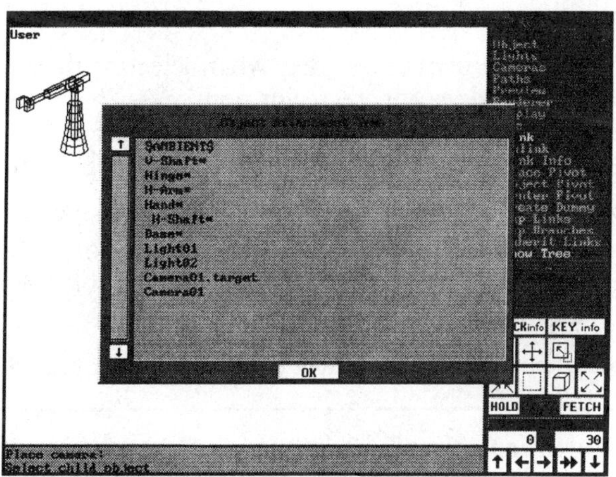

The Object Attachment Tree dialog box displays information about objects and their relationships.

RELATED COMMAND

Hierarchy/Link

Hierarchy
Object
Lights
Cameras
Move
Rotate
Rotate Abs.
Scale
Squash
Morph...
Show Path
Snapshot
Delete
Tracks...
Attributes
Motion Blur

Object/Move

Changes the position of an object along one or multiple axes.

How to Move an Object

1. Select *Object/Move*, then select the object you want to move. When selecting the object to move, you have the following options:

   Select. Clicking on the object creates a position key for the object.

   Shift+Select. Holding down the Shift key when selecting the object will create a clone or copy of the object. You are prompted for a unique name, and whether you want to copy the object's subtree. See *Hierarchy/Link*.

   Alt+Select. Holding down the Alt key when selecting the object updates all of its keys equally, but does not create any new keys. This changes the object's location, but does not change its movement during the animation. Use the Alt key to update the location of an object that has already been animated.

2. As you move the mouse, an outline of the object moves. You can use the Tab key to control horizontal and vertical movement. If you have locked one or more of the axis in the Key dialog box, you won't be able to move the object along those axis. See *Icon-Key Info*.

3. Click to place the object, or right-click to cancel the command.

> **NOTE** Moving an object in key #1 changes the position of the object in both the Keyframer and 3D Editor. Moving the object in any other frame changes the object's Position key at that frame.

Clicking and moving an object in frame 14 creates a position key for the object and makes it a keyframe.

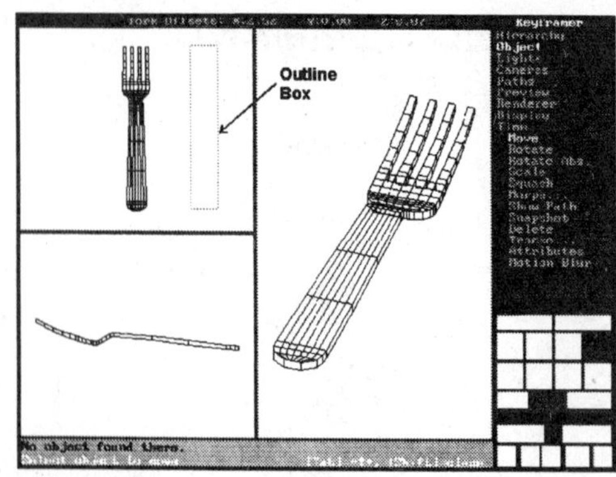

RELATED COMMANDS

Views-Use Snap, Views-Use Grid, Icon-Key Info

```
Hierarchy
Object
Lights
Cameras
  Move
  Rotate
  Rotate Abs.
  Scale
  Squash
  Morph...
  Show Path
  Snapshot
  Delete
  Tracks...
  Attributes
  Motion Blur
```

Object/Rotate

Rotates an object about one of its local axes.

Rotating an Object about Its Local Axis

1. Select *Object/Rotate*, then select the object you want to rotate. When selecting the object to rotate, you have the following options:

   Select. Clicking on the object creates a position key for the object.

   [Shift]+Select. Holding down the [Shift] key when selecting the object will create a clone or copy of the object. You are prompted for a unique name, and whether you want to copy the object's subtree. See *Hierarchy/Link*.

   [Alt]+Select. Holding down the [Alt] key when selecting the object updates all of the object's keys equally, but does not create any new keys. This rotates the object, but does not change it during the animation. Use the [Alt] key to update the location of an object that has already been animated.

2. As you move the mouse, the selected objects are rotated about its local axis. Use the [Tab] key to cycle through the different axis of rotation. See *Hierarchy/ Object Pivot* to modify the object's local axis. If you have locked one or more of the axes in the Key dialog box, you won't be able to rotate the object along those axes. See *Icon-Key Info*.

3. Click to place the object, or right-click to cancel the operation.

> **NOTE** Rotating an object in key #1 changes the position of the object in both the Keyframer and 3D Editor. Rotating the object in any other frame changes the object's Position key at that frame.

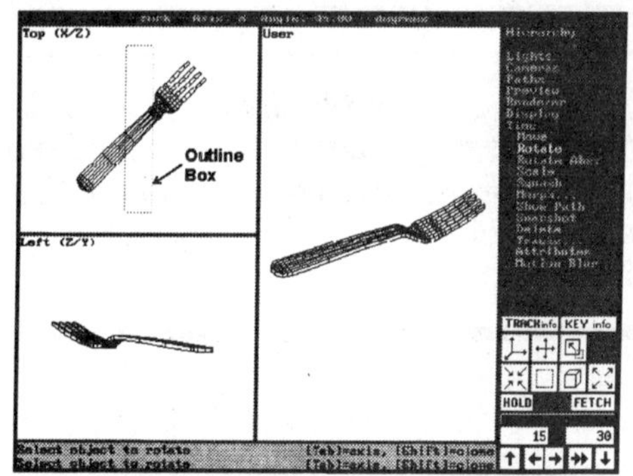

Clicking and rotating an object in frame 15 creates a position key for the object and makes it a keyframe.

RELATED COMMANDS

Views-Use Snap, Views-Use Grid, Hierarchy/Object Pivot, Modify/Object/Abs. Rotate, Icon-Key Info

Hierarchy
Object
Lights
Cameras
Move
Rotate
Rotate Abs.
Scale
Squash
Morph...
Show Path
Snapshot
Delete
Tracks...
Attributes
Motion Blur

Object/Rotate Abs.

Rotates an object about an axes perpendicular to the active viewport.

Rotating an Object

1. Select *Object/Rotate Abs.*, then select the object you want to rotate. When selecting the object to rotate, you have the following options:

Select. Clicking on the object creates a position key for the object.

[Shift]+Select. Holding down the [Shift] key when selecting the object will create a clone or copy of the object. You are prompted for a unique name, and whether you want to copy the objects subtree. See *Hierarchy/Link*.

[Alt]+Select. Holding down the [Alt] key when selecting the object updates all of the object's keys equally, but does not create any new keys. This rotates the object, but does not change it during the animation. Use the [Alt] key to update the location of an object that has already been animated.

2. As you move the mouse, the selected objects are rotated about an axis parallel or perpendicular to the current viewport. Use the [Tab] key to cycle through the different axis of rotation. If you have locked one or more of the axes in the Key dialog box, you won't be able to rotate the object along those axes. See *Icon-Key Info*.
3. Click to place the object, or right-click to cancel the operation.

> **NOTE** Rotating an object in key #1 changes the position of the object in both the Keyframer and 3D Editor. Rotating the object in any other frame changes the object's Position key at that frame.

> **NOTE** The *Modify/Object/Abs.Rotate* command rotates the object about an axis positively perpendicular or parallel to the active orthographic or user viewport. The *Modify/Object/Rotate* command rotates the object about the local axis of the object. Except for this difference, the commands are identical.

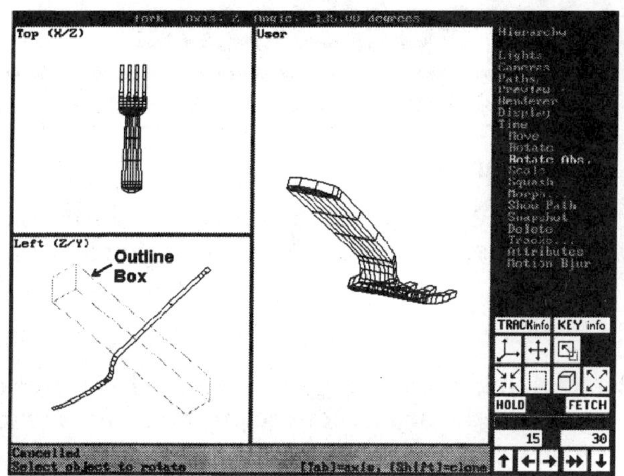

Clicking and rotating an object in frame 15 perpendicular to the Left viewport.

RELATED COMMANDS

Views-Use Snap, Views-Use Grid, Hierarchy/Rotate, Icon-Key Info

Hierarchy
Object
Lights
Cameras
Move
Rotate
Rotate Abs.
Scale
Squash
Morph...
Show Path
Snapshot
Delete
Tracks...
Attributes
Motion Blur

Object/Scale

Scales an object along one or more of its local axes.

Scaling an Object

1. Select *Object/Scale*, then select the object you want to scale. When selecting the object to scale, you have the following options:

Select. Clicking on the object creates a position key for the object.

[Shift]+Select. Holding down the [Shift] key when selecting the object will create a clone or copy of the object. You are prompted for a unique name, and whether you want to copy the object's subtree. See *Hierarchy/Link*.

[Alt]+Select. Holding down the [Alt] key when selecting the object updates all of the object's keys equally, but does not create any new keys. This rotates the object, but does not change it during the animation. Use the [Alt] key to update the location of an object that has already been animated.

2. As you move the mouse, the object is scaled along the local axis of the object. You can use the [Tab] key to control horizontal, vertical, and unidirectional scaling. If you have locked one or more of the axes in the Key dialog box, you won't be able to scale the object along those axes. See *Icon-Key Info*.

3. Click to place the object.

NOTE Scalng an object in key #1 changes the position of the object in both the Keyframer and 3D Editor. Scaling the object in any other frame changes the object's Position key at that frame.

Scaling an object unidirectionally in the Top viewport.

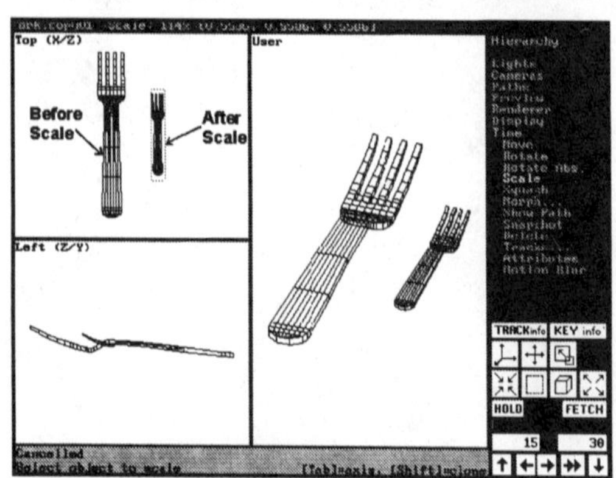

RELATED COMMANDS

Views-Use Snap, Views-Use Grid, Icon-Key Info, Object/Squash

Hierarchy
Object
Lights
Cameras
Move
Rotate
Rotate Abs.
Scale
Squash
Morph...
Show Path
Snapshot
Delete
Tracks...
Attributes
Motion Blur

Object/Squash

Scales an object along one axes and in the opposite direction in the other two axes, maintaining the same volume of the object.

Squashing an Object

1. Select *Object/Squash*, then select the object you want to squash. When selecting the object to squash, you have the following options:

   Select. Clicking on the object creates a position key for the object.

   [Shift]+Select. Holding down the [Shift] key when selecting the object will create a clone or copy of the object. You are prompted for a unique name, and whether you want to copy the object's subtree. See *Hierarchy/Link*.

   [Alt]+Select. Holding down the [Alt] key when selecting the object updates all of the object's keys equally, but does not create any new keys. This rotates the object, but does not change it during the animation. Use the [Alt] key to update the location of an object that has already been animated.

2. As you move the mouse, the object is squashed in one direction, and the opposite direction in the other two axes. The volume of the object remains the same. You can use the [Tab] key to control the axis the squash is performed along.

3. Click to place the object.

> **NOTE** Squashing an object in key #1 changes the position of the object in both the Keyframer and 3D Editor. Squashing the object in any other frame changes the object's Position key at that frame.

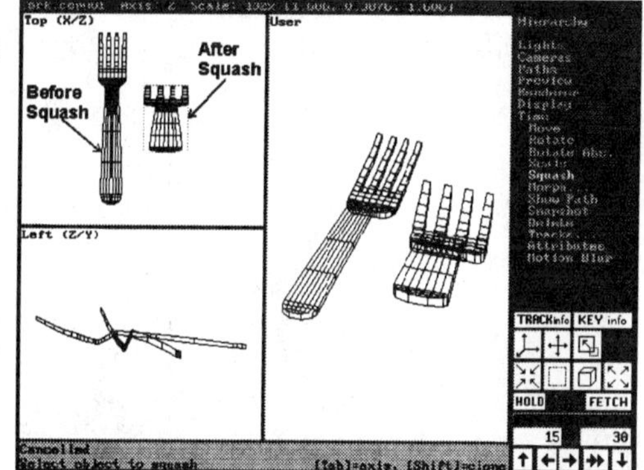

Squashing an object about the Z axis in the Top viewport.

RELATED COMMANDS

Views-Use Snap, Views-Use Grid, Object/Scale

Hierarchy
Object
Lights
Cameras
Move
Rotate
Rotate Abs.
Scale
Squash
Morph...
Show Path
Snapshot
Delete
Tracks...
Assign
Options

Object/Morph/Assign

Changes an object's shape by moving its vertices to the position of a second object's vertices.

Assigning Objects to Morph

1. Change to the frame in which you want the metamorphosis to occur.
2. Select *Object/Morph/Assign*, then select the object you want to morph *from*.
3. In the Select Morph Object dialog box, select the name of the object you want to morph *to*.
4. Click on **OK**. A morph key is created in the current frame. The vertices of the first object are moved to the vertices of the second object. In most cases you will not want the second object to show. Use *Display/Hide/Object* to hide the second object.

To create a successful morph, all objects must have the exact same number of vertices. This can be accomplished by the following:

1. Create two different shapes in the 2D Shaper with the same number of vertices, then loft them in the 3D Lofter with Optimize turned off.
2. Loft the same shape in the 3D Lofter along different paths that have the same number of vertices. Turn Optimize off.
3. Create a copy of an object in the 3D Editor, and modify the copy.

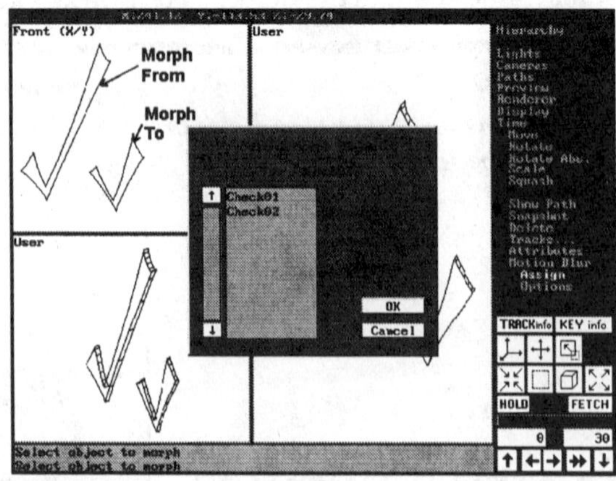

To create a successful morph, both objects must have the exact same number of vertices.

RELATED COMMAND

Object/Morph/Options

Hierarchy
Object
Lights
Cameras
Move
Rotate
Rotate Abs.
Scale
Squash
Morph...
Show Path
Snapshot
Delete
Tracks...
Assign
Options

Object/Morph/Options

Allows you to morph materials and smoothing assignments.

Morphing Options

1. Select the objects you want to morph. See *Object/Morph/Assign*.
2. Select *Object/Morph/Options* and click on a morph object to access the Morph Options dialog box. The available options are:

   Morph Materials: The materials assigned to the first object are morphed to the second and any additional morphed objects.

   Animate Smoothing: As the morph is rendered, new smoothing groups are assigned based on the angle set in the Angle: text box. See *Surface/Smoothing/Object/AutoSmooth.*
3. Click on **OK** to save the morph options settings.

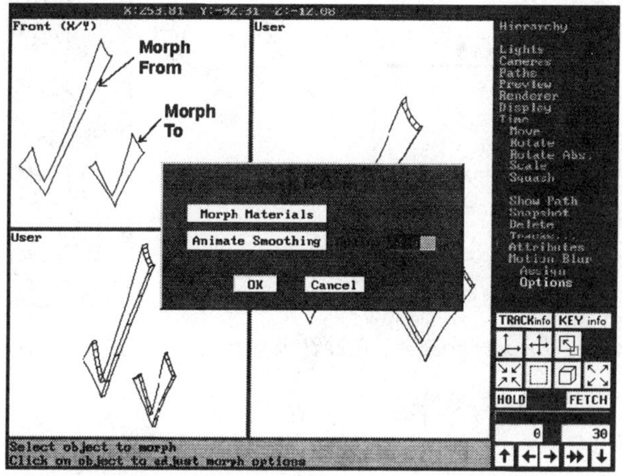

Use the Morph Options dialog box to morph materials from the first object to the second.

RELATED COMMANDS

Object/Morph/Assign, Surface/Smoothing/Object/AutoSmooth

Hierarchy
Object
Lights
Cameras
Move
Rotate
Rotate Abs.
Scale
Squash
Morph...
Show Path
Snapshot
Delete
Tracks...
Attributes
Motion Blur

Object/Show Path

Turns the path display for an object on or off.

Displaying the Path for a Selected Object

1. Select *Object/Show Path* and select an object.
2. The movement path for the object appears. The path movement appears as a red line, the white squares represent the keys, and the yellow dots represent the frames. If only a single yellow square within a square appears, no Position keys have been assigned to the object.
3. To turn off the path display, select *Object/Show Path* and select the object.

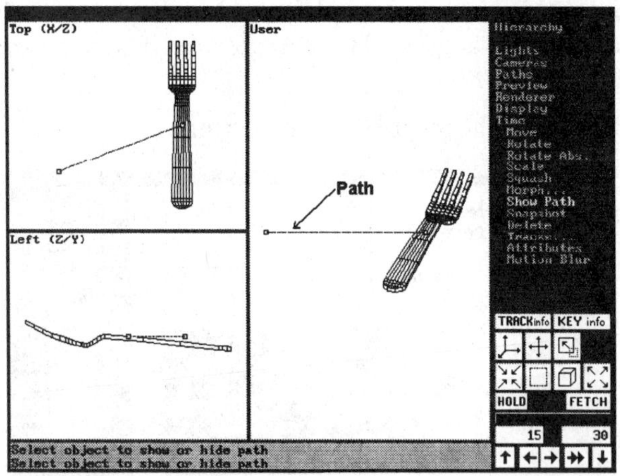

Displaying the path for an object that was moved once in frame 15.

RELATED COMMANDS

None

Hierarchy
Object
Lights
Cameras
Move
Rotate
Rotate Abs.
Scale
Squash
Morph...
Show Path
Snapshot
Delete
Tracks...
Attributes
Motion Blur

Object/Snapshot

Allows you to capture geometry at any frame in an animation and copy it back to the 3D Editor.

Creating a Snapshot of an Object

1. Move to the frame you want to copy the object in and select *Object/Snapshot*.
2. Select the object to copy. The Snapshot dialog box appears with the following options:

   Single: Creates a single snapshot of the object. If the selected object has a subtree, the **Subtree** button appears. Clicking on the **Subtree** button snapshots the parent and subtree objects as well.

   Range: Enter the starting and ending number of the frames you want to snapshot and the number of frames in the **# Copies** text box. If the selected object has a subtree, the **Subtree** button appears. Clicking on the **Subtree** button snapshots the parent and subtree objects as well.
3. New objects are created in the Keyframer as well as the 3D Editor. The names are derived from the name of the source object with a two-digit number.

TIP You can use *Object/Snapshot* to create a variety of animation effects, such as:

1. Combine *Object/Snapshot* with Hide keys to simulate objects that other objects pick up.
2. Use Object/Snapshot to create intermediate morph objects for an animation to look at.

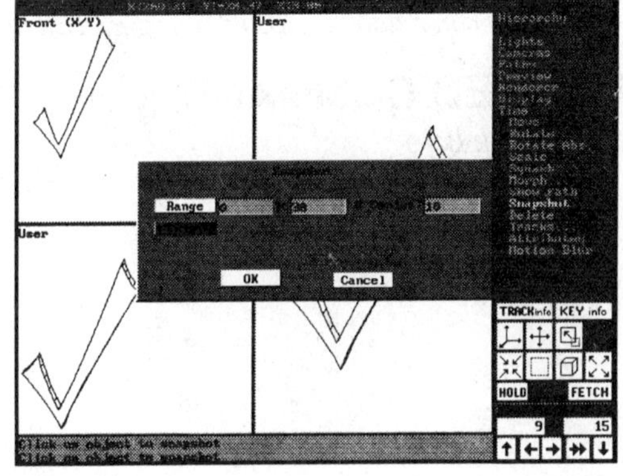

Creating a Snapshot creates a copy of an object at any frame in a animation.

RELATED COMMANDS

None

Hierarchy
Object
Lights
Cameras
Move
Rotate
Rotate Abs.
Scale
Squash
Morph...
Show Path
Snapshot
Delete
Tracks...
Attributes
Motion Blur

Object/Delete

Deletes a selected object and all of its children.

Deleting a Selected Object

1. Select *Object/Delete*, then select the object you want to delete. You can also delete a dummy object or an instance of an object.
2. In the Delete This Object dialog box, select **Yes.**
3. In the Delete subtree also? dialog box, selecting **Yes** will delete the object and all of its children, including hidden objects. Selecting **No** will delete the parent object only.

To make objects disappear and reappear during an animation, use the Hide keys in the Track Info dialog box. See *Icons-Track Info.*

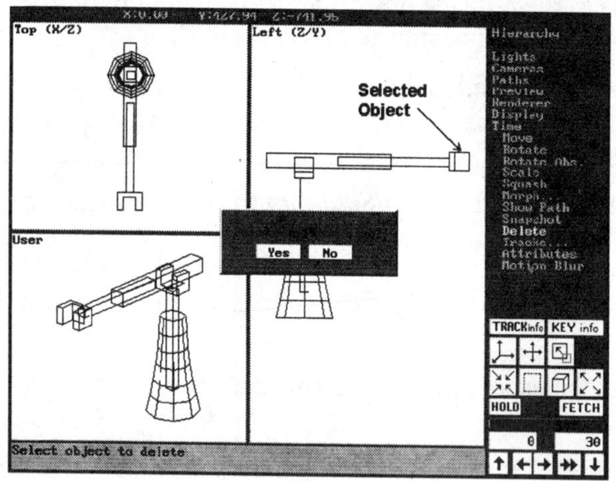

You can delete a selected object and all of its children with Object/Delete.

RELATED COMMAND

Icons-Track Info

Hierarchy
Object
Lights
Cameras
Squash
Morph...
Show Path
Snapshot
Delete
Tracks...
Attributes
Motion Blur
Loop
Copy
Reverse
File Insert

Object/Tracks/Loop

Copies all key settings at frame 0 to the last frame in the animation.

Looping Tracks

1. Press the **Hold** button (Ctrl H) to store the current state of your geometry, viewport configuration, and selection set.
2. Select *Object/Tracks/Loop* and select an object. If the object has a subtree, you will be asked if you want to loop it also.
3. Looping the tracks in an animation makes permanent changes to the last frame of your animation, including:

   Last Frame: Becomes a keyframe if it is not already.

   Key Values: Key values of the first frame of the selected object are copied to the last frame.
4. If the results are not what you wanted, press the **Fetch** button (Ctrl F)to restore the original configuration.

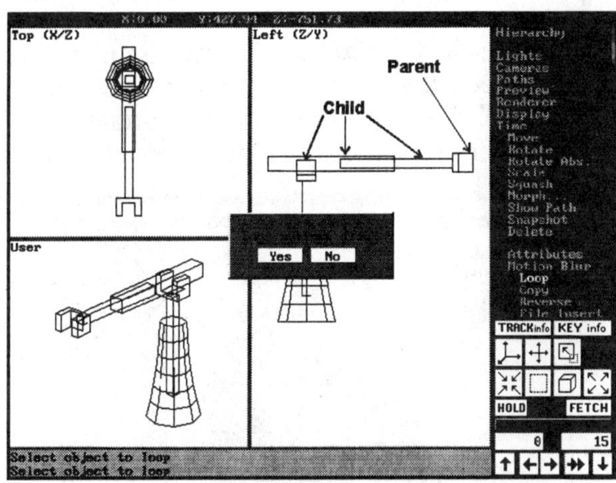

Looping tracks copies all key settings at frame 0 to the last frame in the animation, allowing you to copy all keys for linked children also.

RELATED COMMAND

Icons-Track Info

Hierarchy
Object
Lights
Cameras
Squash
Morph...
Show Path
Snapshot
Delete
Tracks...
Attributes
Motion Blur
Loop
Copy
Reverse
File Insert

Object/Tracks/Copy

Copies the keys from one object to another.

Copying Keys

1. Because the *Object/Tracks/Copy* command does not have an Undo, press the **Hold** button ([Ctrl] [H]) to store the current state of your geometry, viewport configuration, and selection set.
2. Select *Object/Tracks/Copy* and select the source object.
3. Select the Destination Object. The Copy Tracks dialog box appears, with Position, Rotate, Scale, Morph, and Hide buttons. Activating a button copies the related key information from the source to destination object.

   Relative: Applies the motion as an offset from the object's current location.

   Absolute: Relocates the destination object to the same location as the source object.
4. Select OK to copy the keys. If the results are not what you wanted, press the **Fetch** button ([Ctrl] [F])to restore the original configuration.

> **TIP** You can use the *Object/Tracks/Copy* command when you have several objects that all have to be doing the same thing, such as planes flying in formation. To select more than one destination object, press the [H] key when prompted for the destination object to display a list of all objects.

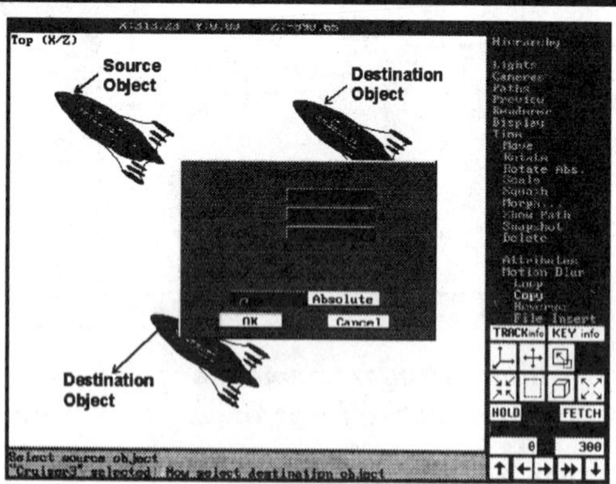

Copying tracks from the source to destination objects to make the cruisers fly in formation.

RELATED COMMAND

Icons-Track Info

Object/Tracks/Reverse

Hierarchy
Object
Lights
Cameras
Squash
Morph...
Show Path
Snapshot
Delete
Tracks...
Attributes
Motion Blur
Loop
Copy
Reverse
File Insert

Takes any motion assigned to a selected object and keys it backwards.

Reversing the Tracks of a Selected Object

1. Because the *Object/Tracks/Reverse* command does not have an Undo, press the **Hold** button (Ctrl H) to store the current state.
2. Select *Object/Tracks/Reverse* and select the object you want to reverse the tracks on. The Reverse Tracks dialog box shows which tracks will be reversed.
3. After selecting which tracks you want reversed, click **OK**. If the results are not what you wanted, press the **Fetch** button (Ctrl F)to restore the original configuration.

> **TIP** Use *Object/Tracks/Reverse* to create assembly animations. Begin with an assembled object, and animate it as the different parts of the object are taken away. Then use *Object/Tracks/Reverse* to reverse the tracks of the animation, so the object begins in pieces and assembles itself during the animation.

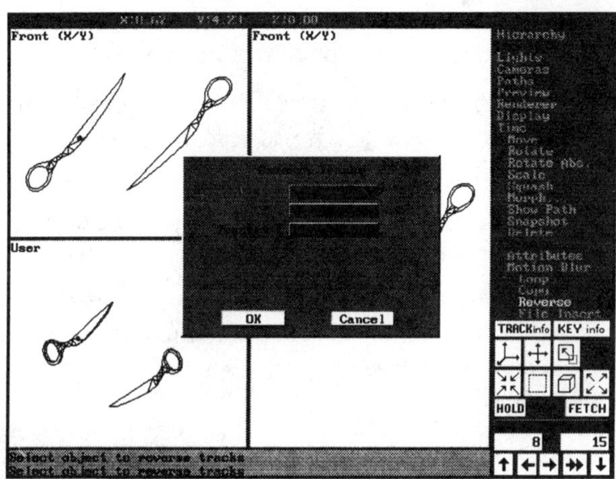

Reversing the tracks of the scissors, so it will begin in pieces and reassemble itself.

RELATED COMMAND

Icons-Track Info

Hierarchy
Object
Lights
Cameras
Squash
Morph...
Show Path
Snapshot
Delete
Tracks...
Attributes
Motion Blur
Loop
Copy
Reverse
File Insert

Object/Tracks/File Insert

Applies the motion from any object in any file to any similar object in the current file.

Inserting Tracks from a File

1. Press the **Hold** button (Ctrl H) to store the current state.
2. Move to the frame where you want the tracks inserted.
3. Select *Object/Tracks/File Insert* and select the destination object you want the keys inserted.
4. Select the source file containing the keys from the dialog box.
5. After the Insert Animation Tracks dialog box appears, select from the following:

   Scope: Object inserts only tracks from the selected source object; **Subtree** selects the tracks from the selected source object and all of its children.

   Method: Use **Relative** to apply the inserted tracks relative to the current tracks. Use **Absolute** to use the absolute values of the source object.

   Source Frames: Specify the frames you want to include from the source object.

   First key to Last key: Click to set the range in the Source Frames box to match up with the frames used by the destination object.
6. After setting the appropriate options, select **OK**. If the results are not what you wanted, press the **Fetch** button (Ctrl F) to restore the original configuration.

The source object and destination object must have the same link hierarchy or the motion keys will not be applied correctly.

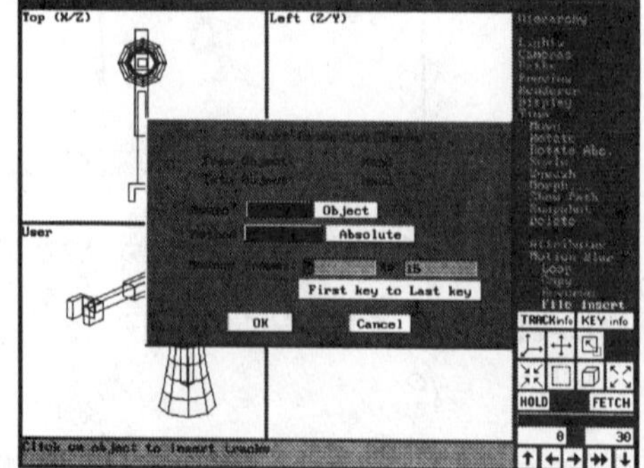

Inserting animation tracks from a selected source file.

RELATED COMMAND

Icons-Track Info

Hierarchy
Object
Lights
Cameras
Move
Rotate
Rotate Abs.
Scale
Squash
Morph...
Show Path
Snapshot
Delete
Tracks...
Attributes
Motion Blur

Object/Attributes

Allows you to alter various attributes of a selected object.

Altering an Object's Attributes

Select *Object/Attributes*. Selecting an object in any viewport accesses the Object Attributes dialog box with the following options:

Old name: Displays the current name of the selected object.

New name: Enter a new unique name to rename the object.

Vertices: Displays the number of vertices in the selected object.

Faces: Displays the number of faces in the selected object.

Matte Object: If active, the object will be invisible when rendering but will block any geometry behind it. It will not block the background, however.

Cast Shadows: Active by default, meaning the object will cast shadows on other objects.

Receive Shadows: Active by default, meaning the object will receive shadows cast by other objects.

External Process

Name: Accesses the AXP Selector dialog box, allowing you to assign an *animated stand-in external process* to the object.

On/Off: If turned on, the AXP process is assigned as an attribute of the object.

Settings: Used to change the settings of selected AXP programs.

Load/Save: Lets you save and reload settings for selected AXP programs.

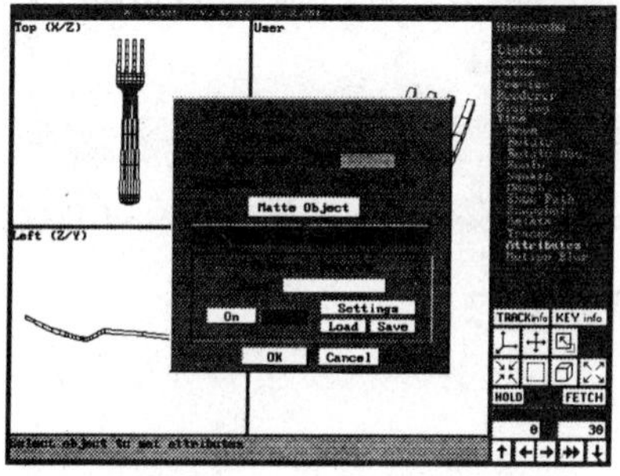

Various attributes of an object can be modified with the Object Attributes dialog box.

RELATED COMMAND

None

Hierarchy
Object
Lights
Cameras
Move
Rotate
Rotate Abs.
Scale
Squash
Morph...
Show Path
Snapshot
Delete
Tracks...
Attributes
Motion Blur

Object/Motion Blur

Assigns motion blur setting to single or multiple objects. Motion blur specifies that 3D Studio render multiple copies of an object on each frame, and dither between the copies of the object.

Assigning Motion Blur to Selected Objects

1. Select *Object/Motion Blur*.
2. Press the [H] key to access the Select Objects to Blur dialog box. Select the objects you want to blur. Selected objects are tagged with an asterisk.
3. Select OK to assign motion blur to the selected objects.

> **NOTE** You must apply motion blur to each object you want blurred. The object must then move during the command to have any effect. See *Render/Setup/Options* for a complete description of the motion blur options.

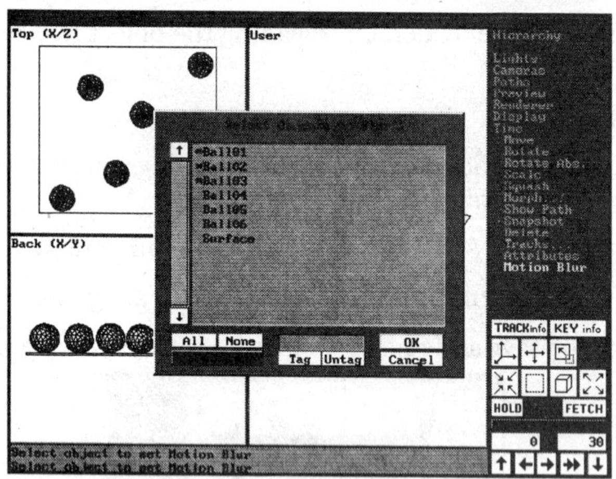

Assigning motion blur to selected objects.

RELATED COMMAND

Render/Setup/Options

Lights/Ambient

Adjusts the color of ambient light.

Changing the Ambient Color Light

1. Select *Lights/Ambient*. The Ambient Light Definition dialog box appears.
2. Make adjustments to the dialog box sliders. Click the + button to increase a value and click − to decrease a value, or click and drag on the slider. All changes to ambient light are displayed in the color box on the right of the dialog box. The dialog box controls are:

R: Adjusts the Red value.
G: Adjusts the Green value.
B: Adjusts the Blue value.
H: Adjusts the Hue (Color) value.
L: Adjusts the Luminance (Brightness) value.
S: Adjusts the Saturation (Purity) value.

3. Select **OK** to accept the settings and close the dialog box. Select **Cancel** to cancel the settings and close the dialog box.

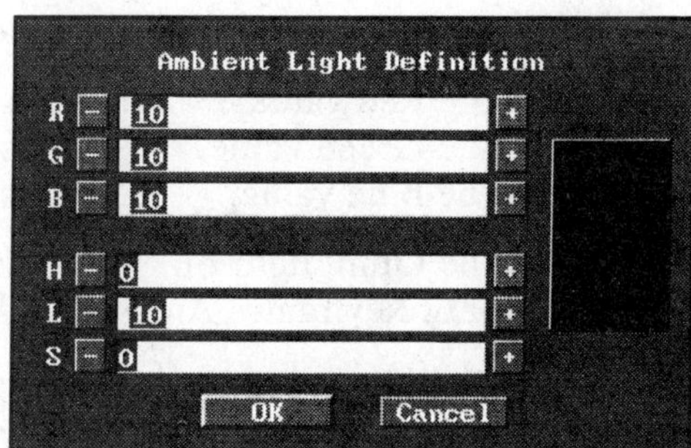

The Ambient Light Definition dialog box.

NOTE If the color of ambient light is changed at frame #1, the changes are reflected in the Keyframer and the 3D Editor. If it is modified on any other frame, that frame becomes a keyframe.

TIP Very rarely will ambient lighting be the only light used in a scene. Use it to increase contrast by decreasing ambient settings. Ambient lighting also can be used to tint an entire scene with a particular color.

RELATED COMMANDS

Lights/Omni/Create, Lights/Spotlight/Create

Hierarchy
Object
Lights
Cameras
Paths
Preview
Ambient
Omni...
Spot...
Tracks...
Create
Move
Place Hilite
Adjust
Show Path
Delete

Lights/Omni/Create

Creates an Omni light for use in the Keyframer and the 3D Editor.

Creating an Omni Light

1. Activate an orthographic or user viewport to receive the Omni light. Move to frame #1, unless the Omni light is to be animated.
2. Select *Lights/Omni/Create*.
3. Click in the active viewport at the location for the light. The Light Definition dialog box appears as shown on page 4-31.
4. Give the Light a unique name in the **Light Name:** input box.
5. Make adjustments to the dialog box sliders. Click the + button to increase a value and click − to decrease a value or click and drag slider. All changes to Omni light are displayed in the color box on the right of the dialog box. All dialog box controls and settings are described below.

R: Adjusts the Red value.
G: Adjusts the Green value.
B: Adjusts the Blue value.

H: Adjusts the Hue (Color) value.
L: Adjusts the Luminance (Brightness) value.
S: Adjusts the Saturation (Purity) value.

On: Turns the Omni light on. When the light is on, it appears yellow in the 3D Editor or Keyframer. An Omni light is on throughout an animation.

Off: Turns the Omni light off. If the light is off, it appears black in the 3D Editor or Keyframer. To turn a light off during an animation, change its luminance value to 0 at the frame where the light is to be turned off.

Multiplier: Amplifies the amount of light. A setting of 2 will double the light value. A setting of -2 will halve the light value. The effective range is from 10 to -10.

Exclude: Used to exclude objects that are receiving light from this particular Omni light. Once this option is selected, the Object Selection dialog box appears. Select those objects to be excluded and click on the **OK** button. The button will appear red if one or more objects have been selected to be excluded.

Attenuation: Determines whether the Omni light's intensity drops off to a value of zero over a predefined range. **On** turns on Attenuation, **Off** turns it off.

Create: Creates the Omni light with the above settings and closes the dialog box. The Omni light icon [*] will now appear in the active viewport.

Cancel: Cancels the command and closes the dialog box.

Omni lights are similar to light bulbs in that light radiates from the source in all directions.

It is important to note that Omni lights do not cast shadows. If you wish to create shadows, use Spotlights instead.

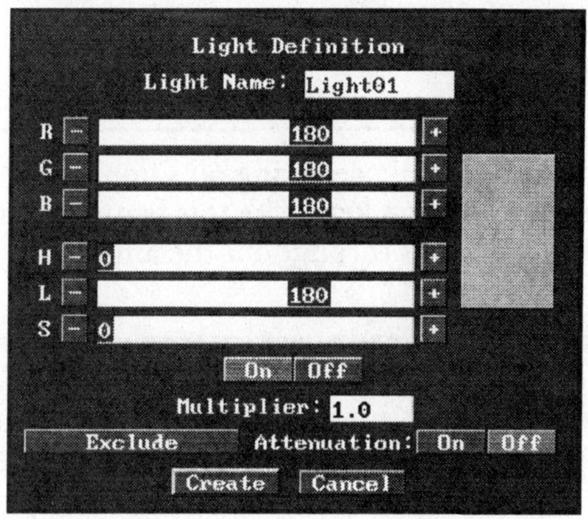

The Light Definition dialog box.

RELATED COMMANDS

Lights/Ambient, Lights/Omni/Create, Lights/Omni/Move, Lights/Omni/Adjust, Lights/Spot/Create

Hierarchy
Object
Lights
Cameras
Paths
Preview
Ambient
Omni...
Spot...
Tracks...
Create
Move
Place Hilite
Adjust
Show Path
Delete

Lights/Omni/Move

Changes the location of an Omni light or allows you to create a clone of an existing light at a new location.

Moving an Omni Light

1. Ensure that an Omni light has been created previously using *Lights/Omni/Create*.
2. Select *Lights/Omni/Move*.
3. Select the orthographic or user viewport that contains the Omni light to be moved. Move the light in frame #1 to change its location in the 3D Editor as well. If the light is moved in any other frame, a position key will be created.
4. Click on the light.
5. Move the light to its new location and click to place or right-click to cancel.

NOTE Pressing [Alt] while selecting an Omni light to be moved will update all position keys. Use this feature to move an animated light and adjust its movements throughout the animation to reflect the animation changes.

TIP To create a clone of an omni light, hold down [Shift] and click on the light. Move the new cloned light to its new location and click to place or right-click to cancel.

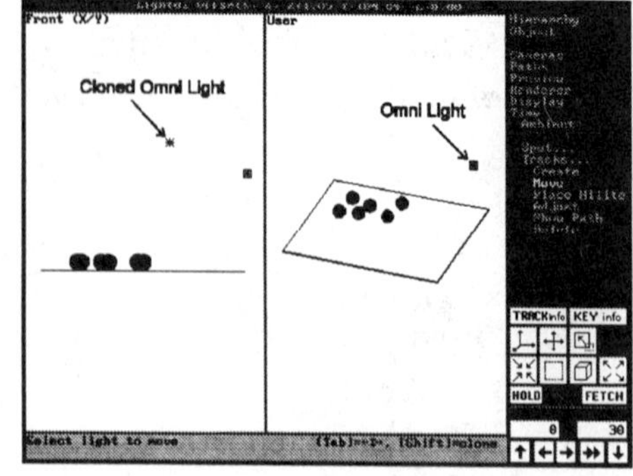

An Omni light appears as an asterisk.

RELATED COMMANDS

Lights/Omni/Create, Light/Omni/Place Hilite, Lights/Spot/Move

Lights/Omni/Place Hilite

Hierarchy
Object
Lights
Cameras
Paths
Preview
Ambient
Omni...
Spot...
Tracks...
Create
Move
Place Hilite
Adjust
Show Path
Delete

Moves a previously created Omni light to a new location that will create a highlight at a specified location on an object.

Placing a Highlight on an Object

1. Ensure that the object to receive the highlight has been created and that an Omni light has been created previously.
2. Select *Lights/Omni/Place Hilite.*
3. Click in the viewport that is best suited for selecting the highlight location. Place the highlight in frame #1 to change its location in the 3D Editor as well. If the light is moved in any other frame, a position key will be created.
4. Click on the object at the location to receive the highlight.
5. Click on the Omni light that is to cast the highlight. The Omni light will be moved to the new location.
6. To verify that the highlight has been placed properly, render that viewport.

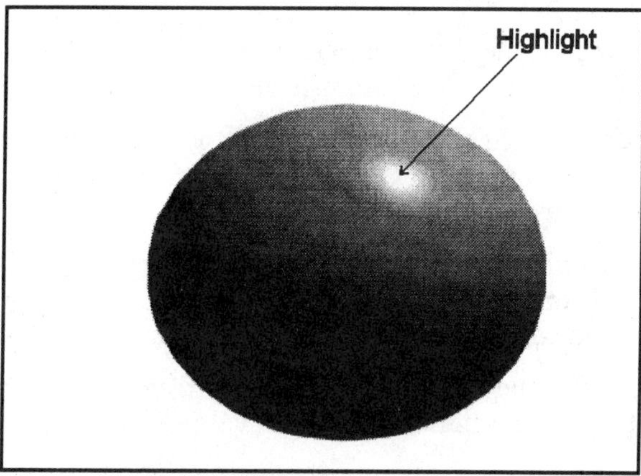

Rendering of a sphere highlighted with an Omni light.

RELATED COMMANDS

Lights/Omni/Create, Lights/Spot/Move

Hierarchy
Object
Lights
Cameras
Paths
Preview
Ambient
Omni...
Spot...
Tracks...
Create
Move
Place Hilite
Adjust
Show Path
Delete

Lights/Omni/Adjust

Changes the values of previously created Omni lights.

Adjusting an Omni Light

1. Ensure that an Omni light has been created using *Lights/Omni/Create*.
2. Select *Lights/Omni/Adjust*.
3. Click in the viewport that contains the Omni light to be adjusted. Adjust the light in frame #1 to change its attributes in the 3D Editor as well. If the light is adjusted in any other frame, a color key will be created.
4. Click on the Omni light to be adjusted. The Light Definition dialog box appears.
5. Make adjustments to the dialog box sliders. Click the + button to increase a value and click − to decrease a value. All changes to Omni light are displayed in the color box on the right of the dialog box. The dialog box controls and settings are:

Light Name: Adjusts the name of the light.

R: Adjusts the Red value.
G: Adjusts the Green value.
B: Adjusts the Blue value.
H: Adjusts the Hue (Color) value.
L: Adjusts the Luminance (Brightness) value.
S: Adjusts the Saturation (Purity) value.

On: Turns the Omni light on. When the light is on, it appears yellow in the 3D Editor or Keyframer. An Omni light has to stay on through an animation if it is to be used.

Off: Turns the Omni light off. If the light is off, it appears black in the 3D Editor or Keyframer. To turn a light off during an animation, change its luminance value to 0 at the frame where the light is to be turned off.

Multiplier: Amplifies the amount of light. A setting of 2 will double the light value. A setting of -2 will halve the light value. The effective range is from -10 to 10.

Exclude: Used to exclude objects that are receiving light from this particular Omni light. Once this option is selected, the Object Selection dialog box appears. Select the objects to be excluded and click on the **OK** button. The button will appear red if one or more objects have been selected to be excluded.

Attenuation: Determines whether the Omni light's intensity drops off to a value of 0 over a predefined range. **On** turns on Attenuation and **Off** turns off Attenuation.

OK: Adjusts the Omni light with the above settings and closes the dialog box.

Cancel: Cancels the command and closes the dialog box.

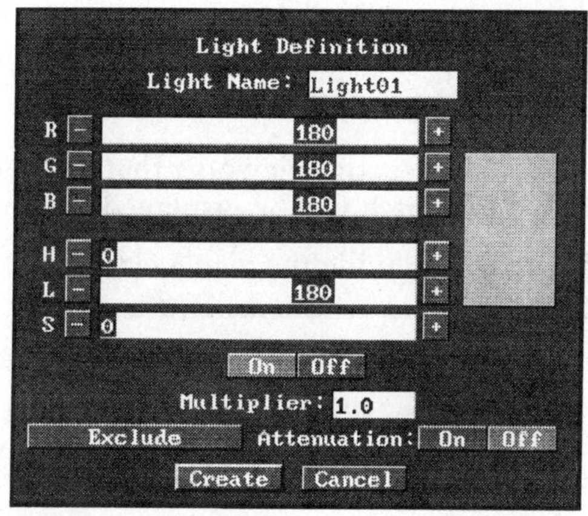

The Light Definition dialog box, used to adjust an Omni light.

RELATED COMMAND

Lights/Omni/Create

Hierarchy
Object
Lights
Cameras
Paths
Preview
Ambient
Omni...
Spot...
Tracks...
Create
Move
Place Hilite
Adjust
Show Path
Delete

Lights/Omni/Show Path

Displays or hides the path assigned to an animated Omni light.

Displaying and Hiding an Omni Light Path

1. Ensure that an Omni light has been created previously and that a path has been assigned to that light.
2. Select *Lights/Omni/Show Path*.
3. Select the Omni light in the active viewport that has been assigned to the path to be displayed. The path will be displayed as shown below.
4. Selecting the light again will hide the displayed path.

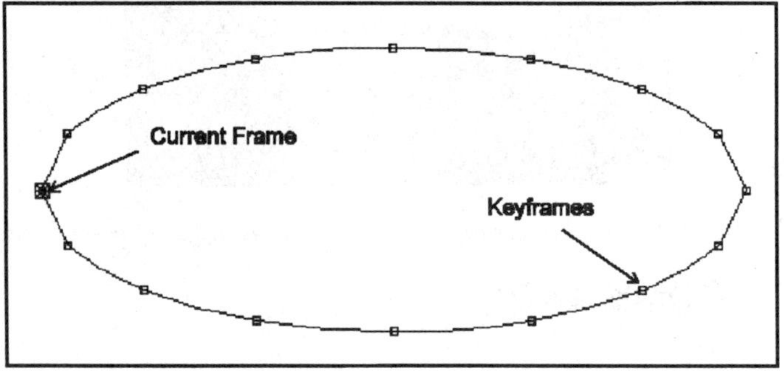

Displaying the path assigned to an Omni light.

RELATED COMMANDS

Lights/Omni/Create, Paths/Get

Lights/Omni/Delete

Deletes a previously created Omni light.

Deleting an Omni Light

1. Ensure that an Omni light has been created previously using the *Lights/Omni/Create* command.
2. Select *Lights/Omni/Delete*.
3. Click on the Omni light to delete in any viewport. The Omni light will be deleted from the scene.

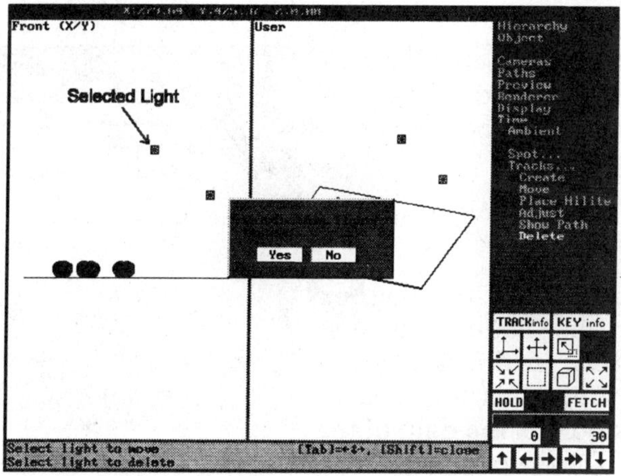

Deleting an Omni light.

RELATED COMMANDS

Lights/Omni/Create, Lights/Spot/Delete

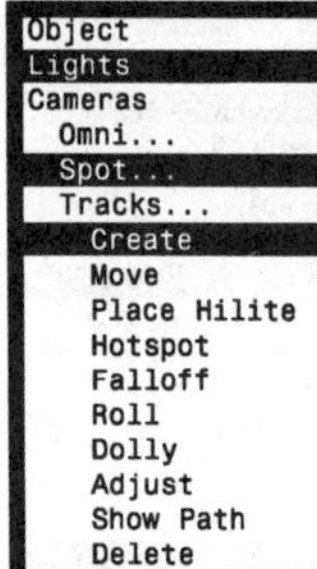

Lights/Spot/Create

Creates a spotlight and target for use in the Keyframer and 3D Editor.

Creating a Spotlight

1. Activate an orthographic or user viewport that is to receive the spotlight.
2. Move to frame #0 unless the spotlight is to be animated.
3. Select *Lights/Spot/Create*.
4. Click in the active viewport at the location for the spotlight.
5. Move the mouse and select the location for the spotlight target. The Spotlight Definition dialog box appears as shown at right.
6. Give the spotlight a unique name in the **Light Name:** input box.
7. Make adjustments to the dialog box sliders. Click the + button to increase a value and click − to decrease a value. All changes to spotlight are displayed in the color box on the right of the dialog box. The dialog box controls and settings are:

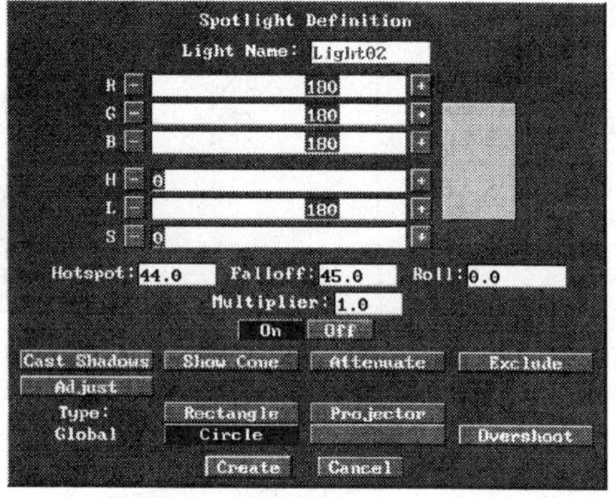

The Spotlight Definition dialog box.

R: Adjusts the Red value.
G: Adjusts the Green value.
B: Adjusts the Blue value.

H: Adjusts the Hue (Color) value.
L: Adjusts the Luminance (Brightness) value.
S: Adjusts the Saturation (Purity) value.

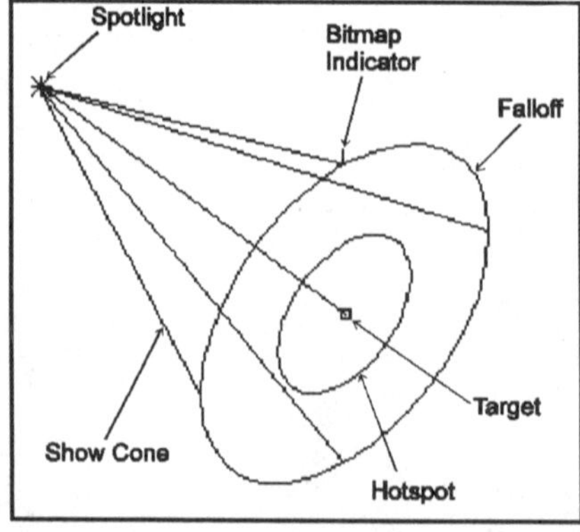

The parts of a spotlight.

Hotspot: Adjusts the value for the hotspot. The hotspot is the angular width of the beam of light thrown. The value range is 1 (narrow beam) to 174.5 (wide beam) degrees. This value can be changed visually using *Lights/Spot/Hotspot*.

Falloff: Adjusts the value for the falloff. The falloff is the angular width of the falloff of light to darkness. The value range is 1 to 175 degrees. This value can be changed visually using the *Lights/Spot/Falloff* command.

Roll: Adjusts the rotation of the spotlight about the center of the falloff area. The value range is -180 (ccw) to 180 (cw) degrees.

Multiplier: Adjusts the power of the light. The effective value range is -10 (low power) to 10 (high power).

On: Turns the spotlight on. When the light is on, it appears yellow in the 3D Editor or Keyframer.

Off: Turns the spotlight off. If the light is off, it appears black in the 3D Editor or Keyframer.

Cast Shadows: Turns on or off the ability of the spotlight to cast shadows. If this option is **On,** the button will be red. The shadows will be cast only on metal or phong materials surfaces.

Adjust: Displays the Local Shadow Control dialog box shown below. Make adjustment to the controls as described below.

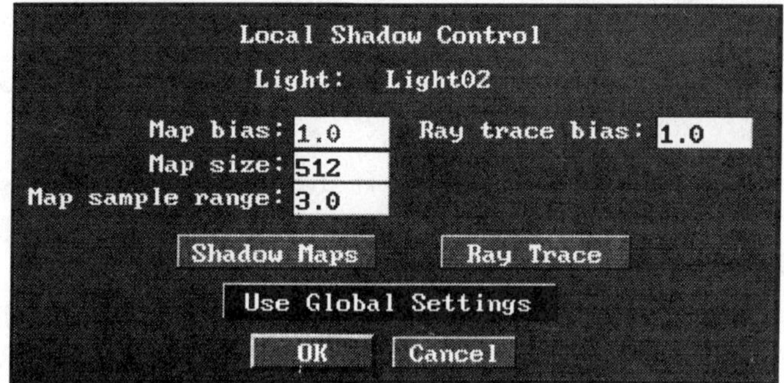

The Local Shadow Control dialog box.

Adjusting the Local Shadow Control Dialog Box

Map bias: Adjusts the shadow map either toward or away from the shadow-casting object(s). The value range is any positive number.

Map size: Adjusts the size of shadow maps. The value range is 10 to 4096 pixels squared. Increasing this value from the default 512 will take up more memory and may not produce more realistic shadows.

Map sample range: Adjusts the sharpness of the edge of a shadow map. The value range is 1 (sharp edges) to 5 (softer edges). Values higher than 5 may be used with unpredictable results.

Ray trace bias: Adjusts the ray trace map either toward or away from the shadow-casting object(s) The value range is any positive number.

Shadow Maps: Selects the shadow maps method of producing shadows from the spotlight using the map settings described above. When this selection is chosen, the button will be red.

Ray Trace: Selects the ray trace method of producing shadows from the spotlight using the Ray Trace Bias setting describe above. When this selection is chosen, the button will be red.

Use Global Settings: Selects whether to use the above shadow settings or the setting specified with *Renderer/Setup/Shadows*.

OK: Accepts the above settings and returns to the Spotlight Definition dialog box.

Cancel: Cancels the above settings and returns to the Spotlight Definition dialog box.

Type: Automatically displays whether **Local** or **Global** shadow-casting methods are used.

Show Cone: Turns show cone on and off. The show cone visually displays the hotspot and falloff of the spotlight either with concentric circles or with rectangles, depending on which option is chosen. A short yellow line is displayed at the edge of the show cone that represents the top alignment of a projector map.

Attenuate: Turns attenuation on or off. If attenuate is on, the light gradually decreases in intensity between the hotspot and falloff. If this option is off, the hotspot and falloff are ignored.

Exclude: Excludes objects that are receiving light from this particular spotlight. Once this option is selected, the Object Selection dialog box appears. Select those objects to be excluded and click on the **OK** button. The button will appear red if one or more objects have been selected to be excluded.

Rectangle/Circle: Click on this button to cycle through both of these options. Choosing **Circle** selects a circular spotlight. Choosing **Rectangle** selects a rectangular spotlight.

Projector: Selects a bitmap to be projected by the spotlight. Once this option is turned on, select the blank button below it. A dialog box will appear. Use this dialog box to select the bitmap to be projected. If you wish to project another animation to be shown within an animation, select *.fli* or *.flc* file to be projected.

Overshoot: Gives the spotlight the characteristics of an Omni light. Light is projected in all directions but all shadows and image projection settings remain intact.

Create: Creates the spotlight with the above settings and closes the dialog box.

Cancel: Cancels the command and closes the dialog box.

NOTE A spotlight contains two objects in the Keyframer, the spotlight itself and its target. The target name will always be the name of the spotlight with the *.target* extension. For example, a spotlight with an object name *FRNTSPOT* will have a target name *FRNTSPOT.target*.

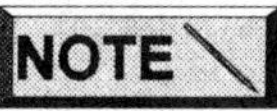

When the spotlight is created, a new position, color, hotspot, falloff, and position key are created.

RELATED COMMANDS

Lights/Omni/Create, Lights/Spot/Adjust

Object
Lights
Cameras
Omni...
Spot...
Tracks...
Create
Move
Place Hilite
Hotspot
Falloff
Roll
Dolly
Adjust
Show Path
Delete

Lights/Spot/Move

Changes the location of a spotlight or allows you to create a clone of an existing light at a new location.

Moving a Spotlight

1. Ensure that a spotlight has been created previously using *Lights/Spot/Create.*
2. Select *Lights/Spot/Move.*
3. Select the orthographic or user viewport that contains the spotlight to be moved. Move the spotlight or target in frame #0 to change its location in the 3D Editor as well. If the spotlight or target is moved in any other frame, a position key will be created.
4. Click on the light or the target. To move both at the same time, hold down [Ctrl] before clicking on the light.
5. Move the light, target, or both to the new location and click to place or right-click to cancel.

NOTE Pressing [Alt] while selecting a spotlight to be moved will update all position keys. Use this feature to move an animated light and adjust its movements throughout the animation to reflect the animation changes.

TIP To create a clone of a spotlight, hold down [Shift] and click on the light. Move the new cloned light to its new location and click to place or right-click to cancel.

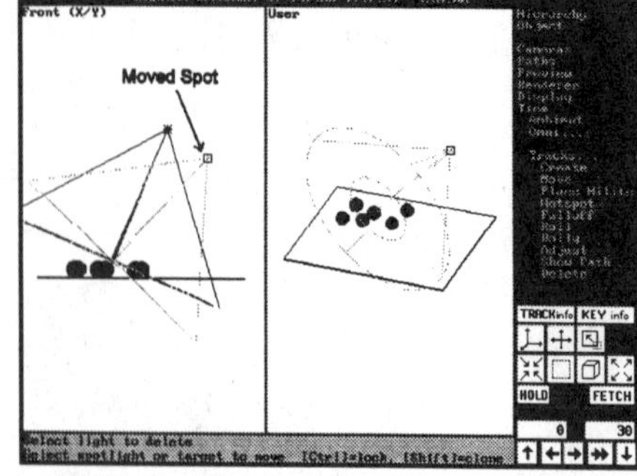

Creating a clone of an existing spotlight.

RELATED COMMANDS

Lights/Spot/Create, Lights/Omni/Move, Light/Spot/Place Hilite

Lights/Spot/Place Hilite

Object
Lights
Cameras
Omni...
Spot...
Tracks...
Create
Move
Place Hilite
Hotspot
Falloff
Roll
Dolly
Adjust
Show Path
Delete

Moves a previously created spotlight to a new location that will create a highlight at a specified location on an object.

Placing a Highlight on an Object

1. Ensure that the object to receive the highlight has been created and that an spotlight has previously been created. See *Lights/Spot/Create.*
2. Select *Lights/Spot/Place Hilite.*
3. Click in the viewport that is best suited for selecting the highlight location.
4. Click at the location of the object to receive the highlight.
5. Click on the spotlight that is to cast the highlight. The spotlight will be moved to the new location.
6. To verify that the highlight has been placed properly, render that viewport.

> **NOTE** If this command is used in frame #0, the change is made in the Keyframer and the 3D Editor.

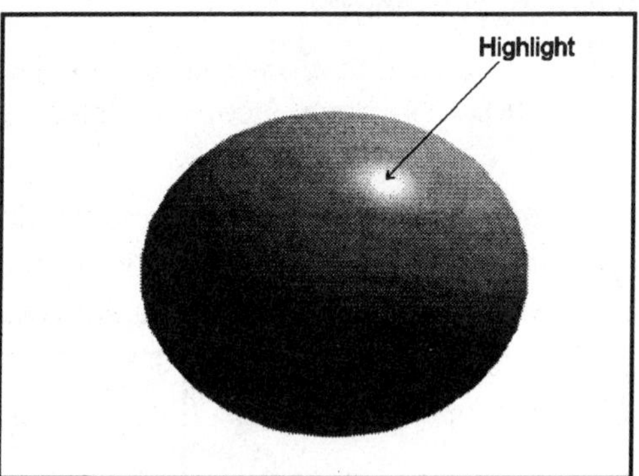

Creating a highlight on an object.

RELATED COMMANDS

Lights/Spot/Create, Lights/Spot/Move

Object
Lights
Cameras
Omni...
Spot...
Tracks...
Create
Move
Place Hilite
Hotspot
Falloff
Roll
Dolly
Adjust
Show Path
Delete

Lights/Spot/Hotspot

Changes the size of the hotspot on a previously created spotlight.

Modifying a Spotlight Hotspot

1. Ensure that a spotlight has been created previously using *Lights/Spot/Create*.
2. Select *Lights/Spot/Hotspot*.
3. Click in the viewport that contains the spotlight with the hotspot to be adjusted.
4. Click on the spotlight asterisk (*) in the spotlight or target. The spotlight cone appears which represents the hotspot and falloff. The hotspot is the inner circle or rectangle. The angle of the hotspot is displayed on the status line.
5. Move the mouse sideways to adjust the angle of the hotspot. The angle of the hotspot can be no more than 0.5 degrees less than the falloff.
6. Once the hotspot is modified to its new angle, click to accept the changes or right-click to cancel the command.

1. To allow for more accurate adjustment of the angle, turn angle snap on by pressing [A].
2. This command also can be used to clone a spotlight. To clone a spotlight, hold [Shift] and complete step 4 above. A copy will also be created in the 3D Editor.
3. Use the spotlight viewport to adjust the hotspot and falloff from the perspective of the spotlight itself. Click in a viewport and press [Shift][$ 4].

The hotspot is the inner circle or rectangle.

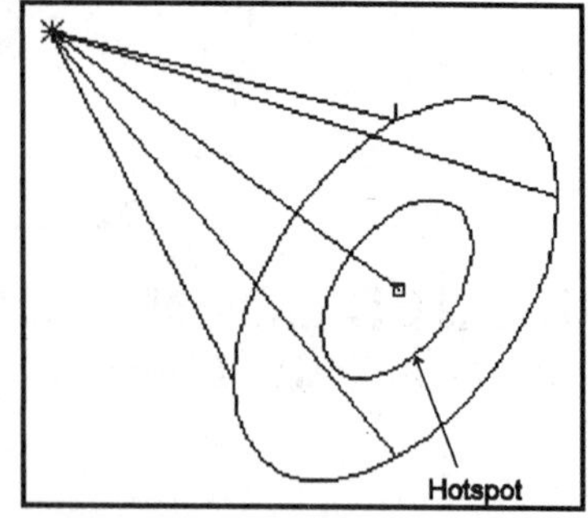

RELATED COMMANDS

Views-Viewports, Lights/Spot/Create, Lights/Spot/Falloff

Object
Lights
Cameras
Omni...
Spot...
Tracks...
Create
Move
Place Hilite
Hotspot
Falloff
Roll
Dolly
Adjust
Show Path
Delete

Lights/Spot/Falloff

Changes the size of the Falloff on a previously created spotlight.

Modifying a Spotlight Falloff

1. Ensure that a spotlight has been created previously using *Lights/Spot/Create.*
2. Select *Lights/Spot/Falloff.*
3. Click in the viewport that contains the spotlight with the falloff to be adjusted.
4. Click on the spotlight asterisk (*) in the spotlight or target. The spotlight cone appears which represents the hotspot and falloff. The falloff is the outer circle or rectangle. The angle of the falloff is displayed on the status line.
5. Move the mouse sideways to adjust the angle of the falloff. The angle can be no more than 0.5 degrees greater than the hotspot.
6. Once the falloff is modified to its new angle, click to accept the changes or right-click to cancel the command.

TIP

1. To allow for more accurate adjustment of the angle, turn angle snap on by pressing [A].
2. This command also can be used to clone a spotlight. To clone a spotlight, hold [Shift] and complete step 4 above. A copy will also be created in the 3D Editor.
3. Use the spotlight viewport to adjust the hotspot and falloff from the perspective of the spotlight itself. Click in a viewport and press [Shift][$ 4].

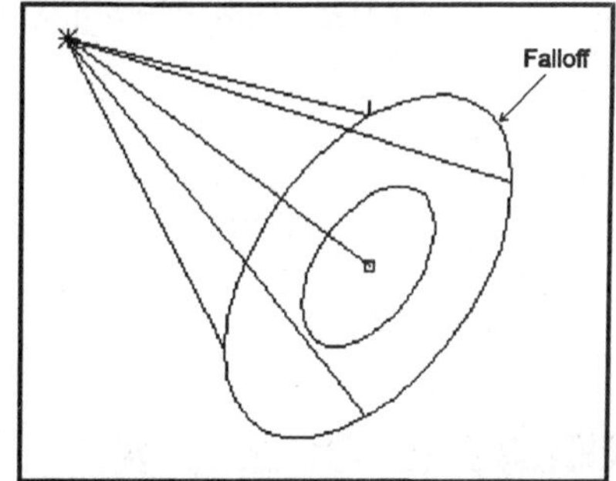

The falloff is the outer circle or rectangle.

RELATED COMMANDS

Views-Viewports, Lights/Spot/Create, Lights/Spot/Hotspot

Object
Lights
Cameras
Omni...
Spot...
Tracks...
Create
Move
Place Hilite
Hotspot
Falloff
Roll
Dolly
Adjust
Show Path
Delete

Lights/Spot/Roll

Adjusts the roll of a spotlight by rotating it clockwise or counterclockwise. Used to adjust the rotation angle of rectangular spotlights and to assist in the proper rotation of projection maps.

Adjusting the Roll of a Spotlight

1. Ensure that a spotlight has been created previously using *Lights/Spot/Create*.
2. Select *Lights/Spot/Roll.*
3. Click in the viewport that contains the spotlight.
4. Click on the spotlight asterisk (*) on camera or target. The spotlight cone appears and the roll angle appears in the status line.
5. Move the mouse sideways to adjust the roll of the spotlight.
6. Once the roll is modified, click to accept the changes or right-click to cancel the command.

TIP

1. To allow for more accurate adjustment of the angle, turn angle snap on by pressing [A].
2. This command also can be used to clone a spotlight. To clone a spotlight, hold down [Shift] and complete step 4 above. A copy will also be created in the 3D Editor.
3. Use the spotlight viewport to adjust the roll from the perspective of the spotlight itself. Click in a viewport and press [Shift][$ 4].

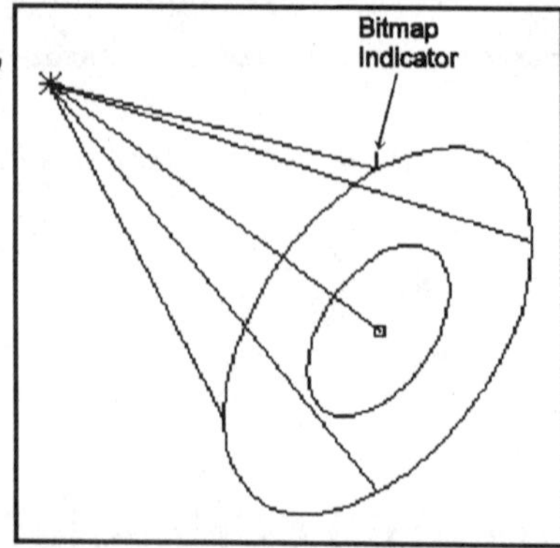

Use the top of the bitmap indicator to visually verify the rotation orientation.

RELATED COMMANDS

Views-Viewports, Lights/Spot/Create, Camera/Roll

Object
Lights
Cameras
Omni...
Spot...
Tracks...
Create
Move
Place Hilite
Hotspot
Falloff
Roll
Dolly
Adjust
Show Path
Delete

Lights/Spot/Dolly

Adjusts the spotlight toward or away from its target location.

Dolly the Spotlight

1. Ensure that a spotlight has been created previously using *Lights/Spot/Create*.
2. Select *Lights/Spot/Dolly*.
3. Click in the viewport that contains the spotlight.
4. Click on the spotlight asterisk (*) in the camera or target.
5. Move the mouse sideways to dolly the spotlight.
6. Click to accept the changes or right-click to cancel the command.

TIP

1. This command also can be used to clone a spotlight. To clone a spotlight, hold down [⇧Shift] and complete step 4 above. A copy will also be created in the 3D Editor.
2. Use the spotlight viewport to dolly the spotlight from the perspective of the spotlight itself. Click in a viewport and press [⇧Shift] [$ 4].

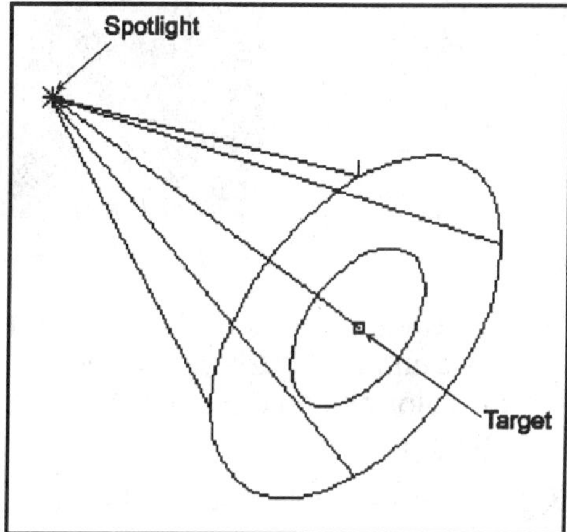

Use Dolly to adjust the spotlight toward or away from its target.

RELATED COMMANDS

Views-Viewports, Lights/Spot/Create, Camera/Dolly

Object
Lights
Cameras
Omni...
Spot...
Tracks...
Create
Move
Place Hilite
Hotspot
Falloff
Roll
Dolly
Adjust
Show Path
Delete

Lights/Spot/Adjust

Changes the settings of a predefined spotlight using the same Spotlight Definition dialog box as *Light/Spot/Create*.

Adjusting Spotlight Settings

1. Ensure that a spotlight has been created previously using *Lights/Spot/Create*.
2. Select *Lights/Spot/Adjust*.
3. Click in the viewport that contains the spotlight. Adjust the light in frame #0 to change its location in the 3D Editor as well. If the light is adjusted in any other frame, a color key will be created and that frame will become a keyframe.
4. Click on the spotlight or target icon. The Spotlight Definition dialog box appears as shown below.

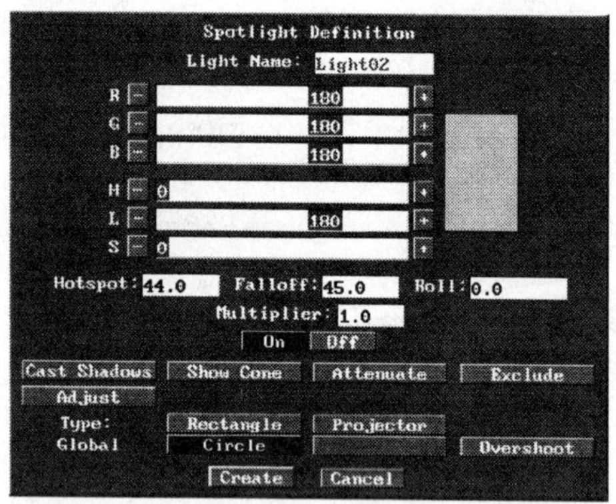

The Spotlight Definition dialog box.

5. Make adjustments to the dialog box sliders. Click the + button to increase a value and click – to decrease a value. All changes to spotlight are displayed in the color box on the right of the dialog box. The dialog box controls and settings are:

R: Adjusts the Red value.
G: Adjusts the Green value.
B: Adjusts the Blue value.
H: Adjusts the Hue (Color) value.
L: Adjusts the Luminance (Brightness) value.
S: Adjusts the Saturation (Purity) value.

Hotspot: Adjusts the value for the hotspot. The hotspot is the angular width of the beam of light thrown. The value range is 1 (narrow beam) to 174.5 (wide beam) degrees. This value can be changed visually using *Lights/Spot/Hotspot*.

Falloff: Adjusts the value for the falloff. The falloff is the angular width of the falloff of light to darkness. The value range is 1 to 175 degrees. This value can be changed visually using *Lights/Spot/Falloff*.

Roll: Adjusts the rotation of the spotlight about the center of the falloff area. The value range is -180 (ccw) to 180 (cw) degrees.

Multiplier: Adjusts the power of the light. The effective value range is -10 (low power) to 10 (high power).

On: Turns the spotlight on. When the light is on, it appears yellow in the 3D Editor or Keyframer. The spotlight is on throughout the animation.

Off: Turns the spotlight off. If the light is off, it appears black in the 3D Editor or Keyframer. To turn a light off during an animation, change its luminance value to 0 at the frame where the light is to be turned off.

Cast Shadows: Turns on or off the ability of the spotlight to cast shadows. If this option is **On**, the button will be red. The shadows will be cast only on metal or phong material surfaces.

Adjust: Displays the Local Shadow Control dialog box shown below. Make adjustment to the controls as described below.

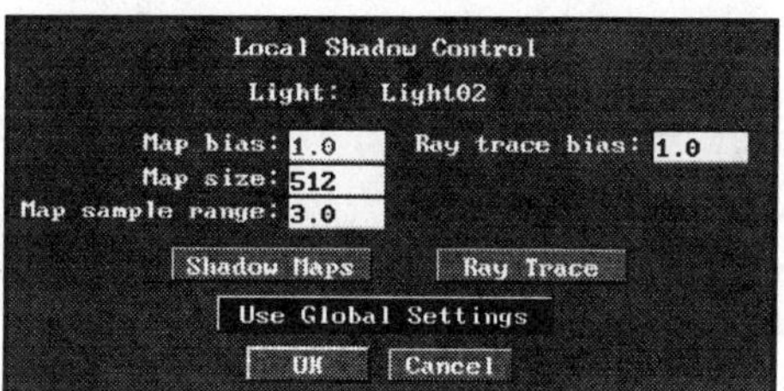

The Local Shadow Control dialog box.

Adjusting the Local Shadow Control Dialog Box

Map bias: Adjusts the shadow map toward or away from the shadow-casting object(s). The value range is any positive number.

Map size: Adjusts the size of shadow maps. The value range is 10 to 4,096 pixels squared. Increasing this value from the default 512 will take up more memory and may not produce more realistic shadows.

Map sample range: Adjusts the sharpness of the edge of a shadow map. The value range is 1 (sharp edges) to 5 (softer edges). Values higher than 5 may be used with unpredictable results.

Ray trace bias: Adjusts the ray trace map toward or away from the shadow-casting object(s) The value range is any positive number.

Shadow Maps: Selects the shadow maps method of producing shadows from the spotlight using the map settings described above. When this selection is chosen, the button will be red.

Ray Trace: Selects the ray trace method of producing shadows from the spotlight using the Ray trace bias setting described above. When this selection is chosen, the button will be red.

Use Global Settings: Selects whether to use the above shadow settings (**Off**) or to use the setting specified with *Renderer/Setup/Shadows* (**On**).

OK: Accepts the above settings and returns to the Spotlight Definition dialog box.

Cancel: Cancels the above settings and returns to the Spotlight Definition dialog box.

Type: Automatically displays whether local or global shadow-casting methods are used.

Show Cone: Turns show cone on and off. The show cone visually displays the hotspot and falloff of the spotlight with concentric circles or with rectangles, depending on which option is chosen. A short yellow line is displayed at the edge of the show cone, which represents the top alignment of a projector map.

Attenuate: Turns attenuation on or off. If Attenuate is on, the light gradually decreases in intensity between the hotspot and falloff. If this option is off, the hotspot and falloff are ignored.

Exclude: Excludes objects that are receiving light from this particular spotlight. Once this option is selected, the Object Selection dialog box appears. Select those objects to be excluded and click on the **OK** button. The button will appear red if one or more objects have been selected to be excluded.

Rectangle/Circle: Click on this button to cycle through both of these options. Choosing circle selects a circular spotlight. Choosing rectangle selects a rectangular spotlight.

Projector: Selects a bitmap to be projected by the spotlight. Once this option is turned on, select the blank button below. A dialog box will appear. Use this dialog box to select the bitmap to be projected. If you wish to project another animation to be shown within an animation, select an *.fli* or *.flc* file to be projected.

Overshoot: Gives the spotlight the characteristics of an Omni light. Light is projected in all directions but all shadows and image projection settings remain intact.

Create: Creates the spotlight with the above settings and closes the dialog box.

Cancel: Cancels the command and closes the dialog box.

NOTE When the spotlight is adjusted, position, color, hotspot, and falloff keys are created or updated.

NOTE See *Light/Spot/Create* for details on all settings in the Spotlight Definition dialog box.

RELATED COMMAND

Lights/Spot/Create

Object
Lights
Cameras
Omni...
Spot...
Tracks...
Create
Move
Place Hilite
Hotspot
Falloff
Roll
Dolly
Adjust
Show Path
Delete

Lights/Spot/Show Path

Displays or hides the path assigned to an animated spotlight.

Displaying or Hiding a Spotlight and Spotlight Target Path

1. Ensure that spotlight and target have been created previously and that a path has been assigned to that light and/or target.
2. Select *Lights/Spot/Show Path.*
3. Select the spotlight or target in the active viewport that has been assigned to the path to be displayed. The path will be displayed as shown below.
4. Selecting the spotlight or target again will hide the displayed path.

NOTE The spotlight and target may both have assigned paths. Displaying the path for one does not automatically display the path for another.

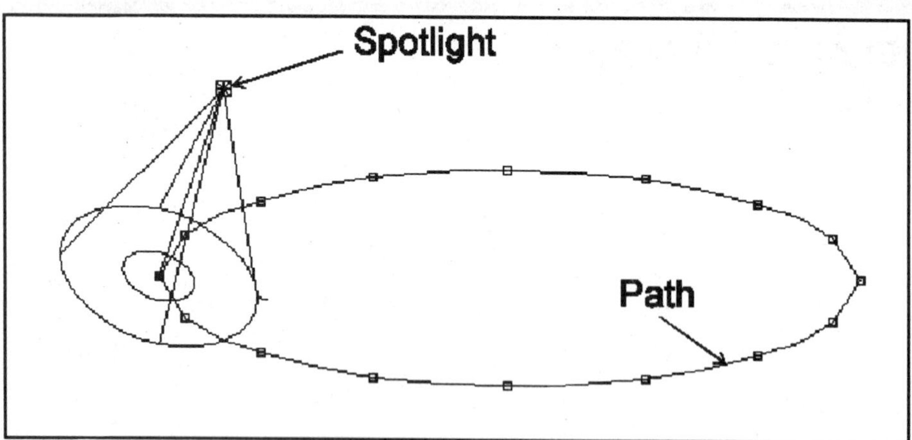

The spotlight, target, and displayed path.

RELATED COMMANDS

Lights/Omni/Show Path, Paths/Get

Object
Lights
Cameras
Omni...
Spot...
Tracks...
Create
Move
Place Hilite
Hotspot
Falloff
Roll
Dolly
Adjust
Show Path
Delete

Lights/Spot/Delete

Deletes a previously created spotlight.

Deleting an Spotlight

1. Ensure that a spotlight has been created previously using *Lights/Spot/Create*.
2. Select *Lights/Spot/Delete*.
3. Click on the spotlight to delete in any viewport. The spotlight will be deleted from the scene.

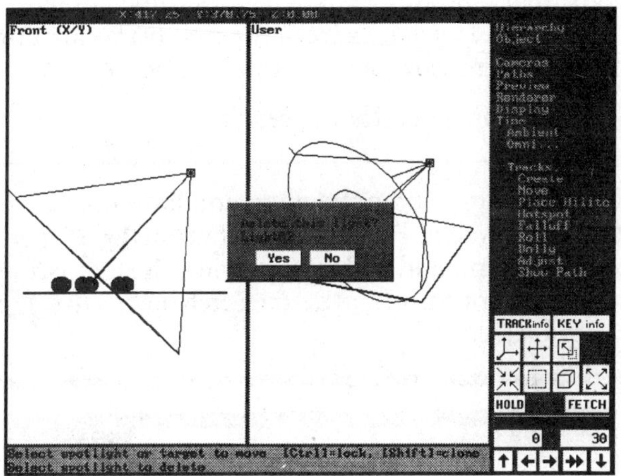

Deleting a spotlight.

RELATED COMMANDS

Lights/Spot/Create, Lights/Omni/Delete

Hierarchy
Object
Lights
Cameras
Paths
Preview
Renderer
Display
Ambient
Omni...
Spot...
Tracks...
Loop
Copy
Reverse
File Insert

Lights/Tracks/Loop

Ensures that an animation begins at the point at which it ends (loops), this command will copy the keys from the first keyframe to the last keyframe for the light selected.

Looping a Lights Animation

1. Ensure that all lights and objects have been created and that the animation is complete.
2. Select *Lights/Tracks/Loop*.
3. Select the light that contains the key values to be copied. The last frame becomes a keyframe. The values from the first frame are copied to the last frame. The **Loop** buttons in the Key Info dialog box is activated.
4. Preview the animation to verify the results.

> **TIP** Use this command only when you have completed the animation and saved it. Press the **Hold** button (Ctrl H) before using the command. Apply the command and then preview the animation to verify the results. If the results are not correct, press the **Fetch** button (Ctrl F) to return the values to their previous settings.

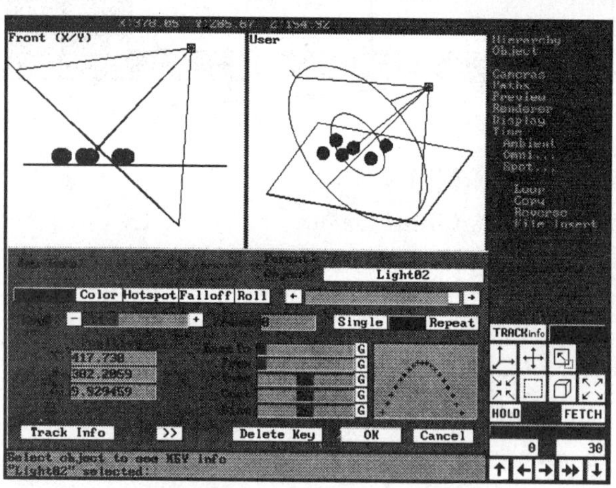

Looping the tracks of a selected light.

RELATED COMMANDS

Object/Tracks/Loop, Cameras/Tracks/Loop

Lights/Tracks/Copy

Copies the common tracks between an Omni light, spotlight, or spotlight target to a selected object.

Copying Common Tracks

1. Ensure that an Omni light, Spotlight, or Spotlight target has been created previously.
2. Select *Lights/Tracks/Copy*.
3. Because this command has no undo, click the **Hold** button (Ctrl H) before selecting the object from which to copy the tracks.
4. Select the object to receive the tracks. The Copy Tracks dialog box appears.
5. One or more of the following options will appear in the dialog box based on their commonality between the two objects selected. Select the appropriate actions, as described below:

   Position: Copies the position tracks.

   Color: Copies the color tracks.

   Roll: Copies the roll tracks.

   Relative: Tracks are applied relative to their key #1 values or spaced away from the object from which the traces were copied.

   Absolute: Tracks are applied absolutely to their key #1 values or on top of the object from which the tracks were copied.
6. Select **OK** to copy the tracks and exit the dialog box. If the results are not correct, press the **Fetch** button (Ctrl F) to return the values to their previous settings.

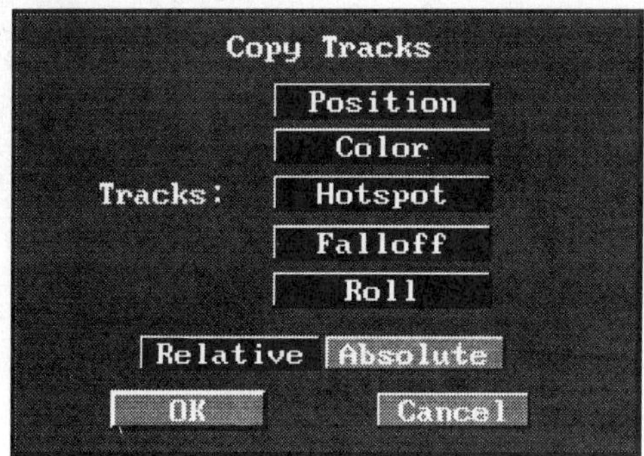

The Copy Tracks dialog box.

RELATED COMMANDS

Objects/Track/Copy, Camera/Track/Copy

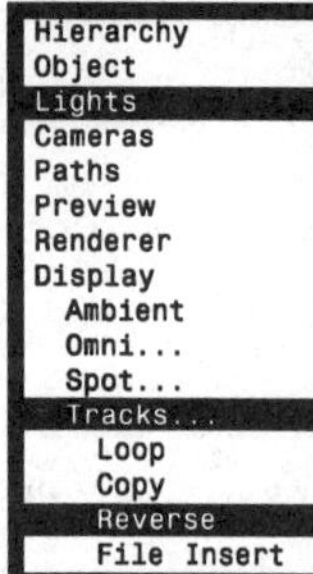

Lights/Track/Reverse

Reverses the order of the keys for an Omni light, Spotlight, or Spotlight target.

Reversing the Order of the Keys for the Active Segment

1. Ensure that an Omni light, Spotlight, or Spotlight target has been created previously.
2. Select *Lights/Tracks/Reverse*.
3. Select the object that contains the keys to be reversed. The Reverse Tracks dialog box will appear as shown below.
4. Make the changes necessary as described below:

   Position: Reverses the position tracks.

   Color: Reverses the color tracks.

   Roll: Reverses the roll tracks.

   Relative: Tracks are reversed relative to their key #1 values.

   Absolute: Tracks are reversed absolutely to their key #1.
5. Select **OK** to copy the tracks and exit the dialog box. Select **Cancel** to cancel the command and close the dialog box.

To undo the changes made, simply repeat the command and reverse the tracks back to their original position.

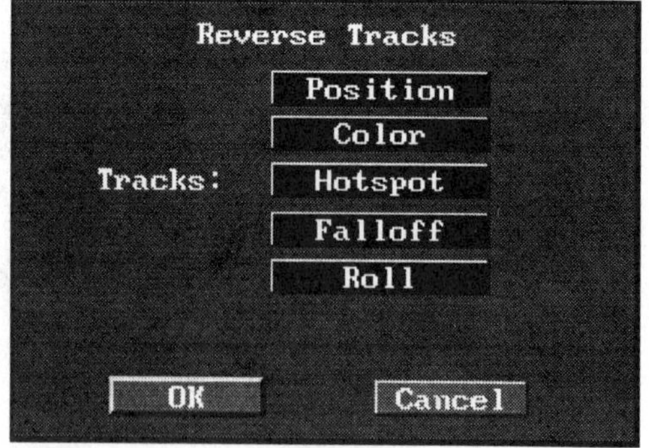

The Reverse Tracks dialog box.

RELATED COMMANDS

Objects/Track/Reverse, Cameras/Track/Reverse

Hierarchy
Object
Lights
Cameras
Paths
Preview
Renderer
Display
Ambient
Omni...
Spot...
Tracks...
Loop
Copy
Reverse
File Insert

Lights/Tracks/File Insert

Inserts or appends all or a range of tracks from lights in other *.3ds* files.

Inserting or Appending Tracks from a File

1. Ensure that a light that is to receive the tracks has been created previously using *Lights/Omni/Create* or *Lights/Spot/Create.*
2. Move to the frame that will be at the end of the inserted tracks.
3. Select *Lights/Tracks/File Insert.*
4. Select the light to receive the inserted tracks (destination light). A file selector will appear.
5. Select the file that contains the tracks to be inserted. The Object Selection dialog box appears.
6. Select the light from which to copy the tracks (source light). The Insert Animation Tracks dialog box appears. Make the selections as described below:

   From Object/Into Object: Displays the source light name and the destination light name.

   Scope: Specifies the scope of the track insertion.

   Subtree: Inserts the tracks of the object and its hierarchies if the hierarchies match.

   Object: Inserts the tracks of the object only.

   Method: Specifies the method of track insertion.

   Relative: Tracks are inserted relative to the current track values.

   Absolute: Tracks are inserted absolutel to the current track values.

   Source frames: Specifies the range of the frames to be inserted.

   First key to Last key: Sets the range of the Source Frames fields to select only those frames from the source object that contain keys.

7. Select **OK** to insert the tracks and exit the dialog box. Select **Cancel** to cancel the command and close the dialog box.

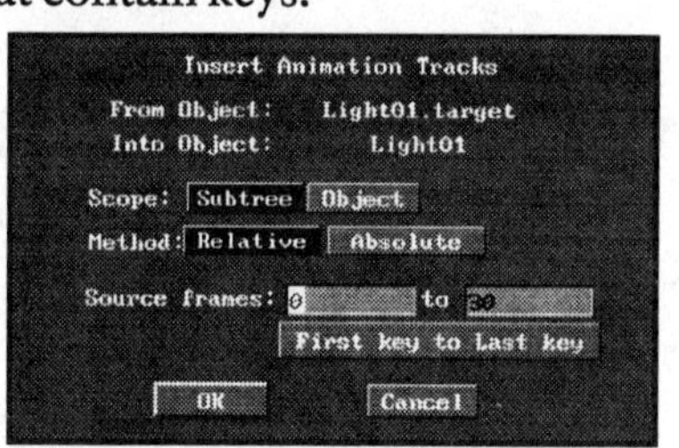

RELATED COMMAND

Objects/Track/File Insert

Hierarchy
Object
Lights
Cameras
Paths
Preview
Create
Move
Roll
FOV
Dolly
Perspective
Adjust
Show Path
Delete
Tracks...

Cameras/Create

Creates a camera.

Creating a Camera

1. Activate an orthographic viewport to place the camera.
2. Select *Cameras/Create.*
3. In the active viewport, select the location of the camera.
4. Select the location of the camera target. The Camera Definition dialog box appears as shown on page 4-59.
5. Adjust settings to the camera using the following options:

Camera: Gives the camera a unique name. The camera name can be up to 10 characters.

Lens: Enters a lens in millimeters (mm) or select a lens size from stock lenses. The range of camera sizes is 9.857142 mm (wide angle) to 10,000,000 mm (narrow angle).

FOV: Enter the camera's Field of View. Field of View is expressed in angles. The range for these angles is 0.00025 degrees to 175 degrees. To determine the corresponding lens, click on the **Calculate** button.

Roll: Used to roll the camera from -180 to 180 degrees. Positive values rotate the camera clockwise; negative values rotate the camera counterclockwise.

Show Cone: Select **On** to turn on the show cone. If **On** is selected, the show cone will be displayed as a cyan pyramid in all viewports. Select **Off** to reject the use of the show cone. If **Off** is selected, only the camera and target are represented by a blue line.

Create: Creates a camera in all viewports with the selected settings.

Cancel: Cancels the command and exits the dialog box.

Hiding the Camera Icon(s)

1. Ensure that a camera has been created using *Camera/Create.*
2. Use [Alt][C] to hide the camera icon(s). Press [Alt][C] again to display the camera icon(s).

Using a Camera Viewport.

1. Click in any viewport.
2. Use [C] to change the viewport to a camera viewport. If there are multiple cameras, a dialog box will be displayed listing the names of all cameras. Select the camera view to be displayed in the active viewport and click on **OK**.
3. Multiple camera viewports can be created by repeating steps 1 and 2 in another viewport.

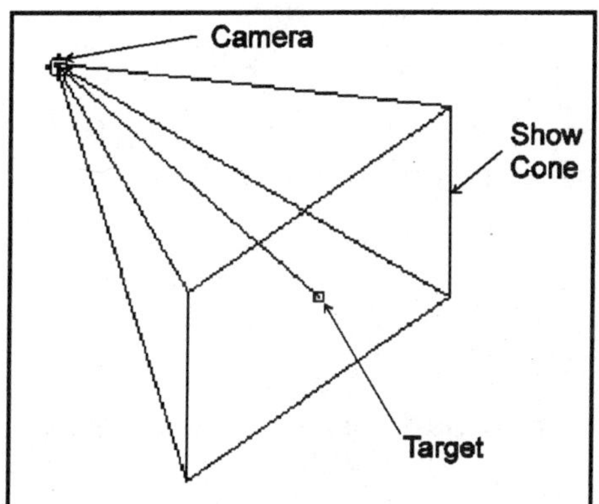

The Camera icon.

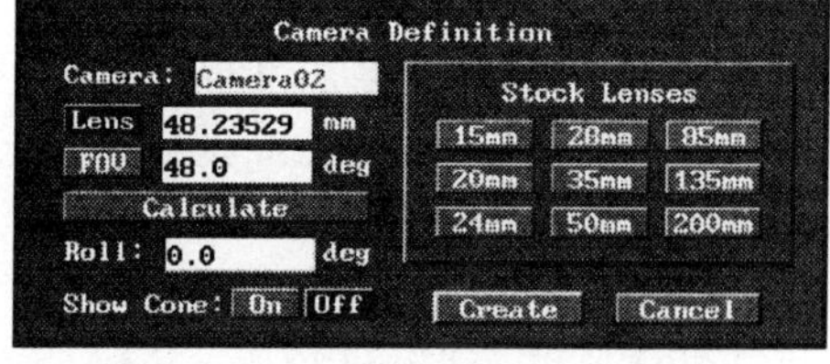

The Camera Definition dialog box.

RELATED COMMANDS

Views-Viewports, Cameras/Move, Cameras/Roll, Cameras/FOV

Hierarchy
Object
Lights
Cameras
Paths
Preview
Create
Move
Roll
FOV
Dolly
Perspective
Adjust
Show Path
Delete
Tracks...

Cameras/Move

Move a previously created camera or camera target or creates a clone of the camera.

Moving a Camera or Camera Target

1. Ensure that a camera has been created previously using *Cameras/Create*.
2. Select *Cameras/Move*.
3. Click in the orthographic viewport where the camera is to be moved.
4. Select either the camera or the target. The camera or the target is displayed in gray while the original position is displayed in blue.
5. Move the camera or target to its new location and click or right-click to cancel the command.

Moving the Camera and Target Simultaneously

1. Ensure that a camera has been created previously using *Cameras/Create*.
2. Select *Cameras/Move*.
3. Click in the orthographic viewport where the camera is to be moved.
4. Hold down [Ctrl]. Select the camera or the target.
5. Move the camera to its new position and click, or right-click to cancel the command.

TIP To create a clone of the camera, first click in the orthographic viewport where the camera is to be cloned. When selecting either the camera or the target to move, hold down [Shift]. Move the cloned camera to its new position and click, or right-click to cancel the command.

Moving the camera and target.

RELATED COMMANDS

Cameras/Create, Cameras/Roll.

Hierarchy
Object
Lights
Cameras
Paths
Preview
  Create
  Move
  Roll
  FOV
  Dolly
  Perspective
  Adjust
  Show Path
  Delete
  Tracks...

Cameras/Roll

Adjusts the roll of a camera by rotating it clockwise or counterclockwise

Adjusting the Roll of a Camera

1. Ensure that a camera has been created previously using *Cameras/Create*.
2. Select *Cameras/Roll*.
3. Click in the viewport that contains the camera.
4. Click on the camera or target. The camera field of view appears in white and the roll angle appears in the status line.
5. Move the mouse sideways to adjust the roll of the camera.
6. Once the roll is modified, click to accept the changes, or right-click to cancel the command.

> **NOTE** This command can also be used to clone a camera. To clone a camera, hold the [Shift] key and complete step 4 above.

> **TIP** To allow for more accurate adjustment of the angle, turn the angle snap on by pressing [A]. Roll can be adjusted in Key info after the key has been created.

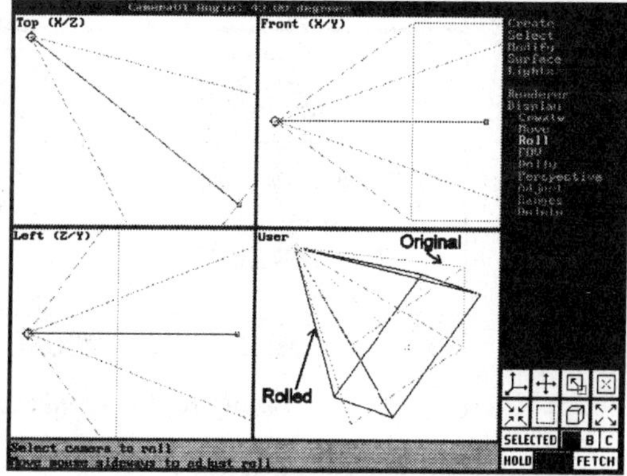

Rolling the camera.

RELATED COMMANDS

Cameras/Create, Cameras/Spot/Roll

Hierarchy
Object
Lights
Cameras
Paths
Preview
Create
Move
Roll
FOV
Dolly
Perspective
Adjust
Show Path
Delete
Tracks...

Cameras/FOV

Adjusts the field of view (FOV) for a previously created camera.

Changing the Field of View

1. Ensure that a camera has been created previously using *Cameras/Create*.
2. Select *Cameras/FOV*.
3. Click in any orthographic viewport.
4. Select the camera or target whose FOV is to be modified. If **Show Cone** is on, the original field of view is displayed in cyan and any new changes are displayed in white. If **Show Cone** is off, the changes for the FOV are displayed in white and no reference to the prior FOV is displayed. The FOV is displayed in the status line.
5. Move the mouse sideways to adjust the FOV.
6. Click to accept the new FOV settings or right-click to cancel the command.

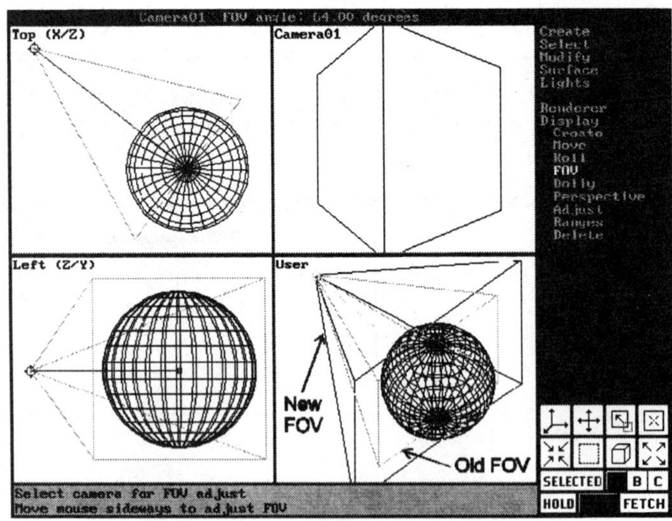

Changing the cameras field of view.

RELATED COMMAND

Cameras/Create

Cameras/Dolly

Adjusts the camera toward or away from its target location.

Dolly the Camera

1. Ensure that a camera has been created previously using the *Cameras/Create* command.
2. Select *Cameras/Dolly*.
3. Click in the viewport that contains the camera.
4. Click on the camera.
5. Move the mouse sideways to dolly the camera.
6. Click to accept the changes, or right-click to cancel the command.

TIP: Use the camera viewport to dolly the camera from the perspective of the camera. Click in a viewport and press [Shift] [$ 4].

NOTE: This command can also be used to clone a camera. To clone a camera, hold down the [Shift] key and complete step 4 above.

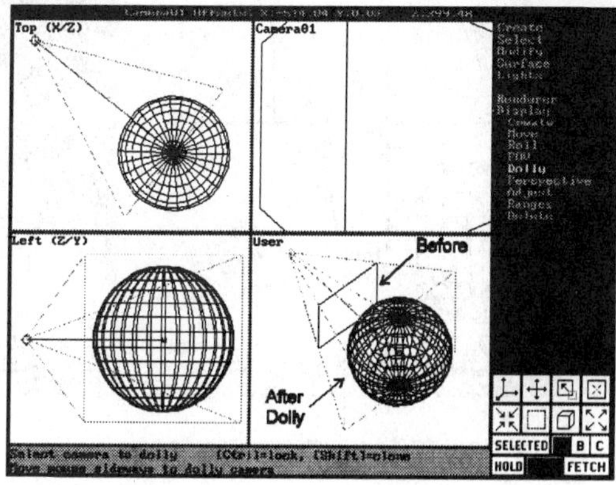

Dolly the camera.

RELATED COMMAND

Cameras/Create

Hierarchy
Object
Lights
Cameras
Paths
Preview
  Create
  Move
  Roll
  FOV
  Dolly
  Perspective
  Adjust
  Show Path
  Delete
  Tracks...

Cameras/Perspective

Adjusts the FOV and dollies the camera to adjust the perspective of a camera composition.

Changing the Camera Perspective

1. Ensure that a camera has been created previously using *Cameras/Create*.
2. Select *Cameras/Perspective*.
3. Click in the orthographic viewport that contains the camera.
4. Click on the camera.
5. Move the mouse sideways to adjust the perspective. As the camera is moved, the FOV remains unchanged.
6. Click to accept the changes or right-click to cancel the command.

> **TIP** Use this command to match the perspective of a scene with that of a bitmap that is being used as a background.

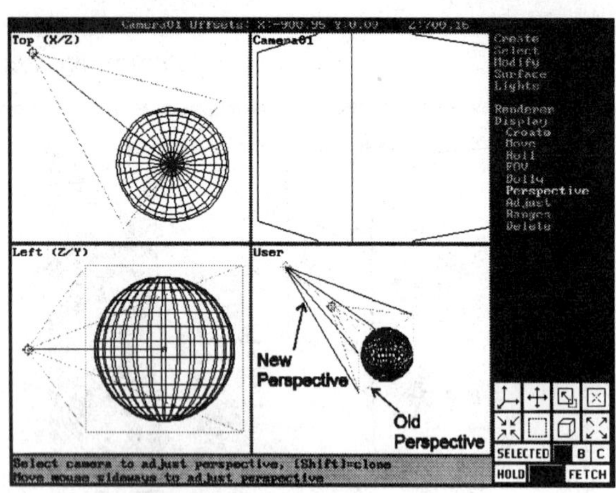

Changing the camera perspective.

RELATED COMMANDS

Cameras/Create, Cameras/Dolly, Cameras/FOV

Cameras/Adjust

Hierarchy
Object
Lights
Cameras
Paths
Preview
Create
Move
Roll
FOV
Dolly
Perspective
Adjust
Show Path
Delete
Tracks...

Adjusts the values of a previously created camera.

Changing the Camera Perspective

1. Ensure that a camera has been created previously using *Cameras/Create*.
2. Select *Cameras/Adjust*.
3. Click in the viewport that contains the camera to be adjusted. Adjust the camera in frame #0 to change its location and the settings in the 3D Editor as well. If the camera is adjusted in any other frame, a roll or FOV key will be created.
4. Click on the camera to be adjusted. The Camera Definition dialog box appears.

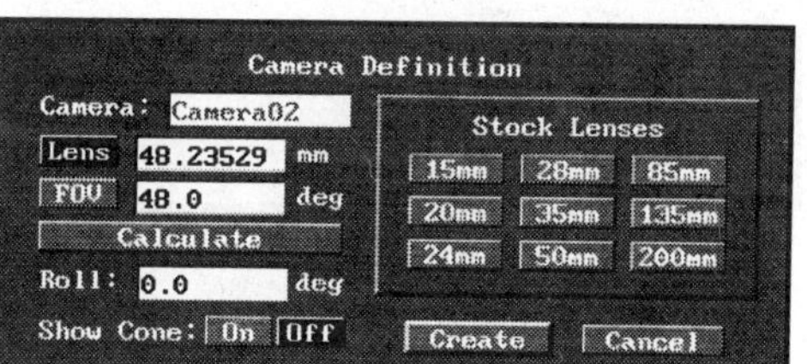

The Camera Definition dialog box.

Camera: Gives the camera a unique name. The camera name can be up to 10 characters.

Lens: Enters a lens in millimeters (mm) or select a lens size from the Stock Lens. The range of camera sizes is 9.857142 mm (wide angle) to 10,000,000 mm (narrow angle).

FOV: Enters the camera's Field of View. Field of View is expressed in angles. The range for these angles is 0.00025 degrees to 175 degrees. To determine the corresponding lens, click on the Calculate button.

Roll: Used to roll the camera from -180 to 180 degrees. Positive values rotate the camera clockwise; negative values rotate the camera counter-clockwise.

Show Cone: Select **On** to turn on the show cone. If **On** is selected, the show cone will be displayed as a cyan pyramid in all viewports. Select **Off** to reject the use of the show cone. If **Off** is selected, the camera will be represented by a blue line.

Create: Creates a camera in all viewports with the selected settings.
Cancel: Cancels the command and exit the dialog box.

RELATED COMMANDS

Camera/Create, Cameras/Move, Cameras/Roll, Cameras/FOV

Hierarchy
Object
Lights
Cameras
Paths
Preview
Create
Move
Roll
FOV
Dolly
Perspective
Adjust
Show Path
Delete
Tracks...

Cameras/Show Path

Displays or hides the path assigned to an animated camera.

Displaying and Hiding a Camera Path

1. Ensure that a camera has been created previously and that a path has been assigned to that camera or target.
2. Select *Camera/Show Path*.
3. Select the camera in the active viewport that has been assigned to the path to be displayed. The path will be displayed as shown below.
4. Selecting the camera or target again will hide the displayed path.

NOTE The camera and target may both have paths assigned. Displaying the path for one does not automatically display the path for the other.

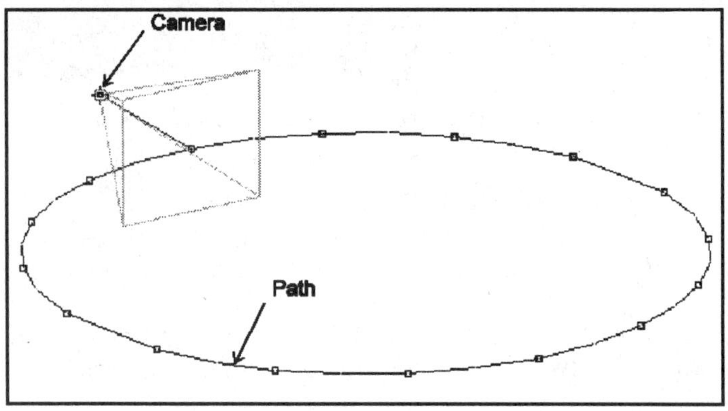

Displaying the path of a camera.

RELATED COMMANDS

Camera/Create, Paths/Get

Hierarchy
Object
Lights
Cameras
Paths
Preview
Create
Move
Roll
FOV
Dolly
Perspective
Adjust
Show Path
Delete
Tracks...

Cameras/Delete

Deletes a previously created camera in the Keyframer and the 3D Editor.

Deleting a Camera

1. Ensure that a camera has been created previously using *Camera/Create*.
2. Select *Camera/Delete*.
3. Click on the camera to be deleted in any viewport. The camera will be deleted from the scene.

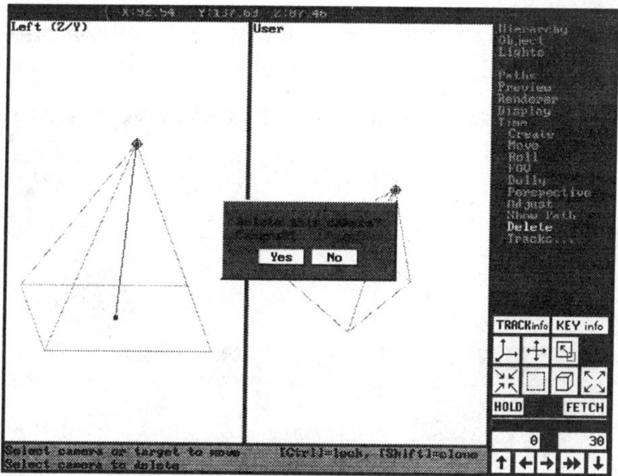

Deleting a camera.

RELATED COMMAND

Cameras/Create

Hierarchy
Object
Lights
Cameras
Paths
Preview
Dolly
Perspective
Adjust
Show Path
Delete
Tracks...
Loop
Copy
Reverse
File Insert

Cameras/Tracks/Loop

Loops a Camera's animation by copying the key values in the first frame to the last frame.

1. Ensure that all cameras and objects have been created and that the animation is complete. Select the **Hold** button (Ctrl H) to save your current configuration.
2. Select *Cameras/Tracks/Loop*.
3. Select the camera that contains the key values to be copied. The last frame becomes a keyframe. The values from the first frame are copied to the last frame. The **Loop** button in the Key Info dialog box is activated.
4. Preview the animation to verify the results. If the results are not correct, select the **Fetch** button (Ctrl F) to return the values to their previous settings.

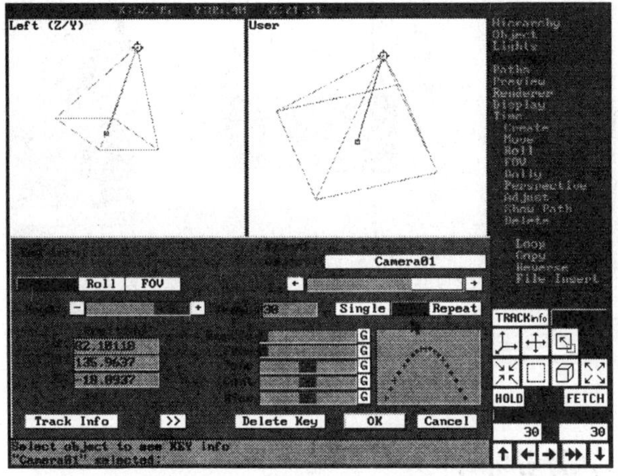

Looping the tracks of a selected camera.

RELATED COMMANDS

Object/Tracks/Loop, Lights/Tracks/Loop

Cameras/Tracks/Copy

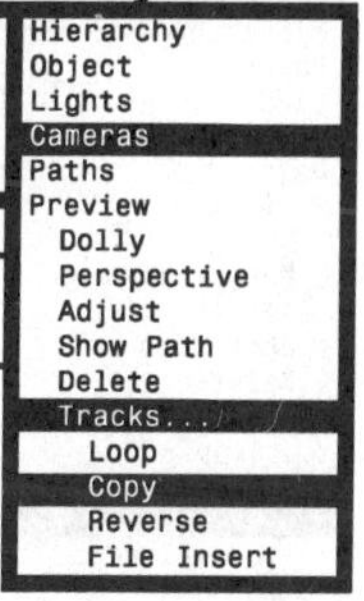

Hierarchy
Object
Lights
Cameras
Paths
Preview
Dolly
Perspective
Adjust
Show Path
Delete
Tracks...
Loop
Copy
Reverse
File Insert

Copies the common tracks between a camera and another selected object.

Copying Common Tracks

1. Ensure that a camera and target have been created previously. Select the **Hold** button (Ctrl H) to save your current configuration.
2. Select *Cameras/Tracks/Copy*.
3. Select the camera from which to copy the tracks.
4. Select the camera to receive the tracks. The Copy Tracks dialog box appears as shown below.
5. One or more of the following options will appear in the dialog box based on the commonality between the two objects selected. Make the changes necessary as described below.

Position: Copies the position tracks.

Roll: Copies the roll tracks.

FOV: Copies the field of view tracks

Relative: Tracks are applied relative to their key #1 values or spaced away from the object from which the tracks were copied.

Absolute: Tracks are applied absolutely to their key #1 values or on top of the object from which the tracks were copied.

6. Select **OK** to copy the tracks and exit the dialog box. If the results are not correct, select the **Fetch** button (Ctrl F) to return the values to their previous settings.

The Copy Tracks dialog box.

Copy Tracks
Tracks: Position
Roll
FOV
Relative Absolute
OK Cancel

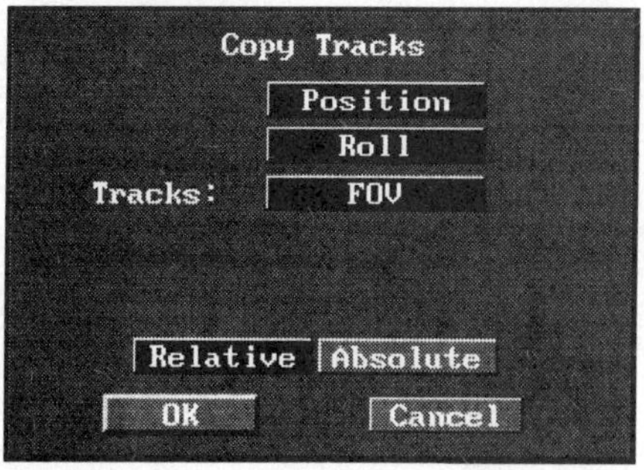

RELATED COMMANDS

Objects/Track/Copy, Lights/Track/Copy

Hierarchy
Object
Lights
Cameras
Paths
Preview
Dolly
Perspective
Adjust
Show Path
Delete
Tracks...
Loop
Copy
Reverse
File Insert

Cameras/Tracks/Reverse

Reverses the order of the keys for a camera.

Reversing the Keys Order for the Active Segment

1. Ensure that a camera has been created previously.
2. Select *Cameras/Tracks/Reverse*.
3. Select the camera that contains the keys to be reversed. The Reverse Tracks dialog box will appear as shown below.
4. Make the changes necessary as described below.

   Position: Reverses the position tracks.

   Color: Reverses the color tracks.

   Roll: Reverses the roll tracks.

   Relative: Tracks are reversed relative to their key #1 values.

   Absolute: Tracks are reversed absolutely to their key #1.
5. Select **OK** to copy the tracks and exit the dialog box. Select **Cancel** to cancel the command and close the dialog box.

To undo the changes made, repeat the command and reverse the tracks back to their original position.

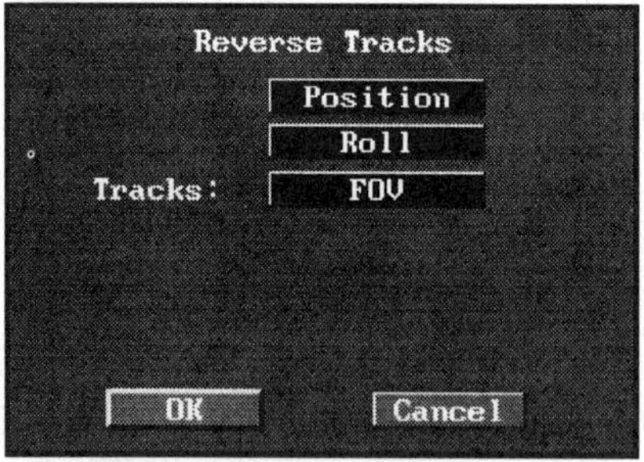

The Reverse Tracks dialog box.

RELATED COMMANDS

Object/Tracks/Reverse, Lights/Tracks/Reverse

Cameras/Tracks/File Insert

Inserts or appends all or a range of tracks from cameras in other *.3ds* files.

Inserting or Appending Tracks From a File

1. Ensure that a camera that is to receive the tracks has been created previously.
2. Move to the frame that will be at the end of the inserted tracks.
3. Select *Cameras/Tracks/File Insert.*
4. Select the camera to receive the inserted tracks (destination camera). A file selector will appear.
5. Select the file that contains the tracks to be inserted. The Object Selection dialog box appears.
6. Select the camera from which to copy the tracks (source camera). The Insert Animation Tracks dialog box appears. Make the selections as described below:

From Object/Into Object: Displays the source camera name and the destination camera name.

Scope: Specifies the scope of the track insertion

Object: Inserts the tracks of the object only.

Subtree: Inserts the tracks of the object and its hierarchies if the hierarchies match.

Method: Specifies the method of track insertion.

Relative: Tracks are inserted relative to the current tracks values.

Absolute: Tracks are inserted absolutely to the current tracks values.

Source frames: Specifies the range of the frames to be inserted.

First key to Last key: Sets the range of the Source Frames fields to select only those frames from the source object that contain keys.

7. Select **OK** to insert the tracks and exit the dialog box. Select **Cancel** to cancel the command and close the dialog box.

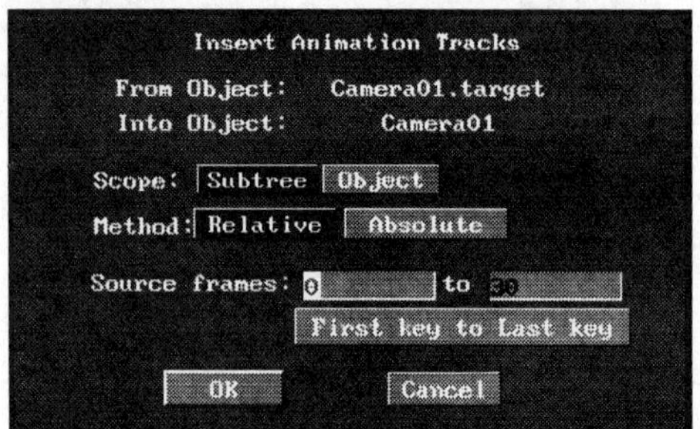

The Insert Animation Tracks dialog box.

RELATED COMMANDS

Object/Tracks/File Insert, Camera/Tracks/File Insert

Paths/Get/Shaper

Cameras
Paths
Preview
Renderer
Get...
Show-Hide
Hide All
Follow
Move Key
Add Key
Delete Key
Adjust TCB...
Adjust...
Shaper
Lofter
Disk

Applies a shape from the 2D Shaper to a selected component in the Keyframer.

Importing a Path from the 2D Shaper

1. Before you can import a path from the 2D Shaper, the shape must exist in the 2D Shaper. See *Shape/Assign* in the 2D Shaper.
2. In the Keyframer, select *Paths/Get/Shaper* and select the object, light, camera, or target you want to assign the path to.
3. When the Get Path dialog box appears, you have the following options:

   Relocate object to path start? Selecting **Yes** will reposition the object to the first vertex of the path. See *Display/First/On* in the 2D Shaper.

   Reverse path direction? Selecting **Yes** will make the object coincident with the first vertex of the path at key #1.

   Adjust keys for constant speed? Selecting **Yes** will space the keys evenly so the object moves at a constant speed.
4. Selecting **OK** will import the path. You can display the path by selecting *Paths/Show-Hide*.

NOTE

When importing paths from the 2D Shaper, keep in mind the following points:

1. Paths from the 2D Shaper are all 2D.
2. The path is imported on the construction plane parallel to the top viewport.
3. You should have at least as many frames in the animation as vertices in the imported path.

TIP

You can display geometry from the 3D Editor in the 2D Shaper to help you create your path by selecting *Display/3D Display/Choose* in the 2D Shaper.

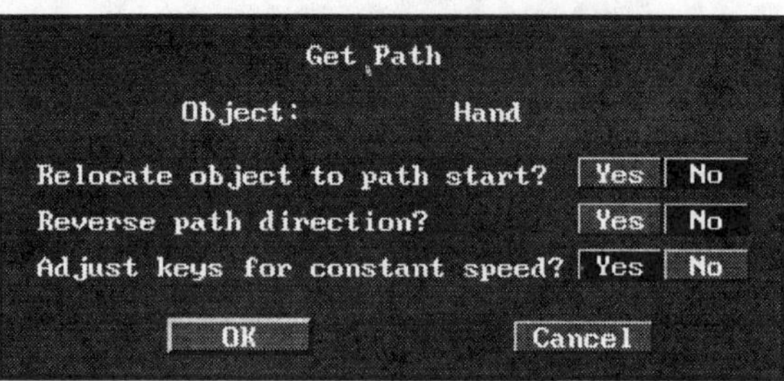

The Get Path dialog box is used to set the options when importing a path from the 2D Shaper.

RELATED COMMANDS

Shape/Assign in the 2D Shaper, Paths/Show-Hide

Cameras
Paths
Preview
Renderer
Get...
Show-Hide
Hide All
Follow
Move Key
Add Key
Delete Key
Adjust TCB...
Adjust...
Shaper
Lofter
Disk

Paths/Get/Lofter

Applies the current path from the 3D Lofter to a selected component in the Keyframer.

Importing a Path from the 3D Lofter

1. Before you can import a path from the 3D Lofter, the shape must exist in the 3D Lofter.
2. In the Keyframer, select *Paths/Get/Lofter* and select the object, light, camera, or target you want to assign the path to.
3. When the Get Path dialog box appears, you have the following options:

   Relocate object to path start? Selecting **Yes** will reposition the object to the first vertex of the path.

   Reverse path direction? Selecting **Yes** will make the object coincident with the first vertex of the path at key #1.

   Adjust keys for constant speed? Selecting **Yes** will space the keys evenly so the object moves at a constant speed.
4. Selecting **OK** will import the path. You can display the path by selecting *Paths/Show-Hide*.

> **TIP** Editing a path in the 3D Lofter that was created in the 2D Shaper will allow you to adjust its vertical positioning. You can display geometry from the 3D Editor in the 3D Lofter by selecting *3D Display/Choose* in the 3D Lofter.

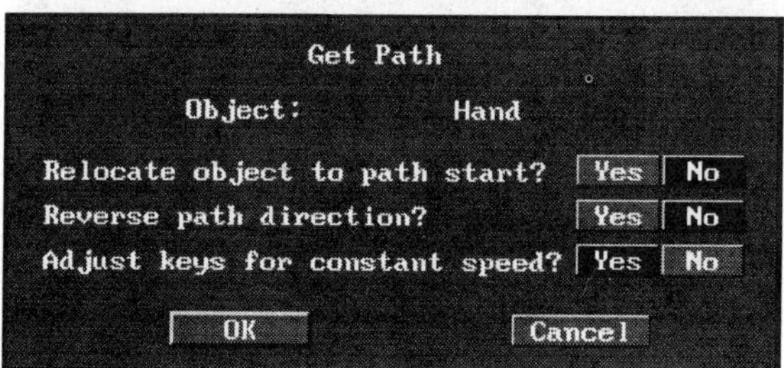

The Get Path dialog box is used to set the options when importing a path from the 3D Lofter.

RELATED COMMAND

Paths/Show–Hide

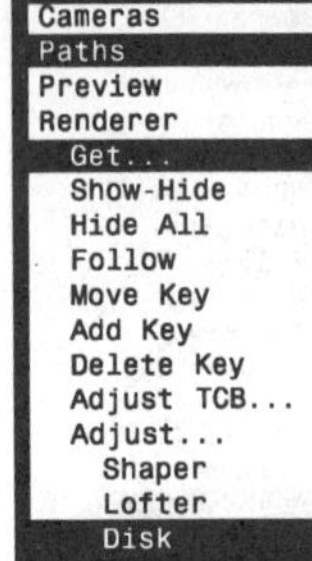

Paths/Get/Disk

Imports a *.*lft* file and assigns its path to a selected component, or loads a *.*dxf* file and assigns a polyline to a selected component.

Importing a Path from Disk

1. Choose *Paths/Get/Disk* and select the object you want to assign the path to.
2. In the Select a Path file to merge dialog box, select the path you want to import. You can import *.*lft* or *.*dxf* files.

   ***.lft* files.** Imports a path that was created in the Lofter.

   ***.dxf* files.** Imports a path that was created in another program, such as AutoCAD.
3. After selecting the name and type of path to import and the Get Path dialog box appears, you have the following options:

   Relocate object to path start? Selecting **Yes** will reposition the object to the first vertex of the path.

   Reverse path direction? Selecting **Yes** will make the object coincident with the first vertex of the path at key #1.

   Adjust keys for constant speed? Selecting **Yes** will space the keys evenly so the object moves at a constant speed.
4. Selecting **OK** will import the path. You can display the path by selecting *Paths/Show-Hide*.

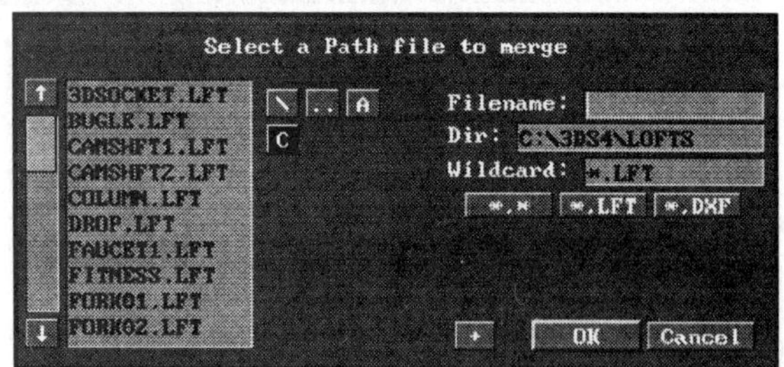

*Importing a *.dxf or *.lft file to use as a path for a selected object*

RELATED COMMAND

Paths/Show–Hide

Hierarchy
Object
Lights
Cameras
Paths
Preview
Renderer
Get...
Show Hide
Hide All
Follow
Move Key
Add Key
Delete Key
Adjust TCB...
Adjust...

Paths/Show-Hide

Turns the path display for an object on or off.

Displaying the Path for a Selected Object

1. Select *Paths/Show-Hide* and select an object.
2. The movement path for the object appears. The path movement appears as a red line, the white squares represent the keys, and the yellow dots represent the frames. If only a single yellow square within a square appears, no Position keys have been assigned to the object.
3. To turn the path display off, select *Paths/Show-Hide* and select the object, or select *Paths/Hide All*.

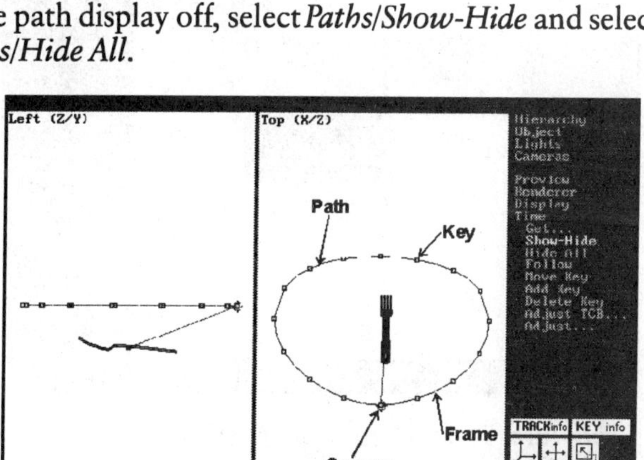

Displaying the path for the camera.

RELATED COMMAND

Paths/Hide All

Hierarchy
Object
Lights
Cameras
Paths
Preview
Renderer
Get...
Show-Hide
Hide All
Follow
Move Key
Add Key
Delete Key
Adjust TCB...
Adjust...

Paths/Hide All

Turns all displayed paths off.

Hiding All Displayed Paths.

1. Select *Paths/Hide All* to access the Hide all paths? dialog box.
2. Select **Yes** to hide all paths. To hide only selected paths, use *Paths/Show-Hide*.

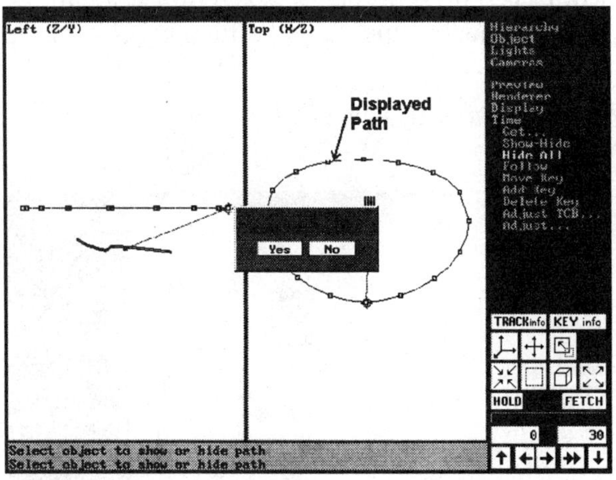

Using Paths/Hide All to turn off all displayed paths.

RELATED COMMAND

Paths/Show-Hide

Paths/Follow

Hierarchy
Object
Lights
Cameras
Paths
Preview
Renderer
Get...
Show-Hide
Hide All
Follow
Move Key
Add Key
Delete Key
Adjust TCB...
Adjust...

Guides a selected object along an inserted path by adding additional rotation keys and modifying existing ones.

Making a Selected Object Follow a Path

1. Create a path for an object to follow with *Object/Move*, or import a path with *Paths/Get/Shaper, Paths/Get/Lofter* or *Paths/Get/Disk.*
2. Make sure the path of the object is displayed. If the path is not displayed, select *Paths/Show-Hide* and select the object.
3. Select *Paths/Follow* and select the object in a non-camera viewport.
4. In the Follow Path dialog box, select from the following options:

   Bank: If you select **Yes**, the object will bank or roll as it follows the path.

   Max Bank Angle: When Bank is turned on, this will be the maximum angle the object will bank as it follows the path. A positive angle makes the object bank into the curve of the path; a negative bank angle makes the object bank away from the path.
5. Select **OK** to apply the options to the selected object.

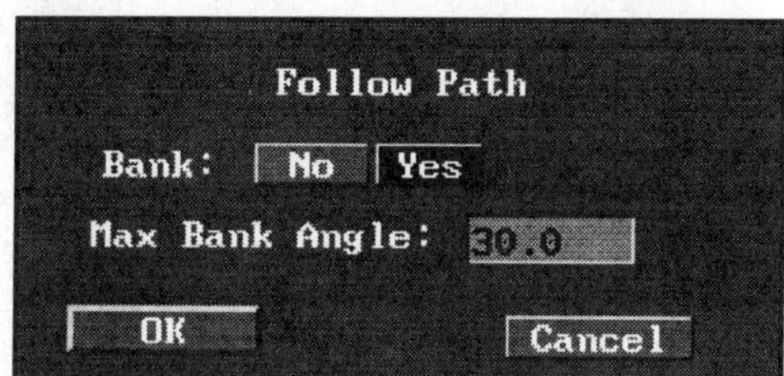

A selected object will align itself to a path and optionally bank as it follows the path.

RELATED COMMAND

Paths/Show-Hide

Hierarchy
Object
Lights
Cameras
Paths
Preview
Renderer
Get...
Show-Hide
Hide All
Follow
Move Key
Add Key
Delete Key
Adjust TCB...
Adjust...

Paths/Move Key

Allows you to position a key anywhere in space.

Moving a Key

1. Make sure the path you want to move the key on is displayed. See *Paths/Show-Hide*.
2. Select *Paths/Move Key*, and select the key you want to move in any non-camera viewport. Pressing the [Alt] key when selecting the key will move the entire path. Pressing the [Shift] key will create an instance copy of the key.
3. After selecting the key, it becomes attached to the mouse. The line representing the original path is red, and the new path is blue. You can use the [Tab] key to restrain movement along the different axis.
4. When you have the key positioned in its new location, click to set it or right-click to cancel the operation.

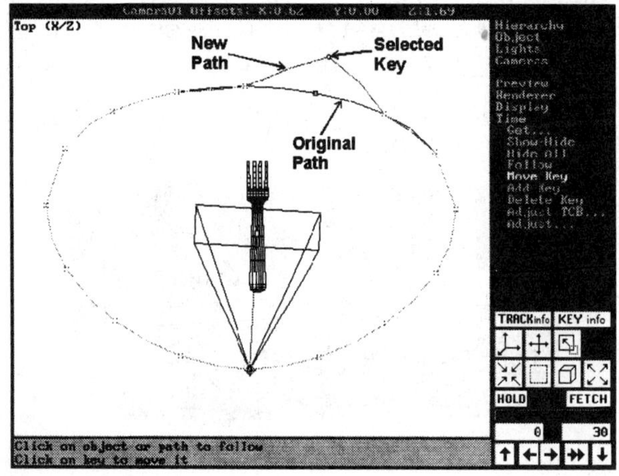

When the key is placed in its new position, the Position values of that key are updated.

RELATED COMMAND

Paths/Show-Hide

Paths/Add Key

Hierarchy
Object
Lights
Cameras
Paths
Preview
Renderer
Get...
Show-Hide
Hide All
Follow
Move Key
Add Key
Delete Key
Adjust TCB...
Adjust...

Inserts a new key into the position track at the frame selected on the path.

Adding a New Key

1. Make sure the path you want to insert the key on is displayed. See *Paths/Show-Hide*.
2. Select *Paths/Add Key*. To add a key, click on any yellow dot on the displayed path.
3. The new key appears as a white square. You can move the key to a new location with *Paths/Move Key*.

> **NOTE** The *Paths/Add Key* command does the same thing as using the Add button in the Track Info dialog box. See *Icons-Track Info*.

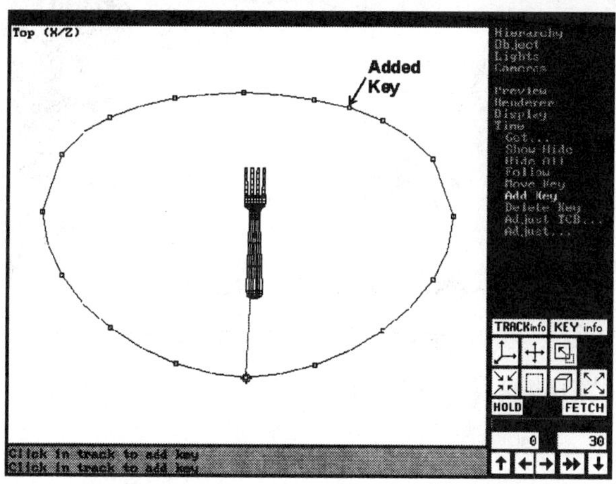

A new key is displayed as a white square.

RELATED COMMANDS

Paths/Show-Hide, Paths/Move Key, Icons-Track Info

Hierarchy
Object
Lights
Cameras
Paths
Preview
Renderer
Get...
Show-Hide
Hide All
Follow
Move Key
Add Key
Delete Key
Adjust TCB
Adjust...

Paths/Delete Key

Removes a selected key from the path.

Deleting a Key

1. Make sure the path you want to delete the key on is displayed. See *Paths/Show-Hide*.
2. To delete a key, select *Paths/Delete Key* and click on the key you want to delete.
3. The selected key is deleted. The only key removed is the key in the Position track. No other keys in other tracks at that frame are affected.

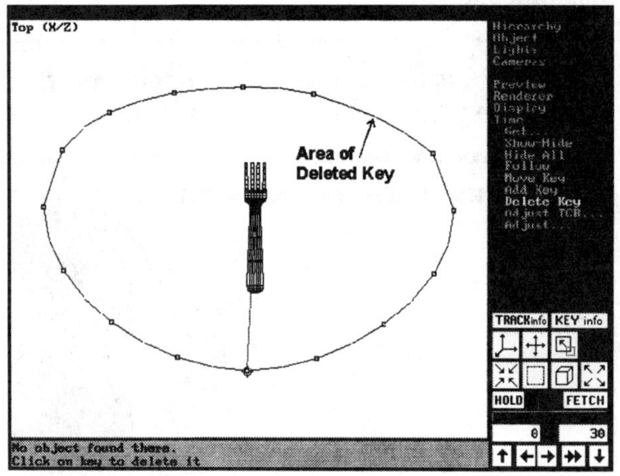

When deleting a key, all keys in other tracks at that frame are not affected.

RELATED COMMAND

Paths/Show-Hide

Cameras
Paths
Preview
Renderer
  Get...
  Show-Hide
  Hide All
  Follow
  Move Key
  Add Key
  Delete Key
  Adjust TCB...
  Adjust...
    Tension
    Continuity
    Bias

Paths/Adjust TCB/Tension

Adjusts the curvature of the path through a selected key.

Adjusting the Tension

1. Make sure the path you want to adjust the tension on is displayed. See *Paths/Show-Hide*.
2. Select *Paths/Adjust TCB/Tension* and click on a key. Moving the mouse horizontally back and forth will increase or decrease the tension.
3. Click to set the new tension.

> **TIP** You can adjust the tension of all keys at the same time by holding down the [Alt] key when selecting the key. You can also adjust the tension in the Key Info dialog box. See *Icon-Key Info*. While adjusting the Tension, you can also switch to adjust the Continuity and Bias by pressing the [C] and [B] buttons, respectively. See *Paths/Adjust TCB/Continuity* and *Paths/Adjust TCB/Bias*.

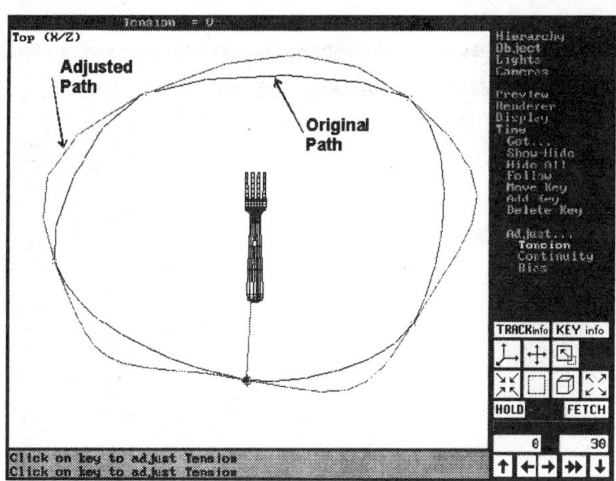

Adjusting the curvature of the path through all keys by holding down the [Alt] key when selecting the key.

RELATED COMMANDS

Paths/Show-Hide, Paths/Adjust TCB/Continuity, Paths/Adjust TCB/Bias

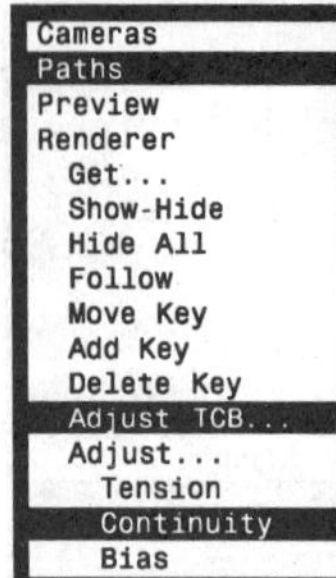

Paths/Adjust TCB/Continuity

Adjusts the angle at which the spline path enters and leaves the selected key.

Adjusting the Continuity

1. Make sure the path you want to adjust the tension on is displayed. See *Paths/Show-Hide.*
2. Select *Paths/Adjust TCB/Continuity* and click on a key. Moving the mouse horizontally back and forth will increase or decrease the angle at which the spline path enters and leaves the selected key.
3. Click to set the new continuity.

> **TIP** You can adjust the continuity of all keys at the same time by holding down the Alt key when selecting the key. You can also adjust the continuity in the Key Info dialog box. See *Icon-Key Info*. While adjusting the Continuity, you can also switch to adjust the Tension and Bias by pressing the T and B buttons respectively. See *Paths/Adjust TCB/Tension* and *Paths/Adjust TCB/Bias*.

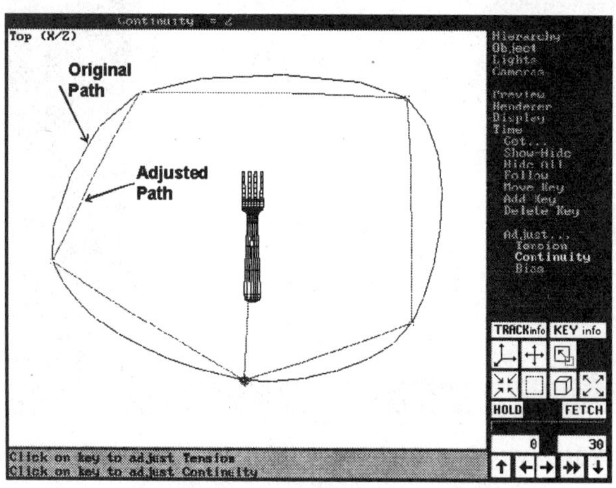

Adjusting the angle at which the spline path enters and leaves all keys by holding down the Alt key when selecting the key.

RELATED COMMANDS

Paths/Show-hide, Paths/Adjust TCB/Tension, Paths/Adjust TCB/Bias

Paths/Adjust TCB/Bias

Adjusts the overshoot or undershoot of the spline path as it enters and leaves the selected key.

Adjusting the Bias

1. Make sure the path you want to adjust the bias on is displayed. See *Paths/Show-Hide*.
2. Select *Paths/Adjust TCB/Bias* and click on a key. Moving the mouse horizontally back and forth will adjust the overshoot and undershoot of the spline path as it enters and leaves the selected key.
3. Click to set the new bias.

> **TIP** You can adjust the bias of all keys at the same time by holding down the [Alt] key when selecting the key. You can also adjust the bias in the Key Info dialog box. See *Icon-Key Info*. While adjusting the Bias, you can also switch to adjust the Tension and Continuity by pressing the [T] and [C] buttons, respectively. See *Paths/Adjust TCB/Tension* and *Paths/Adjust TCB/Continuity*.

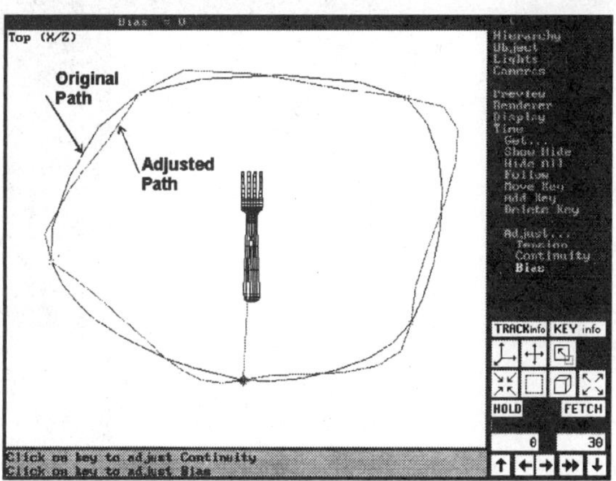

Adjusting the overshoot and undershoot of the spline path for all keys by holding down the [Alt] key when selecting the key.

RELATED COMMANDS

Paths/Show-Hide, Paths/Adjust TCB/Tension, Paths/Adjust TCB/Continuity

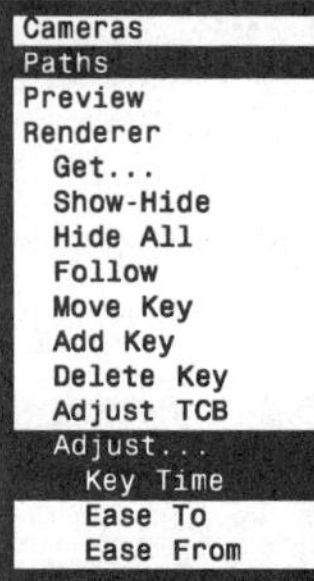

Paths/Adjust/Key Time

Moves a selected key in time along the displayed path.

Moving a Key in Time

1. Make sure the path you want to adjust the key time on is displayed. See *Paths/Show-Hide*.
2. Select *Paths/Adjust/Key Time* and click on a key. The frame the key is currently on is displayed in the status line at the top of the screen.
3. Moving the mouse horizontally back and forth will move the key to a different frame in time. The change is reflected in the status line. Note the spacing of the yellow dots on both sides of the selected key are altered.
4. Click to set the new key time.

TIP Using *Paths/Adjust/Key Time* is the same as using the Move button in the Track Info dialog box. See *Icons-Track Info*. The difference, however, is that with the *Paths/Adjust/Key Time* command you cannot move the selected key beyond the keys on either side of it.

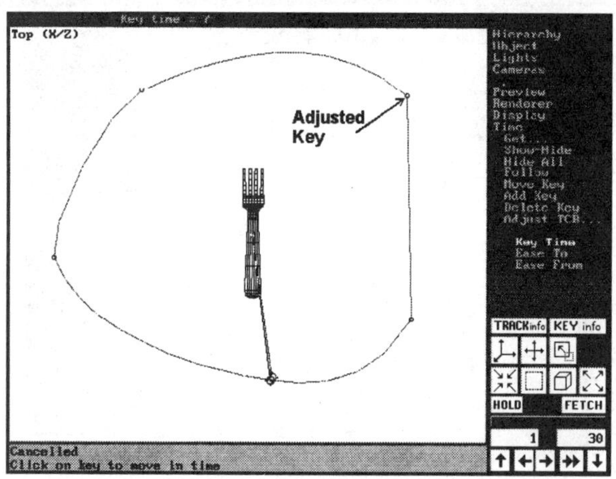

Adjusting the time of the key at frame 13 to frame 7.

RELATED COMMANDS

Paths/Show-Hide, Icons-Track Info

Paths/Adjust/Ease To

Adjusts the ease to value of a key, which affects how quickly an object will approach the selected key.

Adjusting the Ease To Value of a Selected Key

1. Make sure the path you want to adjust the ease to value is displayed. See *Paths/Show-Hide*.
2. Select *Paths/Adjust/Ease To* and click on a key. The ease to value is currently on and is displayed in the status line at the top of the screen.
3. As you move the mouse horizontally, the spacing of the yellow dots before the selected key changes to indicate the velocity of the object approaching the key. The change is reflected in the status line.
4. Click to set the new value, which can range from 0 (no change) to 50.

TIP You can also adjust the ease to value in the Key Info dialog box. See *Icons-Key Info*.

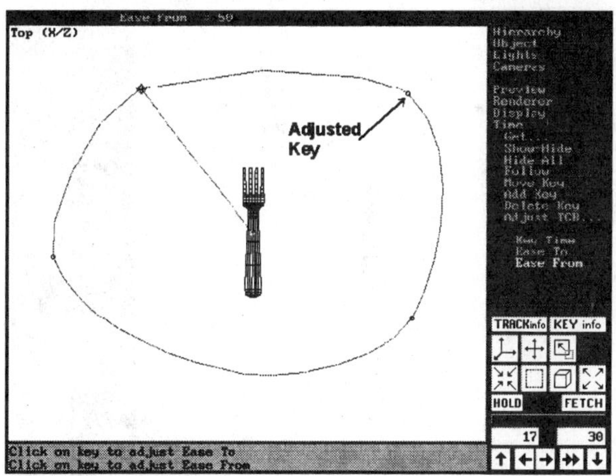

Adjusting the Ease To value for a selected key to 50, the maximum value.

RELATED COMMANDS

Paths/Show-Hide, Icons-Key Info, Paths/Adjust/Ease From

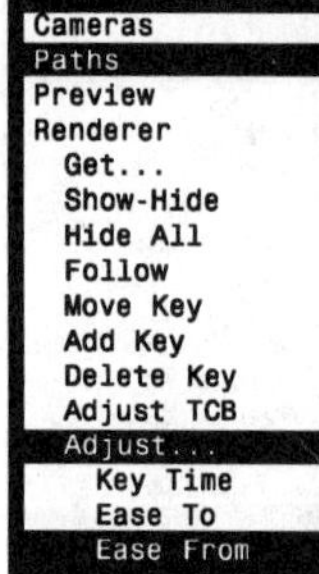

Paths/Adjust/Ease From

Adjusts the ease from value of a key, which affects how quickly an object will leave the selected key.

Adjusting the Ease From Value of a Selected Key

1. Make sure the path you want to adjust the ease from value is displayed. See *Paths/Show-Hide*.
2. Select *Paths/Adjust/Ease From* and click on a key. The ease from value is currently on and is displayed in the status line at the top of the screen.
3. As you move the mouse horizontally, the spacing of the yellow dots after the selected key changes to indicate the velocity of the object leaving the key. The change is reflected in the status line.
4. Click to set the new value, which can range from 0 (no change) to 50.

You can also adjust the ease from value in the Key Info dialog box. See *Icons-Key Info*.

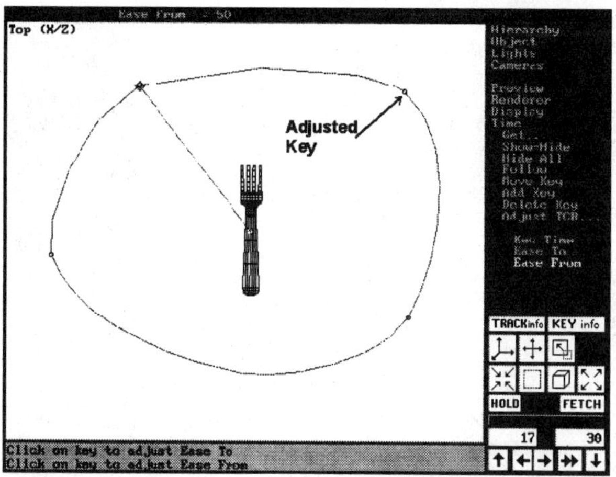

Adjusting the Ease From value for a selected key to 50, the maximum value.

RELATED COMMANDS

Paths/Show-Hide, Icons-Key Info, Paths/Adjust/Ease To

Preview/Make

Hierarchy
Object
Lights
Cameras
Paths
Preview
Renderer
Display
Time
Make
Play
View Flic
Set Speed
Save

Creates a preview animation, using flat shading, a default white material for all objects without shadows, reflections, or maps. All lights are changed to white, non-projecting omni lights.

Making a Preview Animation

1. Select *Preview/Make* and click in any viewport. In most cases it is beneficial to select a Camera viewport, because the Keyframer uses the camera view to calculate depth sorting. Rendering from a non-camera viewport can cause missing faces.
2. The Make Preview dialog box appears with the following options:

Draw:

Faces: Produces flat shaded surfaces.

Faces+Lines: Produces flat shaded surfaces with a wireframe outline superimposed on the surfaces.

Lines: Produces wireframe objects.

Box: Renders only the bounding box of the objects.

Numbers:

No: Does not imprint frame numbering.

Yes: Imprints frame numbering in the upper left-hand corner of each frame. The numbers remain part of the animation.

Two-sided:

No: Renders only the faces whose surface normals face the camera.

Yes: Renders both sides of all faces.

Frames:

All: Renders all frames, from 0 to the total number in the animation.

Segment: Renders all frames in the active segment. See *Time/Define Segment*.

Single: Renders the current frame only.

Range: Renders all frames between and including the frames listed in the text boxes.

Every Nth Frame: Skips the number of frames entered in the text box.

Size: Select the size in pixels of the preview animation, or enter your own in the Size text box. The default is 320/200.

3. Click on Preview to create the preview animation. To stop the rendering process, press the Esc key at any time. The preview is stored as *preview.fli* in the directory specified by PREVIEW-PATH in the *3ds.set* file.

To speed up the creation of the preview animation, set the value in Every Nth Frame to 2, and decrease the Size.

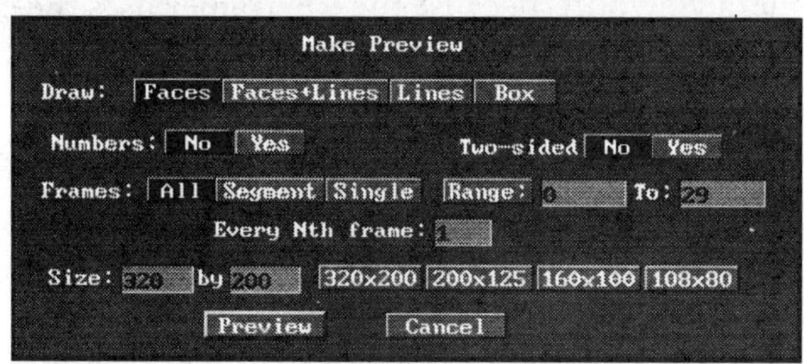

To make preview animation's quicker, set the value in Every Nth Frame to 2, and make the Size smaller than 320 X 200.

RELATED COMMAND

Preview/Play

Preview/Play

Hierarchy
Object
Lights
Cameras
Paths
Preview
Renderer
Display
Time
Make
Play
View Flic
Set Speed
Save

Plays the most recent preview flic created.

Playing a Preview Flic

1. Select *Preview/Flic* and the last preview flic created will be played.
2. Press the [Esc] key or right-click to stop the animation.

> **NOTE** If an alert box appears indicating that the preview animation cannot be played, turn off the Check Speed box in the Preview Playback Speed dialog box. See *Preview/Set Speed*.

A sample frame from a preview animation.

RELATED COMMANDS

Preview/Make, Preview/Set Speed

Hierarchy
Object
Lights
Cameras
Paths
Preview
Renderer
Display
Time
Make
Play
View Flic
Set Speed
Save

Preview/View Flic

Accesses a file selector dialog box, allowing you to select a flic (**.fli* or **.flc*) animation to view.

Viewing a Flic

1. Select *Preview/View Flic* to access the Select Flick file to load dialog box. Select the file to load and press **OK.**
2. When the animation is playing, you can use the following keys to control the playback of the flic:

[→] Increases the playback speed.

[←] Decreases the playback speed.

[↑] Sets the speed to the default of 20 frames per second.

[↓] Pauses the playback. Pressing [→] during a pause will step through the animation one frame at a time.

[Esc] or right-click stops the animation playback.

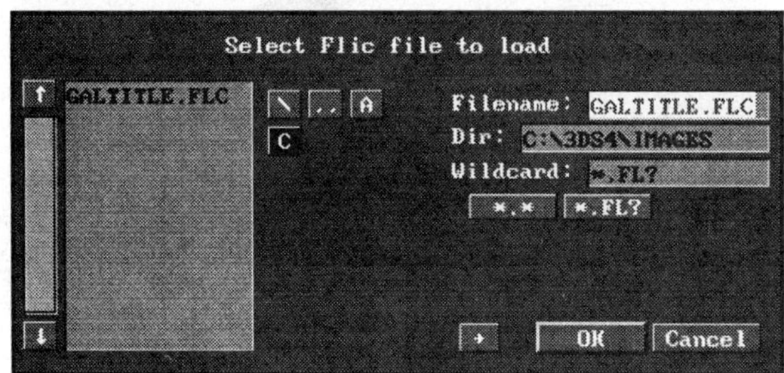

*You can view *.fli or *.flc animation's, selected through a dialog box.*

RELATED COMMAND

Preview/Set Speed

Hierarchy
Object
Lights
Cameras
Paths
Preview
Renderer
Display
Time
  Make
  Play
  View Flic
  Set Speed
  Save

Preview/Set Speed

Allows you to adjust the playback speed of a preview animation.

Setting the Speed of a Preview Animation

1. Select *Preview/Set Speed* to access the Preview Playback Speed dialog box.
2. Enter the frames per second that you want the preview played at. To check the speed for accuracy, click **Yes** beside Check Speed.
3. Click on **OK** to save the settings. When you select *Preview/Play*, the preview will be played back using the defined settings.

> **NOTE** This is intended to preview animations that will be sent to a real-time playback medium. The standard video speed is 30 frames per second. Depending on your hardware, you may not be able to play back an animation at this speed. To simulate 30 frames per second, render the preview to every second frame (set in the Every Nth frame under *Preview/Make*) and set the speed to 15 frames per second.

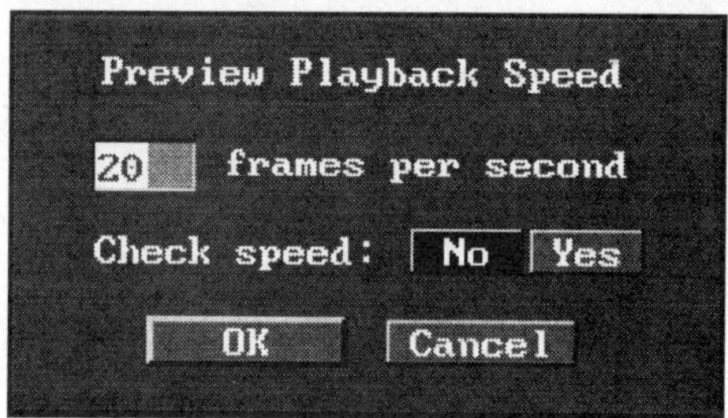

If you are having trouble viewing your preview animation, set the speed to 15 frames per second, and click on No *beside Check speed.*

RELATED COMMANDS

Preview/Make, Preview/Play

Hierarchy
Object
Lights
Cameras
Paths
Preview
Renderer
Display
Time
  Make
  Play
  View Flic
  Set Speed
  Save

Preview/Save

Saves the current preview animation to disk in a **.fli* format.

Saving the Current Preview Animation

1. Select *Preview/Save* to access the Select Flic file to save dialog box.
2. Enter a filename for the saved flic, and click OK.

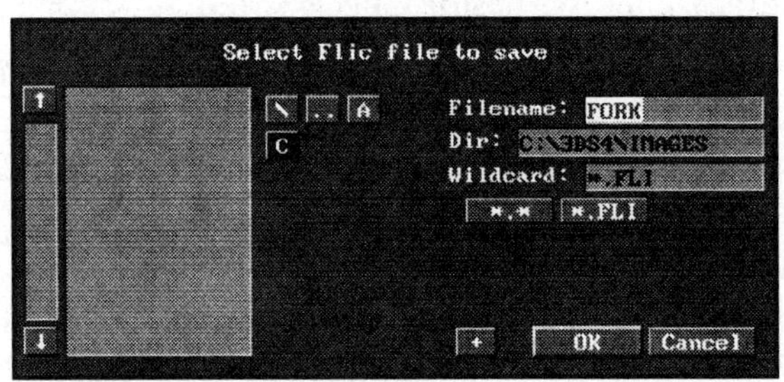

*Saving the current preview animation to disk in *.fli format.*

RELATED COMMAND

Preview/Make

Paths
Preview
Renderer
Display
Time

Render View
Render Region
Render Blowup
Render Object
Render Last
Video Post
Setup...
View...
VTR Control...

Renderer/Render View

Renders an active viewport.

Rendering an Active Viewport

1. Select *Renderer/Render View.*
2. Click in any viewport to render. The Render Animation dialog box appears.

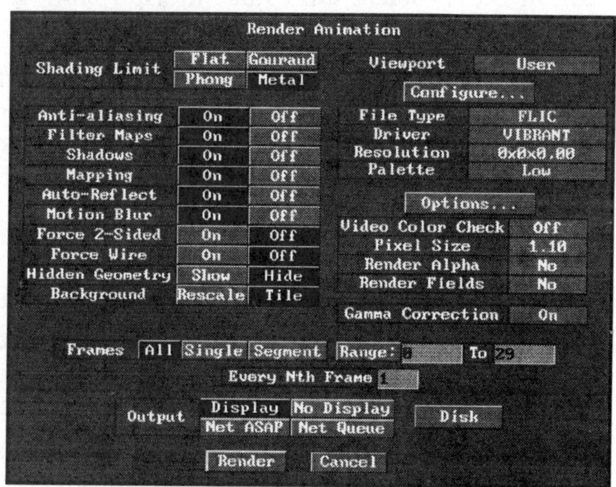

The Render Animation dialog box.

3. Configure the renderer using the following options.

Shading Limit: Select the shading method used in the rendering.

Flat: Renders each face as a single solid color; useful for quick renderings where very little detail is needed.

Gouraud: Renders each face as a color gradient; useful for checking light placement and scene composition. No materials, textures, shades, or shadows are displayed.

Phong: Renders each pixel individually using its given surface properties. Phong is required for shading, shadows, bump mapping, transparency, and reflections.

Metal: Renders each pixel and applies a rendering technique that gives each object a metallic look. Metal is required for shading, shadows, bump maps, transparency, and reflections.

Anti-aliasing: Select **On** to prevent "jaggies" in curved lines and diagonal lines. Select **Off** only to speed up "check" renderings.

Filter Maps: Select **On** to filter mapped materials. Select **Off** when background objects need to appear sharp and defined.

Shadows: Select **On** to cast shadows from spotlights in a scene. Select **Off** if no shadows are needed and to decrease rendering time.

Mapping: Select **On** to use material maps. Select **Off** to ignore map materials and to decrease rendering time.

Auto-Reflect: Select **On** to use reflection maps. Select **Off** to ignore reflection maps and decrease rendering time.

Motion Blur: Select **On** to use motion blur. Select **Off** to turn off motion blur.

Forced 2-Sided: Select **On** to render both sides of the faces in a scene. This is useful if objects do not have their faces "normalized" properly or if the inside of an object needs to be rendered as well as the outside. Select **Off** to ignore 2-sided faces and to dramatically reduce the amount of rendering time.

Force Wire: Select **On** to render all surfaces using a single pixel-width wire attribute. Select **Off** to render all surfaces normally.

Hidden Geometry: Select **SHOW** to render hidden and visible objects. Use this option to ensure that automatic reflection maps are created. Select **HIDE** to render only the objects that are not hidden.

Background: Select **RESCALE** to modify the background bitmap resolution to match that of the rendering resolution. Select **TILE** to keep the existing bitmap resolution, but to repeat the bitmap if its resolution is smaller than that of the rendering resolution.

Configure...: Displays the Device Configuration dialog box. See *Renderer/Setup/Configure* for more information.

Options: Displays the Render Options dialog box. See *Renderer/Setup/Option* for more information.

Output: Determines the output of the renderer

Display: Renders to the screen.

No Display: Selects the **NULL** display driver.

Hard Copy: Renders to a configured hard copy device.

Net ASAP: Places the rendering as the number one priority in a network rendering configuration.

Net Queue: Places the rendering as the lowest priority in the network rendering configuration.

Disk: Renders to a file. When this option is selected and the **Render** button is selected, a file selector will be displayed. Choose the name and location of the file and click on **OK**. The renderer will now proceed.

Frames: Determines the frames to be rendered.

All: Renders all frames.

Single: Renders the current frame.

Segment: Renders all frames specified using *Time/Define Segment*.

Range: Specifies a range by editing the two numbers in the edit boxes.

Every Nth Frame: Skips the specified number of frames between frames. A setting of one will render every frame; a setting of two will render every other frame.

Output: : Determines the output location for the rendering.

Display: Renders to the currently configured display.

No Display: Does not render to the currently configured display. Used to render to resolutions higher than the capabilities of the installed display.

Net ASAP: Renders to the network immediately.

Net Queue: Renders to the network queue.

Disk: Specifies a file and location for the animation. Will render to either a *flic* file or a series of images. When chosen, a file selector will appear.

4. Select **Render** to start the rendering process or **Cancel** to cancel the command and close the dialog box.
5. If **Render** was selected, the Rendering in Progress... dialog box appears as shown on the following page. The rendering progress bar gives a visual indication of how much time is left for the rendering and the rest of the dialog box displays what options were chosen for the rendering. Use the spacebar to toggle between this dialog box and the image being rendered if your video setup supports that option.

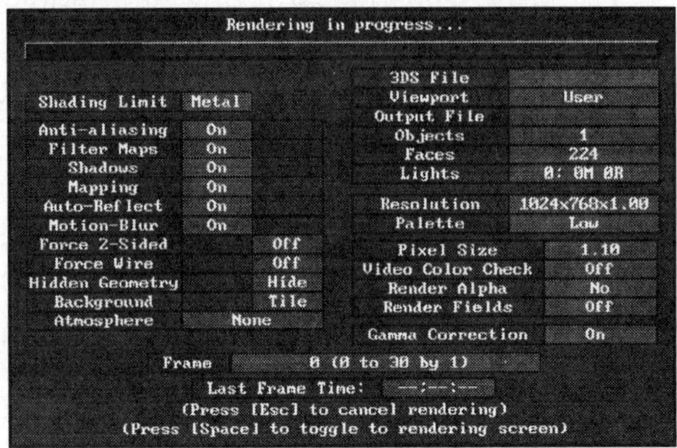

The Rendering in progress... dialog box.

6. To cancel the rendering, press [Esc] or right-click.
7. When the rendering is completed it will be displayed on screen if display was chosen. Press [Esc] or right-click to return to the viewport display.

RELATED COMMANDS

Renderer/Render Last, Renderer/Setup/Configure

Renderer/Render Region

Paths
Preview
Renderer
Display
Time
Render View
Render Region
Render Blowup
Render Object
Render Last
Video Post
Setup...
View...
VTR Control...

Renders a selected region of the active viewport.

Rendering a Region

1. Activate the viewport that contains the region to be rendered.
2. Select *Renderer/Render Region*.
3. In the active viewport, click to specify the beginning corner of the region. Move the mouse diagonally to the opposite corner of the region and click as shown in the figure below. The Render Animation dialog box appears.
4. Repeat the steps as shown in the *Renderer/Render View*. Only the selected region will be rendered as shown below.
5. Press [Esc] to cancel the rendering.

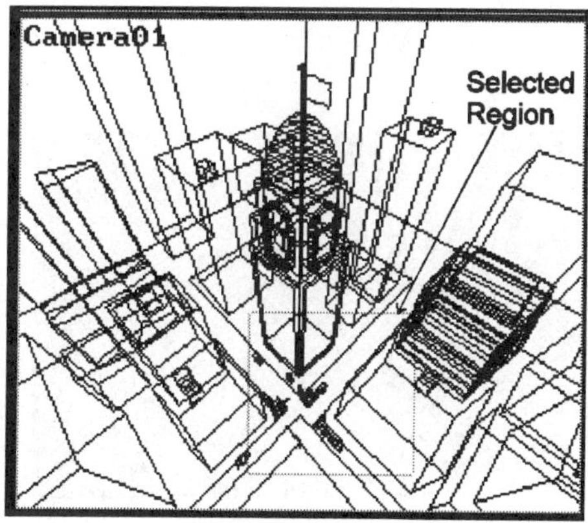

Selecting a region.

Rendering the selected region.

RELATED COMMANDS

Renderer/Render View, Renderer/Render Blowup

Paths
Preview
Renderer
Display
Time
Render View
Render Region
Render Blowup
Render Object
Render Last
Video Post
Setup...
View...
VTR Control...

Renderer/Render Blowup

Renders a region, then scales the region to match that of the rendering resolution.

Rendering a Blowup

1. Activate the viewport that contains the region to be rendered.
2. Select *Render/Render Blowup*.
3. In the active viewport, click to specify the beginning corner of the region, move the mouse diagonally to the opposite corner of the region, and click as shown in the figure below. The Render Animation dialog box appears.
4. Repeat the steps as shown in *Renderer/Render View*. The selected region will be rendered to match the resolution of the rendering device as shown below.
5. Use [Esc] or right-click to cancel the rendering.

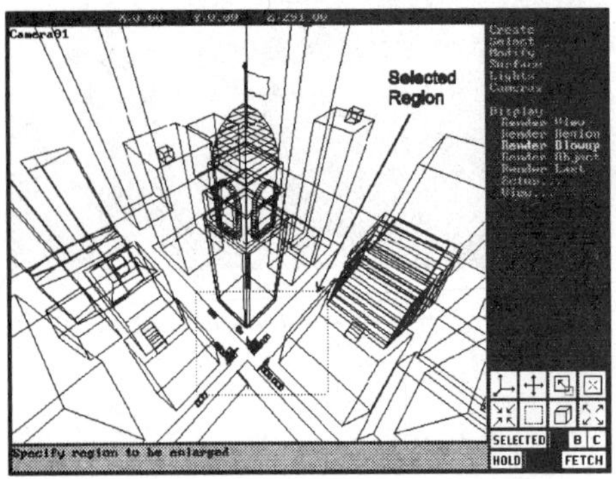

Specifying the region to be enlarged.

Enlarged rendering of the region.

RELATED COMMANDS

Render/Render View, Renderer/Render Region

Paths
Preview
Renderer
Display
Time
  Render View
  Render Region
  Render Blowup
  Render Object
  Render Last
  Video Post
  Setup...
  View...
  VTR Control...

Renderer/Render Object

Renders a single object in a scene.

Rendering a Single Object

1. Create an object in the 3D Editor.
2. Activate the viewport that contains the object to be rendered.
3. Select *Render/Render Object*.
4. In the active viewport, click on the object to be rendered. The Render Animation dialog box appears.
5. Repeat the steps as shown in *Renderer/Render View*. Only the selected object will be rendered as shown below.
6. Use [Esc] or right-click to cancel the rendering.

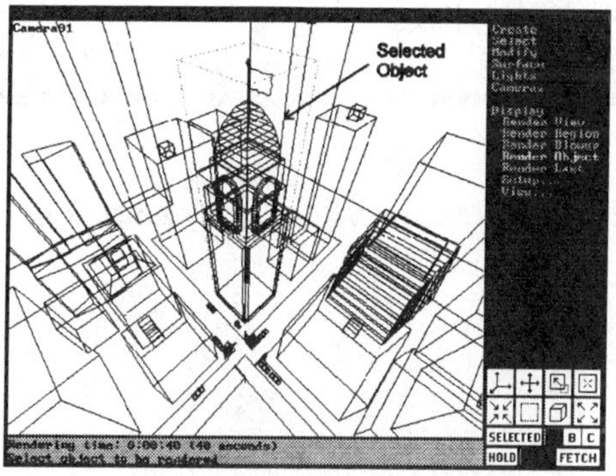

Selecting the object to render.

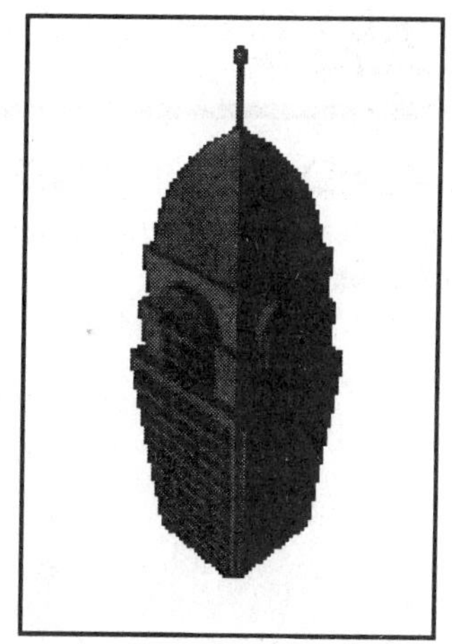

Rendering of the selected object.

> **TIP** Using this command in the Keyframer with a frame buffer will render the object and in the next frame will display the previous placement of the object, leaving a trail or animation path. This path can be used to verify the animation path for the object.

RELATED COMMAND

Renderer/Render View

Paths
Preview
Renderer
Display
Time
Render View
Render Region
Render Blowup
Render Object
Render Last
Video Post
Setup...
View...
VTR Control...

Renderer/Render Last

Repeats the last rendering command using all previous settings.

Using Render Last

1. Ensure that a rendering was created previously using *Render View, Render Region, Render Blowup,* or *Render Object*.
2. Make necessary changes to the scene.
3. Select *Renderer/Render Last*. No dialog box is displayed and the rendering is started immediately using all previous rendering configurations.
4. Use Esc or right-click to cancel the rendering.

This command will not render to disk.

RELATED COMMANDS

Renderer/Render View, Renderer/Render Region, Renderer/Render Blowup, Renderer/Render Object

Renderer/Video Post

Paths
Preview
Renderer
Display
Time
Render View
Render Region
Render Blowup
Render Object
Render Last
Video Post
Setup...
View...
VTR Control...

Displays the Video Post dialog box. This dialog box allow for composite layers of flics and images, creation of transitions for multiple flics, use of alpha channels, application of mattes, and use of image-processing external programs.

Using the Video Post Dialog Box

1. Select *Renderer/Video Post.*
2. Select the viewport to prepare. The Video Post dialog box appears as shown below.

The Video Post dialog box.

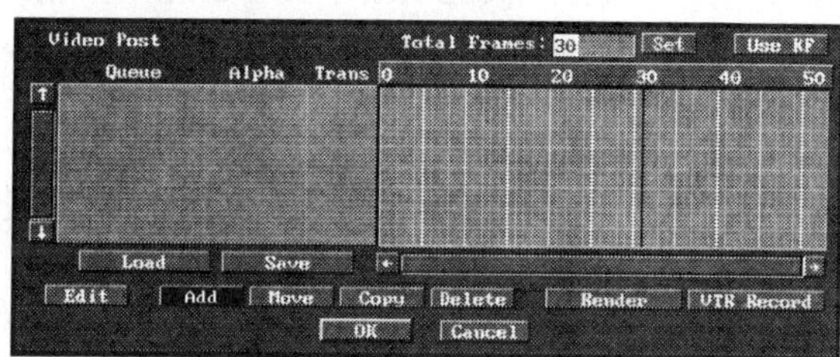

3. Make adjustments to the dialog box as described below:

Total Frames: Specifies the total number of frames to be accessed in the frame grid of the Video Post dialog box. Once this number is selected, click on **Set**. To use the number frames currently defined in the keyframer, click on **Use KF**.

Queue: Displays the names of the entries included for the video post processing.

Alpha: Controls the transparency and opacity of a bitmap entry.

Trans: Assigns a fade-in, fade-out, or image transition to the video post processing entry.

Load: Loads previously defined and saved video post settings from files with the *.vp* file extension.

Save: Saves video post settings to a file with the *.vp* file extension.

Edit: Edits any entry in either the **Queue, Alpha, and Trans** column. Select **Edit** and then click on the entry. The appropriate dialog box will be displayed and you can now edit the settings.

Add: Adds a new entry to either the **Queue, Alpha, and Trans** column. Click on this button then select the column to add an entry. The entry is added beneath the selection point and all other entries are moved down.

Move: Changes the location of a **Queue, Alpha,** or **Trans** entry. Click on this button then select the entry to move. Move the cursor to its new location and click.

Copy: Copies a **Queue, Alpha,** or **Trans** entry. Click on this button then select the entry to copy. Move the cursor to the copies new location and click.

Delete: Deletes a **Queue, Alpha,** or **Trans** entry. Click on this button then select the entry to delete.

Render: Renders all **Queue** entries. The Render Animation dialog box appears. Make all necessary changes and click on **OK.**

VTR Record: Records the entries to the video tape recorder (VTR).

4. Select **OK** to accept all modifications. Select **Cancel** to cancel the modifications and close the dialog box.

> **TIP** The scope of this command's abilities is complex and a complicated concept to understand. Refer to the 3D Studio users manual for more information on its use and functions.

RELATED COMMANDS

Renderer/Render View, Renderer/VTR Control/Record

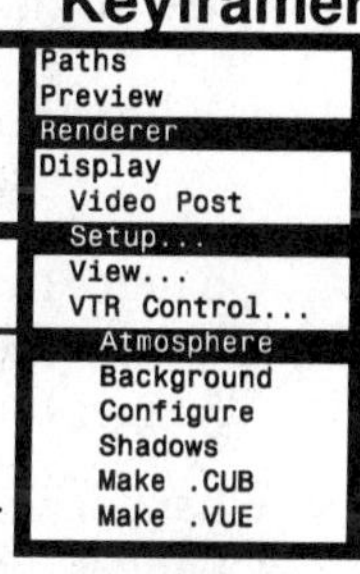

Renderer/Setup/Atmosphere

Modifies the Atmosphere settings.

Modifying Atmosphere Settings

1. Select *Renderer/Setup/Atmosphere*. The Atmosphere Definition dialog box appears as shown below.

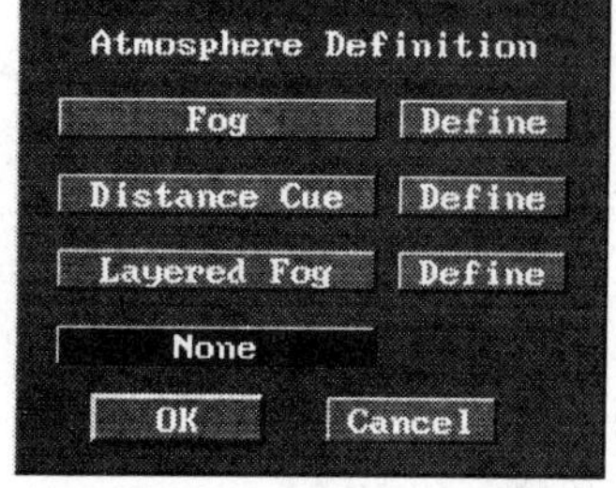

The Atmosphere Definition dialog box.

2. Select the options from the list below:

Fog: Fades the colors of the objects to another color (default is white) to simulate a fog effect in a camera viewport.

Distance Cue: Fades the colors of the objects to black in a camera viewport.

Layered Fog: Creates a layer of fog that is independent from the camera viewport and can be placed based on world coordinates.

None: Deselects all atmosphere effects.

Define: Select the **Define** button to the right of an effect to modify that effect's settings.

OK: Accepts the settings and closes the dialog box.

Cancel: Cancels the command and closes the dialog box.

3. Render the scene to see the new effects.

Modify the Fog Definition

1. Select *Renderer/Setup/Atmosphere*. The Atmosphere Definition dialog box appears.
2. Select **Fog**.
3. Click on the **Define** button next to fog. The Fog Definition dialog box appears as shown below. Make changes to the settings below. Use the color sliders to establish fog color.

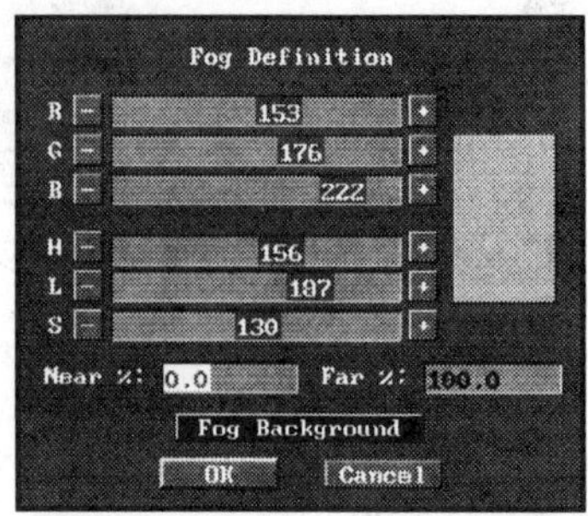

The Fog Definition dialog box.

R: Changes the red color value of the fog.
G: Changes the green color value of the fog.
B: Changes the blue color value of the fog.

H: Changes the hue value of the fog.
L: Changes the luminance value of the fog.
S: Changes the saturation value of the fog.

Near %: Specifies the percentage that the color value will affect the objects near the front of the scene. Zero percent yields no effect; 100 percent changes the color of all objects to the selected color

Far %: Specifies the percentage that the color value will affect the objects in the rear of the scene.

Fog Background: Changes the background to match the color value of the **Far %** value.

OK: Accepts the settings and closes the dialog box.

Cancel: Cancels the command and closes the dialog box.

4. Render the scene to see the fog effect applied.

Modifying the Distance Cue

1. Select *Renderer/Setup/Atmosphere.* The Atmosphere Definition dialog box appears.
2. Select **Distance Cue.**
3. Click on the **Define** button next to distance cue. The Distance-Cueing dialog box appears as shown below. Make changes to the settings below.

The Distance-Cueing dialog box.

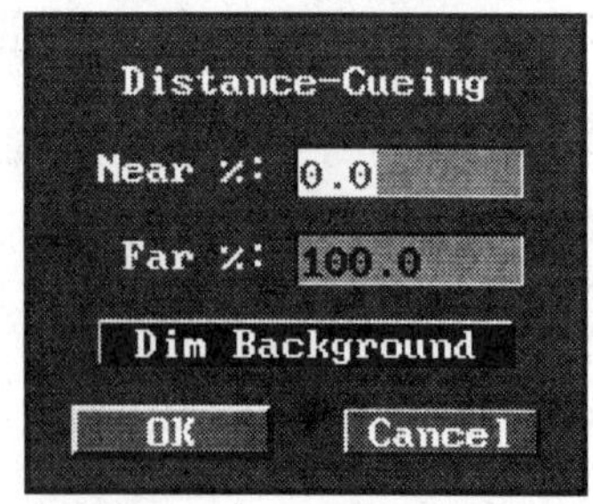

Near %: Specifies the percentage that the objects near the front of the scene will dim. 0 percent yields no effect; 100 percent changes the object to black.

Far %: Specifies the percentage that the objects to the rear of the scene will dim.

Dim Background: Changes the background to match the dim value of the **Far %** value.

OK: Accepts the settings and closes the dialog box.

Cancel: Cancels the command and closes the dialog box.

4. Render the scene to see the fog effect applied.

Modifying the Layered Fog

1. Select *Renderer/Setup/Atmosphere*. The Atmosphere Definition dialog box appears.
2. Select **Layered Fog.**
3. Click on the **Define** button next to distance cue. The Layered Fog Definition dialog box appears as shown below. Make changes to the settings below.

The Layered Fog Definition dialog box.

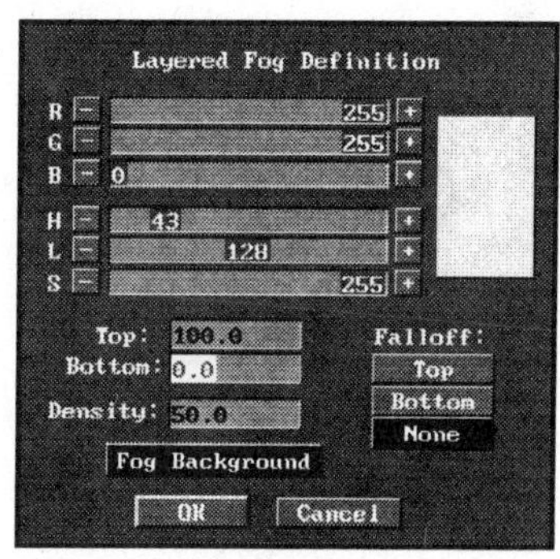

R: Changes the red color value of the fog.
G: Changes the green color value of the fog.
B: Changes the blue color value of the fog.

H: Changes the hue value of the fog.
L: Changes the luminance value of the fog.
S: Changes the saturation value of the fog.

Top: Sets the top altitude, in world coordinates, of the layer of fog.

Bottom: Sets the bottom altitude, in world coordinates, of the layer of fog.

Density: Specifies the opacity of the layer of fog. 100 percent yields a layer of fog that is completely opaque; 50 percent yields a layer of fog that is half as opaque.

Falloff:

Top: When this is selected, the density of the fog at the top altitude drops to 0 percent.

Bottom: When this is selected, the density of the fog at the bottom altitude drops to 0 percent.

None: When this is selected, it produces a layer of fog with the same density from the top altitude to the bottom one.

Fog Background: Changes the background to match the values set in the Layered Fog Definition dialog box.

OK: Accepts the settings and closes the dialog box.

Cancel: Cancels the command and closes the dialog box.

4. Render the scene to see the fog effect applied.

RELATED COMMAND

Renderer/Setup/Background

Renderer/Setup/Background

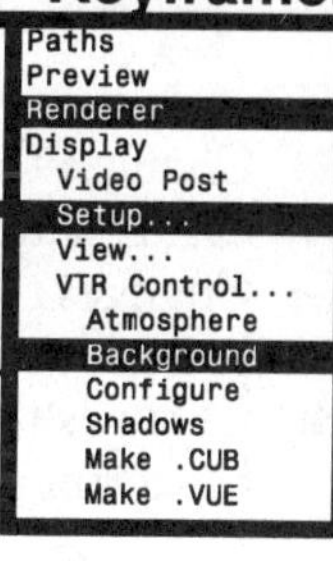

Defines the background of a scene using a solid color, a gradient, or a bitmap.

Setting up a Background

1. Select *Renderer/Setup/Background.* The Background Method dialog box appears as shown below.
2. Select the options from the list below.

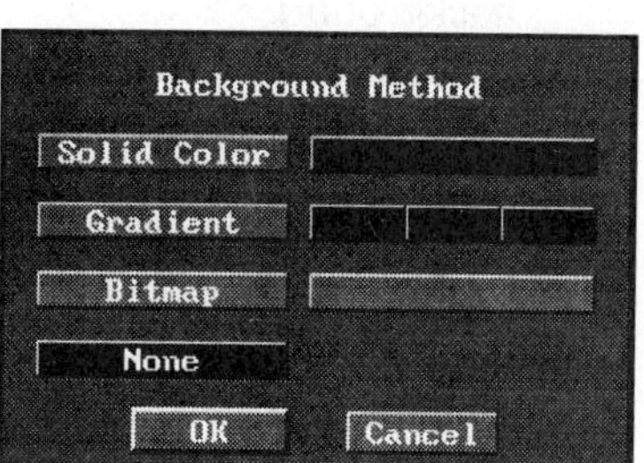

The Background Method dialog box.

Solid Color: Changes the color of the background.

Gradient: Sets a gradient color pattern for the background.

Bitmap: Selects a bitmap to be used as the background.

None: Deselects all backgrounds.

OK: Accepts the settings and closes the dialog box.

Cancel: Cancels the command and closes the dialog box.

3. Render the scene to see the new effects.

Modifying a Solid Background

1. Select *Renderer/Setup/Background.* The Background Method dialog box appears.
2. Select **Solid Color.**
3. Click on the color swatch to the right of the **Solid Color** button. The Define Solid Color dialog box appears as shown below. Make changes to the settings below.

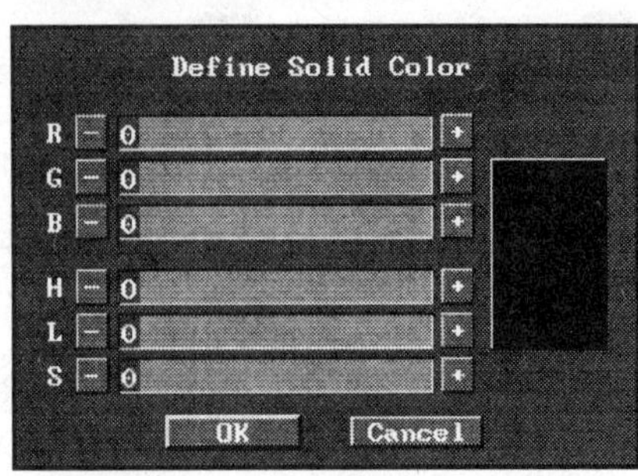

The Define Solid Color dialog box.

R: Changes the red color value of the background.
G: Changes the green color value of the background.
B: Changes the blue color value of the background.

H: Changes the hue value of the back ground.
L: Changes the luminance value of the background.
S: Changes the saturation value of the background.

OK: Accepts the settings and closes the dialog box.

Cancel: Cancels the command and closes the dialog box.

4. Render the scene to see the background effect applied.

Modifying a Gradient Background

1. Select *Renderer/Setup/Background.* The Background Method dialog box appears.
2. Select **Gradient.**
3. Click on the gradient swatch to the right of the **Gradient** button. The Define Gradient Colors dialog box appears as shown below.
4. Select the top, middle, or bottom swatch at the bottom right of the dialog box.
5. Make changes to the gradient color by selecting the swatch and then changing the color sliders. The changes will be shown in the background preview window at the bottom left of the dialog box.
6. Repeat step 5 for the two remaining gradient colors if necessary.
7. Select **OK** to accept the values and close the dialog box. Select **Cancel** to cancel the command and close the dialog box.
8. Render the scene to see the background effect applied.

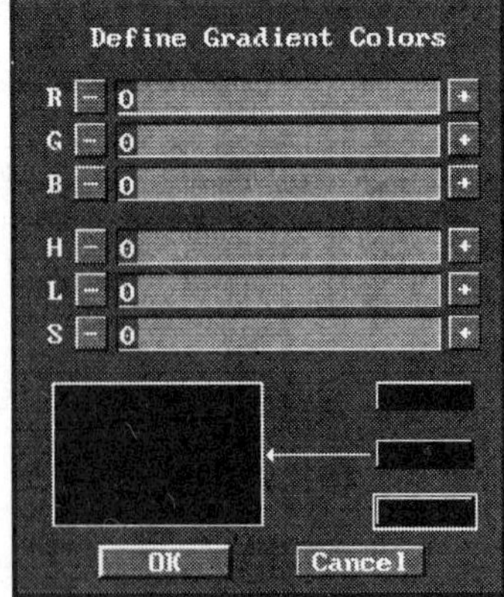

The Define Gradient Colors dialog box.

Selecting a Bitmap Background

1. Select *Renderer/Setup/Background.* The Background Method dialog box appears.
2. Select **Bitmap**.
3. Select the button to the right of the **Bitmap** button. A file selector dialog box appears.
4. Select the bitmap file to used as a background. The Background Method dialog box reappears with the name of the bitmap file on the button.
5. Render the scene to see the bitmap background.

To create interesting animations, use *.flic* files, image file lists, or animated cel files for the background.

TIP

When rendering, if the bitmap resolution does not match the rendering resolution, a warning will be displayed and you will have the option of scaling the background to match the rendering resolution. Scaling the bitmap prior to using it will decrease rendering times.

RELATED COMMAND

Renderer/Render View

Renderer/Setup/Configure

Configures the renderer output device and file type.

Configuring the Renderer

1. Select *Renderer/Setup/Configure*. The Device Configuration dialog box appears as shown below.
2. Make changes as outlined in the sections below.
3. Render the scene to verify the changes.

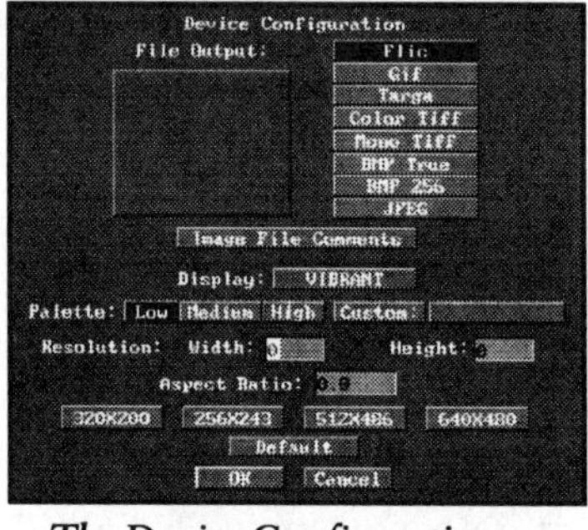

The Device Configuration dialog box.

Configuring the Rendering File Output

1. Select *Renderer/Setup/Configure*. The Device Configuration dialog box is displayed.
2. Make a selection from the **File Output:** options as shown below:

   Flic: Creates a flic file.

   Gif: Creates a graphics interchange format (*.gif*) file.

   Targa: Creates a targa (*.tga*) file.

   Color Tiff: Creates a color tagged image file format (*.tif*) file.

   Mono Tiff: Creates a monochrome tagged image file format (*.tif*) file.

   BMP True: Creates a Microsoft® Windows™ truecolor bitmap (*.bmp*) file.

   BMP 256: Creates a Microsoft® Windows™ 256-color bitmap (*.bmp*) file.

   JPEG: Creates a joint photographic experts group (*.jpg*) file.
3. Click **OK** to accept the selection.

> **NOTE** When saving bitmap files, you have the option of compressing the file. This can degrade the quality of the bitmap if not used properly. Consult the 3D Studio manual for more information on compression.

Adding Comments to a Targa File

1. Select *Renderer/Setup/Configure*. The Device Configuration dialog box is displayed.
2. Select the **Image File Comments** button.
3. Before rendering using *Renderer/Render View* or any other render command, the dialog box shown below will be displayed.
4. Use [Tab] to cycle through the fields to add comments.
5. To view the comments after the rendering has been completed, select **File-File Info.**

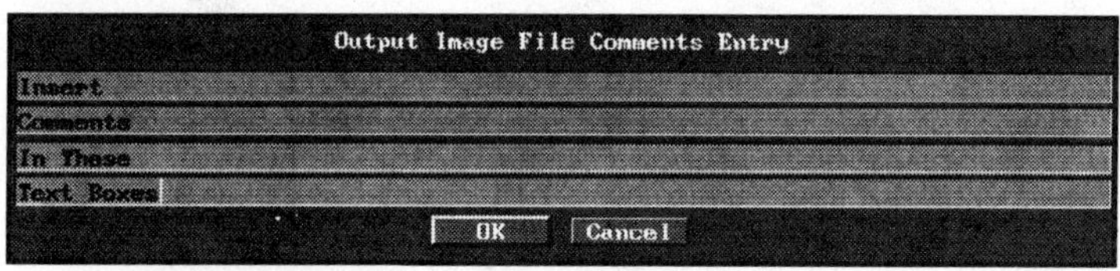

The Output Image File Comments Entry dialog box.

Changing the Rendering Device

1. Select *Renderer/Setup/Configure*. The Device Configuration dialog box is displayed.
2. Select the button to the right of **Display**. The Select Driver dialog box appears as shown below.
3. Select the display device from the list below. The selection will appear in the selection box.

   NULL: Turns off output to the screen. Use this option when rendering to a file with a resolution larger than that of the display. Using the **NULL** settings decreases rendering times.

   RCPADI: Renders to the Autodesk Device Interface combined rendering/display driver.

   RDPADI: Renders to the Autodesk Device Interface rendering display driver.

   VESA: Renders to the VESA display driver.

   VGA320X200: Renders to the VGA320X200 variable graphics array (VGA) driver.

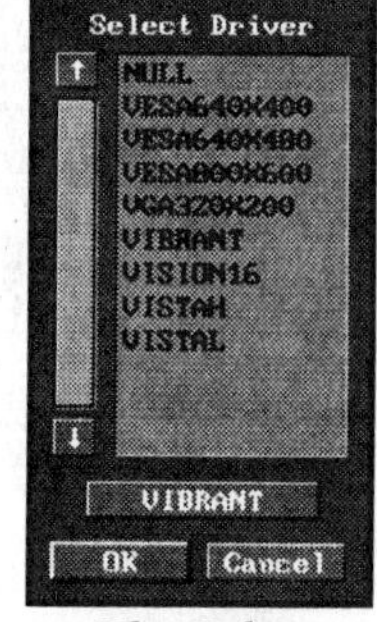

The Select Driver dialog box.

VIBRANT: Renders to the VIBRANT driver.

VISION16: Renders to the Vision Technologies Vision 16 frame grabber.

VISTAH: Renders to the Truevision Vista high-resolution (756x486) frame buffer.

VISTAL: Renders to the Truevision Vista low-resolution (512x468) frame buffer.

4. Click **OK** to accept the selection. The dialog box will be closed and the display device will be shown on the button.

Changing the Palette and Resolution of a Rendering

1. Select *Renderer/Setup/Configure*. The Device Configuration dialog box is displayed.
2. Make the appropriate **Resolution:** settings from the list below.

   Width: Specifies the resolution width of the rendering.

   Height: Specifies the resolution height of the rendering.

   Aspect Ratio: Specifies the aspect ratio for the rendering, which corrects such problems as circles being rendered as ovals.

   320x200: Automatically sets the resolution and aspect ratio for standard VGA devices.

   512x486: Automatically sets the resolution and aspect ratio for Targa devices.

   640x400: Automatically sets the resolution and aspect ratio for VGA.

   600x480: Automatically sets the resolution and aspect ratio for extended mode VGA.

   Default: Changes the resolution and aspect ratio to its default values which are specified in the *3DS.SET* file.

3. Make the appropriate **Palette:** settings as described below. These settings only affect flic files.

   Low: Least accurate but extremely fast, **Low** will create a 256-color palette from the first frame and will apply it to all successive frames.

   Medium: Creates a 256-color palette for each frame of the animation and stores this information. The colors are then averaged to create a final 256-color palette that is applied across the entire animation.

High: Creates a 24-bit color palette for each frame of the animation and stores this information. The colors are then averaged to create a final 256-color palette that is applied across the entire animation. This mode requires a lot of disk space and time.

Custom: Uses a color palette from an existing *.gif*, *.flc* (first frame in the animation), *.cel*, or *.col* file.

4. Click **OK** to accept the selection.

RELATED COMMANDS

Renderer/Render View, Renderer/Setup/Options

Renderer/Setup/Options

Modifies the systems parameters available for rendering.

Modifying Rendering System Parameters

1. Select *Renderer/Setup/Options*. The Render Options dialog box is displayed as shown below.

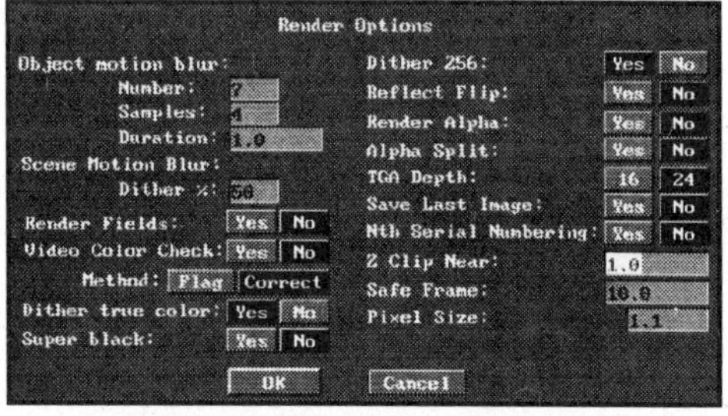

The Render Options dialog box.

2. Make the appropriate changes to the parameters listed below.

Object motion blur: Blurs an object when it is rendered to give it the appearance of movement. Before setting these parameters, ensure that an object has been selected for motion blur with *Object/Motion Blur* in the Keyframer.

Number: Sets the number of copies that the object will be duplicated to produce the blur effect.

Samples: Dithers the motion-blur copies that were specified with the **Number:** setting. The value should be less than or equal to the **Number:** setting.

Duration: Sets the spacing between the original object and its motion-blur copies. This determines the amount of time that the "shutter" is open during the frame.

Scene motion blur: Applies motion blur to the whole scene.

Dither %: Sets the percentage of dither to be used.

Render Fields: Renders to video fields on videotape as opposed to frames in a file.

Video Color Check: Verifies that the color value for pixels is within the safe limits for NTSC and PAL video formats using one of the two methods listed below.

Method:

Flag: Any pixels that fall out of the limits are rendered in black. This allows you to view the incorrect pixels.

Correct: Automatically reduces the pixels to a safe color level.

Dither true color: Performs color and alpha calculation in 64-bit mode before transferring the information to 24- or 32-bit output files.

Super black: Sets the deepest black in the scene to the SUPER BLACK parameter in the *3ds.set* file.

Dither-256: Used only with 256-color VGA, this option dithers colors to smooth out color transitions.

Reflect Flip: When set to **Yes**, reflection maps are flipped.

Render Alpha: Renders Targa files at 32 bits and includes alpha information within file, which increases definition of objects for use with video post.

Alpha Split: Saves the additional information provided by Render-Alpha as a separate file. A rendering with a filename *rocket.tga* would have its alpha information saved in a file with the filename *a_rocket.tga*.

TGA Depth:

16: Creates 16-bit dithered Targa files.

24: Creates 24-bit Targa files.

Save Last Image: Determines whether the last rendering is saved temporarily to disk so that it may be viewed using *Renderer/View/Last* or saved using *Render/View/Save Last*.

Nth Serial Numbering: Sets whether a series of frames rendered with a frame step greater than 1 are sequentially numbered or not.

Z-Clip-Near: Specifies the clipping plane distance from the camera. The value will be determined based on the given units. Change the clipping plane to a value larger than 1 to see inside an object after it is rendered.

Safe Frame: Sets the amount, in percentage, outside the screen for the safe frame. The range of the values is 0 - 100.

Pixel Size: Changes the pixel size from 1.0 to 1.5. A larger value will smooth object edges for use in broadcast-quality renderings.

3. Select **OK** to accept the changes or **Cancel** to cancel the command and close the dialog box.
4. Render the scene.

RELATED COMMANDS

Renderer/Render View, Renderer/Setup/Configure

Paths
Preview
Renderer
Display
Video Post
Setup...
View...
Atmosphere
Background
Configure
Options
Shadows
Make .CUB
Make .VUE

Renderer/Setup/Shadows

Modifies the values of the shadows parameters.

Modifying Shadow Parameters

1. Select *Renderer/Setup/Shadows*. The Global Shadow Control dialog box appears as shown below.
2. Make the appropriate changes to the parameters listed below.

   Map bias: Adjusts the shadow map toward or away from the shadow-casting object(s). The value range is any positive number.

   Ray trace bias: Adjusts the ray trace map toward or away from the shadow-casting object(s) The value range is any positive number.

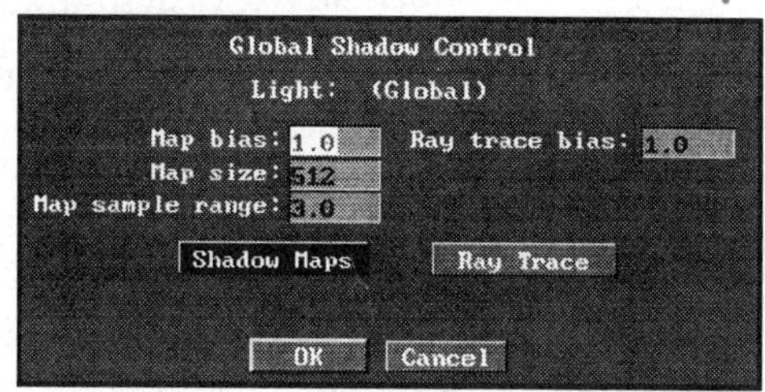

The Global Shadow Control dialog box.

   Map size: Adjusts the size of shadow maps. The value range is 10 to 4096 pixels squared. Increasing this value from the default 512 will take up more memory and may not produce more realistic shadows.

   Map sample range: Adjusts the sharpness of the edge of a shadow map. The value range is 1 (sharp edges) to 5 (softer edges). Values higher than 5 may be used with unpredictable results.

   Shadow Maps: Selects the shadow maps method of producing shadows from the spotlight using the map settings described above. When this selection is chosen, the button will be red.

   Ray Trace: Selects the ray trace method of producing shadows from the spotlight using the **Ray trace bias** setting described above. When this selection is made, the button will be red.

   OK: Accepts the above settings and returns to the Spotlight Definition dialog box.

   Cancel: Cancels the above settings and returns to the Spotlight Definition dialog box.

3. Render the scene to see the adjustments.

RELATED COMMAND

Lights/Spot/Adjust

Renderer/Setup/Make .CUB

Creates six Targa files that make up the cubic environment map from the center of a selected object. It also creates an ASCII file that lists the names of the six Targa files that can be assigned later as a material.

Making a Cubic Environment Map (*.cub*) File

1. Select *Renderer/Setup/Make .CUB*.
2. Click on an object in the active viewport that contains the center of the cubic reflection map. The Generate Cubic Environment Map dialog box appears.
3. Make the appropriate changes to the parameters listed below.

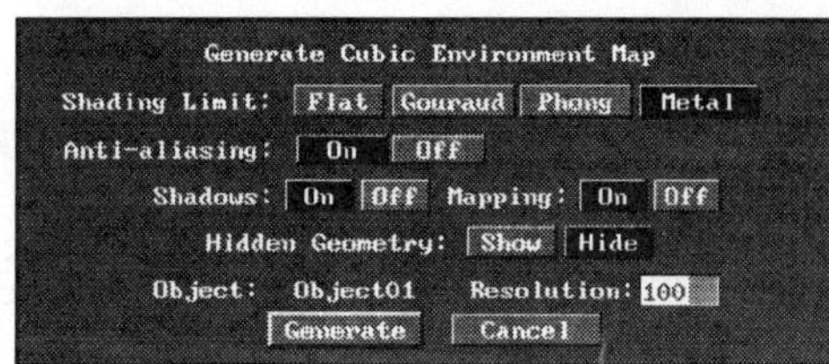

The Generate Cubic Environment Map dialog box.

Shading Limit:

Flat: Renders each face as a single solid color. Useful for quick renderings where very little detail is needed.

Gouraud: Renders each face as a color gradient. Useful for checking light placement and scene composition. No materials, textures, shades, or shadows are displayed.

Phong: Renders each pixel individually using its given surface properties. Phong is required for shading, shadows, bump mapping, transparency, and reflections.

Metal: Renders each pixel and applies a rendering technique that gives each object a metallic look. Metal is required for shading, shadows, bump maps, transparency, and reflections.

Anti-aliasing: Select **On** to prevent “jaggies” in curved lines and diagonal lines in the renderings. Select **Off** only to speed up renderings.

Shadows: Select **On** to cast shadows from spotlights in a scene. Select **Off** if no shadows are needed and to decrease rendering time.

Mapping: Select **On** to use material maps in the reflections. Select **Off** to ignore map materials and to decrease rendering time.

Hidden Geometry: Select **Show** to render hidden objects and visible objects. Use this option to ensure that automatic reflection maps are created. Select **Hide** to render only the objects that are not hidden.

Object: Displays the name of the object selected.

Resolution: Sets the size in pixels of the cubic reflection map. Because this is a cubic reflection map, a value of 200 creates a file with a resolution of 200x200.

4. After setting the parameters, select **Generate.** A file selector will appear.
5. Enter a six-character filename and location for the *.cub* file and click **OK.** The Rendering in Progress dialog box appears and the six files are rendered to disk. They will not appear on the screen. The *.cub* ASCII file is also created.
6. The six files are named using the six characters provided and then ended with the appropriate view descriptions as shown below.

**bk.tga*	Back
**dn.tga*	Bottom (Down)
**ft.tga*	Front
**lf.tga*	Left
**rt.tga*	Right
**tup.tga*	Top (Up)

Using the *.cub* File as a Reflection Map

1. Activate the Materials Editor.
2. Select the **Reflection Map** button for a material. A file selector will appear.
3. Select the *.cub* file as the reflection map and click on.
4. The *.cub* file will appear on the reflection map button.
5. Render the scene.

RELATED COMMAND

Renderer/Render View

Renderer/Setup/Make .VUE

Creates a *.vue* file for an animation or parts of an animation. The *.vue* file is an ASCII file that contains keyframe instructions that can be used during command-line rendering. An example of a *.vue* file is displayed below.

Creating a .VUE file

1. Prepare an animation.
2. Select *Renderer/Setup/Make. VUE.*
3. Select the viewport where the animation will be created. The Render Animation dialog box will appear.
4. Adjust all settings in this dialog box and click on **OK**. The Write Render File: dialog box will appear.
5. Select a filename and a location and click on. The *.vue* file will be created. A sample vue vile is displayed below.

```
VERSION 201

frame 0
light "Light01"" 1093.281 -1229.6401 801.1708 1 1 1
transform "Pole" 1 0 0 0 1 0 0 0 1 -21.0224 -0.0126 168.7838
transform "toprope" 0.2868 0.8997 -0.3292 -0.5134 0.4344
0.7401 0.8088 -0.0432 0.5865 -7.5334 0.7991 426.3702
morph "FLAG0000" 1 "FLAG0000" 1 1 0 0 0 1 0 0 0 1 100 -
0.0175 356.1042
transform "bottomrope" 0.6538 0.5974 -0.4644 -0.5107 -
0.1045 -0.8534 -0.5583 0.7951 0.2368 -12.0565 -0.7304
264.6165
camera 354.0347 -567.3524 148.1592 70.633 -12.9646 343.2453
0 53.2488

frame 1
light "Light01" 1093.281 -1229.6401 801.1708 1 1 1
transform "Pole" 1 0 0 0 1 0 0 0 1 -21.0224 -0.0126 168.7838
transform "toprope" 0.2868 0.8997 -0.3292 -0.5134 0.4344
0.7401 0.8088 -0.0432 0.5865 -7.5334 0.7991 426.3702
morph "FLAG0000" 3 "FLAG0000" 0.4063 "FLAG0001" 0.6875
```

RELATED COMMAND

Renderer/Setup/Configure

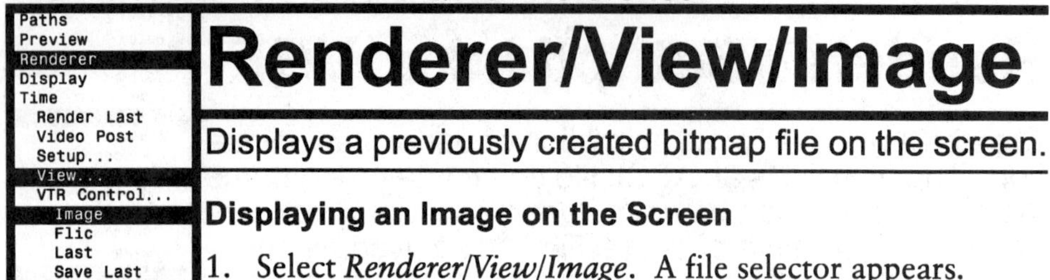

Renderer/View/Image

Displays a previously created bitmap file on the screen.

Displaying an Image on the Screen

1. Select *Renderer/View/Image*. A file selector appears.
2. Select the bitmap file to be viewed and click on **OK**.
3. If the bitmap file resolution matches or is lower than the screen display resolution, it will be displayed on the screen.
4. If the bitmap resolution is greater, the dialog box shown below will be displayed.

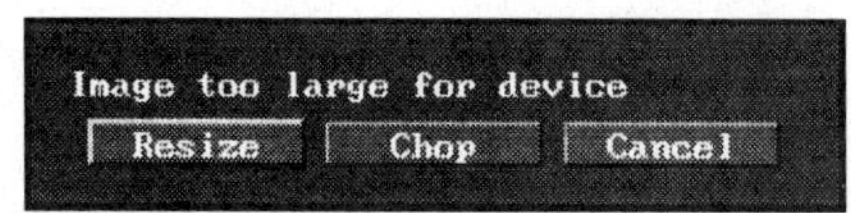

The Image too large for device warning box.

5. Select **Resize** to modify the resolution of the image to match that of the display device resolution.
6. Select **Chop** to display only the upper left corner of the image. Select **Cancel** to quit the command.
7. If the image is not within the map path, the dialog box shown below is displayed. This is a reminder that to display the image in the scene, the assigned bitmap must be in the map path. Use the *Info-Configure* pull-down menu and add the path of the bitmap.

A warning displayed if the bitmap is not found in the map-path or image-path directories.

8. Press [Esc] or right-click to return to the viewport display.

RELATED COMMANDS

Info-Configure, Program-Image Browser, Renderer/View/Flic, Renderer/View/Last

Paths
Preview
Renderer
Display
Time
Render Last
Video Post
Setup...
View...
VTR Control...
Image
Flic
Last
Save Last

Renderer/View/Flic

Displays a previously created animation on the screen.

Displaying and Animation

1. Select *Renderer/View/Flic*. The Select Flic File to Load dialog box appears.
2. Select the animation file to be viewed and click on **OK**. The animation will be played on the screen.
3. Use the following keys to control the animation.

Key	Action
→	Increases playback speed.
←	Decreases playback speed.
↑	Return to default speed (20 fps).
↓	Pause/Resume playback.
→ .	Frame by Frame (during pause only).
Esc	Exit playback and return to viewport display.

TIP To view 320x200 VGA animations without loading 3D Studio, use the *AAPLAY.EXE* program found in the 3DS4 subdirectory.

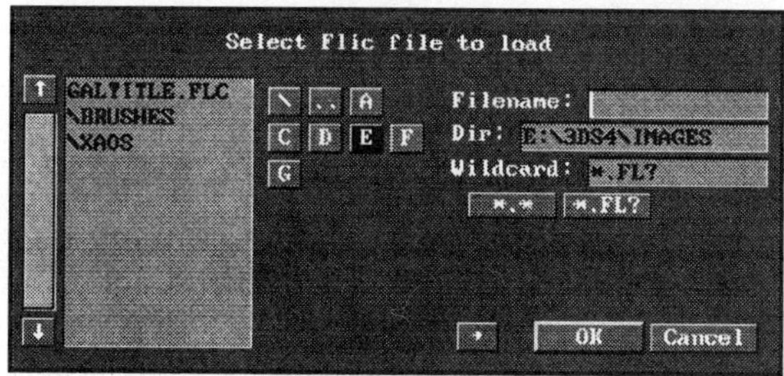

The Select Flic File to Load dialog box.

RELATED COMMAND

Renderer/View/Image

```
Paths
Preview
Renderer
Display
Time
  Render Last
  Video Post
  Setup...
  View...
  VTR Control...
    Image
    Flic
    Last
    Save Last
```

Renderer/View/Last

Displays the last rendered image.

Displaying the Last Rendered Image

1. Ensure that a render has been performed and that the Save-Last-Image parameter is set to **Yes** in the Render Options dialog box displayed using *Renderer/Setup/Options.*
2. Select *Renderer/View/Last.* The last rendering will be displayed on the current configured display device.
3. Press Esc or right-click to return to the viewport display.

RELATED COMMAND

Renderer/View/Flic

Paths
Preview
Renderer
Display
Time
Render Last
Video Post
Setup...
View...
VTR Control...
Image
Flic
Last
Save Last

Renderer/View/Save Last

Saves the last rendered image to a specified filename and location.

Saving the Last Rendered Image

1. Ensure that a render has been performed and that the Save-Last-Image parameter is set to Yes in the Render Options dialog box displayed using *Renderer/Setup/Options*.
2. Select *Renderer/View/Save Last*. The Save last image to file dialog box is displayed.
3. Select the format you want to save the image to. Enter a filename and location for the image file. Choose a file output format and select **OK**. The image file will be saved.

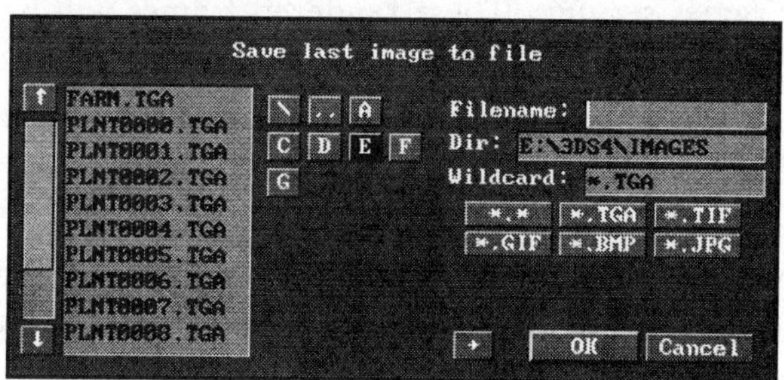

The Save last image to file dialog box.

RELATED COMMAND

Renderer/View/Last

Paths
Preview
Renderer
Display
Time
Video Post
Setup...
View...
VTR Control...
VTR Setup
Set Inpoint
Control
Record
Disk-to-VTR

Renderer/VTR Control/VTR Setup

Initializes a videotape recorder (VTR) and displays the VTR Setup dialog box.

Using the VTR Dialog box

1. Ensure that a VTR is connected to the rendering station.
2. Select *Renderer/VTR Control/VTR Setup*. The VTR Setup dialog box is displayed as shown below.
3. Make adjustments as described below.

   Frame Repeat #: Sets the number of times to repeat the rendering of each frame to videotape.

   Heads: Select **Use** to render the first frame the number of times specified in the **Frames** setting. These rendered frames will be placed at the beginning of the animation.

   Tails: Select **Use** to render the last frame the number of times specified in **Frames.** These rendered frames will be placed at the end of the animation.

   Frames: Specifies the number of times to copy a **Heads** or **Tails** frame.

   Initialize: Initializes the VTR and checks for proper configuration of the VTR device.
4. Select **OK** to accept the settings or **Cancel** to cancel the settings and exit the dialog box.

A videotape recorder must be installed and configured before this command can be used.

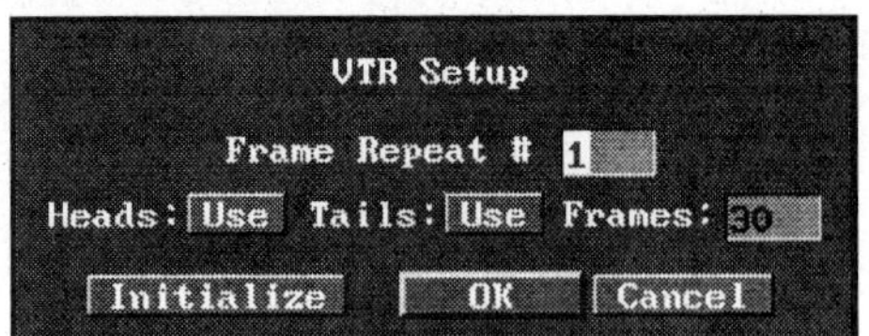

The VTR Setup dialog box.

RELATED COMMAND

Renderer/VTR Control/Record

Renderer/VTR Control/Set Inpoint

Paths
Preview
Renderer
Display
Time
Video Post
Setup...
View...
VTR Control...
VTR Setup
Set Inpoint
Control
Record
Disk-to-VTR

Determines the point in time that the animation is to be recorded on the VTR.

Using the Set Inpoint Option

1. Ensure that a VTR has been installed and configured properly.
2. Select *Renderer/VTR Control/Set Inpoint.*
3. Make settings as described below.

   Hr:Min:Sec: Enter the start point on the video tape in time.

   Current Frame: Click on this button to set the above time from the current frame on the VTR.
4. Select **OK** to accept the settings. Select **Cancel** to cancel the settings and close the dialog box.

RELATED COMMAND

Renderer/VTR Control/Control

Paths
Preview
Renderer
Display
Time
Video Post
Setup...
View...
VTR Control...
VTR Setup
Set Inpoint
Control
Record
Disk-to-VTR

Renderer/VTR Control/Control

Displays the VTR interactive controller dialog box. Use this box to control the attached VTR from 3D Studio.

Using the VTR Control Dialog Box

1. Ensure that a VTR has been installed and configured properly.
2. Select *Renderer/VTR Control/Control.* The VTR Control dialog box appears.
3. Adjust the VTR using the following options.

   Current Location: Displays the current location of the tape in the VTR

   Go to: Modify the settings under this button and then click on this button to jump to that point on the videotape.

   <<<: Rewinds the tape.

   <: Move back one frame.

   >: Move forward one frame.

   >>: Plays the tape.

   >>>: Fast forwards the tape.

   STOP: Stops the current operation.
4. Select **Close** to close the dialog box and return to 3D Studio.

RELATED COMMAND

Renderer/VTR Control/Set Inpoint

Paths
Preview
Renderer
Display
Time
Video Post
Setup...
View...
VTR Control...
VTR Setup
Set Inpoint
Control
Record
Disk-to-VTR

Renderer/VTR Control/Record

Renders the specified animation to the VTR.

Recording the Animation to VTR

1. Ensure that a VTR has been installed and configured properly.
2. Select *Renderer/VTR Control/Record.* The Render Animation dialog box appears. Make all necessary adjustments. See *Renderer/Render/Render View* for a full description of each option.
3. Click on **Render**. The animation is rendered to the VTR.

RELATED COMMANDS

Renderer/VTR Control/Control, Renderer/VTR Control/Set Inpoint

Paths
Preview
Renderer
Display
Time
Video Post
Setup...
View...
VTR Control...
VTR Setup
Set Inpoint
Control
Record
Disk-to-VTR

Renderer/VTR Control/Disk-to-VTR

Transfers a series of bitmap files to videotape.

Transferring Bitmaps to a VTR to create an Animation

1. Ensure that a VTR has been installed and configured properly.
2. Select *Renderer/VTR Control/Disk-to-VTR*. A file selector appears.
3. Select the first sequentially numbered file in the subdirectory that contains all of the sequentially numbered files. For example, the first filename may be *test001.tga*. All other files with the *test* prefix, and the trailing numerical sequence, will be rendered to the VTR. A list of the files might look like this: *test001.tga, test002.tga, test003.tga, test004.tga* and so on. Alternately, you can select an image file list (*.ifl*) file that lists the bitmaps to be transferred to the VTR. Once the files are selected, the Disk-to-VTR Control dialog box is displayed.
4. Specify the number of times the animation is to be "looped" or repeated on the VTR and click **OK**, or click **Cancel** to cancel the command and close the dialog box.

> **NOTE** If you select an image list file, be sure to only list the bitmap file names and not the location. Then be sure that the location of these bitmaps are in the Image and Map path parameters.

RELATED COMMANDS

Renderer/VTR Control/Control, Renderer/VTR Control/Set Inpoint

Preview
Renderer
Display
Time
Hide...
Unhide...
Geometry...
Constr...
Object
All
By Name
By Color
Lights
Cameras

Display/Hide/Object

Hides an object in all viewports.

Hiding an Object

1. Ensure that an object has been created previously.
2. Select *Display/Hide/Object*.
3. In any viewport, select the object to be hidden. That object will be hidden in all viewports. If the object has children, the Hide Object dialog box will appear as shown below. Select **Yes** to hide the children with the parent object, select **No** to hide the parent object only.
4. To redisplay the hidden object, select *Display/Unhide/By Name*.

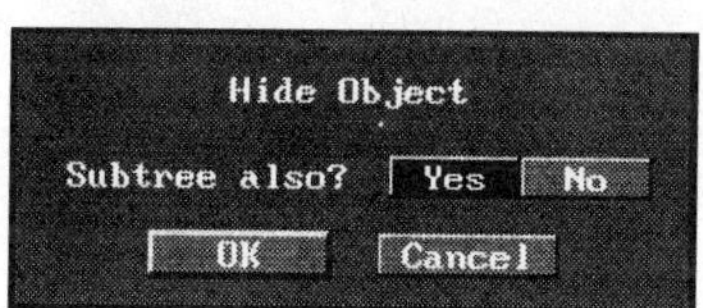

The Hide Object dialog box.

RELATED COMMAND

Display/Unhide/By Name

Preview
Renderer
Display
Time
Hide...
Unhide...
Geometry...
Constr...
Object
All
By Name
By Color
Lights
Cameras

Display/Hide/All

Hides all geometry in all viewports.

Hiding all Objects

1. Ensure that geometry has been created previously.
2. Select *Display/Hide/All*. All geometry is hidden in all viewports.
3. To redisplay the hidden element, select *Display/Unhide/All*.

RELATED COMMAND

Display/Unhide/All

Display/Hide/By Name

Hides objects by selecting their names.

Hiding an Object by Selecting its name

1. Ensure that an object has been created previously.
2. Select *Display/Hide/By Name*. The Hide Objects: dialog box appears as shown below.
3. Select the object(s) in the dialog box to be hidden or use the following: options.

   All: Selects all objects in the list.

   None: Deselects all objects in the list.

   Tag: Place the wild card pattern in the text box above this button. Click on the **Tag** button. All objects that match the wild card will be selected.

   Untag: Place the wild card pattern in the text box above this button. Click on the **Untag** button. All objects that match the wild card will be deselected.

   Subtree: Click on this button to hide the child objects if the object itself is a parent object.
4. Select **OK** to accept the selection and close the dialog box. The objects selected will be hidden in all viewports.
5. Select **Cancel** to cancel the command and exit the dialog box.

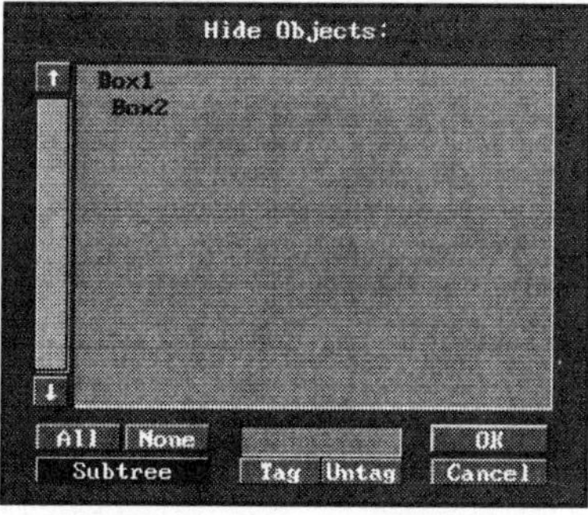

The Hide Objects dialog box.

RELATED COMMAND

Display/Unhide/By Name

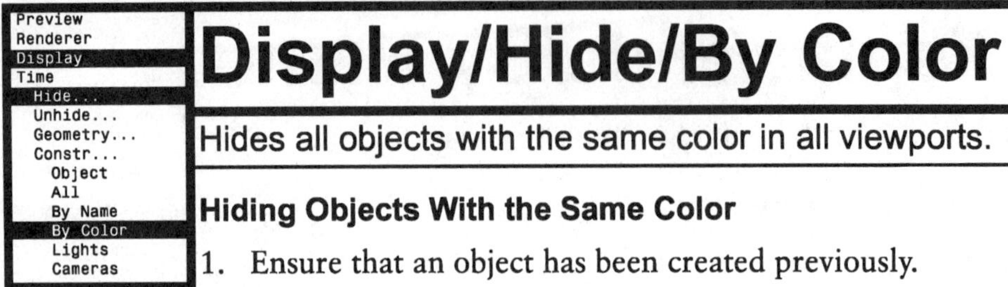

Display/Hide/By Color

Hides all objects with the same color in all viewports.

Hiding Objects With the Same Color

1. Ensure that an object has been created previously.
2. Select *Display/Hide/Color*.
3. In any viewport, select the object to be hidden. That object will be hidden in all viewports as will any other objects that are the same color.
4. To redisplay the hidden objects, select *Display/Unhide/By Color*.

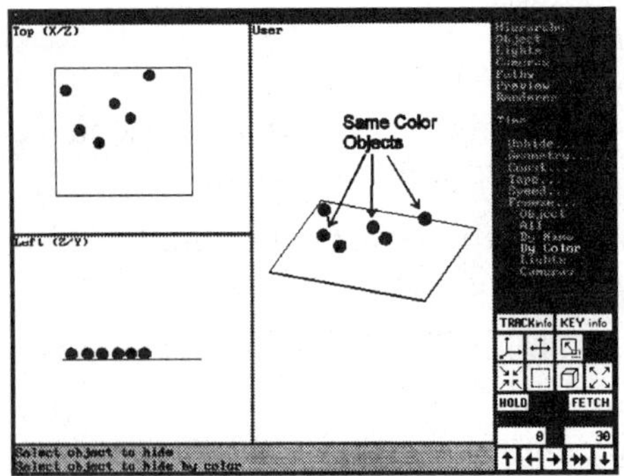

Before hiding by color.

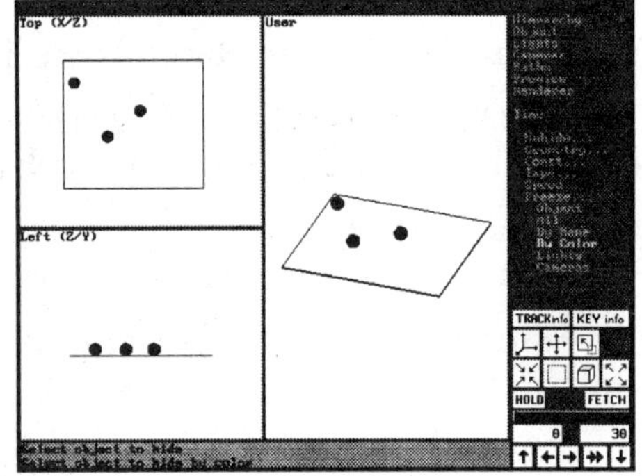

After hiding by color.

RELATED COMMANDS

Display/Unhide/By Color, Modify/Object/Change Color

Preview
Renderer
Display
Time
Hide...
Unhide...
Geometry...
Constr...
Object
All
By Name
By Color
Lights
Cameras

Display/Hide/Lights

Hides all light icons in all viewports.

Hiding Light Icons

1. Ensure that lights have been created previously.
2. Select *Display/Hide/Lights*. All light icons are hidden in all viewports.
3. To redisplay the light icon, select *Display/Unhide/Lights*.

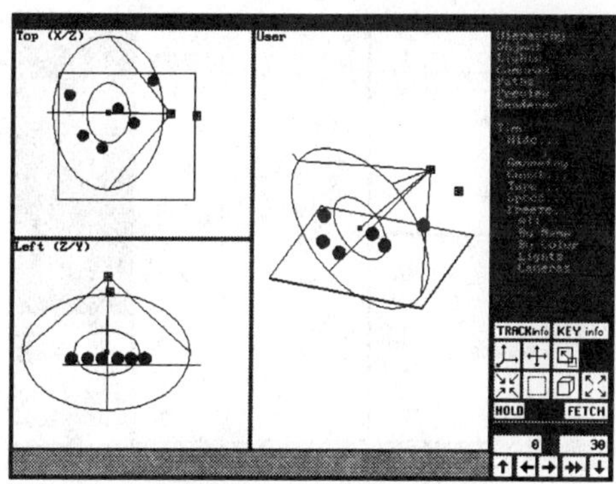

Light icons displayed.

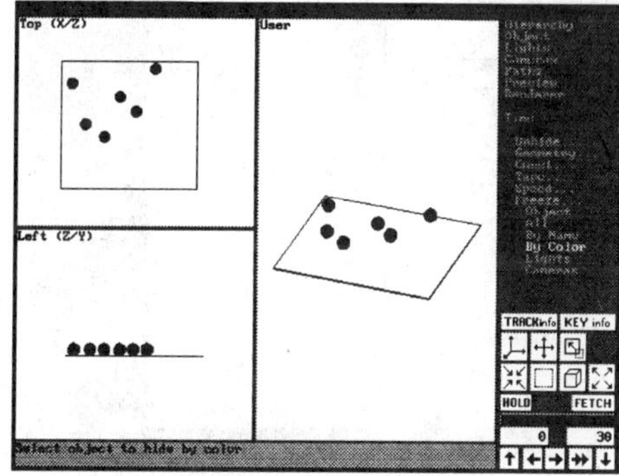

Light icons hidden.

Hiding the light icon does not turn the light off. Use *Lights/Omni/Adjust* or *Lights/Spot/Adjust* to turn off lights.

RELATED COMMAND

Display/Unhide/Lights

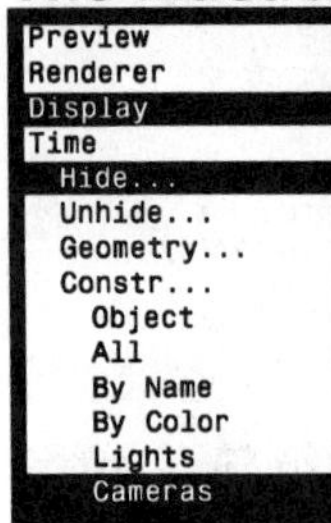

Display/Hide/Cameras

Hides all camera icons in all viewports.

Hiding Camera Icons

1. Ensure that a camera has been created previously.
2. Select *Display/Hide/Camera*. All camera icons are hidden in all viewports.
3. To redisplay the camera icon, select *Display/Unhide/Camera*.

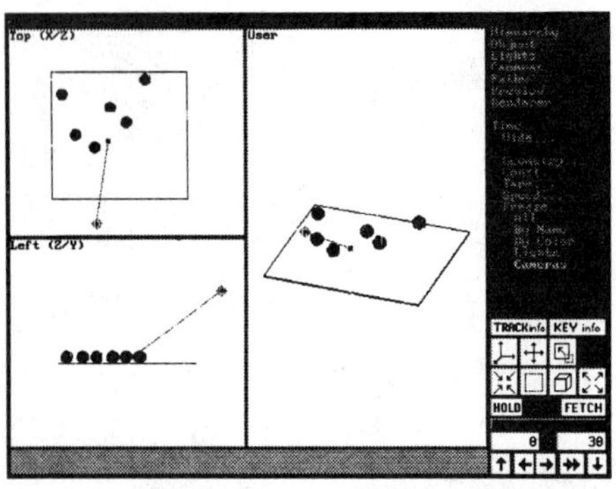

Displaying the camera icon.

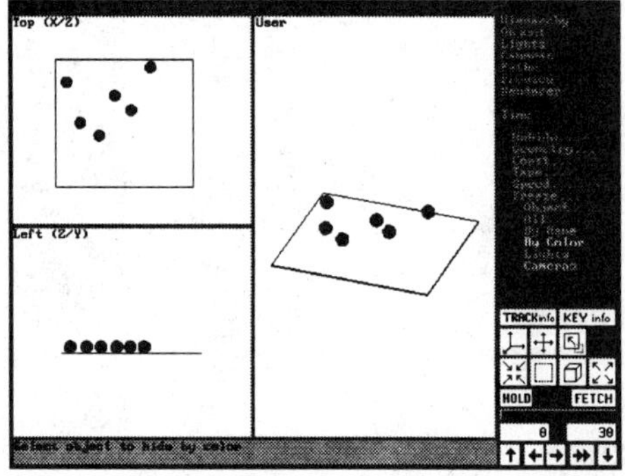

Hiding the camera icon.

Hiding the camera icon does not disable it. The camera view can still be seen in a viewport or used for rendering.

RELATED COMMAND

Display/Unhide/Lights

Display/Unhide/All

Preview
Renderer
Display
Time
Hide...
Unhide...
Geometry...
Constr...
Tape...
All
By Name
By Color
Lights
Cameras

Redisplays all hidden geometry in all viewports.

Unhiding All Objects

1. Ensure that geometry has been previously hidden.
2. Select *Display/Unhide/All.* All geometry is redisplayed in all viewports.

RELATED COMMAND

Display/Hide/All

Preview
Renderer
Display
Time
Hide...
Unhide...
Geometry...
Constr...
Tape...
All
By Name
By Color
Lights
Cameras

Display/Unhide/By Name

Redisplays all hidden geometry by selected its names.

Unhiding an Object by Selecting its Name

1. Ensure that an object has been previously hidden.
2. Select *Display/Unhide/By Name*. The Unhide Objects: dialog box appears as shown below.
3. Select the object(s) in the dialog box to be redisplayed or use the following options:

   All: Selects all objects in the list.

   None: Deselects all objects in the list.

   Tag: Place the wild card pattern in the text box above this button. Click on the **Tag** button. All objects that match the wild card will be selected.

   Untag: Place the wild card pattern in the text box above this button. Click on the **Untag** button. All objects that match the wild card will be deselected.

   Subtree: Click on this button to hide the child objects if the object itself is a parent object.
4. Select **OK** to accept the selection and close the dialog box. The objects selected will be redisplayed in all viewports.
5. Select **Cancel** to cancel the command and exit the dialog box.

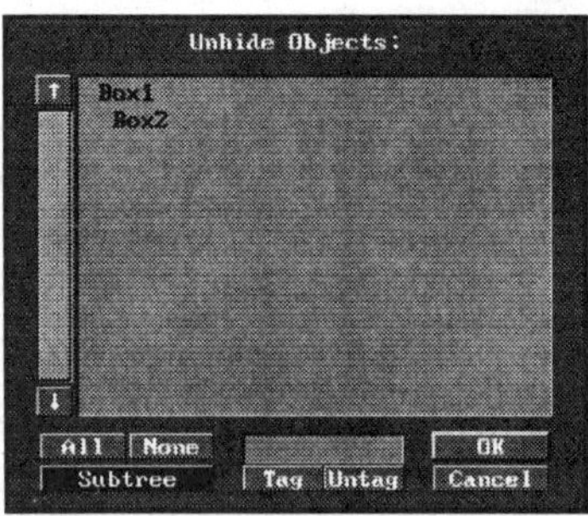

The Unhide Objects dialog box.

RELATED COMMAND

Display/Hide/By Name

Display/Unhide/By Color

Redisplays all objects previously hidden with the same color in all viewports.

Unhiding Objects With the Same Color

1. Ensure that geometry has been created previously.
2. Select *Display/Unhide/By Color*. The Unhide Object(s): object palette dialog box appears as shown below.
3. Select the color that matches the color of the object(s) to be redisplayed.
4. Select **OK** to accept the selection and close the dialog box. All hidden objects that match the color selected will be redisplayed in all viewports.
5. Select **Cancel** to cancel the command and exit the dialog box.

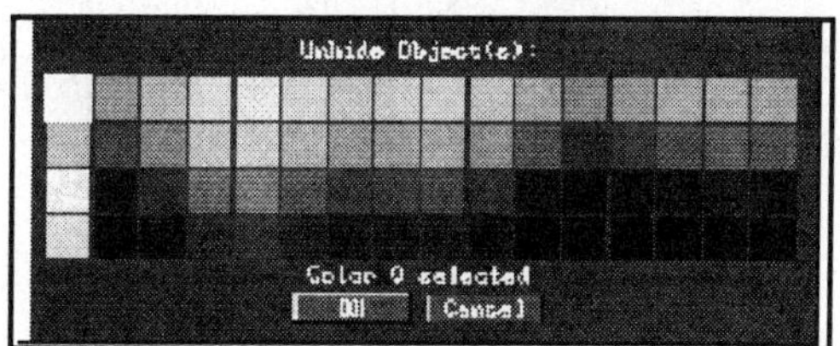

The Unhide Objects dialog box.

RELATED COMMANDS

Display/Hide/By Color, Modify/Object/Change Color

Display/Unhide/Lights

Redisplays all light icons in all viewports.

Unhiding all Light Icons

1. Ensure that lights have been hidden previously.
2. Select *Display/Unhide/Lights*. All light icons are redisplayed in all viewports.

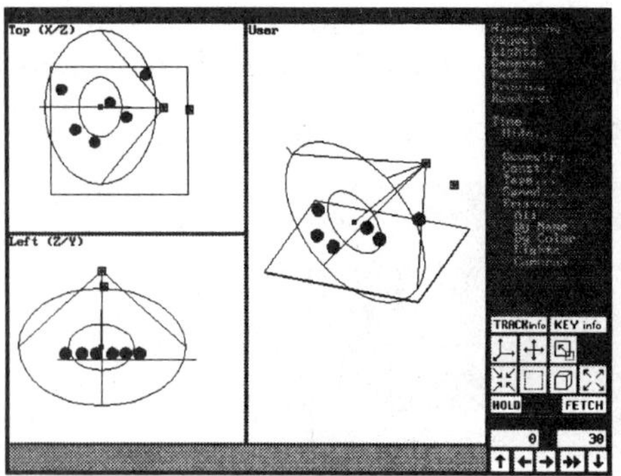

Light icons displayed.

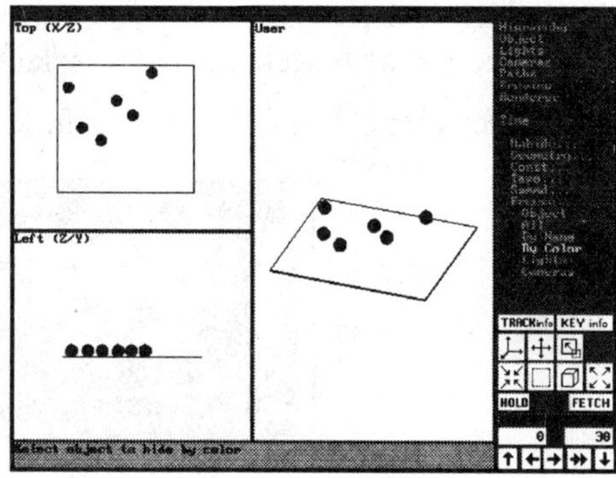

Light icons hidden.

Unhiding the light icon does not turn the light on. Use *Lights/Omni/Adjust* or *Lights/Spot/Adjust* to turn off lights.

RELATED COMMAND

Display/Hide/Lights

Display/Unhide/Cameras

Preview
Renderer
Display
Time
Hide...
Unhide...
Geometry...
Constr...
Tape...
All
By Name
By Color
Lights
Cameras

Redisplays all camera icons in all viewports.

Unhiding all Camera Icons

1. Ensure a camera icon has been hidden previously.
2. Select *Display/Unhide/Camera*. All camera icons are redisplayed in all viewports.

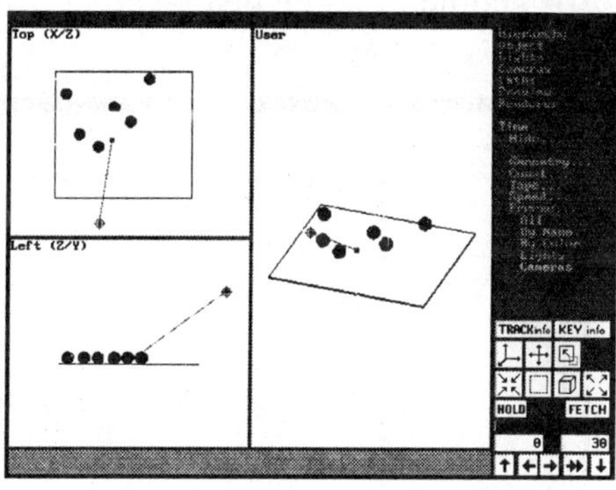

Displaying the camera icon.

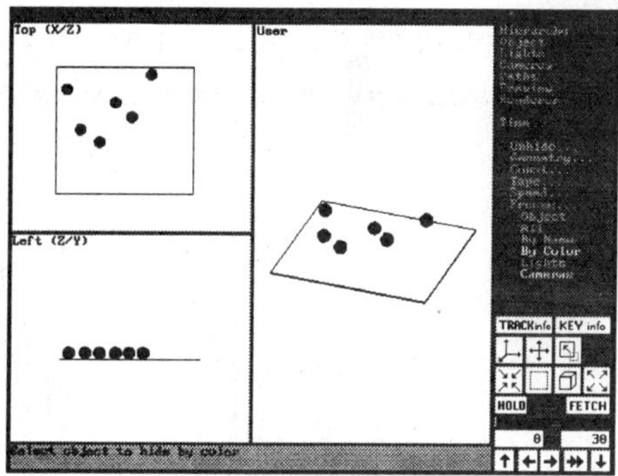

Hiding the camera icon.

RELATED COMMAND

Display/Hide/Cameras

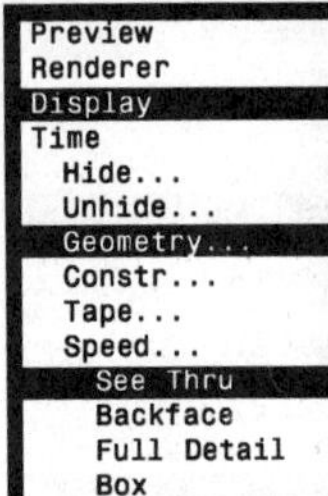

Display/Geometry/See Thru

Displays all edges of all geometry in all viewports.

Displaying the Edges of All Geometry

1. Ensure that geometry has been created previously.
2. Select *Display/Geometry/See Thru.* All geometry will be displayed in the viewports with all backfaces on.

> **TIP** Use *Display/Geometry/All Lines* and *Display/Geometry/Edges Only* to modify the amount of geometry to be displayed and to decrease regeneration time.

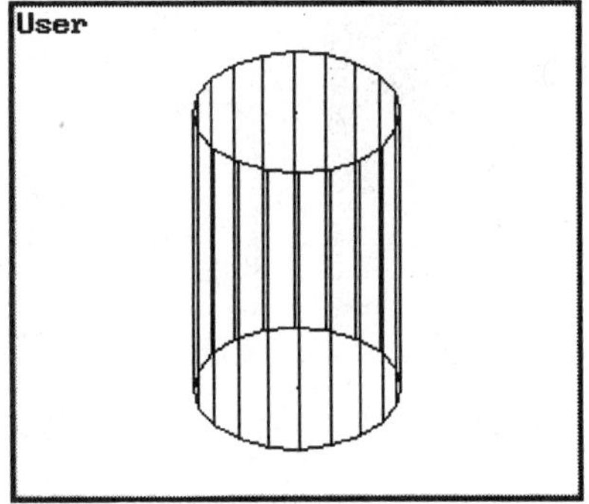

Geometry displayed with all edges shown.

RELATED COMMANDS

Display/Geometry/Backface, Display/Geometry/See Thru

Preview
Renderer
Display
Time
Hide...
Unhide...
Geometry...
Constr...
Tape...
Speed...
See Thru
Backface
Full Detail
Box

Display/Geometry/Backface

Displays all faces that are facing the viewport. Hides all faces that are facing away from the viewport (backfaces).

Hiding the Backface of Geometry

1. Ensure that geometry has been created previously.
2. Select *Display/Geometry/Backface*. All backfaces will be turned off as shown in the figure below.

> **TIP** Use *Display/Geometry/All Lines* and *Display/Geometry/Edges Only* to modify the amount of geometry to be displayed and to decrease regeneration time.

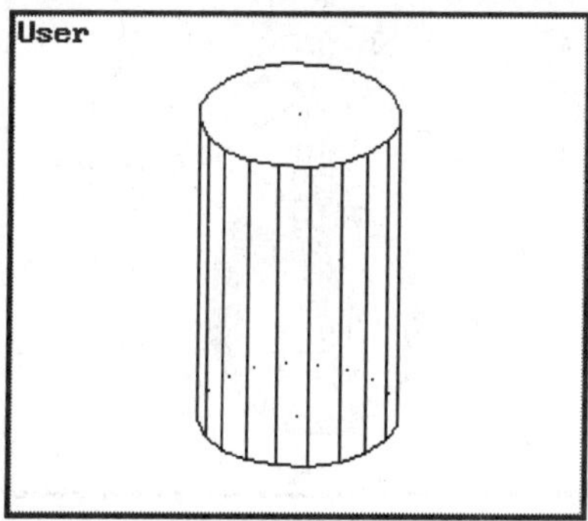

Geometry displayed with backfaces hidden.

RELATED COMMANDS

Display/Geometry/See Thru, Display/Geometry/See Thru

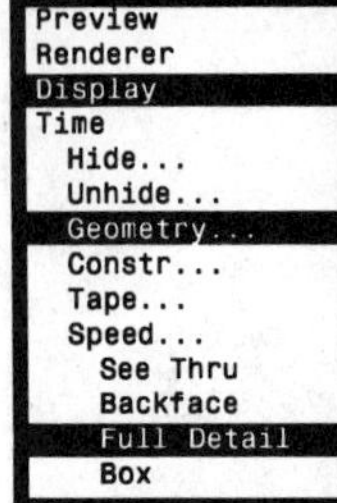

Display/Geometry/Full Detail

Displays geometry with all vertices, edges, faces, and elements.

Displaying Geometry in Full Detail

1. Ensure that geometry has been created previously.
2. Select *Display/Geometry/Full Detail.* The objects are displayed with vertices, edges, faces, and all elements.

Viewing geometry using this mode will increase regeneration times.

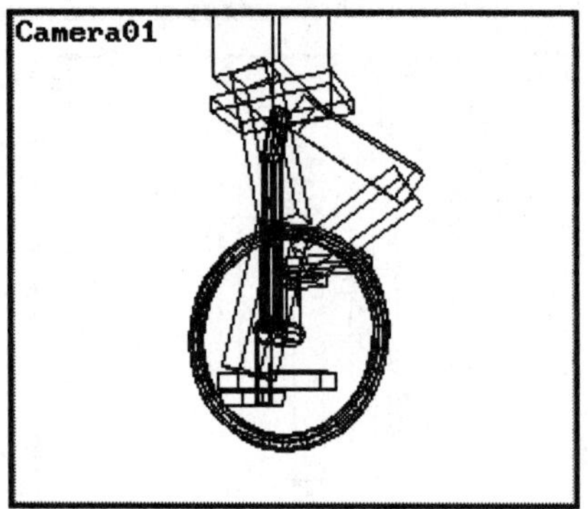

Geometry displayed in full detail.

RELATED COMMANDS

Display/Geometry/Box, Display/Speed

Display/Geometry/Box

Displays geometry in box mode.

Preview
Renderer
Display
Time
Hide...
Unhide...
Geometry...
Constr...
Tape...
Speed...
See Thru
Backface
Full Detail
Box

Displaying Geometry in Box Mode

1. Ensure that geometry has been created previously and is being displayed with vertices, edges, or faces.
2. Select *Display/Geometry/Box*. The objects are displayed in box mode.

NOTE The box represents the bounding box of the object. If the object is rendered it will not be rendered as a box but in its original shape.

TIP Using this mode dramatically decreases regeneration time but does not allow for vertex adjustment or modification. Use this command for tasks that do not require displaying vertices, such as camera/ light placement, arranging objects in a scene, or viewport configuration.

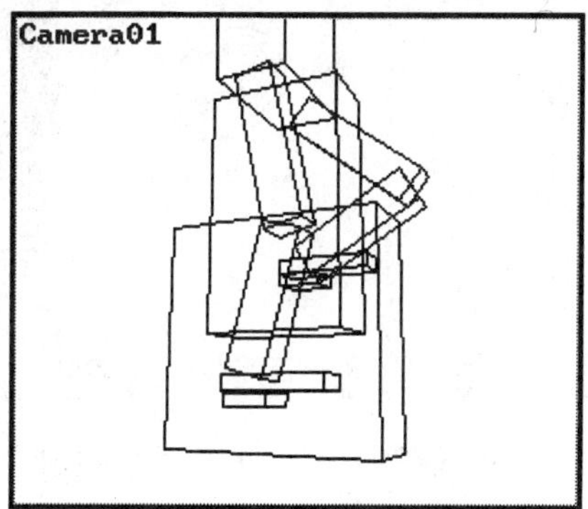

Geometry displayed in the box mode.

RELATED COMMANDS

Display/Geometry/Full Detail, Display/Speed

Preview
Renderer
Display
Time
Hide...
Unhide...
Geometry...
Constr...
Tape...
Speed...
Place
Show
Hide
Home

Display/Constr/Place

Changes the location of the construction planes.

Placing the Construction Plane

1. Select *Display/Constr/Place*.
2. Activate an orthographic viewport where the construction plane is to be moved.
3. Select a point in the viewport to represent the intersection of the two planes being placed. Black crosshairs will appear in all orthographic viewports representing the intersection of the two planes displayed in the appropriate viewport. Example: In the top viewport, the X (horizontal) and Z (vertical) plane intersection is displayed.

This command affects the 3D Editor and the 3D Lofter construction planes.

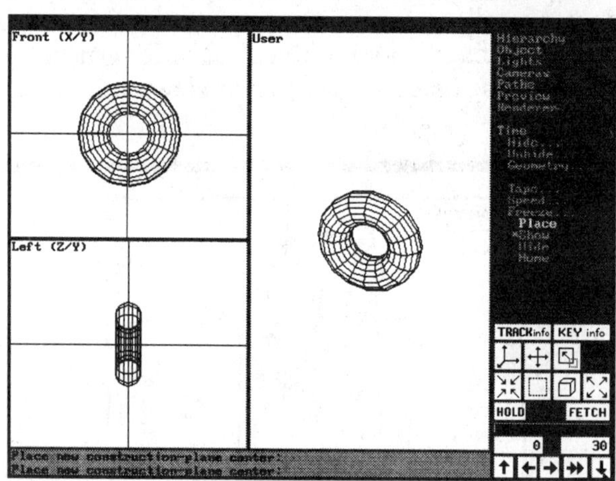

Placing the construction plane in the center of the torus.

RELATED COMMANDS

Display/Constr/Show, Display/Constr/Hide, Display/Constr/Home

Display/Constr/Show

Preview
Renderer
Display
Time
  Hide...
  Unhide...
  Geometry...
  Constr...
  Tape...
  Speed...
    Place
    Show
    Hide
    Home

Displays the construction plane in the orthographic viewports.

Displaying the Construction Planes

1. Use *Display/Constr/Place* to set the location of the construction plane if necessary.
2. Select *Display/Constr/Show*. The construction plan and crosshairs appear in all orthographic viewports and an asterisk (*) appears next to the command.

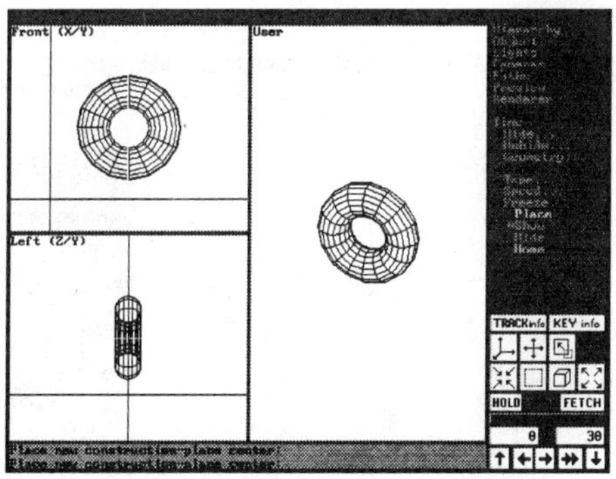

The construction plane is displayed.

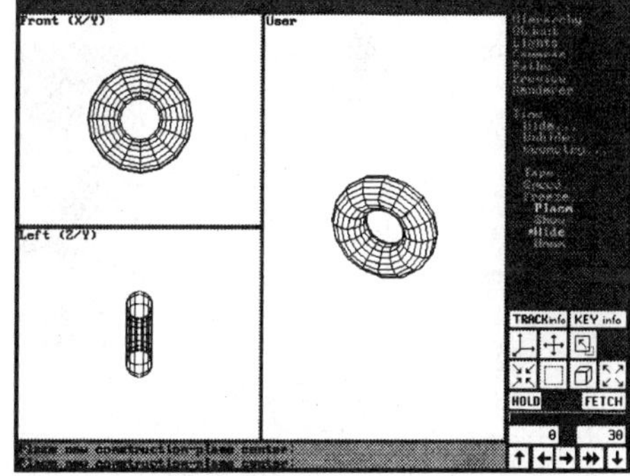

The construction plane is hidden.

RELATED COMMANDS

Display/Constr/Place, Display/Constr/Hide, Display/Constr/Home

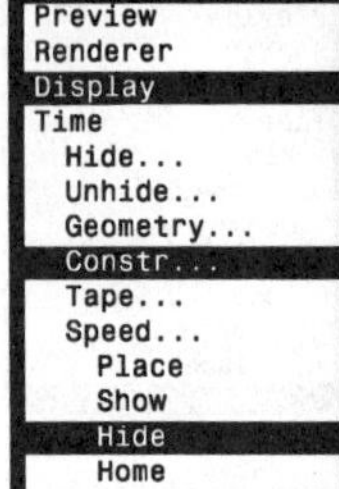

Display/Constr/Hide

Hides the construction plane in the orthographic viewports.

Hiding the Construction Planes

1. Ensure that the construction planes are displayed using *Display/Constr/Show* or that they are placed by using *Display/Constr/Place*.
2. Select *Display/Constr/Hide*. The construction plan crosshairs disappear in all orthographic viewports and an asterisk (*) appears next to the command.

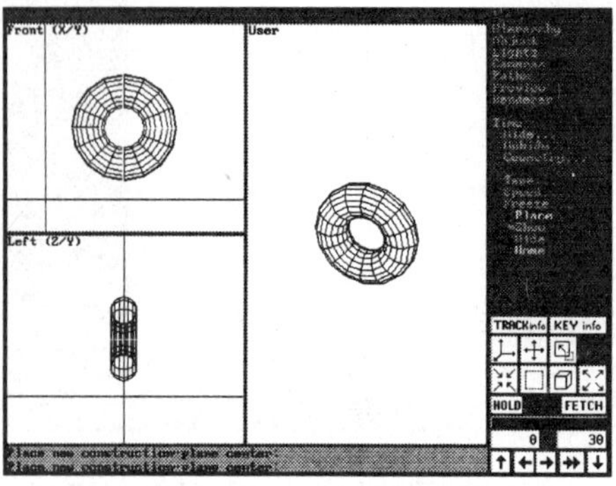

The construction plane is displayed.

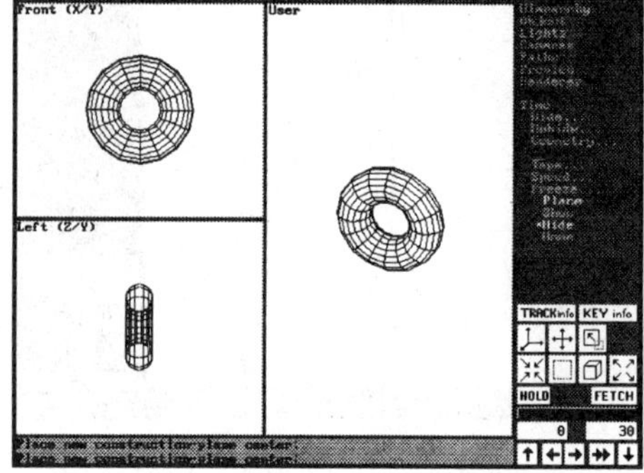

The construction plane is hidden.

RELATED COMMANDS

Display/Constr/Place, Display/Constr/Show, Display/Constr/Home

Display/Constr/Home

Moves the construction plane back to its default (home) position at coordinates 0,0,0.

Moving the Construction Plane to the Default Position

1. Ensure that the construction planes were previously moved from their default location using *Display/Constr/Place*.
2. Select *Display/Constr/Home*. The construction planes crosshairs return to their default position.

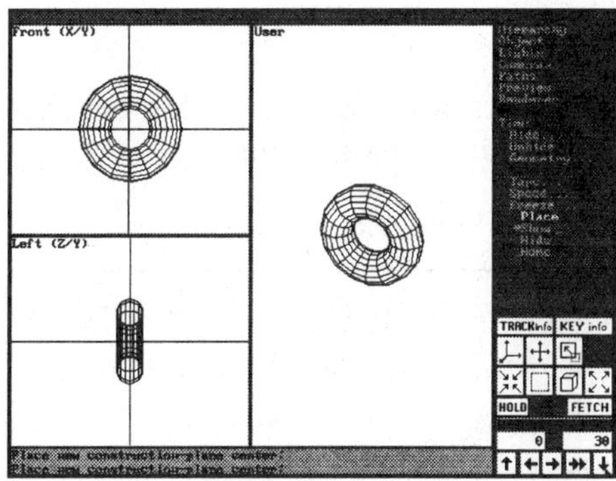

The construction plane located in the center of the torus.

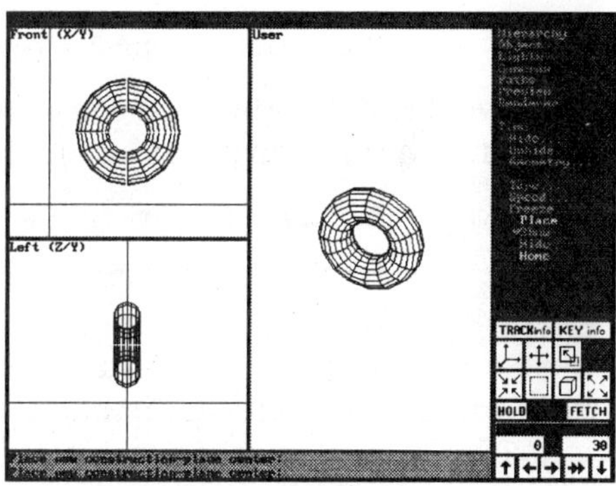

Relocating the construction plane to its home position.

RELATED COMMANDS

Display/Constr/Place, Display/Constr/Show, Display/Constr/Hide

Renderer
Display
Time
Unhide...
Geometry...
Constr...
Tape...
Speed...
Freeze...
Move
Find
Show
Hide
Toggle Vsnap

Display/Tape/Move

Adjusts or moves the Tape Measure icon.

Adjusting the Tape Measure Icon

1. Ensure that the Tape Measure icon is displayed in an orthographic viewport using *Display/Tape/Show*.
2. Select *Display/Tape/Move*.
3. Select the orthographic viewport where the tape measure icon is to be adjusted.
4. Select either end of the Tape Measure icon.
5. Move the end of the Tape Measure icon to its new location and select that point. The tape length and angle are displayed in the status line.
6. Make further adjustments to both ends as necessary.

> **TIP** If exact measurement of objects is needed, use *Display/Tape/ Toggle VSnap*. You can also use [Tab] to constrain movements in the horizontal or vertical direction.

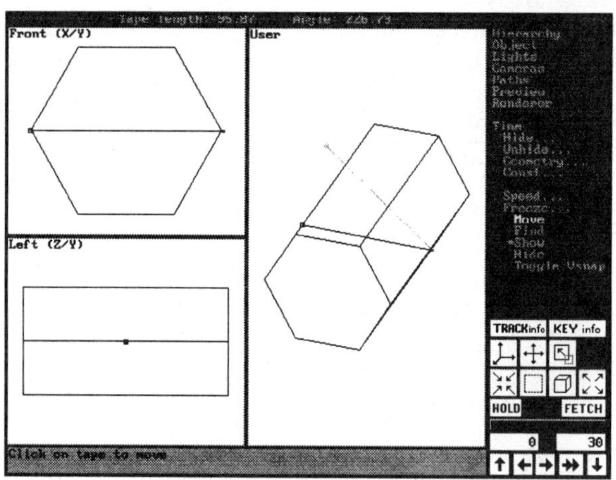

Displaying and moving the tape icon.

Moving the Tape Measure Icon

1. Ensure that the Tape Measure icon is displayed in an orthographic viewport using *Display/Tape/Show*.
2. Select *Display/Tape/Move*.
3. Select the orthographic viewport where the Tape Measure icon is to be moved.
4. Hold down [Ctrl] and select either end of the Tape Measure icon. A white copy of the icon will appear connected to the cursor, and a green reference icon will remain at its beginning location.
5. Move the Tape Measure icon to its new location. The tape length and angle are displayed in the status line.
6. Make further adjustments as necessary.

The settings for the tape in the 3D Editor and the Keyframer are independent of each other.

If you cannot find the Tape Measure icon use *Display/Tape/Find*.

RELATED COMMANDS

Display/Tape/Find, Display/Tape/Show, Display/Tape/Hide, Display/Tape/Toggle VSnap

Renderer
Display
Time
Unhide...
Geometry...
Constr...
Tape...
Speed...
Freeze...
Move
Find
Show
Hide
Toggle Vsnap

Display/Tape/Find

Adjusts the Tape Measure icon in the active viewport so that it may be located easily.

Finding the Tape Measure Icon

1. Select an orthographic or user viewport.
2. Select *Display/Tape/Find.* The Tape Measure icon will be scaled to 80 percent of the active viewport. It also will be centered within that viewport and reset to its default angle of 270 degrees. The tape length and angle are displayed in the status line.

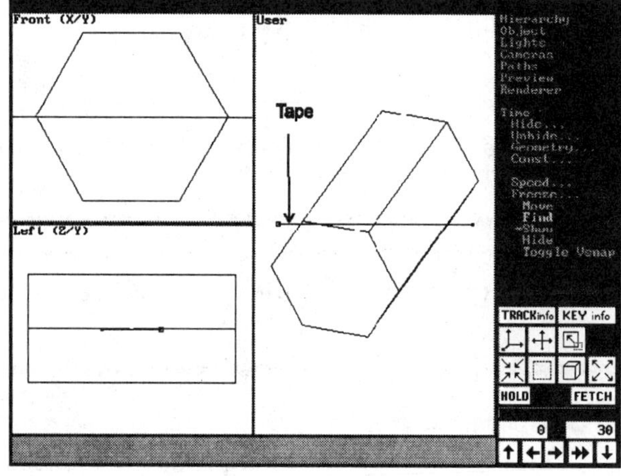

Displaying the Tape Measure icon at its default position and size.

RELATED COMMANDS

Display/Tape/Show, Display/Tape/Hide

Keyframer

Renderer
Display
Time
Unhide...
Geometry...
Constr...
Tape...
Speed...
Freeze...
Move
Find
Show
Hide
Toggle Vsnap

Display/Tape/Show

Displays the Tape Measure icon.

Displaying the Tape Measure Icon

1. Select *Display/Tape/Show.* The Tape Measure icon will be displayed in all orthographic and user viewports at its previously defined location and direction. An asterisk will appear next to the command. The tape length and angle are also displayed in the status line.

2. Use *Display/Tape/Move* to adjust the Tape Measure icon.

Use *Display/Tape/Find* if the Tape Measure icon cannot be seen after using this command.

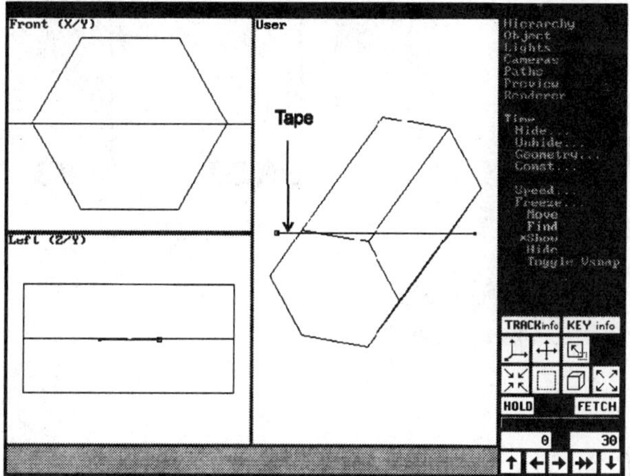

Displaying the Tape Measure icon.

RELATED COMMANDS

Display/Tape/Move, Display/Tape/Find, Display/Tape/Hide

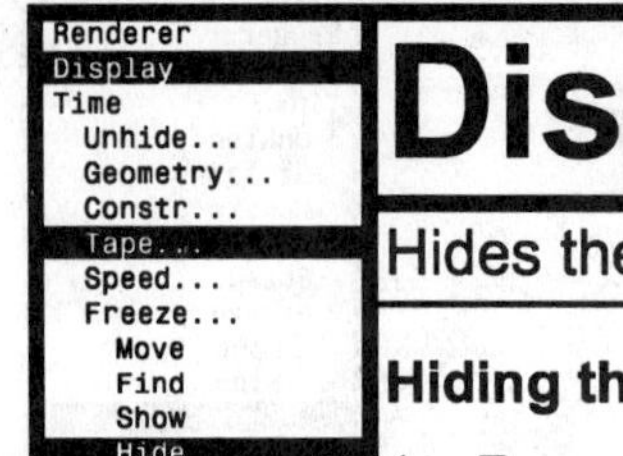

Display/Tape/Hide

Hides the Tape Measure icon.

Hiding the Tape Measure Icon

1. Ensure that the Tape Measure icon has been displayed previously using either *Display/Tape/Show* or *Display/Tape/Find.*
2. Select *Display/Tape/Hide*. The Tape Measure icon will disappear from the orthographic and user viewports and an asterisk (*) will appear next to the command.

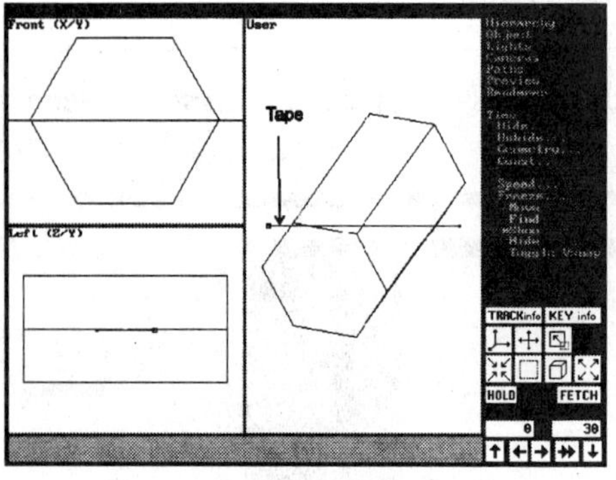

Displaying the tape icon.

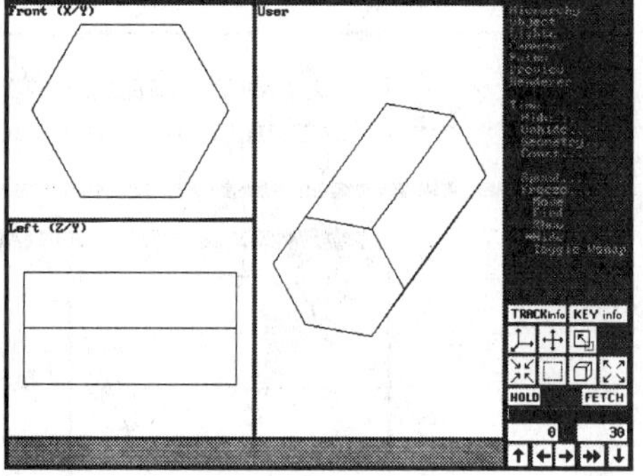

Hiding the tape icon.

RELATED COMMANDS

Display/Tape/Find, Display/Tape/Show

Display/Tape/Toggle VSnap

Toggles the Vertex Tape Snap mode.

Turning on Vertex Tape Snap mode

1. Select *Display/Tape/Toggle VSnap*. An asterisk (*) appears next to the command.
2. Use *Display/Tape/Move* to snap the ends of the Tape Measure icon to any vertex on a line, face, or path.

NOTE For the end of the Tape Measure icon to snap to a vertex, the vertex must be in the pick box when the location of the end of the Tape Measure icon is selected.

TIP Use this command to snap the ends of the Tape Measure icon to a vertex on a mesh object, allowing for a more accurate line measurement.

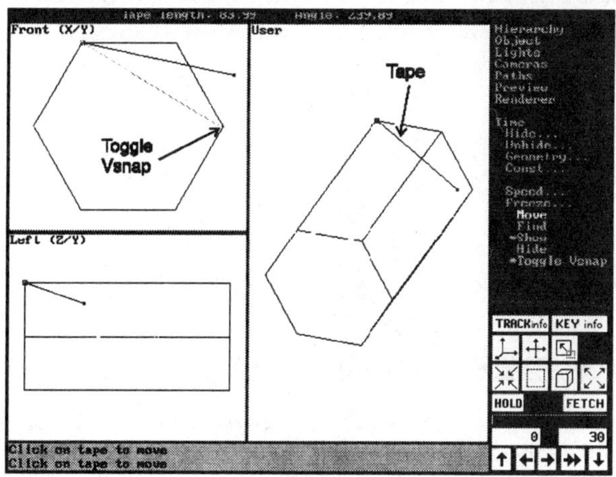

Snapping to a vertex on a mesh object.

RELATED COMMANDS

Display/Tape/Find, Display/Tape/Show

Renderer
Display
Time
Geometry...
Constr...
Tape...
Speed...
Freeze...
Fastdraw
Fulldraw
Set Fast
By Name
By Color
Object

Display/Speed/Fastdraw

Turns on Fastdraw and displays mesh objects with a reduced number of faces to speed redraw times.

Turning On Fastdraw

1. Ensure that geometry has been created previously.
2. Use the *Display/Speed/Set Fast* command to specify the number of faces that will be used to represent mesh objects.
3. Select *Display/Speed/Fastdraw*. An asterisk (*) will appear next to the command and the mesh objects will be displayed with a reduced number of faces.
4. Use *Display/Speed/Fulldraw* to display the mesh objects with all faces.

TIP Using this command can decrease regeneration significantly times on complicated mesh objects with slower systems. It is not necessary to use this command if simple to moderate-size mesh objects are being displayed on medium to fast systems.

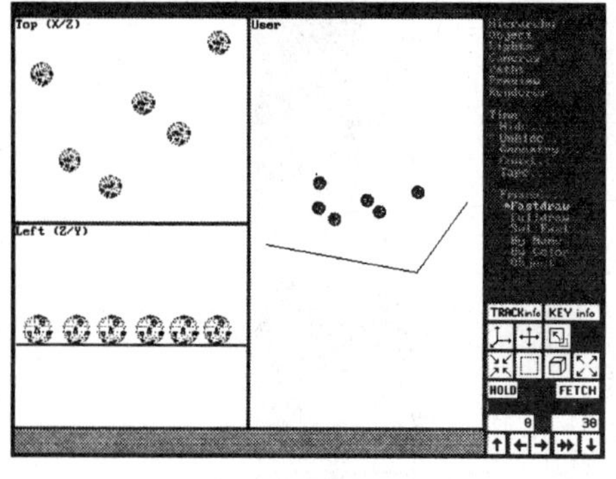

Mesh object displayed with reduced faces.

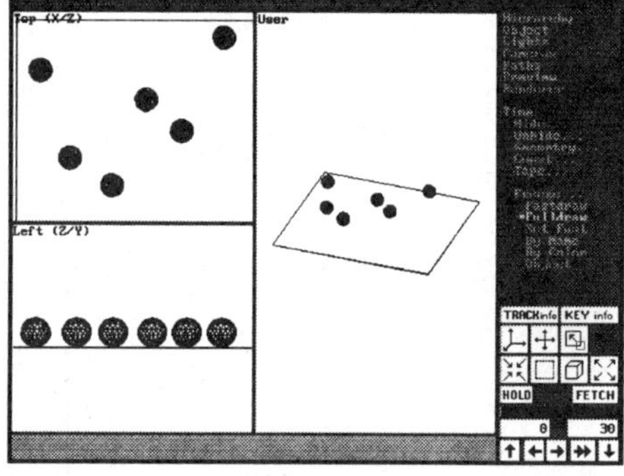

Mesh object displayed with all faces.

RELATED COMMANDS

Display/Speed/Fulldraw, Display/Speed/Set Fast

Renderer
Display
Time
Geometry...
Constr...
Tape...
Speed...
Freeze...
Fastdraw
Fulldraw
Set Fast
By Name
By Color
Object

Display/Speed/Fulldraw

Displays all faces on mesh objects.

Turning On Fulldraw

1. Ensure that geometry has been created previously.
2. Select *Display/Speed/Fulldraw*. An asterisk (*) will appear next to the command and the mesh objects will be displayed with all faces.

Using this command can increase regeneration times significantly on complicated mesh object with slower systems.

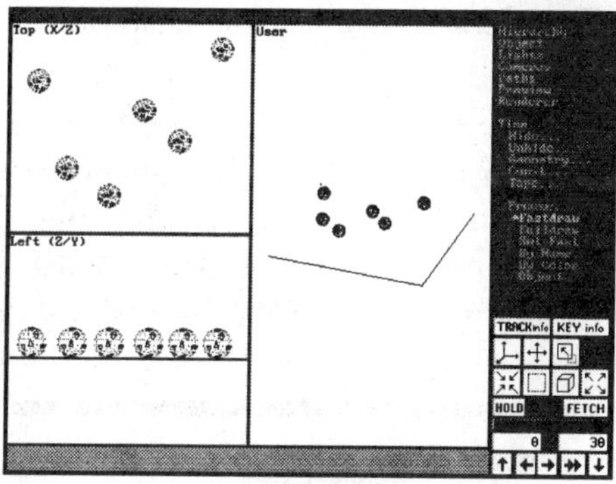

Mesh object displayed with reduced faces.

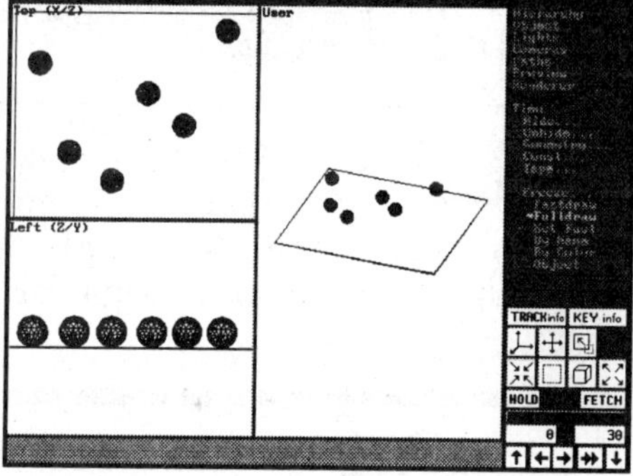

Mesh object displayed with all faces.

RELATED COMMANDS

Display/Speed/Fastdraw, Display/Speed/Set Fast

Display/Speed/Set Fast

Specifies the number of faces used to represent a mesh object.

Changing the Number of Faces for Mesh Objects

1. Select *Display/Speed/Set Fast*. The Set Fastdraw Speed dialog box appears as shown below.
2. Move the slider up or down to specify the number of faces. The range is from 2 to 100. A setting of 2 displays every other face and a setting of 100 displays every 100th face.
3. Click on **OK** to accept the setting or **Cancel** to cancel the command.
4. If **OK** was selected, use *Display/Speed/Fastdraw* to display the mesh object with the new settings.

> **NOTE** Be careful not to specify too high a setting. If the setting is higher than the number of faces in the mesh object, that object will not be seen. If multiple objects are displayed, it is important to make the setting small enough for the object with the fewest number of faces.

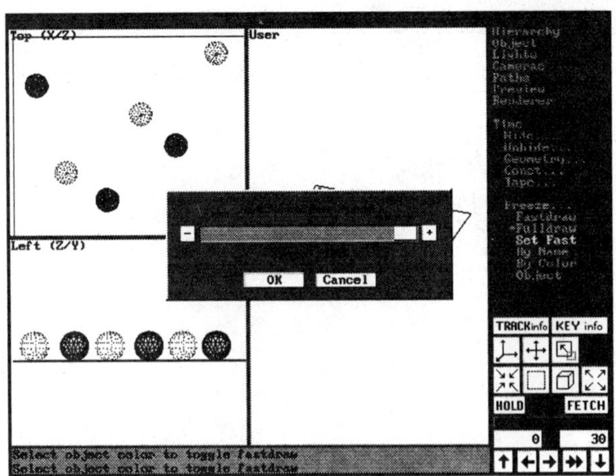

The Set Fastdraw Speed dialog box.

RELATED COMMANDS

Display/Speed/Fastdraw, Display/Speed/Fulldraw

Display/Speed/By Name

Renderer
Display
Time
Geometry...
Constr...
Tape...
Speed...
Freeze...
Fastdraw
Fulldraw
Set Fast
By Name
By Color
Object

Assigns Fastdraw mode to individual objects.

Assigning Fastdraw Mode to Individual Object

1. Ensure that geometry has been created previously.
2. Select *Display/Speed/By Name*. The Select Fastdraw Objects dialog box appears.
3. Select the object(s) in the dialog box or use the following options:

   All: Selects all objects in the list.

   None: Deselects all objects in the list.

   Tag: Place the wild card pattern in the text box above this button. Click on the **Tag** button. All objects that match the wild card will be selected.

   Untag: Place the wild card pattern in the text box above this button. Click on the **Untag** button. All objects that match the wild card will be deselected.
4. Select **OK** to accept the selection and close the dialog box. The objects selected will be redisplayed in all viewports in Fastdraw mode.
5. Select **Cancel** to cancel the command and exit the dialog box.

Display/Speed/Fastdraw overrides this command.

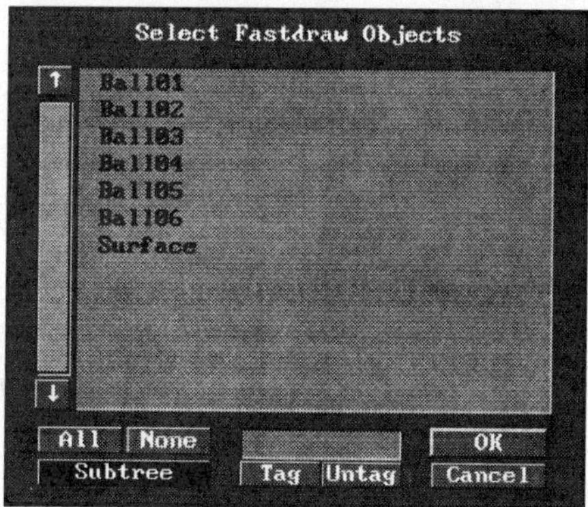

The Select Fastdraw Objects dialog box.

RELATED COMMAND

Display/Speed/Fastdraw

Renderer
Display
Time
Geometry...
Constr...
Tape...
Speed...
Freeze...
Fastdraw
Fulldraw
Set Fast
By Name
By Color
Object

Display/Speed/By Color

Assigns Fastdraw mode to objects with the same color.

Assigning Fastdraw to Objects with the Same Color.

1. Ensure that geometry has been created previously.
2. Select *Display/Speed/By Color.*
3. In any viewport, select the object to receive Fastdraw mode. That object will be redisplayed in Fastdraw mode as will all other objects that are the same color.

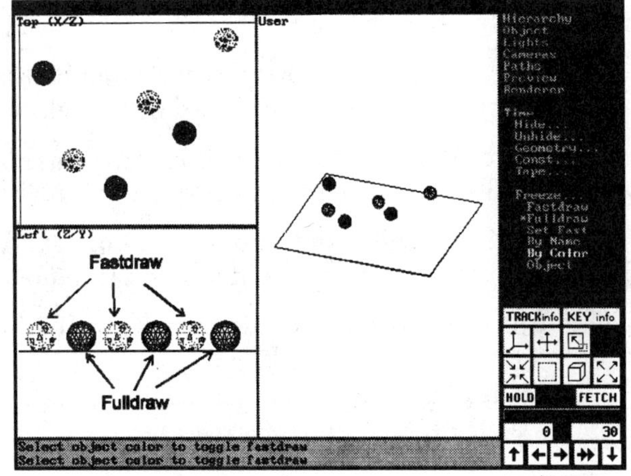

Displaying objects in Fastdraw mode by color.

RELATED COMMAND

Display/Speed/Fast Draw

Display/Speed/Object

Renderer
Display
Time
Geometry...
Constr...
Tape...
Speed...
Freeze...
Fastdraw
Fulldraw
Set Fast
By Name
By Color
Object

Assigns Fastdraw mode to a single object.

Assigning Fastdraw mode to an Object

1. Ensure that an object has been created previously.
2. Select *Display/Speed/Object*.
3. In any viewport, select the object. That object will be redisplayed in Fastdraw mode.
4. Repeating steps 2 and 3 will toggle Fastdraw mode for the object.

Display/Speed/Fastdraw overrides this command.

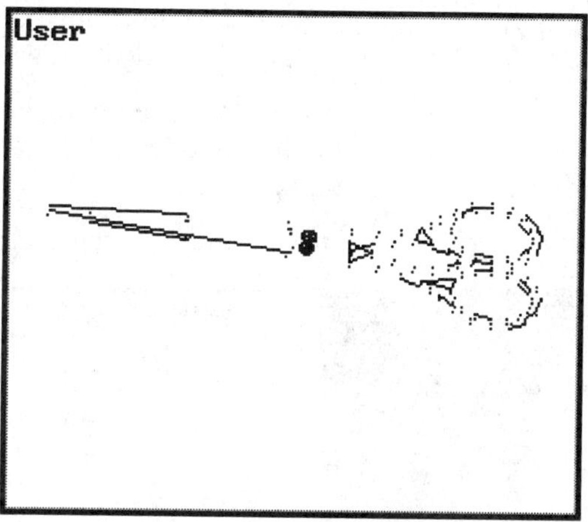

Displaying a selected object in Fastdraw mode.

RELATED COMMANDS

Display/Speed/Fastdraw

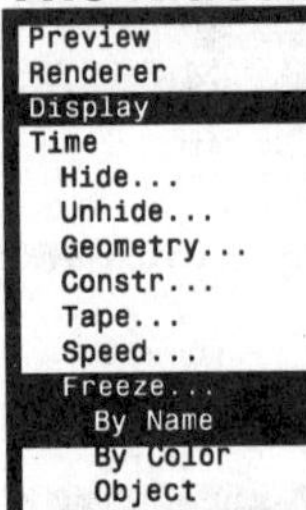

Display/Freeze/By Name

Freezes individual objects so they cannot be edited by some commands.

Freezing Individual Objects

1. Ensure that geometry has been created previously.
2. Select *Display/Freeze/By Name*. The Freeze Objects dialog box appears.
3. Select the object(s) in the dialog box or use the following options:

   All: Selects all the objects in the list.

   None: Deselects all objects in the list.

   Tag: Place the wild card pattern in the text box above this button. Click on the **Tag** button. All objects that match the wild card will be selected.

   Untag: Place the wild card pattern in the text box above this button. Click on the **Untag** button. All objects that match the wild card will be deselected.
4. Select **OK** to accept the selection and close the dialog box. The objects selected will be displayed in gray in all viewports. When frozen, the objects cannot be modified but they can be rendered.
5. Select **Cancel** to cancel the command and exit the dialog box.

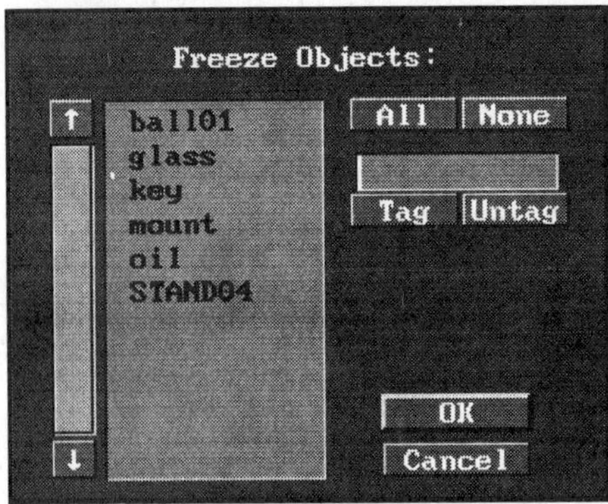

The Freeze Objects dialog box.

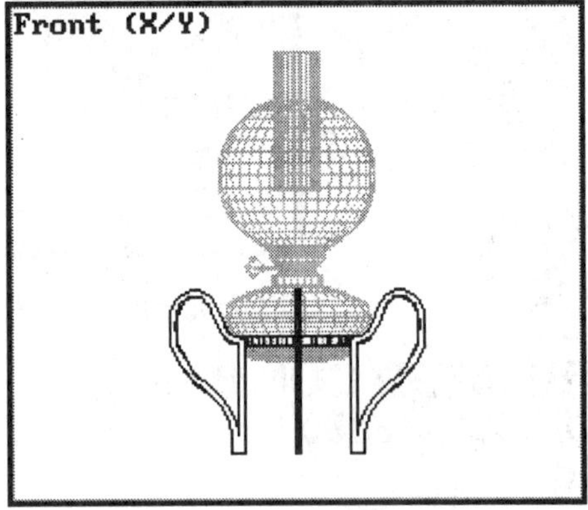

Frozen objects appear lighter.

RELATED COMMANDS

Display/Freeze/By Color, Display/Freeze/Object

Preview
Renderer
Display
Time
Hide...
Unhide...
Geometry...
Constr...
Tape...
Speed...
Freeze...
By Name
By Color
Object

Display/Freeze/By Color

Freezes objects with the same color.

Freezing Objects with the Same Color

1. Ensure that geometry has been created previously.
2. Select *Display/Freeze/By Color*.
3. In any viewport, select an object to freeze. That object will be frozen as will all other objects that are the same color.

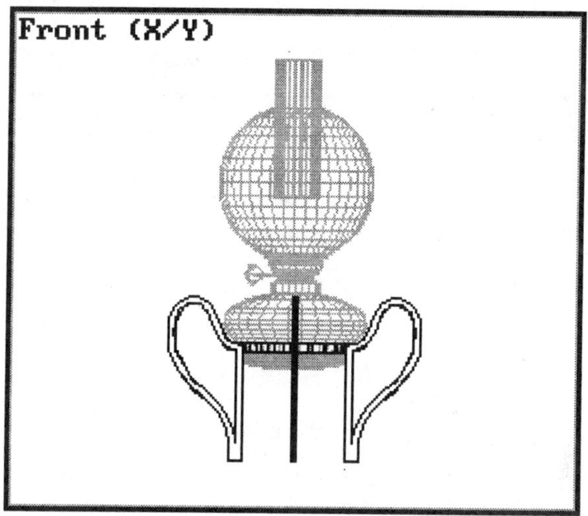

Objects frozen by color.

RELATED COMMANDS

Display/Freeze/By Name, Display/Freeze/Object

Preview
Renderer
Display
Time
Hide...
Unhide...
Geometry...
Constr...
Tape...
Speed...
Freeze...
By Name
By Color
Object

Display/Freeze/Object

Freezes a single object.

Freezing a Single Object

1. Ensure that an object has been created previously.
2. Select *Display/Freeze/Object*.
3. In any viewport, select the object to be frozen. That object will be displayed in gray as shown below. When frozen, the objects cannot be modified but they can be rendered.
4. Repeating steps 2 and 3 will toggle the freezing of an object.

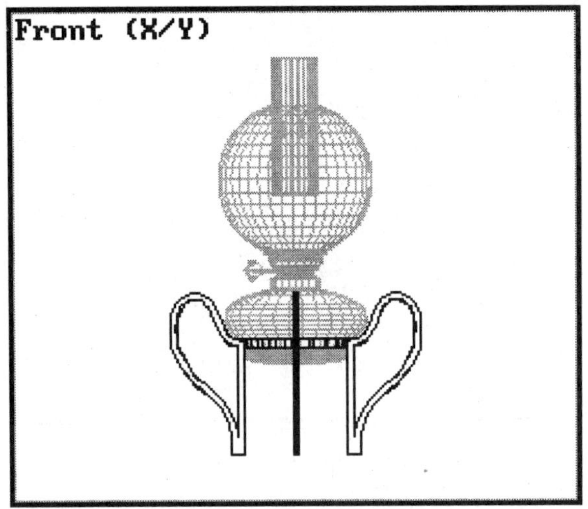

Freezing a selected object.

RELATED COMMANDS

Display/Freeze/By Color, Display/Freeze/By Name

Time/Go to Frame

Moves to a specified frame.

Hierarchy
Object
Lights
Cameras
Paths
Preview
Renderer
Display
Time
Go to Frame
Total Frames
Define Segment
Scale Segment

Moving to Another Frame

1. Select *Time/Go to Frame*. The Go To Frame dialog box appears as shown below.
2. Enter the frame to "go to" in the **Frame:** edit box.
3. Click on **OK** to move to the specified frame, or click on **Cancel** to cancel the command and close the dialog box.

There are two other ways to accomplish this command.

1. Move the frame slider at the bottom of the Keyframer screen.
2. Click on the current frame number on the Keyframer toolbar. The Go To Frame dialog box will be displayed.

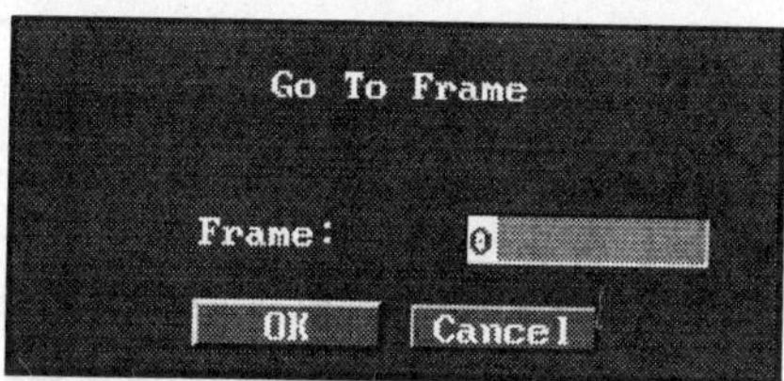

The Go To Frame dialog box.

RELATED COMMAND

Time/Total Frames

Hierarchy
Object
Lights
Cameras
Paths
Preview
Renderer
Display
Time
Go to Frame
Total Frames
Define Segment
Scale Segment

Time/Total Frames

Specifies the total number of frames for an animation.

Setting the Total Number of Frames

1. Select *Time/Total Frames*. The Set Number of Frames dialog box appears as shown below.
2. Enter the number of frames in the **Number:** edit box. If the number entered is smaller than the previously defined number of frames, the excess frames will be ignored and a segment will be activated. Lengthening the animation at a later time will restore these frames.
3. Click on **OK** to choose the specified number of frames, or click on **Cancel** to cancel the command and close the dialog box.

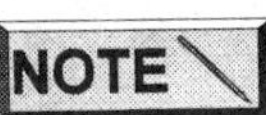

The total number of frames will actually be one more than specified because the Keyframer always begins at frame 0.

Clicking on the total frames on the keyframer toolbar will also display the Set Number of Frames dialog box.

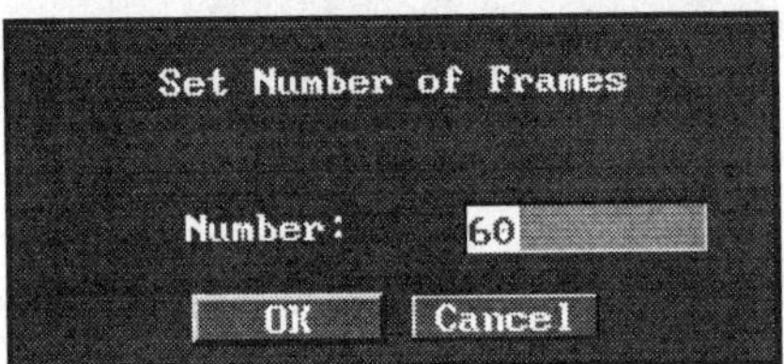

The Set Number of Frames dialog box.

RELATED COMMAND

Time/Go To Frame

Time/Define Segment

Specifies a range for an active segment. When the active segment is created, only those frames within the segment can be edited. All others are ignored until they are included in the segment.

Defining a Segment

1. Select *Time/Define Segment*. The Define Active Segment dialog box appears as shown below.
2. Enter the **Start:** frame and the **End:** frame in their respective edit boxes. **First Key:** displays the frame of the first key in the animation; **Last Key:** displays the frame of the last key in the animation.
3. Click on **OK** to choose the specified frames, or click on **Cancel** to cancel the command and close the dialog box.

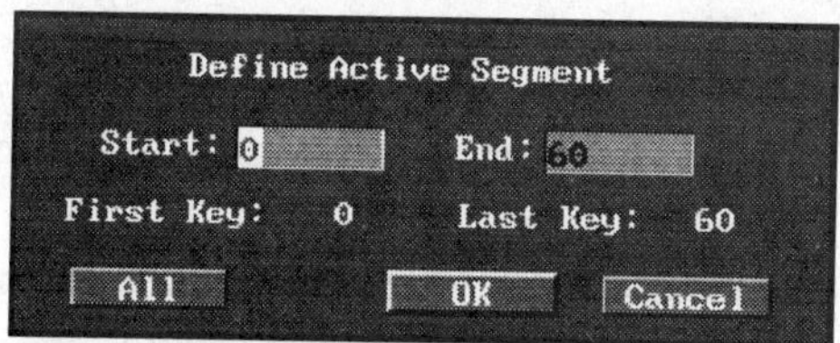

The Define Active Segment dialog box.

RELATED COMMANDS

Time/Total Frames, Time/Scale Segment

Hierarchy
Object
Lights
Cameras
Paths
Preview
Renderer
Display
Time
Go to Frame
Total Frames
Define Segment
Scale Segment

Time/Scale Segment

Increase or decrease the speed at which an animation is played by inserting or deleting frames from the animation between keys.

Scaling a Segment

1. Select *Time/Scale Segment*. The Scale Active Segment dialog box appears as shown below.
2. **Current Segment Length** displays the total number frames within the current defined segment. Enter the number of frames used to scale the active segment in the **Scale to:** edit box.
3. Click on **OK** to scale the specified frames, or click on **Cancel** to cancel the command and close the dialog box.

NOTE If the scale of the segment is reduced, some keys may be combined with other keys in the segment to meet the new scale requirement. These keys cannot be restored at a later time if they are combined.

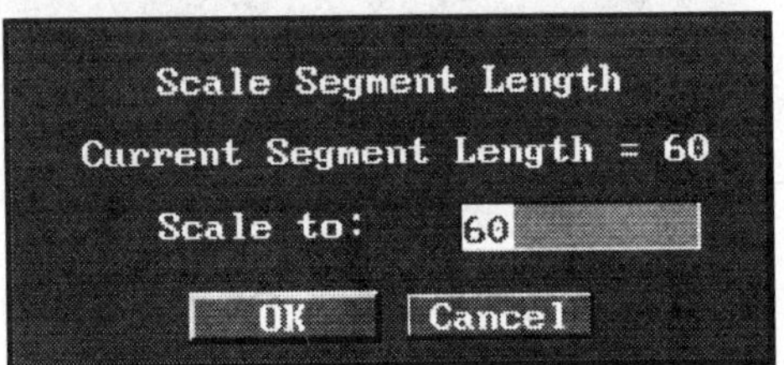

The Scale Segment Length dialog box.

RELATED COMMANDS

Time/Total Frames, Time/Define Segment

Library-New

Library
New
Load Library
Merge Library
Save Library
Delete Library
Quit

Removes all materials in the current library. It allows you to create your own materials and place them in the current library.

Creating a New Materials Library

1. Select New from the Library pull-down menu.
2. In the Remove all materials? dialog box, click **OK**. All materials in the current library are removed from memory.
3. Because there are no materials in memory, you must create your own and place them in the current library. See *Material-Put Material.*
4. After creating and saving your new materials, you can save them as a new materials library. See *Library-Save Library*.

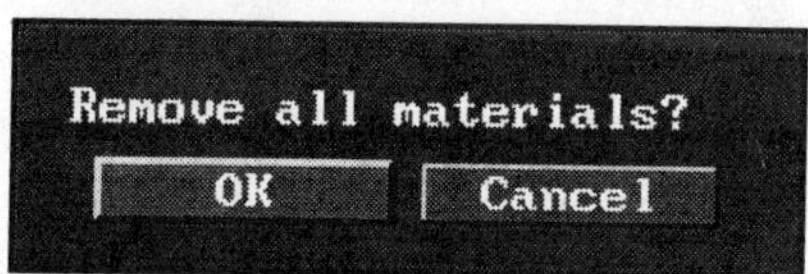

Selecting OK will remove all materials in the current library from memory.

RELATED COMMANDS

Material–Put Material, Library–Save Library

Library-Load Library

Replaces the current materials library with another library from disk.

Loading a New Materials Library

1. Select Load Library from the Library pull-down menu.
2. Select the new library file that you want to load.
3. A warning box will appear, asking you to confirm loading a new library.
4. Click **OK** to load the new materials library.

TIP When you begin 3D Studio, the *3ds.mli* materials library is automatically loaded by default. You can change the materials library that will be loaded by editing the Material–Library option in the *3ds.set* file.

NOTE When you load a new materials library, all materials currently in memory are replaced with materials from the new library. No materials contained in the sample windows are affected, however. Make sure you save any new materials you created before loading a new library.

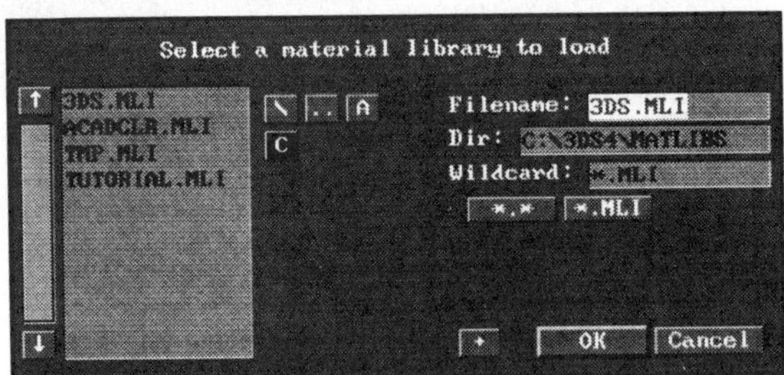

Loading a new materials library replaces all materials currently in memory.

RELATED COMMANDS

Library–Merge, Library–Save, Library–New

Library-Merge Library

Library
New
Load Library
Merge Library
Save Library
Delete Library
Quit

Merges materials in the current library with materials from another materials library on disk.

Merging Two Materials Libraries

1. Select Merge Library from the Library pull-down menu.
2. Select the materials library file that you want to merge with the existing materials library.
3. If a material from the library you are merging has the same name as an existing material, an alert box appears, giving you the option of replacing the existing version.
4. Selecting **OK** will replace the current material with the one from the merged library. Selecting **Cancel** will abort the operation.
5. Select Library-Save Library to save the two merged libraries.

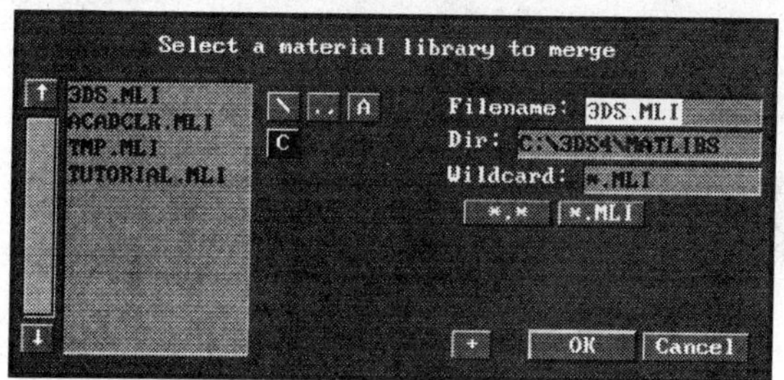

Use Merge Library to combine a materials library on disk with the current materials library.

RELATED COMMANDS

Library–Save Library, Library–Load Library

Library-Save Library

Saves all materials in the current library to disk. All materials in the current library are saved, as well as any materials from libraries that were merged.

Saving the Current Materials Library

1. Select Save Library from the Library pull-down men.
2. To save the library using the current filename, click **OK**. To save the library under a different filename, enter the name in the text box after **Filename.** Select **OK** to save the library.
3. If you are saving the library under an existing library name, an alert box appears. The alert box will say you are about to save the library over an existing library name. If you want to update this library, select **OK.**

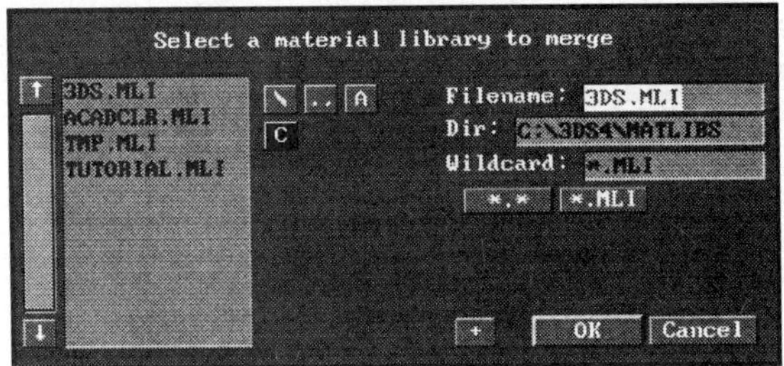

When saving a materials library, all current as well as merged materials are saved.

RELATED COMMANDS

Library–Load Library, Library–Merge Library

Library-Delete Library

Accesses a dialog box that allows you to delete a library file.

Deleting a Library File

1. Select Delete Library from the Library pull-down menu.
2. In the Delete file: dialog box, select the library file you want to permanently remove from disk and click **OK**.
3. An alert box will appear asking you to confirm the deletion of the library file. Select **OK** to remove the library file permanently.

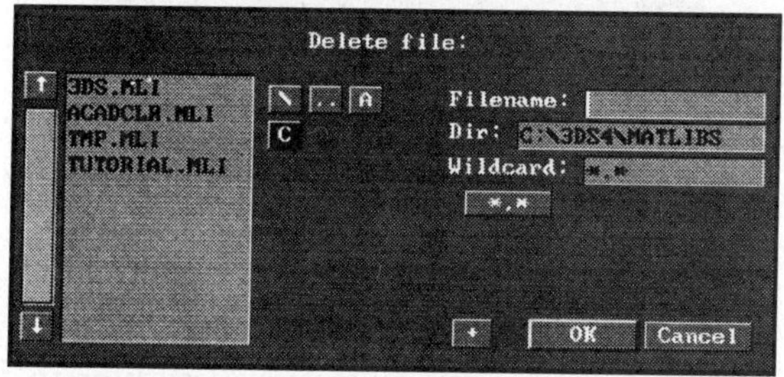

Deleting a library file permanently removes it and all its materials from disk.

RELATED COMMAND

Library–Load Library

Library-Quit

Q

Exits 3D Studio and returns to DOS.

Exiting 3D Studio

1. Select Quit from the Library pull-down menu.
2. If you have unsaved data in any program module, an alert box is displayed showing which modules contain unsaved elements.

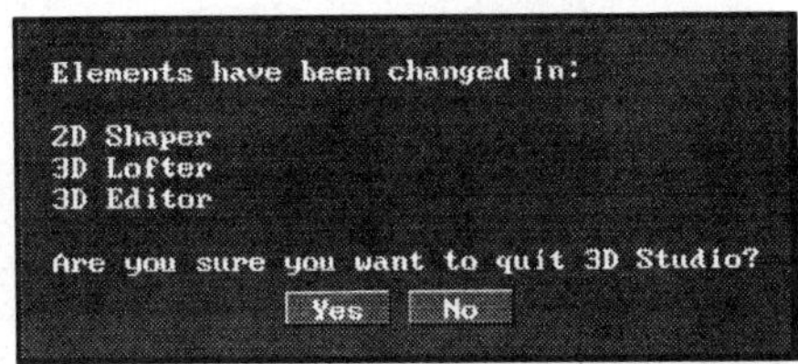

Elements Changed dialog box.

When you Quit 3D Studio, you lose data and program settings for all modules. Before you quit, save everything to disk.

RELATED COMMAND

Library–Save Library

Material-Get Material

Material
Get Material
Put Material
Remove Material
Get From Scene
Put to Scene
Put to Current

Loads a selected material from the current materials library. A sample sphere is rendered in the active rendering window, and all buttons, sliders, and fields are updated to indicate the materials properties.

Getting a Material

1. Because the material must be available in the current materials library, make sure you have the correct materials library loaded. See Library–Load Library.
2. Select Get Material from the Material pull-down menu.
3. Select the material you want to load and click on it. The name of the selected material is displayed in the dialog box. Select **OK** to load the material.
4. After selecting the material, a sample sphere is loaded and the Materials Editor is updated to reflect the materials properties.

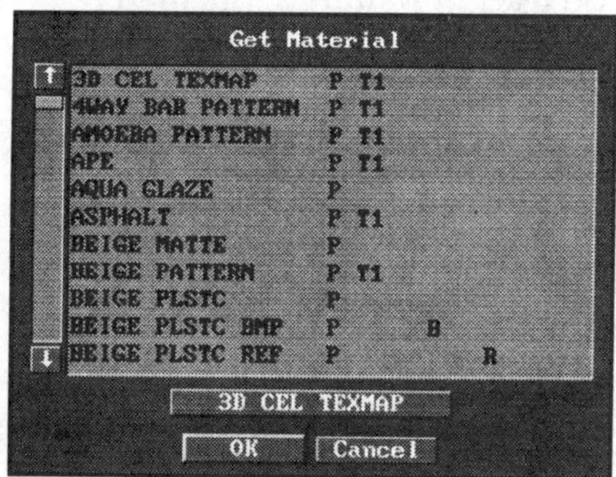

When you get a material, a sample sphere is loaded and the materials editor is updated to reflect the material's properties.

RELATED COMMAND

Library–Load Library

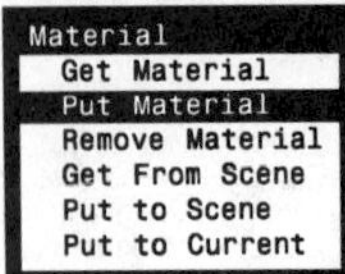

Material-Put Material

Allows you to give the current material a name and insert it into the current material library.

Saving the Current Material

1. Select Put Material from the Material pull-down menu.
2. When the Put Material dialog box appears, the materials name will appear in the text box. To overwrite the material, click **OK**. A warning box will appear, indicating that the name you are giving the material is the same as a name already in the library. Click **OK** to overwrite the existing material.
3. If you want to give the material a different name, enter the name in the text box.

NOTE When you use *Put Material*, the material is added to the current material library. It is not saved to disk. To save the new material to disk, use *Library–Save Library*.

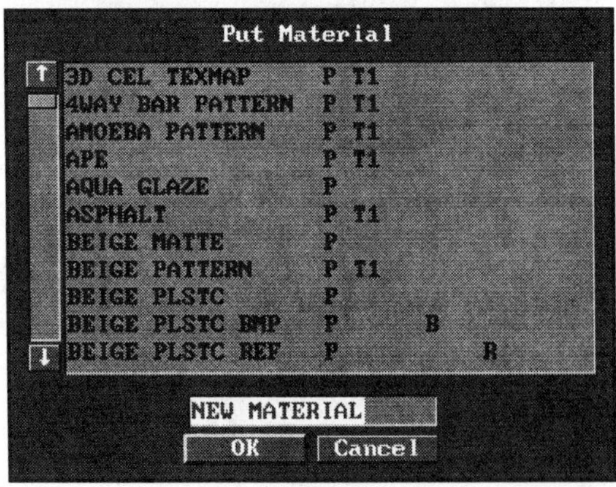

The Put Material option adds the material to the current material library, but does not save it to disk.

RELATED COMMAND

Library–Save Library

Material-Remove Material

Material
Get Material
Put Material
Remove Material
Get From Scene
Put to Scene
Put to Current

Removes one or more selected materials from the current material library.

Removing Selected Materials

1. Select Remove Material from the Materials pull-down menu.
2. Click on the materials you want to remove. Materials selected for removal are tagged with an asterisk.
3. Select **OK** to remove the tagged materials from the current material library.

> **NOTE** When you remove a material, it is removed from the current materials library but is not removed from disk. To remove the material from disk, save the current materials library over the existing one. See *Library–Save Library*.

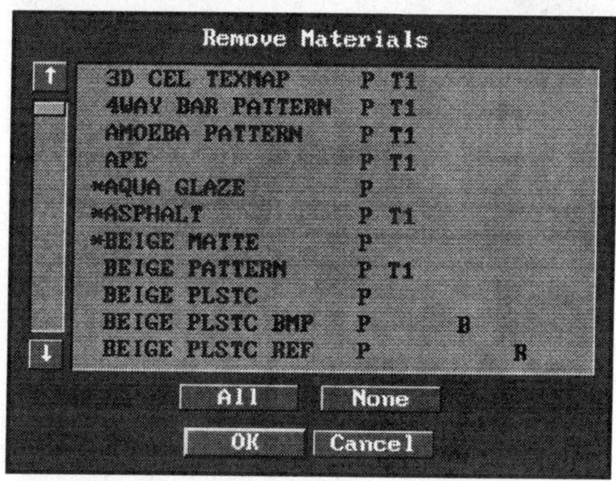

Removing a material from the current materials library does not remove it from disk.

RELATED COMMANDS

Library–Save Library

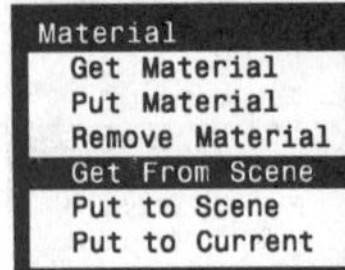

Material-Get From Scene

Accesses a dialog box that lists all materials currently assigned to geometry in the 3D scene. When you select a material, a sample sphere is rendered and the Materials Editor is updated to reflect the material's properties.

Getting a Material from the Current Scene

1. Select Get From Scene from the Material pull-down menu.
2. The Get Material From Scene dialog box appears, listing all materials currently assigned to geometry in the scene.
3. When you select a material, the name is displayed in the dialog box. Click on **OK.**
4. A sample sphere is rendered and the Materials Editor is updated to reflect the material's properties. The material is now available for editing.

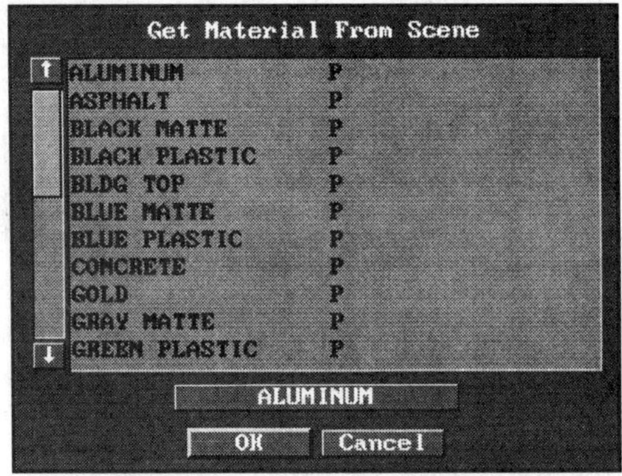

All materials currently assigned to objects in the 3D scene are listed.

RELATED COMMANDS

Material–Put to Scene

Material-Put to Scene

Material
Get Material
Put Material
Remove Material
Get From Scene
Put to Scene
Put to Current

Updates all materials with the same name in the current 3D scene.

Putting a Material Back Into the 3D Scene

1. Before you can put a material back into the scene, you first must have a material defined in the Materials Editor. Define your own material, get a material from the current library with *Material–Get Material*, or acquire a material from the current 3D Scene with *Material–Get From Scene.*
2. Give the material the same name as the material you want to replace in the 3D Scene. See *Options–Current Material.*
3. Select Put to Scene from the Material pull-down menu. An alert box will appear asking you to confirm material replacement. Select **OK** to replace the material.

TIP To make adjustments or modifications to materials in your scene, first use *Material–Get From Scene* to bring the material into the Materials Editor. Make your changes to the material in the Materials Editor, then use *Material–Put to Scene* to update the material in the 3D scene. You can update the material automatically by selecting the **Auto put** button.

NOTE Modifying a material and putting it back into the scene does not update or place it into the current materials library. To put the material in the current library, see *Material–Put Material.*

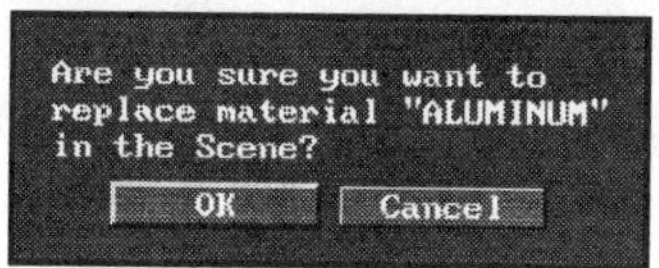

Select OK to apply the property of the current material to all materials with the same name.

RELATED COMMANDS

Material–Get Material, Material–Get from Scene, Material–Put Material

Material
Get Material
Put Material
Remove Material
Get From Scene
Put to Scene
Put to Current

Material-Put to Current

Copies the material currently in the Materials Editor into the 3D Editor and makes it the current material.

Putting the Current Material into the Scene

1. Before you can put a material into the scene, you first must have a material defined in the Materials Editor. Define your own material, get a material from the current library with *Material-Get Material*, or acquire a material from the current 3D Scene with *Material-Get From Scene*.
2. Select Put to Current from the Material pull-down menu. You can **Rename** the material before placing it, or **Replace** the material in the 3D Editor that has the same name.

TIP

You can use *Put to Current* to create a new material and assign it to geometry in the 3D Editor without saving it in a materials library. When you save a **.3ds* or **.prj* file, all materials assigned to geometry are also saved. If you want to save the material in a materials library at a later time, load the **.3ds* or **.prj* file and retrieve the material with *Material–Get From Scene*. Once the material is in the materials editor, use *Material–Put Material*.

When you put the current material to the 3D scene, you can rename it or replace the material.

RELATED COMMANDS

Material–Get From Scene, Material–Put Material, Material–Get Material

Options-Antialias

Options
Antialias
Backlight
Video Color Check
Video File Alpha
View Last Image

Determines how the sphere or cube in the sample window is rendered. When on (an asterisk appears next to the command), the quality of the images is improved.

Turning Antialias On

1. Select a material with *Material-Get Material.*
2. Select Antialias from the Options pull-down menu. An asterisk appears next to the command
3. When you render a sample sphere, the edges will smooth out and the quality of the render will increase. The rendering time will double, however.

> **NOTE** Antialias improves the quality of the image by smoothing out the jagged edges found along the edges of the image. When Antialias is turned on, the edges on the image are smoother, but the rendering time is doubled.

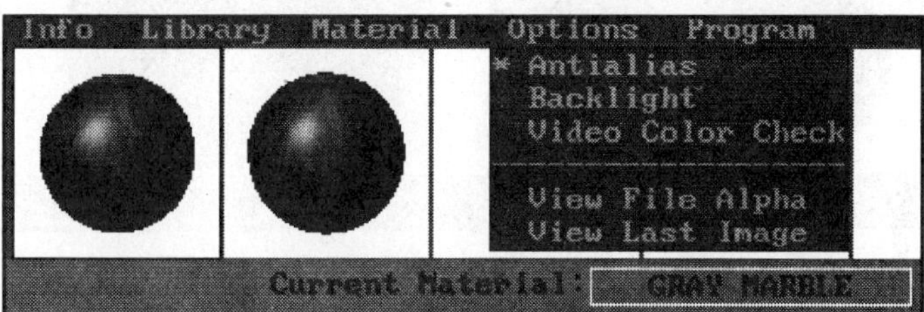

The sphere on the left has Antialias off; the sphere on the right has antialias on.

RELATED COMMAND

Control Panel–Render Sample

Options
Antialias
Backlight
Video Color Check
Video File Alpha
View Last Image

Options-Backlight

Adds a backlight to the sample window. When Backlight is on, an asterisk appears next to the command.

Using the Backlight Option

1. Select a metal material such as Metal Cherry Red with *Material-Get Material.*
2. Select Backlight from the Options pull-down menu. An asterisk appears next to the command.
3. When you render a sample sphere, it will seem as if a light is in back of the sphere.

> **TIP** Turn Backlight on when rendering sample spheres and using metal-shaded materials. The backlight will help you see the specular highlight created by light glancing off the sphere.

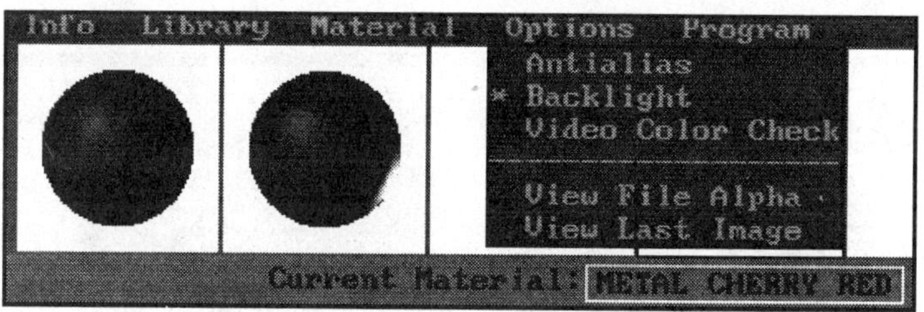

The sphere on the left has the backlight off, the sphere on the right has the backlight on.

RELATED COMMAND

Control Panel–Render Sample

Options-Video Color Check

Options
Antialias
Backlight
Video Color Check
Video File Alpha
View Last Image

When activated (an asterisk appears next to the command), the colors in the sample object are checked to determine whether the object has colors that are beyond safe use for NTSC or PAL video threshold. Pixels that are beyond the safe limit are rendered black on the sample image.

Video Color Check

1. Activate Video Color Check in the Options pull-down menu. An asterisk appears next to the command.
2. Select Render Sample from the Control Panel. If the rendered sample contains any black spots, it means that colors in these areas are beyond safe use for NTSC or PAL video and will be blurry or fuzzy when transferred to videotape.
3. If dark areas appear on the rendered sample, drop the color saturation down below 80 percent and render the sample again.

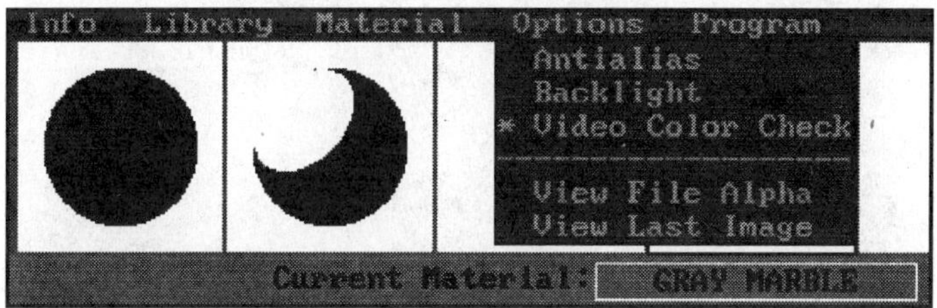

The sphere on the left has video color check off; the sphere on the right has video color check on.

RELATED COMMAND

Control Panel–Render Sample

Options
Antialias
Backlight
Video Color Check
Video File Alpha
View Last Image

Options-View File Alpha

Views a monochrome image of a bitmap. The transparency levels for the image are converted to grayscale intensity values. Black areas represent full transparency, white shows opaque areas, and gray shows semitransparent areas.

Viewing the Alpha Channel for a Selected Object

1. Select View Alpha Channel from the Options pull-down menu.
2. In the View image file dialog box, select the bitmap file you want to display the alpha channel for and click **OK**.
3. The image is rendered on the screen in monochrome, with the intensity levels of the images colors converted into grayscale intensity levels.
4. Click the right mouse button to remove the image from the screen.

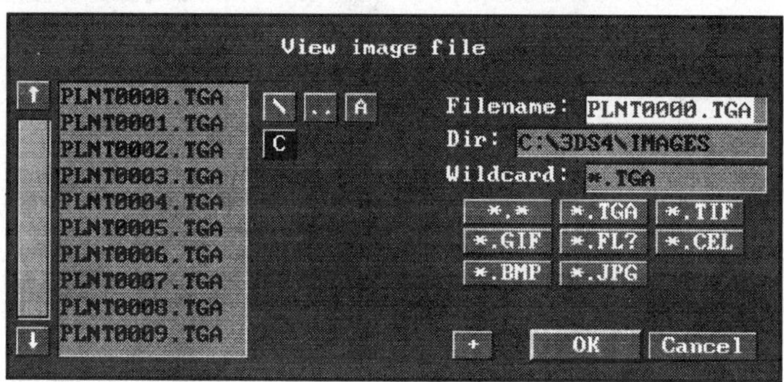

Select the file you want to view the alpha channel for.

RELATED COMMAND

Control Panel-View Image

Options-View Last Image

Options
Antialias
Backlight
Video Color Check
Video File Alpha
View Last Image

Views the last image rendered.

Viewing the Last Image

1. Select View Last Image from the Options pull-down menu.
2. Select **Yes** at the View Last Image prompt.
3. The last image you rendered is displayed.

NOTE You can only view the last image rendered if the following conditions are met:

1. The Save Last Image parameter in the Render options dialog box or in the *3ds.set* file is set to **Yes**.
2. You have previously rendered an image.

RELATED COMMANDS

Renderer/Render View in the 3D Editor, Renderer/Render View in the Keyframer

Sample Windows

A series of seven windows that are used to render samples of materials.

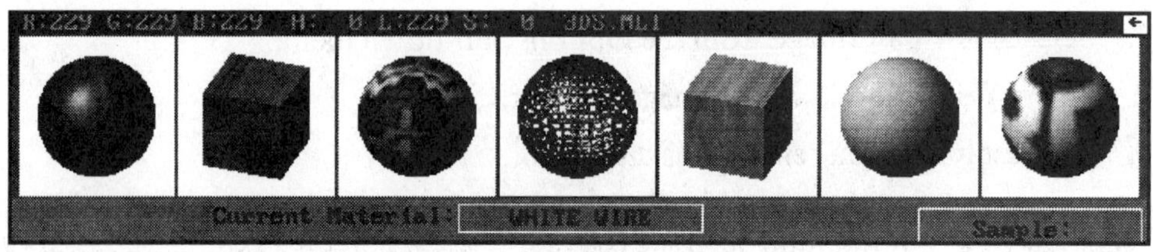

The sample windows, each with a different image.

Using the Sample Windows

1. The outlined window is the current window. If the material in that window has a name, that name appears in the Current Material: box.
2. Selecting Render Sample from the Control Panel renders a sample cube or sphere in the current window using the parameters set up in the materials editor.
3. A sample sphere or box is also rendered when you select *Material-Get Material*.
4. To change current windows, move the cursor to a different window and click.
5. To copy material from one window to another, click in the window you want to copy the material from and hold down the mouse button. Drag the window to the new location, and release the button.

RELATED COMMANDS

Control Panel/Render Sample, Material-Get Material, Control Panel/Background

Current Material

The name of the material in the current sample window is listed after Current Material. If the area is blank, the material does not have a name. Clicking on the material name allows you to rename the material.

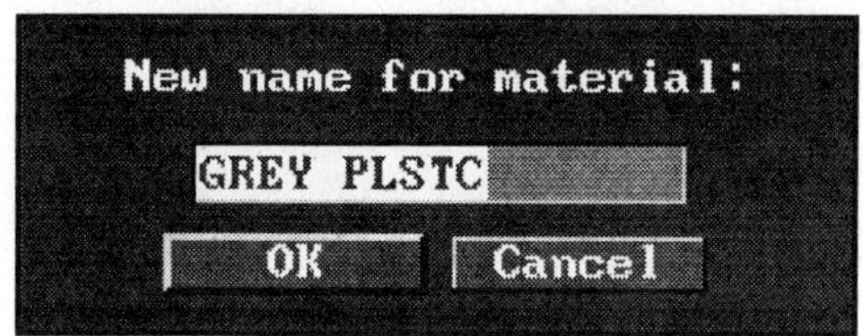

Clicking on the material name allows you to rename the material.

Renaming the Current Material

1. Click on the sample window that contains the material you want to name or rename.
2. Enter the new name for the material in the text box.

NOTE Renaming the material does not put the material into the current library or save the material to disk. To put the material into the current library, see *Material-Put Material*. To save the material to disk, see *Library/Save Library*.

RELATED COMMANDS

Sample Windows, Material-Put Material, Library/Save Library

Sample: Sphere-Cube

Determines the type of object the current material is rendered on in the sample windows. You can render to a sphere or a cube.

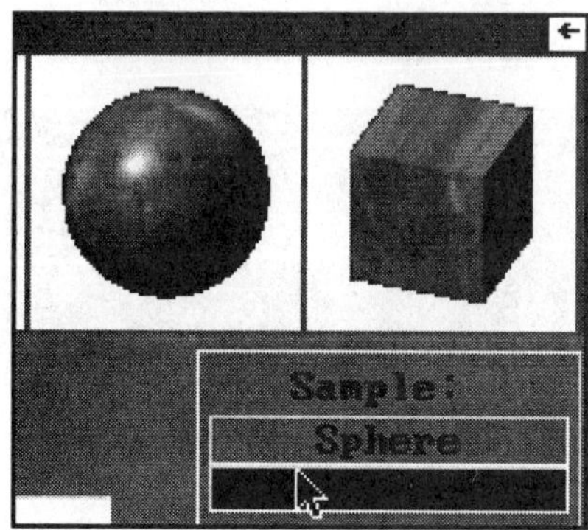

Rendering a material to a sphere and a cube.

Rendering to a Sphere and a Cube

1. In the control panel at the right of the screen, select either the **Sphere** or **Cube** button under Sample.
2. After selecting the appropriate button, the material samples are rendered using the object selected.

To see how the same material sample will look on both a cube and a sphere, perform the following steps:

1. First render the material in one window as a sphere.
2. Click on the widow with the rendered sphere and hold down the left mouse button. Drag the window to a new location and release the mouse button. Answer **Yes** to the Copy material? prompt. This will create a copy of the rendered sphere.
3. Click on the **Cube** button in the control panel.
4. Click on the **Render Sample** button in the control panel. You now have both a cube and sphere rendering of the material.

RELATED COMMAND

Background

Background: Black-Pattern

Determines the type of background used in the sample window. You can select a black or pattern background.

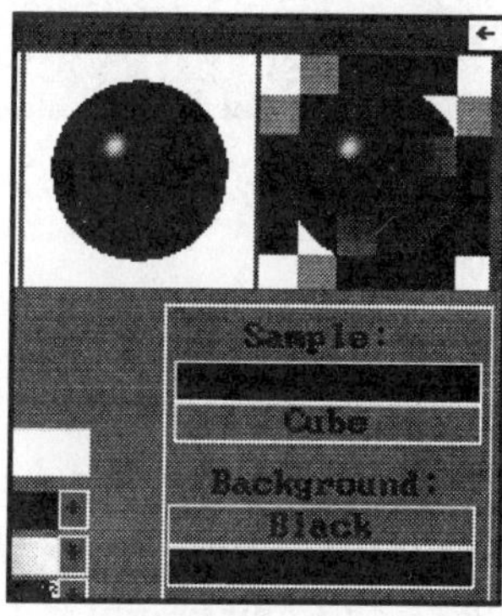

You can select a black or pattern background for the sample window.

Using the Black and Pattern Background

1. In the control panel at the right of the screen, select either the **Black** or **Pattern** button under Background.
2. The Black background renders the sample sphere or cube over a black background.
3. The Pattern background uses a series of different color cubes as a background.
4. Select *Render-Sample* to display the selected pattern.

> **TIP** Selecting a pattern background is especially useful when working with materials that use transparency and opacity mapping. See *Transparency* in the Material Property section and *Opacity* in the Mapping section of the Materials Editor.

RELATED COMMANDS

Transparency, Opacity, Sample

Output

Specifies the output display device used by the sample windows.

The options under Output are determined by your setup and configuration of 3D Studio.

Selecting the Output Device

1. Depending on your setup and configuration of 3D Studio, you can output the sample windows to the display device or a frame buffer.

   Display: Sample windows are rendered to the display device: your monitor.

   Framebuffer: A framebuffer is generally a high-end graphics card and monitor capable of supporting 16 or 32 bit graphics. Depending on the configuration, the framebuffer may use the same graphics card and monitor, a separate graphics card looped back through to the same monitor, or a separate graphics card and monitor.

2. Depending on your configuration and setup, you may have the **Display** button only, or **Display** and **Framebuffer** buttons. If your system is configured to use a framebuffer and the button appears under Output, you have the option of rendering to Display only, Framebuffer only, or both Display and Framebuffer.

3. Your configuration and selection depends on your final output. Configure your system and select the Display or Framebuffer option that will produce the best representation of your final output.

TIP If your system is configured for a framebuffer, you can render the sample windows to both the Display and Framebuffer. This isn't recommended, however, because this significantly increases the rendering time.

RELATED COMMANDS

See the 3D Studio Setup and Configuration manuals for installation and use of a framebuffer.

See Tiling

Controls the number of times a bitmap is repeated on a sample sphere or cube.

Each sphere was rendered with the same bitmap, but used a different tiling value.

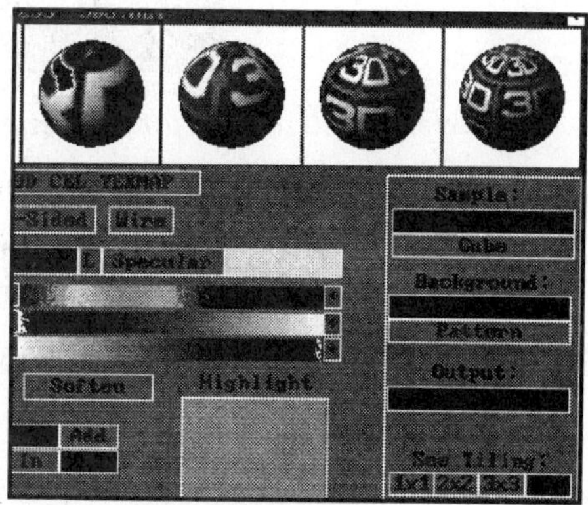

Changing the Tiling Value

1. Changing the Tiling value is primarily used when viewing bitmap images in the sample window. When it is difficult to see the bitmap image, you can change the Tiling value.
2. Selecting one of the Tiling buttons, such as the **1X1** button, repeats the bitmap image once horizontally and once vertically. The **2X2** button repeats the bitmap image twice horizontally and twice vertically.
3. When rendering sample spheres, the number of repetitions cover the entire sphere. Rendering sample cubes shows the tiling on the front of the cube only.
4. If you have difficulty seeing the bitmap image in the sample window, change the Tiling value and then select Render Sample.
5. You can change the Tiling value and use *Render Sample* as often as needed, since it does not change or affect the material.

> **NOTE** Changing the Tiling value only affects the display in the sample window. It does not affect the material, or how the material is applied to the geometry. If you want to tile the bitmap on the geometry, see *Surface/Mapping/Adjust/Tile* in the 3D Editor.

RELATED COMMANDS

Surface/Mapping/Adjust/Tile in the 3D Editor, Texture 1 under Mapping Assignment

Clear Settings

Clears all settings of the current material.

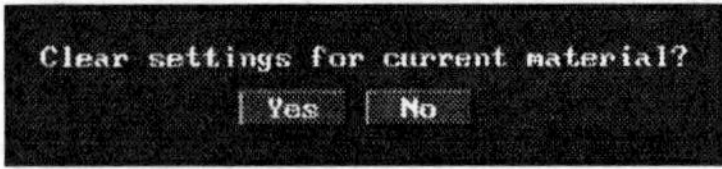

Before clearing all settings for a material, you are asked to confirm the operation.

Clearing the Settings of the Current Material

1. Selecting the **Clear Settings** button accesses a warning box, asking you to confirm the clear settings for the current material.
2. Selecting **Yes** will clear the following:

   Sample Window: Erased.

   Shading Mode: Set to Phong.

   Colors: All colors are set to 0 (black), along with the **Hue Luminance,** and Saturation buttons.

   Material Properties: All attributes, such as Shininess, Shin. Strength, etc., are set to 0.

   Mapping Assignments: All bitmaps are cleared, the **Face Map** button is turned off, and all mapping parameters are returned to their default.

> **NOTE** Clearing the settings for a material does not affect the material stored in the material library. If you want to remove the material from the material library, see *Material–Remove Material*.

RELATED COMMAND

Material–Remove Material.

File Info

Displays information about selected *.TGA, .TIF, .GIF, .FLI, .FLC, .BMP,* and *.JPG* files. The type of information displayed varies, depending upon the graphic file selected.

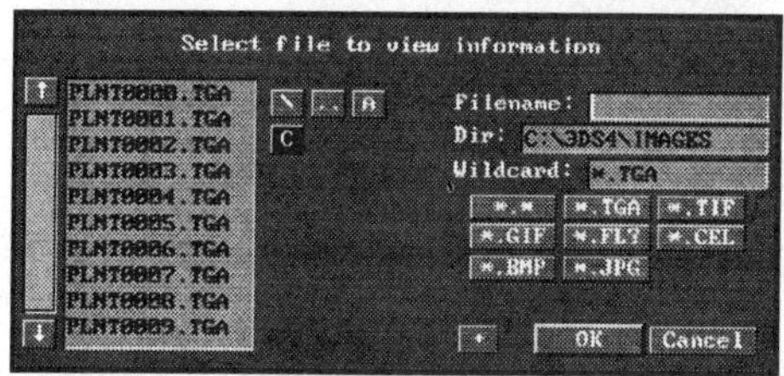

Select the type and the name of the file you want information about.

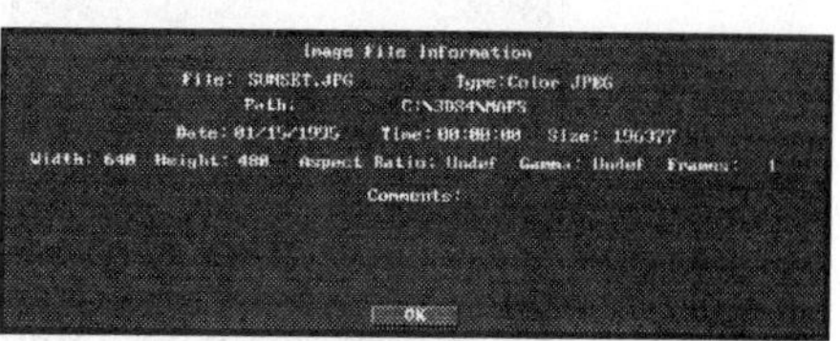

Typical information displayed for a selected bitmap.

Displaying Information about a Selected Graphic File

1. Selecting the **File Info** button accesses the Select file to view information dialog box.
2. Select the type of file, and change to the appropriate drive and directory. Select the file and click on **OK.**
3. The Image File Information box appears. Depending on the file selected, the information will vary. At a minimum the filename, date, time, and size of the file is displayed.

TIP You can easily display information about any file located in any of the mapping buttons. Simply select it and hold the mouse button down. While continuing to hold down the mouse button, drag the filename outline on top of the File Info button and release the mouse button. The Image File Information box appears, showing all available information on the file.

RELATED COMMAND

View Image

View Image

Allows you to display a bitmap image on the current display device.

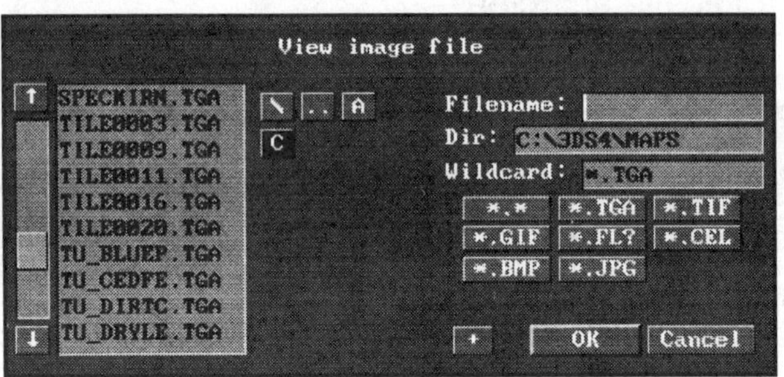

Select the type and the name of the file you want to view.

Viewing a Selected Image

1. Click on the **View Image** button to access the View image file dialog box.
2. Select the type of image file you want to view, and change to the appropriate drive and directory. Select the file and click on **OK**.
3. The selected bitmap is displayed on the current display device.

> **TIP** You can easily view any file located in any of the mapping buttons. Simply select it and hold the mouse button down. While continuing to hold down the mouse button, drag the file name outline on top of the **View Image** button and release the mouse button. The selected bitmap is displayed on the current display device.

RELATED COMMAND

File Info

Auto Put

Used in combination with the Render Last button, the material currently in the materials editor is automatically put to the scene before rendering when the button is activated.

Auto Put

Activating Render Put automatically replaces the same named material in the 3D Scene with the current material in the materials editor.

Using Auto Put

1. Activating Auto Put will automatically replace the same named material in the 3D Scene with the current material in the materials editor. Click on Render Put to activate it.
2. Press the **Render Last** button. With *Render Put* activated, the material is automatically replaced in the current 3D Scene.

When *Render Put* is activated, you are not warned the current material will replace the material with the same name in the 3D Scene.

TIP

If you are modifying several materials from the current 3D Scene, you can update them individually as soon as you have completed changing them. See *Material-Put to Scene.*

RELATED COMMANDS

Render Last, Material-Put to Scene

Render Last

Repeats the last rendering performed in the Keyframer or 3D Editor, using the same settings.

Render Last

Using Render Last in combination with Auto Put can speed up the process of making material adjustments in your 3D Scene.

Rendering the Last Scene

1. To render the last scene while in the Materials Editor, click on the **Render Last** button.
2. If the last rendering you did was in the Keyframer, the current frame is rendered. If the last rendering was in the 3D Editor, the last scene is rendered using the same settings.

Using Auto Put with Render Last

When you are nearing your final renderings and making small adjustments in materials, try the following:

1. Use *Render/Render Object* and select the object you want to make the material adjustment on in the 3D Editor.
2. In the Materials Editor, select *Material-Get from Scene* to get the material from the object you want to change.
3. Activate the **Auto Put** button, and click on Render Last.
4. Because you only rendered one object, rendering time is considerably faster than if you had rendered the entire scene.
5. As long as you leave Auto Put on, you can continue to make adjustments to the material and have it automatically updated in the scene when you select *Render Last*.

RELATED COMMANDS

Render/Render Object, Material–Get from Scene, Auto Put

Render Sample

Uses the current sample window to create a rendering using the settings in the materials editor.

Render Sample

Click to render a sample, using the current material settings.

Rendering a Sample

1. Make sure you are in the sample window where you want the rendering to appear.
2. Clicking on *Render Sample* will create a rendering in the selected window, using the current settings in the material editor.

Pressing the Spacebar or Enter will also render a sample.

RELATED COMMAND

None

Flat

Forces the material to render using the Flat option.

Using Flat Shading Mode

1. Create or load a material.
2. Select the *Flat* shading mode.
3. Make other adjustments to the material as necessary.
4. Render the sample in either the Sample Window or with the *Renderer/ Render View* command.

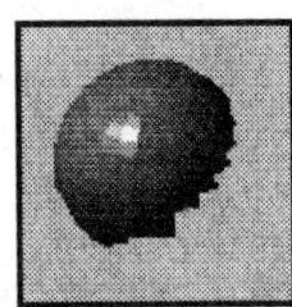

A sphere rendered using Flat shading

All objects that are rendered using the Flat option will have no smoothing on its edges and all objects will appear faceted.

RELATED COMMANDS

Gouraud, Phong, Metal

Gouraud

Forces the material to render using the Gouraud option.

Using Gouraud Shading Mode

1. Create or load a material.
2. Select the *Gouraud* shading mode.
3. Make other adjustments to the material as necessary.
4. Render the sample in the Sample Window or with the *Renderer/Render View* command.

A sphere rendered using Gourand shading.

> **NOTE** All objects that are rendered using the Gouraud option will smooth surfaces by insert colors across the faces based on the colors of the vertices.

RELATED COMMANDS

Flat, Phong, Metal

Phong

Forces the material to render using the Phong option.

Using Phong Shading Mode

1. Create or load a material.
2. Select the *Phong* shading mode.
3. Make other adjustments to the material as necessary.
4. Render the sample in either the Sample Window or with the *Renderer/ Render View* command.

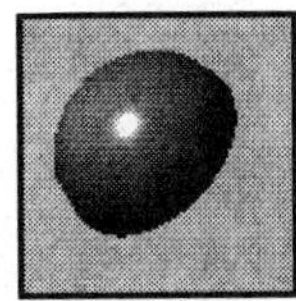

A sphere rendered using Phong shading.

NOTE All objects that are rendered using the Phong option will have its shading produced by modifying each pixel. This and *Metal* are the most time consuming rendering options and must be used to render shadows, bump maps, transparency falloff, and reflection maps.

RELATED COMMANDS

Flat, Gouraud, Metal

Metal

Forces the material to render using the Metal option.

Using Metal Shading Mode

1. Create or load a material.
2. Select the *Metal* shading mode. The **Specular** button and its color swatch will be removed from the Material Editor.
3. Make other adjustments to the material as necessary.
4. Render the sample in either the Sample Window or with the *Renderer/ Render View* command.

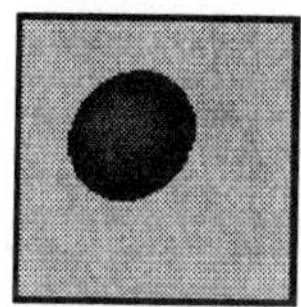

A sphere rendered using Metal shading.

NOTE All objects that are rendered using the Metal option will have its shading produced by modifying each pixel. The difference between the Metal option and Phong is that this option uses the Cool/ Torrance illumination model to create a metallic sheen on the object. This and *Phong* are the most time consuming rendering options and must be used to render shadows, bump maps, transparency fall-off, and reflection maps.

RELATED COMMANDS

Flat, Gouraud, Phong

2-Sided

Forces both sides of the face on the object assigned the material to be rendered.

Using 2-Sided Shading Mode

1. Create or load a material.
2. Select the **2-Sided** button.
3. Make any necessary adjustments to the material.
4. Render the sample in either the Sample Window or with the *Render/Render View* command.

RELATED COMMANDS

Flat, Gourand, Metal

Wire

Forces the material to render using the Wire option.

Using Wire

1. Select the Wire button.
2. The wire frame dialog box will appear.
3. Make adjustments to the dialog box as described:

   Pixels: Renders the thickness of the wire based on the number of pixels.

   Units: Renders the thickness of the wire in real world units.

   OK: Accepts the values and closes the dialog box.

   Cancel: Cancels the settings and closes the dialog box.

A sphere rendered using the Wire option.

RELATED COMMANDS

2-Sides, 3D Editor-Modify/Edge

Ambient

Displays the color of the segment of the object that is not in direct light.

Use this slider to adjust the Ambient value.

Modifying the Ambient Color

1. Click on the **Ambient** button.
2. Change the color controls found below the Ambient color swatch as described below.

   R: Adjusts the Red value.

   G: Adjusts the Green value.

   B: Adjusts the Blue value.

   H: Adjusts the Hue (Color) value.

   L: Adjusts the Luminance (Brightness) value.

   S: Adjusts the Saturation (Purity) value.
3. As the color controls are adjusted, the Ambient color swatch will reflect the changes.

> **NOTE** To modify Ambient and Diffuse at the same time, use the lock feature. Click on the *L* button. Make adjustments as described above. Both color swatches will be changed at the same time. To modify Ambient, Diffuse and Specular at the same time, use both lock buttons.

RELATED COMMANDS

Diffuse, Specular

Diffuse

Displays the color of the segment of the object that is lighted.

Use this slider to adjust the Diffuse value.

Modifying the Diffuse Color

1. Click on the **Diffuse** button.
2. Change the color controls found below the Diffuse color swatch as described below.

   R: Adjusts the Red value.

   G: Adjusts the Green value.

   B: Adjusts the Blue value.

   H: Adjusts the Hue (Color) value.

   L: Adjusts the Luminance (Brightness) value.

   S: Adjusts the Saturation (Purity) value.
3. As the color controls are adjusted, the Diffuse color swatch will reflect the changes.

NOTE To modify Ambient and Diffuse at the same time, use the lock feature. Click on the *L* button. Make adjustments as described above. Both color swatches will be changed at the same time. To modify Ambient, Diffuse and Specular at the same time, use both lock buttons.

RELATED COMMANDS

Ambient, Specular

Specular

Displays the color of the segment of the object that is in the brightest lighted.

Specular

Use this slider to adjust the Specular value.

Modifying the Specular Color

1. Click on the **Specular** button.
2. Change the color controls found below the Specular color swatch as described below.

   R: Adjusts the Red value.

   G: Adjusts the Green value.

   B: Adjusts the Blue value.

   H: Adjusts the Hue (Color) value.

   L: Adjusts the Luminance (Brightness) value.

   S: Adjusts the Saturation (Purity) value.
3. As the color controls are adjusted, the Specular color swatch will reflect the changes.

NOTE To modify Specular and Diffuse at the same time, use the lock feature. Click on the **L** button between the two. Make adjustments as described above. Both color swatches will be changed at the same time. To modify Ambient, Diffuse and Specular at the same time, use both lock buttons.

RELATED COMMANDS

Ambient, Diffuse

Shininess

Adjusts the size of the specular highlight.

Use these two sliders to adjust the Shininess of a material.

Modifying the Size of the Specular Highlight

1. Create or load a material.
2. Select the **Phong** shading mode.
3. Select the **Sphere** sample.
4. Modify the **Shininess** slider. Increasing the value will make the specular highlight smaller and decreasing the value will make the highlight larger. The value will be shown in the highlight graph.
5. Render the sample in either the Sample Window or with the *Renderer/ Render View* command.

Use the Highlight Graph to visually adjust the settings.

When Phong is selected, the Soften button appears. This option will soften the highlight as well as smooth the highlights edges.

RELATED COMMAND

Shin. Strength

Shin. Strength

Adjusts the amount of the specular highlight.

Use these two sliders to adjust the Shininess of a material.

Modifying the Amount of the Specular Highlight

1. Create or load a material.
2. Select the **Phong** shading mode.
3. Select the **Sphere** sample.
4. Modify the **Shin. Strength** slider. Increasing the value will make the specular highlight brighter and decreasing the value will make the highlight dimmer. The value will be shown in the Highlight Graph as shown below.
5. Render the sample in either the Sample Window or with the *Renderer/ Render View* command.

Use the Highlight Graph to visually adjust settings.

RELATED COMMAND

Shininess

Transparency

Adjusts the amount of transparency of a material.

Use this slider to adjust the Transparency of a material.

Adjusting Transparency

1. Create or load a material.
2. Select the **Phong** shading mode.
3. Select the **Sphere** sample.
4. Select the **Pattern** background.
5. Modify the **Transparency** slider. Increasing the value will make the material more transparent and decreasing the value will decrease the amount of transparency.
6. Use the **Sub** option to create a material with glass-like properties. This option will mix the color gray to the objects showing through the transparent material.
7. Use the **Add** option to create a material with light properties. This option will mix the color of the transparent material to the objects showing through the transparent material.
8. Render the sample in either the Sample Window or with the *Renderer/ Render View* command.

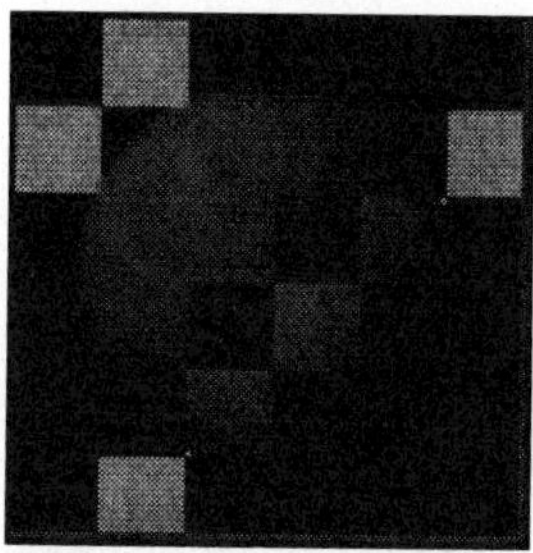

An examaple of a transparent material.

RELATED COMMAND

Trans. Falloff

Trans. Falloff

Adjusts the amount of transparency falloff through a transparent material.

Use this slider to adjust the Transparency Falloff for a material.

Adjusting Transparency

1. Create or load a material.
2. Select the **Phong** shading mode.
3. Select the **Sphere** sample.
4. Select the **Pattern** background.
5. Modify the **Transparency** slider to create a transparent material.
6. Modify the **Trans. Falloff** slider. Changing this slider will adjust the amount of transparency on the outside or inside of the object receiving the material. This command must be used in conjunction with the **Out** and **In** options.
7. Choosing **Out** will transfer the **Trans. Falloff** slider values to the outside of the object.
8. Choosing **In** will transfer the **Trans. Falloff** slider values to the inside of the object.
9. Render the sample in either the Sample Window or with the *Renderer/ Render View* command.

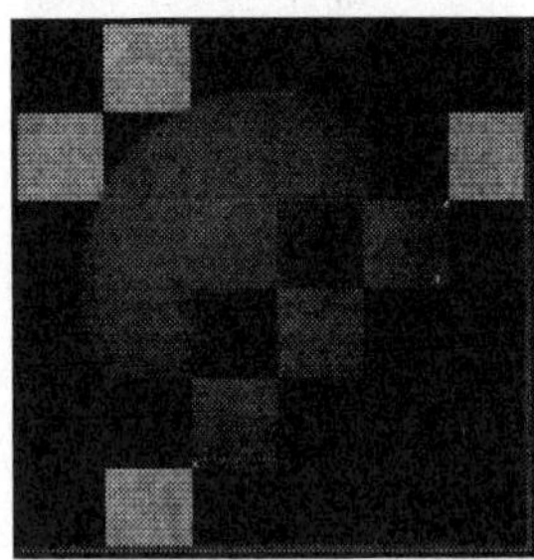

An example of a material using Transparency Falloff.

RELATED COMMAND

Transparency

Reflection Blur

Adjusts the amount of blur that is applied to a reflection map.

Use this slider to adjust the Reflection Blur for a material.

Adjusting the Reflection Blur

1. Create or load a material.
2. Select the **Phong** shading mode.
3. Select the **Sphere** sample.
4. Add reflection mapping using the **Reflection** mapping assignment button.
5. Adjust the **Reflection Blur** slider. Increasing the value softens the reflection map and decreasing the value sharpens the reflection map.
6. Render the sample in either the Sample Window or with the *Renderer/ Render View* command.

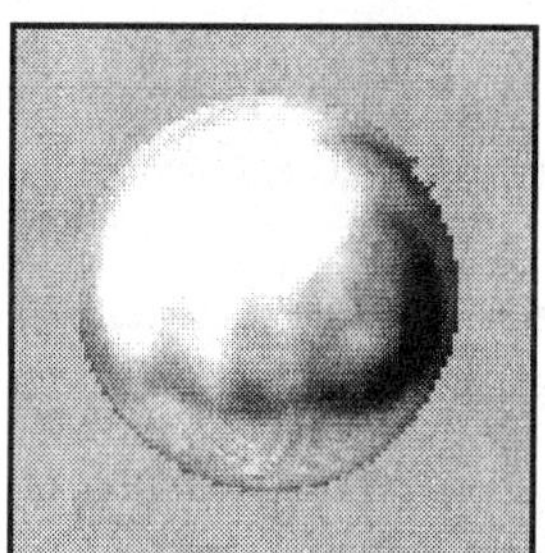

Material with Blur.

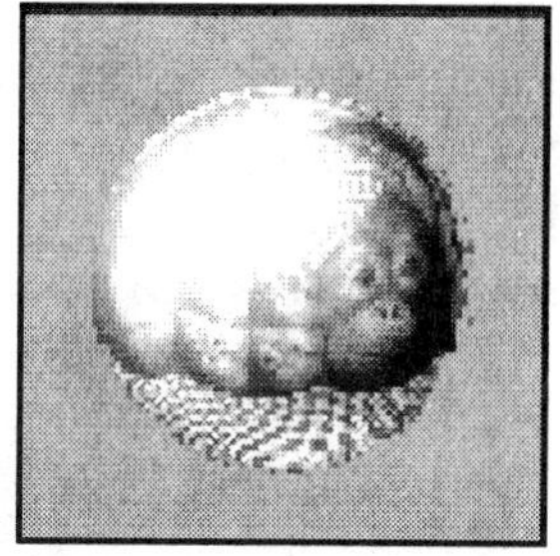

Material without Blur.

NOTE This option has no effect on flat-mirror reflection maps.

RELATED COMMAND

Reflection

Self Illum.

Adjusts the amount of illumination for a self-illuminated material.

Use this slider to adjust the Self Illumination of a material.

Adjusting the Self Illum. Slider

1. Create or load a material.
2. Select the **Phong** shading mode.
3. Select the **Sphere** or **Cube** sample.
4. Ensure that the **Self Illum** mapping is turned off.
5. Adjust the **Self Illum.** slider. Increasing the value will increase the amount of illumination for the material.
6. Render the sample in either the Sample Window or with the *Renderer/Render View* command.

> **NOTE** Use this option to create objects such as parking lights for vehicles, lighted switches and buttons, or add a glow to gems or precious metals.

An example of a material using Self Illumination.

RELATED COMMAND

None

Face Map

Ignores the mapping coordinates for an object. The object will now receive a map on every face of the object.

Face Map

The Face Map button

Assigning a Face Map

1. Select an empty Sample Window.
2. Select the **Texture 1** map button. The button will turn red.
3. Click on the map file slot. The Select Texture Map dialog box appears.
4. Select a bitmapped file for the texture map.
5. Move the amount slider to 100.
6. Click on the **Face Map** button. The button will turn red.
7. Select the **Cube** representation button. The button will turn red.
8. Press the spacebar or select Render Sample. The sample will be rendered in the Sample Window. The texture map will appear on all sides of the cube sample as shown below.

An example of a material using a Face Map.

Do not use a sphere as a representative object for the face map option. This will result in a pattern to small to verify.

RELATED COMMANDS

Texture 1 Map, Cube, Sphere

Map Type: Texture 1

Assigns a bitmap image as the texture for a material.

Use these sliders and buttons to assign a Texture map.

Assigning a Texture Map

1. Select an empty Sample Window.
2. Select a **Sphere** or **Cube** sample.
3. Select the **Texture 1** map button. The button will turn red.
4. Click on the map file slot. The Select Texture Map dialog box appears.
5. Select the bitmap to be used as the texture 1 map.
6. Adjust the amount slider to adjust the effect of the bitmap material. The range for the slider is 0 (less effect) to 100 (full effect).
7. Click on the S button (settings button). The "Mapping Parameters" dialog box appears as shown below.

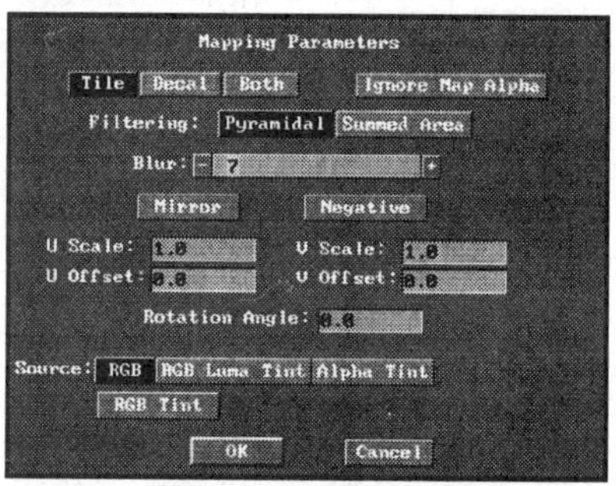

The Mapping Parameters dialog box.

8. Make adjustments to the dialog box as described below.

Tile: Causes the bitmap to repeated along the X and Y axis if the bitmap is smaller than the object. If this option is not selected, the bitmap will be resized to fit the face it is being applied to.

Decal: Place a single instance of the bitmap on a face. This option will also use a portion of the bitmap as a transparent object to allow the ambient and diffuse colors to show. This portion is determined by the use of the Ignore Map Alpha option.

Both: Combines aspects of both **Tile** and **Decal.**

Ignore Map Alpha: Specifies the transparent color by taking a sample pixel from the upper-left corner of the bitmap.

Filtering: Specifies the type of antialias filtering to be applied to the bitmap.

Pyramidal: Use this option for materials that are assigned to surfaces that recede into the distance.

Summed Area: Use this option for small bitmaps or when materials appear to move in animations.

Blur: Changes the value of the slider to effect the sharpness of the bitmap. The range for the slider is from 0 (no blur) to 100 (full blur).

Mirror: Mirrors the bitmap in the horizontal and vertical directions.

Negative: Creates a negative of the bitmap similar to the negatives used in film for photography. This option is good for reversing the effects of a bump map or mask.

U Scale: Changes the horizontal scaling of the texture bitmap. **V Scale:** Changes the vertical scaling of the texture bitmap.

U Offset: Changes the horizontal location of the texture bitmap.

V Offset: Changes the vertical location of the texture bitmap.

Rotation Angle: Changes the rotation angle of the texture bitmap. A positive value rotates the bitmap clockwise.

Source: Specifies the channels to be used by the mapping type.

RGB: Intensity (luminance) value is determined by the color of the bitmap. A white pixel will produce full intensity and a black pixel will yield no intensity.

RGB Luma Tint: When selected, two color swatches will be displayed. Adjust the tint of the bitmap colors will be determined based on the two color swatches.

Alpha Tint: Alpha intensity values, not luminance, is used to specify the tint color of the texture bitmap.

RGB Tint: When selected, three color swatches will be displayed. Adjust these three swatches to change the color value of the red, green, and blue channels of the texture bitmap.

9. Select **OK** to accept the dialog box settings, select **Cancel** to cancel the settings and close the dialog box.

10. Select the **Mask File Slot** if needed. The "Select Texture Mask Map" dialog box appears.
11. Select a mask bitmap if you want to mask the effects of the texture map. It is generally better to use a black and white bitmap for the mask. The white portions of the bitmap will allow the texture map to be displayed where as the black portion will exclude the bitmap effects.
12. If a Mask File is being used click on the Mask File Settings button (S). The Mapping Parameters dialog described above is displayed. The only difference is that there is only **RGB** and **Alpha** for the **Source:** settings. This time the settings will only effect the Mask bitmap.
13. Select **Render Sample** or press the spacebar to see the effects of the texture map in the Sample Window.

> **NOTE** In order to use texture map materials, you must assign mapping coordinates to the object receiving the material unless you select the *Face Map* option or use the *Surface/Material/Box/Assign* command.

RELATED COMMANDS

Texture 2 Map, Face Map

Map Type: Texture 2

Assigns a bitmap image as the texture for a material.

Use these sliders and buttons to assign a second Texture map.

Assigning a Second Texture Map

1. Select an empty Sample Window.
2. Select a **Sphere** or **Cube** sample.
3. Use the **Texture 1** command to assign a texture bitmap.
4. Select the **Texture 2** map button. The button will turn red.
5. Click on the map file slot. The Select Texture Map dialog box appears.
6. Select the bitmap to be used as the texture 2 map.
7. Select the S (settings) button next to the map file slot. The "Mapping Parameters" dialog box appears. Adjust the settings as described in the *Texture 1* option.
8. Adjust the Amount Slider as necessary.
9. Adjust the Mask bitmap if necessary. See **Texture 1** for a description of these options.
10. Select **Render Sample** or press the spacebar to see the effects of the texture map in the Sample Window.

This option will override the *Texture 1* option if the value slider is set to 100. Using any value less than 100 will combine the two texture bitmaps to create a new material.

TIP

Use two texture bitmaps to create effects such as scratches on wood.

RELATED COMMAND

Texture 1 Map

Map Type: Opacity

Adjusts the amount of transparency and opacity for the material based on the assigned bitmap.

Use these sliders and buttons to assign a Opacity mapping.

Assigning an Opacity Map

1. Select an empty Sample Window.
2. Select a **Sphere** or **Cube** sample.
3. Select the **Opacity** map button. The button will turn red.
4. Click on the map file slot. The Select Opacity Map dialog box appears.
5. Select the bitmap to be used as the opacity map.
6. If necessary, select the S (settings) button next to the map file slot. The Mapping Parameters dialog box appears. Adjust the settings as described in the **Texture 1** option.
7. Adjust the Amount Slider as necessary.
8. Adjust the Mask bitmap if necessary. See **Texture 1** for a description of these options.
9. Select **Render Sample** or press the spacebar to see the effects of the opacity map in the Sample Window.

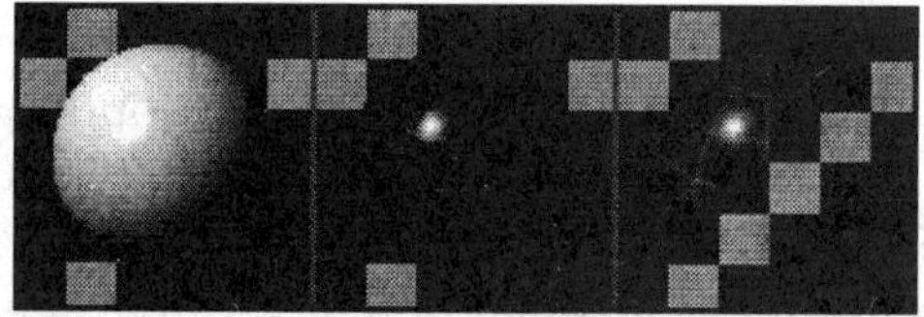

Before - Opacity Map - After

NOTE The amount of opacity is based on the color of the bitmap. The darker the color, the more the material becomes opaque. Use black and white bitmaps to create precisely defined areas of transparency and opacity.

RELATED COMMANDS

Texture 1 Map, Transparency

Map Type: Bump

Adjusts the amount of bumpiness or embossing properties for the material based on the assigned bitmap.

Use these sliders and buttons to assign a Bump map.

Assigning an Bump Map

1. Select an empty Sample Window.
2. Select a **Sphere** or **Cube** sample.
3. Select the **Bump** map button. The button will turn red.
4. Click on the map file slot. The Select Bump Map dialog box appears.
5. Select the bitmap to be used as the bump map.
6. If necessary, select the S (settings) button next to the map file slot. The Mapping Parameters dialog box appears. Adjust the settings as described in the **Texture 1** option.
7. Adjust the Amount Slider as necessary. The amount of bumpiness is not only dependent on this slider but by the bitmap as well. Light colors in the bitmap increase bumpiness and dark colors decrease bumpiness.
8. Adjust the Mask bitmap if necessary. See **Texture 1** for a description of these options.
9. Select **Render Sample** or press the spacebar to see the effects of the bump map in the Sample Window.

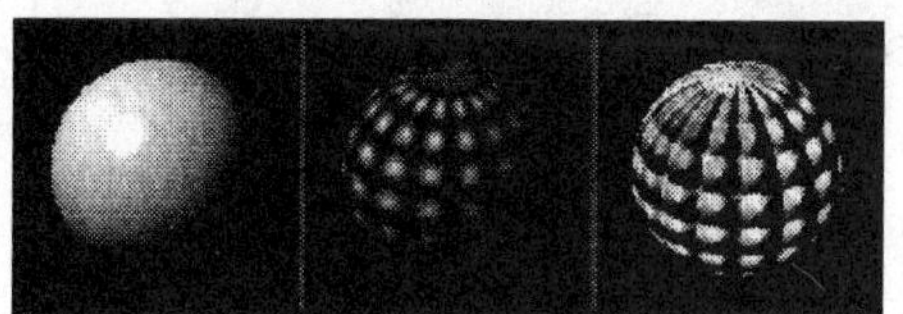

Before - Bump Map - After.

> **TIP** Use black and white bitmaps to create embossed materials because their bumpiness can be defined precisely.

RELATED COMMAND

Texture 1 Map

Map Type: Specular

Places the bitmapped assigned over the specular highlight of an object.

Use these sliders and buttons to assign a Specular map.

Assigning an Specular Map

1. Select an empty **Sample Window**.
2. Select a **Sphere** sample.
3. Adjust the **Shininess** and **Shin. Strength** sliders to create a highlight on the sample sphere.
4. Select the **Specular** map button. The button will turn red.
5. Click on the map file slot. The Select Bump Map dialog box appears.
6. Select the bitmap to be used as the specular map.
7. If necessary, select the S (settings) button next to the map file slot. The Mapping Parameters dialog box appears. Adjust the settings as described in the **Texture 1** option.
8. Adjust the Amount Slider as necessary.
9. Adjust the Mask bitmap if necessary. See **Texture 1** for a description of these options.
10. Select **Render Sample** or press the spacebar to see the effects of the specular map in the Sample Window.

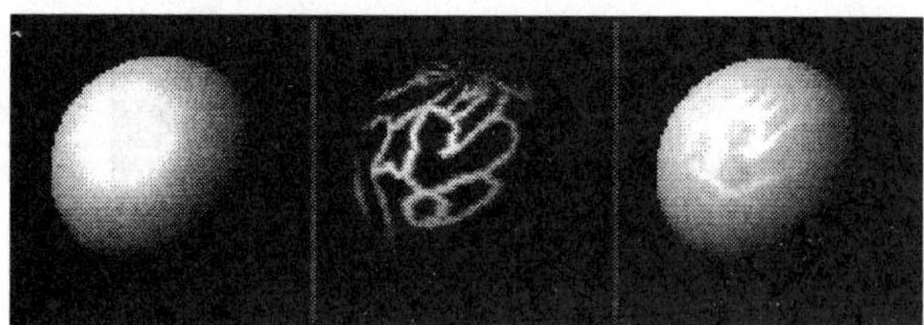

Before - Specular Map - After

RELATED COMMANDS

Phong, Shininess, Shin. Strength

Map Type: Shininess

Modifies the intensity of the specular highlight based on the color values assigned to the selected bitmap.

Use these sliders and buttons to assign Shininess mapping.

Assigning an Shininess Map

1. Select an empty Sample Window.
2. Select a **Sphere** sample.
3. Adjust the **Shininess** and **Shin. Strength** sliders to create a highlight on the sample sphere.
4. Select the **Shininess** map button. The button will turn red.
5. Click on the map file slot. The Select Shininess Map dialog box appears.
6. Select the bitmap to be used as the shininess map.
7. If necessary, select the **S** (settings) button next to the map file slot. The Mapping Parameters dialog box appears. Adjust the settings as described in the **Texture 1** option.
8. Adjust the Amount Slider as necessary.
9. Adjust the Mask bitmap if necessary. See **Texture 1** for a description of these options.
10. Select **Render Sample** or press the spacebar to see the effects of the specular map in the Sample Window.

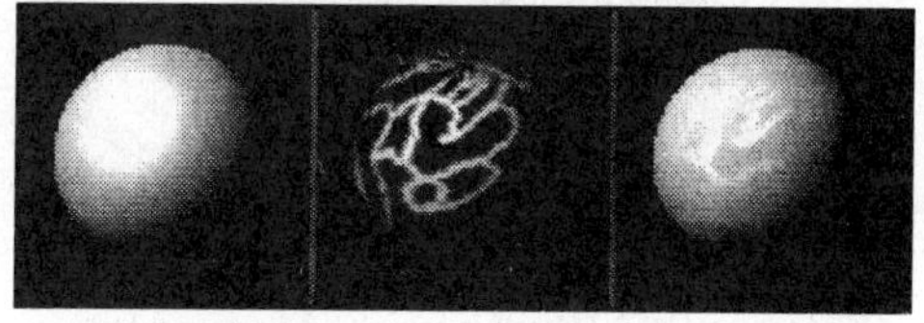

Before - Shininess Map - After

RELATED COMMANDS

Shininess, Shin. Strength, Specular Map

Map Type: Self-Illumination

Adjusts the amount of self-illumination for the material based on the assigned bitmap.

Self Illum - 100 + NONE S NONE S

Use these sliders and buttons to assign Self-Illuminating map.

Assigning an Opacity Map

1. Select an empty Sample Window.
2. Select a **Sphere** or **Cube** sample.
3. Select the **Self-Illumination** map button. The button will turn red.
4. Click on the map file slot. The Select Self-Illumination Map dialog box appears.
5. Select the bitmap to be used as the self-illumination map.
6. If necessary, select the S (settings) button next to the map file slot. The Mapping Parameters dialog box appears. Adjust the settings as described in the **Texture 1** option.
7. Adjust the Amount Slider as necessary.
8. Adjust the Mask bitmap if necessary. See **Texture 1** for a description of these options.
9. Select **Render Sample** or press the spacebar to see the effects of the opacity map in the Sample Window.

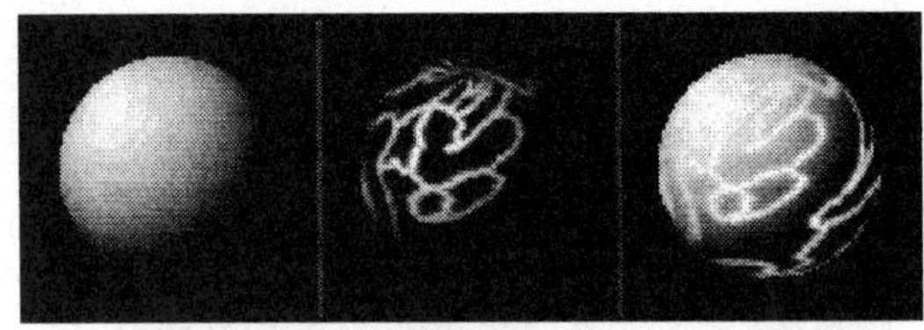

Before - Self-Illumination Map - After

> **NOTE** When using this option, the **Self Illum.** slider values are ignored.

RELATED COMMAND

Self Illum.

Map Type: Reflection

Assigns a bitmap as a reflected image and locks the reflection map to the scene and not the object.

Use these sliders and buttons to assign Reflection mapping.

Assigning an Reflection Map

1. Select an empty Sample Window.
2. Select a **Sphere** or **Cube** sample.
3. Select the **Reflection** map button. The button will turn red.
4. Click on the map file slot. The Select Reflection Map dialog box appears.
5. Select the bitmap to be used as the reflection map.
6. Adjust the Amount Slider as necessary.
7. If you wish to assign automatic reflection mapping click on the **A** button. Automatic will appear in the map file slot and it will turn red.
8. Click on the map file slot. The Automatic Reflection Map dialog box will appear as shown below.

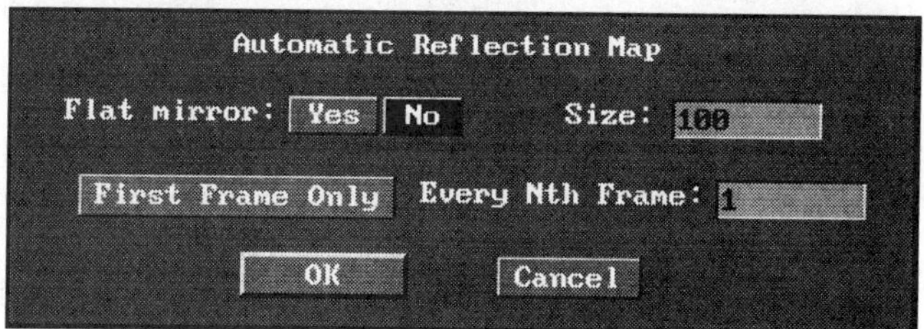

Use this dialog box to make changes to the Automatic Reflection Map.

9. Make adjustments to the dialog box as described below.

Flat mirror: Select **Yes** to create flat mirror maps. Flat mirror maps allow you to easily assign a mirror finish to flat surfaces. Select **No** to use the automatic reflection map settings.

Size: Modifies the size in pixels of the cubic map. Cubic maps are always square and a value of 50 would create a cubic map bitmap at a resolution of 50 x 50 pixels.

First Frame Only: Select this button to create a cubic bitmap only on the first frame of an animation. This is option can save time during rendering because the cubic bitmap will only be calculated in the first frame but will be displayed in all frames. Use this only if the object does not move in an animation.

Every Nth Frame: A value in the edit box to the right of this option will cause the cubic bitmap to be rendered on every Nth frame during an animation. That is, if a value of 2 is chosen, the cubic bitmap will be calculated during every other frame. Use this option for objects that have little movement in an animation.

10. Select **OK** to accept the dialog box settings, select **Cancel** to cancel the settings and close the dialog box.
11. Adjust the Mask bitmap if necessary. See **Texture 1** for a description of these options.
12. To blur the reflection map, use the **Reflec. Blur:** slider.
13. Select **Render Sample** or press the spacebar to see the effects of the opacity map in the Sample Window.

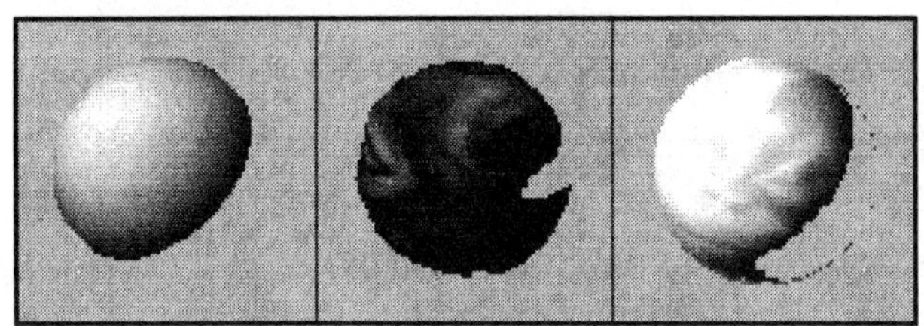

Before - Reflection Map - After.

Unlike the other maps in this section, you cannot use Procedural Maps (SXP) or Procedural Bitmaps (BXP) for reflection maps.

RELATED COMMANDS

Texture 1 Map, Reflec. Blur

Info-About 3D Studio

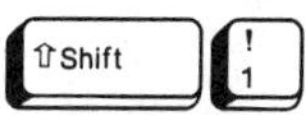

Info
About 3D Studio
Current Status
Configure
System Options
Scene Info
Key Assignments
Gamma Control

Displays the serial and version number of your program.

Displaying Information about Your Program

1. Select *Info-About 3D Studio* to display the serial number, version number, and copyright notice.
2. Pressing any key will remove the display from the screen.

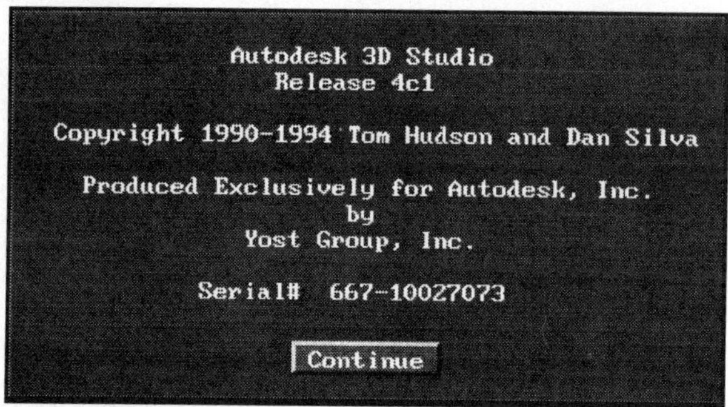

The 3D Studio information box.

RELATED COMMANDS

None

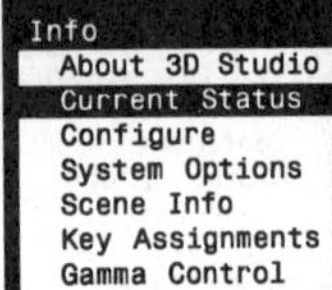

Info-Current Status

Displays the amount of memory used and the amount of memory available, along with additional information about the 3D Editor and 3D Lofter.

Displaying the Current Status of Your Project

The listing in the Current Status display shows the number of current shapes and vertices in the 3D Lofter; the number of current objects, vertices, faces, lights, and cameras in the 3D Editor; information about memory use; and the total time needed to complete the last rendering. Pressing any key will remove the display from the screen.

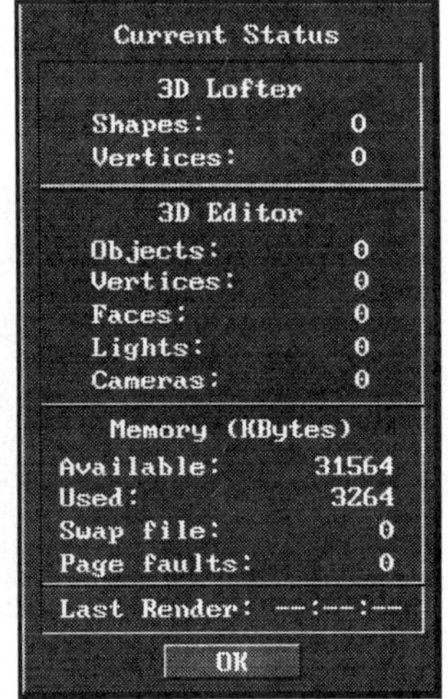

The Current Status box.

TIP To increase speed and performance of 3D Studio, the amount of RAM in your system should exceed the size of the current scene you are working on. When you begin 3D Studio, it instantly takes control of all available RAM. When it runs out of RAM, it builds a virtual swap file on your hard disk. This extends memory space up to the limit of the hard drive space available.

If your system seems to be running slowly, 3D Studio may be using a virtual swap file on your hard disk. To determine if you are swapping to disk, check the Memory section in the Current Status box. If the swap file section is above 0, parts of the current scene are being swapped to disk and performance is significantly degraded. The amount of RAM you need to add to your system to hold the current scene and increase performance should be at a minimum equal to the size of the swap file 3D Studio created. The size of the swap file created is shown in kb after Swap file: in the Current Status box.

RELATED COMMANDS

None

Info-Configure

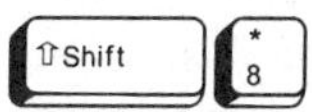

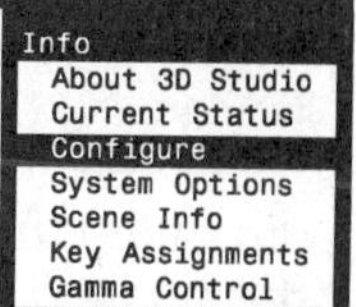

Selects and adjusts the input device and changes the default paths for the Shaper, Lofter, Mesh, Font, and Image. You can also specify up to 250 map paths.

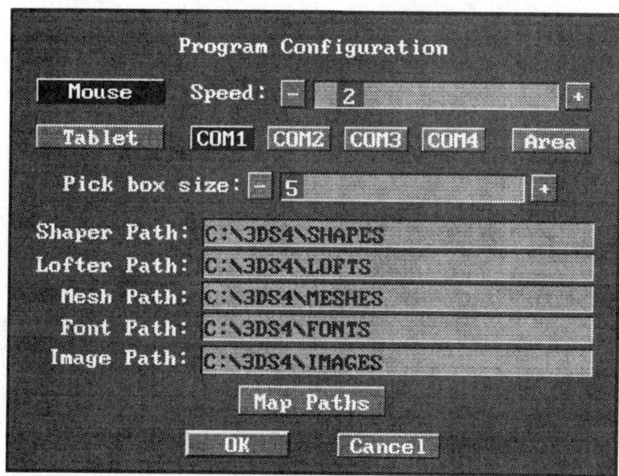

The Program Configuration box.

Mouse/Tablet

You can select *either* a Microsoft-compatible mouse or any pointing device that uses a DGPADI driver.

Speed

Used to change the relationship between the movement of the mouse and screen cursor. The higher the number, the farther you have to physically move the mouse for the cursor to move a given distance on the screen.

COM1-COM4

Used to select the serial (communications) port used by the digitizer.

Area

Used to define the active area of the digitizing tablet. First select the Area button, then select the diagonally opposite corners of the tablet area you want active.

NOTE If you select a com port where no device is connected or click on Area where no device is connected, an alert box tells you 3D Studio cannot find that device. If this occurs, press any key to continue. If neither the mouse or tablet is working, you can use the following keyboard commands:

T	M	1 2 3 4
Tablet	Mouse	COM1-COM4
A	+ -	Enter
Area	Mouse speed	OK

Pick Box Size

Used to adjust the size of the square pick box used to select or place geometry. The greater the slider value, the larger the pick box. While a large cursor is easy to see and work with, it makes it difficult for 3D Studio to distinguish among entities. If you are having trouble selecting or placing geometry, reduce the pick box size or zoom in on the geometry with the Zoom In or Window icons.

Paths

Can be used to edit the default paths for the listed modules, font files, and map and image files. The initial paths listed show the defaults as specified in the *3ds.set* file.

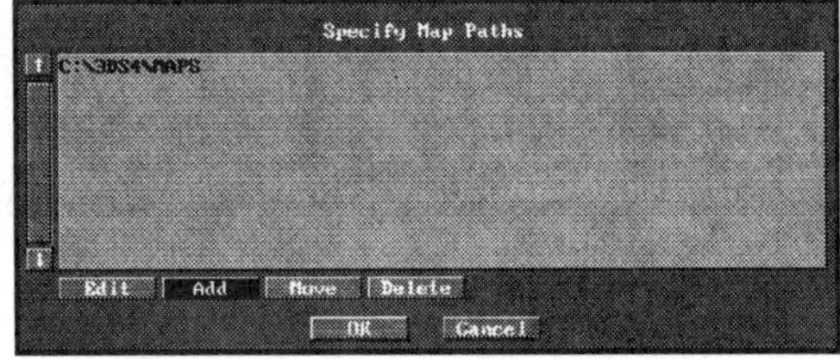

The Specify Map Paths dialog box.

Map Paths

Used to assign up to 250 map paths. These paths are used whenever a graphic file is read by the Renderer.

NOTE Including additional map paths can cause 3D Studio to slow down during rendering, because all of the map paths are searched for the corresponding bitmaps. In addition, if you have two or more bitmaps with the same filename, the Renderer uses the *first* copy of the bitmap it finds.

TIP Any settings changed in the Program Configuration dialog box are restored to their default values every time you restart 3D Studio or select Reset in the File menu. To keep any changes, save your work as a *project*. In addition, you can change any of the default values by permanently editing the *3ds.set* file.

RELATED COMMANDS

None

Info-System Options

Info
About 3D Studio
Current Status
Configure
System Options
Scene Info
Key Assignments
Gamma Control

Allows you to override certain system parameters specified in the *3ds.set* file without exiting 3D Studio.

Backup File

Used when you save a file over an existing file with the same name. When turned **On**, a *.bak* file is created from the old version using the extension name as its prefix. Backup files are created when saving 3DS files (**.3ds*), shape files (**.shp*), library files (**.mli*), and project files (**.prj*).

Region Toggle

Region Toggle affects the way geometry is added to selection sets when the Window or Crossing method is used. It controls whether an object is deselected if chosen twice when using the Window or Crossing method, or if it remains a part of the selection set.

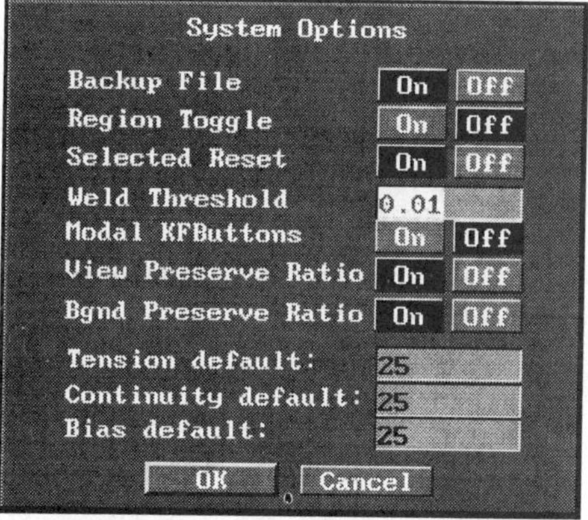

The System Options dialog box.

Selected Reset

Controls whether the **Selected** button is turned off automatically when a new command is chosen from the menu. If Selected Reset toggle is turned to **Off**, the selection set and button remain in effect until a command is chosen that does not use selection sets or it is manually turned off. The commands affected are under the Select options.

Weld Threshold

A value that determines the maximum distance two vertices can be from each other to be welded together with the *Weld* command, or welded together automatically when a *.dxf* file is loaded.

When loading *.dxf* file, set the Weld Threshold value to 0.0001 to weld corresponding vertices together.

Modal KFButtons

Determines whether the **Track Info** and **Scene Info** buttons in the Keyframer remain active or are turned off when exiting the dialog box.

View Preserve Ratio

Controls whether bitmaps automatically fill the screen when using the *Render/View/Image* command in the 3D Editor or Keyframer or whether the aspect ratio is maintained.

Bgnd Preserve Ratio

Affects the proxy image used in viewports when *See Background* (*Views–See Backgrnd*) is active in the 3D Editor or Keyframer. When set to **Yes**, the original aspect ratio of the bitmap is preserved in the proxy image.

Tension default, Continuity default, Bias default

Used to specify the default settings of the key splines in the Key Info dialog box in the Keyframer.

> **TIP** All settings changed in the System Options dialog box are restored to their original values set by the *3ds.set* file every time you restart 3D Studio or select Reset in the File menu. Saving your work as a project file will keep any changes you made.

RELATED COMMANDS

Select/Window, Select/Crossing, Render/View-Image, Views–See Backgrnd, File–Save Project

Info-Scene Info

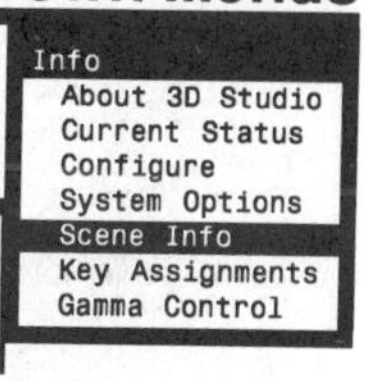

Info
About 3D Studio
Current Status
Configure
System Options
Scene Info
Key Assignments
Gamma Control

Shows text (ASCII) listing of the current scene, including all materials and bitmaps used in the scene.

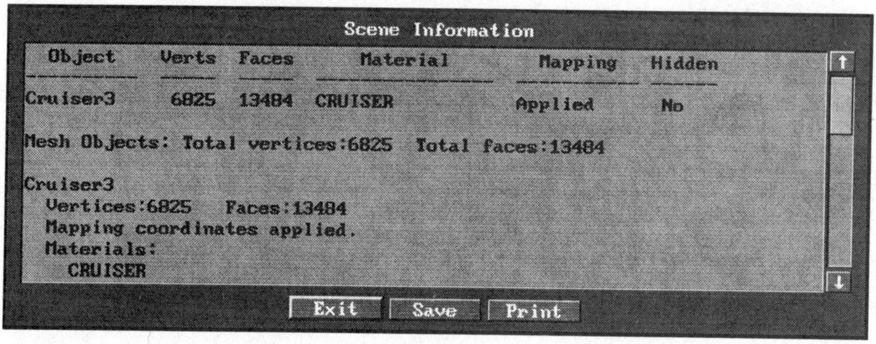

Scene Information

Object	Verts	Faces	Material	Mapping	Hidden
Cruiser3	6825	13484	CRUISER	Applied	No

Mesh Objects: Total vertices:6825 Total faces:13484

Cruiser3
Vertices:6825 Faces:13484
Mapping coordinates applied.
Materials:
CRUISER

Exit Save Print

The Scene Information dialog box.

TIP The Scene Information dialog box can be used to help determine whether mapping coordinates have been assigned to objects, and whether the material assigned to the object requires mapping coordinates.

RELATED COMMANDS

Surface/Material/Choose, Surface/Mapping

Info
About 3D Studio
Current Status
Configure
System Options
Scene Info
Key Assignments
Gamma Control

Info-Key Assignments

Displays and prints the Custom Function Keys dialog box.

Assigning Custom Function Keys

The Custom Function Keys dialog box is *not* used to assign the function keys, only to display and print them. You can assign custom function keys to any program module except the Materials Editor. To create a custom function key, perform the following steps:

1. While in the program module of choice (such as the 3D Editor), hold down the Ctrl key and move the cursor over any command in the column on the right. As you pass the pointing device over the commands, a small K is attached to the cursor indicating you are in the key assignment mode.
2. While holding down the Ctrl key, select the desired command. After selecting a command, the Custom Function Keys dialog box appears.
3. Select any button at the left of the dialog box to assign the command to that function key. After selecting the function key, the command will appear to the right of the button.
4. Select **OK** to exit the dialog box. The assigned command can now be invoked by holding down the Ctrl key and pressing the corresponding function key.

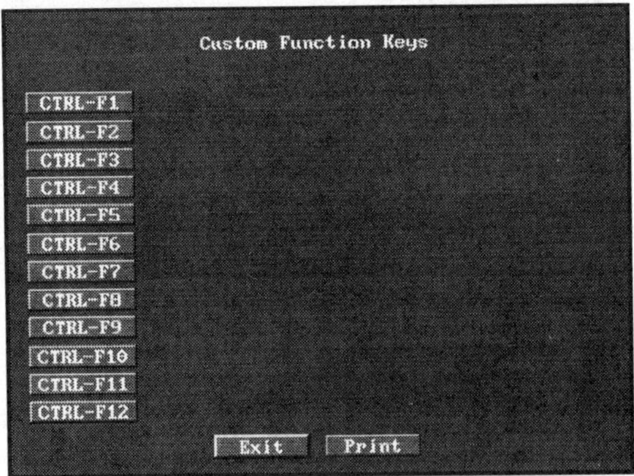

The Custom Function Keys dialog box.

RELATED COMMANDS

None

Info-Gamma Control

Info
About 3D Studio
Current Status
Configure
System Options
Scene Info
Key Assignments
Gamma Control

Allows you to calibrate 3D Studio to your framebuffer and monitor, and specify gamma for file input and output.

Using the Gamma Control Dialog Box

Gamma can be used to calibrate your display screen, framebuffer, input file, and output file so your image will appear the same on all devices. As the gamma of devices varies, the image displayed on one monitor may not look the same on another monitor, depending upon that monitor's gamma values. When you create a rendered image on your computer, your color selections and intensities are based on what you see on your monitor. The Gamma Control dialog box allows you to compensate for changes in gamma among output and display devices and have the image appear the same on all devices.

TIP To set the display gamma for your monitor, select **Set** next to the Display gamma input box. When the Display Gamma dialog box appears, move the slider until both boxes appear to be the same color. The number shown is the proper display gamma for your computer.

NOTE If you are doing network rendering, you must make sure all machines have the gamma parameters set exactly the same, except the Display Gamma. If the settings are not the same, your rendered animation may appear to have color changes among the different frames when rendering. All gamma settings are defaulted in the *3ds.set* file on each machine, so the settings used on the main workstation will not necessarily be the same as the other stations.

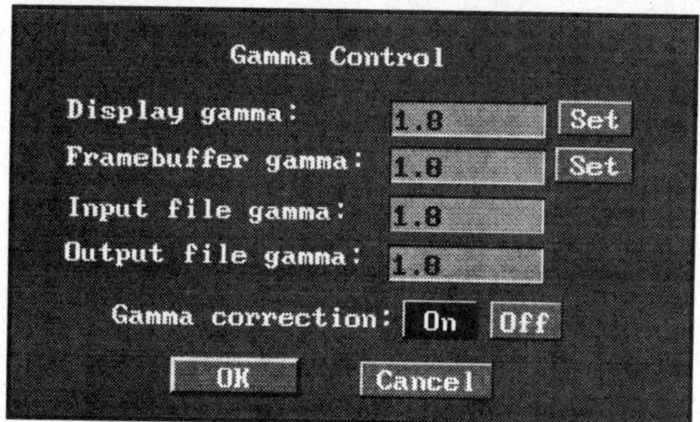

The Gamma Control dialog box.

RELATED COMMANDS

None

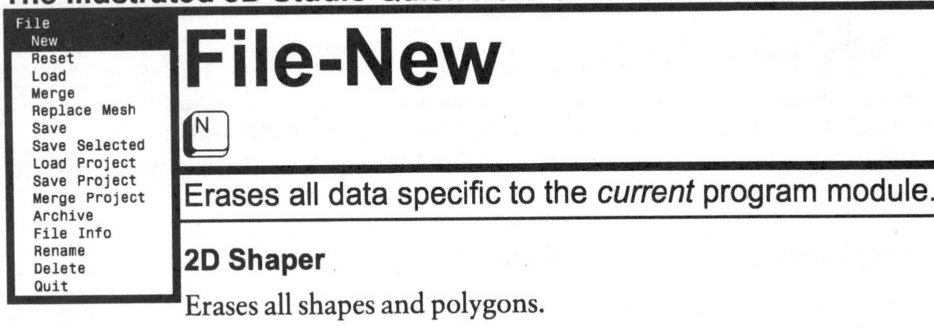

File-New

Erases all data specific to the *current* program module.

2D Shaper

Erases all shapes and polygons.

3D Lofter

Erases all loft shapes and resets the path and all other settings.

3D Editor and Keyframer

Displays the New dialog box with the corresponding options.

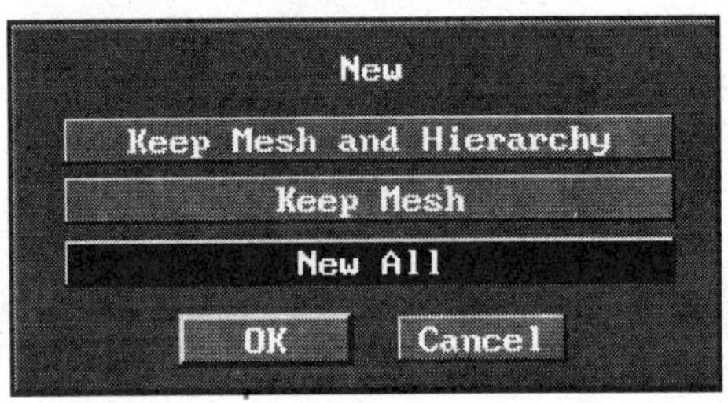

The New dialog box.

Keep Mesh and Hierarchy

Retains all objects, lights, and cameras in both the 3D Editor and Keyframer. Retains all hierarchical links in the Keyframer, but erases all keys and sets new first keys at frame 0.

Keep Mesh

Retains all objects, lights, and cameras in both the 3D Editor and Keyframer. Erases all current key settings and sets new first keys at frame 0 in the Keyframer. Does *not* retain hierarchical links in the Keyframer.

New All

Erases all data, including all mesh objects, lights, cameras, and animation keys from the 3D Editor and Keyframer.

RELATED COMMANDS

None

File-Reset

Resets *all* modules to their default configurations and erases *all* 3D Studio data from the computer's memory.

Resetting 3D Studio

When Reset is selected, an alert box appears asking if you are sure this is what you want to do.

Performing a reset will replace all data in all program modules and reset all settings to their defaults. Are you sure this is what you want?

Yes No

Reset alert box.

Selecting **Yes** in the Reset alert box erases *all* geometry in *all* program modules and restores all system variables to their start-up values.

RELATED COMMANDS

None

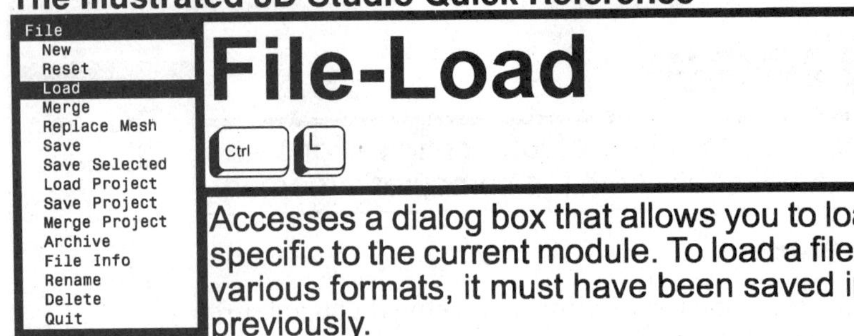

File-Load

Accesses a dialog box that allows you to load a data file specific to the current module. To load a file in one of the various formats, it must have been saved in that format previously.

2D Shaper Loading Options

**.shp* Loads a shape file that consists of either a single assigned shape and its hook or a collection of polygons.

**.dxf* Loads a file that was previously saved in DXF format.

**.ai* Loads a file that was previously saved in Adobe Illustrator (AI) format.

3D Lofter Loading Options

**.lft* Loads a loft file that includes all the components of a single loft. A description of the path contour; the state and configuration of the deformation grids; and the step values of the path, shapes, and fit shapes are included.

3D Editor and Keyframer Loading Options

**.3ds* Loads a scene that contains 3D mesh objects, lights, cameras, animation hierarchy, and keyframer information.

**.asc* Loads an ASCII file containing information about 3D mesh objects, cameras, lights, and any atmosphere settings, materials, mapping coordinates, and smoothing groups.

**.flm* Loads an FLM format filmroll file of a 3D drawing and converts it to a 3DS mesh object.

**.dxf* Loads a file that was saved in DXF format and converts it to a 3DS mesh object.

The default drive and directory for the different file types may be changed under the pull-down menu Info-Configure.

DXF and FLM Loading Options

When loading **.dxf* and **.flm* files in the 3D Editor and Keyframer, the following options are presented:

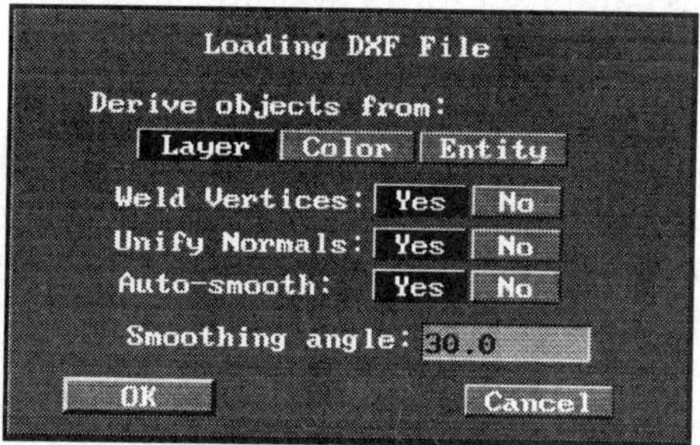

The Loading DXF File dialog box.

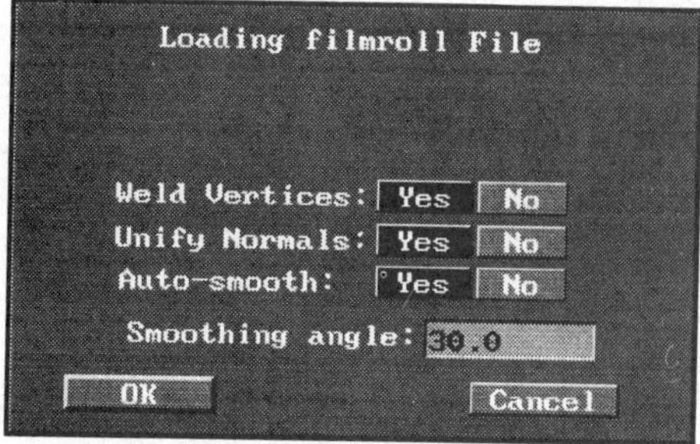

The Loading filmroll File dialog box.

TIP Loading the ACAD.CLR material library before loading a DXF or FLM file will assign materials to the geometry during conversion process that match the colors originally applied to the geometry in AutoCAD. See *Surface/Material/Get Library.*

Derive Objects from Layer, Color, Entity

Each layer with a unique name, each object with a unique color, or each entity will converted into a separate object.

The name of the converted objects may be changed under *Modify/Object/Attributes.*

Weld Vertices

Welds separate vertices that match up point for point into single vertices. The size of the area the vertices must occupy to be welded together is governed by the Weld-Threshold parameter. This can be changed under *Info/System Options.* When importing DXF files, this should be set to 0.0001. This is normally set to **Yes.** If set to **No,** all unwelded objects cannot be unified or smoothed.

NOTE Vertices are welded within each separate object, which were determined by the Layer, Color, or Entity options. Welding is not performed between separate objects.

Unify Normals

Forces the normals of all faces on each object to face in the same direction. When a scene is rendered and certain faces appear transparent, the face normals may be pointing in the wrong direction. Setting this parameter to **Yes** will turn all faces in the converted object the same direction. See *Surface/Normals/Object Flip*.

> **TIP** If you are having difficulty seeing all faces in your object when rendering, activate the **Force 2-Sided** button in the Render still image dialog box. See *Render View, Render Region, Render Blowup, Render Object,* or *Render Last*. You could also apply two-sided materials to the object. See *Shading Mode Options/2-Sided* in the Materials Editor.

Auto–smooth and Smoothing Angle

Applies smoothing to the geometry based on the angle set in the Smoothing angle field. Edges with the included angle greater than the smoothing angle will appear faceted in the rendered image, and edges below the smoothing angle are smoothed. Normally set to **Yes**, with a smoothing angle of 30 degrees. See *Surface/Smoothing/Object/Auto Smooth*.

RELATED COMMANDS

Info-Configure, Surface/Material/Get Library, Modify/Object/Attributes, Info–System Options, Surface/Normals/Object Flip, Surface/Smoothing/Object/Auto Smooth

File-Merge

Combines the current file in memory with the contents of another file.

Merging a File

1. Select Merge from the File pull-down menu.
2. The file being merged must be one that the current module can use. The merge option works slightly differently in each module.

3D Editor and Keyframer Merge Options

1. When you initially select the Merge option, a dialog box appears asking you what you want to merge. Select one or more of the buttons to bring in the components you want.

The Merge dialog box.

NOTE You cannot merge animation data by itself. At least one of the top three buttons must be active.

2. After selecting the type of components you want to merge, a file selector box appears. You can merge **.3ds*, **.dxf*, or **.flm* files. If you selected a **.3ds* type of file to merge, another dialog box appears, listing available objects in the selected file. Select the objects you want to merge, then click **OK**.

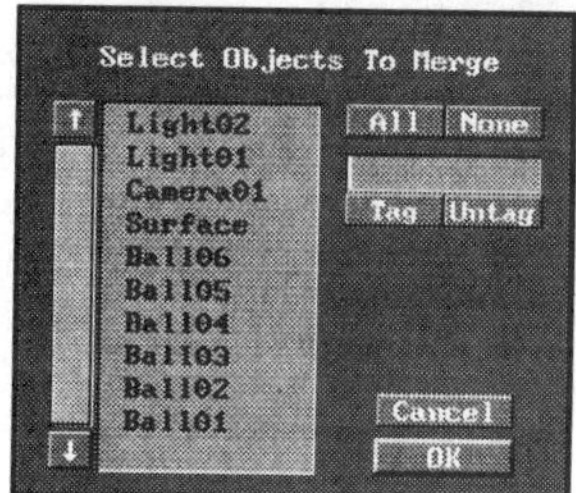

The Select Objects to Merge dialog box.

NOTE If you are merging **.dxf* or **.flm* files, the Loading DXF or Loading FLM dialog box appears. See DXF and FLM Loading Options under *File-Load*.

NOTE If a material in the merging file has the same name as a material in memory, an alert box appears allowing you to replace the material in the scene, or keep the current material in the scene. Each object, light, and camera in 3D space must have a unique name. If any object in the merged file contains a duplicate name, you are given the option of renaming the incoming object.

TIP If you continually use the same or similar lighting and camera setups, you can create the necessary lights and cameras around a simple object and save the file. When you are working on your new scene, you can quickly merge the file containing the lights and cameras and have the scene ready for rendering.

2D Shaper Merge Options

You can merge **.shp, *.dxf*, and **.ai* files into the 2D Shaper module. When merging a valid shape file with a defined shape hook, it is placed according to the position of the hook currently in memory. See *Shape/Hook/Show.*

3D Lofter Merge Options

Although the Merge option is not available in the 3D Lofter, you can load different paths or add additional shapes. See *Path/Get/Disk* and *Shapes/Get Disk.*

RELATED COMMANDS

File-Load, Shape/Hook/Show, Path/Get/Disk, Shapes/Get Disk

File-Replace Mesh

File
New
Reset
Load
Merge
Replace Mesh
Save
Save Selected
Load Project
Save Project
Merge Project
Archive
File Info
Rename
Delete
Quit

Replaces current geometry with geometry that has the same object name from another **.3ds* file.

Using the Replace Mesh Command

When using the *Replace Mesh* command, the imported objects must have exactly the same name as the objects already in the scene. You are given the option of tagging the options you want to replace. After selecting the objects to replace, an alert box appears.

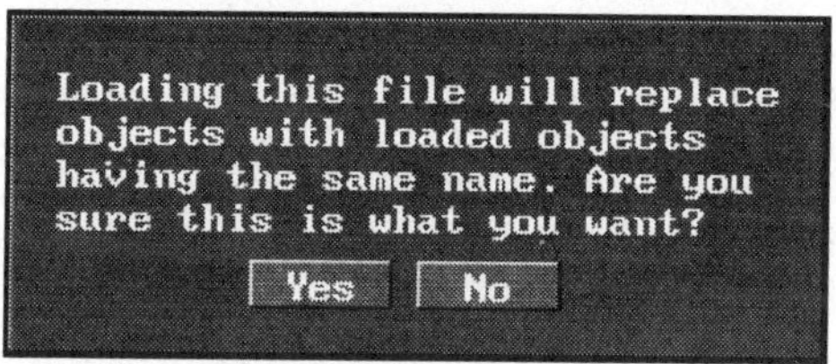

The Mesh alert box.

NOTE All replaced geometry is lost when using the *Replace Mesh* command. If you want to keep the old geometry, save the new file with the merged objects under a different file name.

TIP The *Replace Mesh* command can be used to speed up the scene creation process, especially if complex objects are used. When initially creating a scene, use simple objects, such as a ball or cube, as stand-in objects. When you are ready to complete the scene, replace the stand-in objects with the detailed ones.

RELATED COMMANDS

File-Merge

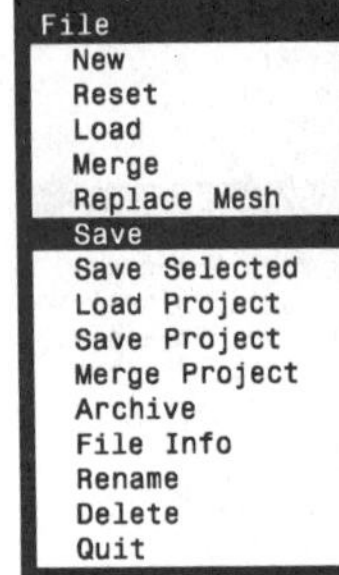

File-Save

Saves the work in the current module.

Saving Your Work

1. If a file with the same name and path exists, an alert box appears.
2. You do not need to enter a filename extension because the corresponding module automatically adds the appropriate extension. The Save option works slightly differently in each module.

3D Editor and Keyframer Save Options

Saves all 3D mesh objects, keys, associated materials, lights, and cameras in a **.3ds* file. Mesh objects alone may be saved as **.dxf* files.

ASCII File Saving

You can also save a scene in ASCII (**.asc*) format. While an ASCII file is larger than a corresponding **.3ds* file, it can be used to convert 3D Studio files into other formats. Another advantage of the ASCII format is that the files can be edited with a standard text editor, then reloaded into 3D Studio.

2D Shaper Save Options

1. You can save polygons as **.shp* or Adobe Illustrator **.ai* files. You are also given the option of saving shapes only, or all polygons.
2. When saving, 3D Studio checks for invalid shapes. A valid shape consists of one or more closed, nonintersecting polygons. If your geometry contains any invalid shapes, an Alert box appears.
3. It may be advantageous to save invalid shapes, because open polygons can be used as a path for the camera in the Keyframer to follow.

The 2D Shaper Save Option box.

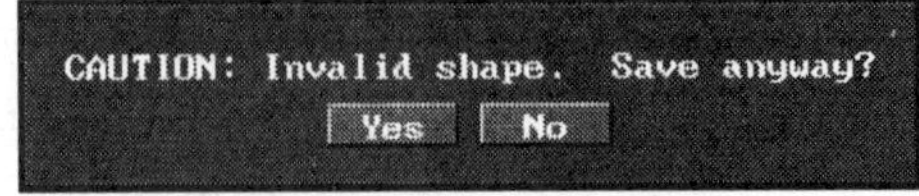

The 2D Shaper alert box.

3D Lofter Save Options

Saves the current loft in a *.*lft* file. The contour of the path, all shapes on the path, the state and configuration of the deformation grids, and the step values of the shapes, path, and fit shapes are all saved.

RELATED COMMAND

File–Save Selected

File
New
Reset
Load
Merge
Replace Mesh
Save
Save Selected
Load Project
Save Project
Merge Project
Archive
File Info
Rename
Delete
Quit

File-Save Selected

Saves objects in the 3D Editor that are part of a selection set.

Saving Selected Objects

1. Before you can use the Save Selected option, you must define a selection set. See the different options for creating a selection set under Select.

2. The following figure shows several objects included in a selection set. All of the highlighted objects are saved when using the Save Selected option.

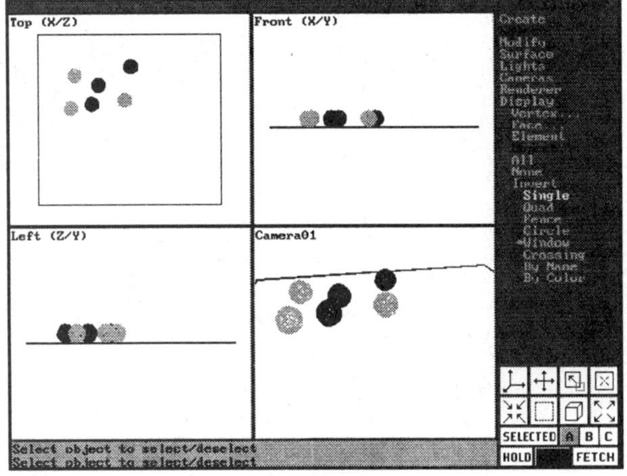

Selected objects are saved when using the Save Selected option.

NOTE All vertices and faces of an object must be included in the selection set for the object to be saved. Along with the object selected, the materials and mapping coordinates are also saved in a *.*3ds* file.

RELATED COMMANDS

Select/Vertex..., Select/Face..., Select/Element..., Select/Object...

File-Load Project

File
New
Reset
Load
Merge
Replace Mesh
Save
Save Selected
Load Project
Save Project
Merge Project
Archive
File Info
Rename
Delete
Quit

Loads the geometry and system configuration saved by the Save Project option.

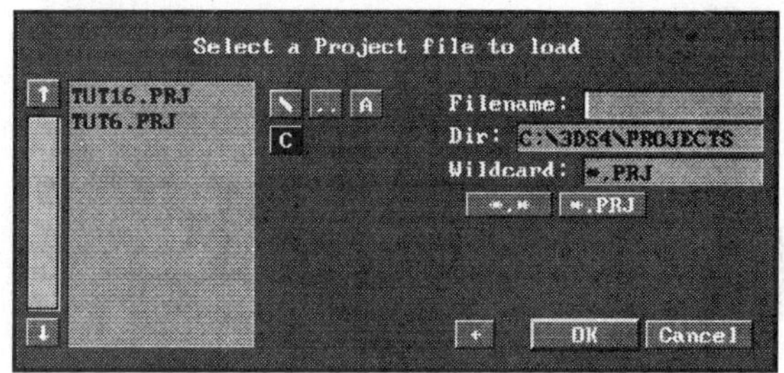

The Load Project File dialog box.

Loading a project file will replace *all* system variables and geometry in *all* program modules.

RELATED COMMAND

File-Save Project

File
New
Reset
Load
Merge
Replace Mesh
Save
Save Selected
Load Project
Save Project
Merge Project
Archive
File Info
Rename
Delete
Quit

File-Save Project

Saves all program module components and all system configurations.

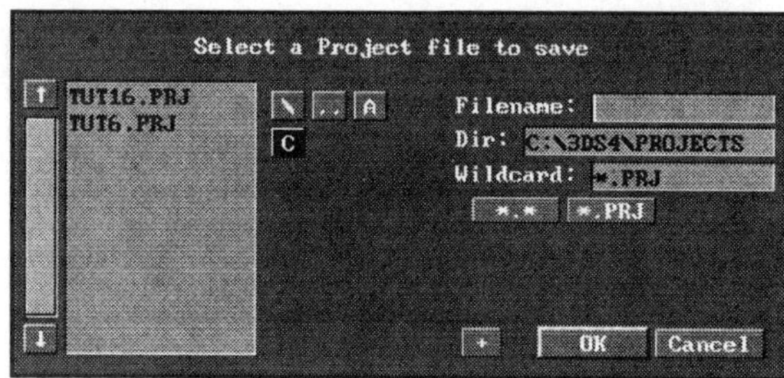

The Save Project dialog box.

TIP You can use the Save Project option to create a template file for 3D Studio, containing various settings commonly used in your scene creation.

1. To begin, set up a general scene configuration of viewports, snap settings, drawing aids, lights, cameras, etc. Do not include any geometry.
2. Save this project file under the directory specified by the Project–Path variable contained in your *3ds.set* file. By default, this is the 3DS4\PROJECTS subdirectory. Save the project filename under the special name *3ds.prj*.
3. The settings contained in your *3ds.prj* file are loaded automatically whenever you start or reset 3D Studio.

RELATED COMMANDS

File–Load Project, File–Save

File-Merge Project

File
New
Reset
Load
Merge
Replace Mesh
Save
Save Selected
Load Project
Save Project
Merge Project
Archive
File Info
Rename
Delete
Quit

Merges 3D objects, lights, cameras, and animation data from a **.prj* file.

Merging a Project

1. When selecting the Merge Project option, the Merge dialog box appears asking you what you want to merge.
2. Select one or more of the buttons to bring in the components you want.

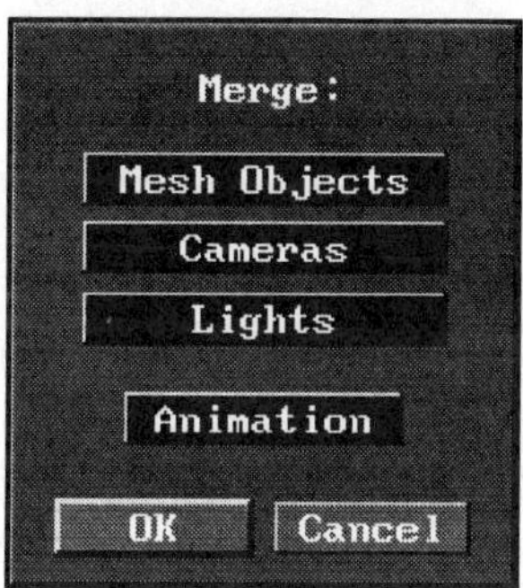

The Merge: dialog box.

NOTE Using the Merge Project option and the Merge: dialog box is similar to using the 3d Editor and Keyframer merge options under *File-Merge*. The difference is that with the Merge Project option all system configurations, as well as the options selected in the Merge: dialog box, will be brought into your scene.

RELATED COMMAND

File–Merge

File
New
Reset
Load
Merge
Replace Mesh
Save
Save Selected
Load Project
Save Project
Merge Project
Archive
File Info
Rename
Delete
Quit

File-Archive

Creates a compressed archive file using an external archiving program such as PKZIP.

Archiving a File

To use the archiving feature of 3D Studio, you must do the following:

1. Have PKZIP installed on your computer, either in the directory where the 3D Studio executables are found, or by using the PATH statement so 3D Studio can find it.
2. Copy the *command.com* file into the 3D Studio directory, or add the following line to your *autoexec.bat* file:

   SET COMSPEC=C:\DOS\COMMAND.COM

   Normally this line is added to the *autoexec.bat* file when DOS is installed. To check this, type **set** at the DOS prompt.
3. Start 3D Studio by typing **3dshell.**

NOTE When you have performed the above steps, you can create an archive file of your current scene. The archive file contains a project file of the current scene and all bitmaps used as maps in any material in the scene.

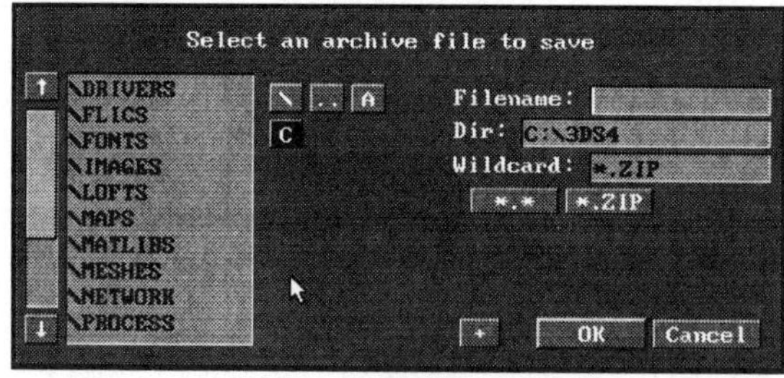

The Archive File dialog box.

RELATED COMMANDS

None

File-File Info

File
New
Reset
Load
Merge
Replace Mesh
Save
Save Selected
Load Project
Save Project
Merge Project
Archive
File Info
Rename
Delete
Quit

Displays information about a selected file, including **.tga, *.tif, *.gif, *.fli, *.flc, *.cel, *.bmp,* and **.jpg* files.

Displaying Information about a File

1. Selecting Info from the File pull-down menu accesses the Image File Information box.
2. Select the file you want information on.
3. Depending on the type of file, a variety of information is displayed. At a minimum, the filename, date, time, and size are shown. Graphic files contain more information, such as the resolution of the file, compression status, etc.

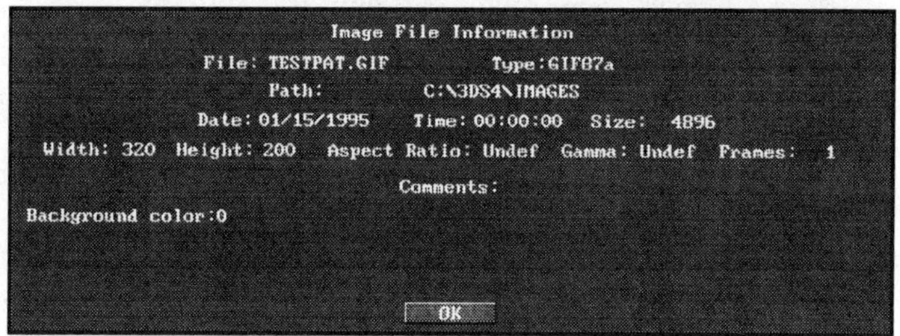

The Image File Information box.

RELATED COMMANDS

None

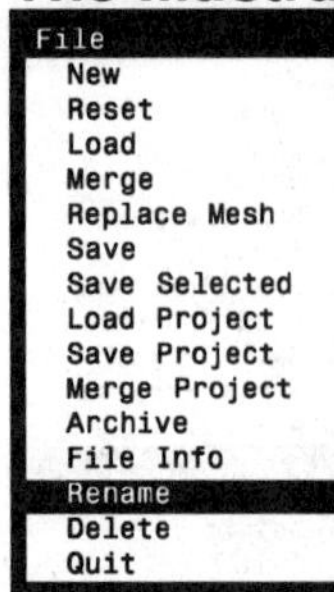

File-Rename

Allows you to rename a file.

Renaming a File

1. Select Rename from the File pull-down menu to access the Rename File Selection dialog box.
2. Once you have selected the file to rename, the Rename File dialog box appears.

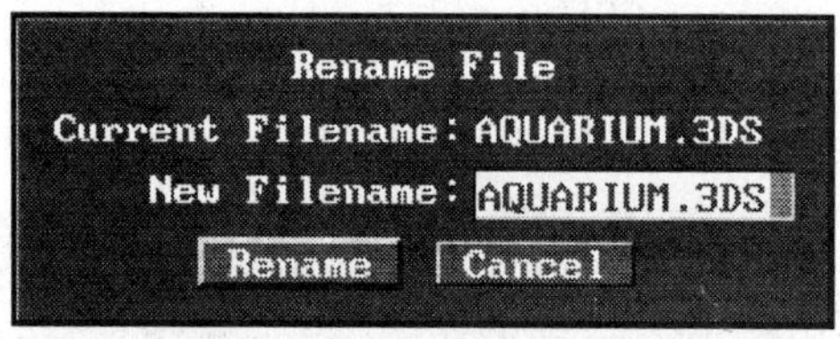

The Rename File dialog box.

3. Edit the New Filename field to change the name of the file, then select Rename.

NOTE When renaming a file, changing the extension of the file does *not* change the type of file. For example, you cannot change a *.gif* file to a *.tif* file simply by giving the filename a different extension. In most cases you should keep the file extension the same, and change only the name.

RELATED COMMANDS

None

File-Delete

File
New
Reset
Load
Merge
Replace Mesh
Save
Save Selected
Load Project
Save Project
Merge Project
Archive
File Info
Rename
Delete
Quit

Permanently deletes a file from the disk.

Deleting a File

1. Selecting Delete from the File pull-down menu accesses the Delete File dialog box.

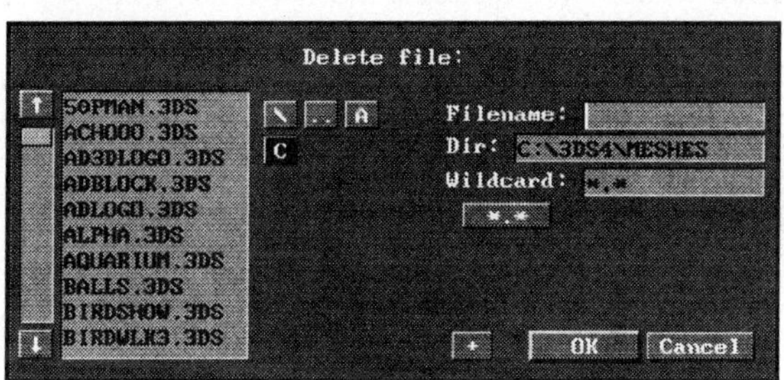

Delete File: dialog box.

2. Select the file you want to delete, then select OK.

> **NOTE** When you delete a file from the disk, it is *permanently* removed. While it is possible to restore a deleted file using special file utility programs, these are not included in 3D Studio.

RELATED COMMANDS

None

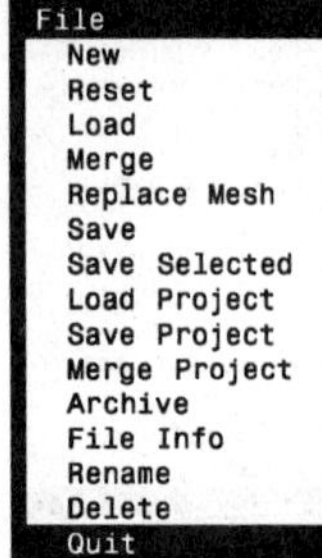

File-Quit

Q

Exits 3D Studio and returns to DOS.

Exiting 3D Studio

1. Select Quit from the File pull-down menu.
2. You will be asked to confirm quitting 3D Studio. Selecting **Yes** will return you to DOS.
3. If you have unsaved data in any program module, an alert box is displayed showing which modules contain unsaved elements.

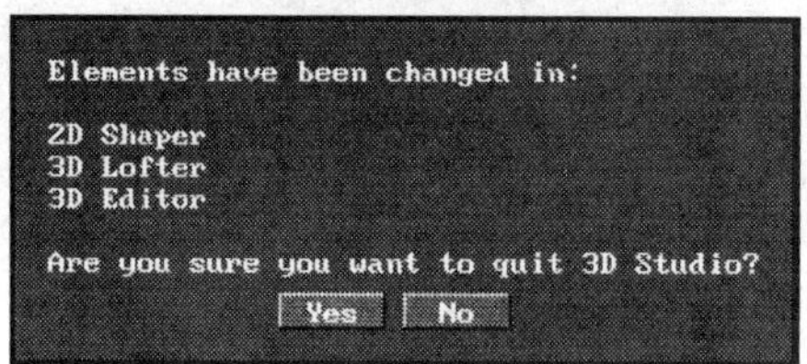

Elements Changed dialog box.

When you Quit 3D Studio, you lose all data and program settings for all modules. Before quitting, make sure you save everything to disk.

RELATED COMMANDS

File-Save, File-Save Project

Views-Redraw

```
Views
  Redraw
  Redraw All         ~
  ----------------------
  Viewports         ^V
  Drawing Aids      ^A
  Grid Extents       E
  Unit Setup        ^U
  ----------------------
  Use Snap           S
  Use Grid           G
  Fast View          V
  Disable            D
  Scroll Lock        I
  Safe Frame        @E
```

Refreshes the current active viewport.

Redrawing the Active Viewport

1. Ensure that the viewport to be redrawn is active.

2. Select *Views-Redraw*. The active viewport will be redrawn and any lines or faces missing from the display will return to the display.

TIP: Complex models require more time to redraw. To reduce the time, use the *Views-Fastview* command.

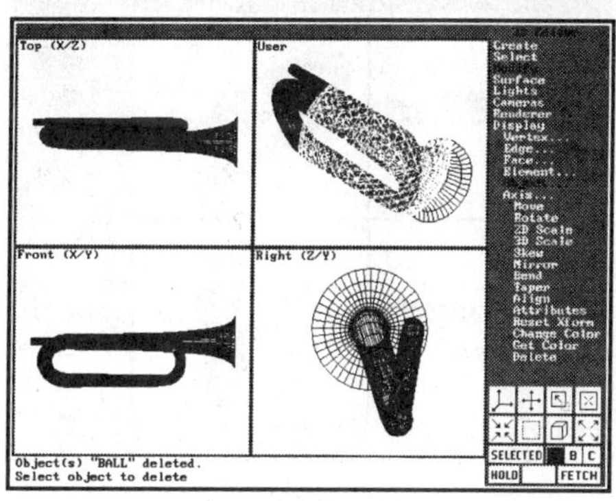

Before Redraw.

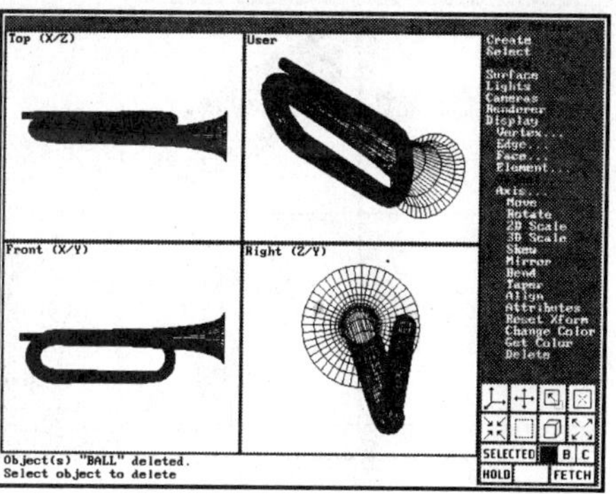

After Redraw.

RELATED COMMANDS

Views-Redraw All, Views-Viewports, Views-Fastview, 3D Display/Speed, Display/Speed

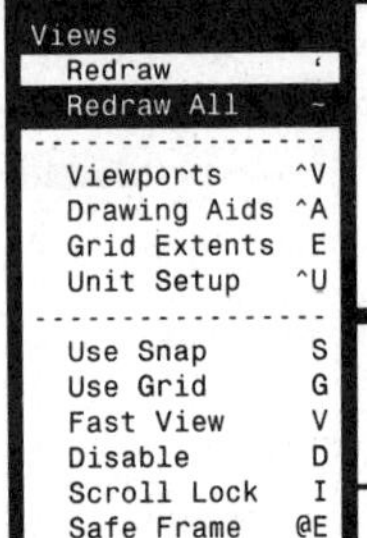

Views-Redraw All

Refreshes all viewports in a predefined viewport configuration.

Redrawing All Viewports

1. Select *Views-Redraw All.* All viewports will be redrawn and any missing lines or faces will return to the display.

Complex models require more time to redraw. To reduce the time, use the *Views-Fastview* command.

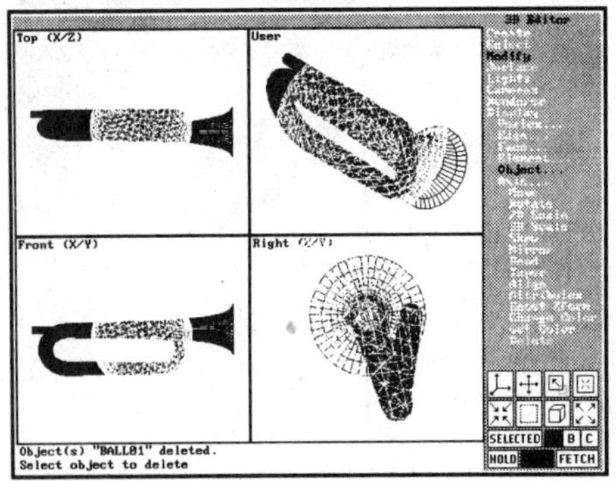

Before Redraw.

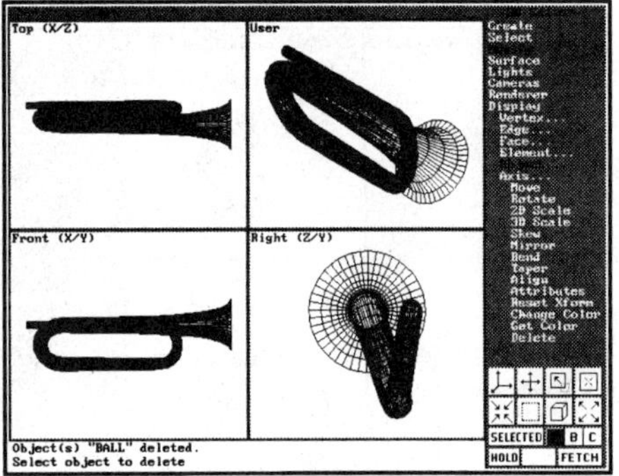

After Redraw.

RELATED COMMANDS

Views-Redraw, Views-Viewports, Views-Fastdraw, 3D Display/Speed, Display/Speed

Views-Viewports

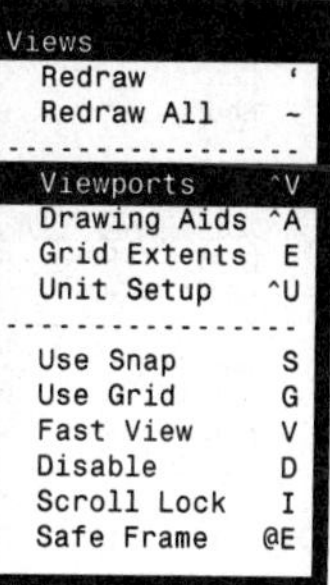

Calls a dialog box that creates and divides the 3D Editor drawing area into one, two, three, or four predefined viewport configurations. Each individual viewport can then receive a specific view of the geometry being created.

Assigning a view

1. Select *Views-Viewports.* The Viewports dialog box will be displayed.

2. Choose one of the views listed below:

   Top: Orients view to top of 3-dimensional space.

   Left: Orients view to left of 3-dimensional space.

   Front: Orients view to front of 3-dimensional space.

   Bottom: Orients view to bottom of 3-dimensional space.

   Right: Orients view to right of 3-dimensional space.

   Back: Orients view to back of 3-dimensional space.

   User: Orients view to the user-adjustable user plane.

   Camera: Orients view as seen through a specified camera.

   None: Turns off view.

   Spotlight: Orients view as seen from position of selected spotlight.

3. Select the viewport representation in the dialog box to activate that view. The first letter of the view should appear in the viewport representation.

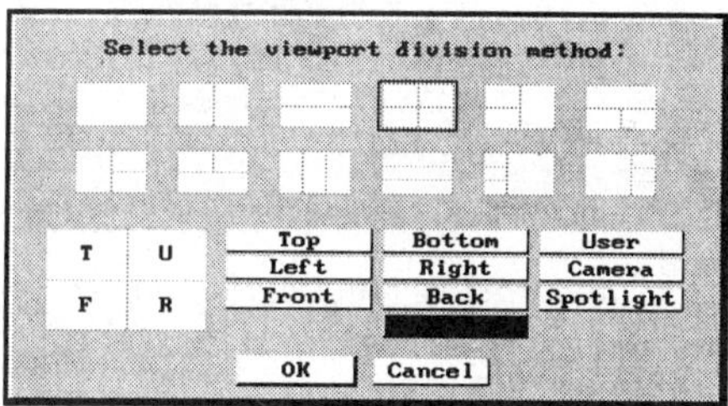

The Viewports dialog box.

RELATED COMMAND

Views-Disable

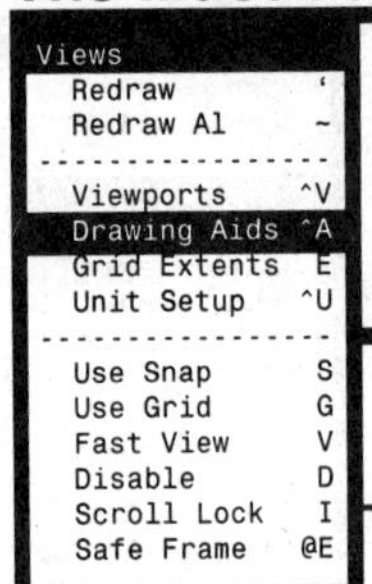

Views-Drawing Aids

Adjusts the snap spacing, grid spacing, grid extents, and angle snap.

Using the Drawing Aids Dialog Box

1. Select *Views-Drawing Aids*.

2. Make the following adjustments to the settings in the Drawing Aids dialog box:

   Snap Spacing: Adjusts the snap increment for the X, Y, and Z spacing.

   Grid Spacing: Adjusts the grid increment for the X, Y, and Z spacing.

TIP You can copy the X value to Y and Z by clicking on the X. To copy the Y value only to Z, click on the Y.

   Grid Extent Start: Adjusts the starting coordinates for the extents.

   Grid Extent End: Adjusts the ending coordinates for the extents.

   Angle Snap: Adjusts the snap angle.

   OK: Accepts the changes made and exits the dialog box.

   Cancel: Cancels all changes and exits the dialog box.

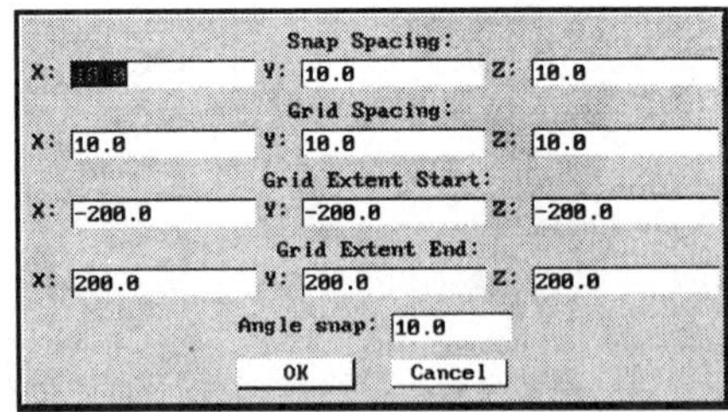

The Drawing Aids dialog box.

RELATED COMMANDS

Views-Use Snap, Views-Use Grid, Views-Grid Extents, Views-Angle Snap

Views-Grid Extents

Views
Redraw '
Redraw All ~
Viewports ^V
Drawing Aids ^A
Grid Extents E
Unit Setup ^U
Use Snap S
Use Grid G
Fast View V
Disable D
Scroll Lock I
Safe Frame @E

Adjusts the visible extents of the grid by entering the coordinates with the mouse.

Using the extents establishes the work area for your geometry. Extents are used as a guide and can be changed at any time during the project.

Setting the Grid Extents

1. Select *Views-Grid Extents.*
2. In the active viewport, click on one corner of the grid extents.
3. In the same viewport, click on the opposite corner of the grid extents.
4. To see the grid extents, select *Views-Use Grid.*

TIP Setting the Grid Extents can also be accomplished with coordinates by using the Drawing Aids dialog box. To use the Drawing Aids dialog box, you must enter the Grid Extents Start and the Grid Extents End coordinates at the keyboard.

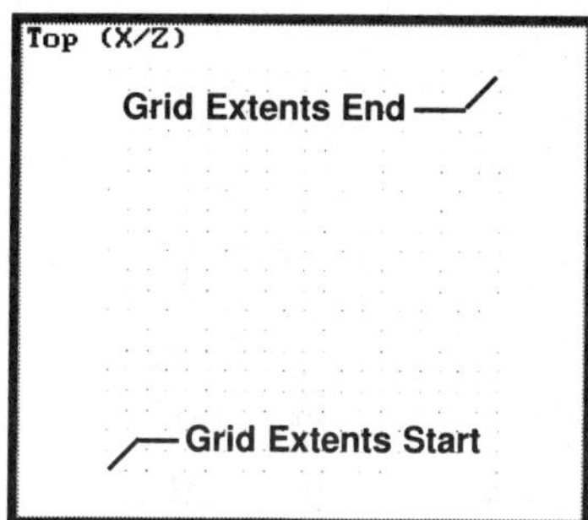

Grid being displayed with extents established.

RELATED COMMAND

Views-Drawing Aids

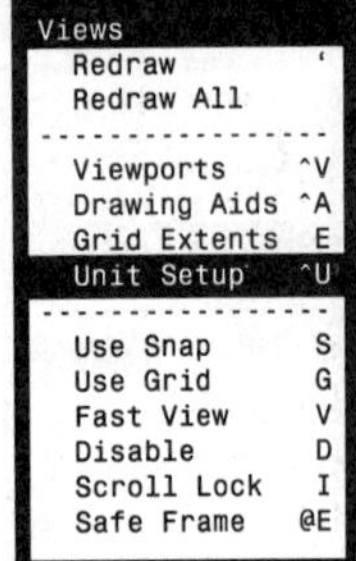

Views-Unit Setup

Selects the type of units for coordinates input and display.

Setting the Units for a Project

1. Select *Views-Unit Setup*. The Unit Setup dialog box appears.

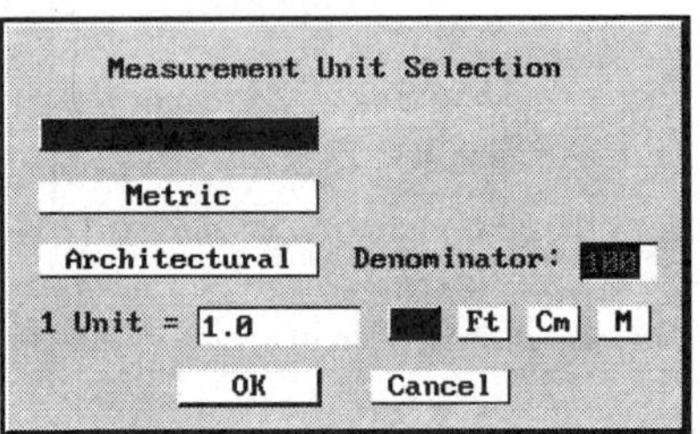

The Units Setup Dialog box

2. Make changes in the Measurement Unit Selection dialog box as shown below.

Decimal: Decimal Units is the default selection. Use this option to enter or view coordinates in a *1.50* English units format.

Metric: Use this option to enter or view coordinates in a *1.500*m metric units format.

Architectural: Use this option to enter or view coordinates in a *1'6"* architectural units format.

Denominator: Use this option to set the value for the denominator of the architectural unit fraction. For example, entering a 4 will produce a fractional denominator of 1/4 inch. In the previous example, the coordinates *1'6"2* would be the equivalent of 1 foot, 6-1/2 inches.

Unit =: Use this option to define the unit scale. The four options are: In=inches, Ft=Feet, Cm=Centimeters, and M=Meters.

OK: Accepts the changes made and exits the dialog box.

Cancel: Cancels all changes and exits the dialog box.

If you use metric notation, be sure that you have selected Cm or M in the 1 Unit = field.

RELATED COMMANDS

None

Views-Use Snap

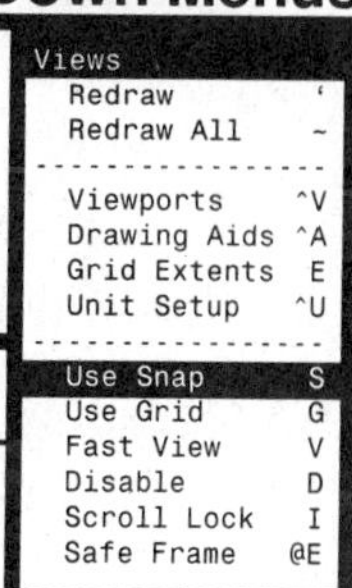

Toggles the snap function on or off.

Snap is used to allow for more accurate placement of geometry within the active viewport. The snap spacing setting is entered in the Views-Drawing Aids dialog box.

Using Snap

1. Select *Views-Use Snap*. A yellow S will appear in the upper right corner of the 3D Studio screen next to the module name and an asterisk will appear next to Use Snap in the Views pull-down menu.

2. As the cross-hairs are moved, they will "snap" to the increment set in the Drawing Aids dialog box.

It is often beneficial to use Snap in conjunction with the grid to allow for a more visual representation of the snap distance.

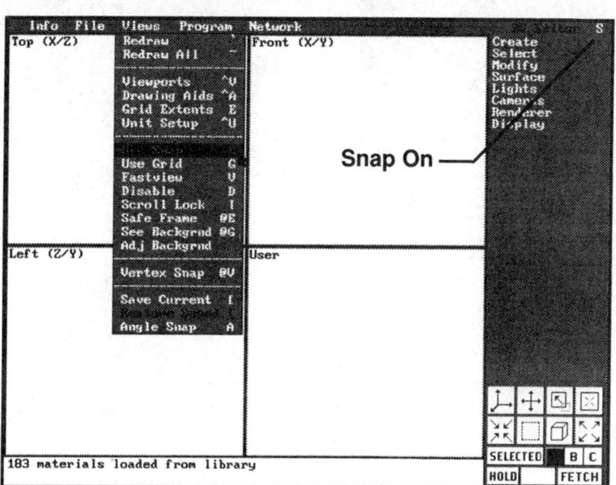

Turning Snap on.

NOTE Snap must be toggled for each viewport in each module.

RELATED COMMANDS

Views-Drawing Aids, Views-Vertex Snap, Views-Grid

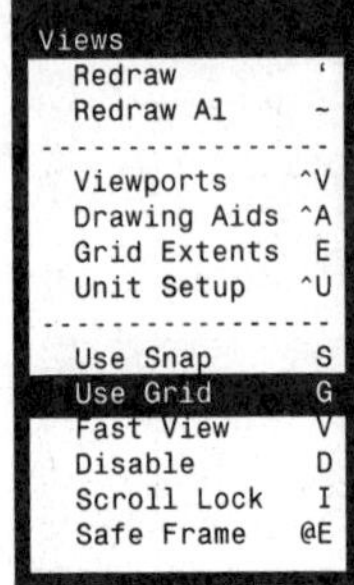

Views-Use Grid

Toggles the grid display on or off.

The grid is used to assist in the accurate placement of geometry and give a quick visual representation of distance. The grid setting is entered in the Views-Drawing Aids dialog box.

Using Grid

1. Select *Views-Use Grid*. The grid will appear in the active viewport and an asterisk will appear next to Use Grid in the Views pull-down menu.

2. To turn the grid off, select Views-Use *Grid* again.

Grid must be toggled for each viewport and module. Grid cannot be used in User, Camera, or Spotlight viewports.

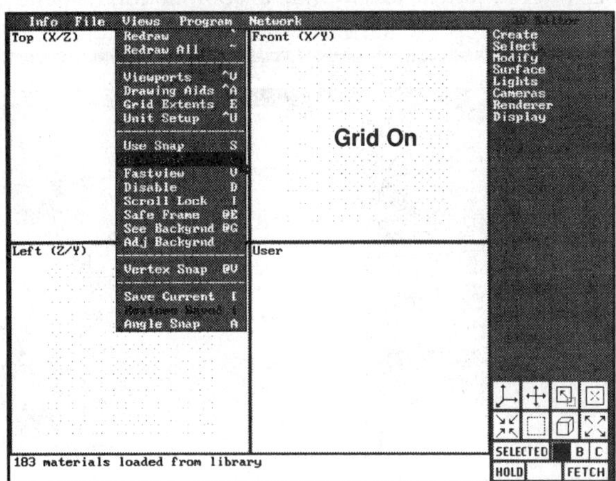

Turning Grid on.

RELATED COMMANDS

Views-Drawing Aids, Views-Grid Extents

Views-Fastview

Views
Redraw `
Redraw All ~
Viewports ^V
Drawing Aids ^A
Grid Extents E
Unit Setup ^U
Use Snap S
Use Grid G
Fast View V
Disable D
Scroll Lock I
Safe Frame @E

Toggles the ability to reduce the number of faces displayed in a viewport to increase drawing speed.

Views-Fastview will affect the current viewport. Use this option with complex models that require long redraw times.

Using Fastview

1. Select *Views-Fastview*. A degradation in model quality will appear in the active viewport and an asterisk will appear next to Fastview in the Views pull-down menu.

2. To turn off Fastview, select *Views-Fastview* again.

NOTE Fastview is not available in either the 2D Shaper or the shape viewport of the 3D Lofter.

TIP It is often useful to use this command in the User, Camera, or Spotlight viewports because these viewports are generally more complex.

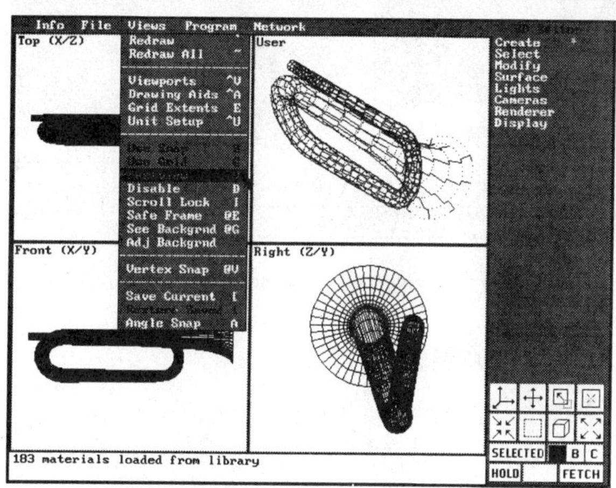

Use Fastview to minimize redraw times.

RELATED COMMANDS

3D Display/Speed/Fastdraw, Views-Redraw

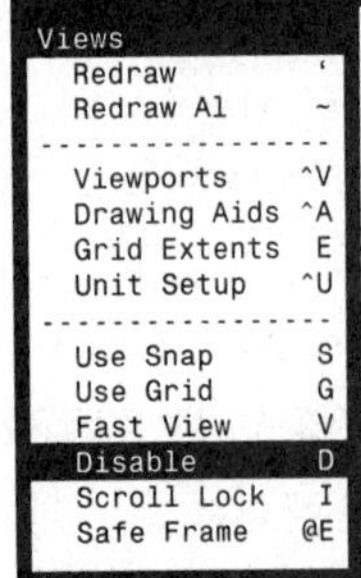

Views-Disable

Toggles the display of the current viewport on or off.

Disable will only affect the current viewport. Use this option to turn off unneeded viewports in complex drawings to increase the redraw speed.

Disabling a Viewport

1. Select *Views-Disable*. An asterisk will appear next to Disable in the Views pull-down menu and Viewport Disabled will appear in the disabled viewport.

2. No geometry can be viewed when the viewport is disabled.

3. To enable a viewport, select *Views-Disable* again.

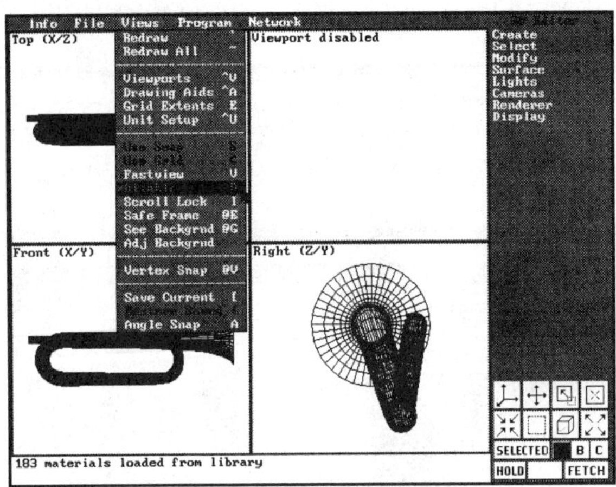

When the viewport is disabled, the model will not be displayed.

RELATED COMMANDS

Display/Hide, Views-Redraw

Views-Scroll Lock

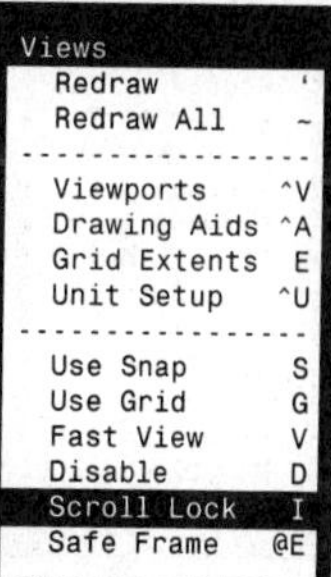

Toggles automatic scrolling of the viewport when the cursor reaches the viewport boundary.

Scroll Lock will only affect the current viewport. Use this option when you do not want the viewport to pan past the cursor when it reaches the boundary of the viewport.

Using Scroll Lock

1. Select *Views-Scroll Lock.* When *Scroll Lock* is activated an asterisk will appear next to *Scroll Lock* in the Views pull-down menu.

2. As the cross-hair is moved toward the edge of the active viewport, automatic scrolling will be disabled.

3. To turn off Scroll Lock, select *Views-Scroll Lock* again.

This command is useful in the 2D Shaper when you want to trace over the 3D display or a bitmap background.

RELATED COMMAND

Icons/Pan

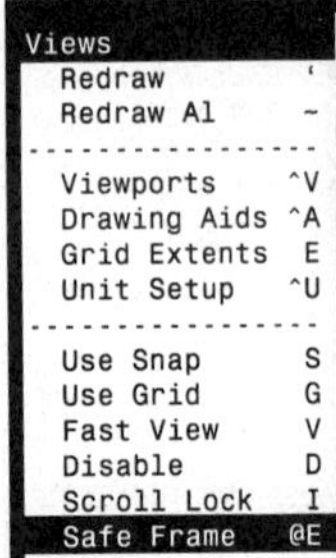

Views-Safe Frame

Displays two rectangles in the current viewport that represent the edges of your output device.

Use *Views-Safe Frame* to see how your project will be placed in a rendering within individual viewports. It is important to use *Views-Safe Frame* to help in the composition of the output of the model. The safe frame is composed of two rectangles: an outer yellow and an inner green. The yellow rectangle represents the outer edges of the rendering display device. The green rectangle represents the outer edge of the safe area. device. Use the Safe-Frame parameter in the Render/Setup/Options dialog box to change the percentage of the outer rectangle and the display in pixels of the rectangles.

Activating the Safe Frame.

1. Select *Views-Safe Frame.* An asterisk will appear next to Safe Frame in the views pull-down menu and the safe frame will appear in the active viewport.

2. To deactivate the safe frame, select *Views-Safe Frame* again.

TIP If a project is being output to videotape, *Safe Frame* can be used to show the overscan region so that no black borders will be seen in the final rendering on an NTSC or PAL television screen. Use the distance between the rectangles to represent the overscan area.

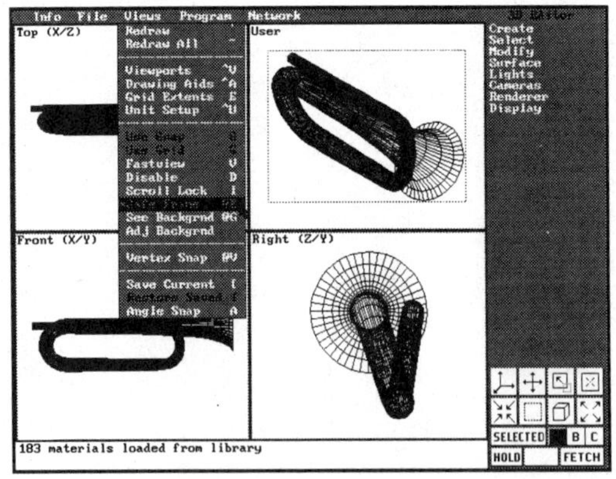

Activating the Safe Frame

RELATED COMMAND

Render/Setup/Options

Views-See Backgrnd

Views
Use Snap S
Use Grid G
Fast View V
Disable D
Scroll Lock I
Safe Frame @E
SeeBackgrnd@G
Adj Backgrnd
Vertex Snap @V
Save Current [
Restore Saved{
Angle Snap A

Toggles the displays of a proxy image of an assigned background in the current viewport.

Use *Views-See Backgrnd* to help position objects in relationship to the chosen background. When *Views-See Backgrnd* is turned on, a three-color proxy image is displayed in the active viewport. The three colors used in the proxy image are dark gray, medium gray, and light gray which represent the contrast of the background.

Viewing the Background in a Viewport

1. Select *Views-See Backgrnd*. An asterisk will appear next to *See Backgrnd* in the Views pull-down menu and a three color-proxy image will be displayed in the active viewport.

2. To turn off the background, select *Views-See Backgrnd* again.

NOTE A background must first be assigned using the *Renderer/Setup/Background* dialog box before any background can be displayed.

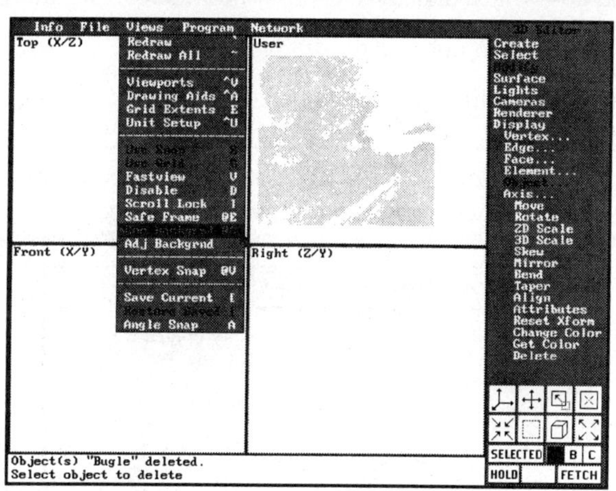

Displaying the Background bitmap.

TIP Use this option in the 2D Shaper to trace over existing bitmaps such as logos to be converted into 3D shapes in the 3D Lofter.

RELATED COMMANDS

Render/Setup/Background, Views-Adj Backgrnd

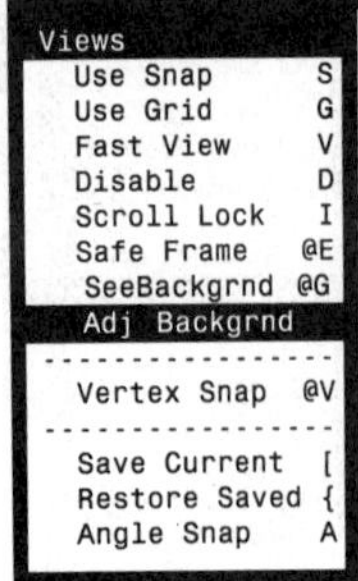

Views-Adj Backgrnd

Adjust the display of the proxy image placed by the *Views-See Backgrnd* command.

Use *Views-Adj Backgrnd* when the proxy background image in the viewport is hard to distinguish. When this command is used, the Background Contrast Control dialog box is displayed.

Adjusting the Background Proxy Image

1. Select *Views-Adj Backgrnd*. The Background Contrast Control dialog box is displayed.

2. Make adjustments as necessary using the following guidelines:

   Dark: Adjust the Dark setting to change the percentage of contrast for the dark gray portion of the image.

   Light: Use the Light selection to change the percentage of light gray. Any percentage left over will be applied to the medium gray portion of the proxy image.

   Display: To preview the settings, click on the **Display** button and a proxy image representation will be displayed in the window above the button.

   OK: Accept the changes and exit the dialog box.

   Cancel: Reject the changes and exit the dialog box.

Views-See Backgrnd must be on in the active viewport to view the adjustments made to the background proxy image.

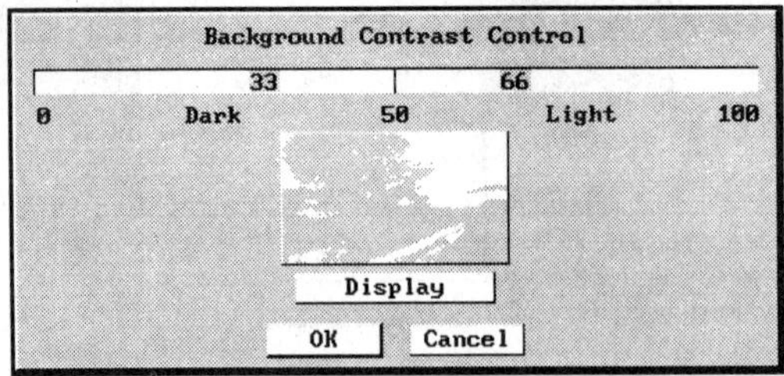

The Background Contrast Control dialog box.

RELATED COMMANDS

Render/Setup/Background, Views-See Backgrnd

Views-Vertex Snap

Views
Use Snap S
Use Grid G
Fast View V
Disable D
Scroll Lock I
Safe Frame @E
SeeBackgrnd @G
Adj Backgrnd
Vertex Snap @V
Save Current [
Restore Saved {
Angle Snap A

Toggles the Vertex Snap option on or off in the 3D Editor.

When Vertex Snap is on, any vertex moved closer to a second vertex will automatically snap to that vertex on a 2D plane. Because it only works on a 2D plane, it may be necessary for this function to be performed again in another orthographic view to connect the two vertices. This function will only work in non-camera, non-spotlight viewports. The two vertices must fall within the pickbox in order for the vertex snap to func-

The size of the pickbox is adjustable in the Program Configuration dialog box.

Using Vertex Snap

1. Select *Views-Vertex Snap.* An asterisk will appear next to Vertex Snap in the Views pull-down menu and a V will appear in the upper right corner next to the module name. If Snap is on, Vertex Snap will overide Snap.

2. Select *Vertex/Move.* Move a vertex close to another vertex. The first vertex will "snap" onto the second.

3. Continue making modifications to the model as needed.

4. To deactivate Vertex gain.

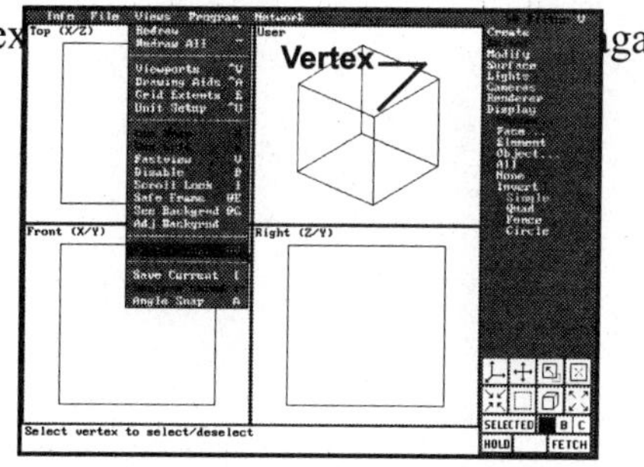

Displaying the Background bitmap.

RELATED COMMANDS

Views-Use Snap, Info-Configure-Pick box size

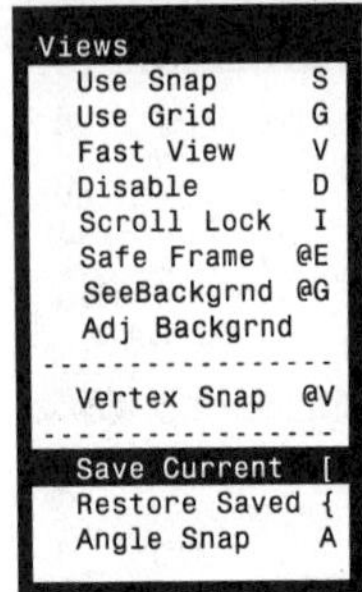

Views-Save Current

Saves the current configuration of the active non-camera, non-spotlight viewport.

When *Views-Save Current* is applied to the active viewport, the view in that viewport is saved to a buffer for retrieval later. Only one viewport configuration can be saved for each program module. This command only works on non-camera, non-spotlight viewports.

Saving a Viewport

1. Make the viewport to be saved the active viewport.
2. Select *Views-Save Current.* The current viewport will be saved.

RELATED COMMAND

Views-Restore Saved

Views-Restore Saved

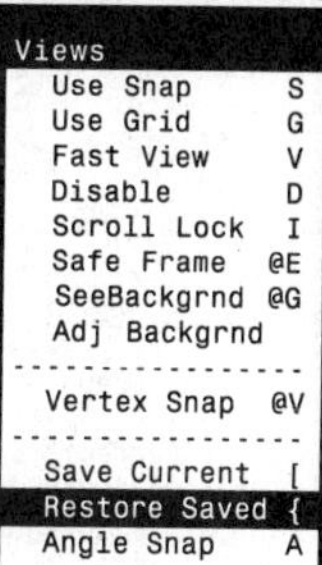

Restores the saved viewport configuration to the active viewport.

When *Views-Restore Saved* is applied to the active viewport, the view in that viewport is replaced with the view saved using the *Save Current* command.

Restoring a Saved Viewport

1. Ensure that a viewport has been saved using the *Views-Save Current* command.
2. Activate the viewport to receive the previously saved view.
3. Select *Views-Restore Saved*. The previously saved viewport will be displayed.

Views-Restore Saved will not replace a shape viewport in the 2D Shaper because a shape view must always be present.

RELATED COMMAND

Views-Save Current

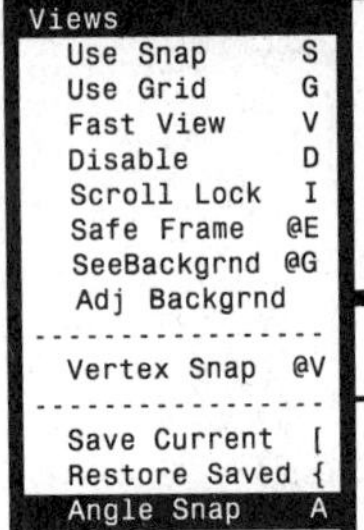

Views-Angle Snap

Toggles Angle Snap on and off.

Views-Angle Snap constrains all angular rotations to the degree specified in the Views-Drawing Aids dialog box. Using *Views-Angle Snap* makes it easier to snap to a specific angle when rotating an object, bending an object, changing camera roll, and using all other rotational commands.

Using Angle Snap

1. Select *Views-Angle Snap*. An asterisk appears next to Angle Snap in the views pull-down menu and a yellow A appears in the upper right-hand corner next to the program module name.

2. Rotate an object in the active viewport. As the object rotates, it will "snap" to the increment specified in the Drawing Aids dialog box.

3. To deactivate angle snap, select *Views-Angle Snap* again.

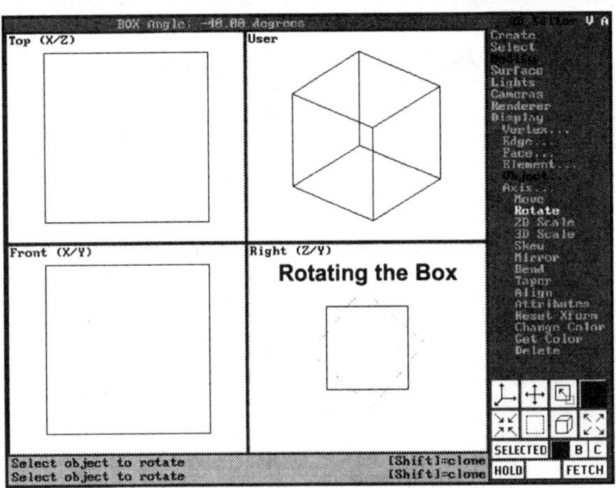

Using Angle Snap to precisely rotate a box.

RELATED COMMANDS

Views-Use Snap, Views-Drawing Aids

Program-2D Shaper

Program
2D Shaper F1
3D Lofter F2
3D Editor F3
Keyframer F4
Materials F5
Browser F6
Camera/PrevuF7
IK F8
Keyscript F9
DOS Window F10
Text Editor F11
PXP Loader F12

Switches to the 2D Shaper program module.

This module is used to create 2D shapes for later use as shapes for lofts and paths. See 2D Shaper for more information on this module.

The 2D Shaper program module.

RELATED COMMANDS

None

Program
2D Shaper F1
3D Lofter F2
3D Editor F3
Keyframer F4
Materials F5
Browser F6
Camera/PrevuF7
IK F8
Keyscript F9
DOS Window F10
Text Editor F11
PXP Loader F12

Program-3D Lofter

F2

Switches to the 3D Lofter program module.

This module is used to loft shapes from the 2D shaper to create complex 3D objects. See 3D Lofter for more information on this module.

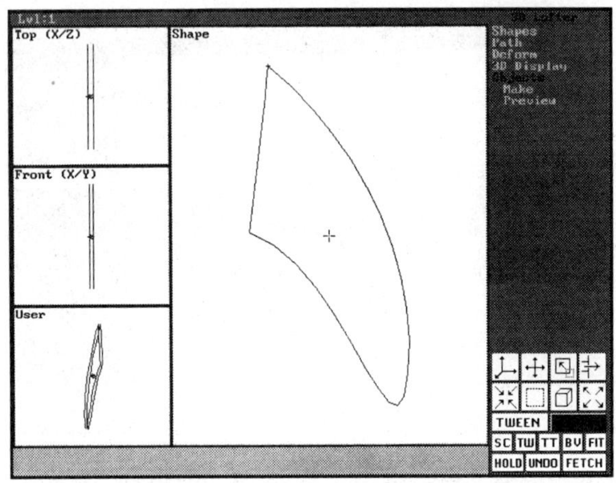

The 3D Lofter program module.

RELATED COMMANDS

None

Program-3D Editor

Program
2D Shaper F1
3D Lofter F2
3D Editor F3
Keyframer F4
Materials F5
Browser F6
Camera/PrevuF7
IK F8
Keyscript F9
DOS Window F10
Text Editor F11
PXP Loader F12

Switches to the 3D Editor program module.

This module is used to create scenes and basic primitive geometric shape geometry. This module can also be used to create still renderings of projects. See 3D Editor for more information on this module.

The 3D Editor program module.

RELATED COMMANDS

None

Program
2D Shaper F1
3D Lofter F2
3D Editor F3
Keyframer F4
Materials F5
Browser F6
Camera/PrevuF7
IK F8
Keyscript F9
DOS Window F10
Text Editor F11
PXP Loader F12

Program-Keyframer

F4

Switches to the Keyframer program module.

This module is used to create complex 3D animations. See Keyframer for more information on this module.

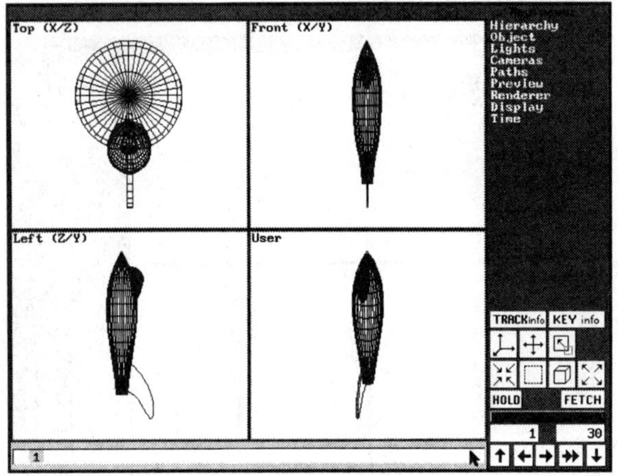

The Keyframer program module.

RELATED COMMANDS

None

Program-Materials

Program	
2D Shaper	F1
3D Lofter	F2
3D Editor	F3
Keyframer	F4
Materials	F5
Browser	F6
Camera/Prevu	F7
IK	F8
Keyscript	F9
DOS Window	F10
Text Editor	F11
PXP Loader	F12

Switches to the Materials program module.

This module is used to create and modify materials. See Materials Editor for more information on this module.

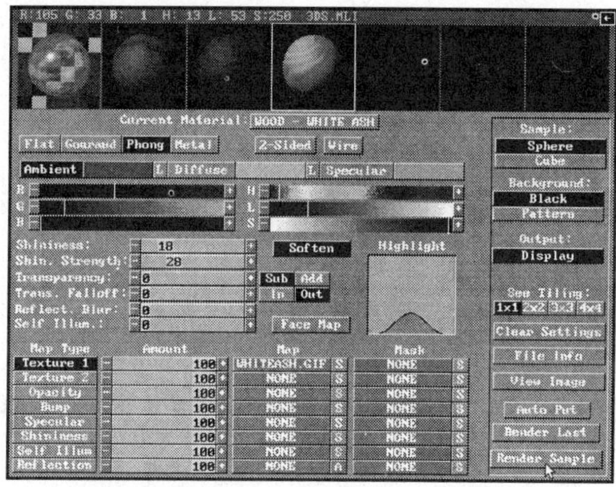

The Materials program module.

RELATED COMMANDS

None

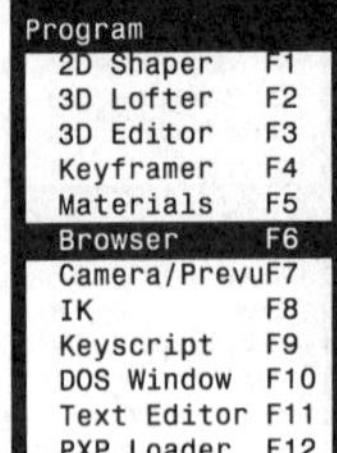

Program-Browser

Switches to the Browser IPAS Plug-In.

The Browser is used to quickly view thumbnail-size images of bitmapped images that may be used as materials or backgrounds.

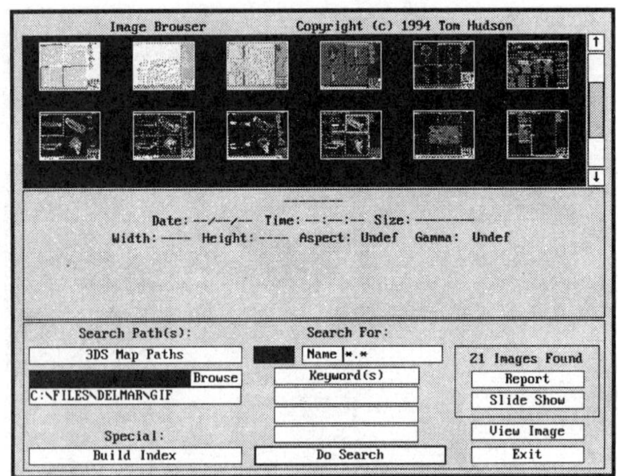

The Browser program module.

RELATED COMMANDS

None

Program-Camera/Prevu

Program
2D Shaper F1
3D Lofter F2
3D Editor F3
Keyframer F4
Materials F5
Browser F6
Camera/PrevuF7
IK F8
Keyscript F9
DOS Window F10
Text Editor F11
PXP Loader F12

Switches to the Fast Preview Plug-In.

The Fast Preview is used to quickly render previews of scenes within the active camera viewport in the 3D Editor or any viewport in the Keyframer.

Using the Camera/Prevu

1. Select a Camera Viewport.
2. Select *Program-Camera/Prevu*. The viewport will render.
3. Select Exit to return to the regular viewport.

NOTE The main display must be set to at least 256 colors in order for Fast Preview to work. Certain graphics cards may cause Fast Preview to fail when set above 256 colors. Setting the main display to 256 colors is recommended when using Fast Preview.

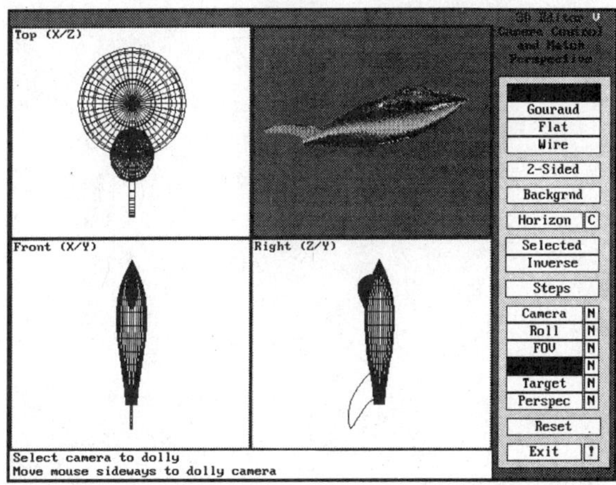

Using the Camera/Prevu on a camera viewport.

RELATED COMMANDS

None

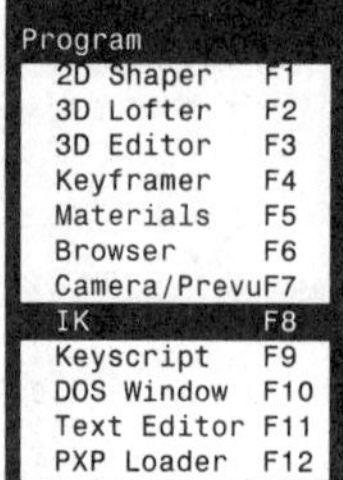

Program-IK

Switches to the Inverse Kinematics (IK) Plug-In.

Use the IK plug-in to link objects to create complex realistic-looking animations. The IK plug-in, like the Keyframer, allows objects to be linked in a parent/child relationship. The IK plug-in allows you to define chains along the hierarchically linked objects. It is these chains that can have either parent or child objects as the start or end of the chain definition. In other words, in the IK plug-in, you can move the child (leaf) object and the parent (branch) object(s) will move with predescribed attributes. The IK plug-in allows for two methods to accomplish this: automatic and interactive. In the automatic mode, calculations for all object positions are made. In the interactive mode, the user manipulates hierarchies in a rendered viewport.

NOTE This selection can only be activated within the Keyframer.

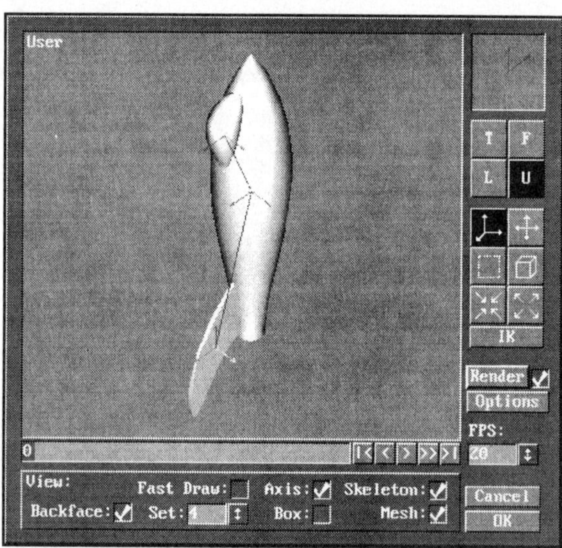

The Inverse Kinematics program module.

RELATED COMMAND

Hierarchy/Link

Program-Keyscript

Program
2D Shaper F1
3D Lofter F2
3D Editor F3
Keyframer F4
Materials F5
Browser F6
Camera/PrevuF7
Program-IK F8
Keyscript F9
DOS Window F10
Text Editor F11
PXP Loader F12

Switches to the Keyframer Scripting Language Plug-In.

The Keyframer Scripting Language Plug-In is used to create scripts using a BASIC-like language to control aspects of animations such as movement, rotation, position, hiding, linking, unlinking, etc.

NOTE The Keyframer Scripting Language Plug-In can only be called from the Keyframer.

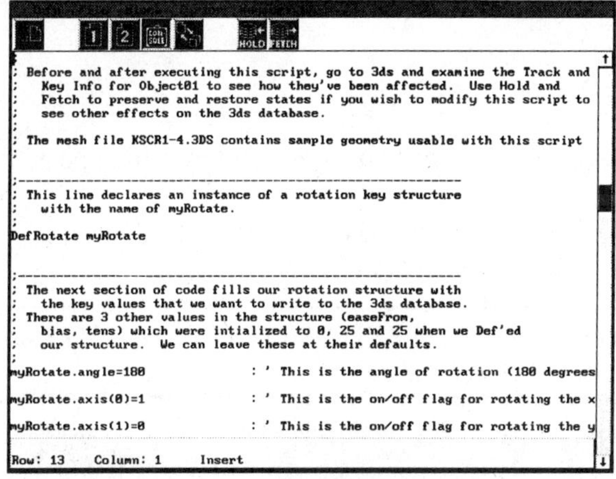

The Keyscript program module.

RELATED COMMAND

Text Editor

```
Program
 2D Shaper    F1
 3D Lofter    F2
 3D Editor    F3
 Keyframer    F4
 Materials    F5
 Browser      F6
 Camera/PrevuF7
 IK           F8
 Keyscript    F9
 DOS Window  F10
 Text Editor F11
 PXP Loader  F12
```

Program-DOS Window

Switches to a DOS window.

Allows DOS commands to be entered without exiting 3D Studio. Other medium to large programs can also be executed if 3D Studio is started using the 3DSHELL.COM command or if Phar Lap has been properly configured to allow this.

Using the DOS Window

1. Select Program-DOS Window. The Exit to DOS Window dialog box will be displayed.
2. Select **Yes** or **No**.
3. If **Yes** is chosen, the DOS prompt shown below will appear.
4. To return to 3D Studio, type EXIT at the command prompt.

> **NOTE** It is important that EXIT be used to return to 3D Studio. Do not type 3DS.EXE to return.

Shelling out to the DOS Window.

RELATED COMMANDS

None

Program-Text Editor

Program
2D Shaper F1
3D Lofter F2
3D Editor F3
Keyframer F4
Materials F5
Browser F6
Camera/PrevuF7
Program-IK F8
Keyscript F9
DOS Window F10
Text Editor F11
PXP Loader F12

Switches to the built-in Text Editor module.

Use the Text Editor to edit and create ASCII files. Generally this module is used to edit Keyframer eXternal Process script files, but it is also useful for

Pressing Ctrl Q will exit the Text Editor.

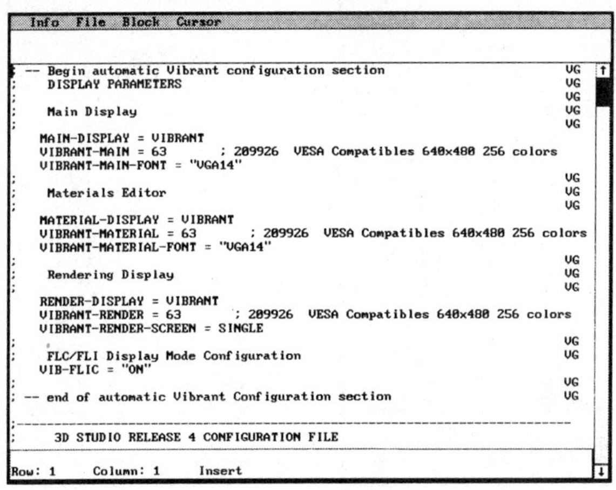

The Text Editor program module.

RELATED COMMANDS

None

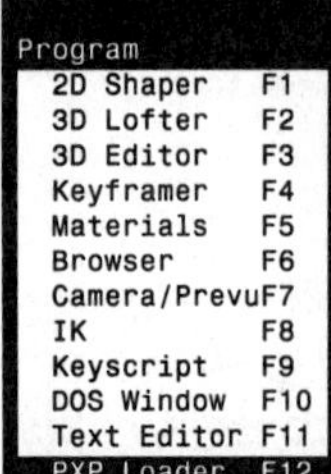

Program-PXP(KXP) Loader

Switches to the PXP or KXP Selector dialog box.

Use the PXP(KXP) Loader to load IPAS routines. Procedural modeling eXternal Process (PXP) routines are called from the 3D Editor only and modify the geometry of objects. Keyframer eXternal Process (KXP) routines are called from the Keyframer only and modify the animation process.

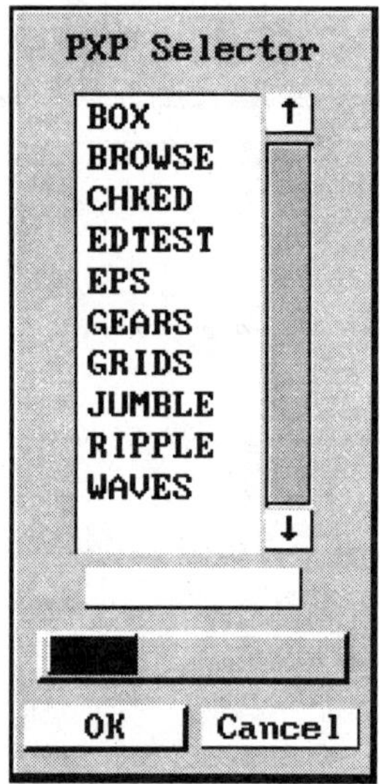

The PXP Loader.

The KXP Loader.

RELATED COMMANDS

None

Network-Slave

Places the local system computer into rendering slave mode.

Slave mode allows the local system to become part of a network-rendering system. Using a network will allow more than one computer to assist in rendering animations and multiple still renderings. Until a local system is placed in slave mode, it cannot become a part of the rendering farm. Slave mode can also be used on a single system not attached to a network. The user would "queue" a series of renderings to be processed unattended.

Using Slave Mode

1. Select *Network-Slave.*
2. A dialog box displaying a warning that all data in all modules will be erased will be displayed. Choose **Yes** to continue and **No** to cancel slave mode.
3. If **Yes** is chosen, the dialog box shown below will be displayed.
4. Press the [Esc] key to exit slave mode. The Exit SLAVE mode dialog box will be displayed. Choose **OK** to exit slave mode, choose **Cancel** to return to slave mode.

When the local system is placed into slave mode, all data in all modules will be lost. Be sure to save any data before executing this command.

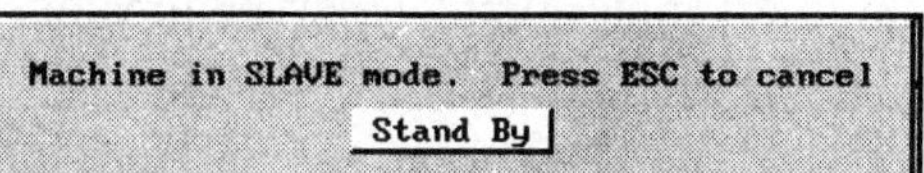

This dialog box will appear when 3D Studio is placed in Slave mode.

RELATED COMMANDS

Network-Configure, Network-Edit Queue, Renderer/View

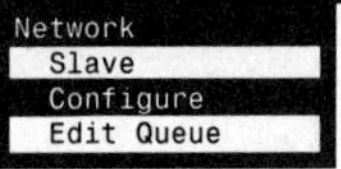

Network-Configure

Switches to the Network Parameters dialog box.

Use this command to configure the local system for use as a rendering station. Each of the following parameters must be set before the local system can be used.

Changing the Network Parameters

1. Select *Network-Configure.* The Network Parameters dialog box (shown below) will be displayed.

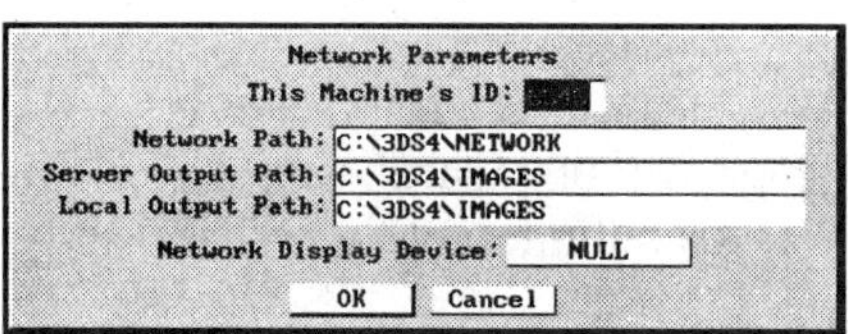

2. Make changes to the parameters using the following guidelines:

This Machine's ID: Use up to four unique digits to numerically identify the local system to the network.

Network Path: Enter the complete network path and directory for the shared directory on the network. The network must have one common directory to allocate rendering files.

Server Output Path: Enter the complete server directory path and directory on the network. This may or may not be the same as the Network Path.

Local Output Path: Enter the complete local path and directory. The local system must have a local directory for output of image files.

Network Display Device: Enter the type of network display device. It is important to use the **NULL** setting if there are various display devices on the network.

OK: Accepts the changes and exit the dialog box.

Cancel: Rejects the changes and exit the dialog box.

NOTE These settings can also be changed in the 3DSNET.SET file using the Text Editor. Changing these settings in the dialog box does not overwrite the default settings in the 3DSNET.SET file.

RELATED COMMANDS

Network-Slave, Network-Edit Queue

Network-Edit Queue

Network
Slave
Configure
Edit Queue

Switches to the Network Queue Control dialog box.

Use this command to modify the current rendering queue on a rendering network. There are five areas that must be considered in the network rendering process; the Name of the Process: the **Owner** of the process, the **Machines** assigned to the process, the **Status** of the process, and the output **Filename** of the process. The pending processes are controlled by clicking on an option and then selecting a process to modify.

Editing the Network Queue

1. Select *Network-Edit Queue*. The Network Parameters dialog box shown below will be displayed.

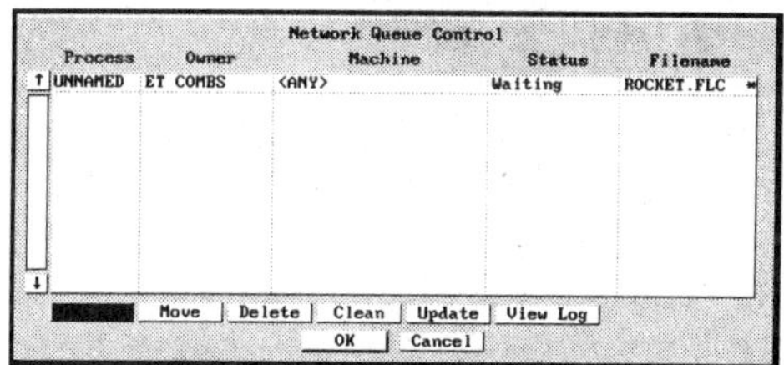

2. Make changes to the parameters using the following guidelines:

Edit: Allows a process to be active or inactive as well as changing the owner's name, the machines assigned, and the output path and filename.

Move: Changes the location of the process. The higher up this is on the list, the higher the priority for that process.

Delete: Deletes a process from the queue.

Clean: Removes any failed conditions that have occurred during the network rendering process.

Update: Updates the queue window by talking to all computers on the network and deterring machine availability and any changes made to the queue control file.

View Log: Displays the Log File Viewer Window.

OK: Accepts the changes and exit the dialog box.

Cancel: Rejects the changes and exit the dialog box.

RELATED COMMANDS

Network-Slave, Network-Configure, Renderer/View/Net ASAP, Renderer/View/Net Queue

Axis Tripod

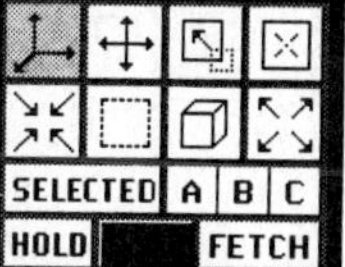

Changes the view angle of the active viewport.

Changing the View Angle of a Viewport with the Mouse

1. Activate the viewport that is to receive the changes in the view angle.

2. Click on the Axis Tripod icon or press [U]. The X,Y,Z axis tripod appears in the viewport, as shown below, and the horizontal and vertical angles of rotation are displayed on the status line.

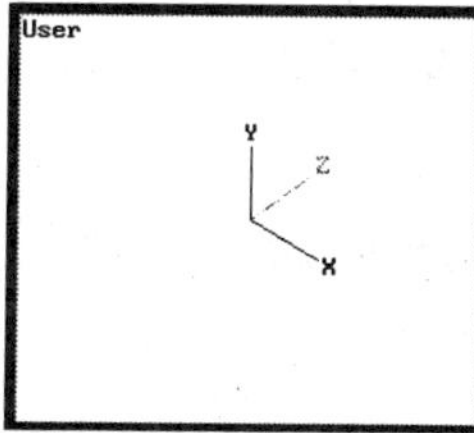

After pressing [U] the Axis Tripod appears.

3. Move the mouse horizontally or vertically to adjust the view angle. The axis tripod moves to reflect the changes made.

4. Once the view angle is correct, click the left mouse button or right-click to cancel the command.

NOTE While adjusting the view angle, you can return to the default setting (20 degrees horizontal and 30 degrees vertical) by pressing [R]. Press [Enter] or right click to accept the default changes.

Changing the View Angle of a Viewport with the Keyboard

1. Activate the user viewport that is to receive the view angle changes.

2. Using the following keys to adjust the view angle. The view angle will change according to the keystrokes selected.

[↑]: Moves the view angle 10 degrees up.

[↓]: Moves the view angle 10 degrees down.

[←]: Moves the view angle 10 degrees to the left.

[→]: Moves the view angle 10 degrees to the right.

[Shift] + cursor key: Moves the view angle at 1- degree increments.

RELATED COMMAND

Views-Viewports

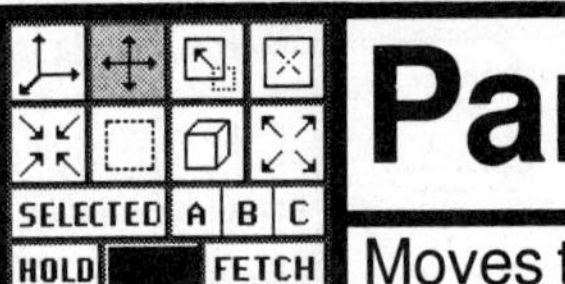

Pan

Moves the view (pans) about the viewport plane in the active viewport.

Panning the Active Viewport.

1. Activate a non-camera/non-spotlight viewport that is to be panned.

2. Select the Pan icon or press [P]. The Pan icon turns red.

3. Click on the first point to pan "from." An arrow appears showing the current direction of the pan.

4. Move and click on a second point to pan "to." The view is panned in the direction and distance specified.

5. To cancel the pan mode, right-click or select another command.

6. To continue panning, repeat steps 3and 4 in the current or any other viewport.

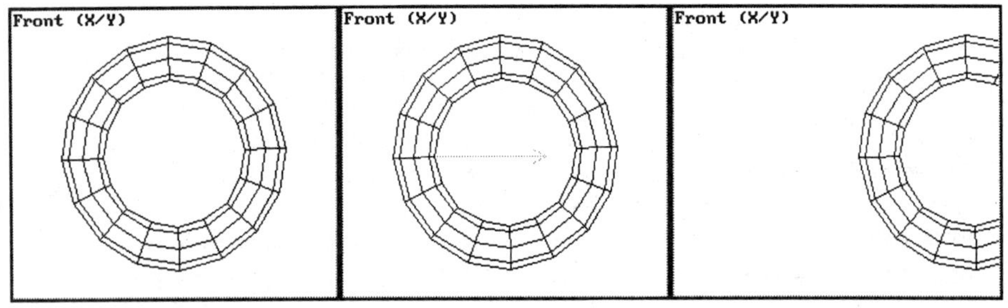

Before the pan. *During the pan.* *After the pan.*

RELATED COMMANDS

Zoom-In, Zoom-Out, Window Zoom

Full-Screen

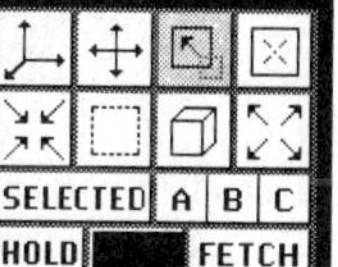

Changes the active viewport from normal to full-screen mode.

Toggling Between Normal and Full-Screen Mode

1. Activate a normal viewport.
2. Select the Full-Screen Toggle icon or press [W]. The viewport toggles from normal mode to full-screen mode as shown in the figure below.
3. To toggle back to normal mode, repeat step 2.

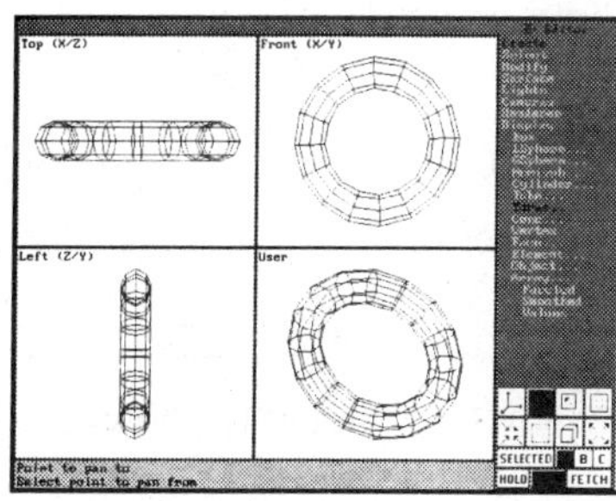

Before full screen.

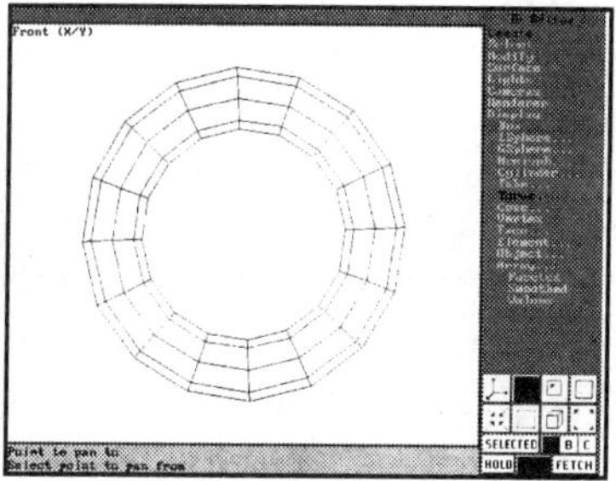

After full screen.

RELATED COMMAND

View-Viewports

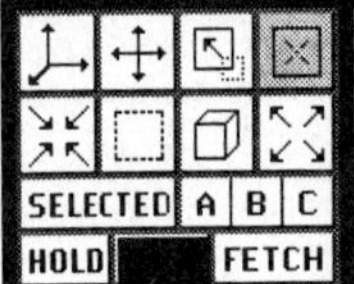

Local Axis

Ensures that the center point is central to any geometry being modified with *Rotate*, *Scale*, *2D Scale*, *3D Scale*, *Skew*, or *Taper* commands.

Using Local Axis

1. Create geometry in the 2D Shaper or 3D Editor.
2. Choose a command that references a center point, such as *Modify/Object/Rotate.*
3. Select the Local Axis icon. The icon will turn red.
4. Rotate the object. It will be rotated about its center point.
5. Turn off the Local Axis.
6. Rotate the object again. Notice that the center rotation point is no longer about the center of the object but about the global axis.

> **NOTE** Using the Local Axis icon when more than once object is selected will result in a center point being placed in the center of the combined object's bounding box.

RELATED COMMANDS

Modify/Axis

Zoom In

⇧Shift Z

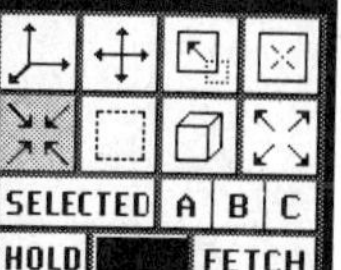

Modifies an orthographic viewport by 50 percent of its present magnification or doubles the focal length of a camera viewport.

"Zooming In"

1. Activate a viewport.

2. Select the Zoom In icon or press ⇧Shift Z. The viewport is "zoomed in" as shown in the figures below.

3. To zoom in on all viewports simultaneously, right-click on the Zoom In icon.

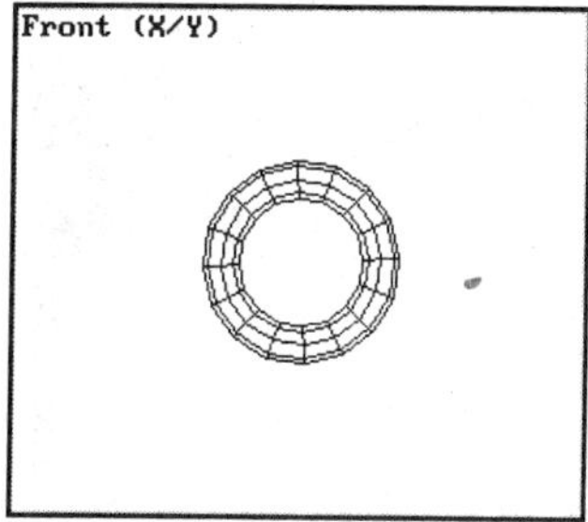

Before full screen.

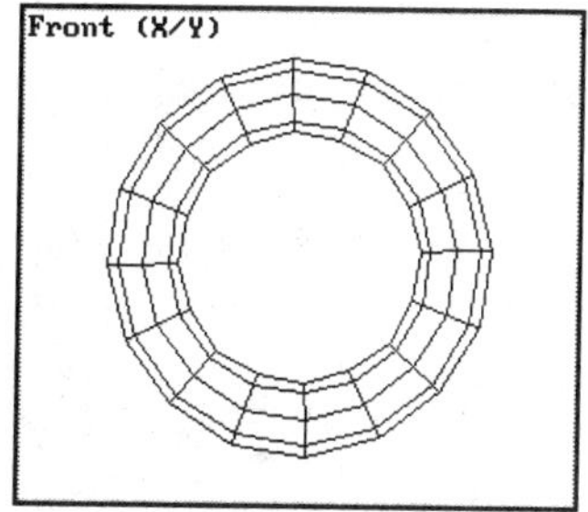

After full screen.

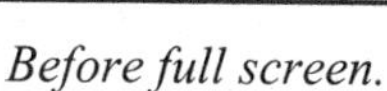

TIP Holding ⇧Shift while selecting the Zoom In icon will change the zoom factor from 50 percent to 10 percent.

RELATED COMMANDS

Zoom Extent, Zoom Out

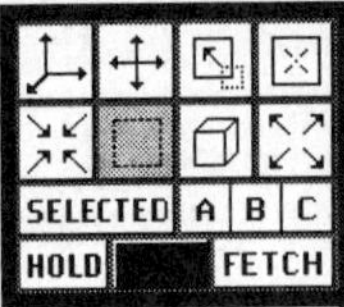

Window Zoom Alt Z

Allows you to enlarge a defined part of the active viewport.

Zooming in the Active Viewport

1. Click on the viewport you want to zoom in on.
2. Selecting the Window Zoom icon will cause the screen crosshairs to appear.
3. Click to set the first corner. Move the mouse diagonally to define a box enclosing the area you want to zoom in on.
4. When the box encloses the area you want zoomed, click to zoom the area or right-click to cancel the operation.

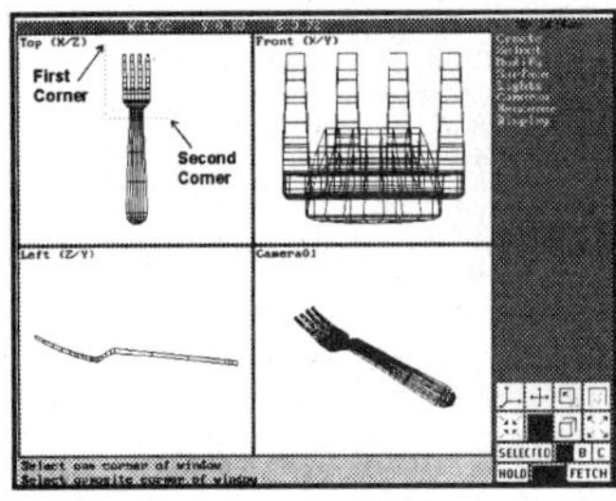

Before window zoom.

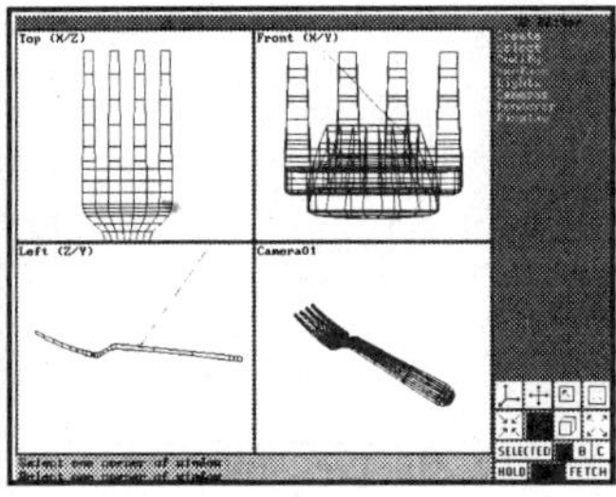

After window zoom.

NOTE You cannot zoom in camera or spotlight viewports.

After selecting the Window Zoom icon, it turns red indicating you can continue to zoom in on selected areas. You can switch active viewports and use any of the other icons except Pan.

RELATED COMMANDS

Zoom Out, Zoom Extent

Zoom Extent

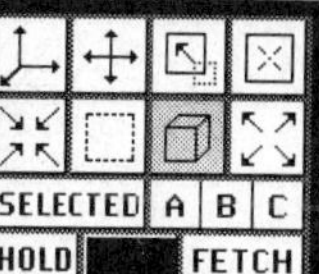

Zooms the active viewport or all viewports so all components are displayed, including objects, cameras, and spotlights.

Zooming All Components

1. Click on the viewport you want to zoom extents on.
2. Selecting the Zoom Extent icon with the *left* mouse button will cause the active viewport to zoom in or out so all components are displayed.
3. Selecting the Zoom Extent icon with the *right* mouse button will cause all viewports to zoom in or out so all components are displayed in each viewport.

3D Editor and Keyframer

Any hidden objects are not zoomed, including lights and cameras.

3D Lofter

Zooms only the path and associated shapes. Any 3D Shapes displayed (see *3D Display/On* in the 3D Lofter) are ignored.

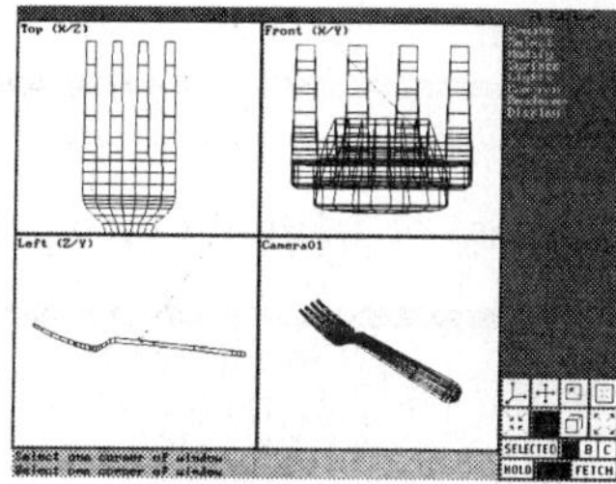

Before zoom extend.

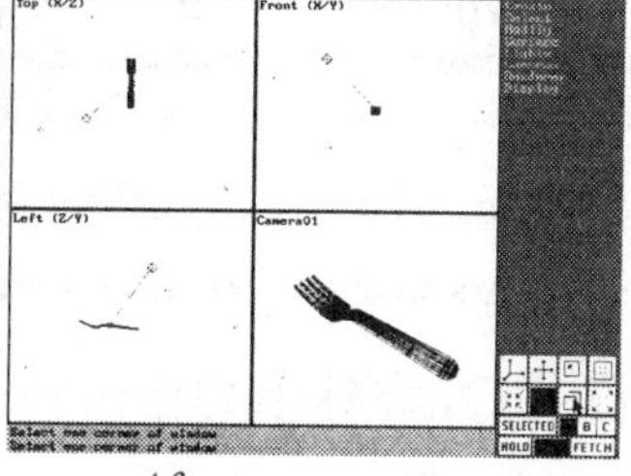

After zoom extent.

NOTE Zoom-Extent has no effect on camera or spotlight viewports.

RELATED COMMANDS

Zoom Out, Zoom In

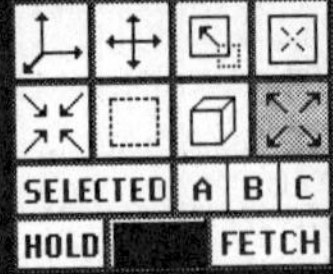

Zoom Out

Zooms out 50 percent on the active viewport or all viewports.

Zooming Out

1. Click on the viewport you want to zoom out on.
2. Selecting the Zoom-Out icon with the*left* mouse button will cause the active viewport to zoom out 50 percent.
3. Selecting the Zoom-Out icon with the*right* mouse button will cause all viewports to zoom out 50 percent.

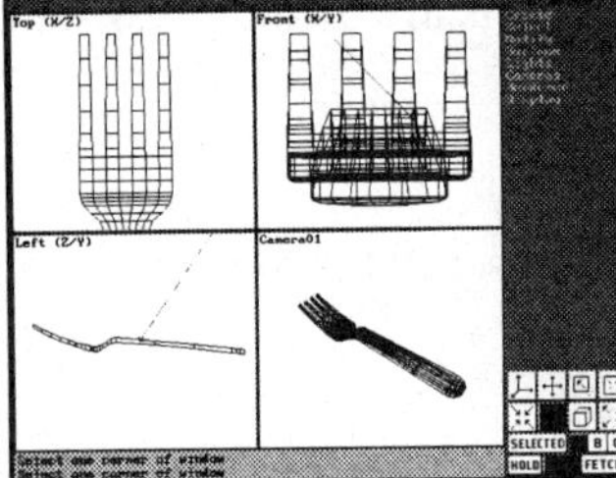

Before zoom-out

After zoom-out

Holding Shift while selecting the Zoom-Out Icon will cause all viewports to zoom out 50 percent.

Zoom-Out has no effect on camera or spotlight viewports.

RELATED COMMANDS

Zoom-Extent, Zoom-In

Selected and A-B-C

Used in combination with selection sets of geometry. Selection sets may be applied to the A-B-C buttons, and activated by clicking on the Selected button.

Using the Selected and A-B-C Buttons

1. Click on the A, B, or C button and create a selection set. Only one of these buttons can be active at a time. Defining or changing a selection set in one letter does not affect the selection sets stored in the remaining letters.

   2D Shaper: see the commands under *Select.*

   3D Lofter: command not available.

   3D Editor: see the commands under *Select.*

   Keyframer: command not available.

2. The objects selected will be applied to the A, B, or C button selected.

3. After selecting a command that prompts you to select an object (such as *Modify/Object/Move* in the 3D Editor or *Modify/Vertex/Move* in the 2D Shaper), click on the **Selected** button. The command function will now be applied to all of the objects defined in the selection set.

This command allows you to keep three different selection sets stored in memory. Choose A, B, or C to activate that selection set.

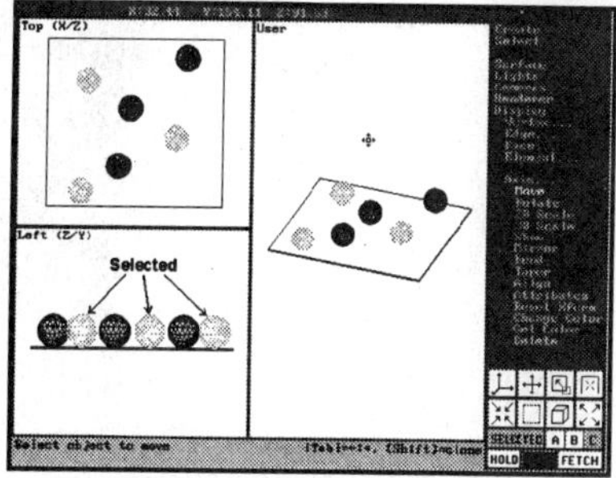

Defining a selection set of objects in the 3D Editor.

RELATED COMMANDS

See the Select commands in the 2D Shaper and 3D Editor.

Hold

Stores the state of the current program module, including the viewport configuration and any defined selection sets.

Storing the State of the Current Program Module

1. Before performing an operation you might want to undo, press the **Hold** button.

    - **2D Shaper:** contains its own hold buffer. You can use the **Hold** button to save a particular configuration. Unlike the Undo button, once you press Hold, the current configuration is saved and is not affected by any further commands.

    - **3D Editor:** shares a hold buffer with the Keyframer. Because the 3D Editor does not have an Undo option, make sure you press the **Hold** button before performing any operation you may want to undo later.

    - **3D Lofter:** contains its own hold buffer. You can use the **Hold** button to save a particular configuration. Unlike the Undo button, once you press Hold, the current configuration is saved and is not affected by any further commands.

    - **Keyframer:** shares a hold buffer with the 3D Editor. Because the Keyframer does not have an Undo option, make sure you press the **Hold** button before performing any operation you may later want to undo.

2. To restore the state of the current program module, press the **Fetch** button.

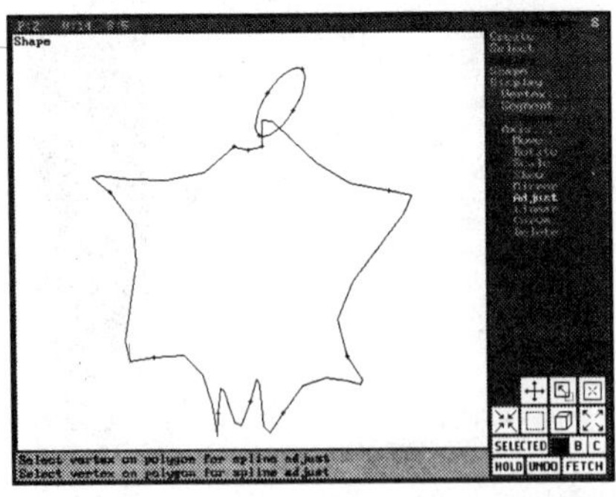

Use the Undo button to cancel the last operation if it is not what you wanted.

RELATED COMMANDS

Fetch, Undo

Fetch

Restores the program configuration saved when the Hold button was used last.

Restoring the Program Configuration

1. To restore the program configuration, it first must have been saved at some point by pressing the **Hold** button.
2. To restore the program configuration stored in the hold buffer, press the **Fetch** button. A dialog box appears, asking you to confirm the operation. Select **Yes** to restore the information stored in the hold buffer.

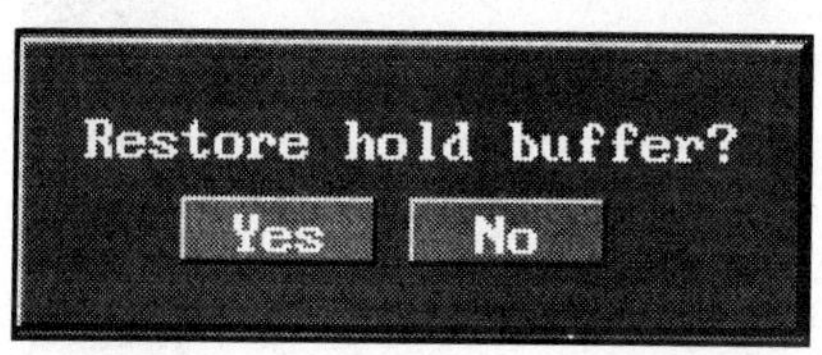

Select Yes to restore the information stored in the hold buffer.

RELATED COMMANDS

Hold, Undo

Undo

Cancels the effect of the last operation. Available in the 2D Shaper and 3D Lofter only.

Undoing the Last Operation

1. Immediately after performing the operation, press the **Undo** button. The previous operation will be undone.
2. Clicking on the **Undo** button again will cancel the undo.

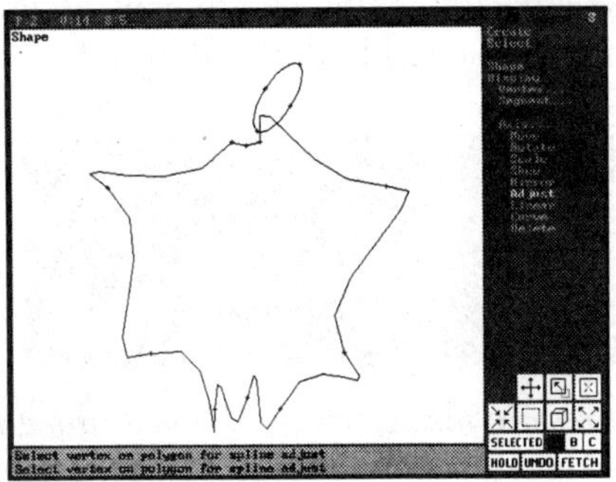

Use the Undo button cancel the last operation if it is not what you wanted.

TIP The **Undo** button will only undo the most recent operation. If you are performing a series of operations, press the **Hold** button before beginning. This will store the current state of the program module, and is not affected by subsequent commands.

RELATED COMMANDS

Hold, Fetch

Create Color

The Create Color button only appears in the 3D Editor between the Hold and Fetch buttons. It is used to set the color for newly created objects.

Setting the Color of New Objects

1. To set the color, click on the Create Color box located between the **Hold** and **Fetch** buttons in the 3D Editor.
2. When the Object Creation Color dialog box appears, select a new color.
3. All newly created objects will have the selected color.
4. To change the color of objects already created, see *Modify/Object/Change Color* in the 3D Editor.

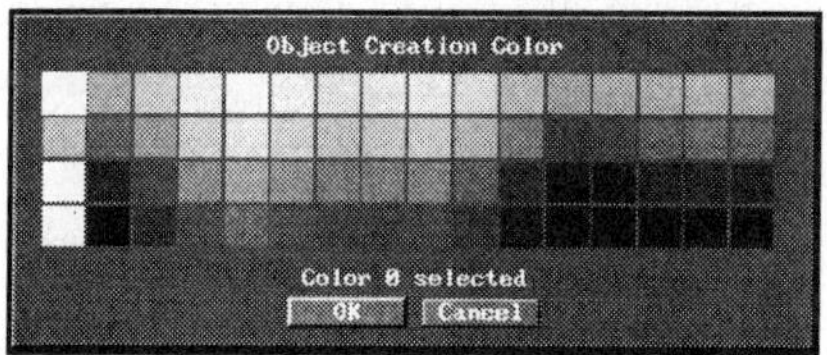

The color selected will be applied to all newly created objects.

The Object Creation Color dialog box will only display a solid white box if your display is not set up to show 256 colors.

RELATED COMMANDS

Modify/Object/Change Color in the 3D Editor

Track Info

Located in the Keyframer, it accesses the Track Info dialog box. You can use the Track Info dialog box to add, delete, or adjust an item's keys.

Accessing the Track Info Dialog Box

1. To access the Track Info: dialog box, click on the **Track Info:** button and select any object.

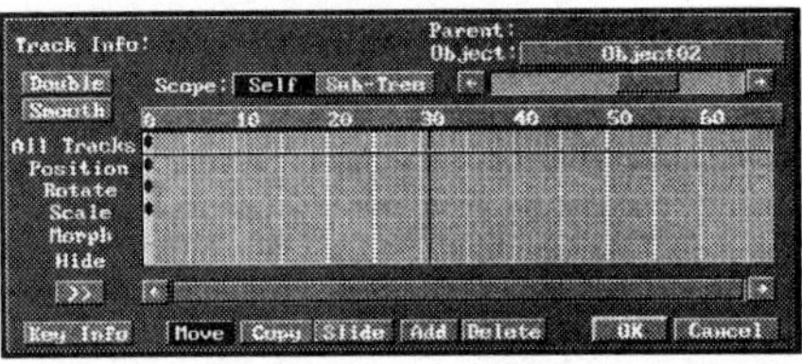

The track info: dialog box can be used to adjust the keys for a selected object.

Understanding the Track Info: Dialog Box

Parent: Object: Displays the name of the parent and corresponding object for which the keys are displayed. To cycle through the different objects in the scene, use the slider bar directly below the Parent: Object:0 bar.

Gridded Window: The middle part of the dialog box contains a gridded window.

Horizontal Rows: Each component in the animation has its own row. *Mesh objects* have a track for position, rotation, scale, morph, and hide. *Cameras* have a track for position, roll, and field of view. *Camera targets* have a single track for position. *Omni lights* have one track for position and one for color. *Spotlights* contain tracks for position, color, hotspot angle, falloff angle, and roll angle.

Vertical Columns: Each vertical column represents one frame in the animation.

Key Dots: Each key in the animation is represented in the grid as a black dot.

All Tracks: The key in this top row represents all keys in the row below it. Modifying a key in the All Tracks column modifies all keys in the row below it.

Hide: Allows you to turn objects on and off during an animation. To hide an object at a specific frame, click on **Add**, then click in the hide row in the frame you want the object to hide in. A black dot appears in the selected row. Cells to the left appear white, indicating that the object is visible. Cells to the right appear gray, indicating that the object is hidden.

Scope: This appears when an object with a parent is active. You can change how the key dots are displayed in the gridded window.

Self: Each key dot is shown representing only the key of the current object.

Sub-Tree: The keys for the current object as well as all of its decendents appear. If you edit a key in the All Tracks row, you are also editing all transformation keys at that frame for all linked objects.

Double: Doubles the pattern of all keys for the selected object. If **Sub-Tree** is active under **Scope**, the keys for all of its descendents are also doubled.

Smooth: The first and last keys remain in their current location. All other keys are repositioned so that they are evenly spaced. This can be used to make the velocity of the object appear constant.

Move: Moves a key from one frame to another. Hold down the ⇧Shift key when selecting it to make a copy. See *Paths/Move Key.*

Copy: Creates a copy of a selected key and allows you to move it to another frame. See *Paths/Add Key.*

Slide: Moves a selected key and all following keys, maintaining the same spacing.

Add: Adds a new key in an empty space on the grid.

Delete: Deletes single or multiple keys in a track. To delete a single key, select **Delete** and click on the key. To delete multiple keys, select Delete and click on a track label, such as Position. See *Paths/Delete Key.*

Key Info: See the Key Info icon.

RELATED COMMANDS

Paths/Move Key, Paths/Add Key, Paths/Delete Key

Key Info

Allows you to adjust key values of a selected object, light, camera, or target at any keyframe.

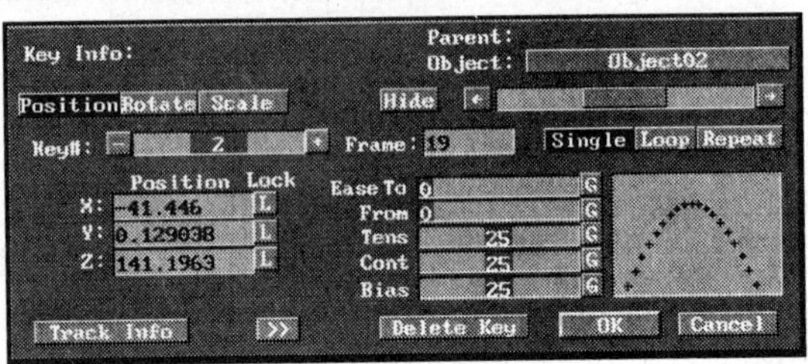

The Key Info dialog box allows you to adjust the key values of a selected object.

NOTE You can access the Key Info dialog box by selecting the **Key Info** button. You can also access it by selecting the **Key Info** button in the Track Info dialog box and clicking on the key to adjust the values.

Using the Key Info Dialog Box

The type and number of radio buttons appearing in the Key Info label section depend on the object selected. The active button under Key Info determines what values are available for modification.

Parent: Object: Displays the name of the parent and corresponding object for which a selected key is displayed. To cycle through the different objects in the scene, use the slider bar directly below the Parent: Object.

Key#: Moving the slider bar back and forth changes the established keys for the selected object. The corresponding frame is displayed in the **Frame:** box.

Frame: As the **Key#** slider is moved, the corresponding frame is displayed.

Single/Loop/Repeat: Selecting **Single** (default) carries out the animation as defined by each frame. Selecting the **Loop** button will copy the key values in frame #1 to the last frame in the animation. See *Object/Tracks/Loop*. Selecting **Repeat** repeats the established pattern of keys thoughout the animation.

Ease To/From: Allows you to adjust the ease to and ease from values. See *Paths/Adjust/Ease To* and *Paths/Adjust/Ease From*.

Tens/Cont/Bias: Allows you to adjust the Tension, Continuity, and Bias for the selected key. See *Paths/Adjust TCB/Tension, Paths/Adjust TCB/Continuity, and Paths/Adjust TCB/Bias.*

> **TIP** Many of the buttons and settings in the Key Info dialog box permanently alter the key values. Before changing any values in the dialog box, press the **Hold** button to store the current configuration of the keyframer module. This also stores the current configuration of all the keys. If the results are not what you wanted after altering the key values, you can restore the keys back to their original setting by pressing the **Fetch** button.

RELATED COMMANDS

Object/Tracks/Loop, Paths/Adjust/Ease To and Paths/Adjust/Ease From, Paths/Adjust TCB/Tension, Paths/Adjust TCB/Continuity, Paths/Adjust TCB/Bias

Define Active Segment

Displays the active segment. Clicking on the segment bar displays the Define Active Segment dialog box.

Setting the Active Segment

1. Click on the Segment Bar to access the Define Active Segment dialog box.
2. By entering values in the text boxes, you can set the beginning and end frames of the active segment. By defining an active segment, you restict access to only the frames in the defined range. This affects the segment bar, playback of the animation, rendering, and the Track Info dialog box.

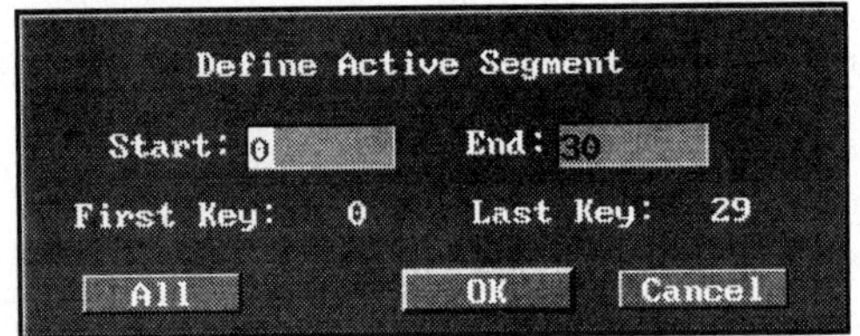

Clicking on the segment bar accesses the Define Active Segment dialog box.

TIP Setting the active segment is especially useful when working on long animations. When you set the active segment, you can work on a smaller portion of a large animation.

RELATED COMMAND

Time/Total Frames

Current Frame

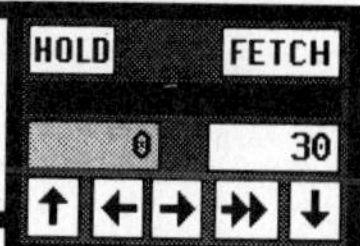

Displays the current frame. Clicking on the Current Frame button displays the Go To Frame dialog box.

Going to a Specific Frame

1. Click on the **Current Frame** button to access the Go To Frame dialog box.
2. Enter the frame number you want to go to, and click **OK**.

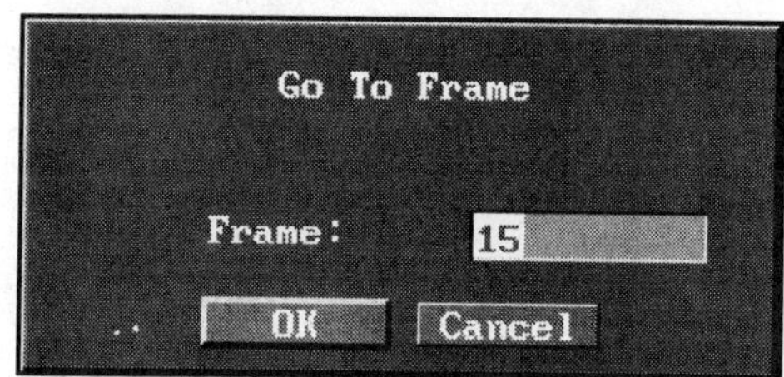

Clicking on the Current Frame button displays the Go To Frame dialog box.

You can also go to a different frame by selecting *Time/Go to Frame*, and by dragging the frame slider at the bottom of the screen.

RELATED COMMAND

Time/Go to Frame

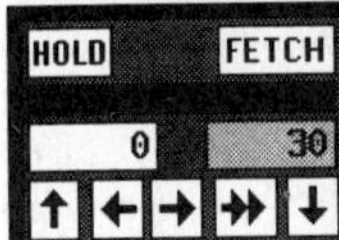

Total Frames

Displays the total number of frames in the animation. Clicking on the Total Frames button displays the Set Number of Frames dialog box.

Setting the Number of Frames in an Animation

1. Click on the **Total Frames** button to access the Set Number of Frames dialog box.

2. Enter the total number of frames you want, and click **OK**. You can have up to 32,001 frames in your animation

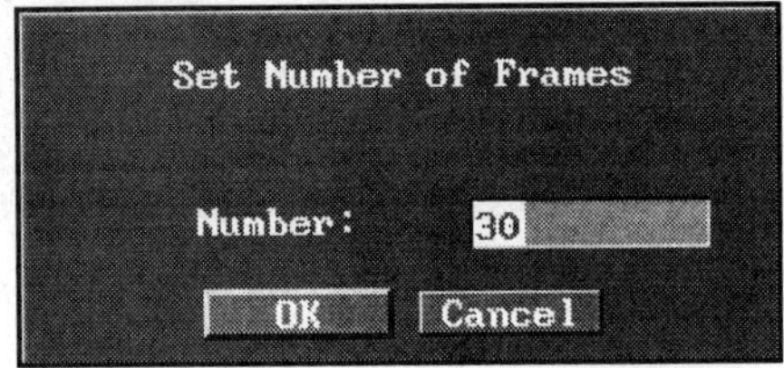

Clicking on the Total Frames button displays the Set Number of Frames dialog box.

TIP You can also set the total number of frames by selecting *Time/Total Frames*. If you shorten an animation, any extra frames are not deleted. They are still displayed in the Track Info dialog box.

RELATED COMMAND

Time/Total Frames

Playback Icons

The different icons control the playback of the animation in the active viewport.

Goes to the first frame in the active segment.

Moves back one frame.

Moves forward one frame.

Plays the animation in a loop.

Goes to the last frame in the active segment.

RELATED COMMANDS

None

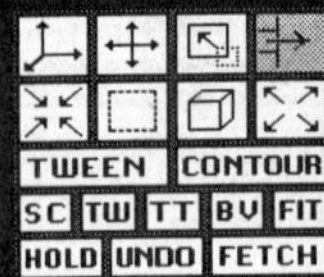

Switch Viewports

Changes the active viewport from small to large viewport mode in the 3D Lofter.

Toggling Between Small and Large Viewport Mode

1. Switch to the 3D Lofter.
2. Activate a small viewport.
3. Select the Switch Viewports icon or press [X]. The small viewport changes places with the large viewport.
4. To toggle back to small viewport mode, repeat step 2.

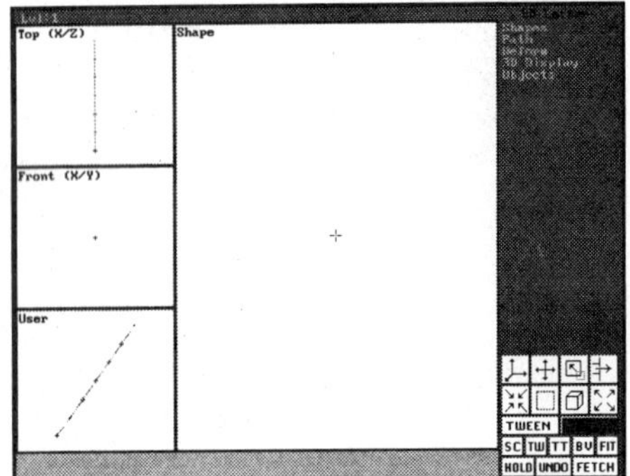

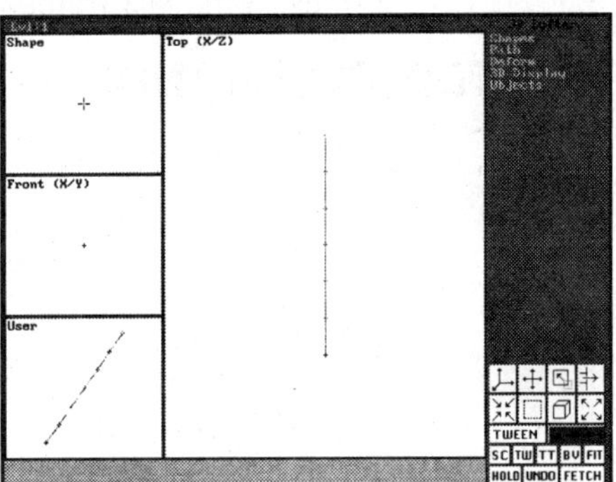

Switching the Top View with the Shape View.

RELATED COMMAND

View-Viewports

Tween Button

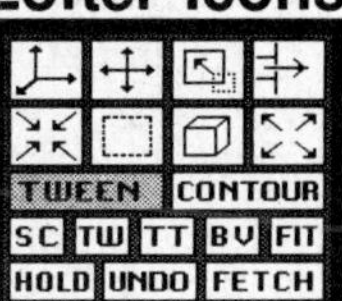

Applies Tween to the object being lofted.

For more information on Tween, refer to *3D Lofter-Object/Make*.

Using Tween

1. Activate the 3D Lofter.
2. Modify or create a shape and a path to be lofted.
3. Select the **Tween** button. The icon turns red.
4. Use *Objects/Make* or *Objects/Preview* to view the results.

RELATED COMMANDS

3D Lofter-Objects/Make, 3D Lofter-Objects/Preview

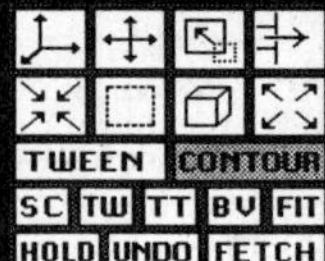

Contour Button

Applies the Contour Deformation grid settings to the object being lofted.

For more information on Contour, refer to *3D Lofter-Deform/Contour* commands.

Applying Twist Deformation Grid Settings

1. Activate the 3D Lofter.
2. Modify or create a shape and a path to be lofted.
3. Adjust the Contour Deformation grid using the *Deform/Contour* commands.
4. Select the **Contour** button. The icon turns red.
5. Use *Objects/Make* or *Objects/Preview* to view the results.

RELATED COMMANDS

3D Lofter-Deform/Contour commands

Scale Button

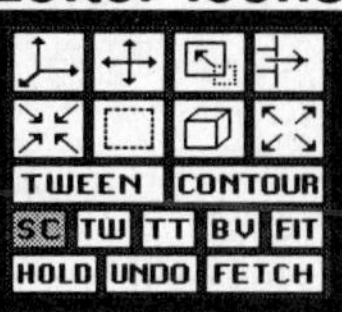

Applies the Scale Deformation grid settings to the object being lofted.

For more information on Scale, refer to the *3D Lofter-Deform/Scale* commands.

Applying Scale Deformation Grid Settings

1. Activate the 3D Lofter.
2. Modify or create a shape and a path to be lofted.
3. Adjust the Scale Deformation grid using the *Deform/Scale* commands.
4. Select the **Scale** button. The icon turns red.
5. Use the *Objects/Make* or *Objects/Preview* to view the results.

RELATED COMMANDS

3D Lofter-Deform/Teeter commands

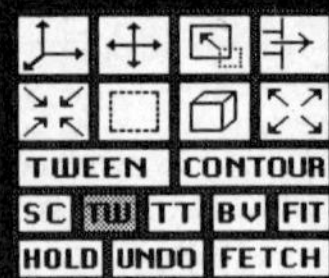

Twist Button

Applies the Twist Deformation grid settings to the object being lofted.

For more information on Twist, refer to *3D Lofter-Deform/Twist* commands.

Applying Twist Deformation Grid Settings

1. Activate the 3D Lofter.
2. Modify or create a shape and a path to be lofted.
3. Adjust the Twist Deformation grid using *Deform/Twist* commands.
4. Select the **Twist** button. The icon turns red.
5. Use *Objects/Make* or *Objects/Preview* to view the results.

RELATED COMMANDS

3D Lofter-Deform/Twist commands

Teeter Button

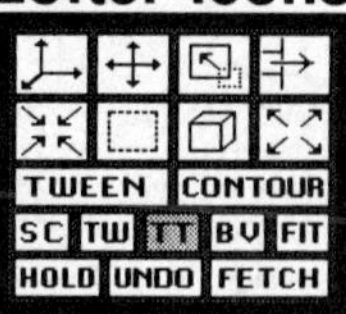

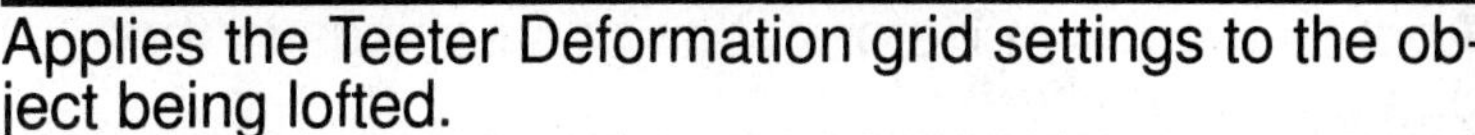

Applies the Teeter Deformation grid settings to the object being lofted.

For more information on Teeter refer to *3D Lofter-Deform/Teeter* commands.

Applying Teeter Deformation Grid Settings

1. Activate the 3D Lofter.

2. Modify or create a shape and a path to be lofted.

3. Adjust the Teeter Deformation grid using *Deform/Teeter* commands.

4. Select the **Teeter** button. The icon turns red.

RELATED COMMANDS

3D Lofter-Deform/Teeter commands

Bevel Button

Applies the Bevel Deformation grid settings to the object being lofted.

For more information on Bevel, refer to *3D Lofter-Deform/Bevel* commands.

Applying Bevel Deformation Grid Settings

1. Activate the 3D Lofter.
2. Modify or create a shape and a path to be lofted.
3. Adjust the Bevel Deformation grid using *Deform/Bevel* commands.
4. Select the **Bevel** button. The icon turns red.
5. Use *Objects/Make* or *Objects/Preview* to view the results.

RELATED COMMANDS

3D Lofter-Deform/Bevel commands

Fit Button

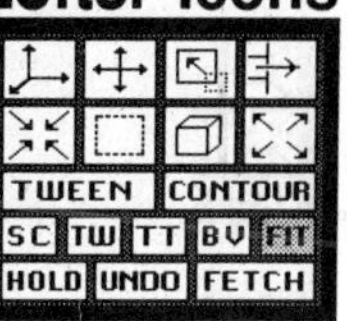

Applies the Fit Deformation grid settings to the object being lofted.

For more information on Fit, refer to *3D Lofter-Deform/Fit* commands.

Applying Fit Deformation Grid Settings

1. Activate the 3D Lofter.
2. Modify or create a shape and a path to be lofted.
3. Adjust the Fit Deformation grid using *Deform/Fit* commands.
4. Select the **Fit** button. The icon turns red.
5. Use *Objects/Make* or *Objects/Preview* to view the results.

RELATED COMMANDS

3D Lofter-Deform/Fit commands

Index

C

M

N

O

S